Urban Education

Many factors complicate the education of urban students. Among them are issues related to population density; racial, ethnic, cultural, and linguistic diversity; poverty; racism (individual and institutional); and funding levels. Although urban educators have been addressing these issues for decades, to place them under the umbrella of "urban education" and treat them as a specific area of practice and inquiry is relatively recent. Despite the wide adoption of the term, a consensus about its meaning exists only at the broadest of levels. In short, urban education remains an ill-defined concept.

This comprehensive volume addresses this definitional challenge and provides a three-part conceptual model in which the achievement of equity for all—regardless of race, gender, or ethnicity—is an ideal that is central to urban education. The model also posits that effective urban education requires attention to the three central issues that confront all education systems: (a) *accountability* of individuals and the institutions in which they work, (b) *leadership*, which occurs in multiple ways and at multiple levels, and (c) *learning*, which is the raison d'être of education. Just as a three-legged stool would fall if any one leg were weak or missing, each of these areas is essential to effective urban education and affects the other issues. Key features of this exciting new book include the following:

- **Conceptual Model**—A three-part model of urban education built around the concepts of account-ability, leadership, and learning helps to define and organize this sprawling and loosely coupled field of study. Further definition is provided by threading the theme of educational equity through each of these organizing concepts.
- **Comprehensive**—The book covers all aspects of urban education and, unlike most books in the field, covers PreK–16 education.
- **Integrates Research and Practice**—All chapters are grounded in the relevant research, while also providing implications for practice.
- **Interdisciplinary and Global**—Chapters cover a wide range of perspectives from leading national and international scholars, and practitioners whose expertise spans diverse settings, student populations, educational systems, and academic fields.
- **Accessible Style**—Although grounded in the latest research, the book's style and tone make it accessible to the textbook, professional development, and reference book markets.

This book is appropriate for university researchers, instructors, and graduate students in schools with an urban education program and as a resource for policymakers at the district, state, and national levels.

Karen Symms Gallagher is Emery Stoops and Joyce King Stoops Dean at the Rossier School of Education, University of Southern California.

Rodney Goodyear is Emeritus Professor of Education (Counseling Psychology) at the University of Southern California, and Professor of Education at the University of Redlands.

Dominic J. Brewer is Associate Dean of Research and Faculty Affairs, and Clifford H. and Betty C. Allen Professor in Urban Leadership at the Rossier School of Education, University of Southern California.

Robert Rueda is Stephen Crocker Professor in Education and Professor of Educational Psychology at the Rossier School of Education, University of Southern California.

Urban Education

A Model for Leadership and Policy

Edited by
Karen Symms Gallagher,
Rodney Goodyear,
Dominic J. Brewer, and
Robert Rueda

Routledge
Taylor & Francis Group

NEW YORK AND LONDON

First published 2012
by Routledge
711 Third Avenue, New York, NY 10017

Simultaneously published in the UK
by Routledge
2 Park Square, Milton Park, Abingdon, Oxon OX14 4RN

Routledge is an imprint of the Taylor & Francis Group, an informa business

© 2012 Taylor & Francis

Library of Congress Cataloging-in-Publication Data
Urban education : a model for leadership and policy / [edited by]
Karen Gallagher ... [et al.].
p. cm.
Includes bibliographical references and index.
1. Education, Urban. 2. Urban schools–Administration. I. Gallagher, Karen S.
LC5131.U665 2011
370.9173'2–dc22
2011012750

ISBN13: 978–0–415–87240–9 (hbk)
ISBN13: 978–0–415–87241–6 (pbk)
ISBN13: 978–0–203–83733–7 (ebk)

Typeset in Minion
by Keystroke, Station Road, Codsall, Wolverhampton

Printed and bound in the United States of America on acid-free paper by Edwards Brothers, Inc.

We dedicate this book both to our spouses (Pat, Karen, Kalvin, and Mary) and to children and adult learners in urban settings.

Contents

Figures

Tables

Contributors

Elpida Ahtaridou
Principal Researcher
Teaching, Learning, Curriculum &
Qualifications Centre
Learning and Skill Network (LSN), London

Gilberto Arriaza
Professor
Department of Educational Leadership
College of Education and Allied Studies
California State University, East Bay

Ron Avi Astor
Richard M. and Ann L. Thor Professor in
Urban Social Development
Schools of Social Work and Education
University of Southern California

Naomi Baum
Director
Resilience Unit
Israel Center for the Treatment of
Psychotrauma
Herzog Hospital, Jerusalem, Israel

Rami Benbenishty
Professor
School of Social Work
Bar-Ilan University, Israel

Estela Mara Bensimon
Co-Director
Center for Urban Education
Professor of Higher Education
Rossier School of Education
University of Southern California

Robin Bishop
Provost Fellow and Research Assistant
Center for Urban Education
Rossier School of Education
University of Southern California

Dominic J. Brewer
Associate Dean of Research and Faculty Affairs
Clifford H. and Betty C. Allen Professor in
Urban Leadership
Rossier School of Education
University of Southern California

Danny Brom
General Director
Israel Center for the Treatment of
Psychotrauma
Herzog Hospital, Jerusalem, Israel

Vichet Chhuon
Assistant Professor
College of Education
University of Minnesota

Charles D. Claiborn
Professor of Counseling and Counseling
Psychology
Arizona State University

David T. Conley
Director
Center for Educational Policy Research
Professor, Educational Policy and Leadership
College of Education
University of Oregon
Chief Executive Officer
Educational Policy Improvement Center

Tara B. Davidson
Doctoral Candidate
Rutgers University-Newark

Mariëtte de Haan
Professor of Intercultural Education
Faculty of Social Sciences
Utrecht University

Kris De Pedro
Doctoral Student
Rossier School of Education
University of Southern California

Alicia C. Dowd
Co-Director
Center for Urban Education
Associate Professor of Higher Education
Rossier School of Education
University of Southern California

Julia Eksner
Research Associate
Department of Education and Psychology
Free University of Berlin

Yrjö Engeström
Professor of Adult Education
Director
Center for Activity, Development and Learning
(CRADLE)
Institute of Behavioral Sciences
University of Helsinki

Karen Symms Gallagher
Emery Stoops and Joyce King Stoops Dean
Rossier School of Education
University of Southern California

Rodney Goodyear
Emeritus Professor of Education (Counseling
Psychology)
University of Southern California
Professor of Education
University of Redlands

Matthew Gutierrez
Doctoral Student
University of Redlands

Guilbert C. Hentschke
Professor and Richard T. Cooper and
Mary Catherine Cooper Chair in Public School
Administration
Rossier School of Education
University of Southern California

Rosemary Henze
Professor of Linguistics & Language
Development
San José State University

David Hopkins
Professor Emeritus
Institute of Education
University of London

Cynthia Hudley
Professor
School of Education
University of California, Santa Barbara

Adrianna Kezar
Associate Professor of Higher Education
Rossier School of Education
University of Southern California

Shayna Klopott
Doctoral Candidate
Teachers College
Columbia University

James W. Lichtenberg
Professor and Associate Dean
School of Education
University of Kansas

Andrew McEachin
Provost Fellow and Doctoral Student
Rossier School of Education
University of Southern California

Douglas E. Mitchell
Professor
Graduate School of Education
University of California, Riverside

Ross E. Mitchell
Assistant Professor
School of Education
University of Redlands

Ruth Pat-Horenczyk
Director
Child and Adolescent Clinical Services
Israel Center for the Treatment of
Psychotrauma
Herzog Hospital, Jerusalem, Israel

Lucinda Pease-Alvarez
Associate Professor of Education (Language,
Literacy and Culture)
University of California, Santa Cruz

Lawrence O. Picus
Professor
Rossier School of Education
University of Southern California

Heather Meyer Reynolds
Mentor, Master of Arts in Teaching
Empire State College

Robert Rueda
Stephen H. Crocker Professor in Education
Rossier School of Education
University of Southern California

John L. Rury
Professor, School of Education and
(by courtesy) Department of History
University of Kansas

Alan R. Sadovnik
Board of Governors Distinguished Service
Professor
Professor of Education, Sociology and Public
Affairs
Rutgers University

Miriam Schiff
Lecturer
The Paul Baerwald School of Social Work and
Social Welfare
Hebrew University of Jerusalem

John Brooks Slaughter
Professor of Education and Engineering
Rossier School of Education and Viterbi School
of Engineering
University of Southern California

Margaret Beale Spencer
Marshall Field IV Professor of Urban Education
Department of Comparative Human
Development
University of Chicago

Petra Stanat
Director
Institute for Educational Quality Improvement
(IQB)
Humboldt University of Berlin

Kenneth A. Strike
Professor Emeritus
Cornell University

Dena Phillips Swanson
Associate Professor of Counseling and Human
Development
Warner School of Education and Human
Development
University of Rochester

Marianne Teräs
Researcher
Center for Activity, Development and Learning
(CRADLE)
Institute of Behavioral Sciences
University of Helsinki

Terence J. G. Tracey
Professor of Counseling and Counseling
Psychology
Arizona State University

Aída Walqui
Director
Quality Teaching for English Learner Project
WestEd, San Francisco

Bruce E. Wampold
Professor and Chair
Department of Counseling Psychology
Clinical Professor of Psychiatry
University of Wisconsin, Madison

Keith Witham
Research Assistant
Center for Urban Education
Rossier School of Education
University of Southern California

Kenneth K. Wong
Chair
Department of Education
Walter and Leonore Annenberg Professor in
Education Policy
Brown University

Michelle D. Young
Professor of Educational Leadership and Policy
University of Virginia

Acknowledgments

Any book requires the efforts of multiple people to bring it to fruition. This is especially true of an edited book. We want, therefore, to begin by thanking all the contributors. The quality of this book is a direct result of their good work.

We want to thank as well several colleagues for their important help in conceptualizing the book and directing us to contributors. In particular, we thank Estela Bensimon for her help conceptualizing the central role that equity would play in this book; Adrianna Kezar for her work helping us to conceptualize the Leadership section; and Larry Picus for his work helping us to conceptualize the Accountability section. We thank all three for their help identifying the very strong roster of contributors.

We are grateful as well to Kris Gutierrez who was instrumental in conceptualizing and structuring the Learning section of the volume. Her ideas and contributions were invaluable in helping to broaden the ranges of issues related to learning, and her assistance in helping to shape the diverse but exciting list of contributors is greatly appreciated.

This acknowledgment would be incomplete if we did not also thank Lane Akers, our Routledge Editor, for his support; most of all, for his patience with a project that took much longer to complete than any of us had anticipated.

I
Foundation

The chapters in this section address definitional, contextual, and disciplinary issues related to urban education. They are intended to establish the foundation for the remainder of the book.

1

Introduction

Karen Symms Gallagher, Rodney Goodyear, Dominic J. Brewer, and Robert Rueda

McEachin and Brewer (Chapter 6, this volume) document that the majority of the U.S. population now lives in urban areas. In fact, this has become true world-wide and the proportion of those living in cities *continues* to grow (Cohen, 2003). Urbanization, though, is a relatively recent historical development. As a result, the very concept of "urban education" only really has begun to evolve over the past half century.

This is usefully illustrated in Figure 1.1, which draws from Google data. Its project of scanning over 5.2 million books has permitted scholars to track the rise and fall of interest in a topic across more than 200 years (see http://ngrams.googlelabs.com) by examining the proportion of times it is mentioned. Authors first began to use the term "urban education" in books at about the turn of the last century, but infrequently so until roughly 1960. Since then, interest in the topic has grown consistently, in a roughly linear upward manner, as indicated by the line we added; this, despite the upward spike in the 1970s (see Figure 1.1). Whereas Rury (Chapter 2, this volume) provides a more elaborated history, the Google data provide a reminder of how new the topic really is.

Urbanization has created a demand for educators who are able to provide urban students with a quality and equitable education. But a number of issues can complicate the work of those educators, including high levels both of population density and diversity (racial, ethnic, cultural, and linguistic), poverty, institutional racism, social segmentation and socioeconomic inequalities, unequal distribution of qualified teachers, and problematic funding levels. To make matters more complicated, these issues typically exist in some combination and with important interaction effects.

Although urban centers tend to be associated with negative factors, they can also offer a wealth of cultural, social, and economic resources, presenting unique opportunities as well as challenges for educators. Among the educational resources available to educators in urban settings are often business and intellectual centers, including universities and the university faculty to whom educators can turn for their expertise. It is important to note, in fact, that in some parts of the world, urban education is superior to what is available in other areas.

Nevertheless, the complicating issues we mentioned above help to locate much of urban education in the category of a "wicked problem." This concept, developed by Rittel and Webber (1973) and later elaborated by others (e.g., Conklin, 2006; Horn & Weber, 2007), has been usefully applied to social problems, particularly some economic and political issues; lately, it has been used with respect to global warming (Lazarus, 2009).

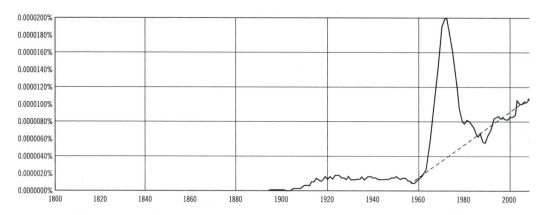

Figure 1.1 Mention of Urban Education in Books, 1800–2008

Kazdin (2009) compiled from the literature the attributes of a wicked problem. These included:

- There is no single, simple, or definitive formulation, for the problem is ill-structured. In fact, one problem is in the formulation of the problem.
- No single solution will get rid of the problem.
- There are multiple stakeholders, and "this fact leads to multiple formulations of what 'really' is the problem and therefore what are legitimately appropriate solutions" (Kazdin, 2009, p. 343).
- The problem is intertwined with and affected by other problems, some of which are themselves wicked problems.
- It is unlikely that the problem will be completely resolved.
- The uniqueness and complexity of the problem, along with the extent to which it is intertwined with other problems means that information and data that can guide action always will be incomplete.

These attributes describe much of urban education. What educators can gain by employing this conceptual frame "is clarity about the fact that [the wicked problem] require[s] novel ways of thinking in relation to problem formulation, evaluation, and intervention strategies" (Kazdin, 2009, p. 342). We hope that this book will be useful in encouraging that novel thinking while promoting greater consideration of the possible assets that might be appropriated for educational excellence.

There are some large handbooks (Kincheloe, Hayes, Rose, & Anderson, 2006; Noblit, Noblit, & Pink, 2008) available as resources, but few books provide a foundational examination of the range of urban education issues, overviewing the important literature in the field and its practice implications. Our purpose in editing this book was to provide that. In so doing we made sure that we addressed two particular issues of scope, recognizing that:

1. Urban education is not unique to any one country. Importantly, then, this volume addresses urban education issues in Britain, Finland, Germany, Israel, the Netherlands, and the United States, with contributors from each of those countries.
2. Urban education is not restricted to the K–12 level, but in fact ranges from pre-kindergarten through college and university levels. Several chapters, therefore, specifically address urban higher education.

Book Organization

We used the conceptual model depicted in Figure 1.2 to organize the book. The conceptual model is intended to provide urban education scholars and practitioners with a lens through which to view and understand a construct that has remained ill-defined, despite its unquestioned importance.

In this model, equitable access and opportunity for all students—regardless of their race or ethnicity, gender, linguistic background, and so on—is central. The model also posits that effective urban education requires attention to the three issues of (a) accountability of individuals and the institutions in which they work, (b) leadership, which occurs in multiple ways and at multiple levels, and (c) learning, which is the raison d'être of education. Just as a three-legged stool would fall if any one leg were weak or missing, each of these areas is essential to effective urban education and affects the others. The model also suggests that what separates one urban education setting from another is the specific sociocultural context in which it resides. This model informs the organization of the book. Its first, introductory section provides foundational information about urban education. This is followed by sections focusing on leadership, accountability, and learning.

Sociocultural Context

The issues related to education in urban settings do not occur as isolated phenomena. In fact, one thing that makes urban settings unique is the distinctive constellation of social, political, economic, and historical forces which have shaped their creation and which impact their functioning and ongoing dynamics. Whereas we use the word "sociocultural context" to describe these influences, it should be understood that our usage extends well beyond the simple physical setting. The complex

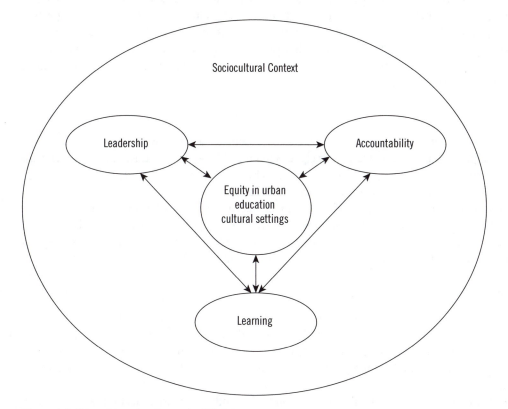

Figure 1.2 Urban Education Conceptual Model

ecologies created and re-created on an ongoing basis by these influences form the backdrop for the factors considered in Figure 1.2, and these forces are intertwined in complex and continually shifting ways in each of the areas. As the reader will note, the chapters in each of the sections refer to or focus on different aspects of these influences in different ways and at different levels of their analysis and discussion. We would claim that any attempt to promote understanding of urban education needs to explicitly incorporate attention to these areas as foundational concepts.

Equity

Equity is a multidimensional theoretical construct derived from concepts of fairness, social justice, and human agency articulated in several disciplines. Equity requires (Bensimon, 2007):

- Being color-conscious (as opposed to color-blind) in an affirmative sense. To be color-conscious means noticing and questioning patterns of educational outcomes that reveal unexplainable differences for minority students, viewing inequalities in the context of a history of exclusion, discrimination, and educational apartheid.
- Being aware that beliefs, expectations, and practices can result in negative racialization. Examples of racialization include attributing unequal outcomes to students' cultural predispositions and basing academic practices on assumptions about the capacity or ambitions of minority students.

Whereas much of the conversation about equity has focused on opportunities, it is at least as important to focus on equitable outcomes. In fact, equitable opportunity is a prerequisite for equitable outcome, which really is the gold standard (Benasimon, Rueda, Dowd, & Harris, 2007).

Chapters in the book address the current status of equity and issues related to helping urban educators more closely approximate this ideal. In urban contexts, which often are characterized by great inequalities, it is critically important to have a means to make these inequalities transparent in order to raise awareness of their existence among educational leaders and practitioners. Without evidence, there is less urgency to act on the problem.

Leadership

Leadership in urban settings requires specific skills, competencies, and awareness. The Leadership section of the book includes chapters that help to better understand these distinctive capacities, needs, and challenges. Urban leaders, in particular, need to be aware of issues of equity (and learning and accountability?) and how they play out in educational settings.

Equity-minded leaders ask some of the following questions: How do issues of equity impact on the students, parents, teachers, and community in which our school is located? Have I included all the stakeholders in decision-making so that decisions reflect multiple constituencies? How do schools' processes, funding, and policies reflect beliefs about equity? Are they fair and just?

Accountability

Accountability is a key force shaping the work of urban educational leaders at all levels.

Chapters in the Accountability section of the book address accountability in urban schools and colleges that serve large numbers of low-income and racial/ethnic minority groups, addressing the implications and challenges of the enhanced focus on accountability that education at all levels is facing.

They also address the competing accountability demands in urban education, accountability issues in the education of minority students, English language learners, and special education students in the era of No Child Left Behind (NCLB, 2002). Some of these chapters examine the organizational life of urban institutions, considering accountability as a tool for improving organizational improvement, focusing on developing a culture of inquiry, building internal capacity, benchmarking, and using data to obtain more equitable outcomes. The ethical issues that are increasingly being raised in the current era of accountability are also addressed.

Learning

Learning and motivation underlie the core work of educational institutions. Urban schools present both special challenges and opportunities to expand the frameworks that have traditionally guided teaching and learning practices. The increasing diversity in urban school settings along racial, ethnic, linguistic, and social class lines has provided special impetus to examine core concepts and theories that have often been assumed to reflect universal factors.

Culture, contextual influences, and related factors have assumed increasing importance and have helped expand traditional notions of teaching and learning. Chapters in this section examine the variety of ways that current work on teaching, learning, and motivation is tackling the special issues confronting urban schools. We adopt a dynamic view of learning that encompasses multiple layers— from individual cognitive and motivational factors to interpersonal factors to the social and community factors—and that emphasizes the social, contextual, and cultural roots which impact learning. This view provides the foundation for the multiple lenses through which teaching, learning, and motivation are explored here.

Conclusion

Demographic trends reflect the continuing growth of cities and so urban education will continue to increase in importance. But this is a complex terrain that requires not only specific knowledge but a map to navigate it. The contributors to this volume provide essential knowledge and we intend our organizating conceptual framework as a map. We hope, therefore, that this volume will be helpful to urban education practitioners and scholars alike.

References

Bensimon, E. M. (2007). The underestimated significance of practitioner knowledge in the scholarship of student success. *Review of Higher Education, 30*(4), 441–469.

Bensimon, E. M., Rueda, R., Dowd, A. C., & Harris III, F. (2007). Accountability, equity, and practitioner learning and change. *Metropolitan, 18*(3), 28–45.

Cohen, J. E. (2003). Human population: The next half century. *Science, 302,* 1172.

Conklin, J. (2006). *Dialogue mapping: Building shared understanding of wicked problems.* West Sussex, UK: Wiley.

Horn, R. E., & Weber, R. P. (2007). *New tools for resolving wicked problems: Mess mapping and resolution mapping processes.* Retrieved March 23, 2009, from: www.strategykinetics.com//New_Tools_For_Resolving_Wicked_Problems.pdf

Kazdin, A. E. (2009). Psychological science's contributions to a sustainable environment: Extending our reach to a grand challenge of society. *American Psychologist, 64,* 339–356.

Kincheloe, J. L., Hayes, K., Rose, K., & Anderson, P. M. (Eds.) (2006). *Praeger handbook of urban education.* Westport, CT: Greenwood Press.

Lazarus, R. J. (2009). Super wicked problems and climate change: Restraining the present to liberate the future. *Cornell Law Review, 94*(5), 1153–1234.

NCLB (2002). No Child Left Behind Act of 2001. P.L. 107-110. Washington, DC: U.S. Congress.

Noblit, G., Noblit, G. W., & Pink, W. T. (Eds.) (2008). *International handbook of urban education.* New York: Springer.

Rittel, H. W. J., & Webber, M. M. (1973). Dilemmas in a general theory of planning. *Policy Sciences, 4,* 155–169.

2

The Historical Development of Urban Education

John L. Rury

Urban schools are widely believed to represent the most vexing problems in American education today. Just the mention of urban education can conjure images of disorder, discipline issues, and low academic achievement. Middle-class urbanites often send their children to private institutions or to magnet or charter schools to avoid the city schools, which are seen as serving students left with no alternatives. In recent years education has become an important focal point of urban revitalization campaigns, aiming to reorganize institutions that customarily have been unresponsive to change. Whereas such reforms offer hope for thousands of children, the historical record does not suggest that great optimism is warranted for most of the nation's urban schools in the immediate future.

Things were not always so bad. Just 50 years ago these school systems were often held up as models, especially in the largest cities. Urban school systems have always had problems seemingly endemic to the diverse constituencies they serve and have long been marked by great extremes in quality (Rury & Mirel, 1997), but because of their size, such districts historically also possessed greater resources than their counterparts in smaller communities. Features of modern schooling taken for granted today started in urban settings: age grading, uniform textbooks, specialized classes, and summer school, among many others. Historically, big-city schools offered a wider range of courses and sometimes specialized programs such as college prep or vocational training. Teachers were paid better in the city; as a result, these schools generally got the most experienced educators. Because they often were seen as good, big-city schools attracted gifted students, many from modest backgrounds. Even if some of the worst schools were in the city, so were the very best, and most were not considered to be bad (Angus, Mirel, & Vinovskis, 1988; Mirel, 1993; Rury & Cassell, 1993).

These conditions changed, however, for reasons that were rooted in a sweeping historical process, one that also transformed many other aspects of urban life. The problems that grew from this change, moreover, have proven impervious to numerous reform campaigns. Because of this, it is crucial to understand the social and economic forces that have shaped the development of urban education in the United States and cities elsewhere in the world as well. It also is advisable to examine the changing structure of urban institutions, as they too have evolved over time. The multifaceted problems of urban schools today are the products of a continuing process of change.

This chapter examines these questions in history. What follows is a brief account of broad trends in education and urban development in the United States and other countries, with particular reference to the 20th century. As such, it is intended to preface the remainder of the book. Forces that have affected education historically, after all, have affected particular settings and shaped debates around particular issues in different ways, and this will be evident in the chapters that follow.

The Origins of Urban School Systems

To fully appreciate the changes that have occurred in city schools, it is important to begin at an earlier stage of history. Most schools today are public institutions funded by local, state, and federal governments, but the very first urban schools were private or connected to churches. In Europe, schools were concentrated in cities, towns, and villages during the medieval and early modern eras, as they were principally sponsored by the Church and located in or near cathedrals and monasteries. By and large, these institutions served a relatively small fraction of the children in these settings, although there was a great deal of variation from one national setting to another. In the countryside, the options for formal education were even more limited, and illiteracy was quite high. The advent of Protestantism began to change this pattern in the 16th and 17th centuries, as basic literacy skills became more highly valued in the wake of religious conflict and struggle. But even as schools became more numerous, they were generally urban and religious in orientation (Maynes, 1985a, 1985b).

These patterns were evident in the New World. During the North American colonial era, cities were much smaller, and all types of institutions were correspondingly diminutive in scale. Governmental obligations were few, and education was widely considered to be a religious or personal concern, depending on the colony in question. The earliest schools in North American cities appear to have been church-sponsored or were conducted by individual masters who taught for a fee. New England had the longest tradition of schools established by community or governmental authority, and these too were predominantly religious in purpose. Even in Boston, with its staunch heritage of public support for schools, private institutions of one sort or another proliferated. In most colonial cities, small proprietary schools served all segments of the population, although there certainly were distinctions in wealth and status that characterized both students and institutions. When available, public funding was intended to assist the education of the poorest students. By the time of the American Revolution, the largest cities had acquired loosely structured systems of private, church-sponsored, and publicly supported schools linked to different classes of the population. The vast majority of these institutions served White males, the sons of the middling classes. Wealthy families often employed private tutors, especially in the South. Special schools existed for Blacks and for women, but they were few in number. In the 18th century, formal education was largely a patriarchal preserve, and the best schooling was reserved for boys. All of this would change in the years to come (Grubb, 1992; Kaestle, 1973a; Rury, 2009; Schultz, 1973).

In the decades following the American Revolution and leading up to the Civil War, cities grew rapidly, propelled by incipient industrialization, improved transportation, and a rising tide of immigration. As cities became larger and more diverse, dramatic new developments reshaped education. At the start of the period, private masters and philanthropic charity schooling organizations ran urban schools, but reformers exerted considerable pressure to create public institutions so as to broaden the reach of popular education. There also was resistance to this development, particularly in the South, as traditions of popular support for formal schooling varied considerably from one region of the country to another. With time, however, industrialization and the growth of trade transformed the social profile of these and other cities, rendering the small-scale private institutions of the past seemingly archaic. The growing number of children who could not afford private schooling—running in the streets and creating mischief—made schooling a compelling issue for a growing segment of the public. In most large cities, such problems meant that the logic of tax-supported public education was difficult to resist, especially as crime began to mount and popular concerns about safety became widespread. The appearance of more poor and unskilled working-class city dwellers gave rise to a new atmosphere of diversity and cultural dissonance. The arrival of newcomers, many of them foreign-born, contributed to perceptions of growing social disquiet and discord. Schools came to be seen as an important way to reach out to these new members of the urban polity and to train their children to be useful citizens (Kaestle, 1983; Schultz, 1973).

Over time, community pride and competitive (or isomorphic) impulses helped to spread institutional forms, policies, and educational practices from one city to another. By and large, the 19th century was an era of institution building, and urban schools were in the forefront of campaigns to ensure greater social stability through education. Whether maintained by private charity groups (such as the New York Public School Society) or public agencies (like the public schools in Boston), "free" (no tuition) primary schools were first established to serve the children of the indigent classes and to teach them correct behavior and proper morality. Eventually, these institutions developed into fully articulated public educational systems, complete with high schools and sometimes even colleges, intended for all elements of the population. In some places, such as New York, the transition from charity schooling for the poor to public education for all spanned the 19th century, and was fraught with difficulty. In places that were settled later, such as St. Louis or Chicago, the transition was less abrupt, as reform advocates could point to the schools in other cities. By the end of the century, urban school systems across the country were beginning to appear quite similar in their organization and operating principles (Kaestle, 1973a; Ravitch, 1974; Rury, 2009; Troen, 1975).

Enrollments expanded rapidly as cities grew during these years, and school leaders struggled to build schools to meet escalating demand for education. As a number of studies have demonstrated, however, not all groups made full use of the opportunities afforded by the urban schools. Even when there was broad public support for these institutions, it was families in the social and cultural mainstream that came to embrace the schools most enthusiastically. Working-class children regularly left the schools when they were old enough to get jobs. There also was considerable conflict on cultural and religious grounds, especially concerning the Catholics, who eventually decided to form their own educational systems. African Americans and other racial minority groups were often excluded altogether or relegated to schools of inferior quality. Taxpayers objected to rising costs; they challenged expensive new institutions, such as public high schools, and other reforms. Gradually, however, continued agitation by reformers and shifting public attitudes resulted in change in most places. Larger numbers of families were persuaded to enroll their children in public institutions, even if many did not remain in the schools very long. Following the Civil War, the political question of public support for city schools was eventually largely resolved in favor of local school taxes, much like the larger common school movement on the national stage. Reformers continued to agitate for greater public support of the expanding school systems, both urban and rural, and new professional standards for all educators. City schools paved the way for these developments, laying the foundation for today's highly evolved educational institutions (Lazerson, 1971; Moss, 2009; Tyack, 1974).

Similar patterns were evident in other countries too, although the route to state-sponsored schools was often more direct and immediate than in the United States and less reliant upon local willingness to levy taxes to support them. In Great Britain, early sponsors of "charity schools" promoted the educational methods of Joseph Lancaster, a schoolmaster who developed a system of instruction that permitted a single adult to manage hundreds of pupils by using student "monitors" to assist with lessons for smaller groups. Such approaches helped to control costs and reinforced the socializing purposes of schooling for the masses of poor children who bedeviled cities during early industrialization. Lancaster's "monitorial" methods became popular in the United States for a time but were less appealing in countries where industrial development did not produce such widespread extremes in child welfare, such as France and Germany. State-sponsored schools had become a prevailing norm in much of Europe by the latter 19th century, although churches also remained important patrons of formal education, particularly in southern and eastern Europe. By and large, cities were centers of culture and institutional advancement, and urban schools were better developed than their rural counterparts across the continent (Goodenow & Marsden, 1992; Kaestle, 1973b; Müller, Ringer, & Simon, 1990).

In the United States, cities continued to give rise to educational innovation in the latter 19th century, as new institutional forms were developed to address changing circumstances. A new class of administrators came to lead the urban schools—professional superintendents who strove to build systems in keeping with the latest innovations sweeping the country. These men (and just a few women) created professional networks whereby information and ideas were constantly exchanged, helping to stimulate institutional development. As David Tyack and Elisabeth Hansot have noted, these leaders came from similar backgrounds in middle American culture and shared a common commitment to building orderly and efficient school systems. The challenges they faced were legion, especially the task of addressing the multifarious educational requirements of the nation's rapidly evolving urban industrial society (Tyack & Hansot, 1982). Accordingly, as city school systems grew, they became more complex and differentiated, featuring institutions for various levels of education and a growing array of specialized purposes. By 1900, for instance, most large urban school systems had established kindergartens for the youngest pupils, and grammar and high schools for those seeking higher levels of instruction, along with schools for manual training, commercial education, and any number of other particular purposes. Special schools or classes also were designated for children deemed "slow" or prone to chronic misbehavior. Innovations such as these spread quickly as administrators from different cities exchanged ideas through their nascent professional networks, and districts recruited candidates for leadership positions from other urban school systems (Beatty, 1995; Kliebard, 1995; Lazerson, 1971; Tyack, 1974).

Inevitably, institutions in the new urban systems became important sources of credentials and markers of social status, especially as schools became more integral to the economy. Perhaps the most important was the rapidly growing high school. Only a fraction of students attended secondary schools, less than 25% in most cities at the turn of the century, but these institutions came to be seen as important repositories of learning and culture. In setting entrance requirements, usually by examination, the high schools also helped raise academic standards across the districts, as lower schools strove to keep pace with shifting expectations. The most academically successful students could compete for jobs in business or prepare for a professional career. Manual training institutions and commercial high schools served different purposes, preparing youth for the skilled trades or providing basic business and clerical skills. Some big-city school districts established normal schools (basic pedagogical colleges) to meet the rapidly growing demand for teachers. In other cases, "normal departments" were attached to high schools, to provide staffing for the burgeoning elementary institutions. Curricular innovation, often under the banner of "progressive" reform, created programs of study to link schools to the job market. It was an age of increasing specialization in many spheres of life, and the urban schools helped prepare students for new roles. These institutions offered credentials that conferred status in the expanding, increasingly differentiated urban economic and social system (Kantor, 1988; Labaree, 1989; Reese, 1999; Rury, 1991).

Industrialization, Urbanization, and Bureaucracy

The later 19th and early 20th centuries were a time of especially rapid growth for most American cities, particularly in the industrial Northeast but elsewhere too. This was an era of surging industrial and urban development in American history, and the effects were manifold. The pace of immigration picked up after 1890, with as many as a million new arrivals per year, the vast majority heading to the cities. In Chicago, one of the period's great boom towns, the population doubled every decade, approaching 3 million by the 1920s. Other places expanded nearly as quickly. In the wake of such growth, simply keeping pace with enrollments was a major challenge for school districts. Questions of social and cultural diversity became ever more important, as a veritable kaleidoscope of languages and customs eventually dotted the urban landscape. New educational controversies erupted over matters of curriculum and various mechanisms for the control of schools, often affecting local political arrangements. Early teacher organizations recurrently were embroiled in such debates, fighting to increase the scope and efficacy of public education. At the same time, parochial (religious) school systems grew in parallel development to the public schools. Educating as many as 25% of the population in some cities, these schools represented an important alternative to state-sponsored institutions, particularly in the industrial Northeast. All of these developments, coupled with continuing differentiation and organizational change, made for a period of considerable ferment (Sanders, 1977; Tyack, 1974).

Among the great educational issues of the age was the political organization of urban school districts. In most cities, public schooling was originally structured in a decentralized fashion, with control often focused at the local level (usually the city ward). Eventually, in the wake of frenetic building campaigns to accommodate rising enrollments, this led to an atmosphere rife with conflict and the possibility of corruption. Local politicians doled out teaching jobs to friends and associates; other positions went to the highest bidders; and textbook publishers and suppliers offered kickbacks for lucrative orders. Practices such as these led to drastic changes in the way schooling was organized. Reformers aimed to take the schools "out of politics" by instituting highly centralized bureaucratic administrative systems. The creation of the modern superintendency in the early 20th century marked the apogee of this reform impulse, creating an ideal of impartiality, efficiency, and operational control for school leaders everywhere. In the wake of these developments—as rules and regulations were established to govern behavior of teachers and other employees, and students and parents as well—bureaucracy became the dominant ethos of educational administration. Strict financial controls and accounting procedures were devised to monitor expenditures and combat corruption; social relations were formalized as well. Standards of performance were refined for employees, and "professional" expectations of behavior came to govern day-to-day interaction at all levels of these growing systems. As these practices spread from one part of the country to another, facilitated by emergent networks of educators, they became important cultural norms (Callahan, 1962; Reese, 2002; Tyack, 1974; Tyack & Hansot, 1982).

By the early 20th century, a particular mode of organizational behavior, eventually designated as "the one best system," was becoming evident in a growing number of urban school districts. If there was an instructional corollary to these administrative changes, it was evident in the rising use of standardized testing to identify differences in student performance and to differentiate curricula in order to prepare youth for various occupational goals. Intelligence tests were introduced on a wide scale in the 1920s, and a host of other instruments to measure reading skills, mathematical competence, and even vocational preferences had become commonplace by the middle of the century. Students in city schools were assigned to tracks on the basis of such assessments, resulting in patterns of curricular differentiation that often reflected social and ethnic characteristics of the population. Children from middle- and upper-class backgrounds, most of them White and with parents born in the United States, were most prevalent in the academic tracks associated with college attendance. Other children were often assigned to vocational courses, where they prepared for the job market. This was a key element of what became known as "social efficiency," a matter of carefully aligning the curriculum to the perceived demands of the expanding economy (Garrison, 2009; Tyack, 1974).

This new bureaucratic ethos in urban education spread quickly but was hardly uniform in its impact. Reform was irregular at first, and corruption and political conflict continued to be problems in many cities. Political battles raged in some districts, as dissenting groups challenged the newly dominant management ethos. This was the case in Chicago, where teachers publicly denounced businesses that did not pay their share of school taxes and confronted administrators who turned a blind eye. In Los Angeles, teachers resisted the adoption of intelligence testing, which they depicted as an unnecessary intrusion on their professional judgment. Similar battles occurred in other places. The path of resistance was hard to sustain, however, and the newly professionalized district leaders gradually consolidated their authority. Although it was seriously tested at times—as during the financial crisis of the Great Depression, when school budgets in many cities were slashed—the prevailing "progressive" model of school administration throve in most city school systems well into the second half of the 20th century (Hogan, 1985; Mirel, 1993; Raftery, 1992; Tyack, Lowe, & Hansot, 1987; Wrigley, 1982).

In the 1920s, large American cities began to assume some of the dimensions of their contemporary form, with modern transportation systems, bureaucratic government services, and the very first stages of suburbanization. At about this time, many of the nation's city school systems entered into a prolonged period of stability in leadership and organizational character, in certain respects a golden age of urban education. As the population base of the larger cities leveled off, the educators became less preoccupied with continuing expansion and focused on gradual improvements in the quality of education, especially expanding access to secondary and higher education. It was an era characterized by high levels of public confidence in the schools, as the bureaucratic rules and standards established in the earlier period helped to ensure wide access to the schools and at least the appearance of equity in the outcomes. As greater numbers of youth graduated from high school, approaching 50% by 1950, the education system came to be seen as a vital engine of economic development, providing opportunities for advancement to children from all segments of the population. At the same time, many schools still were viewed as neighborhood institutions, and teachers and administrators who worked in them over the years came to assume an endearing familiarity. Even if minority groups were largely excluded from benefiting from the best of these schools, it was a time of considerable consensus about the purposes of public education and widespread public confidence in city schools (Dougherty, 2004; Mirel, 1993; Monkkonen, 1988; Neckerman, 2007). There was little question who was in charge of the nation's urban schools. Highly professionalized school administrators, their expertise certified by specialized university training and credentials, were rulers of the roost. It would not be long, however, before the social and political context of urban education changed profoundly, heralding a new era in the history of city schools.

Social Change and Urban Education: The Postwar Era and Beyond

As suggested earlier, the most basic factors in the development of urban school systems were demographic and economic. In the years following World War II, the social and financial profile of American cities shifted significantly. Whereas the proportion of Americans living in large cities changed little, the thrust of metropolitan development was altered by suburbanization—population movement to communities ringing the urban core. At the same time, the central cities received successive waves of new residents, many of them members of racial and ethnic minority groups and most living in poverty. Despite their relatively stable population size, in that case the nation's larger cities underwent a dramatic process of social change. The urban population was still culturally diverse, but its composition shifted and vast segments of the urban landscape were transformed by destitution and associated problems of crime and physical deterioration.

The period of relative stability in urban schooling, interrupted by the Great Depression and World War II, did not last very long. Following a hiatus during the Depression, urban development resumed with the war years. Renewed industrial expansion fueled migration, notably among African Americans from the South, although central city growth was moderated by rapidly accelerating suburbanization in the 1950s. Suburban development became one of the iconic features of the post-war era, as it occurred on an unprecedented scale. Made possible by the popular ownership of auto-mobiles and a boom in home building, suburbanization became a driving force in metropolitan development. At the same time, the introduction of mechanized farming in the South in the 1940s contributed to massive movement among the region's large rural African American population, stimulating migration to the cities. Within two decades of the war's end, about 5 million Blacks left the South to find employment in the urban centers of the North as well as the Midwest and Pacific states, and millions more moved to southern cities (Kantor & Brenzel, 1992; Kantor & Lowe, 1995, Rury, 1999).

Black migration to urban areas continued in the 1960s, and so did suburban development. Large ghetto communities developed in most major American cities, and when suburbanization accelerated in these years, it became known as "White flight." Urban school systems became highly segregated because of changing residential patterns in the cities. This led to glaring disparities within many urban districts, and dramatic protests erupted over the unequal educational resources available to various groups of students. As ever, larger numbers of middle- and upper-class Whites left their old urban neighborhoods for suburban communities, the tax base of city governments and school systems began to decline. Many of the newcomers to the cities were poor and could hardly afford to support the rising costs of high-quality urban schools. As a result, urban educational systems began to face dire budget shortfalls in the 1960s and 1970s, just as their student populations became predominantly African American or Hispanic. Schools serving poor children from these communities required a growing level of support from such external sources as state and federal grants just to maintain services. The process of suburbanization thus created two different kinds of problems for city schools. The first was the matter of segregation, or racial and cultural "isolation," which resulted from minority groups settling in certain urban neighborhoods while Whites departed. The other was financial: the declining tax base that suburbanization entailed. Consequently, at the same time that urban schools had larger numbers of disadvantaged children to teach, educators had to look farther afield to acquire the necessary resources. These issues have continued to bedevil urban districts up to the present (Rury & Mirel, 1997).

Urban school districts too often were slow to respond to the changing conditions affecting the cities they served, thus compounding these problems. Even though board members and administrators were supposed to be impartial and nonpartisan, they habitually enforced policies that reinforced existing patterns of racial and ethnic inequity in the provision of educational resources. In the South, school leaders actively opposed desegregation; even when efforts were made to improve Black schooling, true equality of education for children of all races almost never was achieved in segregated systems. In response to these conditions, activists organized hundreds of demonstrations against school inequity in cities across the country, involving tens of thousands of community members and students. These developments occurred across the decade of the 1960s and into the 1970s, marking it as an age of conflict and confrontation. The bureaucratic organization of large urban districts, however, made it difficult for school leaders to react effectively to events such as these. Long-standing rules and regulations, established to prevent corruption and fraud, often prevented school leaders from responding immediately to demands for change. Whereas organizational norms often provided convenient excuses for recalcitrant administrators and board members, they also hampered the efforts of well-intentioned reformers. Proposals for change often were stymied by procedural requirements. Meaningful reform was painfully slow to achieve, and this led to even greater frustration for poorly served urban constituencies. By the end of the decade, despite years of protest, it was clear that the schools had declined significantly in their ability to address the needs of these communities (Katznelson & Weir, 1988; Mirel, 1993; Nelson, 2005; Patterson, 2002; Ravitch, 1983).

The 1970s saw a number of developments that further aggravated these problems. First, government-enforced desegregation plans and middle-class fears about crime and deteriorating urban neighborhoods contributed to ongoing suburbanization in many parts of the country. District efforts to stem these losses with enhanced services and specialized "magnet schools" aimed at attracting academically able middle-class students produced mixed results, although many such institutions did provide clear examples of high achievement, showing that this was indeed possible in urban settings. But the general trend of declining enrollments continued. Second, although Black migration from the South slowed, new immigrant groups began to appear in major American cities in large numbers, a process facilitated by the Immigration and Naturalization Act of 1965. Like previous newcomers, many members of these groups were poor and unskilled, and they too experienced cultural and linguistic exclusion in their new homeland. The largest groups of new immigrants were those who spoke Spanish, most coming from Mexico, Central America, or the Caribbean (Puerto Rico in particular). These groups had been important minorities in American cities during earlier times, but their numbers grew especially quickly in the late 1960s and 1970s. By 1980, nearly one-fifth of New York's population was Spanish-speaking, and Chicago counted more than 400,000 residents of Hispanic heritage. Even larger numbers settled in Los Angeles, Houston, and other cities in California and the Southwest. This posed yet a new challenge to the urban schools: one of educating a diverse population of recent immigrants while also dealing with long-standing problems of racial segregation and poverty (Portes & Rumbaut, 1990, 2001).

In addition to these changes, the economic base of major cities began to shift as well. In the 1960s, manufacturing employment began to decline substantially, a process often described as "deindustrialization," and it accelerated in the 1970s and 1980s. It was concentrated in cities and occurred for a number of reasons, some of them linked to growing industrial competition from abroad. Consequently, unemployment in inner-city communities increased significantly. As social scientists have noted, the movement of industry out of American cities, whether to locations overseas or simply to the suburbs, has resulted in historically unprecedented social dislocation. The resulting loss of employment brought a host of other problems, many with dire implications for education. Since 1970, as marriages became difficult to sustain in the wake of rising unemployment, the number of female-headed households in American cities has grown enormously. Illegal drug sales, violent crime, and teen pregnancy also have increased sharply in the wake of these developments. And as the popular media have amply documented, these are issues that have had a direct bearing upon children and youth (Bluestone & Harrison, 1982; Chicago Tribune, 1988; Moran, 2005; Wilson, 1987, 1996).

An International Crisis of Urban Education

Although these developments in American cities have given rise to a host of problems in urban schools, there is evidence that institutions in other countries have been subjected to similar social and economic forces. Many larger European cities have witnessed a parallel process of urban development, which also has contributed to difficulties in the schools. In the immediate aftermath of World War II, there was extensive damage to cities across the continent. Whereas much of this was quickly repaired or restored, the rebuilding process contributed to population movement out of the central cities to nearby suburban communities. The circumstances of this shift were somewhat different from those in the United States, as Europeans constructed mass transit systems rather than highways to foster metropolitan expansion, but the effects were analogous. As native residents moved out of the cities, immigrant families moved into them, or at least into certain neighborhoods. Immigration from Africa, the Middle East, and Eastern Europe was fueled by the demand for low-wage workers in the industrial and service sectors of western European economies. By the 1970s, the result was a rising minority population, greater cultural and linguistic diversity, and escalating problems in city schools across much of the Continent. Although perhaps not quite as dramatic as the questions facing inner-city schools in many American communities, the issues confronting urban educators in many European countries became major challenges to their national systems of education (Driessen, 2000; Grace, 1984; Osborn, Broadfoor, Planel, & Pollard, 1997; van Daele & van Pouke, 1984).

Given these developments, it would not be inaccurate to speak of a global crisis in urban education in the closing decades of the 20th century. As massive population movement has brought millions of new residents to cities around the world, manifold educational questions have arisen. Poor and culturally disparate children have challenged the ability—and willingness—of existing institutions to prepare them to be productive members of their urban and national communities. And the conditions they have encountered in many instances have been quite similar. It is telling, after all, that inner-city teachers in France demonstrate the same tendency to leave their schools as exhibited by their urban counterparts in the United States. Research has confirmed that popular depictions of urban schools in a number of countries follow parallel lines, often featuring images of violence and disorder (Broadfoot, Osborn, Gilly, & Paillet, 1988; Osler & Starkey, 2005). Although much attention has been devoted to the United States and Europe, the circumstances are even more ominous in developing countries, as newcomers to the cities are often forced to live in vast squatter settlements, with virtually no public services and only the barest of educational opportunities. Whereas good urban schools exist in all large cities, many of them private schools or public institutions serving well-to-do neighborhoods, those available to the migrants and their children—going back several generations in some cases—are almost invariably poor by comparison. Insofar as education is functioning today as a global resource that is critical both to individual and collective advancement, these disparities contribute materially to the perpetuation of inequity and the economic stagnation of vast segments of the urban community (Hoffman & Centeno, 2003; Johnson, 1993; Palen, 1992; Potts, 1995; Robinson, 1991).

Given the relatively high level prosperity of the United States, it is particularly deplorable that conditions in inner-city communities here have continued to reflect these tendencies. By the 1990s, more than half of all Black children in large American cities were born in poverty, most of them in female-headed families. With the virtual collapse of urban industrial employment, Black communities that traditionally relied upon the factory for successive generations of employment found themselves in a state of crisis. These changes have had a palpable impact on urban schooling. Whereas suburbanization changed the economic and demographic profile of the city, problems once restricted to only the poorest areas became far more ubiquitous in urban America. Like their predecessors in poor immigrant areas some 60 years earlier and their counterparts in countries around the world more recently, educators in high-poverty schools worked with children contending with deprivation and neglect every day in their home lives. But because of unemployment, crime, racial discrimination, and a host of other factors, the problems today are far worse than those faced by earlier generations of urban children. In many inner-city communities of the 1990s, destitution and isolation contributed to an atmosphere of nihilistic self-destruction, where gang membership and a host of illegal activities became important elements of indigenous peer culture. Dropout rates among urban teenagers came to be as high as 50% in many large American cities, with thousands of adolescents turning to the street in the absence of any real prospects of stable and meaningful employment. Historically, the number of poor single-parent families and the severity of crime and social dislocation in these communities can be directly linked to the duration and severity of unemployment. In this fashion, the crisis in education can be linked to the economic crisis in inner-city minority communities. This remains a great challenge facing the leaders of urban educational institutions in the years ahead (Goldsmith & Blakely, 1992; Jargowsky, 1997; Lipman, 2003).

With these circumstances, the democratic tenet of the American public school tradition that education is to be shared by all members of the society is considerably less viable in today's cities than it was for previous generations of urban children. It is possible to say that there are two systems of public education in many metropolitan areas today: one for the disadvantaged and disenfranchised in the cities and the other for those who can afford to live in the suburbs or to send their children to a "good" school (Glazer, 1992; McClain, 1995; Sigelman & Henig, 2001). The cries for reform have grown increasingly strident in recent decades, with proposals ranging from voucher programs (to support the development of private alternatives to the public schools) to sweeping accountability systems based on systematic testing of student learning on a massive scale. Chicago has represented the latter strategy of reform, combining decentralization of school leadership with a strict account- ability program. Milwaukee and Cleveland have charted a different path to reform with controversial voucher plans. Creative student exchange programs between urban and suburban schools have existed on a small scale in St. Louis and other cities for many years, and the decline of desegregation campaigns may eventually encourage additional programs of this sort. Finally, charter schools have proven to be a popular strategy for urban school renewal in the past decade, reminiscent in certain respects of the magnet schools from the desegregation era, although the results of these alternative institutional forms have been uneven. As these different approaches to reform suggest, the challenges to urban schools are many and varied, and it is unclear just what the solutions to their problems ultimately will be. Without doubt, however, it will require all of the inventiveness and resources of the next generation of educators to deal with these issues (Henig, 2009; Hess, 2005; Payne, 2008; Vander Weele, 2004; Witte, 2001).

Conclusion

Urban schools in the United States have come a long way from the 18th century, when city children, if schooled at all, were educated in private schools run by individual teachers on a proprietary basis. During the 19th century public schools were established to help assimilate immigrants and the working class as well as to teach proper morality and the habits of industry. Later, these institutions were organized along the lines of bureaucratic efficiency, even while they were continually immersed in political controversy. In the later 20th century, schools were buffeted by the tides of urban change, particularly suburbanization—the movement of White middle-class families beyond the city limits. Those who remained in the inner cities have been disproportionately disadvantaged, both economi- cally and in educational terms. With the appearance of larger numbers of poor and minority students in their classrooms, urban schools have acquired an unenviable reputation for low academic achievement and high failure rates. They also have become associated with myriad social problems, ranging from drug addiction to teenage pregnancy. These generally are not issues stemming directly from the policies of urban school districts or the behavior of educators. Rather, it appears that the troubles of the big cities have become the problems of the schools.

Other factors that affected urban education in the 20th century, such as curricular reform and organizational change, have been less important than social context. These factors have affected most public schools in the United States, even those that most observers have agreed were good schools. People generally do not find the present state of urban schools to be acceptable, however. Once the proud sentinels of academic standards and vehicles of opportunity for generations of students, urban schools eventually came to represent the biggest problems in American education. Despite federal support, funding levels in urban schools continued to lag behind those in suburban school districts. Teachers have tended to choose school systems with better working conditions and more highly motivated students. And gross inequities in American education continued to sharpen as the 20th century came to an end (Lewis & Nakagawa, 1995). Similar trends have become evident in cities around the world in recent decades.

Looking at the history of urban education, it is clear that city schools have changed owing to the consequences of a historic transformation of urban life, a process that appears to have affected cities around the world. As indicated throughout the chapters that follow in this book, it is a process that has certainly shaped the development of schools in many settings and one that may lie beyond the power of individual urban communities to remedy. Given this, it seems safe to say that ending the current crisis in urban education will require monumental national resolve and a momentous change in policy to effect basic changes in the metropolitan social structure. Although education would no doubt play a vital role in such a transformation, fundamental questions of social and economic inequality must also be addressed. This is the great unfinished task facing the nation's metropolitan regions and the ongoing challenge to educators concerned with improving the lives of urban children.

References

Angus, D. L., Mirel, J., & Vinovskis, M. (1988). Historical development of age stratification in schooling. *Teachers College Record, 90,* 211–236.

Beatty, B. (1995). *Preschool education in America: The culture of young children from the colonial era to the present.* New Haven, CT: Yale University Press.

Bluestone, B., & Harrison, B. (1982). *The deindustrialization of America: Plant closings, community abandonment, and the dismantling of basic industry.* New York: Basic Books.

Broadfoot, P., Osborn, M., Gilly, M., & Paillet, A. (1988). What professional responsibility means to teachers: National contexts and classroom constants. *British Journal of Sociology of Education, 9,* 265–287.

Callahan, R. C. (1962). *Education and the cult of efficiency.* Chicago: University of Chicago Press.

Chicago Tribune (1988). *Chicago's schools: Worst in America.* Chicago: Tribune Books.

Dougherty, J. (2004). *More than one struggle: The evolution of black school reform in Milwaukee.* Chapel Hill: University of North Carolina Press.

Driessen, G. (2000). The limits of educational policy and practice? The case of ethnic minorities in the Netherlands. *Comparative Education, 36,* 55–72.

Garrison, M. J. (2009). *A measure of failure: The political origins of educational testing.* Albany: State University of New York Press.

Glazer, N. (1992). The real world of urban education. *Public Interest, 106,* 57–75.

Goldsmith, W. W., & Blakely, E. J. (1992). *Separate societies: Poverty and inequality in U.S. cities.* Philadelphia: Temple University Press.

Goodenow, R. K., & Marsden, W. E. (Eds.). (1992). *The city and education in four nations.* Cambridge, UK: Cambridge University Press.

Grace, G. (Ed.) (1984). *Education and the city: Theory, history and contemporary practice.* London: Routledge.

Grubb, F. (1992). Educational choice in the era before free public schooling: Evidence from German immigrant children in Pennsylvania, 1771–1817. *Journal of Economic History, 52,* 363–375.

Henig, J. R. (2009). *Spin cycle: How research is used in policy debates: The case of charter schools.* New York: Russell Sage Foundation.

Hess, F. M. (Ed.) (2005). *Urban school reform: Lessons from San Diego.* Cambridge, MA: Harvard Education Press.

Hoffman, K., & Centeno, M. A. (2003). The lopsided continent: Inequality in Latin America. *Annual Review of Sociology, 29,* 370–373.

Hogan, D. J. (1985). *Class and reform: School and society in Chicago, 1880–1920.* Philadelphia: University of Pennsylvania Press.

Jargowsky, P. A. (1997). *Poverty and place: Ghettos, barrios and the American city.* New York: Russell Sage Foundation.

Johnson, P. L. (1993). Education and the "new" inequality in Papua New Guinea. *Anthropology & Education Quarterly, 24,* 183–204.

Kaestle, C. F. (1973a). *Evolution of an Urban School System: New York, 1750–1850.* Cambridge, MA: Harvard University Press.

Kaestle, C. F. (1973b). *Joseph Lancaster and the Monitorial School Movement.* New York: Teachers College Press.

Kaestle, C. F. (1983). *Pillars of the republic: Common schools and American society, 1780–1860.* New York: Hill and Wang.

Kantor, H. A. (1988). *Learning to earn: School, work and vocational reform in California, 1880–1930.* Madison: University of Wisconsin Press.

Kantor, H., & Brenzel, B. (1992). Urban education and the "truly disadvantaged": The historical roots of the contemporary crisis, 1945–1990. *Teachers College Record, 94,* 278–314.

Kantor, H., & Lowe, R. (1995). Class, race, and the emergence of federal education policy: From the New Deal to the Great Society. *Educational Researcher, 24,* 4–11.

Katznelson, I., & Weir, M. (1988). *Schooling for all: Class, race and the decline of the democratic ideal.* Berkeley: University of California Press, 1988.

Kliebard, H. M. (1995). *The struggle for the American curriculum, 1893–1958.* New York: Routledge.

Labaree, D. F. (1989). *The making of an American high school: The credentials market and the central high school of Philadelphia, 1838–1939.* New Haven, CT: Yale University Press.

Lazerson, M. (1971). *The origins of urban education: Massachusetts, 1870–1930.* Cambridge, MA: Harvard University Press.

Lewis, D. A. & Nakagawa, K. (1995) *Race and educational reform in the American metropolis: A study of school decentralization.* Albany: State University of New York Press.

Lipman, P. (2003). *High stakes education: Inequality, globalization, and urban school reform.* New York: Routledge.

Maynes, M. J. (1985a). *Schooling for the people: Comparative local studies of schooling history in France and Germany, 1750–1850.* New York: Holmes & Meier.

Maynes, M. J. (1985b). *Schooling in western Europe: A social history.* Albany: State University of New York Press.

McClain, P. D. (1995). Thirty years of urban policies: Frankly, my dears, we don't give a damn! *Urban Affairs Review, 30,* 641–644.

Mirel, J. E. (1993). *The rise and fall of an urban school system, Detroit, 1907–1980.* Ann Arbor: University of Michigan Press.

Monkkonen, E. H. (1988). *America becomes urban: The development of U.S. cities & towns, 1780–1980.* Berkeley: University of California Press.

Moran, P. W. (2005). *Race, law and the desegregation of public schools.* New York: LFB Scholarly Publishing.

Moss, H. J. (2009). *Schooling citizens: The struggle for African American education in antebellum America.* Chicago: University of Chicago Press.

Müller, D., Ringer, F., & Simon, B. (Eds.) (1990). *The rise of the modern educational system: Structural change and social reproduction, 1870–1920.* Cambridge, UK: Cambridge University Press.

Neckerman, K. M. (2007). *Schools betrayed: Roots of failure in inner city education.* Chicago: University of Chicago Press.

Nelson, A. (2005). *The elusive ideal: Equal educational opportunity and the federal role in Boston's public schools, 1950–1985.* Chicago: University of Chicago Press.

Osborn, M., Broadfoot, P., Planel, C., & Pollard, A. (1997). Social class, educational opportunity and equal entitlement: Dilemmas of schooling in England and France. *Comparative Education, 33,* 375–393.

Osler, A., & Starkey, H. (2005). Violence in schools and representations of young people: A critique of government policies in France and England. *Oxford Review of Education, 31,* 195–215.

Palen, J. J. (1992). *The Urban World* (4th ed.). New York: McGraw Hill.

Patterson, J. T. (2002). *Brown v Board of Education: A civil rights milestone and its troubled legacy.* New York: Oxford University Press.

Payne, C. M. (2008). *So much reform, so little change: The persistence of failure in urban schools.* Cambridge, MA: Harvard Education Press.

Portes, A., & Rumbaut, R. G. (1990). *Immigrant America: A portrait.* Berkeley: University of California Press.

Portes, A., & Rumbaut, R. G. (2001). *Legacies: The story of the immigrant second generation.* Berkeley: University of California Press.

Potts, D. (1995). Shall we go home? Increasing urban poverty in African cities and migration processes. *The Geographical Journal, 161,* 245–264.

Raftery, J. R. (1992). *Land of fair promise: Politics and reform in Los Angeles schools, 1885–1941.* Stanford, CA: Stanford University Press.

Ravitch, D. (1974). *The great school wars, New York City, 1805–1973; A history of the public schools as battlefield of social change.* New York: Basic Books.

Ravitch, D. (1983). *The troubled crusade: American education, 1945–1980.* New York: Basic Books.

Reese, W. J. (1999). *The origins of the American high school.* New Haven, CT: Yale University Press.

Reese, W. J. (2002). *Power and the promise of school reform: Grass roots movements during the Progressive Era.* New York: Teachers College Press.

Robinson, J. C. (1991). Stumbling on two legs: Education and reform in China. *Comparative Education Review, 35,* 177–189.

Rury, J. L. (1991). *Education and women's work: Female schooling and the division of labor in Urban America, 1870–1930.* Albany: State University of New York Press.

Rury J. L. (1999). Race, space and the politics of Chicago's public schools: Benjamin Willis and the tragedy of urban education. *History of Education Quarterly, 39,* 117–142.

Rury, J. L. (2009). *Education and social change: Contours in the history of American Schooling.* New York: Routledge.

Rury, J. L., & Cassell, F. (Eds.) (1993). *Seeds of crisis: Public schooling in Milwaukee since 1920.* Madison: University of Wisconsin Press.

Rury, J. L., & Mirel, J. (1997). The political economy of urban education. *Review of Research in Education, 22,* 49–110.

Sanders, J. W. (1977). *The education of an urban minority: Catholics in Chicago, 1833–1965.* New York: Oxford University Press.

Schultz, S. K. (1973). *The culture factory: Boston's public schools, 1790–1860.* New York: Oxford University Press.

Sigelman, L., & Henig, J. R. (2001). Crossing the great divide: Race and preferences for living in the city versus the suburbs. *Urban Affairs Review, 37,* 3–18.

Troen, S. (1975). *The public and the schools: Shaping the St. Louis system, 1838–1920.* Columbia: University of Missouri Press.

Tyack, D. B. (1974). *The one best system: A history of American urban education.* Cambridge, MA: Harvard University Press.

Tyack, D. B., & Hansot, E. (1982). *Managers of virtue: Public school leadership in America, 1820–1980.* New York: Basic Books.

Tyack, D. B., Lowe, R., & Hansot, E. (1987). *Public schools in hard times: The Great Depression and recent years.* Cambridge, MA: Harvard University Press.

van Daele, H., & van Poucke, J. (1984). Urban education in Belgium. *European Journal of Education, 19,* 385–395.

Vander Weele, M. (2004). *Reclaiming our schools: The struggle for Chicago school reform.* Chicago: Loyola Press.

Wilson, W. J. (1987). *The truly disadvantaged: The inner city, the underclass, and public policy.* Chicago: University of Chicago Press.

Wilson, W. J. (1996). *When work disappears: The world of the new urban poor.* New York: Knopf.

Witte, J. F. (2001). *The market approach to school reform: An analysis of America's first voucher program.* Princeton, NJ: Princeton University Press.

Wrigley, J. (1982). *Class, politics and Chicago's public schools, 1900–1950.* New Brunswick, NJ: Rutgers University Press.

3

Prototypic Features of Urban Education

Rodney Goodyear, Terence J. G. Tracey, Charles D. Claiborn,
James W. Lichtenberg, Bruce E. Wampold, and Matthew Gutierrez

Some concepts are difficult to define, yet we still "know" what they mean. This was the point of Justice Potter Stewart's opinion in *Jacobellis* v. *Ohio*, which included the assertion that "I shall not today attempt further to define the kinds of material I understand to be embraced within that shorthand description [hard-core pornography]; and perhaps could never succeed in intelligibly doing so. *But I know it when I see it*, and the motion picture involved in this case is not that."

Most concepts—pornography in that particular case—have certain recognizable, characteristic features. This is the basis for prototype theory, which cognitive psychologists (e.g., Rosch, 1973; for reviews, see Hororwitz & Turan, 2008; Mervis & Rosch, 1981) have developed to address difficult-to-define concepts, of which urban education is one. It "remains a difficult concept to truly define" (Obiakor & Beachum, 2005, p. 9).

Many university programs prepare teachers and administrators to work with students in urban schools (i.e., those in cities of more than 250,000 population) (U.S. Department of Education, 2009). As well, urban education is the focus both of a growing literature and of policy and research work being conducted in more than 18 university-based centers or institutes. All this requires some consensus about what urban education is, even if only at an implicit level. That consensus likely would be around some of urban education's attributes, which include schools that "typically are diverse, characterized by large enrollments and complexity, many struggling with growth . . . [and those schools] often serve students representing many ethnic minorities, multiple languages, and have a greater concentration of the poor" (Heindel, 2005, p. 1).

It is hard to move beyond this description of context to an actual definition of urban education, for it is a fuzzy concept. By this, we mean that its boundaries are not fixed and most of its features are also apparent to some degree in categories that are "not urban education." This is not to say, though, that we agree with Kress's assertion that "'Urban education' means something different to everyone based on their gender, race, sexual orientation, nationality, culture, socioeconomic status, age, or profession" (Kress, 2006, p. 324). This stance precludes a coherent body of knowledge that might guide urban educators, researchers, and policymakers, but in making that assertion, she clearly underscores the definitional challenges that the concept of urban education poses.

We have therefore employed a prototype perspective as a means of illuminating urban education as a concept. To do this, we asked urban education experts to identify urban education prototypes—

that is, to present its "clearest cases or best examples" (Russell & Fehr, 1994, p. 187). An advantage of this approach is that prototypes reflect how people think and talk about concepts and so are "experience near." This is an approach that Hofsess and Tracey (2010) recently used, for example, to examine the psychotherapeutic concept of countertransference.

Prototype Analysis

Cognitive psychologists note that a concept can have two levels of prototypes: one is the level of *exemplars* and the other that of *features*. To illustrate, consider the concept of "dog." Exemplars (also known as examples, instances, cases, or members) might include specific breeds of dogs: Doberman, dachshund, cocker spaniel, and poodle, for example. In the classic study of exemplars-as-prototype, Rosch (1973) used apples, figs, pears, and oranges as exemplars of the category "fruit" and found that people rated apples as better examples of that category than figs; that is, they were more prototypical of fruit.

The second level of prototype is that of *features* (also known as elements, indicators, and characteristics). Prototypic features of "dog" might be either physical or behavioral. Physical features would include being four-legged carnivores, having a tail, being furred, and having a keen sense of smell. Behavioral features would include, for example, running in packs in which there are clearly defined social hierarchies and having evolved to behave interdependently with humans. Fehr (2004) provides an example of a feature-as-prototype study in a study of intimacy expectations in same-sex friendships. It was found, for example, that both men and women regarded as prototypic of that concept such behaviors as "If I need to talk, my friend will listen," "If I am in trouble, my friend will help me," and "If someone was insulting me or saying negative things behind my back, my friend would stick up for me." On the other hand, those students regarded as much less prototypic such behaviors as "If I need money, my friend will lend it to me," and "If I am sad, my friend is sad too."

Prototypes, whether at the level of exemplars or of features, will differ in how central they are to the concept they represent: they will range from those that are highly characteristic, or prototypic, of the concept through those that are less so—and eventually so much less so that they become nonprototypic. Put more simply, exemplars and features vary in their degree of membership in the particular category (see, e.g., Russell & Fehr, 1994).

It also is possible for a particular concept to have features that one group of experts would consider prototypic of their particular domain but also that experts in another domain would consider prototypic of *their* domain. For example, as we show in the data we report further on, whereas persistent poverty is often considered a characteristic of urban education, it is *also* a characteristic of rural education. When this sort of thing occurs, the particular feature cannot actually be considered a characteristic of the prototype. This is a familiar concept in the measurement literature, where a measure is said to have construct validity if it (a) correlates highly with other measures of that construct (convergent validity) but (b) does *not* correlate substantially with an unrelated construct (discriminant validity) (Campell & Fiske, 1959). The relationship of persistent poverty to both urban and rural education violates the second of those assumptions.

In summary, our purpose in this chapter is to use prototype analysis as a means to characterize urban education. We accomplished this by submitting various features to two panels, one consisting of urban educators and the other of rural educators. Each panel was asked to rate each of the listed features in terms of its prototypicality for their particular domain. As a contrast and in order to examine discriminant validity, we also employed some features that we believed would be characteristic of rural education and then asked rural education experts to rate the prototypicality of all items for their domain.

Method

We employed two groups of participants. The first were experts in urban education; the second, experts in rural education.

Urban Education Expert Panel

The 37 (15 female, 22 male) urban education experts reported that their current positions were as follows: Professor ($N = 18$), presidential professor ($N = 1$), associate professor ($N = 4$), assistant professor ($N = 8$), clinical professor ($N = 2$), postdoc ($N = 1$), K–12 program manager ($N = 1$), former large-city superintendent ($N = 1$). One provided no information about their current position. In addition, one of these reported being a dean and another the director of an urban education research center. Most ($N = 27$) were European American, the rest reported that they were Latino ($N = 5$), African American ($N = 1$), Asian American ($N = 1$), and other ($N = 3$).

Rural Education Expert Panel

This panel of 20 (9 female, 11 male) comprised 13 university faculty at various ranks in disciplines including rural sociology, mathematics education, special education, and education leadership, 5 K–12 administrators (1 superintendent, 3 principals, 1 "administrator"), 1 director of a nonprofit consulting firm, and one provided no job information. One was "Australian"; 19, European American.

Measure

Participants were asked to respond to 55 features, rating each in the extent to which it seemed indicative of either urban or rural education. Those ratings were on an 8-point scale, anchored by 1 = "Not at all a manifestation of urban education" at one end and 8 = "Definitely a manifestation of urban education" at the other (for the rural panel, the word *urban* in these scale anchors was replaced by *rural*). Refer to Table 3.1 for a list of these features.

We developed a list of features that we believed would be prototypic of urban education, but to control for acquiescence (i.e., the tendency to respond affirmatively to items), we also generated peripheral and unrelated features. Creating a measure with a range of features in terms of their prototypicality enabled both the generation of the prototype and participant discernment of the prototype, which was essential to assess individual differences in the availability of the prototype. We were guided by Rosch's (1973, 1975) method in developing these items.

Features Predicted to be Prototypic of Urban Education

We first generated a list of features of urban education by sampling the extant literature and consulting a small group of urban educators. Tables of contents of the past decade of the journal *Urban Education* were examined for examples. This was done as well with the two *Handbooks* (Kincheloe, Hayes, Rose, & Anderson, 2006; Noblit, Noblit, & Pink, 2008). In addition, specific articles and chapters provided their own lists of topics addressed by urban educators.

To ensure that we captured behaviors of urban educators that might not have received attention in the literature we had reviewed, we obtained input from five people who were deemed urban education experts on the basis of either their publication record or their leadership of a university-based urban education training program, institute, or center. Each completed a demographic form and an open-ended questionnaire in which they were asked to (1) review the 36 features we so far had generated from the literature and (2) suggest others that they thought would be important. This resulted in the elimination of some features, the modification of others, and then the addition of several others. These processes resulted in 26 of the final set of 55 features (those indicated as prototypical in Table 3.1).

Features Predicted to be Peripheral to Urban Education

In addition, a list of examples was generated that could be considered peripheral examples using the criterion that the example must reflect a possible but not overtly obvious manifestation of urban education. For example, examples were included that were considered to be indicative of urban education in some circumstances. Such peripheral examples included "Working under the pressures of high-stakes testing," and "Working in a district in which student bullying of all types (emotional, verbal, physical) is a notable problem." Fifteen of the final 55 features were those we predicted would be peripheral. Those are so indicated in Table 3.1.

Features Predicted to be Unrelated to Urban Education

Items characteristic of rural education were used in the development of unrelated items, i.e., items expected to be low in prototypicality. These were identified via a Google search, using the terms *rural education problems, rural education issues,* and *rural education characteristics,* and from material in published articles (e.g., Herzog & Pittman, 1995; Johnson & Strange, 2009). As well, we consulted with a rural education expert who suggested several additional items. This process resulted in 14 features that we anticipated would be unique to rural education and nonprototypic of urban education (see Table 3.1 for a list of those features). Examples included "Working in a district in which class sizes are small" and "Working in a district in which teachers know their students personally."

Procedure

The pool of urban education experts included all who were authors in this text as well as faculty in university centers and academic programs that were explicitly claiming urban education focus. The pool of rural education experts included people serving on editorial boards of rural education journals as well as some rural school administrators. Each was sent an email explaining the purpose of the study and asking his or her participation. The message included a link to our web-based survey. One follow-up email was sent as a reminder in order to increase the response rate.

Results

For each of the 55 features, means and standard deviations were calculated for the prototypicality ratings made by (1) the urban and (3) the rural education experts. Effect size (Cohen's d) was calculated for the urban versus rural ratings for each feature. These results are presented in Table 3.1, which is organized by urban educator ratings, so that the feature they rated as most prototypic of urban education (*Teaching in linguistically diverse classrooms*) is listed first and then other features, following in decreasing order of magnitude of ratings.

There are no set rules for determining where on the rating continuum to decide which features no longer qualify as prototypic. One logical strategy would be to look for a natural break in the data, but when the data were plotted, the trend was generally linear, with no distinct break until about item 50. Therefore, given no clear break in the data, it probably is safe to assert that features above the median are prototypic of urban education. The median rating by urban education experts was 5.38 (M = 5.09; SD = 1.93).

In general, features that were rated as highly prototypic for urban education were rated as low in prototypicality for rural education and vice versa. Moreover, the differences between the two groups were greatest at the extremes of the urban education scores. Thus when effect sizes were considered as the measure of difference, the 10 items that were *most* prototypic of urban education had a mean effect size of 1.78 (i.e., of comparisons of urban versus rural education) and the 10 items that were

Table 3.1 Descriptive Statistics for Ratings of Prototypicality of Items to Urban and Rural Education

	Urban			Rural			Effect size[1]	Initial prediction
	N	M	SD	N	M	SD		
Teaching in linguistically diverse classrooms	37	6.67	1.62	20	2.50	1.64	2.55	Prototypic
Teaching in racially and ethnically diverse classrooms	37	6.47	2.09	20	3.05	1.70	1.80	Prototypic
Teaching students who are at high risk of dropping out before graduation	37	6.47	1.86	20	3.35	1.87	1.67	Prototypic
Teaching students whose parents are non-English-speaking	37	6.42	1.73	20	2.95	1.47	2.16	Prototypic
Working in a district in which it is difficult to attract qualified teachers	37	6.36	1.91	20	4.95	2.11	2.24	Prototypic
Working in a district with a large central bureaucracy	37	6.33	2.03	19	2.26	1.73	2.16	Prototypic
Working in a community with relatively high levels of persistent poverty	37	6.31	2.16	20	5.40	2.09	0.43	Peripheral
Working in a district with relatively high rates of suspensions and expulsions	37	6.28	1.47	20	2.50	1.50	2.55	Prototypic
Working in a district in which it is difficult to retain qualified teachers	37	6.28	2.09	20	4.60	2.44	0.74	Peripheral
Working in a district where African American students are overidentified for special education	37	6.25	1.90	19	3.11	2.31	1.48	Peripheral
Working in a community in which many students live in overcrowded conditions	37	6.22	1.87	20	2.60	1.27	2.25	Prototypic
Working in a district in which there are relatively high levels of student mobility	37	6.19	2.05	20	4.10	2.00	1.03	Prototypic
Working with students whose families are immigrants	35	6.17	1.95	20	3.60	1.73	1.40	Prototypic
Working in a district with high levels of teacher burnout	37	6.17	1.98	20	3.65	1.46	1.45	Prototypic
Working in a highly regulated bureaucracy	36	6.11	2.13	20	3.05	1.67	1.60	Prototypic
Working in a district with relatively high rates of truancy	36	6.03	1.54	14	3.00	1.66	1.95	Prototypic
Working with students with irregular school attendance	37	5.94	1.74	20	3.30	1.75	1.51	Prototypic
Working in a district in which physical violence (gang and otherwise) is a notable problem	37	5.89	1.82	20	2.40	1.47	2.11	Prototypic
Working in a district in which class sizes are large	37	5.86	1.85	20	2.25	1.55	2.11	Prototypic
Working in a district in which there is an achievement gap between the races	37	5.72	2.28	20	3.60	2.26	0.93	Peripheral
Working in a district in which administrators oversee a large staff	37	5.61	2.00	20	2.70	2.15	1.39	Prototypic
Working with students who live in single-parent households	37	5.56	2.01	20	3.70	1.59	1.02	Peripheral
Working in a district with complex, collectively bargained terms and conditions	35	5.50	2.26	20	2.70	1.92	1.34	Prototypic
Teaching in a district that is inadequately funded	37	5.47	2.47	20	4.75	2.38	0.29	Peripheral
Working with outdated, insufficient resources	35	5.46	1.79	20	4.65	2.01	0.42	Prototypic
Working in a district with low college enrollment rates	35	5.43	2.09	20	4.75	2.12	0.32	Prototypic
Working in a district with a higher-than-average rate of superintendent turnover	37	5.39	2.14	20	3.70	2.08	0.80	Prototypic
Working in a district in which parental involvement is limited	37	5.39	1.87	20	3.15	1.39	1.36	Prototypic
Working in a setting with relatively high levels of teacher absenteeism	35	5.29	1.79	20	2.30	1.34	1.89	Prototypic
Working in a district that shows the effects of institutional racism	37	5.19	2.08	19	3.95	1.96	0.61	Peripheral
Working under a highly politicized school board	35	5.17	2.16	20	4.35	2.52	0.39	Peripheral
Working with students whose families are unemployed	37	5.17	2.04	20	3.70	1.87	0.75	Prototypic

Table 3.1 Continued

	Urban			Rural			Effect size[1]	Initial prediction
	N	M	SD	N	M	SD		
Working in a district in which teen pregnancy is a notable problem	37	5.11	2.07	20	3.55	1.82	0.80	Peripheral
Working under the pressures of high-stakes testing	35	5.03	2.60	20	4.30	2.13	0.31	Peripheral
Teaching students who often behave disrespectfully	37	4.92	1.96	20	2.80	1.58	1.19	Peripheral
Teaching within the context of a narrowing curriculum	37	4.86	2.27	20	4.05	1.82	0.39	Peripheral
Teaching students who lack confidence in their ability to be successful	37	4.81	1.86	20	3.30	1.87	0.81	Prototypic
Working in a community where students have limited access at home to Internet and digital resources	37	4.78	1.97	20	5.05	1.32	0.16	Prototypic
Working in a district that offers students limited exposure to the broad range of careers	37	4.61	1.86	20	5.50	1.67	0.51	Unrelated
Working in a district in which student substance abuse is a problem	37	4.53	1.83	19	4.11	1.73	0.24	Peripheral
Working in a district in which student bullying of all types (emotional, verbal, physical) is a notable problem	37	4.47	1.90	20	3.35	2.03	0.57	Peripheral
Working in a district in which administrators have multiple roles	37	4.36	2.29	20	6.20	1.85	0.88	Unrelated
Working in a district that is slow to incorporate technological innovations	37	4.25	1.70	20	4.20	1.94	0.03	Peripheral
Working in a district with relatively few social service agencies to serve troubled students	37	4.14	2.06	20	5.10	2.00	0.48	Unrelated
Working in a district in which students live far apart from each other and the school	37	4.11	2.01	19	6.89	1.05	1.74	Unrelated
Teaching students who have a sense of connection to or roots in their community	37	3.94	1.90	20	6.30	1.59	1.34	Unrelated
Working in a district in which school buildings are used by the community	37	3.86	2.09	20	5.75	1.86	0.95	Unrelated
Working with a school board that has a narrow conception of what education should include	35	3.71	1.95	20	5.15	1.46	0.84	Unrelated
Working in a district in which teachers know their students personally	37	3.69	1.82	19	7.32	1.00	2.48	Unrelated
Working in a district geographically removed from cultural institutions in the arts and sciences	35	3.29	1.92	20	6.15	1.98	1.46	Unrelated
Working in a district in which athletics are central to school life	37	3.28	1.91	19	5.21	2.32	0.91	Unrelated
Working in a district in which there are high levels of parental involvement	37	3.03	1.36	20	4.25	1.77	0.77	Unrelated
Working in a community dominated by conservative religious traditions	37	2.81	1.97	20	5.30	1.95	1.29	Unrelated
Working in a district in which class sizes are small	35	2.17	1.25	20	5.80	1.79	2.34	Unrelated
Working in a district in which students are predominantly White	37	1.72	0.85	20	6.00	1.89	2.92	Unrelated

Note. Urban signifies ratings done by urban education experts of the degree of prototypicality of each feature to the concept of urban education; *rural* signifies ratings done by rural education experts of the degree of prototypicality of each feature to the concept of rural education.

1 Effect size = Cohen's *d*.

least prototypic of urban education had a mean effect size of 1.53. But the 10 items from the middle of the grouping (items 23 to 32) had a mean effect size of 0.76, indicating much less difference between the two groups. In short, when items were scored as highly prototypic of urban education, they generally were scored as having low prototypicality for rural education, and vice versa.

Also, the ratings generally corresponded to our predictions with respect to whether the features would be prototypic, peripheral, or unrelated to urban education. There were, though, a few items that we predicted would be peripheral that turned out to be more prototypic (e.g., "Working in a district in which there is an achievement gap between the races") and others which we predicted would be prototypic but that turned out to be more peripheral (e.g., "Working in a community where students have limited access at home to Internet and digital resources").

The items most prototypic of urban education were generally low in prototypicality for rural education. One notable difference was the feature "Working in a community with relatively high levels of persistent poverty." Its relatively small effect size (.43) within the context of this study suggests that even though this item was rated by our experts as highly prototypic of urban education, it is *also* perceived as generally prototypic of rural education as well, and so by definition could not be considered a prototypic feature of either. Otherwise, the data provided relatively clear evidence that rural and urban education can be relatively clearly differentiated. The obtained between-group (urban versus rural) correlation for the items' mean scores was −.66.

The features most prototypic of rural education, which were at the same time rated low in prototypicality for urban education, were as listed below:

- Working in a district in which teachers know their students personally.
- Working in a district in which students live far apart from each other and the school.
- Teaching students who have a sense of connection to or roots in their community.
- Working in a district in which administrators have multiple roles.
- Working in a district geographically removed from cultural institutions in the arts and sciences.

Discussion

In many respects, this was a very simple study. But it is the first to employ an empiric approach to examine the nature of urban education. Its unique contribution was to establish that urban education experts *were* able to discriminate prototypic features of urban education; whereas experts may struggle to define urban education, they *do* recognize it when they see it.

It is possible to discern several intuitive clusters of urban education features. For example, racial, ethnic, and linguistic diversity were among the most prototypic features of urban education (contrasted with rural education, whose experts ascribed a relatively high prototypic score to working in a district where students are primarily White). Another cluster concerned working with students whose families are immigrants and who live in overcrowded conditions. Two other intuitive clusters were (1) difficulties attracting and retaining qualified teachers owing to teacher burnout and (2) working in highly regulated large central bureaucracies.

The obvious caveats had to do with sample size and then representativeness. This is particularly true of the smaller sample of rural education experts, but for both groups there is the reasonable question of how much a larger sample would have increased reliability or changed the results. As well, we used particular sampling strategies, and perhaps different strategies would have resulted in samples with different perspectives about what is prototypic about urban or rural education.

It can be useful as well to consider those features that had the smallest urban-versus-rural effect sizes, as these could be understood as the features that were most similar across the two settings.

Working (1) under the pressures of high-stakes testing and (2) within the context of a narrowing curriculum were two such issues, ones that no doubt are related. There also were similarities with respect to the adequacy of resources, Internet access, and adoption of technological innovations. And the two areas were similar as well, with two student-related issues: concerns about substance abuse and about relatively low college enrollment rates. It would be interesting to examine the proto-typicality of these features to suburban schools as well to see how common they are across this third major setting.

We do want to address one important caveat: Whereas urban education is a global issue, our study really generalizes only to the United States. Therefore, one extension of this study would be to address those features of urban education that generalize more globally. For example, two of the three highest-rated items in this study concerned linguistic diversity (among parents as well as within the classroom), which probably has special salience because the United States traditionally has been thought of as a melting pot. In the Los Angeles Unified School District, for example, students speak approximately 90 languages. Diversity would have varying degrees of salience to European urban education but probably only minimally so in China, which has huge urban areas.

Haberman (undated) observed that, "In American parlance, 'God's country' is used to refer to rural areas or nature preserves, not cities . . . [and] negative associations with the term urban profoundly affect education and shape the nature of urban schooling." As is true with most generalizations, this one oversimplifies, for urban education has positive features as well as negative ones—and rural education has negative features as well.

It is true that many of the prototypic features of urban education that we found did seem to have negative connotations. In fact, several of our respondents offered the criticism that our list of features seemed grounded in a deficit model. It is true that there were potential positive features that did not make it to our list. For example, the relatively low score for urban typicality for "Working in a district geographically removed from cultural institutions" could be seen as affirming that urban educators *do* have access to cultural institutions.

However, we would note that our focus was on that which is *characteristic* of urban education versus what is desirable. For example, as much as we would like to believe that it is prototypic of urban education that teachers are challenging racism and its effects or are working to involve parents in their children's schooling, this seems at this point to be aspirational rather than typical.

A follow-up study would be to examine what urban educators *should* be doing (i.e., ideal behavior). We could imagine that such a list might include providing culturally responsive pedagogy and curricula, combating racism and sexism and their effects, being an advocate for marginalized groups, instilling hope and resilience in students who have been marginalized, working to prevent school violence and bullying, working to counteract the personal and educational effects of poverty, helping students develop positive racial and ethnic identities, exercising leadership in school desegregation, facilitating school involvement in families of diverse populations, and so on.

These are the sorts of things that we hope effective urban educators will do, i.e., we want urban educators "To create urban schools which really teach students, which reflects the pluralism of the society, which serve the quest or social justice—this is a task which will take persistent imagination, wisdom, and will" (Tyack, 1974, p. 291).

Author Note

Appreciations to Panel 1 consultants whose feedback helped refine the items: David Bloomfield (City University of New York), Jennifer Brooks (Texas Christian University), Myron Dembo (University of Southern California), Pedro Noguera (New York University), and Jana Noel (California State University, Sacramento).

References

Campell, D. T., & Fiske, D. W. (1959). Convergent and discriminant validation by the multitrait-multimethod matrix. *Psychological Bulletin, 56,* 81 –105.

Fehr, B. (2004). Intimacy expectations in same-sex friendships: A prototype interaction-pattern model. *Journal of Personality and Social Psychology, 86,* 265–284.

Haberman, M. (undated). Urban education: Students and structure, special challenges, characteristics of successful urban programs. In *Education Encyclopedia.* StateUniversity.com. Retrieved February 21, 2010 from: http://education.state university.com/pages/2524/Urban-Education.html

Heindel, A. J. (2005). Urban education defined. Unpublished document. Retrieved February 21, 2010 from: http://myweb.usf. edu/~aheindel/UE_UrbanEducationDefined.doc

Herzog, M. J. R., & Pittman, R. B. (1995). Home, family, and community: Ingredients in the rural education equation. *Phi Delta Kappan, 77,* 113–118.

Hofsess, C. D., & Tracey, T. J. G. (2010). Countertransference as a prototype: The development of a measure. *Journal of Counseling Psychology, 57,* 52–67.

Hororwitz, L. M., & Turan, B. (2008). Prototypes and personal templates: Collective wisdom and individual differences. *Psychological Review, 115*(4), 1054–1068.

Johnson, J., & Strange, M. (2009). *Why rural matters 2009: State and regional challenges and opportunities.* Arlington, VA: Rural School and Community Trust. Retrieved March 24, 2010 from: http://files.ruraledu.org/wrm09/WRM09.pdf

Kincheloe, J. L., Hayes, K., Rose, K., & Anderson, P. M. (Eds.). (2006). *The Praeger handbook of urban education.* Westport, CT: Greenwood Press.

Kress, T. (2006). Purple leaves and charley horses: The dichotomous definition of urban education. In J. L. Kincheloe, K. Hayes, K. Rose, & P. M. Anderson (Eds.), *The Praeger handbook of urban education* (pp. 324–329). Westport, CT: Greenwood Press.

Mervis, C. B., & Rosch, E. (1981). Categorization of natural objects. *Annual Review of Psychology, 32,* 89–115.

Noblit, G., Noblit, G. W., & Pink, W. T. (Eds.) (2008). *International handbook of urban education.* New York: Springer.

Obiakor, F. E., & Beachum, F. D. (2005). Urban education: The quest for democracy, equity, and excellence. In F. E. Obiakor & F. D. Beachum (Eds.), *Urban education for the 21st century: Research, issues, and perspectives* (pp. 3–19). Springfield, IL: Charles C. Thomas.

Rosch, E. H. (1973). Natural categories. *Cognitive Psychology, 4,* 328–350.

Rosch, E. H. (1975). Cognitive representation of semantic categories. *Journal of Experimental Psychology General, 104,* 192–233.

Russell, J. A., & Fehr, B. (1994). Fuzzy concepts in a fuzzy hierarchy: Varieties of anger. *Journal of Personality and Social Psychology, 67,* 186–205.

Tyack, D. B. (1974). *The one best system: A history of American urban education.* Cambridge, MA: Harvard University Press.

U.S. Department of Education (2009). *Digest of education statistics: 2008.* Washington, DC: National Center for Education Statistics, Institute for Education Sciences. Retrieved February 27, 2010 from: http://nces.ed.gov/programs/digest/d08/index.asp

4

The Sociology of Urban Education

Alan R. Sadovnik and Tara B. Davidson

Urban education has been the subject of ongoing discussion over the last 40 years, with vigorous debate over policies aimed at urban school improvement. As urban areas became increasingly poor and segregated (see Chapter 14, this volume), their school systems have come to mirror the problems of urban poverty, including low student achievement, high student mobility, high dropout rates, and high levels of school failure. A significant percentage of urban schools have been identified as in need of improvement under federal No Child Left Behind Act (2002) guidelines, with large city school systems having dropout rates at or above 40% and student achievement well below 50% proficiency in mathematics and reading (U.S. Department of Education, 2009a, 2009b). Although rural and many suburban schools have similar problems, urban schools represent the most serious challenges.

Over the past four decades, affluent White families have either moved to the suburbs or sent their children to private schools. This is clear from data presented in Table 4.1, obtained from the National Center for Education Statistics interactive Web site (NCES, available at: http://nces.ed.gov/pub search/pubsinfo.asp?pubid=2009020) for eight of the largest U.S. cities. Proportions of the various ethnic minority groups differ from city to city, so that African Americans make up the largest group in some cities (e.g., Baltimore, Detroit, and Washington, DC) and Hispanics the largest group in others (e.g., Los Angeles and Miami). However, the low representation of White students characterizes all eight cities.

Given the salience of race, ethnicity, and socioeconomic status (SES) to urban education, we begin this chapter by documenting the achievement and educational attainment gaps as well as investment gaps that exist as a function of these two variables. We then draw from the sociology of education literature to explore factors that seem to affect these gaps and then offer suggested remedies. We conclude by invoking a sociological lens to consider both the limits and possibilities of reform.

Achievement and Attainment Gaps by Ethnicity and SES

The gaps include higher academic achievement by high-income students compared with low-income students; White and Asian American students compared with African American and Hispanic students, even when controlling for SES; and male students compared with female students. There have been some improvements since the 1960s, with the gender gap closing dramatically. In some

Table 4.1 Enrollments of Eight U.S. City School Districts by Student Ethnicity, 2006–2007

	% Asian	% African American	% Hispanic	% White
Baltimore	0.7	89.2	2.1	7.7
Chicago	3.3	49.1	39.2	8.3
Detroit	0.8	90.0	6.4	2.4
Houston	3.1	29.2	59.3	8.3
Los Angeles	6.2	11.1	73.5	8.8
Miami	1.2	27.2	62.0	9.5
New York	13.7	32.2	39.4	14.2
Philadelphia	5.7	64.4	16.4	13.2
Washington, DC	1.8	82.1	10.3	5.7

cases, women have been outperforming men, while social class, race, and ethnic differences lessened, at least until 1988. However, the social class, race, and ethnic achievement gap widened thereafter, despite continued educational policies aimed at reducing them. Data from the National Assessment of Educational Progress (U.S. Department of Education, 2009b) illustrate these achievement gaps.

Achievement Gaps and Ethnicity

Gaps in achievement test score began to narrow between Whites and both African American and Hispanic students on the National Assessment of Educational Progress (NAEP) reading and math tests during the early 1970s through the mid- to late 1980s. But then they began once again to widen. For example, the gap between African American and White 17-year-olds on the reading test was 21 points in 1988 but rose to 32 points in 1999. A similar trend occurred with respect to math scores, where the gap between African American and White 17-year-olds was 20 points in 1990 but then rose to 31 points in 1999 (U.S. Department of Education, 2000). Based on 2009 data from the NAEP, African American and Hispanic 17-year-olds do math at the same levels as White 13-year-olds, and African American and Hispanic 17-year-olds read at the same levels as White 13-year-olds.

There is some more recent positive news in that between 1999 and 2008, the gap between White students and African American and Hispanic 4th-grade students narrowed to less than 20 points on the NAEP reading and math exams (Education Trust, 2010a), and at the 8th-grade level, the gap narrowed slightly in reading and narrowed for all groups in math.

Unfortunately, reading and math scores of 17-year-olds have remained flat and even declined slightly since 1996. In fact, the achievement gaps at the 12th-grade level in reading have widened since 1988 while remaining mostly flat in math.

Achievement Gaps and SES

With respect to social class differences, on grade 4 reading achievement in 2004, the average scale scores of poor and nonpoor students were approximately 196 and 232, respectively; on grade 8 mathematics achievement, these scores were 259 and 286 (Education Trust, 2004).

The good news is that between 1996 and 2007, the percentage of low-income students scoring at the proficient or advanced proficient level has increased from 7% to 22%, and the number of students scoring below the basic level has decreased from 60% to 30% on the 4th-grade math NAEP exam (Education Trust, 2009, 2010b). In 2009, in all states except Connecticut, the gap between lower- and higher-income groups was smaller or not measurably different from the U.S. national average on the 8th-grade NAEP math exam (Education Trust, 2010a, 2010b, 2010c). Overall, national student achievement increased from 2003 to 2009 on the 8th-grade NAEP math exam for both lower- and higher-income students (Education Trust, 2010a, 2010b).

Educational Attainment Gaps by Ethnicity and SES

In 2001, the four-year high school graduation rate for all students was 70%, but there were considerable differences between ethnic groups. Graduation rates broken out by group were: Asian, 79%; White, 72%; Native American, 54%; Hispanic, 52%; and African American, 51% (Education Trust, 2004).

The story of college graduation rates is similar. For all students who began college as freshmen, 55% graduated in 2002. But broken out by group, these rates were: Asian, 64%; White, 59%; African American, 40%; and Hispanic, 36%. When graduation rates were considered for the longer term of six years, those rates were: Asian, 94%; White, 90%; African American, 81%; and Hispanic, 63% (U.S. Bureau of the Census, 2002).

Table 4.2 provides a summary of several levels of educational attainment reached by African American, Hispanic, and White 24-year-olds. The reported percentages were based on those in each group who had entered the educational system in kindergarten.

SES is also a predictor of attainment, for at age 26, some 60% of young people from high-income families graduate from college, versus 7% of young people from low-income families (Mortenson, 1997). The reasons for the differences in achievement and educational attainment are complex, including factors both outside and inside the schools. Rothstein (2004) argued that much of the achievement gap can be accounted for by factors related to poverty, including inadequate housing, health care, and environmental problems, including lead paint and other toxins in the urban environment. Although this is the case, it is undoubtedly also true that factors within urban schools contribute to low achievement. These include unequal funding, unqualified teachers, low expectations and dumbed-down curricula, as well as high turnover of teachers and principals.

Investment Gaps

In 2001, the United States had an effective funding gap of $773 per student between the highest and lowest poverty districts and a gap of $1,122 between high-minority and low-minority school districts (Education Trust, 2010d). These gaps exist country-wide: across the country, the highest-poverty districts in 36 states receive less funding than the lowest-poverty districts (Education Trust, 2009, 2010d). These gaps vary by state, with some, such as Illinois and New York, having the largest funding gaps at more than $2,000 per student, and Alabama, Arizona, Louisiana, Michigan, Pennsylvania, and Texas at more than $900 per student (Education Trust, 2009). These funding gaps are most pronounced between urban and suburban districts. Whereas some states, most notably New Jersey, have eliminated these differences through court intervention, children in most U.S. cities receive considerably less funding than their suburban neighbors.

Table 4.2 Relative Rates of Educational Attainment Achievement by Ethnicity at Age 24, 2002

For every 100 kindergarteners who . . .	At age 24		
	Were high school graduates %	Had completed some college %	Had attained a bachelor's degree %
African American	87	51	17
Hispanic	63	32	11
White	93	65	32

Source: Data are from the U.S. Bureau of the Census (2002).

Over the past 40 years, theory and research in the sociology of education have played an important role for understanding urban educational problems and policies aimed at their solution. This chapter examines the contributions of the sociology of education and provides an overview of these problems and policies.

Sociology of Education Research and Theory Bearing on these Gaps

The study of education and inequality has been a central theme in the sociology of education since the 1960s. Sociological studies have focused on several broad questions. First, what does the empirical evidence tell us about the nature and extent of achievement gaps in relation to social class, race, ethnicity, and gender? Second, what are the causes of these educational inequalities (e.g., are they caused by factors inside and/or outside schools)? Third, what do the answers to these questions tell us about the role of education in ameliorating or reproducing existing inequalities?

Numerous sociological studies have documented the extent of achievement gaps, both in the United States and internationally. Some of the socioeconomic data are presented above. In the simplest terms, they can be summarized as follows: students from higher social classes have higher achievement levels than students from lower social classes, and students from dominant racial and ethnic groups outperform those from subordinate groups.

The case of gender is more complicated. Girls have been closing the gap over the last 30 years and are now outperforming boys in almost all categories except mathematics and the sciences. Longitudinally, gaps in terms of social class, race, and ethnicity, at least in the United States, declined from the 1970s to the late 1980s, at which point they rose again into the late 1990s. Since 2000, these gaps have decreased slightly (see Education Trust (www.edtrust.org) for detailed data on achievement gaps).

These findings can be broken down into those that emphasize factors external to schools and those that emphasize school-based factors. In 1966, the Coleman Report concluded that forces outside of schools, especially neighborhood and peer-group effects, were more important than measures of school or teacher quality and other within-school variables. At a time when liberal educational reforms—as a result of Lyndon Johnson's Great Society programs—produced optimism in the United States, the Coleman Report (1966) cast doubt on the ability of schools to ameliorate inequalities on their own. In the 1970s, the work of political economists Bowles and Gintis (1976) and sociologist Jencks (Jencks et al., 1972), which concluded that schools reproduced inequalities or had little effect on them, furthered this skeptical orientation.

This tradition continues today, with Anyon (2005) arguing that educational inequalities are caused by political–economic conditions, often related to poverty, and that without significant economic transformations, school-based reforms are doomed to failure.

In response to this pessimistic perspective, a number of researchers have argued that schools, often independent of the demographic characteristics of their students, had the potential to reduce inequalities. Edmonds's (1979) work on effective U.S. urban schools comprising low-income and African American students indicated that schools could avoid perpetuating social and class disadvantage. More recently, proponents of "no excuses" schools such as the Knowledge Is Power Program (KIPP) (Thernstrom & Thernstrom, 2003), argue that schools can compensate for societal problems.

In the 1970s, sociologists of education argued that it was imperative to examine the process of schooling (i.e., what goes inside schools and classrooms) to fully understand its limits and possibilities in ameliorating or reproducing inequalities. Studies of school inputs—including school funding (Tractenberg, Liss, Moscovitch, & Sadovnick, 2006), teacher quality (Ingersoll, 2003), school processes such as tracking (Oakes, 2005), and teacher expectations (Rist, 1977)—analyzed the ways in which schooling contributed to social stratification or provided ways of reducing it. In Europe, researchers analyzed the connections between family and school. They demonstrated that social class advantages resulted in different educational and communication codes (Bernstein, 1971, 1973, 1975) and in social and cultural capital (Bourdieu, 1973), thus leading to educational inequalities.

Based upon the evidence, two competing sociological theories on education and inequality have dominated over the past four decades (Sadovnik, 2010). The first, *functionalism*—tracing its roots to the 19th-century French sociologist Emile Durkheim and 20th-century U.S. sociologist Talcott Parsons—has argued that although schooling has not eliminated inequalities, it has on balance provided an important vehicle for upward mobility, at least in the United States. The second, *conflict theory*—tracing its roots to 19th-century social theorist Karl Marx, 19th-century sociologist Max Weber, and 20th-century sociologists such as Randall Collins—has argued that, on balance, schools have tended to reproduce existing social inequalities.

Approaches to Reform

Over the past decade, two different approaches to urban school reform have developed. The first, represented by the Education Equity Project, stresses the independent power of schools in eliminating the achievement gap for low-income students. The second, represented by the Broader Bolder Approach, stresses that school-level reform alone is necessary but insufficient and that societal and community-level reforms are necessary. Much of the political debate over urban educational reform has been ideological and often with no reliance on empirical evidence. The importance of sociological theory and research is to provide more objective, empirical evidence to inform these debates.

In creating the Education Equality Project (EEP), Joel Klein, Chancellor of the New York City Public Schools, and the Reverend Al Sharpton sought to eliminate the achievement gap by "working to create an effective school for every child." To create effective schools, the EEP works to ensure that every school has a highly effective principal as well as skilled teachers; to create system-wide accountability; to empower parents as well as to encourage them to demand more from their schools and from themselves; and to constantly focus on what will be the best decision for students (Education Equality Project, 2010). Their efforts to do this may require some ruffling of union feathers, since the group believes that in order to eliminate the achievement gap, failing teachers and principals should no longer be protected (Toppo, 2008).

The society/community-based approach of the Broader Bolder Approach founded by Pedro Noguero and Helen Ladd was built upon the works of Jean Anyon and Richard Rothstein and others who argued that schools have only a limited ability to eradicate the effect of poverty and its consequences for children. In Anyon's radical approach, "an all-out attack on poverty and racial isolation that by necessity will affect not only the poor, but the more affluent as well, will be necessary in order to remove the barriers that currently stand in the way of urban educational change" (1997, p. 13). This approach suggests that economic and social differences between races and classes affect academic achievement at all levels, from prenatal to early childhood, and that they damage the overall health, welfare, and living environments of children (Rothstein, 2004).

There are inequalities that can affect children even before they are born. Low-SES mothers, for example, and to some extent low-SES fathers, are associated with low-birth-weight babies and greater infant mortality (Fiscella & Williams, 2004). Twice as many low-birth-weight African American than White children are born, and children of low birth weight typically have lower IQ scores, mild learning disabilities, and attention deficit disorders (Hack, Klein, & Taylor, 1995; Hoffman, Llagas, & Snyder, 2003). Children from low-income families face a greater risk of death from sudden infant death syndrome (SIDS); they are also more likely to experience child abuse and higher rates of exposure to lead poisoning and secondhand smoke. They are more likely to suffer from asthma, developmental delays, and learning disabilities, and are more often exposed to violence and drug trafficking (Fiscella & Williams, 2004).

Minority and lower-class children have more visual, hearing, and dental health problems than do White children, which can affect their ability to focus and learn in school. For example, twice as many poor children have severe visual impairments, which are, of course, likely to interfere with their academic work (Starfield, 1982). In many cases such problems are not diagnosed, owing to the lack of adequate health care, available doctors, and time for parents to take their children to be examined. Physicians serving low-SES patients have greater logistical and financial burdens as well as problems communicating because of differences in language, culture, and health literacy as well as inadequate resources to deal with all of these problems (Fiscella & Williams, 2004). Children who receive normal optometric services have been shown to improve in reading beyond what would normally be expected for their age (Rothstein, 2004).

Within the home environment, there also are inequalities that can indirectly affect a child's ability to learn. Asthma can be triggered by factors in the home environment, such as dust, mold, and cockroaches. This is important to consider in developing health policies, because asthma is the main cause of chronic school absence and also causes low-SES children to be overclassified for special education (Corburn, Osleeb, & Porter, 2006; Hilts, 2000).

There also are neighborhood health and environmental factors that influence the health of the community. Typically, there is a disparity in the number of health facilities, with fewer facilities being located in high-poverty neighborhoods (Komaromy et al., 1996). There are also fewer good-quality grocery stores, exercise facilities, parks, and recreational areas.

Therefore, "[F]ully closing the black-white achievement gap is both desirable and feasible, but will first require social and economic reforms that would result in distributing black and white students equally between the social classes" (Rothstein, 2004, p. 18). To do that, the federal government must aim reforms at the urban system as a whole, initiating economic and social reforms for all citizens (Anyon, 1997). The Coleman Report (1966) highlighted the importance of neighborhood and social class variables for education. The greater integration of social classes can lead to improvements in educational achievement (Wells, Duran, & White, 2004).

Constructing new social and economic policies that address family, community, and neighborhood inequities—such as raising the poverty line, fully funding affordable housing programs, offering rental subsidies, providing assistance to families to find units in nicer neighborhoods, enforcing fair housing laws, building more mixed-income housing, and changing local zoning laws that prevent public housing from being built in better neighborhoods—will help to eliminate the differences between groups in the United States, and ultimately equalize and improve the educational level of our society as a whole.

School-based Educational Reform and Effects Accountability: No Child Left Behind

Beginning in the 1990s, educational policymakers implemented accountability-based reforms to improve schools and student achievement. In 2001, President George W. Bush, with bipartisan support, signed the No Child Left Behind (NCLB) law aimed at eliminating the nation's achievement gap. The key components of NCLB were as follows (Karen, 2008, pp. 16–17):

1. Requiring annual testing of students in grades 3 through 8 in reading and math, plus at least one test in grades 10 through 12, with science testing to follow. Graduation rates were to be used as a secondary indicator of success for high schools.

2. Requiring states and districts to report school-by-school data on students' test performance, broken down by whether the students were African American, Latino, Native American, Asian American, White non-Hispanic, special education, limited English proficiency (LEP), and/or from low-income families.

3. Requiring states to set "adequate yearly progress" (AYP) goals for each school. To meet AYP goals, not only must each subgroup make progress in each year in each grade in each subject but 95% of each subgroup must participate in testing. AYP goals must be constructed so that 100% of the students reach proficiency by 2014.

4. Labeling schools that fail to meet AYP goals for 2 years "in need of improvement" (INOI). Initially, this requirement means that schools must offer students opportunities to attend other public schools and/or to receive federally funded tutoring. Funds would also be provided for teachers' professional development. A school that failed to meet future AYP targets would be subject to "restructuring" (firing of the teachers and the principal, the takeover of the school by the state or a private company, and so forth).

5. Requiring schools to have "highly qualified" teachers for the "core academic subjects" (English, reading or language arts, math, science, foreign languages, civics and government, economics, arts, history and geography) by 2005–2006.

After nearly a decade, social science research indicates that although there have been some improvements, by and large the achievement gap has not been substantially diminished (Sadovnik, O'Day, Bohrnstedt, & Borman, 2008). Moreover, this research also indicates that NCLB's goals of eliminating the gap by 2014 will not be achieved.

In addition, sociologists of education and other researchers have argued that because of problems in the law, especially its failure to include value-added measures of school improvement to its flawed definition of AYP, the law has disproportionately labeled urban schools, with their low-income students, as failing. Recognizing the limitations of NCLB, President Barack Obama and his Secretary of Education have proposed a major overhaul of NCLB in the reauthorization of the Elementary and Secondary Education Act of 1965 (ESEA). Their approach would maintain strong accountability measures but focus on college and career readiness and other reforms in their Race to the Top competition, including linking teacher evaluation to student achievement and increasing the number of charter schools. Most importantly, sociologists of education continue to point out that such school-based educational reforms will have limited success unless they are accompanied by policies aimed at the factors outside of schools that contribute to the achievement gap, especially in urban schools.

Teacher Quality

NCLB's requirement that all schools have highly qualified teachers in every classroom has highlighted the problem of unqualified teachers in urban schools. But whereas most teachers meet the "highly qualified standards" of NCLB, the data indicate that significant numbers of classrooms are staffed by teachers who are not highly qualified in the particular subject they teach. This is the result of the practice called out-of-field teaching, whereby teachers are assigned to teach subjects that do not match their training or education. This is a crucial issue, because highly qualified teachers actually may become highly unqualified in that circumstance.

At the secondary school level, about one-fifth of classes in each of the core academic subjects (math, science, English, social studies) are taught by teachers who do not hold teaching certificates in the subject taught. The data also show that more out-of-field teaching occurs in urban schools, especially low-income ones, than in others. Urban schools with high levels of minority students also typically have a larger percentage of novice teachers (Education Trust, 2010c). Ingersoll (1999, 2003) asserts that problems in staffing urban schools have less to do with teacher shortages and more to do with organizational issues inside schools. Principals often find it easier to hire unqualified teachers than qualified ones, and the absence of status and professionalism, as well as poor working conditions in teaching, leads to high dropout rates in the first five years of teaching. Therefore, urban districts are constantly replacing teachers on an ongoing basis. This has significant consequences, since it takes years to become an expert teacher. Rates of teacher attrition and misassignment are more prevalent in urban and high-poverty schools (Ingersoll, 1999, 2003).

Ingersoll's research suggests that programs aimed at solving urban school staffing problems at the supply level through alternative teacher education programs—such as Teach for America, the New York City Teaching Fellows Program, and New Jersey's Alternative Certification Program (all which allow college graduates with majors in their teaching field to enter teaching without traditional certification through a college teacher education program)—fail to address the organizational problems within schools that are responsible for high turnover rates.

Recently, reformers have stressed the existence of teacher tenure, seniority-based transfers, and layoff provisions in union contracts as a primary factor in preventing improvements in teacher quality. A number of provisions in the Race to the Top funding and new contracts like the one in Washington, DC, have addressed some of these issues.

School Quality

Data from the Education Trust (2004) indicate that many urban schools do not have rigorous academic curricula for all of their students, often track a significant number into nonacademic programs, and have low expectations for success for a majority of their students. Bryk, Lee, and Holland (1993) argued that one reason urban parochial schools are more successful in teaching low-income students of color is because these schools require all students to follow a rigorous academic college preparatory curriculum.

Research on effective urban schools has been conducted since the 1970s. Over the past 30 years, scholars have analyzed the characteristics of effective and high-performing schools serving low-income students. Edmonds (1979) was one of the preeminent scholars of the effective schools movement and stressed equity and the "mastery of basic skills" as an important component in producing effective schools. The effective schools movement, however, evolved in response to the 1966 Coleman Report, which argued that schools had little to do with student achievement. Coleman maintained that family background was critical and more significant than schools in making a difference in students' academic achievement.

Ron Edmonds, one of the founders of the research on effective schools, rejected this conclusion and argued that equity and the "mastery of basic skills" was crucial to creating effective schools. As Andrews and Morefield (1991) note:

> The early research findings of Ron Edmonds, Larry Lezotte, and others (Edmonds, 1979, 1980, 1983; see Murphy, Weil, Hallinger, & Mitman, 1985) challenged the genetic/familial explanations of differences in outcomes [espoused by Coleman, 1966]. [Thus] by identifying schools that were effective with children, regardless of family income or ethnic status, the effective school research ... attributed differences in children's performance to schools themselves. (p. 271)

Over the past three decades, researchers have analyzed the characteristics of effective and high-performing schools serving predominantly low-income populations. Several studies have examined the characteristics of effective schools and the effective school movement (Andrews & Morefield, 1991; Bell, 2001; Bliss, Firestone, & Richards, 1991; Edmonds, 1979, 1980, 1982, 1983; Good &

Brophy, 1986; Marzano, 2003; Peterson & Lezotte, 1991; Purkey & Smith, 1983). Their findings suggest that there are common factors essential to the basic tenets of school effectiveness. These include strong principal leadership, a quality instructional program, high expectations of students, and a structured and safe school environment. Edmonds, for example, argued that equity, instructional leadership, teacher expectations, and school climate are key factors to student achievement (Edmonds, 1979, 1980, 1982, 1983).

Whereas research on the effective school challenged the Coleman Report's findings, much of the sociological research (Anyon, 1997; Lareau, 2003; Lee & Burkam, 2002; Rothstein, 2004) suggests that poverty and family *do* have significant effects on student achievement. While acknowledging this fact, reformers who focus on school improvement argue that effective schools have the potential for mitigating, if not overcoming, these effects.

Despite these problems, there are also numerous examples of highly successful urban schools (Education Trust, 2009). For example, in Newark, New Jersey—which was taken over by the New Jersey Department of Education in 1995 for, among other things, low student achievement—there are a number of district and public charter schools with high poverty and high minority populations that perform not only above the state averages but at the same levels as those in the highest SES districts (Barr, 2004a, 2004b).

School Choice

Beginning with the publication of Chubb and Moe's *Politics, Markets and America's Schools* (1990), school choice advocates have pushed for the introduction of free markets into K–12 public education. Arguing that public education is dominated by a public bureaucracy dominated by teacher unions, choice advocates believe that only through the introduction of market competition will public schools, especially in urban areas, be forced to improve.

Charter Schools

Passage of the first state-legislated charter law in Minnesota in 1991 has spawned enactment of charter laws in 41 states as well as the District of Columbia and Puerto Rico. This fledgling movement has produced nearly 3,700 charter schools serving 1,076,964 students nationwide (Center for Educational Reform, 2005). Demand for charter schools remains high, as evidenced by the 70% of charter schools with waiting lists for admission (RPP International, 1998, 1999, 2000, 2001).

States are responding to this demand by authorizing more charters and amending charter laws to accommodate the desire for growth, while other states without charter laws consider their enactment (Center for Educational Reform, 2005; Finn, Manno, & Vanourek, 2000; RPP International, 1998, 1999, 2000, 2001). Charter schools are public schools that are free from many of the regulations applied to traditional public schools; in return, they are held accountable for student performance. In essence, they swap red tape for results, also referred to as an "autonomy for accountability" trade within the movement. The "charter" itself is a performance contract that details the school's mission, program, goals, students served, methods of assessment, and ways to measure success. It is a formal, legal document between those who establish and run a school ("operators") and the public body that authorizes and monitors it ("authorizers"). Charter schools are, in theory, autonomous. They work in the ways they think best, for charter schools are self-governing institutions with wide control over their own curricula, instruction, staffing, budget, internal organization, calendar, and so on (Finn, Manno, & Vanourek, 2000).

As a public school, a charter school is paid for with tax dollars (no tuition charges) and must be open to all students in the district. And whereas charter schools can be started by virtually anyone (teachers, parents, nonprofit agencies, for-profit organizations, community members, etc.), charters are supposed to demonstrate results to the public agencies that review and approve their charters as well as monitor and audit their progress. Authorization may be handled by a single agency, such as the state Department of Education in New Jersey, or a state may have multiple authorizing agencies, including local school boards, community colleges, state colleges, and universities (Hill et al., 2001). Accountability is a critical component of the charter movement; if a charter school fails to meet the provisions of its charter, it can lose its funding and be forced to shut its doors.

Proponents of charter schools have long argued that they provide a more effective and efficient alternative for low-income children, especially in urban areas. Often tied to the school choice and voucher movements, advocates believe that charter schools, freed from the bureaucratic constraints of traditional urban public schools, will provide a better education at lower cost. However, in 2004, the American Federation of Teachers (AFT), long a skeptic if not an opponent of charter schools, issued a statistical report finding that district public schools outperformed charter schools nationally (Nelson, Rosenberg, & Van Meter, 2004). Immediately following the release of this document, a group of education researchers, some long associated with the school choice and voucher movements, were signatories to a full-page advertisement in the *New York Times* condemning the AFT study for sloppy research. It argued that the study failed to control sufficiently for student background variables, used one year of data rather than multiyear data sets, and did not measure the value-added effects of charter schools on their students, many of whom came to charters far below state proficiency levels (*New York Times*, 2004).

In 2006, the National Center for Educational Statistics released its report on charter schools. Its study design satisfied some of the criteria for acceptable research outlined in the *Times* advertisement and concluded that, after controlling for student demographic characteristics, students in traditional public schools had higher overall achievement in 4th-grade reading and mathematics. These differences were not statistically significant for charter schools affiliated with a public school district, while unaffiliated charter schools scored significantly lower than traditional public schools (U.S. Department of Education, 2006). These findings were confirmed by a comparison of achievement in public, private, and charter schools (Lubienski & Lubienski, 2006).

Charter school advocates (see Center for Educational Reform, 2005), however, argue that charter schools often admit students who have not performed well in public schools and that it takes time for charter schools to have an impact. Given the lack of statewide student-level data, however, the Department of Education and Lubienski studies could not examine the value-added effects of district and charter schools when controlling for student background factors. C. M. Hoxby (2004), a leading proponent of charter schools and school choice, released studies that compared charter schools nationally with their neighboring district schools (as a way of controlling for student background factors and comparing them to the schools where the charter school students would have remained if they did not have choice); and compared students in these charter schools with students who applied but were on waiting lists and who remained in the neighboring district schools. Both studies indicated that students in charter schools showed higher achievement than those who remained in the neighboring district schools, even after controlling for student background variables. Miron and Nelson (2001, 2002) argue that we still do not know enough about student achievement in charter schools and often do not have the type of data needed to effectively evaluate charter school performance. In 2009, The Center for Research on Educational Outcomes (CREDO) at Stanford released its national charter school report, which indicated that there were wide variations in the quality of charter schools in the United States and that, on the whole, charter school students performed below district public school students (Center for Research on Educational Outcomes, 2009a). At the same time, Hoxby (2009) issued a report on New York City charter schools that, while controlling for a variety of variables, including family background, showed that the students in these schools outperformed students in New York City district schools. Additionally, she issued a critique of the CREDO study, which resulted in a series of written debates between CREDO and Hoxby (see Center for Research on Educational Outcomes, 2009b).

Vouchers

In the 1990s, a number of states, including Wisconsin, Ohio, and Florida, implemented school voucher programs, all of which were challenged in state courts for violating the separation of Church and state. In 2002, the U.S. Supreme Court in *Zelman* v. *Simmons-Harris* ruled that the Cleveland voucher program did not violate the establishment clause of the First Amendment. Specifically, it ruled that because the vouchers went directly to families rather than to religious schools and could be used in either religious or secular private schools, the voucher program did not violate the constitutional prohibition against public money being used for religious purposes.

Following this decision, many policy experts believed that there would be widespread adoption of new voucher programs. Although Washington, DC, adopted a voucher program in 2004, there has not been a significant increase in new programs. In 2006, the Florida Supreme Court ruled against the constitutionality of its voucher program based on the state's constitutions requirement that the state have a uniform educational system (Robelen, 2006). In 2009, Congress voted to stop the DC voucher program, resulting in protests from pro-voucher groups (*Washington Times*, 2009).

Voucher advocates argue that school choice will have three important educational impacts. First, it will provide low-income parents with the same choices as middle-class parents and lead to increased parental satisfaction with their children's schools. Second, given the absence of the large educational bureaucracy of urban school systems, charter and voucher schools will provide better learning environments for low-income students and result in higher student achievement. Third, owing to the market effects of competition from charter and voucher schools, urban public schools will be forced to improve or close their doors. This will result in higher student achievement in urban public schools.

Over the past decade, there has been considerable controversy over whether the empirical evidence supports the claims of choice advocates, particularly with respect to the voucher programs in Milwaukee and Cleveland. J. F. Witte and colleagues—controlling for socioeconomic status, race, and ethnicity—found that voucher students did not perform significantly better in either math or reading than students in public schools (Witte et al., 1995). Instead, they found statistical significance for negative effects on reading scores for students attending choice schools in the second year of the program, 1991–1992 (Carnoy, 2001). J. P. Greene and colleagues found that those students who applied and won vouchers made significant gains in both math and reading compared with those who applied for vouchers but ended up in public schools (Greene, Peterson, Du, Boeger, & Frazier, 1998). Rouse (1998) compared annual gains for a larger sample of voucher students with both general Milwaukee public school students and students who applied for vouchers but did not enter the program. She found a gain of only 1.5 to 2.3 percentile points per year in math for voucher students but no statistically significant differences in reading scores. Although her research methods overcame some of the limitations of Greene's methods, some argue that her study was still limited in selection bias and accounting for the possibility of other factors, such as students' families and home practices that would have contributed to math score gains (Fuller et al., 1999; Hess, 2002).

In 1995, Wisconsin ended its assessment of the Milwaukee voucher program; since then, few data have been available for analyzing the effects of the program on student achievement. Van Dunk and Dickman (2003) argue that the data required for a systematic accounting of the Milwaukee program do not exist, and until they do, choice advocates and critics do not have the evidence necessary to support their claims.

The Ohio State Department of Education commissioned Metcalf (Metcalf et al., 1998, 1999, 2001, 2003) to study the voucher program. Controlling for socioeconomic background and other variables, he found that no significant difference in achievement between voucher students and their public school peers. After four years of longitudinal research, Metcalf (Metcalf et al., 2004) provided some cautionary observations, including the points that operational procedures are crucial; that parents cite safety, academic quality, and classroom order as the main reasons for their choice; that public and private school classrooms are similar; and that overall conclusions about voucher effects are elusive.

Hoxby (2000, 2001) found that competition leads to higher test scores and lower costs of neighboring public school systems. Hoxby (2001) argues that test scores from Milwaukee public schools subject to voucher and charter school competition increased more rapidly compared with test scores of similar schools elsewhere in Wisconsin that did not face school choice competition.

Voucher advocates cite a growing body of literature showing how voucher programs increase student achievement, empower low-income families, increase parental satisfaction, improve public education through competition, and offer a more cost-effective method for financing schools. School choice and voucher advocates claim that low-income and minority students will increase their academic achievement at private and parochial schools because they will not be confined to low-performing neighborhood schools but rather be free to select more effective schools. With this freedom of choice, parents will increase their satisfaction with and involvement in their children's schooling.

Proponents also argue that by injecting market competition into the education system, low-performing urban schools will be forced to deliver higher quality education at a lower cost. And schools that are clearly not producing positive effects or that are operating at a high cost, will simply be put out of business, i.e., private schools supported by public funds actually do a better job than public schools, while also improving the quality of public schools by introducing competition.

Critics of voucher programs argue that proponents' claims have underlying assumptions and limited methods of analysis; they also say that such programs drain resources from public schools and cause further inequality of education. They argue that there simply is not enough evidence to validate the claims made by proponents. In some cases, they point to contradicting evidence. For instance, the critics argue that there is no conclusive evidence that learning opportunities at private and parochial schools actually lead to higher test scores. As far as parental satisfaction goes, there is only limited understanding of the relationship between parental satisfaction and student achievement.

Ladd (2002), in a balanced and exhaustive review of the literature, concluded that policymakers need to balance the choices of parents with overall societal priorities, in a way that does not advantage these families.

Societal, Community, and School-based Reforms

School Finance

Following the Supreme Court's 1973 decision in *Rodriguez* v. *San Antonio*, which declared that there is no constitutional right to an equal education, school finance equity and adequacy advocates litigated at the state level. Even before *Rodriguez*, *Robinson* v. *Cahill* was filed in 1970 against the state of New Jersey, citing discrimination in funding for some school districts, which prosecutors believed was creating disparities in urban students' education by failing to provide all students with a "thorough and efficient" education, as guaranteed under the New Jersey State Constitution. Although the state enacted an income tax in accordance with the ruling of this case in 1973, the program was never fully funded. By 1980, more evidence had been accumulated regarding the inequality of education in urban areas, and the Education Law Center filed *Abbott* v. *Burke* on behalf of several urban school districts, also due to a violation of the "thorough and efficient" clause.

The court ruled in 1990 that more funding was needed to serve the children in the poorer school districts. In order to provide a "thorough and efficient" education in urban districts, funding was equalized between urban and suburban school districts. It was also determined that extra funding was to be distributed to provide additional programs in order to eliminate disadvantages within poorer school districts.

In 1998, the state was required to implement a package of supplemental programs, including preschool, as well as a plan to renovate urban school facilities. The *Abbott* v. *Burke* ruling implemented additional entitlements for urban schools, including whole-school reform, full-day kindergarten, preschool for all 3- and 4-year-olds, a comprehensive managed and funded facilities program to correct code violations; plus a plan to eliminate overcrowding and provide adequate space for all educational programs at Abbott schools.

Other supplemental programs included social services, increased security, a technology-alternative education, as well as school-to-work, after-school, and summer-school programs (Education Law Center, 2010; Yaffe, 2007). What made *Abbott* different from other school finance decisions is that, in addition to equalizing funding, the court recognized that factors outside of schools had to be addressed as well. Its requirement for the funding of mandatory preschool and supplemental services illustrated this approach.

In 2009, the New Jersey Supreme Court ruled as constitutional a new funding formula, the School Funding Reform Act (SFRA), which eliminated the *Abbott* remedies and implemented a formula for allocating funding to all districts based on student needs. According to the state, this "money follows the child" approach would distribute funding more equitably to all "at risk" children in the state, including those in its rural and lower-income urban rim districts. The Education Law Center (2010), in its legal challenge, argued that the new formula would take necessary funding away from the urban districts. School finance researchers are currently studying the law's effects.

Other states, including Kentucky, Massachusetts and New York, had similar litigation. In 1993, New York State began its own 16-year battle for equity in education. A group of concerned parents and advocates banded together under the nonprofit group called the Campaign for Fiscal Equity (CFE) to challenge the state to provide a "sound basic" education for all students that would prepare them to participate in society. A "sound basic" education was defined according to Justice DeGrasse as "high school graduates [who] must be able to evaluate complex issues that may arise in jury service or voting and they must also be able to obtain and hold competitive employment" (New York State United Teachers, 2003). In *CFE* v. *State of New York*, the State Supreme Court found in 2001 the state's school-funding formula to be unconstitutional. Following a series of appeals, the state was ordered to provide New York City public schools with additional funding for their annual operating budgets. CFE continues its advocacy work to ensure that the implementation of reforms and distribution of money is meeting the needs of the lowest-performing students in the schools with the highest need.

Full-service and Community Schools

Another way to attack education inequity is to examine and plan to educate not only the whole child, but also the whole community. Dryfoos's model of full-service schools (Dryfoos, 1994), Geoffrey Canada's Harlem Children's Zone (Tough, 2008), and Newark's Broader Bolder Approach are three models of community-based reforms. Full-service schools focus on meeting students' and their families' educational, physical, psychological, and social needs in a coordinated and collaborative fashion between school and community services (Dryfoos, 1994). In this model, schools service as community centers within neighborhoods that are open extended hours to provide a multitude of services such as adult education, health clinics, recreational facilities, after-school programs, mental health services, drug and alcohol programs, job placement and training programs, and tutoring services.

Specifically designed to target and improve at-risk neighborhoods, full-service schools aim to prevent problems, as well as to support them. Whereas this model supports Anyon's (1997) argument to repair the larger social and economic problems of society as a means of improving public education, there is no evidence that full-service schools affect student achievement.

Harlem Children's Zone

Growing up in the south Bronx and an-all Black community on Long Island did not prepare Geoffrey Canada, the founder of the Harlem Children's Zone, for the academic and social challenges he faced at Bowdoin College in Maine. As a result, he wanted to ensure that other African American children were prepared. The aspect of Canada's approach that is unique as compared with other philosophies from boarding schools, charities, and social service agencies is that he wants to leave children where they are, simultaneously changing them and their neighborhoods, instead of removing them from their familiar surroundings (Tough, 2008).

Canada hopes that children can positively "contaminate" New York City's Harlem community. He said that

> when you've got most of the kids in a neighborhood involved in high-quality programs, you begin to change the cultural context of that neighborhood. If you are surrounded by people who are always talking about going to college, you're going to end up thinking, "Hey, maybe this is something I could do, too." You can't help but get contaminated by the idea. It just seeps into your pores, and you don't even know that you've caught the virus. (Tough, 2008, p. 125)

It is more common for educated parents to read to their children when they are younger as well as to encourage them to read more independently when they are older (Bianchi & Robinson, 1997; Hoffereth & Sandberg, 2001). White parents typically have spent more time educating their child at home than Black parents; therefore, African American children are often behind from the beginning of the school process (Rothstein, 2004). Black children are more likely than White children to watch television for long periods of time (Rothstein, 2004). Providing quality early childhood education helps minority and low-income children to be successful when they begin formal schooling.

Canada therefore provides programs for parents in Harlem before their children are even born in an attempt to infuse the knowledge that middle-class parents are likely to do for their children in a "sensitive way." Participants of "Baby College" are recruited from every corner of Harlem to participate in the program, where instructors of color teach them how to have academic conversations with their children as well as how to provide them with a healthy home environment and acceptable forms of discipline. Baby College even purchases items that parents need and cannot afford for their homes.

Canada expresses hope that all parents will pass along the "Harry Potter values" to their children in order for them to be academically successful. Canada's formula, along with an extended school day and tutoring for at-risk students, paid off in 2007, when a significant number of his middle-school students improved their state test results to meet grade-level requirements in math and reading, and the middle school earned an "A" on the New York City Department of Education school report card evaluation process.

In Newark, education reformer and New York University Professor of Education, Pedro Noguero, is implementing the Broader Bolder Approach, an adaptation of the Harlem Children's Zone as a pilot program in six K–8 feeder schools into Central High School, located in one of the lowest-income communities in Newark, the ward of the 1967 Newark riots.

Although supporters laud reforms such as the Harlem Children's Zone and "no excuses" schools—those in the KIPP (the Knowledge Is Power Program)—as evidence of the positive effects of high expectations and strong discipline on student achievement, critics point to their cultural deficit model and highly disciplinarian processes as problematic, although at the same time praising their impact (Sadovnik, 2010).

Limits and Possibilities of Reform: A Sociological Analysis

Four decades of sociological research have resulted in a number of recommendations for urban educational reform and improvement:

- Put all children—not just some—in a demanding high school core curriculum.
- Teachers matter—make sure they are of high quality and supported.
- Focus on improving low-performing schools.
- Motivate more students and prepare more students for higher education.
- Principals matter—focus on effective leadership.
- Focus on instructional time.

Although these educational reforms have the potential to improve urban schools, by themselves they are limited in reducing the achievement gaps (Anyon, 2005; Rothstein, 2004; Tractenberg, Sadovnik, & Liss, 2004) unless they also address the factors outside of schools responsible for educational inequalities.

Rothstein (2004) calls for economic programs to reduce income inequality and to create stable and affordable housing as well as the expansion of school-community clinics to provide health care and counseling. He also warns that although school finance suits are necessary to ensure that all children receive an adequate education, they will not be sufficient if they do not address the economic forces outside of schools. Rothstein, a liberal, and Anyon (2005), a radical, both conclude that school reform is necessary but insufficient to reduce the achievement gaps without broader social and economic policies aimed at reducing the effects of poverty. Therefore, school-based reforms have the following significant shortcomings:

- Failure to address problems associated with replication and "scaling up" for both district and charter schools.
- Failure to address outside school factors (community, peer group, health, and environmental factors).
- Failure to address economic factors (labor force and wage issues).
- Often, the perpetuation of a simplistic "no excuses" ideology of school improvement.

Based on the sociological evidence, successful urban school improvement will require systemic reform aimed at the school, students, and community as well as addressing economic and societal factors, which include the following.

At the school level:

- Equity in school finance reform.
- Equitable distribution of high-quality teachers and principals.
- School-level reforms based on research findings on effective schools and comprehensive school reform.

- District-level reform based on the best practices research of more successful urban districts (i.e., Austin, Boston, Charlotte, and New York City).

At the student, community, economic, and societal levels:

- Address student and family health, environmental, and social-psychological needs.
- Implement research-based best practices family involvement programs (i.e., Comer, 2010; Epstein, 2001).
- Implement research-based best practices gang prevention programs.
- Link school reform to urban community and economic development.
- Develop urban revitalization programs.
- Promote school-level economic integration through affordable housing programs and magnet school choice programs.
- Address the pernicious effects of poverty through urban social and economic policies.

Sociological research indicates that although many of the reforms discussed above have promise, they need to be part of a more systemic approach that links schooling to the factors outside schools that are affecting them. This includes the need for:

- More sociological research to inform urban educational policy.
- Continued focus on reducing the achievement gap.
- Emphasis on equal opportunity to learn.
- Emphasis on building the capacity of schools and districts in need of improvement.
- Emphasis on factors beyond schools, including poverty, community, and neighborhood variables.

Reforming urban schools will be difficult. Based on the sociological research, urban school reformers seeking quick and politically palatable solutions will resist my message as too slow and unfeasible. At a forum during my first year at Rutgers-Newark on the Newark, Jersey City, and Paterson state takeovers (see Tractenberg, Holzer, Miller, Sadovnik, & Liss, 2002), a panelist, the Assistant Commissioner of Education in New Jersey, a man committed to improving urban schools in his state, was asked to comment on the perspective that unless we treat causes of school failure such as poverty, school-based reforms are doomed to fail. He cryptically replied that such analyses are just more excuses for urban school failure and that what we do not need is more excuses. Although I understood his impatience with the slowness of reform and his insistence that we deal with the schools, the sociological research on urban educational reform suggests that we do this at our own peril.

References

Andrews, R. L., & Morefield, J. (1991). Effective leadership for effective urban schools. *Education and Urban Society, 23,* 270–278.

Anyon, J. (1997). *Ghetto schooling: A political economy of urban educational reform.* New York: Teachers College Press.

Anyon, J. (2005). *Radical possibilities: Public policy, urban education and a new social movement.* New York: Routledge.

Barr, J. (2004a). *A statistical portrait of New Jersey's schools.* Newark, NJ: Cornwall Center for Metropolitan Studies.

Barr, J. (2004b). *A statistical portrait of Newark's schools.* Newark, NJ: Cornwall Center for Metropolitan Studies.

Bell, J. (2001). High performing, high poverty schools. *Leadership, 31* (September/October), 8–11.

Bernstein, B. (1971). *Class, codes, and control: Vol. 1.* London: Routledge.

Bernstein, B. (1973). *Class, codes, and control: Vol. 2.* London: Routledge.

Bernstein, B. (1975). *Class, codes, and control: Vol. 3.* London: Routledge.

Bianchi, S. M., & Robinson, J. (1997). What did you do today? Children's use of time, family composition, and the acquisition of social capital. *Journal of Marriage and the Family, 59,* 332–344.

Bliss, J. R., Firestone, W. A., & Richards, C. E. (Eds.) (1991). *Rethinking effective schools: Research and practice.* Englewood Cliffs, NJ: Prentice Hall.

Bourdieu, P. (1973). Cultural reproduction and social reproduction. In R. Brown (Ed.), *Knowledge, education, and cultural change* (pp. 71–112). London: Tavistock.

Bowles, S., & Gintis, H. (1976). *Schooling in capitalist America.* New York: Basic Books.

Bryk, A., Lee, V., & Holland, P. (1993). *Catholic schools and the common good.* Cambridge, MA: Harvard University Press.

Carnoy, M. (2001). *School vouchers: Examining the evidence.* Washington, DC: Economic Policy Institute.

Center for Educational Reform (2005). About charter schools. Retrieved June 1, 2011 from: www.edreform.com/Issues/ Charter_Connection/?All_About_Charter_Schools

Center for Research on Educational Outcomes (CREDO) (2009a). National Charter School Study. Palo Alto, CA: CREDO, Stanford University. Retrieved December 25, 2009 from: http://credo.stanford.edu

Center for Research on Educational Outcomes (CREDO) (2009b). The Hoxby-CREDO debates. Palo Alto, CA: Stanford. Retrieved August 18, 2010 from: http://credo.stanford.edu

Chubb, J., & Moe, T. (1990). *Politics, markets and America's schools.* Washington, DC: Brookings Institution.

Coleman, J. S. et al. (1966). *Equality of educational opportunity.* Washington, DC: U.S. Government Printing Office.

Comer, J. (2010). Comer School Development Program. New Haven, CT: Yale University Medical School. Retrieved July 12, 2010 from: http://medicine.yale.edu/childstudy/comer

Corburn, J., Osleeb, J., & Porter, M. (2006). Urban asthma and the neighborhood environment in New York City. *Health Place, 12,* 167–179.

Dryfoos, Joy G. (1994). *Full service schools: A revolution in health and social services for children, youth, and families.* San Francisco, CA: Jossey-Bass.

Edmonds, R. (1979). Effective schools for the urban poor. *Educational Leadership, 37,* 5–24.

Edmonds, R. (1980). *Search for effective schools.* Speeches/meeting papers sponsored by the Horace Mann Learning Center, Washington, DC.

Edmonds, R. (1982). Programs of school improvement: An overview. *Educational Leadership, 40*(3), 4–11.

Edmonds, R. (1983). An overview of school improvement programs. Reports sponsored by the National Institution of Education (ED), Washington, DC.

Education Equality Project (2010). *What we stand for: Our mission.* Retrieved April 1, 2010 from: www.educationequality project.org

Education Law Center (2010). *History of Abbott.* Retrieved April 1, 2010 from: www.edlawcenter.org/ELCPublic/ AbbottvBurke/AbbottHistory.htm

Education Trust (2004). *Education watch: Achievement gap summary tables.* Washington, DC: Education Trust.

Education Trust (2009). *How it's being done: Urgent lessons from unexpected schools.* Washington, DC: Education Trust.

Education Trust (2010a). *Education watch: The nation.* Washington, DC: Education Trust.

Education Trust (2010b). *Education watch: Achievement gap summary tables.* Washington, DC: Education Trust.

Education Trust (2010c). *Achievement in America: How are we doing? What comes next?* Washington, DC: Education Trust. Retrieved April 1, 2010 from: www.edtrust.org/dc/resources/presentations

Education Trust (2010d). *Close the hidden funding gaps in our schools.* Washington, DC: Education Trust. Retrieved April 1, 2010 from: www.edtrust.org/dc/publication/close-the-hidden-funding-gaps-in-our-schools

Epstein, J. (2001). *School, family and community partnerships: Preparing educators and improving schools.* Boulder, CO: Westview Press.

Finn, C. E., Manno, B. V., & Vanourek, G. (2000). *Charter schools in action.* Princeton, NJ: Princeton University Press.

Fiscella, K., & Williams, D. R. (2004). Health disparities based on socioeconomic inequities: Implications for urban health care. *Academic Medicine, 79,* 1139–1147.

Fuller, B. et al. (1999). *School choice: Abundant hopes, scarce evidence of results.* Berkeley, CA: Policy Analysis for California Education, University of California. Retrieved June 1, 2011 from: http://eric.ed.gov/PDFS/ED476193.pdf

Good, T. L., & Brophy, J. E. (1986). School effects. In M. C. Wittrock (Ed.), *Handbook of research on teaching* (3rd ed., pp. 570–602). New York: Macmillan.

Greene, J. P., Peterson, P., Du, J., Boeger, L., & Frazier, C. L. (1998). *The effectiveness of school choice in Milwaukee: A secondary analysis of data from the program's evaluation.* Occasional Paper 96–3. Cambridge, MA: Harvard University Program in Educational Policy and Governance.

Hack, M., Klein, N. K., & Taylor, H. G. (1995). Long-term developmental outcomes of low birth weight infants. *The Future of Children, 5,* 176–196.

Hess, F. M. (2002). *Revolution at the margins: The impact of competition on urban school systems.* Washington, DC: Brookings Institution.

Hill, P., Lake, R., Celio, M. B., Campbell, C., Herdman, P., & Bulkley, K. (2001). *A study of charter school accountability.* Jessup, MD: U.S. Department of Education, Office of Educational Research and Improvement.

Hilts, P. J. (2000). Study finds most states lack system for monitoring asthma. *New York Times,* May 22.

Hoffereth, S. L., & Sandberg, J. F. (2001). How American children spend their time. *Journal of Marriage and the Family, 63,* 295–308.

Hoffman, K., Llagas, C., & Snyder, T. (2003). *Status and trends in the education of Blacks.* NCES 2003–2004. Washington, DC: U.S. Department of Education, Office of Educational Research and Improvement.

Hoxby, C. M. (2000). Does competition among public schools benefit students and taxpayers? *American Economic Review, 90,* 5.

Hoxby, C. M. (2001). Rising tide: New evidence on competition and the public schools. *Education Next, 1,* 4.

Hoxby, C. M. (2004). *Achievement in charter schools and regular public schools in the United States: Understanding the differences.* Cambridge, MA: Harvard University and the National Bureau of Economic Research. Retrieved June 1, 2011 from: www.innovations.harvard.edu/cache/documents/4848.pdf

Hoxby, C. M. (2009). *The New York City Charter School Evaluation Project.* Cambridge, MA: National Bureau of Economic Research. Retrieved December 12, 2009 from: www.nber.org/~schools/charterschoolseval

Ingersoll, R. (1999). The problem of underqualified teachers in American secondary schools. *Educational Researcher, 28,* 26–37.

Ingersoll, R. (2003). *Who controls teachers' work?: Power and accountability in America's schools.* Cambridge, MA: Harvard University Press.

Jencks, C., Smith, M., Acland, H., Bane, M., Cohen, D., Gintis, H., et al. (1972). *Inequality: A reassessment of the role of families and schools.* New York: Basic Books.

Karen, D. (2008). No Child Left Behind? Sociology ignored! In A. R. Sadovnik, J. A. O'Day, G. W. Bohrnstedt, & K. M. Borman (Eds.), *No Child Left Behind and the reduction of the achievement gap* (pp. 13–24). New York: Routledge.

Komaromy, M., Grumbach, K., Drake, M., Vranizan, K., Lurie, N., Keane, D., et al. (1996). The role of Black and Hispanic physicians in providing health care for underserved populations. *New England Journal of Medicine, 334,* 1305–1310.

Ladd, H. F. (2002). *Market-based reforms in urban education.* Washington, DC: Economic Policy Institute.

Lareau, A. (2003). *Unequal childhoods: Class, race, and family life.* Berkeley, CA: University of California Press.

Lee, V. E., & Burkam, D. T. (2002). *Inequality at the starting gate: Social background differences in achievement as children begin school.* Washington, DC: Economic Policy Institute.

Lubienski, C., & Lubienski, S. T. (2006). Charter schools, academic achievement and NCLB. *Journal of School Choice, 1*(3), 55–62.

Marzano, R. J. (2003). *What works in schools: Translating research into action.* Alexandria, VA: Association for Supervision and Curriculum Development.

Metcalf, K. K. et al. (1998). *Evaluation of the Cleveland scholarship and tutoring program, Second Year Report, 1997–1998.* Bloomington, IN: Indiana Center for Evaluation.

Metcalf, K. K. et al. (1999). *Evaluation of the Cleveland scholarship and tutoring program 1996–1999.* Bloomington, IN: Indiana Center for Evaluation.

Metcalf, K. K. et al. (2001). *Evaluation of the Cleveland scholarship and tutoring program 1998–2000.* Bloomington, IN: Indiana Center for Evaluation.

Metcalf, K. K. et al. (2003). *Evaluation of the Cleveland scholarship and tutoring program 1998–2001.* Bloomington, IN: Indiana Center for Evaluation.

Metcalf, K. K. et al. (2004). *Evaluation of the Cleveland scholarship and tutoring program 1998–2004.* Bloomington, IN: Indiana Center for Evaluation.

Miron, G., & Nelson, C. (2001). *Student academic achievement in charter schools: What we know and why we know so little.* Kalamazoo, MI: Western Michigan University, Evaluation Center.

Miron, G., & Nelson, C. (2002). *What's public about charter schools? Lessons learned about choice and accountability.* Thousand Oaks, CA: Corwin.

Mortenson, T. (1997). *Research seminar on public policy analysis of opportunity for post secondary education.* Washington, DC: Education Trust. Retrieved May 25, 2005 from: www.edtrust.org

Nelson, F. H., Rosenberg, B., & Van Meter, N. (2004). *Charter school achievement on the 2003 National Assessment of Educational Progress.* Retrieved April 1, 2020 from: http://archive.aft.org/pubs-reports/downloads/teachers/NAEP CharterSchoolReport.pdf

New York State United Teachers (2003). Court of Appeals rules for Campaign for Fiscal Equity, *NYSUT Briefing Bulletin,* No. 03–12, June 26. Retrieved April 2, 2010 from: http://nysut.org/research/bulletins/20030627cfe.html

New York Times (2004). Advertisement against AFT Charter School Study. July 28.

No Child Left Behind Act of 2001 (NCLB) (2002). P.L. 107–110. Washington, DC: U.S. Congress.

Oakes, J. (2005). *Keeping track.* New Haven, CT: Yale University Press.

Peterson, K. K., & Lezotte, L. W. (1991). *Educators, researcher, and the effective schools movement.* In J. R. Bliss, W. A. Firestone, & C. E. Richards (Eds.), *Rethinking effective schools: Research and practice* (pp. 128–137). London: Prentice Hall International (UK).

Purkey, S. C., & Smith, M. S. (1983). Effective schools: A review. *Elementary School Journal, 83*(4), 427–452.

Rist, R. (1977). On understanding the processes of schooling: The contributions of labeling theory. In J. Karabel, & A. H. Halsey (Eds.), *Power and ideology in education* (pp. 292–305). New York: Oxford University Press.

Robelen, E. W. (2006). Florida voucher ruling roils school choice waters, *Education Week.* Retrieved October 17, 2010 from: www.edweek.org/login.html

Rothstein, R. (2004). *Class and schools: Using social, economic, and educational reform to close the Black–White achievement gap.* New York: Teachers College Press.

Rouse, C. (1998). Schools and student achievement: More on the Milwaukee Parental Choice Program. *Economic Policy Review, 4,* 61–78.

RPP International (1998). *The state of charter schools 1998.* Washington, DC: U.S. Department of Education, Office of Educational Research and Improvement.

RPP International (1999). *The state of charter schools 1999.* Washington, DC: U.S. Department of Education, Office of Educational Research and Improvement.

RPP International (2000). *The state of charter schools 2000.* Washington, DC: U.S. Department of Education, Office of Educational Research and Improvement.

RPP International (2001). *Challenge and opportunity: The impact of charter schools on school districts.* Washington, DC: U.S. Department of Education, Office of Educational Research and Improvement.

Sadovnik, A. R. (2010). *Sociology of education: A critical reader* (2nd ed.). New York: Routledge.

Sadovnik, A. R., O'Day, J. A., Bohrnstedt, G. W., & Borman, K. M. (2008). *No Child Left Behind and the reduction of the achievement gap.* New York: Routledge.

Starfield, B. (1982). Child health and socioeconomic status. *American Journal of Public Health, 72,* 532–534.

Thernstrom, A., & Thernstrom, S. (2003). *No excuses: Closing the racial gap in learning.* New York: Simon & Schuster.

Toppo, G. (2008). Sharpton, education plan may tear union ties. *USA Today,* June 11. Retrieved April 2, 2010 from: www.usatoday.com/news/education/2008-06-11-race-equality_N.htm

Tough, P. (2008). *Whatever it takes: Geoffrey Canada's quest to change Harlem and America.* New York: Houghton Mifflin.

Tractenberg, P., Sadovnik, A., & Liss, B. (2004). *Tough choices: An informed discussion of school choice.* Newark, NJ: Institute on Education Law and Policy, Rutgers University. Retrieved July 10, 2010 from: www.ielp/rutgers.edu

Tractenberg, P., Liss, B., Moscovitch, R., & Sadovnik, A. R. (2006). *Don't forget the schools: Legal considerations for school finance reform.* Newark, NJ: Institute on Education Law and Policy, Rutgers University. Retrieved July 10, 2010 from: www.ielp/rutgers.edu

Tractenberg, P., Holzer, M., Miller, G., Sadovnik, A., & Liss, B. (2002). *Developing a plan for reestablishing local control in the state-operated districts.* Newark, NJ: Institute on Education Law and Policy, Rutgers University. Retrieved July 10, 2010 from: www.ielp/rutgers.edu

U.S. Bureau of the Census (2002). Current population reports. *Educational attainment in the United States.* Washington, DC: Bureau of the Census.

U.S. Department of Education (2000). *The condition of education: National assessment of educational progress.* Washington, DC: National Center for Educational Statistics, Office of the Under Secretary and Office of Elementary and Secondary Education.

U.S. Department of Education (2006). *A closer look at charter schools using hierarchical linear modeling.* Washington, DC: National Center for Educational Statistics, National Assessment of Educational Progress. Retrieved April 1, 2007 from: http://nces.ed.gov/nationsreportcard//pdf/studies/2006460.pdf

U.S. Department of Education (2009a). *Characteristics of the 100 largest public elementary and secondary school districts in the United States: 2006–2007.* Washington, DC: National Center for Education Statistics. Retrieved April 1, 2010 from: http://nces.ed.gov/pubs2009/100_largest/tables/table_a09.asp?referrer=report

U.S. Department of Education (2009b). *The nation's report card.* Washington, DC: The National Assessment of Educational Progress. Retrieved April 1, 2010 from: http://nces.ed.gov/nationsreportcard

Van Dunk, E., & Dickman, A. M. (2003). *School choice and the question of accountability: The Milwaukee experience.* New Haven, CT: Yale University Press.

Washington Times (2009). Senate kills GOP voucher bid. *Washington Times,* March 11. Retrieved from: www.washington times.com/news/2009/mar/11/senate-kills-gops-dc-vouchers-bid

Wells, A. S., Duran, J., & White, T. (2004) Refusing to leave segregation behind: From graduates of racially diverse schools to the Supreme Court. *Teachers College Record, 106*(10), 2032–2056.

Witte, J. F. et al. (1995). *Fifth-year report on the Milwaukee Parental Choice Program.* Madison, WI: University of Wisconsin. Retrieved March 10, 2004 from: http://dpls.dacc.wisc.edu/choice/choice_rep95.html

Yaffe, D. (2007). *Other people's children: The battle for justice and equality in New Jersey's schools.* New Brunswick, NJ: Rutgers University Press.

5

Politics of Urban Education
Equity, Accountability, and Innovation

Kenneth K. Wong and Shayna Klopott

This chapter focuses on school politics in the intergovernmental system, urban district governance reform, and the new politics of innovation and accountability. Analytically, for each of these topics, we provide the research context for the current debate and try to specify relevant lessons learned from the appropriate body of work. Taken as a whole, this chapter offers the analytical foundation for students who are interested in the politics of urban schools.

School Politics in the Intergovernmental System: Policy Implementation as a Subfield

Federalism has shaped our understanding of urban school politics in one major arena, namely the challenge of implementing reform that promotes equity. Since the Great Society Reform of the 1960s, the federal government has clearly focused on social equity issues by promoting racial equality, protecting the educational rights of the handicapped, funding compensatory education, and assisting those with limited English proficiency (Peterson, Rabe, & Wong, 1986). These programs are seen as allocating resources (and legitimacy) to address inequities that primarily arise from class, status, and racial cleavages (Lowi, 1964; Ripley & Franklin, 1984). Earlier studies of the implementation of Title I and other federal programs for disadvantaged students suggested local resistance (Murphy, 1971; Pressman & Wildavsky, 1973).

As federal programs mature, researchers find increasing organizational accommodation (Peterson et al., 1986). With the passage of time, a tendency toward increasing intergovernmental accommodation seems to have gradually emerged, as suggested by studies that employed a longitudinal analysis (Jung & Kirst, 1986; Kirst & Jung, 1982 on Title I; Singer & Butler, 1987 on programs for the handicapped; also see the four-stage process developed by Huberman & Miles, 1984). The compensatory education program, for example, has evolved through three distinct phases (Peterson et al., 1986). Originally, it was little more than a general federal school aid, with virtually no stipulations attached to the use of funds. Extensive local misuses of these resources prompted the federal government to write tighter regulations. Throughout the 1970s, the program had acquired an exceedingly well-defined set of rules and guidelines that many state and local officials had difficulty putting into place. Intergovernmental conflict seemed to have tempered by the late 1970s and early 1980s, when federal, state, and local administrators worked out their differences.

This gradual shift from institutional conflict to accommodation has been facilitated by several factors. At the district and school level, a new professional cadre more identified with program objectives was recruited to administer special programs, and local officials became more sensitive to federal expectations. At the federal level, policymakers began to doubt whether detailed regulations, tight audits, and comprehensive evaluations were mixed blessings. With the state agency serving as an active mediator, appropriate changes and adjustments were made. Over time, administrators developed program identifications that transcended governmental boundaries, and a commitment to a coordinated effort gradually emerged. As institutional accommodation occurred, local professionals began to direct more attention to instructional issues, such as whether pullout practices were educationally sound (Hill, 1977; Knapp, Turnbull, David, Stearns, & Peterson, 1983; National Institute of Education, 1977). The pace of moving toward federal-local cooperation in the management of special programs was not uniform. Wong (1990) found that local reform in redistributive services depended on the district's fiscal conditions, political culture, and the policymaking autonomy of the program professionals.

Understanding NCLB Implementation

Clearly, the enactment of the No Child Left Behind Act (NCLB, 2001), the reauthorization of the Elementary and Secondary Education Act, has generated an enormous amount of interest in the politics of implementation. From the district and state perspective, NCLB established a number of new mandates, such as annual testing, but did not provide full funding. Consequently, a number of districts in three states—Michigan, Texas, and Vermont—joined the National Education Association in filing a suit against the U.S. Department of Education (National Education Association, 2005). The state of Connecticut also sued the U.S. Department of Education, arguing that it had failed to provide funding to administer the NCLB-mandated assessments, and was, therefore, unconstitutional. In addition, two districts in Illinois filed suit, arguing that NCLB violated the Individuals with Disabilities Education Act. While both the Connecticut and the Illinois school districts' suit were thrown out by the judge, the conflict demonstrated the degree to which districts and states were concerned about the requirements established in NCLB.

Districts have also found NCLB quite difficult to implement. Lewis (2003) describes four challenges districts faced in the initial phase. Data for this study were taken from interviews conducted with district staff from school districts around the country, and with national and regional education organizations. WestEd, the study's sponsor, also "convened a group of district leaders from Arizona, California, Nevada and Utah" (p. 1). Four areas of concern over NCLB implementation were identified:

1. how to fulfill the choice and supplemental service option;
2. how to ensure that all teachers were highly qualified;
3. how to collect, use, and report data effectively; and
4. how to finance all of the NCLB requirements.

Recent studies on NCLB have focused on how districts managed to meet the federal NCLB expectations. In a 2008 report on restructuring in Georgia, the Center on Education Policy detailed the intergovernmental policy implementation process (Duffrin & Scott, 2008). Initially, NCLB restructuring in Georgia consisted primarily of schools being told to write and implement restructuring plans, but little assistance was offered by the state to support such implementation. After schools complained to Georgia Department of Education, the department began providing principal mentors, classroom coaching, and professional development. It also created a monitoring system to hold individual schools accountable for making the changes outlined in their restructuring plans.

Until the 2007–2008 school year, however, much of the support and monitoring was done for the schools directly by the state. In 2007–2008, the state gave districts more responsibility for the planning process, requiring that a district representative be involved in the planning process at each school and in the monitoring of implementation. The state aimed to get districts to think more systematically about how their policies and practices affect their restructuring schools, and to make necessary changes/adjustments to provide increased support for such schools.

In Atlanta, school restructuring was already underway when NCLB was passed into law. The case study suggests that the district has continued to focus more on its own accountability practices than those affiliated with NCLB, but that the added resources provided under NCLB have been quite useful. However, the district officials interviewed for the case study indicated that NCLB did require a lot of additional paperwork, which hampers the district's efforts to actually help the schools in restructuring, and that the "one-size-fits-all" criteria for making Adequate Yearly Progress (AYP) are problematic, citing the difficulty of bringing students in their alternative high school up to standard by the end of freshman year. Thus, while NCLB has provided some support for Atlanta, it has also been a source of frustration for district officials trying to provide support for the district's struggling schools. The application of a single model of accountability from the federal government on individual districts does not take into account local district needs or the needs of individual students (Duffrin & Scott, 2008).

Another Center for Education Policy study illuminates intergovernmental conflict in Ohio (Kelleher & Scott, 2009). This report looks at "the effects of differentiated accountability and related policies" (p. 1). The data for this report were drawn from interviews with two Ohio Department of Education officials, over 20 local administrators, teachers, and other staff, as well as a review of restructuring documents and state and district test data. Local interviews were conducted in four districts: Cincinnati, Cleveland Metropolitan, Mansfield City, and Mount Vernon City. All data were collected in the fall and winter of 2008–2009. The Ohio study highlights intergovernmental conflict primarily between the state and districts, but also between the state and federal government and, to some extent, between the federal government, as represented through the state, and individual schools. State officials, though working to fully implement NCLB, were skeptical of its premise: "that school improvement and district improvement can be addressed separately" (p. 1). As a result, the state's strategy is to provide support primarily to districts, with the hope that it will trickle down to the individual schools. As part of the Ohio Improvement Plan (the state's differentiated account-ability process), all schools in the district are expected to move through improvement together. Moreover, the researchers found that district and school officials have a much better understanding of, and give more weight to, Ohio's performance ratings than to NCLB accountability status. In fact, many school personnel interviewed asked questions of the researchers suggesting that they didn't have an understanding of the NCLB accountability system. This was quite evident in the Cleveland case study, where the researchers noted that school principals were unfamiliar with NCLB restructuring and instead focused on the district's student achievement goals and restructuring plans. It is unclear from the case study whether this was intentional or not—it could be that the district was trying to protect principals from an added layer of complication and paperwork, or there could just be poor communication from the district to the schools around NCLB restructuring. Intergovernmental conflict was again evident in Cleveland's high school restructuring effort, which seems to be primarily to open new high schools. Parents and students expressed satisfaction with the new schools; however, according to principals and teachers, the existing high schools lost enrollment as a result of students enrolling in the new schools, and were, therefore, left with less funding to undertake restructuring. While the state suggests opening new schools as one means to meeting AYP, it does not seem to suggest a strategy for dealing with the existing schools, and students left in them, in restructuring.

A third Center for Education Policy study (Scott, 2009) demonstrates how state level political decisions and actions affect the implementation of NCLB at the district and school level. The data for this report were taken from document reviews, interviews with state and local officials, as well as with technical assistance providers that worked with districts, and four district case studies (and nine schools in them)—Oakland Unified, Palmdale Elementary, Tahoe-Trukee Unified, and Twin Rivers Unified. All data were collected in the fall and winter of 2008–2009.

The report highlights two key political issues that arose during the study period. First, the state legislature had been slow to pass the funding bill, so money for restructuring was not dispersed to districts until after school had started in the fall of 2008. The failure of the legislature to act in a timely fashion meant that districts and schools were unable to use the extra money well because it was too late to hire additional teachers, revise union contracts, or to get high-quality coaches. In some schools, principals weren't even aware that the state money existed. Furthermore, the funds were only provided one year at a time, so schools and districts were not able to make long-term hires or to base restructuring practices on the additional funding because there was no guarantee that they would get it again the following year. Second, California focuses its funding and technical assistance on the most severe cases of school and district failure. While seemingly making sense, district personnel interviewed suggested that the amount of funding associated with this strategy was not sufficient for school turnaround.

State Efforts to Turn Around Low Performance

In response to growing public demand for academic accountability, state governments are increasingly ready to take more direct action to address low performance. Not surprisingly, the state activist approach has generated state-district conflict. Stringfield and Yakimowski-Srebnick (2005) examine three periods of state-imposed accountability reform efforts in the Baltimore City Public School System (BCPSS). The authors use student data, semi-structured interviews, document analysis, and observations of key informants to understand how state accountability practices affected BCPSS organization and student achievement in a longitudinal mixed-method case study.

The three periods examined are 1992–1997 (Phase I), 1997–2001 (Phase II), and 2001–2003 (Phase III, though that was just the end of the study as the phase is ongoing). Phase I was characterized by a state mandate that schools give the Maryland School Performance Assessment Program (MSPAP) test and that the aggregate school and district-level results be made public. However, during this phase, there was very little support for schools to change. Over the course of Phase I, BCPSS actually fell further behind the rest of the state, ushering in Phase II. Phase II began with the passage of Senate Bill 795, which completely overhauled the governance of BCPSS, gave control of the school system to a new board, appointed by the mayor and governor, increased funding for the district, laid out specific proposals to improve and address failures, and created both a transition and a master five-year plan to improve the school system. The new board imposed numerous curricular, structural, and personnel changes. Over the course of Phase II, student test scores on both the MSPAP and the nationally normed Terra Nova improved, as did high school graduation rates. While Phase II was not a complete success, it was successful enough to be renewed by the state legislature for an additional five years. However, the passage of the No Child Left Behind Act ushered in Phase III, which is ongoing. As of the publishing of this paper, Phase III showed BCPSS schools continuing to improve, though still lagging behind the rest of the state (at least they were no longer a significant outlier). Phase III also forced the state to create better guidelines for how schools would come out of improvement, and, as of 2003, eight schools had done so. Phase III accountability also highlighted some weaknesses of NCLB, particularly with regard to the provision that a state department of education may reconstitute a school, but fails to provide solutions for the failure of an already reconstituted school. Overall, the authors conclude that the Maryland accountability experiment demonstrated that without support for accountability reform, accountability testing may be an empty reform.

In 2000, the Pennsylvania state legislature passed the Education Empowerment Act, which allowed the state to take over districts in financial or academic distress. The following year the state used that power to take control of the Philadelphia Public Schools. The key feature of the state's takeover was the involvement of private contractors—initially, Edison Schools—to take control of the district. Though ultimately a compromise was reached with the district that substantially scaled back Edison's role and left the district central administration in charge of the district, a new model of schooling, the diverse provider model (DPM), was put in place. While it was not the first time such a model had been suggested (see Hill, 2006; Hill, Campbell, & Harvey, 2000), it was one of the first occasions to see it in practice. Hill (2006) and Hill et al. (2000) suggested that DPM would entail districts building portfolios of schools which include district-run schools, charters, and schools managed by external partners; districts being responsible for provider selection and assignment; districts writing and monitoring provider contracts that laid out clear outcome goals; districts providing providers with a fixed per-pupil-based budget, but allowing providers to have full budgetary discretion; providers employing teachers and principals; and parents and students having choice among all schools in the district's portfolio. Essentially, districts under DPM districts would become portfolio managers.

In Philadelphia, the model developed more organically and the district retained control over many more aspects than Hill and his colleagues would have suggested. Nonetheless, the state intervention created a new model of schooling in Philadelphia (Gold, Christman, & Herold, 2007). After three years of implementation, test scores in Philadelphia seemed to be improving, at least as measured by the percentage of fifth and eighth graders scoring proficient or advanced on the Pennsylvania System of School Assessment (PSSA). Moreover, over the course of the first three years of implementation the number of schools making AYP under No Child Left Behind increased (though that figure fell a little after tougher AYP targets were implemented in 2005). Gold et al. (2007) note that while DPM seems to be relatively successful, it is hard to discern whether its success is related to the new governance arrangements or to the district's new core curriculum and regular benchmarking, increased professional development, and increased focus on math and literacy. While state intervention can lead to some improvement in school outcomes, it remains to be seen if such improvements are sustainable and are particularly significant. Under NCLB, states have the option to take over consistently failing districts, yet few have used that option so far. Many critics argue that states are no more adept at running schools than are districts, and that state takeover may not have the desired effect.

Urban Governance Reconsidered: Evolving Centers of Power

Political scientists have contributed to our understanding of power distribution both inside the school district as well as the larger polity within which the school system is embedded. Building on the literature on whether city decisions are made by a closed elite power structure or influenced by organized interests in both public and private sectors, recent studies focus on coalitional politics that involve informal and formal arrangements among multiple power centers. Stone (1989) argues that urban regimes, comprised of both "public bodies and private interests [that] function together in order to be able to make and carry out governing decisions" (p. 6), are crucial to governing in urban environments (see also Shipps, 2003). While private interests are likely to include businesses, they may also include grassroots interests, such as religious and community organizations. Stone, Henig, Jones, and Pierannunzi (2001) conclude that coalitions of stakeholders from multiple constituencies are necessary to change educational policy, and that the business community is particularly important to such coalitions. Government, they argue, is best suited for generating a sense of collective purpose and creating civic mobilization, but that it is the mobilization of multiple stakeholders that will ultimately affect change. Henig (1999) argues that the building of such coalitions is confounded by race, particularly around issues of education. In many urban communities, schools have been a source of middle-class mobility and patronage jobs for Blacks, making school reform that would result in Black job loss a contentious political issue.

Shipps (2003) asks how civic engagement and the substance of school reform interact and how that interaction affects the scaling-up of school reform. Using Chicago as an example, Shipps builds on Stone et al.'s (Stone, 1989; Stone et al., 2001) urban regime theory for understanding school reform. She conducted 180 semi-structured interviews with Chicago elites in 1991, 1994, and 1997, and looked at documentary evidence on the effects of the reform and the politics behind the two Illinois school reform laws. She found that the Chicago Public Schools (CPS) were dominated by a "dysfunctional employment regime" in the 1980s, which provided good jobs for adults, but poor education for low-income children. The 1988 reform, which created Local School Councils (LSCs), challenged the employment regime with an empowerment regime, which sought to shift power from the central office to individual schools and to increase the variety of actors involved in school governance. While the LSCs had some success, in racially mixed schools the LSCs exacerbated existing racial tensions and were themselves poorly functioning. Importantly, Shipps notes that the 1988 reform threatened African Americans who had, albeit shortly, been the primary stakeholders in the previous employment regime, as they believed that their professionalism was being undermined. Ultimately, Shipps argues, the 1988 reform failed to institutionalize because the coalition that had brought them into existence could not institutionalize to provide ongoing support. Corporate leaders became disenchanted with community activists, whom they saw as being too focused on getting funding, and with "passive resistance from the central office administrators" (Shipps, 2003, p. 863). Likewise, community activists were frustrated because they could not get funding from the corporate leaders, which they perceived as a lack of support. As the hopes of the 1988 reform began to fade, a new group of activists was working on building a coalition with foundation leaders in order to participate in the Annenberg Challenge. The Chicago Annenberg Challenge (CAC) sought performance reform, but because of internal union bickering, was unable to build a performance regime. Again, the failure to institutionalize the reform coalition led to failure. The final reform effort that Shipps discusses is the transfer of power to the mayor's office. In 1995 the state legislature gave Mayor Daley control of the CPS, solidifying the market-based approach for which Daley had been advocating. The school system was restructured to resemble a corporation, with a focus on the economic value of good schools and a concern for the bottom line. While the research for the article ended before conclusions could be drawn about the stability of this regime, it seems clear now that the market regime led by Daley has been relatively stable and has resulted in some improvements in the CPS.

Interest Groups as Autonomous Actors

The argument that the school system is capable of accommodating external interests generally undermines the fact that the latter can become autonomous power centers. At times, these actors may threaten the school's interest in organizational maintenance. One major interest is the teachers' union (McDonnell & Pascal, 1979). Grimshaw's (1979) study of the Chicago Teachers Union suggested that the union has gone through two phases in its relationship with the city and school administration. During the formative years, the union largely cooperated with the administration (and the mayor) in return for a legitimate role in the policy-making process. Cole (1969) also found that union recognition was a key objective in the 1960 teachers' strike in New York City. In the second phase, which Grimshaw characterized as "union rule," the union became independent of both the local political machine and the reform factions. Instead, it looked to the national union leadership for guidance and engaged in tough bargaining with the administration over better compensation and working conditions. Consequently, Grimshaw argued that policymakers "no longer are able to set policy unless the policy is consistent with the union's objectives" (1979, p. 150). Shipps (2003) might add a caveat to Grimshaw's conclusion, however. She argues that the 1995 Chicago school reform, which prohibited the union from striking and eliminated previous workplace agreements, was passed without much union resistance because of union infighting. The resulting period, which continues today, might be characterized as union cooption, i.e., the Chicago Teachers Union has developed its own reform organization and works relatively well with the district to accomplish reform goals.

An interesting turn of events has been the reform union. Under reform unionism, or professional unionism (as opposed to industrial unionism), teachers work with school management—i.e., principals, superintendents, and the school board—to improve schools and to take responsibility for student learning (Kerchner, Koppich, & Weeres, 1997). According to Kerchner et al. (1997) "the vision of a union of knowledge workers [their term for how teachers need to be considered] is a vision that builds upon changes in the processes of teaching and learning" (p. 37). This plays out in unions that are less confrontational and that negotiate contracts around topics that would improve student learning, not just teacher working conditions. For example, new contracts included language around "shared decision making, peer assistance and review, professional development, changes in the reward and incentive system, charters and other kinds of semiautonomous schools intervention in low-performing schools, and educational standards" (Kerchner & Koppich, 2007, p. 352). It also includes flexibility in the division of labor (Kerchner et al., 1997), including teacher career ladders, in which teachers have opportunities to grow, becoming mentor teachers, master teachers, and even take on some managerial responsibilities, such as teacher review (Johnson & Kardos, 2000). Johnson and Kardos (2000) show that reform bargaining—i.e., bargaining in which the management and labor collaborate and share interests, where there is "flexibility and site-based discretion built into the contract, [and where] varied roles and status are recognized" (p. 28)—leads to educational reform, whereas contracts negotiated in an industrial style did not.

While reform unionism was actively pursued during the 1980s and 1990s, the last decade has shown how difficult it is to use collective bargaining as a means of school reform. A number of districts and local unions have embraced the concepts inherent in reform unionism and continue to collaborate, but overall, nationally, most unions "spend their working days attending to the nuts and bolts of conventional unionism: representing teachers in grievance processes, negotiating contracts, training teachers for union leadership posts, and attending to the union organization itself" (Kerchner & Koppich, 2007, p. 354). Before discussing other interest groups, we will briefly discuss a few examples of reform unionism in action.

Performance-based pay, or merit pay as it is often called, is one reform that has begun to make some headway in school districts around the country. Odden and Kelley (2002) suggest that performance-based pay can be used to encourage better teaching and learning (both by the students and the teachers), to create a desirable school culture by aligning practices and goals, and to attract and retain good teachers. Moreover, performance-based pay is seen as a means to motivate teachers who might not be performing to the best of their ability. Performance-based pay can also be used as a way to make teaching more professional. The incorporation of the performance-based pay plan into the existing career ladder encourages teachers to see teaching as a career that could vary over time (Johnson & Kardos, 2000).

Denver has implemented an extensive performance-based pay system, the Professional Compensation Plan (ProComp). ProComp replaces the district's single salary schedule with one that rewards teachers for meeting students' growth objectives as measured by the state assessment, receiving satisfactory professional evaluations, increasing their own knowledge and skills, and serving in hard-to-serve schools and positions. ProComp is aligned with district reform goals (http://techtraining.dpsk12.org/ProComp/Welcome/Welcome.html). Importantly, academic growth is measured on a student-by-student basis. The Colorado Department of Education groups students with the same baseline year test score and looks at the change in their score the next year as a percentile group scores in the subsequent year. Teachers who have at least ten students who exhibit growth qualify for the student growth bonus (http://techtraining.dpsk12.org/ProComp/4Exceeds Expectations/4ExceedsExpectations.html). Also, it is important to note that while teachers earn higher salaries if their students do very well, they can also lose those bonuses if their students underperform at a later date. Early data indicate that teachers participating in ProComp only raised their students' score slightly, as compared to their non-participating peers. However, it also indicates that teachers are earning more money, seeking to work in hard-to-staff schools at higher rates, and applying for jobs in the district at higher rates than they did prior to implementation in January, 2006 (*Education Week*, 2007).

Although performance-based pay is often touted as a means for improving teaching, researchers have discovered that many teachers do not respond to extrinsic incentives (Johnson, 1986). Researchers also point out that another difficulty with performance-based pay is that it has not had the consensus of entire staffs and the plans have not been replicable across districts, especially urban districts. A final and considerable problem is that of evaluation (Murnane & Cohen, 1986). If it is done by student performance on standardized tests, they fear that the tests are not fair or that schools may institute policies of teaching to the test. If administrators do the evaluations, they have reservations about the administrators' ability to

1. judge fairly;
2. find time to do sufficient evaluations; or
3. have adequate subject area expertise.

While the Denver Teachers Association and the Denver Public Schools seem to have come to an agreement about how to deal with these concerns, it remains to be seen if other districts will adopt such a comprehensive performance-based salary schedule.

Other districts have demonstrated reform unionism through their acceptance of and participation in school choice. New York City's United Federation of Teachers (UFT), for example, opened its own charter school in the fall of 2005 (secondary school opened in 2006) in order to completely involve teachers in the school leadership, and to demonstrate that unions are not a hindrance to student learning (www.pbs.org/wnet/wherewestand/blog/the-ufts-charter-schools/293). In the summer of 2009, UFT signed a contract with Green Dot Charter Schools, which opened a school in the Bronx. Green Dot Charter Schools believes that teachers need to be treated as professionals and that unions help encourage that behavior (Green, 2009). The UFT's willingness to participate in school choice, both through the creation of their own school and their efforts to bring modified contracts to charter schools—both protecting teachers and encouraging teacher professionalism—demonstrates a new wave of reform unionism that was not likely predicted when the concept became popular in the 1990s.

Parental Empowerment in Practice

The best example in which parents are indeed the key decision-makers is found in the LSCs in the CPS. Following a long legislative process, the 1988 Chicago School Reform Act (P.A. 85-1418) mandated comprehensive reforms in school governance. The 1988 school reform in Chicago represented an opportunity for parents, school staff, and community groups to work together on educational improvement. The reform was designed to restore public confidence by granting parents substantial "ownership" over schools. To enhance accountability, the central office decentralized policymaking to locally elected parent councils and the principal at the school site. The 11-member council consists of six parents (i.e., the majority), two community representatives, two teachers, and the principal. There is also one student member at the high school level.

Members of the LSC were given substantial authority—they could hire and fire the principal, allocate school funds, and develop school improvement plans. With training and support from business and public interest groups, LSCs wrote their bylaws, approved school budgets, and successfully reviewed the principals' contract. The first major exercise of parental power was demonstrated in the decision on the 276 principals (representing half of the schools in the system) who were up for review in March 1990; 82% were retained on a new four-year contract (see Designs for Change, 1990). Councils that were dominated by minorities retained their White principals at a high rate of 78%. However, principals who failed to get contract renewal were more likely to hold "interim" positions in predominantly Hispanic schools. In these neighborhoods, community groups seemed particularly active in pushing for the selection of candidates who promised to be more responsive to their needs, such as solving the problem of overcrowding in the classroom.

The 1988 implementation of LSCs in the CPS gave parents dramatically more power than in previous forms of local control. The LSCs were not only majority parent members, but the chair also had to be a parent. The LSCs's role in hiring and firing the principal and approving the budget and School Improvement Plan gave parents real control of school policy (Bryk, Thum, Easton, & Luppescu, 1998). The parents on the LSCs are more educated and have higher occupational status than do the average adult in Chicago, but even in the lowest income schools, the "education level of LSC members is almost equal to that of the general Chicago population" (Ryan et al., 1997, p. 7). According to a study on the early implementation of the reform (Ryan et al., 1997), the 1988 reform was relatively successful, with 50–60% of LSCs functioning well and another quarter to a third functioning but with a need for improvement. Only about 10–15% of the councils exhibited serious problems.

More than 20 years after they were established, LSCs endure, albeit with significantly less power, even though the CPS have undergone numerous additional reform efforts. In 1995 the Illinois state legislature gave control of the CPS to the mayor. The 1995 reform also required that LSC members attend training, and limited the amount of Chapter 1, i.e., federal money associated with impoverished students, that the district had to distribute to schools, thus limiting the discretionary spending of the LSCs. The provision of training for LSC members was considered crucial, after the initial years of the experiment showed that many LSC members didn't have the knowledge or skills to govern a school. The training that was implemented after 1995 proved to be quite useful to LSC members, though some argued that even more training would have been helpful, particularly in the principal selection (*Catalyst Chicago*, 2004a). After Mayor Daley took control of the schools, the LSCs gradually began to lose some of their power due to the practices of school probation and intervention, both of which allowed the CEO to dissolve an LSC. Even if the LSC wasn't dissolved, probationary status allowed the district to take over many of the duties of the LSC, notably the development and oversight of corrective action/school improvement plans and the right to approve school budgets (*Catalyst Chicago*, 1997). The CPS CEO also had the right to remove principals in schools placed on probation (*Catalyst Chicago*, 2004b). In addition, in 1996 the state legislature gave the CPS CEO veto power over LSCs's decisions to renew (or fail to renew) a principal's contract. Likewise, a 1997 law gave the CEO the ability to intervene in an LSC if he deemed the LSC to be ineffective in his financial duties (*Catalyst Chicago*, 1997). LSCs lost further power after a 1999 law was passed allowing principals to appeal to an independent hearing officer if the LSC didn't renew his or her contract (www.catalyst-chicago.org/guides/?id=59).

As a whole, LSCs began to lose relevance when the district began implementing schools that were not required to have councils (by an exception to the law passed in 1996)—namely small schools and alternative schools (*Catalyst Chicago*, 2004b). In addition, over time, though there was a slight improvement in 2000, the number of candidates and voters for LSC positions diminished substantially from the high point, immediately following LSCs implementation in 1989. In 1989, there were 17,256 candidates for 5,420 seats, or about three candidates per seat. That year, 227,622 parents, staff members, and community members voted, as did 66,561 high school students, who voted for high school representatives to the LSCs (www.catalyst-chicago.org/guides/index.php?id=71). In 2004, in contrast, there were only 6,900 candidates, and only three-quarters of the schools had contested elections. That year, two schools did not field enough candidates to get a quorum on their councils (www.catalyst-chicago.org/guides/index.php?id=52). While their power to govern schools has been limited by more recent school reforms, Chicago's LSCs have stood the test of time, and in schools where they function well, they have been of significant benefit to their schools. However, given the importance of mayoral control in Chicago, it is difficult to assess the distinct contribution of LCSs in school improvement.

A similar experiment was attempted in New Jersey as part of the Abbott legislation. In 1998, schools in all Abbott districts were required to implement school management teams. As in Chicago, the school management teams were responsible for developing a reform plan, choosing a school reform model and guiding the school through implementation. They were also responsible for making sure that the school's curriculum was aligned with the New Jersey Core Curriculum Content Standards; for conducting a needs assessment process based on a review of student data; for developing a professional development plan for the schools' teachers; for creating a technology plan which was submitted to the New Jersey Department of Education (NJDOE) for approval; for ensuring that all program and activities were driven by content standards; and for developing a rewards system for parents and teachers who help students meet standards. Finally, management teams, with the NJDOE's approval, could be responsible for the school budget and the appointment of school staff, including the principal. Although Abbott required site-based management (SBM) that balanced control between parents and school staff (called the control form of SBM), the schools reported that their management teams were leaning toward teacher-dominated SBM. Furthering the strength of the finding, the schools in the first cohort of Abbott implementation were more likely to be moving toward teacher dominance, suggesting that over time the schools were moving away from the state-imposed balanced approach. The schools reported that they were somewhat unsure of their ability to operate well. While they were nearly all committed to the work and most thought that they worked well together, about a third were unclear about their role/responsibilities and another third reported that they had trouble communicating with the school community, particularly in larger school districts. In addition, though the management teams were required by the state to work in subcommittees, more than a third reported that they did not do so and that the ineffectiveness of the subcommittees hampered the team's work as a whole. The teams also reported that they were not particularly well prepared to take on all of the responsibilities required by the state. Less than half of the management team members had experience in the areas of work, though between half and three-quarters reported having some minimal knowledge of most of the areas of responsibility. Finally, about a third of the teams reported not getting any training in many of the areas of responsibility. While the parents on the management teams wanted to be involved in the decision-making and the state-required activities, Walker (2000) suggests that they were not adequately prepared to do so.

Two studies on parent involvement in school choice also provide some insight into parent empowerment. Neild (2005) uses data from semi-structured interviews with parents of eighth graders in public schools in Philadelphia to ascertain what parents knew, or thought they knew, about their children's school choices. The author also investigated the source of parents' information, what influenced their decisions, and their strategies for dealing with the school application process. Neild (2005) found that parents, particularly those without a college education, not only lacked information because it was not provided or made readily accessible by the school district, but also because they did not have the social networks or the knowledge of the school system to obtain such information. Instead of getting information from the district, most parents relied on information from friends, relatives, and the school guidance counselors. The interviews indicated that parents did not have data on school admissions or school quality. As a result, parents were often unable to help guide their children through the high school choice process and they were unable to advocate on their children's behalf when doing so might have made a significant difference in which high school they were accepted.

Buckley (2007) seeks to understand the "effects of schools of choice on parental involvement" (p. 2). He develops a maximum simulated likelihood model, using data drawn from the 2003 Parent and Family Involvement in Education component of the National Household Education Survey to estimate "the selection of the type of school by parents and the effect of this selection on measures of involvement or participation" (p. 2). Buckley finds that while parents of children in public schools of choice do not attend more meetings or activities, they do volunteer more than parents of traditional public school children. Likewise, private secular school parents may increase their volunteer hours, but they actually attend meetings and events less frequently than traditional public school parents. Most interestingly, Buckley finds that after controlling for the fact that private religious school parents have chosen to send their kids to a private religious school, those parents actually participate in the school less than they would have, had their children been in a local public school. While he offers a number of possible explanations for this, he concludes that this suggests that we should not assume that public schools of choice will create "strong school communities by increasing parental engagement" (p. 13).

Governance Innovation to Raise Performance

In the last 20 years, numerous innovations have been suggested and tried as a way to improve urban education. This section highlights how a few of these new governance structures have affected urban politics.

Mayoral Accountability Gains Prominence

Speaking before a gathering of mayors and superintendents in March 2009, U.S. Secretary of Education Arne Duncan urged the mayors to assume greater responsibility for improving public education (Quaid, 2009). He took the position that mayors can provide steady and strong leadership to raise school performance in urban schools. Secretary Duncan's remarks came at a time when there is growing public interest in mayoral accountability as a viable strategy to improve public school governance. In 2006 and 2007 the Gallup Poll surveyed the public's view on mayoral control in schools. In 2006, only 29% were in favor, but in 2007 that number had jumped to 39%, with 42% of parents in favor (Rose & Gallup, 2007). The Obama Administration's support for mayoral involvement is likely to broaden local interest in this new strand of district governance. As a governance framework, mayoral accountability integrates school district performance and the electoral process at the system-wide level. The education mayor is ultimately held accountable for the system's performance, including academic, fiscal, operational, and management. For too long and in too many large urban districts, governance constitutes a structural barrier for progress. Many urban districts are exceedingly ungovernable, where fragmentary centers of power tend to look after their own particularistic interest (Wong, 2002; Ravitch & Viteritti, 1997). Consequently, the independently elected school board has limited leverage to advance collective priorities, and the superintendent lacks the institutional capacity to manage the policy constraints established in state regulations and the union contract. Mayoral accountability aims at addressing the governing challenges in urban districts.

As an institution, mayor-led districts don't insulate education from the city's social, civic, and economic sectors. The education mayor identifies public education as a core component in improving the city's quality of life as well as its long-term economic growth. The education mayor also expands both formal and informal learning opportunities for school children through multiple partnerships with cultural and civic organizations. Aside from these functional benefits, mayors, like any elected politicians, are keenly interested in leaving behind an institutional legacy. Fixing dysfunctional schools and building district capacity enables mayors to advance long-term institutional purposes. In other words, the education mayor is not simply a vote maximizer to get re-elected but also an institution builder.

Currently, several urban districts are under formal mayoral leadership. These include New York, Chicago, Boston, Cleveland, Washington, DC, Providence, New Haven, and Harrisburg. Baltimore and Philadelphia are jointly governed by the mayor and the governor. In recent years, mayors and mayoral candidates in Milwaukee, Dallas, Houston, Memphis, Seattle, St. Paul, Rockford (Illinois), Rochester, and Stafford (Texas), among others, have expressed an interest in more formal involvement in public education. In Detroit, the newly elected mayor, David Bing, endorsed the notion of mayoral control during his electoral campaign. In Nashville, mayoral interest in school reform has never been stronger. In his state of the city address in April 2009, Mayor Karl Dean of Nashville highlighted education reform as his top priority. He has supported Teach for America and the New Teacher Project for recruiting teachers to the district. He also wanted to expand alternative schooling options for students who are over-aged and under-credited. In advocating for a more "aggressive" reform agenda, Mayor Dean told the city that "I think about and work on our schools every single day, and I'm not going to stop until I'm convinced that we have a system that gives all of our students, regardless of race and economic status, an opportunity to graduate from our schools ready to succeed in college and careers."

Growing interest in mayoral accountability is informed by measurable progress in urban districts that are under mayoral control. In *The Education Mayor: Improving America's Schools*, the research team (Wong, Shen, Anagnostopoulos, & Rutledge, 2007) has completed the most comprehensive empirical analysis to date on the effects of mayoral control on student outcomes and management performance. The study examines 104 big-city school systems (including 12 that were under mayoral control) located across 40 states, and synthesizes standardized achievement data from thousands of schools between 1999 and 2003. The study examines multiple years of data by using a mixed methods approach, applying both statistical models and conducting in-depth case studies that connect the macro policy conditions to the micro level practices in a sample of urban classrooms. The analysis found that mayor-led school systems are positively related to standardized elementary reading and math achievement, even after statistically controlling for previous achievement and a host of demographic background variables. The results of the statistical analysis suggested that if a district moved from an elected board to a board with a majority of its members appointed by the mayor, that district would see, relative to other districts in the state, an increase of approximately 0.15–0.19 standard deviations in elementary reading and math. While not likely to move the district above the state mean in the short run, these improvements are nonetheless significant.

A promising effect of mayoral accountability lies in the academic improvement of the district's lowest performing schools, such as the lowest 25th-percentile schools. To be sure, these schools consist of a higher concentration of students eligible for free and reduced-price lunches. In most cases, these schools are also educating greater percentages of African American students than the overall district average. Despite these structural challenges, lowest 25th-percentile schools in mayor-controlled districts show steady progress in the percentage of students who were tested proficient in the state annual benchmarking-grade assessment during 1999 and 2003. For example, the lowest 25th-percentile schools in Baltimore's third-grade reading improved from 5.6% to 32.7%. In math, Chicago's fifth-grade math improved from 10.4% to 27.5% in the lowest performing schools. Further, as New York City (NYC) completed its seventh year of mayoral control in June 2009, student performance showed progress. While there seems to be general agreement on the city's academic gains in state assessment, there is disagreement on the NAEP assessment (Ravitch, 2009). However, an analysis of NYC's NAEP assessment suggests this mayoral district has been making measurable progress on narrowing the achievement gap.

Charter Management and Education Management Organizations

New management models have emerged as the number of charter schools continues to grow. Charter Management Organizations (CMOs) oversee a network of charter schools, which may locate in several districts and states. Education Management Organizations (EMOs) may operate charter schools, or have contracts with districts to operate regular or choice schools within a district, but they may also run particular services for schools/districts. In the latter case, districts and/or schools can contract with the EMO to provide its particular service.

Bulkley (1999) examined the implementation of charter schools in Michigan and Arizona by three very active chartering authorities, Central Michigan University (CMU) and the two boards created in Arizona, during the initial years of charter school implementation. She uses case studies to explore how these authorities have developed their practices from their origination to mid-1998. She also uses an institutional analysis to understand why the chartering authorities in the two states developed to become such different organizations. Data for the case studies come from interviews, conducted between September 1996 and January 1998, with legislators, governor's staff, state department of education staff, board members and staff of charter school sponsors, and representatives from research organizations and interest groups that study and advocate for charter schools. Bulkley examined the forces at play in the creation of the charter authorizers in the two states and found that they developed differently largely because of the political context from which they were created. In Arizona, a Republican governor and state legislature that favored market-based reform created two sponsoring agencies that had a great deal of leeway and which were not required to provide much oversight of the schools they sponsored. Instead, because of their strong belief in the market, policymakers in Arizona believed that parental choice would regulate the schools. In contrast, in Michigan charter school creation was somewhat of a compromise that faced considerable opposition. In response, the CMU sponsoring organization was required to provide much more oversight. Bulkley (1999) also argues that the sponsoring organizations in the two states hired different types of personnel as a response to the ways in which the two types of organizations were expected to operate. In Michigan, CMU was created with a much larger staff to provide increased oversight, and therefore hired more professional educators. In contrast, the Arizona boards were small and, as a result, were able only to hire people from outside of traditional education.

The Philadelphia diverse provider model experiment discussed earlier has been a source of much research on the effectiveness of EMOs. As was discussed previously, after three years the DPM seemed to be having at least a slightly positive effect on student achievement (Gold et al., 2007). However, when schools run by EMOs were looked at alone, the data are more cautious. In a study of how DPM affected PSSA scores over the first three years of implementation, Useem (2005) found that while fifth- and eighth-grade PSSA scores improved over the course of the first three years of implementation, when the data were disaggregated by school type, schools run by the district's Office of Restructured Schools did better than those run by the EMOs. Similarly, MacIver and MacIver (2006) found that eighth graders in Edison schools did not do any better than those in district-run schools. Moreover, eighth graders in non-Edison EMOs did significantly worse than their peers in the district-run schools. Thus, while EMOs seem to offer the promise of improving student achievement because they can work outside of union contracts and/or because they can benefit from being schools of choice, the evidence thus far suggests that they may not actually do so.

One issue that is raised by the use of these organizations, particularly when they run multiple schools in one city, is whether they are acting like a district, in essence replacing the government bureaucracy with a third-party bureaucracy. Bulkley (2004) examined schools that had relationships with three different types of EMOs. She concluded that it really depended on the relationship between the EMO and the school. In the school-EMO relationship in which the EMO provided loose guidance for school structure, the answer was pretty clearly no. However, in other relationships, where the EMO provided much more hands-on guidance and tight structure, the answer might be yes. Clearly, then, if CMOs and EMOs begin to resemble school districts, they might start to experience many of the same problems of urban school bureaucracies. Should they become large enough, they may even serve as a source of competition for urban school bureaucracies. If the public perceives the CMO/EMO as accomplishing the same job as the district with fewer resources and/or with better results, it might rebel against the existing government structure.

Turnaround Challenges

Turnaround Strategy is a method used to completely overhaul failing schools. Creating the right policy environment is critical to successful school turnaround. The studies discussed in this section examined the conditions under which school change has been successful. In addition, two of the studies look specifically at accountability policies, which are a critical component of the Turnaround Strategy. From his experience working with schools as well as from his research, Fullan (2005) argued that leadership changes and improvement cannot be made in isolation; they needed to be done in the context of district-wide capacity building and district efforts to improve all schools. He found that singling out failing schools for restructuring only serves to alienate the school leaders and the teachers; by working on school improvement district-wide, district leaders can improve achievement across the board and provide individual schools with additional supports as necessary. Rhim, Kowal, Hassel, and Hassel (2007) identified environmental context as one of the two key aspects to successful turnaround (the other being leadership, as discussed above). Their review of the literature suggested that an accelerated "timetable [with big changes coming early in the process], the freedom to act, support and aligned systems, performance monitoring, and community engagement" are associated with successful turnarounds. Likewise, Arkin and Kowal (2005), Kowal and Hassel (2005), and Colby, Smith, and Shelton (2005) found that district support and capacity building for leadership changes is critical. They argued that in order for turnaround to be successful, the environment within which schools operate must be changed. In addition to giving school leaders more autonomy, districts that create strong monitoring systems, provide sufficient time for planning and implementing school restructuring plans, and that provide support, including funding and regular budget reports, training in instructional and business leadership skills, technical assistance, moving unwanted faculty members, and in some cases new/repaired facilities, are more successful at spurring school turnaround.

In addition to Kowal and Hassel's (2005) findings on leadership discussed in the first section, they found that five governance components and two environmental components were critical. Their most important finding about governance was that districts must be in charge, i.e., someone in the district office must be responsible for the schools being changed. As part of that, the district must select good turnaround leaders, set expectations for an accelerated change timeline and hold school leaders and staff accountable for those expectations, provide support and aligned systems (including, but not limited to, project managers, ongoing communication with district offices, business management so that turnaround leaders can focus on instructional leadership, etc.), and give turnaround leaders flexibility to implement necessary changes at the school level, such as scheduling, transportation, discipline, and curriculum. Kowal and Hassel (2005) found that community engagement and an accelerated timetable were necessary environmental factors. Communities that felt put upon were not supportive of turnaround and, therefore, it is necessary for the community to be engaged from the beginning of the process. In addition, an accelerated timetable that is focused on implementation and results establishes credibility with naysayers and, in the community, creates momentum for further change and decreases resistance. Kowal and Hassel found that many of the unsuccessful turnarounds they examined failed because change did not occur fast enough.

Similarly, Kowal and Arkin's (2005) study of external management providers found that three system-level governance components and four environmental components were key to successful employment of external education management providers. As in the charter school study, using a formalized process for choosing an external management was crucial to successfully employing such an organization. By using a fair and formalized process, districts could minimize conflict over this highly controversial method of school governance. Such a process includes looking at financials, organizational expertise, and the contacting of several references. In addition, districts that included the community in the decision-making process were able to stave off considerable conflict. Finally, districts that provided ongoing oversight and accountability were more successfully able to employ external management providers. Oversight and accountability includes having a common language and ensuring that the district has the capacity to oversee the partner organizations. Likewise, the environmental factors highlight the importance of clear expectations aligned with adequate support for external management organizations. First, districts that provided adequate time between choosing management organizations and the reopening of schools experienced more success. Second, clear contract terms that provide management organizations with flexibility from the districts' regulations made EMO takeover more successful. Similarly, a clear delegation of responsibilities between the EMO and the district led to more successful employment of EMOs. Finally, clear, measurable expectations from the district for the EMO made for more successful implementation. Such expectations included having a performance-based relationship with narrowly defined objects that could easily be measured, a timeline for improvement, and results balanced to give the EMO time to improve the school without removing all of the district's control (typically five years), public reporting of results, consequences for nonperformance, and fiscal incentives for success.

A clear example of a district setting the proper environment for reform is Boston, Massachusetts. The Center for Collaborative Education's study of Boston Pilot Schools (Tung, Ouimette, & Rugen, 2006) suggests that when the district provides strong support as well as a clear model for change, turnaround schools can be successful. The Boston Pilot Schools outperform district averages across all indicators of student engagement and performance, including attendance, disciplinary actions taken, Massachusetts Comprehensive Assessment System (MCAS) scores, college attendance rates, and lower rates of transfer. The pilot schools have five autonomies: budget, staffing, curriculum/instruction/assessment, governance/policies, and school schedule. They are small, vision-driven schools with the same budget as regular Boston Public Schools (BPS). In contrast to regular BPS schools, however, they have small class sizes/low student–teacher ratios, longer instructional periods, and significant collaboration among the teachers. All pilot schools require graduation by demonstrating competency/mastery (at the end of eighth or twelfth grade). In return for their flexibility, the pilot schools endure a five-year cycle high-stake review process, which, if they "fail," can result in their termination. The program has been so successful that Superintendent Payzant has begun to make many of the autonomies available to regular BPS schools in return for making accountability requirements, and the state has adopted the program as a turnaround option for failing schools.

Good accountability is a cornerstone of the Turnaround Strategy. In return for offering schools increased flexibility and autonomy, the strategy requires that districts and states hold schools accountable for student performance and that if schools fail to meet their performance goals, districts and states will take action. Mintrop and Trujillo (2005) looked at what could be learned from states that had NCLB-like accountability systems prior to NCLB. They examined Kentucky, Maryland, North Carolina, California, Florida, New York, and Texas's accountability systems. In addition, they looked at Chicago and Philadelphia's accountability systems. In all nine systems, they focused on the corrective action and further restructuring stages. They gathered data from existing studies and reports, information on Web sites and used interviews and personal communications to fill any gaps. The article focuses on the lessons learned from these accountability systems.

The most common features of the pre-NCLB accountability systems were school improvement grants, professional development, new instructional materials, programmatic prescriptions, extended learning periods (longer days or summer/weekend school), on-site instructional specialists, evaluations or audits, intervention teams or individual change agents, bureaucratic pressures, market pressures, school reorganization or reconstitution, teacher recruitment incentives, teacher quality policies, school construction and repair, and change of governance and authority (Mintrop & Trujillo, 2005, pp. 3–4). Mintrop and Trujillo (2005) identify eight lessons that can be learned from the pre-NCLB accountability systems studied. First, sanctions/increased pressure alone do not work. When pressure was coupled with incentives to change they were at least somewhat effective, but when teachers/administrators simply felt threatened, student achievement continued to falter. Second, there is no single solution to low-performing schools. Third, stages of corrective action need to be flexible. When the stages of reform are inflexible, they appear to schools as the same thing that has been tried before. However, when the reform system is flexible, schools can go through more organic/developmental reform and find what works best for them. Fourth, intensive capacity building is necessary for real change. Mintrop and Trujillo (2005) found that when states gave schools and districts ambitious goals that were not supported by increased capacity, improvement did not occur. Likewise, when goals were less ambitious and state involvement was still minimal, results were quite mixed. Only when states provided substantial capacity-building structures, preferably coupled with clear goals, did the authors find that schools were consistently able to improve over time. Fifth, a comprehensive set of strategies makes a significant difference in successful school change. When schools and districts implemented comprehensive changes (rather than the piecemeal changes previously used), they were more successful than they had been in the past and it did not feel like "just another passing reform." Sixth, school redesign strategies need to be coupled with changes to the professional environment of schools. When teachers felt well supported and as if they were part of a community, redesign was more effective. Seventh, competent leaders and teachers reduce conflict over school change. Finally, the state needs to commit to school change. Thus, states need to find ways to finance school redesign and the comprehensive school reform strategies that are associated with it.

Of course, the most extensive accountability policy is the No Child Left Behind Act. In 2006 the Center on Education Policy (CEP) conducted a 50-state survey and case studies of 38 districts and 42 schools to understand the effects that NCLB has had on schools (Rentner et al., 2006). CEP surveyed 299 representatives of school districts and conducted a number of national forums to collect additional data. The study found that teaching and learning have been affected by NCLB in a variety of ways: that student achievement has generally improved, but that at the same time states are using more flexible definitions of "proficient"; that over time the effects of NCLB have been relatively stable with regard to the percentage of schools in some stage of restructuring and the percentage of students taking advantage of the tutoring and/or choice provisions; and that urban school districts disproportionately feel the effects of NCLB. With regard to teaching and learning, the study found that while school curricula are better aligned to state standards and that schools are making better use of student data than they were prior to NCLB, they are also using narrower curricula and more prescribed instruction. In addition, although there are now more "highly qualified" teachers, it is not clear that better teaching is occurring. Clearly, states seeking to implement some form of school turnaround must be attuned to the effects that accountability policies can have on schools and student performance.

Conclusion

Two decades ago, urban school politics was dominated by racial tension, regulatory conflict, and an inputs-oriented decision-making process. Since the 1990s, new strands of politics of urban education have gained prominence. We now focus on outcome-based accountability, public and non-public strategies to turn around low performance, and the redrawing of the jurisdictional boundary between district and city hall.

Projecting the trend of current reforms into 2030, what will urban school politics look like? Who will be in charge? Will city politics turn into metropolitan-wide challenges? In terms of interest groups, will unions become less influential than taxpayers on resource allocation? And will mayoral accountability become the dominant governance paradigm? While these issues can be approached from many perspectives and methodologies, it is clear that urban school politics will continue to be an important condition for the success or failure of innovative ideas.

References

Arkin, M. D., & Kowal, J. M. (2005). *School restructuring options under no child left behind: What works when? Reopening as a charter school.* Naperville, IL: Learning Point Associates.

Bryk, A. S., Thum, Y. M., Easton, J. Q., & Luppescu, S. (1998). *Examining productivity: Ten-year trends in Chicago public schools.* Consortium on Chicago School Research, University of Chicago. Retrieved February 1, 2010 from: http://ccsr.uchicago.edu/downloads/775academicproductivity_summary.pdf

Buckley, J. (2007). *Choosing schools, building communities? The effect of schools of choice on parental involvement.* New York: National Center for the Study of Privatization in Education Teachers College, Columbia University.

Bulkley, K. E. (1999). Charter school authorizers: A new governance mechanism? *Educational Policy, 13*(5), 674–697.

Bulkley, K. E. (2004). Balancing act: Educational management organizations and charter school autonomy. In K. E. Bulkley and P. Wohlstetter (Eds.), *Taking account of charter schools: What's happened and what's next* (pp. 121–141). New York: Teachers College Press.

Catalyst Chicago (1997). Law, policy changes dilute LSC power. September. Retrieved February 23, 2010 from: www.catalyst chicago.org/news/index.php?item=649&cat=23

Catalyst Chicago (2004a). Lessons that experience taught. March. Retrieved February 23, 2010 from: www.catalyst-chicago.org/news/index.php?item=1236&cat=23

Catalyst Chicago (2004b). Where councils lost ground. March. Retrieved Feburary 23, 2010 from: www.catalyst-chicago.org/news/index.php?item=1234&cat=23

Colby, S., Smith, K., & Shelton, J. (2005). *Expanding the supply of high-quality public schools.* San Francisco, CA: The Bridgespan Group.

Cole, S. (1969). *The unionization of teachers: A case study of the United Federation of Teachers.* New York: Praeger.

Designs for Change (1990). *Chicago principals: Changing of the guard. A research analysis.* Chicago: Designs for Change.

Duffrin, E., & Scott, C. (2008). *Uncharted territory: An examination of restructuring under NCLB in Georgia.* Washington, DC: Center on Education Policy.

Education Week (2007). ProComp's promise: What the rest of the country can learn from Denver's performance-pay plan. November 19.

Fullan, M. (2005). Turnaround leadership. *Educational Forum, 69*(2), Winter, 174–181.

Gold, E., Christman, J., & Herold, B. (2007). Blurring the boundaries: A case study of private sector involvement in Philadelphia public schools, *American Journal of Education 113*(2), 181–212.

Green, E. (2009). At long last, Bronx Green Dot finalizes (tenure-free) contract. Gotham Schools. Retrieved March 2, 2010 from: http://gothamschools.org/2009/06/24/at-long-last-bronx-green-dot-finalizes-tenure-free-contract

Grimshaw, W. (1979). *Union rule in the schools,* Lexington, KY: D. C. Heath.

Henig, J. R. (1999). *The color of school reform.* Princeton, NJ: Princeton University Press.

Hill, P. T. (1977). *Compensatory education service.* Report prepared for the US Office of Education. Washington, DC: Department of Health, Education and Welfare.

Hill, P. T. (2006). *Put learning first: A portfolio approach to public schools.* Progressive Policy Institute Policy Report. Washington, DC: Public Policy Institute.

Hill, P. T., Campbell, C., & Harvey, J. (2000). *It takes a city: Getting serious about urban school reform.* Washington, DC: Brookings Institution.

Huberman, M., & Miles, M. (1984). *Innovation up close.* New York: Plenum.

Johnson, S. M. (1986). Incentives for teachers: What motivates, what matters. *Educational Administration Quarterly, 22*(3), 54–79.

Johnson, S. M., & Kardos, S. M. (2000). Reform bargaining and its promise for school improvement. In T. Loveless (Ed.), *Conflicting missions? Teachers' unions and educational reform* (pp. 7–46). Washington, DC: Brookings Institution.

Jung, R., & Kirst, M. (1986). Beyond mutual adaptation, into the bully pulpit: Recent research on the federal role in education. *Educational Administration Quarterly, 22*(3), 80–109.

Kelleher, M., & Scott, C. (2009). *Beyond restructuring: Ohio retools state support for high-need districts through differentiated accountability.* Washington, DC: Center on Education Policy.

Kerchner, C. T., & Koppich, J. E. (2007). Negotiating what matters most: Collective bargaining and student achievement, *American Journal of Education, 113*(3), 349–365. Retrieved March 3, 2010 from: www.jstor.org/stable/10.1086/523736

Kerchner, C. T., Koppich, J. E., & Weeres, J. G. (1997). *United mind workers: Unions and teaching in the knowledge society.* San Francisco, CA: Jossey-Bass.

Kirst, M., & Jung, R. (1982). The utility of a longitudinal approach in assessing implementation: A thirteen-year review of title I, ESEA. In W. Williams, R. F. Elmere, J. S. Hall et al. (Eds.), *Studying implementation: Methodologies and administrative issues* (pp. 119–148). New York: Chatham House.

Knapp, M., Turnbull, B., David, J., Stearns, M., & Peterson, S. (1983). *Cumulative effects of federal education policies on schools and districts.* Menlo Park, CA: SRI International.

Kowal, J. M., & Arkin, M. D. (2005). *School restructuring options under no child left behind: What works when? Contracting with external education management providers.* Naperville, IL: Learning Point Associates.

Kowal, J. M., & Hassel, E. A. (2005). *School restructuring options under no child left behind: What works when? Turnarounds with new leaders and staff.* Naperville, IL: Learning Point Associates.

Lewis, J. (2003). *Policy notes: District implementation of No Child Left Behind.* San Francisco, CA: WestEd.

Lowi, T. (1964). American business and public policy, case studies and political theory. *World Politics,* July, 677–715.

MacIver, M. A., & MacIver, D. J. (2005). Which bets paid off? Preliminary findings on the impact of private management and K–8 conversion reforms on the achievement of Philadelphia students. Paper presented at the annual meeting of the American Political Science Association, Washington, DC.

McDonnell, L., & Pascal, A. (1979). *Organized teachers in American schools.* Santa Monica, CA: RAND.

Mintrop, H., & Trujillo, T. (2005). Corrective action in low performing schools: Lessons for NCLB implementation from first-generation accountability systems. *Education Policy Analysis Archives, 13*(48). Retrieved July 12, 2011 from: http://epaa.asu.edu/ojs/article/view/153

Murnane, R. J., & Cohen, D. K. (1986). Merit pay and the evaluation problem: Why most merit pay plans fail and a few survive. *Harvard Educational Review, 56*(1), 1–17.

Murphy, J. (1971). Title I of ESEA: The politics of implementing federal education reform. *Harvard Educational Review, 41* February, 36–63.

National Education Association (2005). Your rights: No Child Left Behind: The basics and the lawsuits.

National Institute of Education (1977). *Administration of compensatory education.* Washington, DC: US Department of Health, Education and Welfare.

Neild, R. C. (2005). Parent management of school choice in a large urban district. *Urban Education, 40*(3), 270–297.

NCLB (2001). No Child Left Behind Act. Pub. L. No. 107–100, 115 Stat. 1425 (2002). Retrieved September 14, 2010 from: www.ed.gov/policy/elsec/leg/esea02/index.html

Odden, A., & Kelley, C. (2002). *Paying teachers for what they know and do: New and smarter compensation strategies to improve schools* (2nd ed.). Thousand Oaks, CA: Corwin Press.

Peterson, P. E., Rabe, B., & Wong, K. K. (1986). *When federalism works.* Washington, DC: Brookings Institution.

Pressman, J. L., & Wildavsky, A. (1973). *Implementation.* Berkeley: University of California Press.

Quaid, L. (2009). School chief: Mayors need control of urban schools. Associated Press, March 31.

Ravitch, D. (2009). Student achievement in New York City: The NAEP results. In A. Kjellberg & L. Haimson (Eds.), *NYC schools under Bloomberg and Klein: What parents, teachers and policymakers need to know* (pp. 23–29). New York: Lulu.

Ravitch, D., & Viteritti, J. (Eds.) (1997). *New schools for a new century: The redesign of urban education.* New Haven, CT: Yale University Press.

Rentner, D. S., Scott, C., Kober, N., Chudowsky, N., Chudowsky,V., Joftus, S., & Zabala. D. (2006). *From the capital to the classroom: Year 4 of the No Child Left Behind Act.* Washington, DC: Center on Education Policy.

Rhim, L.M., Kowal, J. M. Hassel, B. C., & Hassel, E. A. (2007). *School turnarounds: A review of the cross-sector evidence on dramatic organizational improvement.* Chapel Hill, NC: Public Impact, and Lincoln, IL: Academic Development Institute.

Ripley, R., & Franklin, G. (1984). *Congress, the bureaucracy, and public policy.* Homewood, IL: Dorsey Press.

Rose, L. C., & Gallup, A. M. (2007). The 30th Annual Phi Delta Kappa/Gallup Poll of the Public's Attitudes Toward the Public Schools. *Phi Delta Kappan, 89*(1), p. 38.

Ryan, S., Bryk, A. S., Lopez, G., Williams, K. P., Hall, K., et al. (1997). *Charting reform: LSCs—local leadership at work.*

Consortium on Chicago School Research, University of Chicago. Retrieved May 20, 2011 from: http://ccsr.uchicago.edu/publications/ChartingReform_LSCs_LocalLeadershipAtWork.pdf

Scott, C. (2009). *Top down, bottom up: California districts in corrective action and schools in restructuring under NCLB.* Washington, DC: Center on Education Policy.

Shipps, D. (2003). Pulling together: Civic capacity and urban school reform, *American Educational Research Association, 40*(4), 841–878. Retrieved December 28, 2009 from: jstor.org/stable/3699410

Singer, J., & Butler, J. (1987). The education of all handicapped children act: Schools as agents of social reform. *Harvard Educational Review, 57*(2), 25–38.

Stone, C. N. (1989). *Regime politics: Governing Atlanta, 1946–1988.* Lawrence: University Press of Kansas.

Stone, C. N., Henig, J. R., Jones, B. D., & Pierannunzi, C. (2001). *Building civic capacity: The politics of reforming urban schools.* Lawrence: University Press of Kansas.

Stringfield, S. C., & Yakimowski-Srebnick, M. E. (2005). Promise, progress, problems and paradoxes of three phases of accountability: A longitudinal case study of the Baltimore city public schools. *American Educational Research Journal, 42*(1), 43–75. Retrieved December 21, 2009 from: http://jstor.org/stable/3699455

Tung, R., Ouimette, M., & Rugen, L. (2006). *Progress and promise: A report on the Boston pilot schools.* Boston: Center for Collaborative Education.

Useem, E. (2005). *Learning from Philadelphia's school reform: What do the research findings show us so far?* Philadelphia, PA: Reseach for Action.

Walker, E. (2000). Decentralization and participatory decision-making: Implementing school-based management in the Abbott districts. *Research Brief, 1*(1), 1–21. Center for Urban Leadership, Renewal and Research, Department of Educational Leadership Administration and Supervision: Seton Hall University. Retrieved May 20, 2011 from: www.state.nj.us/education/archive/abbotts/wsr/cull.htm

Wong, K. K. (1990). *City choices: Education and housing.* Albany: State University of New York Press.

Wong, K. K. (2002). The new politics of urban schools. In J. Pelissero (Ed.), *Cities, politics, and policy: A comparative analysis* (pp. 283–311). Washington, DC: Congressional Quarterly.

Wong, K. K., Shen, F. X., Anagnostopoulos, D., & Rutledge, S. (2007). *The education mayor: Improving America's schools.* Washington, DC: Georgetown University Press.

6

Economics of Urban Education

Andrew McEachin and Dominic J. Brewer

Over the past 30 years, in the mass media and educational stakeholder and research communities, there has been increased interest in urban education. A controversial report, *A Nation At Risk* (National Commission on Excellence in Education, 1983), fueled the current discussion about the underperformance of American schools, especially in urban areas. The attention of countless policies, billions of dollars, and innumerable person hours have been spent trying to fix urban schools. Since the Industrial Revolution, there has been a population boom in America's urban cities. The majority of individuals now live in urban areas, and these areas have unique economic environments— environments that have adverse effects on education. Considering that economic growth and prosperity are tied to the quality of education within a country (Hanushek & Kimko, 2000), special attention must be given to the unique economic environments that surround students, families, and other education stakeholders in urban areas.

Education researchers are particularly concerned with the lower academic achievement of urban students; but this discussion cannot occur without a finer understanding of the economic and social conditions of these communities. The salient characteristics of urban centers include population diversity and poverty, which also relate to challenges in employment, housing, and educational attainment. A significant portion of education research suggests that family and student charac- teristics—e.g., ethnicity, language status, socioeconomic status, and housing stability—are signifi- cantly related to student achievement (Hanushek, 2003; Rothstein, 2004). The relationship between these variables and education outcomes are typical questions in research on the economics of education.

The agenda of this chapter is not to provide a primer on the theoretical or mathematical under- pinnings of urban economics, nor do we exhaustively cover the research on the economics of edu- cation. Instead, we provide an overview of the economics of urban areas and its relevance to education at a descriptive and conceptual level. First, we present the characteristics of urban centers compared with suburban and rural areas. We offer descriptive data that describe the unique features of urban communities, including population characteristics, economic inequality, labor market, economy, housing, health, and educational attainment. Throughout the discussion we offer com- parative data of these indicators across major metropolitan areas. Second, we present an overview of research in urban education. Numerous studies explore characteristics such as race, socioeconomic status, teacher labor markets, and housing as related to student achievement. Finally, we explore the interrelationships between the economy of urban areas and education opportunities.

The Economics of Urban Areas in the United States

Prior to the Industrial Revolution, towns clustered around trading routes, typically near waterways. Transportation was both expensive and resource-intensive. As new technologies increased the efficiency of transportation (e.g., trains and motorboats) and production (the cotton gin, machines, and internal combustion engines), cities and firms specialized in a few goods and created comparative advantages (O'Sullivan, 2007). From 1900 to 1990, the geographic destination of choice drastically shifted. The total urban population more than tripled, increasing from 54 million to 184 million, while the rural population increased only 33%, from 45 million to 61 million. The diverse economic, social, cultural, and ethnic nature of urban areas makes them both dynamic and mandatory areas of study for education researchers, specifically in population diversity, poverty, and education attainment.

Defining an urban area is a difficult and often arbitrary matter. The stereotypical metropolitan areas such as New York City, Los Angeles, Detroit, and Chicago are clear examples of urban cities. However, the term encompasses a wide array of communities. According to O'Sullivan (2007), the U.S. Census Bureau designates urban areas as places with high population density. The Census Bureau makes the distinction between an urbanized area and urban clusters. Urbanized areas are census block groups with a density of 1,000 people per square mile. These communities may also encompass surrounding areas of less density, but the total population for an urban area is typically more than 50,000 residents. The census also designates urban clusters as smaller communities between 2,500 and 50,000 people. Census areas not designated as urbanized or as an urban cluster are designated as being *rural*.[1] To complicate matters still more, the U.S. Census Bureau does not utilize *suburban* as a geographic classification, although the educational research community often writes about the urban, rural, and suburban triad.

Using these distinctions, 79% of the U.S. population were living in urban areas and 20% in rural areas in the year 2000 (O'Sullivan, 2007). That such a significant proportion of the country's population is designated as "urban" necessitates particular attention to the challenges faced in these communities. It also implies that the term *urban* may be too general for rigorous research and conversation, and that deeper, more meaningful labels are needed. Using U.S. Census designations, urban areas are further broken down into five subgroups. Table 6.1 shows the percent of the population in rural and urban areas and the percent of people living in the four urban subdesignations.

Nearly 70% of the population lived in urban areas with at least 50,000 people, implying that the majority of the population lives in densely populated urban pockets. Even though one urban area can have vastly different characteristics than another, urban areas share enough common characteristics (e.g., higher poverty rates, diverse populations, and health and housing issues) to warrant special attention from educational researchers.

Population Diversity

Urban centers are areas of densely packed racial and economically diverse populations. Descriptive data from eight well-known cities—Los Angeles, New York City, Atlanta, Detroit, Milwaukee, Dallas, Chicago, and Philadelphia—highlight this population diversity. Table 6.2 displays the racial demographics for the eight major urban cities. These cities characteristically have overrepresented *minority* populations. These populations differ significantly from the national average; Detroit is at the extreme, with 90% of its inhabitants belonging to a non-White racial category. This population diversity adds one layer to the complex nature of large urban areas.

Table 6.1 Percentage of U.S. Population Living in Urban vs. Rural Areas, 2000

	Total population	Percent of U.S. total
U.S.	285,230,516	100.00
Urban	225,956,060	79.22
Rural	59,274,456	20.78
Urbanized area >200,000 population	166,215,889	58.27
Urbanized area 50,000–199,999	29,584,626	10.37
Urban clusters 5,000–49,999	25,438,275	8.90
Urban clusters 2,500–4,999	4,717,270	1.65

Source: U.S. Department of Transportation (2011)

Table 6.2 Population Demographics in Geographic Boundaries of Urban Districts, 2006

	Population	Percent Minority Non-White	Percent White	Percent African American	Percent of American Indian or Native Alaskan	Percent Asian	Percent Native Hawaiian or Pacific Islander	Percent Hispanic or Latino
Los Angeles	4,554,163	53.62	46.38	10.02	0.54	9.78	0.20	47.67
New York City	8,214,426	56.12	43.88	25.10	0.28	11.73	0.03	27.61
Atlanta	442,887	62.76	37.24	55.66	0.15	2.32	0.05	5.89
Detroit	834,116	90.00	10.00	83.08	0.29	1.11	0.00	6.19
Milwaukee	563,173	56.38	43.62	39.60	0.64	3.39	0.08	14.94
Dallas	997,737	46.09	53.91	22.89	0.44	1.66	0.05	52.18
Chicago	2,749,283	63.45	36.55	35.29	0.19	4.90	0.05	28.15
Philadelphia	113,127	35.91	64.09	8.34	0.21	2.66	0.00	34.12
United States	299,398,484	33.62	66.38	12.80	0.97	4.40	0.17	14.80
Urban	245,506,756	39.10	60.90	14.20	0.60	5.30	0.20	18.80
Rural	53,891,728	15.70	84.30	6.20	1.40	1.20	0.10	6.80

Source: State Education Data Center (2009)

Poverty and Economic Opportunity

Urban areas often see higher rates of poverty compared to suburban communities. In 2000, some 19.9% of people in central cities lived in poverty, while only 7.5% of those in the suburbs did so (Glaeser, Kahn, & Rappaport, 2008). In 2006, the overall percentage of urban residents in poverty was approximately 13.9%, compared with 13.3% overall in the United States. However, one must note that the percent of individuals living in poverty in urban areas closely mirrors the national average, because urban areas largely skew the mean. When central cities and suburbs are compared, principal cities of metropolitan areas in 2006 have much higher poverty rates (17.7%) than the national average and suburbs of metropolitan areas (9.6%) (U.S. Census Bureau, 2006).

Poverty rates are also highly correlated with unemployment. According to the tables in Appendix A, individuals living below the poverty line in our reference cities are much more likely to be unemployed. The situation is dire in Detroit, where 38% of working-age individuals living below the poverty line are out of work, whereas the national average is approximately 5%.[2] Individuals living in poverty have less access to human capital, such as education or job training, over their lifetimes (see Ehrenberg & Smith, 2008). Their diminished skill sets lead to lower wages in the job market, all else being equal, thus perpetuating the poverty cycle.

Patterns of housing and home ownership also indicate differences in economic status among urban residents. Home ownership is not randomly distributed; in fact, the opposite is true: large pockets of rental property exist primarily in urban areas and principal cities. We highlight a few key housing differences among urban residents, rural residents, and national averages (U.S. Census Bureau, 2006):

- In 2006, 14.4% of urban residents (16.1% for principal cities) lived in a different house within the same state as they did in the year before—13.5% and 10.4% for United States and rural averages respectively.
- In 2006, the median house price for urban areas was $203,700 ($195,600 for principal cities)—$185,200 and $146,500 for the United States and rural averages respectively.
- In 2006, some 63% of urban housing was owner-occupied (53% for principal cities)—67% and 82% for United States and rural averages respectively.
- In 2006, some 38% of residents with mortgages in urban areas (40% for principal cities) spent more than 30% of their household income on monthly living expenses—37% and 33% for United States and rural averages respectively.
- In 2006, some 48% of renter-occupied units in urban areas (50% for principal cities) spent more than 30% of their household income on rent and utilities—46% and 33% for United States and rural averages respectively.

We can see that there are stark housing differences between urban (especially principal cities) and rural areas. These differences are less extreme between urban areas and the national average, although the national averages are skewed, since four times as many people live in urban areas than rural ones. Urban residents are more likely to rent and to spend more than 30% of their household income on living expenses. Home ownership has many benefits, including a stronger sense of community, an increased propensity to vote, and a decrease in transience and mobility (Rothstein, 2004).

Educational Attainment

Educational attainment is a gateway to higher-paying jobs and is related to an increase in positive outcomes, such as the propensity to vote, own a home, and pursue a healthier lifestyle (Oreopoulos, 2007; Rothstein, 2004). The aggregate attainment for individuals in urban and rural areas appears to be approximately equal across geographic areas (see Table 6.3). However, within urban areas there are clear attainment demarcations where the impoverished and minority populations attain lower levels of education (see Appendix A). This poses a problem. Parent education level, especially the mother's education, is highly correlated with student achievement and is often one of the best predictors of this (Rothstein, 2004). Furthermore, individuals with higher levels of education amass more wealth over the course of their lives than those with lower levels of education (Hanushek & Lindseth, 2009).

The Economics of Urban Education

Indicators such as population diversity, poverty, and socioeconomic status have commonly been associated with a variety of educational outcomes. The variables have particular relationships to student achievement, resources, and teacher allocation. In the following sections we explain how scholars conceptualize the economics of education. We explain the statistical models (commonly referred to as production function models) that researchers use to analyze how social and economic factors relate to public schooling and achievement. We then examine some of the extant research that is salient in understanding the particular challenges of education in urban settings.

Table 6.3 Educational Attainment, Urban vs. Rural, 2006

	Percent age 25+ who have completed high school	Percent age 25+ who have completed a bachelor's degree	Percent age 25+ who have completed an advanced degree
United States	84	27	10
Urban	84	29	11
Rural	84	20	7
In metropolitan statistical area	85	29	11
In principal city	82	30	11
Not in principal city	86	29	10
In micropolitan statistical area	82	18	6
In principal city	82	20	8

Source: State Education Data Center

An Economic Paradigm Applied to Education Research

Economists often conceptualize production functions (PFs) that hypothesize some relationship between inputs and outputs (Varian, 1999). For example, one might reasonably hypothesize that the more a student studies (the input), the more likely it is that he or she will achieve higher test scores (the output). Education researchers and economists build on this simplistic example, using more complex relationships to measure the effect of student, family, and school inputs on student achievement. The following equation is an example of a traditional educational PF where a student's achievement is a function of four key areas of input:

$$\text{Achievement} = f(H, P, T, S)$$

where H represents the student's home environment, P represents the student's peer group, T represents the quality of a student's teachers, and S represents the student's school environment (Gottfried, 2009; Hanushek, 1979; Varian, 1999). The sum of a student's inputs influences his or her achievement in school. The previously discussed characteristics of urban areas (i.e., diversity, poverty, socioeconomic status) are potential inputs in the production function. However, as discussed later, urban areas also exhibit differing levels of teacher quality and school resources. Such inputs are areas of controversy and debate for researchers and education reformers.

Race and Education

Race and ethnicity are significant factors in understanding educational outcomes. Diverse student bodies typically characterize public schools in urban areas. The exit of White students from urban schools is one particular concern. Betts and Fairlie (2003) found that for every four immigrants who arrive in U.S. public high schools, on average one student—usually a White student—transfers to a private school, further compounding the racial achievement gap. The relationship between *White flight* and immigration was strongest for immigrants who speak a language other than English at home (Betts & Fairlie, 2003). School choice reforms, such as charter schools, also show evidence of segregation in some states. For example, Ladd, Clotfelter, and Vigdor (2003) found that open enrollment in North Carolina led to *more* segregation by both race and class than when students were assigned to schools by catchment zones. The increase in immigrant students and decrease in White students leave schools with segregated populations.

A major concern among educators, policymakers, and researchers is the persistent racial gap in student achievement (Clotfelter, Ladd, & Vigdor, 2009; Fryer & Levit, 2004; Hanushek & Rivkin,

2006; Lee, 2002; Phillips & Chin, 2004). Traditionally, the debate centers on what to do about the White–Black achievement gap (Rothstein, 2004), although noticeable gaps exist between other minority groups as well. There is evidence that the White–minority gap increases as students progress through school (Fryer & Levit, 2006; Hanushek & Rivkin, 2006), and the differences also vary by racial subgroups (Clotfelter et al., 2009[3]) and ability (Reardon & Galindo, 2009). The achievement gap between White and minority students is estimated to be between 0.5 and 1.0 standard deviations in math and slightly less in reading (Clotfelter et al., 2009).

Table 6.4 displays the achievement gaps between White and Black and White and Hispanic students on the 2007 National Assessment of Educational Progress (NAEP) assessment. This simplistic snapshot parallels the trends in previous research: the Black–White achievement gap tends to be larger than the Hispanic–White gap, and the Black–White gap appears to be growing over time while the Hispanic–White gap remains fairly constant.

The gap also exists when we extend the analysis to educational attainment for populations 25 years of age and older. Hispanic and Black individuals, on average, are less likely to attain post-high school education (see Table 6.5). Considering that there is a strong correlation between parental education level and college-going rates for children (Hanushek & Lindseth, 2009; Keane & Roemer, 2009), the achievement gaps are likely to be perpetuated without some intervention. Appendix B denotes two more important trends: more schooling leads to higher earnings and minority individuals earn less than Whites and Asians, even when they have equal education levels. In the next section, the effects

Table 6.4 Achievement Gaps between Students, NAEP Fourth (Eighth) Grade, 2007

English	White–Black	White–Hispanic	Not eligible for free lunch–Eligible for free lunch	Non-English language learner–English language learner
LAUSD[1]	1 (43)	37 (34)	24 (14)	35 (40)
Washington, DC	67 (NA)	52 (NA)	28 (18)	−1 (NA)
New York	26 (30)	28 (29)	31 (26)	28 (43)
Chicago	33 (27)	26 (11)	23 (19)	22 (34)
Boston	25 (25)	26 (34)	18 (19)	18 (47)
Math				
LAUSD	32 (40)	31 (32)	18 (16)	25 (38)
Washington, DC	54 (NA)	42 (NA)	20 (20)	5 (23)
New York	22 (30)	18 (26)	17 (26)	24 (38)
Chicago	31 (39)	25 (22)	22 (23)	16 (22)
Boston	24 (42)	19 (34)	13 (19)	7 (37)

1 Los Angeles Unified School District

Source: National Center for Education Statistics (2008)

Table 6.5 Educational Attainment by Race (Age 25 Years and Older), 2007

	Percent at least high school	Percent at least some college	Percent at least bachelor's degree	Percent at least advanced degree
Total	85	54	28	10
White	89	59	30	11
Black	80	46	17	6
Hispanic	61	32	13	4
Asian	86	68	50	20

Source: U.S. Census Bureau (2007)

of socioeconomic indicators—primarily parent education and poverty levels—on student achievement are discussed.

Effects of Socioeconomic Indicators on Education

An important part of the education production function is the student's *out-of-school* experience, and a student's socioeconomic status (SES) is a key proxy for the quality of that. One's SES influences the amount of human and social capital accumulated over one's lifetime. Research consistently shows that a student's socioeconomic indicators are the strongest determinant of future education achievement (Coleman, Campbell, & Hobson, 1966; Hanushek, 2003; Rothstein, 2004). We discuss two main indicators below: parental education levels and living in poverty.

A common socioeconomic input variable is parental education level in an education production function (Hanushek, 2003). Beginning with the Coleman report, numerous research findings suggest that parental education level is among the best predictors of student achievement (Coleman et al., 1966; Rothstein, 2004). In particular, higher-education attainment for mothers is strongly related to higher achievement in their children. Various theories may help to explain this relationship. The concept of human capital, or habitus, is one common discussion point. Parents may transmit prior experiences and knowledge that are critical for the academic success of their children. Thus, parents with higher levels of human capital (i.e., education attainment) may influence the success of their child's academic achievement (Altonji & Dunn, 1996; Ehrenberg & Smith, 2008).

The idea of social capital might also explain the relationship between parents and students (see Dika & Singh, 2002; Portes, 1998). Parents with higher social capital have wider networks of relationships to whom they can turn for assistance as their children progress through schooling. Regardless of theoretical underpinnings, parental education level is a commonly used socioeconomic variable in the economics of education. The levels of human and social capital have a palpable differentiating effect on student achievement, as seen in Figure 6.1, which, using the 2007 eighth-grade reading NAEP scores as a snapshot, shows clear demarcations.

Urban, lower-SES students also enter school with a smaller skill set than their higher-SES counterparts. Although all students learn some basic numeracy and literacy skills at home, the quality of *out-of-school* exposure is not equally dispersed (Entwisle, Alexander, & Olson, 1994; Slaughter & Epps, 1987). These out-of-school differences lead to different learning rates. Alexander, Entwisle, and Olson (2001) found that SES predicted the seasonal learning curves of urban elementary school students. While in school, students, regardless of SES, learned at similar rates, keeping the achievement gap between classes static. However, the class achievement gap widened over the summer as the upper-SES children made moderate gains while the lower-SES children remained stagnant (see also Cooper, Nye, Charlton, Lindsay, & Greathouse, 1996, for a literature review of the effects SES have on seasonal learning).

The effects of poverty also manifest themselves in two related areas: childhood nutrition and health. In a study of the effects of malnourishment on early childhood academic achievement, Glewwe, Jacoby, and King (2001) found that individual learning endowments, home environment, and parental characteristics did not fully explain the variation in academic outcomes between nourished and malnourished students. Stopping short of causality, their findings imply that proper nourishment has a positive effect on student achievement.

Another nutritional phenomenon affecting low-income children is *food insecurity*—e.g., when a child is not sure where his or her next meal will come from. In 1999, some 42% of children in impoverished households were food-insecure, and there are stronger negative effects of food insecurity among Hispanic and African American children than among other groups (Winicki & Jemison, 2003). Although the association between food insecurity and academic achievement may

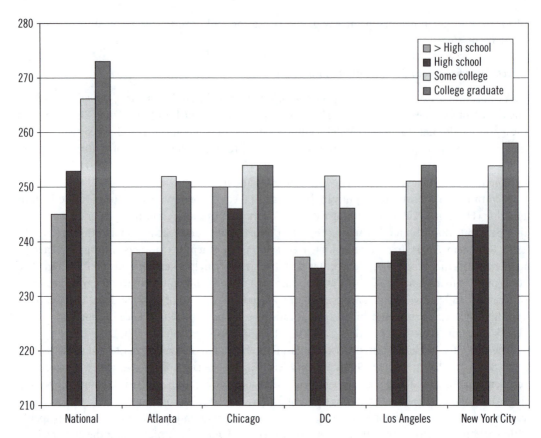

Figure 6.1 Eighth-grade Reading NAEP Scores by Parent Education, 2007

Source: National Center for Education Statistics (2008)

represent a spurious correlation (e.g., other home, environmental, or parental characteristics may play a role), research indicates that food insecurity can have lasting developmental consequences for children (Jyoti, Frongillo, & Jones, 2005). Food insecurity is also associated with lower income and lower levels of education among pregnant women (Laraia, Siega-Riz, Gundersen, & Dole, 2006). Poor health or poor health decisions are also associated with lower levels of education attainment (Hurre, Aro, Rahkonen, & Komulainen, 2006).

School Resources and Finance

The previous sections reviewed the literature on *out-of-school* inputs of a student's production function, but what about the *within-school* inputs? How do inputs within a student's school and district influence his or her performance? Do disparities in funding levels—which theoretically affect school inputs such as class sizes and teacher salaries—differentially affect student achievement? In this section we review the literature on the relationship between school resources and finances, and student achievement.

Over the past three decades, school spending in the United States has approximately quadrupled, while student achievement has remained constant. Over the same time period, student–teacher ratios have decreased, and the average experience of teachers has increased, along with the percent of teachers with at least a master's degree and teachers' salaries (Hanushek & Lindseth, 2009). On the surface, these improvements seem beneficial for student achievement, especially in urban areas, where districts receive more per-pupil funding than suburban schools to compensate for their disadvantaged student populations (Rubenstein, Schwartz, Stiefel, & Amor, 2007). Decreases in student–teacher ratios, however, are associated with rent-seeking teachers' unions, which have a negative impact on student achievement (Eberts, 1983; Hoxby, 1996; Moe, 2009). Furthermore, teachers' education levels, salaries, and years of experience are poor proxies for teacher quality (Goldhaber & Brewer, 2000; Hanushek, 2003). Tacit assumptions that seem logical on the surface actually lead to equivocal results.

Research consistently suggests that the amount of school funding is not related to increases in student achievement. The *level* of funding is not a condition of student achievement; *quality* is (Hanushek, 2003; Rubenstein et al., 2007). Teacher quality is the strongest within-school determinant of student achievement (Hanushek, 2003), but it is also very difficult to define. Typical methods of categorizing teacher quality—experience, credentials, education—have little effect on student achievement (Goldhaber & Brewer, 2000). Instead of emphasizing the levels in school inputs, production function research has shown that policymakers and education stakeholders should focus on the quality of the inputs.

Teacher Quality and Distribution

Although the level of school inputs has a negligible effect on students, the quality of the inputs, especially teacher quality, is a strong determinant of student achievement (Hanushek, 2003). Thus, questions pertaining to teacher attrition, retention, and recruitment become critical (Boyd, Grossman, Lankford, Loeb, & Wyckoff, 2006; Glazerman, Mayer, & Decker, 2006; Rockoff, 2004). A similarly important consideration is the distribution of teachers with respect to quality. Are *good* teachers spread evenly over geographic areas, regardless of the population's race, SES, and other background characteristics? Is the concentration of certain teachers conditioned on school, community, and student characteristics? Empirical research suggests that the dispersion of teachers is not random (Clotfelter, Ladd, & Vigdor, 2006; Lankford, Loeb, & Wyckoff, 2002; Rivkin, Hanushek, & Kain, 2005). In general, urban and low-performing districts struggle to recruit and retain teachers (Hanushek, Kain, & Rivkin, 2004).

Research findings suggest that urban, minority, and lower-achieving students often receive less experienced and less qualified teachers (Clotfelter et al., 2006; Jacob, 2007; Lankford et al., 2002). Such distribution patterns among teachers occur for several reasons. Lankford et al. (2002) find that teachers often leave difficult teaching environments (e.g., urban and low-performing schools) for more appealing schools. The palpable trend of teacher flight has led to the creation of philanthropic and social endeavors (e.g., Teach for America, The New Teacher Project, and the New York City Teaching Fellows) that attempt to increase the demand for hard-to-staff schools (Boyd et al., 2006; Glazerman et al., 2006). These last investigators also find that teachers prefer to work closer to where they live, so that schools in the suburbs and wealthier communities have an easier time hiring higher-quality teachers.

Although possibly less visible, the problem of teacher sorting can also occur within schools. As suggested by Clotfelter et al. (2006), more experienced teachers can influence their placements by leveraging their seniority, often avoiding more difficult positions. In effect, the more experienced teachers avoid the less able students, yet these are the students who need these teachers the most (Rivkin et al., 2005). In turn, placing inexperienced teachers with the neediest students leads to higher attrition rates among new teachers (Murnane & Steele, 2007). These distributional effects make addressing issues of student achievement and teacher recruitment and retention in urban schools very difficult.

Conclusion

In this chapter we highlight the unique characteristics of urban areas and their implications for public schools. Urban schools have diverse student bodies from different cultural, language, and learning backgrounds. Students are also more likely to experience hardships related to lower economic and educational opportunities. These out-of-school factors of urban centers play a significant role in the academic success of schools and students. For education researchers, social and economic variables are significant variables in education production functions. For educators and district leaders, the characteristics of urban settings are unique challenges that must be addressed if schools are to be successful in educating students.

Public schools can make a difference in helping to improve the academic achievement of urban students. However, research in the economics of education suggests that the amount of money and resources put into public schools does not relate to student achievement. In lay terms, merely throwing money at the problem will not lead to improved student outcomes. Rather, how districts use their funding to improve the quality of education promises to have more positive effects. In particular, improving teacher quality and distributing effective teachers to needy urban areas are two strategies that may improve student achievement.

As researchers and educators consider the lessons from research on the economics of education, one must also remember the interconnected quality of variables. Population diversity, poverty, SES, and education attainment are interrelated factors. These variables do not function in isolation from one another. Economic opportunity, social and cultural contexts, and educational outcomes combine to create a cycle of hardship and lower achievement among urban students. Similarly, education reforms that aim to improve student achievement must address the complex challenges posed by urban centers. Policymakers and educators must consider strategies to address the learning needs of diverse student populations and distribute high-quality resources such as effective teachers to areas of need. While these recommendations sound straightforward, such educational change will undoubtedly fly against the established politics, organizational culture, and policies that currently govern public education. The challenges are significant, but scholarly work in the economics of education also teaches us that the benefits of successfully educating urban students can be great.

Appendix A

Table 6.6 Employment Statistics (Age 16 Years and Older) for Atlanta, 2006

	Percent total population	Percent in the labor force	Percent employed	Percent unemployed
Education (25–64)				
High school	11	66	60	11
High school graduate	24	76	70	8
Some college	26	82	76	6
At least BA/BS	38	86	83	3
Below poverty (20–64)	10	56	41	27
(16+)				
White	52	70	66	5
Black	33	72	63	12
Hispanic	9	76	71	6
Asian	5	69	65	5

Source: U.S. Census Bureau (2010).

Table 6.7 Employment Statistics (Age 16 Years and Older) for Chicago, 2006

	Percent total population	Percent in the labor force	Percent employed	Percent unemployed
Education (25–64)				
High school	13	64	57	11
High school graduate	25	75	67	8
Some college	27	81	76	7
At least BA/BS	35	86	83	3
Below poverty (20–64)	10	50	35	30
(16+)				
White	57	68	64	5
Black	19	61	51	17
Hispanic	18	71	65	8
Asian	6	68	64	6

Source: U.S. Census Bureau (2010)

Table 6.8 Employment Statistics (Age 16 Years and Older) for Dallas, 2006

	Percent total population	Percent in the labor force	Percent employed	Percent unemployed
Education (25–64)				
High school	20	70	65	7
High school graduate	23	77	71	7
Some college	27	82	78	5
At least BA/BS	30	85	83	3
Below poverty (20–64)	12	56	44	22
(16+)				
White	51	69	66	5
Black	16	69	60	13
Hispanic	27	73	68	7
Asian	5	67	63	6

Source: U.S. Census Bureau (2010)

Table 6.9 Employment Statistics (Age 16 Years and Older) for Detroit, 2006

	Percent total population	Percent in the labor force	Percent employed	Percent unemployed
Education (25–64)				
High school	11	54	43	21
High school graduate	28	70	62	12
Some college	32	79	73	8
At least BA/BS	29	84	81	4
Below poverty (20–64)	12	49	30	38
(16+)				
White	67	65	60	8
Black	25	59	47	20
Hispanic	3	68	59	14
Asian	3	68	64	6

Source: U.S. Census Bureau (2010)

Table 6.10 Employment Statistics (Age 16 Years and Older) for Los Angeles Urbanized Area, 2006

	Percent total population	Percent in the labor force	Percent employed	Percent unemployed
Education (25–64)				
High school	23	67	62	7
High school graduate	22	74	70	6
Some college	25	79	75	5
At least BA/BS	29	84	81	4
Below poverty (20–64)	12	49	40	20
(16+)				
White	34	64	60	5
Black	7	61	54	11
Hispanic	41	68	63	7
Asian	15	61	58	5

Source: U.S. Census Bureau (2010)

Table 6.11 Employment Statistics (Age 16 Years and Older) for Milwaukee Urbanized Area, 2006

	Percent total population	Percent in the labor force	Percent employed	Percent unemployed
Education (25–64)				
High school	11	60	51	14
High school graduate	28	76	70	8
Some college	29	82	77	5
At least BA/BS	32	87	84	3
Below poverty (20–64)	12	52	37	28
(16+)				
White	72	68	64	5
Black	16	62	51	18
Hispanic	8	70	63	10
Asian	3	67	63	7

Source: U.S. Census Bureau (2010)

Table 6.12 Employment Statistics (Age 16 Years and Older) for New York City Urbanized Area, 2006

	Percent total population	Percent in the labor force	Percent employed	Percent unemployed
Education (25–64)				
High school	14	60	55	10
High school graduate	27	74	69	6
Some college	22	80	75	6
At least BA/BS	38	85	82	3
Below poverty (20–64)	11	43	32	25
(16+)				
White	52	63	60	5
Black	17	63	56	11
Hispanic	20	65	60	9
Asian	9	65	62	5

Source: U.S. Census Bureau (2010)

Table 6.13 Employment Statistics (Age 16 Years and Older) for Philadelphia Urbanized Area, 2006

	Percent total population	Percent in the labor force	Percent employed	Percent unemployed
Education (25–64)				
High school	10	54	47	13
High school graduate	31	74	69	7
Some college	25	82	78	5
At least BA/BS	35	86	84	3
Below poverty (20–64)	11	43	34	15
(16+)				
White	68	66	63	5
Black	21	60	52	14
Hispanic	6	63	57	9
Asian	4	66	62	5

Source: U.S. Census Bureau (2010)

Appendix B

Refer to Table 6.14 on page 80.

Notes

1. *Metropolitan areas* include at least one urbanized area with at least 50,000 people, and *micropolitan areas* include at least one urban cluster of between 10,000 and 50,000 people. Also, the largest principal city in each metropolitan or micropolitan area is known as a principal city (O'Sullivan, 2007).
2. Unemployment rates capture only people who are actively seeking employment; thus, these rates are likely a lower bound to the true estimate of out-of-work individuals.
3. Clotfelter, Ladd, & Vigdor (2009) found that the White–Hispanic gap remained stagnant over time, whereas the White–Black gap grew by 11% over a six-year span.

References

Alexander, K. L., Entwisle, D. R., & Olson, L. S. (2001). Schools, achievement, and inequality: A seasonal perspective. *Educational Evaluation and Policy Analysis, 23*(2), 171–191.

Altonji, J. G., & Dunn, T. A. (1996). The effects of family characteristics on the return to education. *The Review of Economics and Statistics, 78*(4), 692–704.

Betts, J. R., & Fairlie, R. W. (2003). Does immigration induce "native flight" from public schools into private schools. *Journal of Public Economics, 87*, 987–1012.

Boyd, D., Grossman, P., Lankford, H., Loeb, S., & Wyckoff, J. (2006). How changes in entry requirements alter the teacher workforce and affect student achievement. *Education Finance and Policy, 1*(2), 176–216.

Clotfelter, C. T., Ladd, H. F., & Vigdor, J. (2006). Teacher–student matching and the assessment of teacher effectiveness. *The Journal of Human Resources, 41*(4), 778–820.

Clotfelter, C. T., Ladd, H. F., & Vigdor, J. (2009). The academic achievement gap in grades 3 to 8. *Review of Economics & Statistics, 91*(2), 398–419.

Coleman, C. T., Campbell, E., & Hobson, C. (1966). *Equality of educational opportunity.* Washington, DC: Department of Health, Education, and Welfare.

Cooper, H., Nye, B., Charlton, K., Lindsay, J., & Greathouse, S. (1996). The effects of summer vacation on achievement test scores: A narrative and meta-analytic review. *Review of Educational Research, 66*(3), 227–268.

Dika, S. L., & Singh, K. (2002). Applications of social capital in educational literature: A critical synthesis. *Review of Educational Research, 72*(1), 31–60.

Eberts, R. W. (1983). How unions affect management decisions: Evidence from public schools. *Journal of Labor Research, 4*(3), 239–247.

Ehrenberg, R. G., & Smith, R. S. (2008). *Modern labor economics: Theory and public policy.* New York: Addison-Wesley.

Entwisle, D. R., Alexander, K. L., & Olson, L. S. (1994). The gender gap in math: Its possible origins in neighborhood effects. *American Sociological Review, 59*, 822–838.

Fryer, R. G., & Levit, S. D. (2004). Understanding the Black–White test score gap in the first two years of school. *Review of Economics and Statistics, 86*(2), 247–281.

Table 6.14 Median Earnings for Workers (Age 25 Years and Older) by Education, Sex, and Race and Hispanic Origin, 2007 (Earnings in Dollars)

Characteristic	Total		Not a high school graduate		High school graduate		Some college or associate's degree		Bachelor's degree		Advanced degree	
	Earnings	Margin of error[1] (±)	Earnings	Margin of error[1] (±)	Earnings	Margin of error[1] (±)	Earnings	Margin of error[1] (±)	Earnings	Margin of error[1] (±)	Earnings	Margin of error[1] (±)
All workers	33,452	65	19,405	84	26,894	52	32,874	82	46,805	103	61,287	113
Sex												
Male	40,481	52	22,602	137	32,436	63	41,035	83	67,397	227	77,219	347
Female	27,276	46	14,202	116	21,219	64	27,046	69	38,628	156	50,937	133
Race and Hispanic origin												
White	35,609	49	20,192	86	28,253	99	34,291	92	47,904	198	61,496	125
Non-Hispanic White	36,763	51	21,311	120	29,052	99	34,663	101	48,667	193	61,681	130
Black	28,071	180	16,163	197	23,322	225	30,034	193	41,972	290	54,527	912
Asian	37,940	610	19,640	447	24,639	347	32,160	277	46,957	463	70,280	777
Hispanic (any race)	24,602	123	18,804	125	23,836	197	30,801	162	40,068	346	52,268	561
Full-time, year-round workers	41,568	48	24,964	121	32,882	105	40,769	60	56,118	136	75,140	243
Sex												
Male	46,789	84	27,180	111	37,632	167	46,562	121	65,011	272	88,840	454
Female	35,769	61	20,341	110	27,477	90	34,745	122	47,333	137	61,229	180
Race and Hispanic origin												
White	43,731	103	26,125	108	34,903	111	41,793	60	58,288	323	76,578	281
Non-Hispanic White	45,690	69	30,381	161	36,647	76	42,081	62	59,644	195	77,617	304
Black	34,671	202	23,446	382	28,690	273	35,236	212	47,163	410	61,174	466
Asian	47,336	393	24,220	551	30,106	347	39,800	700	65,279	688	82,200	707
Hispanic (any race)	29,749	213	22,040	100	27,838	288	36,218	217	45,396	401	61,395	624

1. A margin of error is a measure of an estimates variability. The larger the margin of error in relation to the size of the estimate, the less reliable the estimate. When added to and subtracted from the estimate, the margin of error forms the 90% confidence interval

Source: U.S. Census Bureau (2007)

Fryer, R. G., & Levit, S. D. (2006). The Black–White test score gap through third grade. *American Law and Economics Review,* 8(2), 249–281.

Glaeser, E. L., Kahn, M. E., & Rappaport, J. (2008). Why do the poor live in cities? The role of public transportation. *Journal of Urban Economics, 63,* 1–24.

Glazerman, S., Mayer, D., & Decker, P. (2006). Alternative routes to teaching: The impacts of Teach for America on student achievement and other outcomes. *Journal of Policy Analysis and Management,* 25(1), 75–96.

Glewwe, P., Jacoby, H. G.,& King, E. M. (2001). Early childhood nutrition and academic achievement: A longitudinal analysis. *Journal of Public Economics, 81,* 345–368.

Goldhaber, D., & Brewer, D. J. (2000). Does teacher certification matter? High school teacher certification status and student achievement. *Educational Evaluation and Policy Analysis,* 22(2), 129–145.

Gottfried, M. A. (2009). Excused versus unexcused: How student absences in elementary school affect academic achievement. *Educational Evaluation and Policy Analysis, 31,* 392–419.

Hanushek, E. A. (1979). Conceptual and empirical issues in the estimation of educational production functions. *Journal of Human Resources,* 14(3), 351–388.

Hanushek, E. A. (2003). The failure of input-based school policies. *Economic Journal¸ 113,* F64–F98.

Hanushek, E. A., & Kimko, D. D. (2000). Schooling, labor-force quality, and the growth of nations. *The American Economic Review,* 90(5), 1184–1208.

Hanushek, E. A., & Lindseth, A. A. (2009). *Schoolhouses, courthouses, and statehouses: Solving the funding-achievement puzzle in America's public schools.* Princeton, NJ: Princeton University Press.

Hanushek, E. A., & Rivkin, S. G. (2006). School quality and the black–white achievement gap. NBER working paper no. 12651.

Hanushek, E. A., Kain, J. F., & Rivkin, S. G. (2004). Why public schools lose teachers. *The Journal of Human Resources, 39,* 326–354.

Hoxby, C. M. (1996). How do teachers unions affect education production? *Quarterly Journal of Economics, 111,* 671–718.

Hurre, T., Aro, H., Rahkonen, O., & Komulainen, E. (2006). Health, lifestyle, family and school factors in adolescence: Predicting adult educational level. *Educational Research,* 48(1), 41–53.

Jacob, B. (2007). The challenges of staffing urban schools with effective teachers. *The Future of Children,* 17(1), 129–153.

Jyoti, D. F., Frongillo, E. A., & Jones, S. J. (2005). Food insecurity affects school children's academic performance, weight gain, and social skills. *The Journal of Nutrition,* 135(12), 2831–2839.

Keane, M. P., & Roemer, J. E. (2009). Assessing policies to equalize opportunity using an equilibrium model of educational and occupational choices. *Journal of Public Economics, 93,* 879–898.

Ladd, H. F., Clotfelter, C. T., & Vigdor, J. (2003). Segregation and resegregation in North Carolina's public school classrooms. *North Carolina Law Review,* 81(4), 1463–1511.

Lankford, H., Loeb, S., & Wyckoff, J. (2002). Teacher sorting and the plight of urban schools: A descriptive analysis. *Educational Evaluation and Policy Analysis,* 24(1), 37–62.

Laraia, B., Siega-Riz, A., Gundersen, C., & Dole, N. (2006). Psychosocial factors and socioeconomic indicators are associated with household food insecurity among pregnant women. *The Journal of Nutrition, 136,* 177–182.

Lee, J. (2002). Racial and ethnic achievement gap trends: Reversing the progress toward equity? *Educational Researcher, 31,* 3–12.

Moe, T. M. (2009). Collective bargaining and the performance of the public schools, *American Journal of Political Science,* 53(1), 156–174.

Murnane, R., & Steele, J. (2007). What is the problem? The challenge of providing effective teachers for all children. *The Future of Children,* 17(1), 15–43.

National Center for Education Statistics (2008). Home page. Retrieved July 24, 2008 from: http://nces.ed.gov/nations reportcard/

National Commission on Excellence in Education (1983). A nation at risk: The imperative for educational reform (ED 226 006). Washington, DC: National Center on Excellence in Education.

Oreopoulos, P. (2007). Do dropouts drop out too soon? Wealth, health, and happiness from compulsory schooling. *Journal of Public Economics, 91,* 2213–2229.

O'Sullivan, A. (2007). *Urban economics.* New York: McGraw-Hill.

Phillips, M., & Chin, T. (2004). School inequality: What do we know? In K. Neckerman (Ed.), *Social inequality.* New York: Russell Sage Foundation.

Portes, A. (1998). Social capital: Its origins and applications in modern sociology. *Annual Review of Sociology, 24,* 1–24.

Reardon, S. F., & Galindo, C. (2009). The Hispanic–White achievement gap in math and reading in the elementary grades. *American Education Research Journal,* 46(3), 853–891.

Rivkin, S. G., Hanushek, E. A., & Kain, J. F. (2005). Teachers, schools, and academic achievement. *Econometrica,* 73(2), 417–458.

Rockoff, J. (2004). The impact of individual teachers on student achievement: Evidence from panel data. *American Economic Review,* 94(20), 247–252.

Rothstein, R. (2004). *Class and schools: Using social, economic, and educational reform to close the black–white achievement gap.* Washington DC: Economic Policy Institute.

Rubenstein, R., Schwartz, A. E., Stiefel, L., & Amor, H. B. H. (2007). From districts to schools: The distribution of resources across schools in big city school districts. *Economics of Education Review, 26,* 532–545.

Slaughter, D., & Epps, E. (1987). The home environment and academic achievement of black children and youth: An overview. *The Journal of Negro Education,* 56(1), 3–20.

State Education Data Center (Dist.) (2009). Student demographics and achievement. Washington, DC: Council of Chief State School Officers. Retrieved October 1, 2009 from: www.SchoolDataDirect.org

U.S. Census Bureau (2006). *2006 Population estimates, detailed tables.* Retrieved May 17, 2011 from: http:factfinder.census.gov/servlet/DTGeoSearchByListServlet?ds_name=PEP_2006_EST&_lang=en&_ts=323353710288

U.S. Census Bureau (2007). *Income, earnings, and poverty data from the 2007 American community survey.* Retrieved May 17, 2011 from: www.census.gov/prod/2008pubs/acs-09.pdf

U.S. Census Bureau (2010). *American fact finder: 2006 American community survey, custom tables.* Retrieved June 1, 2010 from: http://factfinder.census.gov/servlet/CTGeoSearchByListServlet?ds_name=ACS_2006_EST_G00_&_lang=en&_ts=328456927996

U.S. Department of Transportation (2011). *Census 2000 populations statistics.* Retrieved 17 May, 2011 from: www.fhwa.dot.gov/planning/census/cps2k.htm

Varian, H. R. (1999). *Intermediate microeconomics: A modern approach.* New York: W. W. Norton.

Winicki, J., & Jemison, K. (2003). Food insecurity and hunger in the kindergarten classroom: Its effect on learning and growth. *Contemporary Economic Policy, 21*(2), 145–157.

II
Leadership

Leadership in urban settings requires particular competencies as well of an awareness of issues of equity and how they play out in educational settings. Chapters in this section address knowledge, skills, and perspectives that should ground the work of a leader in urban education.

7

Thoughts on Educational Leadership

John Brooks Slaughter

Many years ago I was asked to list what I thought were the 10 most important attributes, skills, or traits that make a leader a leader. After some reflection I developed a list consisting of the following unranked items: courage, compassion, tenacity, knowledge, initiative, integrity, ability to listen, sense of humor, energy, and insight. Over the years, I have thought about that list, and although I might change a few of the items, I have concluded that the most important asset of a leader is the presence of followers.

My definition of a good leader is one who demonstrates the capacity to bring about positive change through the effective employment of people, capital, and material resources, and who has followers. That last phrase is most important; one cannot be a leader if there are no followers. True leaders do not designate themselves leaders; leaders must have others make the endorsement by becoming followers. Gardner (1995) said it best by asserting that such persons "can be given subordinates, but they cannot be given a following. A following must be earned" (p. 186).

Some individuals who have been given titles and authority believe that those things make them leaders. They do not. People are not leaders because of their titles. Their title may be principal, provost, or president; in itself, it does not make them leaders. Such people may be managers or supervisors, but not leaders. The distinction is extremely important. Only followers can give credence to the title "leader." Individuals become leaders only when their behaviors, thoughts, and values, as seen or perceived by those they would lead dictate that they are deserving of their roles. They must hold a vision for the institution and people that they lead and must be able to describe it in ways that inspire trust and elicit the commitment of followers. It is not surprising that the Bible expresses this same thought by asking the question, "For if the trumpet give an uncertain sound, who shall prepare himself for battle?" (1 Corinthians, 14: 8).

One of the most glaring problems of schools and school districts is that they are often over-managed and under-led. It is also often said that the difference between management and leadership is that managers do things right, while leaders do the right thing. It is the doing of the right things that attracts and retains followers and is the essence of good leadership. James McGregor Burns, in his book *Leadership* (1978), said it much more elegantly:

Leadership is leaders inducing followers to act for certain goals that represent the values and the motivations—the wants and needs, aspirations and expectations—of both leaders and followers. The genius of leadership lies in the manner in which leaders see and act on their own and their followers' values and motivations. (p. 19)

Note the emphasis on "values" in Burns's definition of leadership. Leadership is the crucial catalyst needed to mobilize positive and necessary change. Leadership inspires; it provides a sense of meaning and significance to our endeavors. It promotes community and commitment to purpose.

Winston Churchill is purported to have said, "Of all the qualities of leadership, courage is the most important, because courage guarantees all the rest." Today, perhaps more than at any previous period in our nation's history, we need individuals and institutions with the courage to provide leadership—transformative leadership that produces meaningful, sustainable, and positive change. We need courageous leaders who are willing to stand on the side of justice and fairness and not cower in fear or shirk their responsibilities. We need strong leaders who understand the inseparability of equity and excellence. We need wise and visionary leaders who see the demographic changes occurring in our urban schools and campuses as opportunities to educate themselves and their followers and, by so doing, to transform their institutions and ultimately demonstrate to America how to develop and sustain inclusive and pluralistic communities—communities with shared values and goals, common purposes, and hopes.

Leaders must convey the sense that what is important is not race, ethnicity, class, or any other distinction that differentiates one person or group from another. Instead, it is about the inherent worthiness of all people. In the words of Martin Luther King, Jr., they must be individuals who live by the following creed: "We must use time creatively and always remember that the time is ripe to do right." Nowhere is this more important than in education.

A universal characteristic of educational institutions, at all levels, is the presence of ambivalences, differences of opinion, tension, and even hostility. The transformative leader is one who does not shy away from these forces but uses them to motivate followers and to promote growth and constructive change. Burns (1978), well known for his groundbreaking scholarship on political leadership, reminds us that those who would be leaders "do not shun conflict; they confront it, exploit it, ultimately embody it" (p. 39). It is this ability and willingness to deal with strife and conflict, combined with empathy and a passion for positive results, that is the mark of the transformative leader.

Burns, who coined the phrase "transforming leadership," associated an undertone of morality with the expression. He described transforming or transformative leadership as a process that "ultimately becomes moral in that it raises the level of human conduct and ethical aspiration of both leader and led, and thus has a transforming effect on both" (p. 20).

Transforming leadership is the overarching theme of each of the four chapters on leadership in this book on urban education. Transforming the way we teach, learn, and interact with one another, both locally and globally, is the challenge facing educational leaders and their institutions in a world that is becoming increasingly complex, pluralistic, and rife with interdependencies. As a nation, we are confronted with severe economic instability, momentous demographic changes, declining confidence in corporate executives and government officials, and a gnawing sense of insecurity on many fronts.

In addition, the dynamic effects of global developments in science and technology are changing the way we work: they call for new and different skills than were required of workers a few years ago. Each of these concerns, and many others, have serious and predictable consequences for our urban communities and the schools, higher education institutions, service providers, and businesses within them.

We find ourselves in a period of constant change. Institutions of all types are undergoing significant and, in some cases, cataclysmic changes. Our hospitals, schools, courts, and government agencies are being required to adjust to new realities. Change is all around us. Progress is accompanied by change.

Some of it we may like. Most certainly, some of it we will not like. Robert F. Kennedy said, "Progress is an important word. But change is its motivator, and change has its enemies." We are seeing the truth in Kennedy's observation everywhere.

Change brings both challenges and opportunities, the elements of the interesting times foretold by the well-known Chinese curse. Both the challenges and opportunities offer exciting and potentially transforming possibilities. This is particularly true for our educational systems. They must prepare themselves and those they are charged with educating to respond to a set of ever-changing and dynamic environments, domestically and globally. They must also recognize their responsibility to encourage and, in some cases, to initiate positive and substantive changes. They cannot relegate themselves to a passive and completely apolitical role with respect to the great issues and grand challenges facing our communities, our nation and the world. Leadership opportunities and responsibilities abound. These are the unifying aims of the chapters in this section on urban education leadership principles and practice.

References

Burns, J. M. (1978). *Leadership*. New York: Harper & Row.

Gardner, J. W. (1995). Leaders and followers. In J. T. Wren (Ed.), *The leader's companion: Insights on leadership through the ages*. New York: The Free Press.

8

Mutuality and Reciprocity in Urban Renewal Through Shared Leadership

Adrianna Kezar

Diverse demographics, contested and difficult politics, large business communities, weak democratic infrastructures in neighborhoods, important cultural resources and institutions, vastly different value systems, extensive human resources, lack of collective community, enormous intellectual capital, high poverty, wealthy and philanthropic interests, and violence—these are the dichotomous conditions of urban education. Aspects of the community can enrich the research and learning, while other aspects make the role of an urban education leader extremely challenging.

In higher education, the types and roles of urban institutions vary considerably. There are liberal arts colleges, community colleges, research universities, and regional comprehensive universities that all find their home in urban areas. Although many institutions of higher education are located in urban areas, a symbiotic relationship with the metropolitan context does not always exist without intentional effort. For example, many large public or private research universities tend to consider themselves to be national or international institutions in their scope, not closely affiliated with the issues of their urban environment beyond practical issues of property development, parking, and their own workforce. Being in an urban area does not necessarily mean that an educational institution is engaging with the urban community and its assets and challenges.

Perhaps most often, higher education institutions ignore their responsibility to address some of the challenges of urban areas and merely try to take advantage of their assets. However, there is a set of institutions that has formally declared that their missions are shaped by their urban histories and location: the Coalition of Urban and Metropolitan Universities (CUMU), which was founded in 1990 and has approximately 90 members. Most are state universities with a comprehensive blend of teaching and research agendas, but recently some private colleges and universities have also joined. Because they strongly identify with their urban location, these universities and colleges have strategic agendas for engagement with community through partnerships and active participation in community collaborations to build the urban core and capacity. Although this coalition is one identifiable group, some individual community and liberal arts colleges have also developed deep connections to their urban communities.

There is an irony in the higher education community. Although K–12 schools are locally governed and therefore define themselves through place and have quite distinctive identities because of their location, colleges and universities do not necessarily develop the same local identity. Campus location often has little impact on the institutional resources, structure, culture, or almost any aspect of such an institution's operations. Colleges and universities often operate to a large degree in isolation from the broader environments. They often see their mission as serving a broader national or even international mission.

Prestige accrues with institutions that have a national and international presence, which reinforces a more "macro" location affiliation. For many institutions, rural, suburban, or urban is a very small component of the institution's identity. Location is a peripheral issue that emerges only if there are difficult "town and gown" relationships or if a catastrophic event strikes the community. Certainly, there are institutions that do engage their locations (such as the CUMU members), but a central underlying tension in higher education is its lack of identification with urban location or location at all. In this chapter, I want to focus on the lessons we can learn from institutions that have a deeply entrenched history of engaging with the urban environment. Although many institutions are located in urban areas, I will argue that responsible place-oriented leadership within urban higher education institutions is often missing from many campuses. What I mean by responsible leadership is that institutions not only take advantage of the assets within urban areas, but also contribute to overcoming their challenges and help to build capacity; there should be reciprocity. Furthermore, leaders develop an ethic of mutuality in which they listen to the urban community as they engage with them. Reciprocity and mutuality are the core concepts for urban post-secondary leaders to hone as they develop partnerships.

Urban and metropolitan universities have a long tradition of engaging in activities such as community partnerships, service learning, K–16 partnerships, and a variety of other functions that help build the community. However, in order to conduct this type of leadership well and to practice mutuality, it must be done in a shared leadership fashion in which the community is part of the campus leadership team, which I call community-informed leadership.[1] Community-informed leadership is necessary because the challenges that urban areas face, including the building of community capacity, involve complex and multifaceted issues that require diverse expertise to be harnessed and applied, whether that expertise is internal to academia or external from the community. In this chapter, I draw on research from shared leadership that suggests why shared leadership is beneficial for campuses as well as specific strategies needed by leaders on urban campuses in order to be successful using this in engaging with community. I provide specific models and ideas for enacting a community-informed leadership model. Faculty, staff, students, and other individuals should also be included in shared leadership on campus. I focus on the need for greater involvement of community members in leadership, as they are particularly important within an urban setting.

Last, I describe some of the challenges that emerge in using community-based leadership, such as differing interests and values, politics, and power; I also offer strategies to address these from the research on shared leadership. Community-informed leadership is quite different from the tradition of shared governance, which is a part of the academy. Shared governance is based on a wider circle of input into decision-making processes but usually involves mostly internal stakeholders (the exception being the College Board). Boards of trustees typically do not mirror the average members of the community and their interests, and this distinction is where community-informed leadership is unique.

Why Engage the Urban Community as a Leader?

What are the motivations that drive some universities to be more involved in their cities than others? Communities certainly need universities. The history of higher education demonstrates that communities prosper when colleges are located within them—from jobs, new businesses, community events, professional development and training, and healthcare and services. In fact, colleges were so important to community development that in the early 1800s too many were opened in the hope of increasing the economic and social development of the community; but there simply were not enough students to sustain the number of institutions and many of them failed (Lucas, 1994).

Do universities need communities? Their enlightened self-interest will convince many universities of the need to work with other urban stakeholders and to form partnerships. Institutions in cities that have gone into decline (Detroit, Cleveland, and Philadelphia, for example) recognize the importance of working to sustain the viability of the city. As a city goes into decline, it affects the college or university; therefore, the challenges we noted in the introduction (poverty, violence, and unrest) become more visible and apparent to faculty and administrators. Other institutions have faced significant crises such as urban riots (Los Angeles) or natural catastrophes (New Orleans). However, many leaders recognize the need to partner and work with community stakeholders well before a crisis occurs.

Some campuses recognize that they have an interdependent relationship with their communities (prior to some crisis) and that their own goals can be furthered or hampered by the future directions of those communities. Portland State University, for example, recognizes that as Portland changes (both in its growth and the nature of the city environment), this change will likely shape the nature of student interest, research possibilities, and partnership opportunities coming to their institution. The Pacific Northwest is well known for its green and sustainable habits. Because the city has invested in policies and programs that support a green future, this investment has resulted in many research opportunities and grants for faculty and has increased the number of students with a "green" interest coming to their institution. Through the connection with their community, they can create synergistic relationships that further their own goals as well as the goals of the community. They have been able to attract scientists with more prominent backgrounds to their campus, which has increased their prestige. At the same time, these scholars can now work with policymakers in the area to improve practices around sustainability.

Many campus leaders recognize that the challenges or new conditions they face on campus can benefit from expertise and knowledge brought in from the community. The community can also help leverage important changes that leaders are trying to make. This support can be especially useful when leaders face resistance from internal campus stakeholders. Urban campuses have become increasingly diverse over the last 20 years, and the predominantly White faculty and administration often do not have the expertise to adequately help students access and succeed in post-secondary institutions. Community groups possess insight about the motivations, backgrounds, and life experiences of students of color. They can provide relevant, real-world examples to inform curriculum design, and help recreate teaching and learning environments that are more appropriate and responsive to a diverse student body. Campus leaders often face resistance from faculty in their efforts to better support underrepresented minorities on campus (Kezar, 2007). However, successful leaders, who have campuses supportive of students of color, use external groups to pressure faculty into rethinking their teaching methods and approaches (Kezar, 2007). College presidents leverage powerful business communities (such as engineering firms) to gain faculty attention and change behavior. Presidents invite engineering firms to campus to talk about their interest in having more underrepresented minorities in the workplace, and the businesses describe successful practices they have used to retain minority candidates in the workplace and make them successful (Kezar, 2007).

Some scholars have identified how engaging with the community can be a form of organizational learning, where the leaders of urban colleges and universities think of their institutions as part of a larger system and begin to rethink their work and create a stronger organization (Anderson, 2005). Organizational learning helps institutional actors to think from a systems perspective, identifying problems and dysfunctions that they can address. It also helps individuals within the institution to view work across divisions as interrelated and to examine the relationships between the institution, its surrounding community, and external influences. Studies of campus–community partnerships, for example, have demonstrated some of the bureaucratic structures that are difficult for anyone, including students, to navigate (Anderson, 2005). Only when the campus sees itself in relationship to the broader system will some of these inherent problems within the campus become apparent. Another concept of organizational learning is "double-loop learning," where the system is open to information that questions underlying assumptions and behaviors. In her study of community and university partnerships, Anderson (2005) found that universities can receive information that challenges their underlying norms by interacting with community groups. The university may perceive that the faculty are student-oriented but discover that members of the community, who are more in touch with students, do not have the same perception. A university can perceive that an outreach office is meeting its goals, but the community may provide feedback to the contrary and note that the office is creating poor relationships in the community.

Policymakers in particular should want to engage campus leaders to work more with community leaders to enhance urban environments, because research demonstrates that certain urban environments become centers of creativity and innovation, and will be the key to the new economy (Florida, 2002). Having entrepreneurial and creative individuals to create innovations can further economic interests and the new knowledge economy. Florida (2002) predicts that more jobs will be created for the creative class and that the areas that have these workers will have the greatest wealth and prosperity. He found that these creative and entrepreneurial individuals tend to cluster in certain communities (often urban) and typically in a hub of colleges and universities. The conditions that make up these creative communities include tolerance, technology, and talent. Florida discusses how universities are critical to developing these three conditions.

Clearly, whereas universities develop talents and skills in people, they also typically have a goal of creating more tolerance (usually beyond tolerance to celebration and understanding) for diversity, and most campuses are centers for technology. Therefore, community leaders and policymakers should see the central role that universities and colleges can play in building capacity and developing the creative class. State policymakers likely want to encourage partnerships between community leaders and campuses to try to create these kinds of environments, which are the economic engines of the future. Both nationally and internationally, policymakers will also want to examine more "macro" policies, which can help to encourage more communication and connection between campuses and communities.

A counterargument to focusing on the urban community is that the entire notion of community is being changed in the global economy and environment. The land-grant institution, community college, and urban or metropolitan college were developed during a certain historical time period where "place" was more central. Today, we may have moved beyond those times. Universities and colleges that reach internationally are simply ahead of the curve and represent the future; these institutions appropriately have moved beyond limited notions of place. What has made college campuses premiere throughout the world is their attention to a broader international scene rather than a parochial community or local view.

Many institutions are thinking about community in wholly different ways than have been conceptualized in the past. Through technology, our communities can be anywhere and may have nothing to do with physical location. Certainly, this redefining of community is a trend based on the global economy, but I contend that the notion of local community and the urban context will still be meaningful in the future. Rhoades (2008, 2009) argues that professors in the future will be connected both internationally and locally, and will resemble what he calls "local cosmopolitans." Faculty will conduct research with colleagues in India, but they also will be deeply involved in research and service within their local area.

Rhoades also suggests policies for moving faculty in this direction, such as providing incentives for faculty who volunteer and play a leadership role in the local community. Also, the opportunity to develop an international scholarly reputation may not be financially feasible. Most of America's middle- and lower-ranked universities must define success in more local and regional terms because that is their context and opportunity.

Fifteen years ago, many people believed that physical campuses would no longer be necessary because of the power of the Internet and technology. Yet the physical space of the campus remains as central a concept within post-secondary education as it ever has been. Experiments into technology usage for educational purposes have demonstrated that it has very limited capacity for professional schools, programs that have an apprentice element, for teaching research, or for deep learning (Toma & Kezar, 1999; Zemsky, Massey, & Wegner, 2005).

Rote learning activities are best conducted through technology, but human interaction and guidance (thought passé 10 years ago), have proven essential to learning outcomes (Toma & Kezar, 1999). In a similar vein, I argue that while notions of place and community are dynamic and changing, urban spaces and local context will still remain significant conditions that leaders need to consider as they plan the future of their institutions. We cannot and should not try to escape the significance of location.

Engaging the Community: Assets and Challenges

As noted in the Introduction, we can learn from institutions that strongly identify with their urban mission and developed a variety of practices that build community capacity. Perhaps the distinctive area where urban and metropolitan universities have significantly contributed to building community capacity is through partnerships. For many years Housing and Urban Development (HUD) has awarded Community Outreach Partnership Center (COPC) grants that promote universities actively working with various community groups and organizations to solve a mutually agreed upon community problem. The Community-Campus Partnerships for Health (CCPH) is another major program that has successfully created deep partnerships across the country, between colleges and community organizations.[2]

One of the largest scale and best known campus and community partnerships is Marquette University's Campus Circle Project, which invested $50 million in neighborhood redevelopment. The project renovated 188 housing units and constructed 88,000 square feet of rented commercial space, both processes providing jobs. Among many other outcomes, the project surpassed its self-imposed Minority/Women/Disadvantaged Business participation goal of 20–25% in construction and professional services; it also established a Community-Oriented Policing project in cooperation with the Milwaukee Police Department, which has resulted in a 34% decrease in crime. Over 20 universities and cities across America have viewed Campus Circle as a model for neighborhood revitalization, with over half of that number sending delegations to spend time with Campus Circle staff and Marquette University representatives to share and learn about solutions to issues facing urban neighborhoods.

Urban campus leaders can contribute to improving K–12 education. A recent effort toward urban school reform, called the Urban Educators Corps, is composed of urban education school deans and faculty members from 39 public urban research universities (Howey, 2007a). This group works together to enhance the quality of urban education by focusing on teacher quality, student retention and success, and the creation of systemic partnerships. Colleges and universities take responsibility for urban school challenges: student dropout, teachers unwilling to teach in the area, and lack of resources. The federally funded program known as GEAR UP (Gaining Early Awareness and Readiness for Undergraduate Programs) also has been embraced by many urban institutions that are now working closely with school systems. They adopt classrooms and work to create reform efforts while also helping to improve access to college.

College campuses have also become involved in another major effort: increasing access to post-secondary education through school and university partnerships. Many colleges and universities have established outreach programs that work with urban schools to create college-going cultures (see summary in *Metropolitan Universities Journal, 18*(4)). Some of the outreach programs become specialized and focus on particular areas, such as enhancing students' math skills, creating culturally relevant curriculum, or enhancing English as a second language. Another common practice is working with P-16 councils established at the state level. Many colleges and universities are sending campus leaders to participate in these councils, and to create policy for the state that can improve the access of all students attending secondary institutions.

One of the fastest growing trends on campuses is the development of service learning programs where students work on community volunteer projects while learning course material through a class related to their volunteer opportunity. Students work at a homeless shelter or a community agency, providing their time and talent in helping to build community capacity while still learning about real-life problems such as poverty or environmental hazards. Although many campuses have these programs, institutions committed to their urban mission more intentionally develop these programs in communication with community leaders and to address community-defined needs.

Although all colleges and universities that are part of the metropolitan and urban coalition actively engage in all these types of practices, they may not always systematically include community members in campus leadership and planning; they may lack mutuality. My contention is that in order to build community capacity and to more efficiently and effectively channel human and fiscal resources, the community must be brought into campus leadership processes. We must become universities that are systematically community informed, particularly those institutions that seek to meet an urban mission. Many of the efforts (outreach, service learning) created by campuses are the inspiration of a faculty member or administrator.

Although partnerships may serve in an important role, they may not always represent the best use of campus time and resources to address the community need. More communication with the community and creating programs with the community will likely lead to better outcomes. Furthermore, colleges without an urban mission may have service learning or outreach programs. Service learning and outreach have become common practice at colleges and universities. However, it is my contention that many of these efforts do not build community capacity or substantially assist the community, because they are conceived exclusively by college campuses for their own benefit rather than that of the community. The research literature on campus and community partnerships is clear that effective collaboration for campus and community partnerships is built on mutuality between a secondary institutions and community groups, and that this is typically lacking within partnerships.[3]

Some Definitions: Shared Leadership, Shared Governance, Team-based Leadership, Community-informed Leadership

Throughout this chapter, certain terms are used that may seem similar but are slightly different. Below, I briefly describe the difference for clarification. All of these new definitions for leadership emerged because the term *leadership* has become so closely associated with authority-based, top-down, individualistic models of leadership that any deviation from this form has tended to take on some new classification in order to separate it from this traditional understanding or notion (Kezar, Carducci, & Contreras-McGavin, 2006).

First, *shared leadership* is a process where leadership is broadly distributed to a group of leaders who act in the role traditionally reserved for supervisors or managers (Pearce & Conger, 2003). It is conceptualized as an activity that is shared or distributed[4] among members of a group or organization. This leadership is bidirectional between what has traditionally been called leaders and followers. Traditional models of leadership focus only on the downward influence of leaders on subordinates and on a single individual in authority who plays a leadership role. Shared leadership examines both downward and upward hierarchical influence.

Shared governance is a form of shared decision-making but may not be a form of shared leadership. Shared governance is the decision-making process present in some higher education institutions (not the majority) in which different groups (administrators, faculty, and sometimes staff and students) provide input into the development campus policies and practices in areas they are considered to have the greatest expertise (Kezar & Eckel, 2004).

However, the presence of shared governance does not necessarily mean that campus administrators conceptualize faculty as leaders and look to them for innovative solutions or the creation of change on campus. It also does not mean that they distribute leadership (or create mechanisms for them to play a leadership role) to this group. Yet shared governance might make a campus more likely to consider faculty as part of a shared leadership process and encourage them to participate in leading various efforts. Also, shared leadership suggests that people can contribute to problems that are in areas outside their expertise, so it differs from shared governance in this way as well (Pearce & Conger, 2003).

Team-based leadership is one of the major forms of shared leadership that has emerged within organizations. As people in positions of authority tried to grapple with ways to foster leadership throughout an organization, leadership teams emerged as one such vehicle for enhancing and building the leadership capacity more broadly throughout the organization. Other forms of shared leadership exist, but the team-based model is the most prominent one for capturing greater expertise and expanding the knowledge base within the leadership process. However, other researchers describe team-based leadership models as the broader category and shared leadership as a property within or which emerge from team-based models (Mayo, Meindl, & Oastor, 2003). Leadership teams and shared leadership are highly interrelated.

Community-informed leadership, which I am proposing in this article, is a form of shared leadership that looks beyond the internal organization for stakeholders to be included in the leadership process. Although *shared leadership* can be used as the term to describe this phenomenon, almost all conceptualizations of shared leadership (or shared governance) have been internally based, focusing on faculty or staff. To ensure that readers understand that community-informed leadership is a distinctive argument, I have chosen to create a new term.

There is little, if any, direct research on community-informed leadership, but since it is a derivative of shared leadership, I review this literature base. In the next section of the chapter, I describe the research data supporting the notion that the inclusion of additional stakeholders in campus leadership is likely to be beneficial.

The Promise of Shared and Community-informed Leadership: Data on Expanding Leadership Processes to Include More Stakeholders

A variety of research studies support the need to expand leadership from the hands of a few leaders to a broader group of stakeholders in organizations in general and in educational institutions in particular. In fact, Pearce and Conger (2003) demonstrate how studies over the past 100 years have pointed in this direction, but the overwhelming bias toward heroic, individual, and hierarchical leaders prevented scholars and practitioners from conceptualizing and adopting the outcomes of these numerous studies. In other words, bias toward singular leadership caused many to ignore the results of numerous studies illustrating the efficacy of involving multiple individuals, outside positions of authority, and working in collectives as related to important leadership outcomes such as problem solving, change, innovation, and strategic decision-making.

Outcomes supported by shared leadership include increased problem-solving abilities, greater creativity, organizational effectiveness, effectiveness of groups, more motivation and dedication by members of leadership groups, satisfaction with decision-making, greater social integration and more positive relationships within organizations, and collective efficacy (Pearce & Conger, 2003).

Historic studies that support shared leadership models include the law of situation (Follett, 1924); social systems leadership theories (Mayo, 1933); role differentiation by group (Benne & Sheats, 1948); coleadership (Solomon, Loeffer, & Frank, 1953); social exchange theory (Festinger, 1954); emergent leadership (Hollander, 1961); mutual leadership (Bowers & Seashore, 1966); team member exchange (Berger, Cohen, & Zelditch, 1972); participative decision-making (Vroom & Yetton, 1973); leader–member exchange (Graen, 1976); substitutes for leadership (Kerr & Jermier, 1978); self-leadership (Manz & Sims, 1980); shared cognition (Resnick, 1991); and, more recently, research on organizational learning (Senge, 1990) and self-managing work teams (Manz & Sims, 1987).

I comment on these two more recent sources of support (organizational learning and work teams) for the importance of shared leadership and broadening the leadership process to a more collective and diverse group of experts, but it should be noted that studies throughout the last 100 years have supported this perspective. Yet only recently were these data implemented and leadership practices changed to reflect what has been identified as more effective approaches to leadership. I highlight the more general leadership literature first and then describe some studies within higher education that support this perspective.

One of the major areas of research supporting shared leadership is organizational learning (Heifetz, 1994; Senge, 1990). Organizations that are able to overcome significant challenges and operate more effectively depend on the knowledge and expertise throughout an organization (and beyond the organization) rather than relying on the knowledge, decision-making, and leadership of a select few leaders (Kezar et al., 2006; Senge, 1990). Various studies showed that centralizing decision making and problem solving at the higher levels of the organization missed key data at lower levels that created better solutions to problems or better products for customers (Kezar et al., 2006; Senge, 1990). Total quality management and other decentralized models of organization emerged as a result of these findings.

One of the leadership models that developed out of the research on organizational learning is the adaptive leadership model (Heifetz, 1994). Heifetz proposes that the work of leadership is what he termed "adaptive challenges" that require experiments, new discoveries, and adjustments from numerous places in an organization or society. Much of the past research on leaders focused on more routine fixes for technical problems—where an individual expert can apply a solution—what Heifetz (1994) might term management or daily decision-making. Heifetz's work found that these complex challenges (much like the challenges that urban areas face) require mobilizing the expertise of the entire community and that the work of leaders is the ability to bring people together, to have constructive dialogues and problem solving, to engage in reflection and come up with very different solutions, not just applying technical and routine solutions.

In higher education, several researchers have provided evidence about the benefits that accrue when post-secondary institutions engage a broad array of constituents in a learning activity and overcome major challenges. Bauman (2005) demonstrates how campus teams with leadership from divisions across the campus identified performance gaps (that they had not realized before) between White students and students of color, and developed solutions and interventions to students performing poorly. These performance gaps have long plagued campuses, and people had formerly not been able to develop solutions. The key elements of organizational learning are having data and information, a broad-based team that could understand different parts of the system, and the ability for diverse members to solve problems together, which relied on team building and socialization.

Team-based (also referred to as *shared*) approaches to leadership have demonstrated the benefits of working groups and cross-functional teams for decisions and more effective operations (Pearce & Conger, 2003). The studies documented how work teams take on the roles that were previously reserved for management and how they can be extremely effective in developing solutions to organizational problems. Studies demonstrate that when a leader emerges within the group, they are more effective than a designated or assigned leader, again suggesting the value of leaders throughout the organization, not just those in authority (Pearce & Sims, 2002).

There has been no equivalent study in higher education of individual decision-making compared with groups or teams (as there has been in business and government). Bensimon and Neumann (1993) examined leadership teams, but without any comparison group. Instead, they demonstrated how to create more functional or effective presidential teams or cabinets, and how to truly draw on the expertise of multiple members of the group. I (Kezar, Gallant, & Lester, 2011) have demonstrated how campuses that foster grassroots leadership among faculty and staff create a much broader array of change efforts that make the institutions more effective and build the leadership capacity and skills of individuals throughout the organization. Because higher education has a tradition of shared governance, it may be that few researchers feel it necessary to demonstrate that the greater number of stakeholders may lead to the better decisions and stronger leadership.

Although shared leadership seems to be more effective for solving complex problems and addressing the complexity of leadership, it is also fraught with challenges that, if not overcome, can lead to a compromise in outcomes and benefits (Pearce & Conger, 2003). As a result, the majority of recent research on shared leadership has been working to develop principles about how team leadership works most effectively, such as understanding shared cognition (Pearce & Conger, 2003). Researchers have been fine-tuning and understanding what conditions and factors enhance the development of shared leadership, and I draw on this literature later to address challenges faced by community-informed leadership (see Pearce and Conger (2003) for a major summary of research on shared leadership).

It is not the intent of this article to suggest that shared leadership is a panacea for urban educators. Instead, this article suggests that shared leadership is particularly well matched to the challenge of building community capacity, engaging the urban mission, and enacting mutuality. In fact, recent studies have begun to explore how some combination of individuals and collectives, hierarchical and nonhierarchical, and centralized and decentralized forms of leadership can be combined to create a leadership environment that best supports organizations and communities. There are campus issues that will best be handled through other forms of leadership.

Community-informed Leadership: Models and Examples

As noted in the Introduction, higher education has a tradition of sharing leadership in decision-making within the institution called shared governance. This tradition provides a platform for thinking about a more community-informed leadership that includes important external stakeholders in the leadership process. Shared governance suggests that important stakeholders should have input into the decision-making process, particularly where they have noted expertise.

On college campuses, this idea has translated into faculty participating in decision-making and playing a leadership role around curriculum and matters of teaching and learning. Yet the stakeholders involved in campus decision-making and leadership are typically quite limited, and they are always internal (beyond the board of trustees).

What would community-informed leadership look like in action? Community-informed leadership would include members of the local community (particularly related to preexisting or planned community partnerships, and related to community assets and challenges) in planning, change efforts, and key decision-making junctures. Here I review a few principles and then provide examples of avenues for including community members in leadership processes.

First, it is important that community stakeholders represent the diverse communities in the area and more marginal groups such as local nonprofits and neighborhood groups, making sure that those included represent the racial and economic diversity of the area. There is a tendency for broader stakeholder efforts to merely bring in more of the powerful voices—those that already have a voice such as the institution's board of trustees. If leadership and decision-making are expanded but only continue to include the most powerful members of the community, then what you have is still not community-informed leadership.

Second, it is important that community groups have avenues to present partnerships to campuses and provide vehicles for this to happen. Typically, post-secondary institutions decide that they want a partnership to serve an institutional interest, but community-led partnerships have little chance of finding a champion or a process so that a campus might consider working on the partnership. If the institution develops a committee or group that invites and vets community partnership ideas, this step can encourage more mutual development of initiatives. Such committees need to include members of the community.

Third, community members need to be invited to talk about campus issues such as the curriculum, teaching and learning, and not only issues that relate to community development and renewal. Community-informed leadership is unlikely to work if the community is not seen as having any expertise to contribute to the university's own mission and goals. Studies on campus and community partnerships have found that community partnerships can lead to meaningful changes in campus operations and improve its core function (Anderson, 2005). This principle is particularly important because it demonstrates that the campus sees the value in the community perspective and treats them as equal partners with mutuality.

Community-informed leadership can be created through a variety of ways and models. When members form campus-wide planning and strategic teams, the relevant community partners can be invited to join such teams. Individual schools and colleges (such as social work or public policy) often develop leadership groups to create strategic plans and invite community members to join these entities. In fact, academic program-specific examples of community-informed leadership (where community partners are involved in some dimension of the decision-making process) comprise a majority of the examples, such as a school of dentistry bringing in local health nonprofits to inform curricular objectives for relevancy.

Yet it is important to build upon these academic program-specific examples; campuses should also involve the community in campus-wide strategic decisions that have a community impact. Because many of the metropolitan and urban institutions work closely with community groups through partnerships, and already have a tradition of including them in campus decision-making structures, they provide some existing examples of this process. For example, the University of Minnesota established a Council on Public Engagement. This council is an institution-wide body charged with strengthening the public mission and practice across the full range of university activities, and it involves community members in discussions about scholarship and research, curricular contents, student learning outcomes (such as preparing affected citizens), and addressing critical social and public problems.

Trinity College, like the University of Minnesota, has taken a broad approach to involving community groups in campus leadership. Unlike most campus Web sites, they have a portal specifically for community members, which is an artifact of their commitment to engaging community. They offer a host of services and resources for community members, and they are involved in shaping how these services are conceived and delivered. For example, community members have decision-making input on athletics, the arts center, special and public events, career services, community learning initiatives, Hartford Studies Project, and Office of Community and Institutional Relations.

The Office of Community and Institutional Relations builds upon strong existing college and community partnerships, while simultaneously promoting new student and faculty/staff civic engagement and community service. This office acts as a hub for obtaining community input for various programs and initiatives. Many other campuses are following this model of an office for community and institutional relationships that can act as an official liaison. This office does more than outreach; it creates service learning or campus partnerships as it brings in the community to inform institutional affairs.

Another model is slightly more decentralized, but creates the same campus-wide level of involvement. Wagner College created a strategic effort called Civic Innovations. The campus-wide initiative encourages departments to connect to communities, and communities to connect with departments or units on college. The departments work to discover community needs, and the agency learns about student learning outcomes and goals. The groups jointly create learning opportunities for students and/or faculty (sometimes a service learning and other times a research project).

Wagner College has taken a further step, and moved from the community informing departmental learning to community informing the overall campus curriculum. Members met with community leaders from the most underserved areas in Staten Island, and developed a campus-community plan for addressing community needs through curricular and cocurricular learning experiences. The community is a true partner in the formation of campus direction, curriculum planning, and strategy.

Another example of community-informed leadership is the University of Milwaukee's development and implementation of its nonprofit management program. Although this example is not a campus-wide approach as at Minnesota, Trinity, or Wagner, it demonstrates the depth of involvement that the community might have in decisions and how they can take a leadership role in starting a campus-based program. The program itself was conceived of by local community members, philanthropies, and foundations. Community members approached the campus and developed the program in partnership; the community was active in hiring the first director and participated in crafting the curriculum and teaching courses. This establishment set a precedent for the community to have an active role in the operations of the program. The community leaders continue to play an active role in the program through teaching, but they are also part of the governance process when decisions are made about the program.

Although it is important to expand formal decision-making structures to include community groups, it is also important to think about including them in ad hoc and problem-solving leadership groups. This approach also demonstrates the expertise of the community that can help the campus, not just faculty experts helping the community. Cuyahoga Community College was having difficulty retaining Latina women. Many women were dropping out after a few semesters at college, and campus leaders became alarmed at the very high attrition rates. The college president was dedicated to making students from underrepresented backgrounds successful at her institution—a factor she understood to be part of the commitment and responsibility of urban leaders.

Institutional leaders conducted interviews and focus groups with the women. They were able to understand that part of the problem had to do with social pressures not to attend college but to remain in the home and support their family. The women felt that they were also not being good Christians in pursuing post-secondary education. The president realized that this was not an issue that the campus could solve on its own, and that it would be necessary to work with the community to attempt to resolve the issue.

College leaders went out into the community and spoke with Church leaders, family organizations, and nonprofits. They presented the problem of retaining Latina women in college and asked for an open conversation about community views on the issue. Through various dialogues, the community became committed to relieving the pressure that women were feeling to leave school. The Church leaders noted they would reinforce the importance of education and work to change family views, particularly the fathers in the community (Kezar, 2007).

Another example of this issue comes from LaGuardia Community College. This institution is extremely diverse, with immigrants from over 169 countries coming together on a single campus. Campus leaders realized that they could not provide services that were culturally responsive to their students' needs, so they went to the community to ask for help. A variety of community-based organizations that support various ethnicities, whether El Salvadorean or Greek, have creative partnerships with the campus to support students from that particular background by forming clubs, creating mentoring organizations, offering psychosocial counseling and assistance for issues that may be particular to a given culture, and even providing scholarship support. The college has received feedback from students indicating that these support systems have been greatly improved by this partnering and working more closely with the community.

Although the beginning of this chapter addresses the importance of urban institutions engaging more deeply with their urban location and urban stakeholders, the latter part of it deals with some of the issues and concerns that emerge in expanding leadership to include a community-informed model. The following section will therefore be instructive to institutions that already actively identify with the urban community and are working to overcome some of the challenges that emerge in a broader leadership process.

Addressing Different Values and Interests: Research on Diverse Voices and Values in Campus Leadership

As more stakeholders are brought into decision-making and leadership, differing interests and politics are more likely to emerge. The fear (and actuality, in some cases) of differing interests and values dramatically slowing down governance processes or leading to paralysis has led many campus administrators to shy away from including a broader array of people in governance; in fact, it has led to a decrease in input from stakeholder groups in higher education in recent years (Bensimon & Neumann, 1993; Kezar & Eckel, 2004). The concerns that administrators have with faculty deliberation processes must be separated from concerns with interactions with community groups.

Community groups are quite different from faculty in terms of their understanding of leadership and decision-making processes; they often operate in more agile and small organizations, and understand that decisions need to be made deliberately, yet quickly. However, even if community groups can operate more quickly, this factor does not alleviate the differing interests and values they bring to the table.

Studies of leaders from diverse backgrounds demonstrate that they tend to have very different perspectives on leadership (some view it as hierarchical, some see it as collective, some see it as relational), the important issues that leadership should address (strategy, politics, relationships, structures), and how to go about addressing issues and problems (Kezar, 2000). In other words, leaders have very different mental models and underlying assumptions. The more diverse (in terms of race, gender, social class, and cultural differences) the group of leaders studied, the more they varied in their perspectives of leadership (Bensimon & Neumann, 1993; Kezar, 2000).

Although leadership diversity brings in important ideas that lead to the cognitive complexity that teams often develop and which can be harnessed to solve problems, this variance can also create a difficult situation where different viewpoints cannot be reconciled. Diversity of views or mental models is one of the reasons that shared cognition has become such a significant area of research within team leadership. Shared cognition refers to the extent to which team members have similar mental maps regarding their internal work as well as the external environment. Shared cognition is an important aspect of team dynamics and has been identified as important to team effectiveness (Knight et al., 1999). If the mental models of various stakeholders are too different, then team leadership will be fraught with problems.

Burke, Fiore, and Salas (2003) have developed a model of the key constructs that enable shared cognition within shared leadership teams with four main foundational concepts: mental models, situation assessment, metacognition, and attitudes. The first element is metacognition. Team members are aware of their own cognitive processes and are able to understand and manipulate their own cognitive process. In other words, they need to be aware of their own biases and perspectives, be open to others, and be able to shift their view because of new information.

In terms of mental models, Burke et al. (2003) describe the importance of creating shared mental models around two key factors: the team and the situation. Members of a leadership team might differ greatly on a variety of mental models but, as long as they believe that the group has the same goal and role, and as long as they can agree to the situation that exists (say, for example, that they can agree on the problem), then other differences are likely to be worked out. However, if they cannot agree on these two foundational issues, it is unlikely that they will be able to move on to complex cognitive thinking.

The researchers also suggest that shared cognition is more likely to happen when there are some general shared beliefs such as collective efficacy (through working together they can improve the problem at hand), fluid leadership (emerging within different members of the group), and a collective orientation to problem solving. If these attitudes are missing among members of the group, then shared cognition is also difficult to create.

Some researchers have suggested that shared mental models, while desirable, are not absolutely necessary for teams to effectively work together. Bensimon and Neumann (1993) describe the importance of creating a team culture, through building relationships over time and trust, and that teams do not have to shift to think alike to work effectively, but need to feel that there is a safe and productive culture to conduct their work. Their work suggests the importance of group processes that can make shared leadership more successful from carefully choosing people to participate in shared governance process, orientation sessions, group development, and spending time developing relationships and thinking prior to making decisions. Diverse leadership groups are undone by the pressure to make decisions quickly before people understand each other and their perspectives. A campus will not be able to move to community-informed leadership quickly. It will take time and a long-term commitment to arrive at a different way of operating.

In addition to identifying processes that help in team building, Bensimon and Neumann (1993) also highlight roles that people can play to support shared leadership processes. For example, successful shared leadership processes have an individual that is the task monitor who strives to remove obstacles to the team's thinking. Teams also have an emotional monitor who helps maintain the interpersonal relationships developed early through team building. Teams also have a person who elicits and synthesizes diverse perspectives of the group, helping to bring consensus.

Successful teams also have a critic who redefines and analyzes issues so that the shared process does not result in groupthink. One major difference that these researchers saw between effective teams and ineffective teams is that effective teams have members who are sensitive to accept the fact that different people are likely to see the same reality in different ways. The teams are not afraid of the conflict that can be inherent in cognitively diverse teams. Individuals who shape shared leadership processes, such as college presidents, need to articulate their appreciation for different viewpoints.

They need to model this behavior in their interaction with people during shared governance processes.

Another way that they managed these differences is through the careful socialization process teams undergo and having members enact certain important roles (e.g., synthesizer) that were already described. Some have also suggested that as leadership is distributed, more accountability structures need to be put in place because of the likelihood of miscommunication and lack of consensus over values (Spillane & Diamond, 2007). While there are not many examples to provide related to shared governance, the concept is that as more people are invited to be a part of a leadership process, there need to be structures put in place so that people understand what is at stake in their decision-making processes. Within team leadership models, the accountability structures put in place are strict performance measures and regular reporting. This type of accountability remains a challenge for shared governance processes, and more research and ideas are needed on appropriate accountability structures.

Confronting Power and Politics

Research suggests that status differentials and power make shared leadership difficult and traditional leadership emerges instead (Pearce & Conger, 2003). Bensimon and Neumann (1993) suggest that a key part of any shared leadership model is addressing power and status differentials. Part of the group development process needs to be an acknowledgment of the fact that certain individuals hold privileged positions by virtue of their power, authority, expertise, or membership in the dominant group. As a result, they may not understand how less powerful members feel alienated, or have blinders to their own privilege and how this makes them see the world differently. Bensimon and Neumann (1993) suggest that leaders within shared governance processes need to be perceptive of power differences and mediate power differentials. If more privileged group members are alienating others, the team leader needs to pull these members aside and point out some of these issues to ensure that the team continues to move forward together with positive relationships. Research on campus and community partnerships demonstrates that community partners value and feel more comfortable in partnerships where leaders openly addressed status, privilege, and power differences (Leiderman, Furco, Zapf, & Goss, 2004).

Community partners express that they feel a mutual relationship is in place if the leadership group discusses racial, ethnic, and economic inequalities and their causes with candor, and incorporate those discussions into their leadership work. If formal discussions do not happen, community members look for certain indicators of parity in their working relationships with colleges. For example, they look to see if they are treated as equal partners in decision-making processes, if campuses ask for community-driven initiatives or if all discussions are driven by campus priorities, if campus leaders know the expertise held by community members, and in partnerships if leaders distribute authority and funding fairly. So, either through words or through deeds, campuses need to address issues of power to be successful in the shared leadership process.

In order to have candid discussions, I (Kezar, 2002) provide a tool for leaders who want to enact community-informed leadership and become aware of status and power differences (as well as dealing with different values and interests). As I note, leadership development has always acknowledged the importance of understanding oneself, both strengths and weaknesses. However, self-reflection often has left out issues of gender, race, sexual orientation, social class, and other power differences.

I outline three principles of becoming a pluralistic leader:

1. developing an awareness of how identity and power impact leadership beliefs and perspectives;

2. acknowledging multiple interpretations of institutional leadership and personal philosophies of leadership; and

3. taking opportunities for negotiation among multiple interpretations of institutional
leadership and personal philosophies of leadership.

Leaders become adept at seeing the different leadership perspectives, presenting them to the group, and helping people negotiate different perspectives with civility.

I note that these principles are unlikely to be developed through reading, a lecture, or attending a conference. Instead, it requires both personal reflection and experiential learning through case story techniques. Case stories are highly personal, written accounts of real events that include intriguing analysis and reflection.[5] This is an important tool for campus leaders who want to develop a community-informed approach to leadership, and to address the likely problems of power differences and politics that can emerge.

Conclusion

Responsible urban post-secondary leadership is imperative for both urban renewal and the continued success of colleges and universities in the global economy. This chapter argues that urban leaders need to practice reciprocity where they engage both the assets and challenges of the urban environment. For those committed institutions that are already involved reciprocally in the urban environments, I argue for the importance of more mutual forms of leadership through the model of community-informed leadership. There is ample research to support the benefits of such new directions.

Urban leaders must also realize the challenges inherent in acquiring these benefits, which include navigating differing interests and values, and confronting power and politics. Entering this terrain without understanding some of the likely pitfalls can lead to disillusionment and problems.

State and local policymakers can help address this issue of institutional identity by encouraging institutions to contribute to and see themselves as part of their local (and in this case urban) communities. There is precedence for policymakers to encourage colleges and universities to support and identify with their local area. The land-grant movement of the late 1800s was based on the notion that regional areas should have colleges or universities located in them that would be economic, political, and social engines for that area. Land was given and state money provided to help institutions meet this mission. The recent GEAR UP legislation provided money for colleges and schools to partner, enhancing alignment between the two institutions, especially urban institutions.

The new Carnegie Classification scheme for post-secondary institutions now includes community engagement as a category, and over 80 institutions have this new designation. This classification can be used as a lever to obtain more involvement with the urban environment across various institutional types. Policymakers need to build on these traditions and continue to encourage institutions to identify with and support the local community. Some recent initiatives suggest community-informed leadership will become more important as urban city leaders and federal bureaus make this an increasing priority, including the CEOs for Cities effort, Hartford's Collaborative Education Council, Cincinnati's cross-university urban partnership, and Pittsburgh's mayor announcing a new urban collaborative with three universities and various community groups working together.

Notes

1.   It might also be argued that community-informed leadership is not enough and that authentically engaged leadership would be a full collaboration between community and campus. Community-informed leadership acknowledges the community voice and sees the community as a partner in the education enterprise. But community–collaborative leadership would mean that community members are equal players at the table with educational leaders on issues

involving campus affairs. Although this is conceptually consistent with shared leadership, it does not fully make sense in view of the role that community members play, being stakeholders but not full members of the community. Therefore, community-informed leadership is a stronger model that fits the relationship and role that that community plays in relation to educational institutions.

2. CCPH's Web site lists best practices for partnerships and has case studies of successful university and campus partnerships; available at: www.ccph.info

3. This chapter does not address the effective components of campus and community partnerships. There is a large literature base on this topic. (See Holland, 2005; Leiderman, Furco, Zapf, & Goss, 2004; Sandy & Holland, 2006.)

4. Distributed leadership is a particular model of shared leadership in which those in authority set up mechanisms to distribute leadership to other levels of the organization, and leadership is conceptualized as a practice that is an interlinking web throughout the organization (see Spillane & Diamond, 2007).

5. In my article "Capturing the promise of collaborative leadership in becoming a pluralistic leader: Using case stories to transform beliefs" (Kezar, 2002), I provide a detailed case story for leaders to use in personal reflection or for trainers teaching leadership.

References

Anderson, J. (2005). Community service as learning. In A. Kezar (Ed.), *Organizational learning and higher education* (pp. 37–49). New Directions for Higher Education, no. 131. San Francisco, CA: Jossey-Bass.

Bauman, G. (2005). Promoting organizational learning in higher education to achieve equity and educational outcomes. In A. Kezar (Ed.), *Organizational learning and higher education* (pp. 23–36). New Directions for Higher Education, no. 131. San Francisco, CA: Jossey-Bass.

Benne, K., & Sheats, P. (1948). Functional role of group members. *The Journal of Social Issues, 4*, 41–49.

Bensimon, E., & Neumann, A. (1993). *Redesigning collegiate leadership: Teams and teamwork and higher education.* Baltimore, MD: Johns Hopkins University Press.

Berger, J., Cohen, B., & Zelditch, M. (1972). Status characteristics and social interaction. *American Sociological Review, 37*, 241–255.

Bowers, D., & Seashore, S. (1966). Predicting organizational effectiveness with a four factor theory of leadership. *Administrative Science Quarterly, 11*, 283–263.

Burke, C., Fiore, S., & Salas, E. (2003). The role shared cognition in enabling shared leadership and team adaptability. In C. Pearce & J. Conger (Eds.), *Shared leadership* (pp. 103–117). Thousand Oaks, CA: Sage.

Festinger, L. (1954). A theory of social comparison process. *Human Relations, 7*, 117–140.

Florida, R. (2002). *The rise of the creative class.* New York: Perseus Book Group.

Follett, M. (1924). *Creative experience.* New York: Longmans Green.

Graen, G. (1976). Rule-making process is within complex organizations. In M. Dunnette (Ed.), *Handbook of industrial and organizational psychology* (pp. 1201–1245). Chicago: Rand McNally.

Heifetz, R. (1994). *Leadership without easy answers.* Cambridge, MA: Belknap Press.

Holland, B. (2005). Reflections on campus and community partnerships: What has been learned? In P. Pasque, E. Smerek, B. Dwyer, N. Bowman, & B. Mallory (Eds.), *Higher education collaboratives for community engagement and improvement* (pp. 10–17). Ann Arbor, MI: The National Forum of Higher Education for the Public Good.

Hollander, E. (1961). Some effects of perceived status on responses to innovative behavior. *Social Work with Groups, 3*(4), 19–29.

Howey, K. (2009). Challenges for the urban educators corps. *Metropolitan Universities Journal, 19*(4), 3–14.

Kezar, A. (2000). Pluralistic leadership: Incorporating diverse voices. *Journal of Higher Education, 71*(6), 722–743.

Kezar, A. (2002). Becoming a pluralistic leader: Using case stories to transform beliefs. *Metropolitan Universities Journal, 13*(2), 95–104.

Kezar, A. (2007). Tools for a time and place: Phased leadership strategies for advancing campus diversity. *Review of Higher Education, 30*(4), 413–439.

Kezar, A., & Eckel, P. (2004). Meeting today's governance challenges: A synthesis of the literature and examination of a future research agenda. *The Journal of Higher Education, 75*(4), 371–400.

Kezar, A., Carducci, R., & Contreras-McGavin, M. (2006). *Rethinking the "L" word in leadership: The revolution of research on leadership.* San Francisco, CA: Jossey-Bass.

Kezar, A., Gallant, T., & Lester, J. (2011). Everyday people making a difference on college campuses: The tempered grassroots leadership strategies of faculty and staff. *Studies in Higher Education*, n.p.

Kerr, S., & Jermier, J. (1978). Substitutes for leadership: Their meaning and measurement. *Organizational Behavior and Human Performance, 22*, 374–403.

Knight, D., Pearce, C., Smith, K. G., Olian, J. D., Sims, H. P., Smith, K. A., & Flood, P. (1999). Top management team diversity, group process, and strategic consensus. *Strategic Management Journal, 20*, 445–465.

Leiderman, S., Furco, A., Zapf, J., & Goss, M. (2004). *Building partnerships with college campuses: Community perspectives.* Washington, DC: Council for Independent Colleges.

Lucas, C. (1994). *American higher education: A history.* New York: St. Martin's Press.

Manz, C., & Sims, H. (1980). Self-management as a substitute for leadership: A social learning process. *Academy of Management Review, 5*, 361–367.

Manz, C., & Sims, H. (1987). Leading workers to lead themselves: The external leadership of self-managing work teams. *Administrative Science Quarterly, 32*, 106–128.

Mayo, E. (1933). *The human problems on industrial civilization.* New York: Macmillan.

Mayo, M., Meindl, J., & Oastor, J. (2003). Shared leadership in teams. In C. Pearce & J. Conger (Eds.), *Shared leadership* (pp. 193–214). Thousand Oaks, CA: Sage.

Pearce, C., & Conger, J. (Eds.) (2003). *Shared leadership: Reframing the hows and whys of leadership.* Thousand Oaks, CA: Sage.

Pearce, C., & Sims, H. P., Jr. (2002). Vertical versus shared leadership as predictors of the effectiveness of change management teams: An examination of aversive, directive, transactional, transformational and empowering leader behaviors. *Group Dynamics, 6,* 172–197.

Resnick, L. (1991). Shared cognition: Thinking as social practice. In L. Resnick, J. Levine, & S. Teasley (Eds.), *Perspectives on socially shared construction* (pp.1–19). Washington, DC: American Psychological Association.

Rhoades, G. (2008). The centrality of contingent faculty to academe's future. *Academe, 94*(6), 12–15.

Rhoades, G. (2009). Carnegie, DuPont circle, and the AAUP: (Re)shaping a cosmopolitan, locally engaged professoriate. *Change, 41,* 8–15.

Sandy, M., & Holland, B. (2006). Different worlds and common ground: Community partner perspectives in campus-community partnerships. *Michigan Journal of Committee Service Learning, 13*(1), 30–43.

Senge, P. (1990). *The fifth discipline.* New York: Doubleday.

Solomon, A., Loeffer, F., & Frank, G. (1953). An analysis of cotherapist interaction in group therapy. *International Journal of Group Psychotherapy, 3,* 171–180.

Spillane, J., & Diamond, J. (Eds.) (2007). *Distributed leadership in practice.* New York: Teachers College Press.

Toma, D., & Kezar, A. (Eds.) (1999). *The collegiate ideal: The current state and future prospects of the idea of campus.* New Directions for Higher Education, no. 105. San Francisco, CA: Jossey-Bass.

Vroom, V., & Yetton, P. (1973). *Leadership in decision-making.* New York: Wiley.

Zemsky, R., Massey, W., & Wegner, G. (2005). *Remaking the American university: Market-smart and mission-centered.* Baltimore, MD: Johns Hopkins University Press.

9

Preparing Urban Leaders
The UCEA Urban Leadership Development Initiative

Michelle D. Young

The primary focus of federal education policy is the improvement of education in all contexts and for all children. Achieving these goals is in part dependent upon the capacity of state and local governments to leverage federal policies and to implement appropriate and well-resourced programs delivered by highly qualified staff. Education leaders at all levels and in all contexts are finding these increasingly difficult goals to realize. The urban context, however, presents particularly daunting challenges for both new and seasoned educational leaders.

Urban schools are often characterized as "dropout factories," where chronic absenteeism, high rates of failure, and low student achievement run rampant (Fine, 1994). Moreover, teacher turnover, staffing policies, and the quality of the teaching pool present consistent challenges to urban school leaders (Guarino, Santibañez, & Daley, 2006; Ingersoll, 1999)—challenges that are further complicated by the fact that urban leaders are often called to confront prescriptive policy requirements that dictate reform initiatives, curricular offerings, achievement benchmarks, and programmatic requirements (Leithwood & Riehl, 2003), thus limiting their autonomy and influence. Until recently, school leadership was an often overlooked aspect of increasing teacher quality, decreasing the inequality across schools and improving student achievement. However, with the introduction of improved research designs and statistical methods, a growing body of empirical evidence demonstrates that principals have an important impact on schools, teachers, and student achievement (Hallinger & Heck, 1996; Leithwood & Jantzi, 2000, 2005, 2008; Robinson, Lloyd, & Rowe, 2008; Waters, Marzano, & McNulty, 2003). Specifically, research has found that principals indirectly influence student achievement through several key "avenues of influence": people, purposes and goals of the school, structure of the school and social networks, and organizational culture (Hallinger & Heck, 1996, p. 171; Leithwood, Seashore, Anderson, & Wahlstrom, 2004; Supovitz, Sirinides, & May, 2010).

With growing recognition of the importance of school leadership has come increased concern regarding how leaders are prepared, particularly leaders who work in urban schools. Some have expressed serious concern about whether leadership preparation has kept pace with the needs of today's schools and whether a "one size fits all" approach to preparation is appropriate (Young, Petersen, & Short, 2002). Today, a focus on developing leaders who can work within challenging contexts to promote quality teaching and learning for all students is central to many reform agendas

(Bottoms & O'Neill, 2001). The University Council for Educational Administration (UCEA) shares this focus. Through its Urban Leadership Development Initiative, the UCEA has convened a group of leadership faculty from urban universities to develop rigorous and relevant leadership development curriculum and learning experiences for aspiring leaders who plan to work within urban contexts to promote powerful teaching and learning for all students.

An essential element of school improvement is the development of effective school leaders. This chapter charts efforts within the university community to improve the preparation of urban school leaders, highlighting, in particular, the work of the UCEA Urban Leadership Development Project (UCEA ULDP) in developing rigorous and relevant leadership preparation curriculum and learning experiences specifically for aspiring leaders of urban schools. The initiative—which is grounded in recent research on effective leadership, urban school improvement, features of effective preparation programs, and adult learning theory—seeks to substantially enhance the quality of leadership preparation and practice in urban schools.

Program Improvement

University-based programs are the primary source of preparation for school- and district-level leaders. An estimated 500 programs in schools and colleges of education offer leadership preparation (Baker, Orr, & Young, 2007), a number that has grown substantially over the last decade. There are two primary aims of university leadership preparation programs: to develop the leadership skills and capacities of candidates as future leaders and to develop their aspirations and capacities to seek advancement and become educational leaders.

In recent years, many education leadership faculty members have redesigned the content and delivery of their preparation programs to have a stronger influence on their graduates' leadership practices and school effectiveness. Indeed, significant attention has been directed to innovation and best practice in leadership preparation programs, both university- and non-university-based (Jackson & Kelley, 2002; McCarthy, 1999; Milstein, 1993; Orr, 2006; U.S. Department of Education, 2004; Young, Crow, Ogawa, & Murphy, 2009). According to Orr (2006), program innovations can be identified in five areas:

> (1) a reinterpretation of leadership as pivotal for improving teaching and learning; (2) new insights into how program content, pedagogy, and field-based learning experiences can be designed to be more powerful means of preparing leaders; (3) the redesign of the doctorate as an intensive midcareer professional development activity; (4) the use of partnerships for richer, more extensive program design opportunities; and (5) a commitment to continuous improvement. (pp. 492–493)

The drive for these program innovations emanated from a variety of sources. State requirements through standards, assessment and accreditation, national accreditation recognition, and other factors are influencing program improvement and redesign work (Sanders & Simpson, 2005). In fact, across the nation, many scholars, policymakers, policy analysts, school leaders, professional associations, and foundations have been working to improve leadership preparation (Young, Crow, Orr, Ogawa, & Creighton, 2005). Recent years have witnessed focused and effective efforts to improve leadership preparation, led by professional associations as well as states, foundations, and other key players in educational leadership. Many of these reforms have already led to updates and improvements in the preparation of both school and school system leaders.

To illustrate, the national standards movement in leadership preparation has developed sets of standards currently being used in many states and institutions to reform and assess preparation programs. Many of these involved collaborations between professional associations and universities. The most prominent is the Interstate School Leaders Licensure Consortium (ISLLC), a consortium of 32 educational agencies and 13 education administration associations that developed a set of criteria and standards for administrative practice (NPBEA, 2008). In 2002, the ISLLC standards were integrated into the National Council for Accreditation of Teacher Education (NCATE)/ Educational Leadership Constituent Council (ELCC) Program Standards for evaluating leadership preparation programs for national accreditation, and are used as the basis for standardized leadership tests. The ELCC is made up of both professional associations and university groups, such as the UCEA and the National Council for Professors of Educational Administration (NCPEA). States and other organizations have expanded these standards to further improve their impact—these include the Southern Regional Education Board (SREB), the National Association of Elementary School Principals (NAESP), and the Mid-continent Research for Education and Learning (McREL).

Additionally, a number of states (e.g., Iowa, Delaware, Mississippi, and North Carolina) have instituted creative reforms in preparation and certification. According to the Education Commission of the States, 24 policy changes in 17 states regarding school leadership licensure/certification have occurred since 2000. Some state-level reforms were spurred by the State Action for Educational Leadership Preparation (SAELP) grants, funded by the Wallace Foundation. Simultaneously, the National Commission for the Advancement of Educational Leadership Preparation (NCAELP), sponsored by the UCEA and the National Policy Board for Educational Administration (NPBEA), developed a series of studies based on changes in school leaders' roles, identified recommendations for reforming preparation programs and professional development, and advanced a national research taskforce on educational leadership preparation. Moreover, organizations like SREB and the Texas Lighthouse Initiative supported important conversations and partnerships between universities and school district personnel, developed curricular modules, and supported a number of program development opportunities (Young et al., 2005).

At the same time, the field itself is undertaking substantial self-assessment—through state and national accreditation processes, a Taskforce on Evaluating Leadership Preparation Programs, some state requirements, and individual program initiatives. Similarly, an increasing number of scholars, many affiliated with the UCEA-Learning and Teaching in Educational Leadership (LTEL) Evaluation Research Taskforce and the UCEA-American Educational Research Association (AERA)-NCPEA Joint Research Taskforce on Educational Leadership Preparation, have been engaged in individual and joint research on leadership preparation during the last decade. Their work, along with expert opinion, provided insight into a set of essential core program attributes, including: a well-defined, leadership-for-learning focus, coherence, challenging and reflective content, student-centered instructional practices, competent faculty, positive student relationships, a cohort structure, supportive organizational structures, and substantive and lengthy internships (Darling-Hammond, Meyerson, LaPointe, & Orr, 2007; Orr & Pounder, 2008).

Similarly, educational researchers have made concerted efforts to determine the relationship between leadership preparation and practice. Extensive reviews of research on exemplary leadership preparation programs and quality program features (Davis, Darling-Hammond, Meyerson & LaPointe, 2005; Jackson & Kelley, 2002; McCarthy, 1999; Orr, 2006; Young et al., 2009) indicate that certain program features are associated with more positively impactful leadership practice. Additionally, researchers have made concerted efforts to measure the impact of leadership preparation (Fuller, Young & Baker, 2011; Orr, 2011; Orr & Pounder, 2008). As a result, the question of whether educational leadership preparation matters, has been answered: It most certainly does matter. Current research on leadership preparation suggests that highly effective leadership preparation programs are distinguishable by their features and by their influence on their graduates' learning and career advancement (Orr & Pounder, 2008). Moreover, this influence is independent of candidates' prior experience and initial aspirations. Relationships between programs' standards-based curriculum and learning strategies and graduates' learning and intermediate career outcomes have been validated and the evidence of this relationship continues to grow (Darling-Hammond et al., 2007; Orr & Pounder, 2008).

Preparing Leaders for Urban Schools

State and national policymakers expect all schools to ensure that all children meet or exceed state academic performance standards (NCLB, 2002). Given the urgency of this policy expectation and the threat of severe sanctions, such as state takeover, reconstitution or closing, more attention has been given to the leadership of chronically low-performing urban schools.

Although much has been written about the preparation of school leaders over the last few decades (Young et al., 2009), little of this literature has focused directly on the preparation of leaders for urban schools. Indeed, there has been a long-standing image of school administrators as generalists (Culbertson, 1962), regardless of the level, size, or context of the school an administrator leads. Yet the increasing challenges facing public school principals can be even more intense in urban districts, where school staff and students have higher rates of mobility, the distribution of teacher quality tends to be less equitable, and issues outside of school compete significantly with learning time (Fine, 1994; Gordon, 1999; Lankford, Loeb, & Wyckoff, 2002).

The argument here is not that no school leadership programs exist that focus on the preparation of urban leaders. That is not the case. Each of the programs involved in the UCEA ULDP have principalship programs with an urban focus, and there are many programs located in urban areas that prepare leaders for urban schools. Rather, my contention is that programs that prepare urban leaders should be designed with that specific population in mind. The complexity of leading urban schools continues to increase, while external pressures to perform continue to mount, making preparation programs that at one time appeared very influential in their graduates' leadership seem diminished, and raising questions about the quality and relevancy of the programs that various providers are offering.

Over the course of its 55-year history, the UCEA has been consistently engaged in program development and improvement efforts. Its activities have focused around the development of cases, simulations, and standards; fostering research, publications, and research utilization; and supporting collaboration around program improvement. The curriculum initiative described below illustrates the benefits of interuniversity collaboration around program design and innovation.

The Initiative

The UCEA ULDP is a collaborative initiative involving the faculty and district partners of 14 public and private urban leadership preparation programs in the United States, including Temple University, University of Texas-Austin, University of Buffalo, Bank Street College, Duquesne University, New Mexico State University, New York University, University of Wisconsin-Milwaukee, the University of Cincinnati, the University of Massachusetts-Boston, Lehigh University, the University of Texas-San Antonio, the University of Utah, and Claremont Graduate School of Education. Sponsored and facilitated by the UCEA, the UCEA ULDP was developed in 2007 to collaboratively rethink how K–12 leaders should be prepared specifically for urban leadership in the 21st century. Since its inception, initiative faculty have met each summer for three days of facilitated deliberation, discussing research, sharing their program features, and engaging in program design and critical reflection.

The group has been particularly interested in addressing the following three questions:

1. What are the theories of action operating in urban leadership preparation programs?
2. What are the distinguishing characteristics of urban leadership preparation programs that set them apart from other programs?
3. What is the signature pedagogy used to prepare candidates to lead in urban contexts?

As noted above, research has identified a set of essential core program attributes associated with effective leadership practice, including a well-defined leadership-for-learning focus, coherence, challenging and reflective content, student-centered instructional practices, competent faculty, positive student relationships, a cohort structure, supportive organizational structures, and substantive and lengthy internships (Darling-Hammond et al., 2007; Orr & Pounder, 2008). We used this research to guide our work around the above three questions.

In this chapter, I share some of this work in progress. I begin with a discussion of notion of a theory of action for the preparation of urban leaders and how this informed the work of ULDP participants. I then share the features of effective leadership preparation and what they look like in redesigned urban leadership programs. I then turn to the issue of signature pedagogy. By the end of the 2009 work session, ULDP participants had defined their signature pedagogy around the concept of Powerful Learning Experiences (PLE).

Features of Effective Urban Leadership Preparation

Those who prepare education leaders have a series of implicit and explicit beliefs about why they teach what they teach in the way they teach it. These beliefs are essentially their "theories of action" concerning leadership preparation (Argyris & Schön, 1996). Programs that are organized around a theme or purpose also have theories of action. ULDP participants worked together to identify both their own personal theories of action for the preparation of education leaders and then examined the relationships among them to see how they could be integrated into a unified theory that could provide a set of foundational theories of action for the UCEA Urban Leadership Curriculum. Appendixes A and B at the end of the chapter contain the two exercises used to facilitate this process. The first involves the identification of core beliefs concerning leadership in urban schools. The second involved the development of if-then statements that reflected several theories of action about candidate learning. One key theory of action undergirding the curriculum development work of this project is as follows: If leadership preparation programs incorporate research-based features into their programs designed with urban leadership in mind, then the candidates graduating from such programs will be prepared to have a powerful, positive impact in their schools. From this theory of action, ULDP participants redesigned the following program features: purpose, partnerships, selection, curriculum, and pedagogy. Throughout the process, we drew on relevant research about leadership preparation and leadership in urban schools as well as the expertise of the faculty and practitioners participating in the ULDP.

Purpose

One of the most salient changes evident in recent program improvement initiatives is a focus on program purpose—that is, program faculty members have dedicated more energy to designing programs to specifically develop particular kinds of leaders for certain types of contexts. This contrasts with conventional programs, which tend to be designed around more generic forms of leadership. According to Darling-Hammond et al. (2007), effective preparation programs have explicit program purposes that are then articulated in program descriptions, vision statements, and curriculum.

The majority of programs engaged in the ULDP have very distinctive purposes articulated for the preparation of urban leaders, and they have begun to reexamine and revise their programs' content, pedagogy, and other program features to better align to the positions their students take after graduation. For example, Temple University's New Democratic Ethical Educational Leaders (New DEEL) program for urban principals has redesigned the preparation experiences—including the content, practical experiences, and internship—around democratic and ethical educational leadership. New York University redesigned its program around leadership and advocacy. Master's students work on problems of practice as a group, within educational and community contexts. Program faculty at the University of Texas redesigned their program to produce educational leaders who can support social justice in their schools. Specifically, they used collaborations with major urban districts in the state to collaboratively redesign a more coherent program around district needs and the tenets of social justice leadership. Similarly, with the support of a Wallace Foundation grant, New Mexico State University designed a principalship program for urban border school leaders. All aspects of the program, from content to pedagogy, were redesigned to ensure that leaders were prepared to work effectively within the border context.

As a group, ULDP participants articulated that the purpose of any urban leadership program should focus around developing the intellectual, performance, and moral capacity of leaders who will be serving in urban schools and districts, and developing leaders who can work collaboratively in their roles as leader, teacher, researcher, and advocate. Using this broad purpose, participants considered how other program features would need to be redesigned to better realize such a purpose.

Partnerships

A second important feature of effective urban leadership preparation programs is strong partnerships with urban districts. In fact, partnerships between universities and school districts have produced a number of positive changes in education leadership preparation generally, reflecting local contexts and assumptions about how leadership can improve schools and positively impact communities. The University of Texas-San Antonio, for example, formed a district partnership for customized leadership preparation for predominantly Hispanic and African American schools. Bank Street College has partnered with New York City schools, and the University of Buffalo has a strong partnership with the Buffalo School District.

In these partnerships, districts are playing a larger role in shaping program content, coursework, and experiences. Moreover, programs are shaped with district needs in mind. For example, in the second year of the ULDP, the University of Texas-Austin expanded its urban partnerships outside of the Austin area to include several other major urban districts in Texas. Based on a needs assessment of the districts as well as collaborative discussions around program purpose with district partners, the programs were collaboratively designed to specifically meet the needs of secondary principals of high needs schools. Their district partners benefit both from the careful needs assessment, the deliberative shaping of program purpose, and the development of aspiring leaders to address district needs in their practice. Moreover, collaborative partnerships, like this one, tend to extend beyond purpose articulation and curriculum development to also include candidate selection, program governance, grant writing, coteaching, coaching, student evaluation, and supporting full-time internships.

Selection

As noted above, the redesign of programs has not been relegated to what occurs once a candidate begins his or her preparation program. Rather, innovations must also occur in the area of selection. In traditional programs, students tend to apply for admission to a leadership preparation program primarily through self-initiation, encouragement by friends and family, or referral by supervisors, and programs' selection criteria focus on a variety of academic and leadership-related attributes that are assessed through letters of recommendation, statements of purpose, and, less often, through interviews (Black, Bathon, & Pointdexter, 2007; Lad, Browne-Ferrigno, & Shoho, 2005; Young et al., 2002). In redesigned programs, faculty members are aligning their selection criteria and processes to their program focus.

All ULDP participants have restructured their programs in this area. One example is the approach used by the University of Texas. As noted earlier, this principalship program is focused around social justice leadership. Thus, when they review candidates for their programs, they provide opportunities for candidates to demonstrate skills and beliefs around problem framing, collaboration, instructional expertise, leadership, diversity, and equity. One of the theories of action that guides this program is articulated as follows: In order to be a strong social justice leader, a principal must also be a strong educational leader who understands and can support excellent instructional practice. Although faculty feel that they can build the capacity of an excellent educator to supervise and support high-quality instruction, their program is not designed to build excellent educators. Thus, after evaluating students' portfolios and their analysis of a school data set, faculty members visit applicants' classrooms, observe them teaching, and subsequently discuss the lesson with the applicant.

For the participants in the ULDP and other program faculty who have engaged in redesign, student selection has become an important way for programs to select students who they believe will benefit most from participation in their program and who will be effective in the field. It is also a way for faculty to ensure that program components are aligned with its purpose.

Curriculum

Until quite recently there has been little common agreement about the appropriate foundation for administrator preparation (Murphy, 2002) and especially for the "holistic, focused, and integrative design" (Pounder, Reitzug, & Young, 2002, p. 285) that some scholars and practitioners believe is needed. As noted in an earlier section, the 1997 release of the ISLLC standards brought with it a sea change of curriculum redesign. These standards specify the nature of leadership to be developed—in vision building, curriculum and instruction, management and operations, parent and community involvement, ethics and policy—and outline key attributes for a quality internship. Program faculty members used curriculum audits to identify content and experiential areas in their programs where the ISLLC standards were not present and used that information to renew coursework. By 2005, a total of 46 states had adopted leadership standards for administrator certification and preparation programs, and 41 had adopted the ISLLC standards or standards that were aligned with these standards (Sanders & Simpson, 2005). In some programs, the redesign included but moved beyond the ISLLC standards to purposefully refocus around school improvement, social justice, or democratic community (Murphy, 2002; Orr, 2006).

For the programs engaged in the ULDP, the ISLLC standards and, in some cases, state standards provided a baseline for their curriculum. However, faculty did not feel that the ISLLC standards provided adequate coverage of the leadership practice and knowledge specific to the context and work of urban leadership. Specifically, ULDP participants identified the following themes as essential to the development of urban school leaders:

1. The Centrality of Race;
2. Social Justice, Equity, and Cultural Diversity;
3. Systems Thinking;
4. Leading Change;

5. Data Use and Inquiry;
6. Learning and Pedagogy;
7. Teacher Selection and Development;
8. Collaboration and Community Building;
9. Politics, Advocacy, and Activism;
10. Integrity and Ethics;
11. Commitment to Self-Knowledge and Professional Learning.

Thus far, ULDP participants have deliberated on and described six of these themes (data analysis and inquiry, leading change, learning and pedagogy, politics and advocacy, systems, and social justice and equity), how they interrelate with one another, and how they should be reflected in urban leadership preparation curriculum. For example, in describing the social justice and equity theme, participants noted:

> Urban educational leaders address the inequitable distribution of resources and opportunities for all children regardless of race, culture, language, or creed. They must be advocates for changing policies and practices so that educational outcomes promote equitable social changes. School leaders must be able to analyze data so that issues of equity and justice emerge and can be monitored as change is implemented. This is the role of a change agent. Schools are embedded in a larger social, political and economic milieu. This awareness must be integrated into the larger picture of how school inequities affect larger social issues, i.e., familial, communal, national and global contexts. Understanding the relationship between individual and social inequities and individual school data is critical (e.g., examining the equitable deployment of resources—human, fiscal, instructional, and technological and interrogating and interrupting the overrepresentation of particular student groups in suspensions, expulsions and special education). The education of urban leaders must take place in diverse racial and economic settings. (ULDP Thematic Work, 2009)

Participants explained that this curriculum theme is deeply connected to themes of race, cultural, and linguistic differences, systems, politics and advocacy, leading change/inquiry, data, and pedagogy. The identification of other interrelated themes was important to the group's work in that they were trying to move away from the notion of stand-alone courses and toward the possibility of an integrated curriculum. Other issues that were identified as related to social justice and equity included community involvement, activism, communication for advocacy to multiple publics, integrity and ethics, the selection and development of staff, and understanding self.

Once curriculum themes were developed, ULDP participants revisited their program purpose to ensure consistency and alignment. The focus on consistency readied participants to turn their attention to the work of operationalizing the themes within a curriculum framework.

Just as participants had identified their theories of action at the program level, subsequent to the development of the curriculum themes, participants developed theories of action for each curriculum area. A sample theory of action for the data analysis and inquiry theme was, "If we want future school leaders to use data for school improvement, then we should provide real life problem-based situations where they have to read and analyze data and formulate recommendations for schools." A theory of action for the social justice and equity theme was, "If educational leaders experience environments of injustice outside of education (e.g., homeless shelters, battered women, immigrant services), they will have a deeper understanding of the larger social culture and its connection to school data." Subsequently, participants began fleshing out an array of experiences and knowledge that they believed would support their theories of action in each of the six theme areas.

Pedagogy

The short history of preparation for educational leaders is punctuated by research and development activity around the issue of pedagogy. The UCEA archives are full of simulation and case study materials dating back to the late 1950s. Interest in reflective practice emerged in the early 1990s (Hart, 1993; Short & Rinehart, 1993), the UCEA developed a *Journal of Cases in Educational Leadership* in the mid-1990s, providing peer-reviewed contemporary cases for use in educational leadership classrooms, and by the late 1990s, Ed Bridges and Phil Hallinger introduced the idea of problem-based learning into educational leadership preparation (Bridges & Hallinger, 1997; Copland, 2000). In fact, the interest in pedagogy within the higher education preparation community led to the development of the Teaching in Educational Administration special interest group, which was recently renamed Teaching and Learning in Educational Leadership.

These achievements notwithstanding, many questioned whether the pedagogy used within educational leadership preparation enables leadership candidates to connect knowledge and theory to practice (Black & Murtadha, 2007; Bridges & Hallinger, 1997; Young et al., 2009). These questions along with the Carnegie Foundation's (2010) interest in identifying a signature pedagogy in educational leadership, spurred the UCEA signature pedagogy project, in which UCEA members sought to identify pedagogical practices—such as action learning, action research, simulations, and reflection—that support powerful learning for aspiring leaders (Black & Murtadha, 2007). Interestingly, recent research reveals that experiential learning, reflective practice, structured dialogue, problem-based learning, and case study are just a few of the more dynamic learning experiences used in educational leadership preparation programs to foster student reflection on their role as leaders and to enable them to incorporate new knowledge and skills into their practice (Orr, 2006). Indeed, programs are increasingly using processes to intentionally structure individual and group reflective practice (i.e., self-assessments, reflective journals, portfolio development, exit interviews) to challenge students to think critically and reflect on their practice and assumptions (Young et al., 2009).

For ULDP participants, the following question emerged: "If we are to fulfill our theories of action around the preparation of urban educational leaders, what pedagogical approaches must we use?" It was through deliberations around this question that the group's signature pedagogical approach emerged: Powerful Learning Experiences (PLE). PLEs have the following nine features:

1. They are authentic, meaningful, relevant, problem-finding activities.
2. They involve sense-making around critical problems of practice.
3. They involve exploration, critique, and deconstruction from an equity perspective (e.g., race, culture, language).
4. They require collaboration and interdependence.
5. They develop confidence in leadership.
6. They place both the professor and the student in a learning situation.
7. They empower learners and make them responsible for their own learning.
8. They shift the perspective from classroom to school, district or state level.
9. They have a reflective component.

Having these tenets clearly spelled out facilitated subsequent development work. These nine features reflect research on optimal learning for adults, especially adults that have rich experiential backgrounds (Edelman & Tononi, 2000; Kolb, 1984; Lehrer, 2009).

Each PLE identifies one or more theory of action, describes the learning experience, describes key features of the experience, and provides teaching notes and/or advice for the instructor, including suggestions for authentic evaluation. The following is an example of a PLE designed for the systems theme, entitled Breaking School Rules:

Title: Breaking School Rules

Description: A case study of students who protested against unfair treatment in the school and were suspended by the school principal according to discipline policy.

Key Features: The school systems highlighted in this case include policies, procedures, and practices developed to achieve educational goals. The purpose of this case study is to help students see that systems are constructed and that they reflect both our beliefs and our prejudices. In this case study, students discover their own beliefs and attitudes about school systems and rules as well as the beliefs and prejudices they hold about issues of race and racism.

Theories of Action:

- If we teach students that systems are constructed, then they will know that they have the power to shape and change the systems they lead.
- If we teach students how to evaluate the systems they lead, then they will have the skills and abilities to monitor their systems, and create needed change.
- If we teach students that systems are an agreement among people about how we will work together, then they will bring people together to collaborate on needed systems, policies, and practices.
- If we engage students in case studies that immerse them in examining and discussing issues of race, then they will be more likely to have the language needed to raise and address the issue of race with others in the work place.

Teaching Notes/Advice: Students are given the case study and they are asked to assume the role of the school principal. Students need to examine the case and all of the evidence presented, identify key issues and problems to be addressed, decide how to handle the situation, and be prepared to explain their reasoning. After they have shared their approach, they learn that the pursued solution was considered unacceptable by their school community. The students must decide what to do next and, again, explain their reasoning.

The above PLE has many of the nine core features. The case, which is based on a real-life situation, involves sense making, problem finding, and deconstruction from an equity perspective; it also has a reflective component. Such techniques offer situated learning and the means to think through problems of practice from a variety of perspectives (Hart, 1993; Holyoak & Thagard, 1999; Kolb, 1984). Research on pedagogy in educational leadership programs indicates that leadership candidates perceive that they benefit more from authentic, problem-based pedagogies than the typical lecture-and-discussion formats of coursework (Young et al., 2009).

Although the PLEs developed together by ULDP participants have thus far focused on distinct "lessons," faculty and district partners at the University of Texas used the PLE framework to identify theories of action and design a larger-scale and longer-term project. The PLE (or set of PLEs) is set up to begin during the students' first semester in the preparation program. The new cohort of students designs (with faculty guidance) and conducts an in-depth case study of a school, engages in problem finding, problem framing, and identifying solutions that are then shared with school and district personnel. The cohort revisits the school and their data throughout the program through a variety of problem-finding and framing lenses.

One of the most serious critiques of leader preparation focuses on the belief that it does not reflect the realities of the workplace (Hess & Kelly, 2005; Lakomski, 1998; Murphy, 2002; Young et al., 2002). The goal of the UCEA ULDP is to develop a full-scale urban leadership curriculum, with fully developed themes, modules, and PLEs, that reflects the reality of leadership in urban contexts. What I have shared is some of the work in progress of this group, work that provides thoughtful examples of how program features—such as purpose, partnerships, selection, curriculum, and pedagogy— might be redesigned to more powerfully support leadership in urban schools.

Conclusion

Over the last quarter century, reviewers have provided an often "dismal evaluation" (Shakeshaft, 1999, p. 237) of the preparation of future school leaders. Taken together, critiques built an image of a system of preparing school leaders that was seriously flawed and that was found wanting in nearly every aspect (Griffiths, Stout, & Forsyth, 1988; Murphy, 1999), including:

1. the ways students were recruited and selected into training programs;
2. the education they received once there, including the content emphasized and the peda- gogical strategies employed;
3. the methods used to assess academic fitness; and
4. the procedures developed to certify and select principals and superintendents.

However, considerable energy is currently flowing into the improvement and enhancement of preparation programs in educational leadership (Young et al., 2009).

This chapter charts efforts within the university community to improve the preparation of urban school leaders, highlighting, in particular, the work of the UCEA ULDP in redesigning key com- ponents of preparation and developing rigorous and relevant leadership preparation curriculum and learning experiences specifically for aspiring leaders of urban schools. Although the work highlighted does not exhaust the variety of innovations that can be found in educational leadership preparation programs, it offers compelling examples of the kinds of things that programs across the country are doing to improve and make their programs more impactful.

Perhaps one of the most significant aspects of this work is that these programs have been able to rebuild themselves within the context of higher education (Orr, 2006). There are multiple challenges to reform in schools of education, not least of which are the complacency of some faculty members, the lack of support or recognition from within their institutions, and a failure of the university to meet new resource needs (Young et al., 2002). University norms typically do not support either program development or partnership work. Regardless, a growing number of university programs are incorporating new understandings of educational leadership and better understandings of how to integrate PLEs into program design, content, and delivery to develop leadership capacities.

Opportunities for collaboration, like those provided by the UCEA ULDP, appear to be an impor- tant catalyst for educational leadership preparation programs across the examples of improvement shared in this chapter. Possibly, collaboration created both the opportunity and the means to redesign programs despite institutional norms to the contrary (Orr, 2006).

Much is yet to be learned about how effective these new approaches to leadership development will be. Coupling a commitment between preparation and evaluation research will be important. Through continued collaboration and joint inquiry, we can focus and strengthen university preparation and revitalize the field.

References

Argyris, C., & Schön, D. (1996). *Organizational learning II*. Reading, MA: Addison-Wesley.

Baker, B., Orr, M. T., & Young, M. D. (2007). Academic drift, institutional production and professional distribution of graduate degrees in educational administration. *Educational Administration Quarterly, 43*(13) 279–318.

Black, W. R., & Murtadha, K. (2007). Toward a signature pedagogy in educational leadership preparation and program assessment. *The Journal of Research on Leadership Education, 2*(1). Retrieved from: www.ucea.org/jrle_2007_2_1

Black, W. R., Bathon, J., & Pointdexter, B. (2007). *Looking in the mirror to improve practice: A study of administrative licensure and master's degree programs in the state of Indiana.* Indianapolis: Center for Urban and Multicultural Education (CUME), Indiana University-Indianapolis.

Bottoms, G., & O'Neill, K. (2001). *Preparing a new breed of school principals: It's time for action.* Atlanta, GA: Southern Regional Education Board.

Bridges, E. M., & Hallinger, P. (1997). Using problem-based learning to prepare educational administrators. *Peabody Journal of Education, 72*(2), 131–146.

Carnegie Foundation (2010). Carnegie project on the education doctorate (CPED). Retrieved from: www.carnegiefoundation.org/education-doctorate

Copland, M. A. (2000). Problem-based learning and prospective principals' problem-framing ability. *Educational Administration Quarterly, 36*(4), 585.

Culbertson, J. (1962). New perceptions: Implications for program change. In J. Culbertson and S. Hencley (Eds.), *Preparing administrators: New perspectives* (pp. 151–173). Columbus, OH: UCEA.

Darling-Hammond, L., Meyerson, D., LaPointe, M., & Orr, M. T. (2007). *Preparing leaders for a changing world.* Palo Alto, CA: Stanford University.

Davis, S., Darling-Hammond, L., Meyerson, D., & LaPointe, M. (2005). *Review of research. School leadership study. Developing successful principals.* Palo Alto, CA: Stanford University, Stanford Educational Leadership Institute.

Edelman, G. M., & Tononi, G. (2000). *A universe of consciousness: How matter becomes imagination.* New York: Basic Books.

Fine, M. (1994). Chartering urban school reform. In M. Fine (Ed.), *Chartering urban school reform* (pp. 5–30). New York: Teachers College Press.

Fuller, E. J., Young, M. D., & Baker, B. (2011). The relationship between principal preparation and a leader's influence on teacher–team qualifications and student achievement: An exploratory analysis. *Educational Administration Quarterly, 47*(1), 173–216.

Gordon, G. (1999). Teacher talent and urban schools. *Phi Delta Kappan, 81*(4), 304–307.

Griffiths, D. E., Stout, R. T., & Forsyth, P. B. (Eds.) (1988). *Leaders for America's schools: The report and papers of the National Commission on Excellence in Educational Administration.* Berkeley, CA: McCutchan Publishing Company.

Guarino, C. M., Santibañez, L., & Daley, G. A. (2006). Teacher recruitment and retention: A review of the recent empirical literature. *Review of Educational Research, 76*(2), 173–208.

Hallinger, P., & Heck, R. (1996). Reassessing the principal's role in school effectiveness: A review of empirical research, 1980–1995. *Educational Administration Quarterly, 32*(1), 5–44.

Hart, A. W. (1993). Reflection: An instructional strategy in educational administration. *Educational Administration Quarterly, 29*(3), 323–338.

Hess, F. M., & Kelly, A. (2005). An innovative look, a recalcitrant reality: The politics of principal preparation reform. *Educational Policy, 19*(1), 155–180.

Holyoak, K., & Thagard, P. (1999). *Mental leaps: Analogy in creative thought.* Cambridge, MA: MIT Press.

Ingersoll, R. (1999). The problem of underqualified teachers in American secondary schools. *Educational Researcher, 28*, 26–37.

Jackson, B. L., & Kelley, C. (2002). Exceptional and innovative programs in educational leadership. *Educational Administration Quarterly, 38*(2), 192.

Kolb, D. (1984). *Experiential learning: Experiences as the source of learning and development.* Englewood Cliffs, NJ: Prentice Hall.

Lad, K., Browne-Ferrigno, T., & Shoho, A. (2005). Leadership preparation admission criteria: Examining the spectrum from open enrollment to elite selection. Paper presented at the University Council of Educational Administration, Nashville, TN.

Lakomski, G. (1998). Training administrators in the wild: A naturalistic perspective. *UCEA Review, 34*(3), 1, 5, 10–11.

Lankford, H., Loeb, S., & Wyckoff, J. (2002). Teacher sorting and the plight of urban schools. *Educational Evaluation and Policy Analysis, 24*(1), 37–62.

Lehrer, J. (2009). *How we decide.* New York: Houghton Mifflin Harcourt.

Leithwood, K., & Jantzi, D. (2000). The effects of transformational leadership on organizational conditions and student engagement with school. *Journal of Educational Administration, 38*(2), 112–129.

Leithwood, K., & Jantzi, D. (2005). A review of transformational school leadership research. Paper presented at the American Educational Research Association, Montreal, April.

Leithwood, K., & Jantzi, D. (2008). Linking leadership to student learning: The contributions of leader efficacy. *Educational Administration Quarterly, 44*(4), 496–528.

Leithwood, K., & Riehl, C. (2003). *What we know about successful school leadership.* Philadelphia, PA: AERA Division A Task Force on Developing Research in Educational Leadership.

Leithwood, K., Seashore, K., Anderson, S., & Wahlstrom, K. (2004). *How leadership influences student learning.* Toronto, Canada: Center for Applied Research and Educational Improvement & Ontario Institute for Studies in Education.

McCarthy, M. M. (1999). The evolution of educational leadership preparation programs. In J. Murphy & K. S. Louis (Eds.), *Handbook of research on educational administration: A project of the American Educational Research Association* (pp. 119–139). San Francisco, CA: Jossey-Bass.

Milstein, M. M. (1993). *Changing the way we prepare educational leaders: The Danforth Experience.* Newbury Park, CA: Corwin Press.

Murphy, J. (1999). Changes in preparation programs: Perceptions of department chairs. In J. Murphy & P. B. Forsyth (Eds.), *Educational administration: A decade of reform* (pp. 170–191). Thousand Oaks, CA: Corwin Press.

Murphy, J. (2002). Reculturing the profession of educational leadership: New blueprints. *Educational Administration Quarterly, 38*(2), 176–191.

NPBEA (National Policy Board for Educational Administration) (2008). *Educational leadership policy standards: ISLLC 2008.* Austin: University of Texas-Austin.

NCLB (2002). No Child Left Behind Act of 2001. P.L. 107–110. Retrieved February 2, 2007 from: www.ed.gov/policy/elsec/leg/esea02/index. html

Orr, M. T. (2006). Mapping innovation in leadership preparation in our nation's schools of education. *Phi Delta Kappan, 87*(7), 492–499.

Orr, M. T. (2011). How graduate-level preparation influences the effectiveness of school leaders: A comparison of the outcomes of exemplary and conventional leadership preparation programs for principals. *Educational Administration Quarterly, 47*, 114–172.

Orr, M. T., & Pounder, D. (2008). Comparing leadership education from pipeline to preparation to advancement: A study of multiple institutions' leadership preparation programs. Paper presented at the annual meeting of the American Educational Research Association, New York.

Pounder, D., Reitzug, U., & Young, M. D. (2002). Preparing school leaders for school improvement, social justice, and community. In J. Murphy (Ed.), *The educational leadership challenge: Redefining leadership for the 21st century* (pp. 261–288). Chicago: University of Chicago Press.

Robinson, V. M. J., Lloyd, C. A., & Rowe, K. J. (2008). The impact of leadership on student outcomes: An analysis of the differential effects of leadership types. *Educational Administration Quarterly, 44*(5), 635–674.

Sanders, N. M., & Simpson, J. (2005). *State policy framework to develop highly qualified administrators.* Washington, DC: CCSSO.

Shakeshaft, C. (1999). The struggle to create a more gender-inclusive profession. In J. Murphy & K. S. Louis (Eds.), *Handbook of research on educational administration* (2nd ed.) (pp. 99–118). San Francisco, CA: Jossey-Bass.

Short, P., & Rinehart, R. (1993). Reflection as a means of developing expertise. *Educational Administration Quarterly, 29*(4), 501–521.

Supovitz, J., Sirinides, P., & May, H. (2010). How principals and peers influence teaching and learning. *Educational Administration Quarterly, 46*(1), 31–56.

U.S. Department of Education (2004). *Innovations in education: Innovative pathways to school leadership.* Washington, DC: U.S. Department of Education.

Waters, J. T., Marzano, R. J., & McNulty, B. A. (2003). *Balanced leadership: What 30 years of research tells us about the effect of leadership on student achievement.* Aurora, CO: Mid-continent Research for Education and Learning. Retrieved February 2, 2007 from: www.mcrel.org/topics/productDetail.asp?topicsID=7&productID=144

Young, M. D., Petersen, G. J., & Short, P. M. (2002). The complexity of substantive reform: A call for interdependence among key stakeholders. *Educational Administration Quarterly, 38*(2), 137–175.

Young, M. D., Crow, G., Ogawa, R., & Murphy, J. (2009). *The handbook of research on leadership preparation.* New York: Routledge.

Young, M. D., Crow, G., Orr, T., Ogawa, R., & Creighton, T. (2005). An educative look to educating school leaders. *UCEA Review, 47*(2), 1–5.

Appendix A

Each urban leadership preparation program is based on a series of implicit and explicit beliefs about leadership for urban schools. Please list at least three and no more than five core beliefs about leadership for urban schools (as is true for you).

Appendix B

An urban educational leadership preparation curriculum explicitly or implicitly reflects a Theory of Action of how to prepare leaders who can effectively improve and sustain quality education in urban schools. This theory of action, or program theory, is most explicit when stated as a "theory"—in a series of if_____, then_____ statements (if we do [example of broad strategy], then our candidates will be able to [example outcome]). Each theory includes a strategy or set of strategies and leads to measurable outcomes.

Please outline two to four broad theories of action that you would recommend or believe are critical for an urban leadership preparation program in order to accomplish your beliefs.

If we _____,
then _____.

If we _____,
then _____.

If we _____,
then _____.

If we _____,
then _____.

10

Transformative Leaders and Urban Education[1]

Gilberto Arriaza and Rosemary Henze

In this chapter we posit that to successfully engage the challenges of today's urban public schools, a new type of education leadership will be in high demand. First, leadership must shift from charismatic, positional, and transactional approaches to an approach grounded on a twin vision that includes both equity and adequacy. We argue that, for our emerging multiethnic democracy, a floor condition must be present in all schools: the unequivocal provision of a basic, high-quality education for all youth and children. Specifically, fully adequate education must be put in place for youth and children who—owing to racialized conditions, economic poverty, and gender, linguistic, and cultural discrimination—have been rendered disadvantaged in today's school systems.

Second, as our society moves forward in the 21st century, issues that have not been entirely resolved, such as those mentioned above, coupled with entirely new ones, have come to take central stage in the national debates on the future of education. Globalized trade and production of goods and services, new communication and transportation technologies, the ever-expanding production of scientific knowledge, and a fragile natural environment have created tremendous opportunities and unfathomable challenges for our society's entire education system.

The state of today's health system, international conflicts, and the sorry state of party politics pale in comparison with the centrality of the U.S. economy and economic progress. More importantly, the social consensus that the economy of a society very much depends on the quality of its citizens' formal education could not be more relevant. The task before educational reformers may be daunting or even impossible unless it is viewed as a synergy of key elements. In this chapter we attempt to address one of the most significant of these elements: education leadership.

As stated above, the U.S. historical debt to Native Americans, African American, Latinos, and women—owing to discriminatory practices that have systematically placed these populations at a disadvantage—must be resolved. This debt has been amply documented by historians of education (e.g., Brown, 2005; Kozol, 1991; Lieberson, 1980; Tyack, 1974). According to Lieberson (1980), provisions for free elementary education in the South were nonexistent at the time of the Civil War, yet they had been widespread in northern and western states for quite a long time. High schools in the South began their expansion only in the first decade of the 20th century, whereas in the North this process had taken place much earlier.

Along the same lines, in the North, compulsory school attendance laws and their strict enforce-ment were fully in place by 1900, "but the enactment and enforcement of this type of legislation took place considerably later in the South" (Lieberson, 1980, p. 122). In historical terms, certain regions of the country have not provided adequate education. These substandard conditions gave rise to the five legal cases consolidated under *Brown* v. *Board of Education* (Kluger, 1977).

The remedies created by the Brown decision have ameliorated some of the most egregious manifestations of deep societal inequities. Yet vexing educational imbalances continue to this day. School reform efforts of late have focused on closing the achievement gap, gauging its closing mostly through standardized test scores. However, we argue that this narrow focus, which defines equity/adequacy only in terms of closing the academic achievement gap, may render schools incapable of making the advances required to deliver equitable education for all children, thus making it impossible to improve their life chances.

The narrow focus misguides resources and may have the unintended effect of supporting historic and present-day injustices. Add to this picture newer layers of context—such as the deep inter-dependencies brought about by a global economy, the lamentable state of our natural environment, and rapidly advancing communication technologies and scientific knowledge—and we have a situation in which each new factor can multiply the effects of inequality ad infinitum. For example, as globalization continues and expands, it can create more opportunities for those who are "global citizens"; but it can also restrict global citizenship to the elite and leave the urban poor even more marginalized.

In the next section of this chapter, we define equity and adequacy and their relation to a multi-ethnic democracy. After that, we focus on four approaches for urban leadership in these new times:

1. debunking deficit approaches and instead building social, cultural, and intellectual capital;
2. building healthy, positive intergroup relations;
3. committing to a simultaneous focus on both the local and the global; and
4. integrating academic and applied preparation.

Equity, Adequacy, and Multiethnic Democracy

Equity

Equity in the United States traces its roots to the English legal tradition, which describes it as a system that attempts to supplement the ordinary legal rules where their application would operate harshly in a particular case (Keigwin, 1930). In rendering decisions, judges are instructed to apply both the rules of strict law and the principle of equity in reaching their decisions (Legal Information Institute, 2005). The *Random House Dictionary* (1983) refers to equity as a "particular set of remedies and asso-ciated procedures" (pp. 656–657) established to amend social disparities.

For important segments of the education community, equity has primarily come to mean closing the achievement gap. Advocates for equity understand that closing the achievement gap necessarily implies the allocation of money, time, and teacher talent and skill where most needed. The reduction or, as some proponents argue, the elimination of the achievement gap is considered a benchmark of a higher egalitarian system, captured in the aphorism, "equity is the strategy; equality is the goal."

The focus on equity as allocation of resources where most needed suggests a radical departure from equality as the framing concept of reform. Equality has usually meant the equal treatment of students regardless of their background. This way, disadvantaged children will have the same access to knowledge, skills, and resources as children from privileged backgrounds. To close the gap, though, it is now understood that the former have accumulated academic deficits that, for instance, make it impossible for them to benefit from free access to coursework such as advanced placement physics or honors English in high school. Additionally, equity-oriented educators critique the education system for having preemptively closed these children's access by subjecting them to substandard education from early elementary school onward.

Equity actions may lead, notwithstanding, to a paradoxical treatment: while purporting to create a more equal society, these actions could provide some students with a different and unequal service—more or different resources (monetary, material, and human) where most needed—which goes directly against the meritocratic ideal in which all students have an equal opportunity to rise and become successful; those who do succeed do so through their own merit. From Thomas Jefferson's time until now, it has been assumed that schools should exert an equalizing effect on society; ergo, no distinction ought to be made as to students' opportunity to attain knowledge and skills. That is, in a system based on equal access for all, each individual's merit should determine the end results: some will succeed while others will not (Michelli & Keiser, 2005; Oakes, 1994; Tyack, 1974).

Experts distinguish between horizontal and vertical equity. When children are "equally situated" and receive equal treatment in terms of learning inputs, horizontal equity exists (Berne & Stiefel, 1999). In other words, equals are treated equally (Auerbach & Hassett, 2002). Horizontal equity also involves individuals and groups from the same income bracket, gender, and linguistic and/or cultural background. Inputs are supposed to be the same for these children, and it follows that they are expected to produce the same outputs. But this is not always the case. Equal treatment has produced diverse levels of academic achievement within horizontally located groups.

For instance, a subgroup of low-socioeconomic-status students (who may be racially or ethnically diverse) is said to be horizontally located. The horizontal equity approach may mean that those students who are racially/ethnically different but economically poor, receive the same teaching content delivered by the same teachers. They should theoretically produce the same results. Yet we know that most of the time this is not the case.

Vertical equity means that children who are differently situated receive different treatment in terms of learning inputs (Berne & Stiefel, 1999). This may translate into the purposeful infusion of resources for particular groups of children in order to bring those performing at a low level up to par with the ones performing at a high level; more targeted inputs, it is assumed, will produce higher outputs among lower-performing subgroups. However, reforms based strictly on this assumption have not succeeded in eliminating the achievement gap.

Adequacy

Adequacy plays a role similar to that of horizontal equity; it requires absolute results that complement the more relative results of vertical equity. For instance, from an adequate financial perspective, all inputs must provide the necessary support to increase the academic achievement of all children. From a vertical equity perspective, higher inputs must be provided for an underperforming subgroup, so that this group aligns its performance to that of the higher-performing subgroups. Legal language may further explain the definition of adequacy here.

In her rulings, the New York Court of Appeals Chief Judge Judith Kaye (2003) succinctly defined adequacy as "the process of determining the actual cost of providing a sound basic education" (p. 21). Adequacy litigation seeks to remedy inequity in the resources required to ensure a sound, basic education for every child.

Critics of adequacy-based school reform observe that providing basic education does not eliminate society's inherent injustices stemming from its hierarchical organization. Adequacy may only perpetuate the existing academic gaps, since providing adequate education does not address accumulated learning deficits among disadvantaged children and communities. Additionally, the argument against adequacy-based reform questions who defines what *adequate* means and how should it be measured.

In 1978 *adequate* was interpreted to mean that schools should be funded in a manner that allowed them—as Minorini and Sugarman (1999) put it in reviewing the 1978 *Seattle* v. *State of Washington* case—to "equip our children to function as citizens and as potential competitors in today's market as well as in the marketplace of ideas" (p. 193). According to the authors, a broader definition was delivered in West Virginia in the 1979 *Pauley* v. *Kelley* case "as best the state of education expertise allows, the mind, bodies and social morality of its charges to prepare them for useful and happy occupations, recreation and citizenship, and does so economically" (p. 194).

A case that started as litigation over inequitable finances among school districts ended up as a case addressing inadequate resources that prevented children from obtaining a sound, basic education (Picus & Blair, 2004). Indeed, the *Rose* v. *Council for Better Education* case in Kentucky made its way up to the state supreme court, which in 1989 ruled that the entire state school system was unconstitutional. It violated both the education section and the equal protection clause of the state's constitution. A total revamping of the funding structure ensued immediately, from the enactment of the Kentucky Education Reform Act to a more direct involvement of the state at the local level, including a substantial increase of state funds for education. Litigation spurred by the new focus increased considerably thereafter throughout the United States.

By 2005, about 32 states had faced adequacy lawsuits (Griffith, 2005); overall, 25 of these cases had been decided in favor of the plaintiffs (National Access Network, 2005). An example of this new trend is the *Williams et al.* v. *the State of California* case. It was filed in 1999 in San Francisco County Superior Court by about 100 students from low-socioeconomic and low-performing schools in the county of San Francisco and resolved in 2004.

The plaintiffs argued that the state had failed to provide qualified teachers and safe and decent facilities, thus depriving students of their right to basic, good-quality education. As a result of the court's ruling in 2004, children and youth in low-performing schools that serve low-socioeconomic-status populations will potentially benefit from extra state funds, about $2.3 billion, earmarked to redress poor conditions.

In early January 2006 and just two months after the Supreme Court of Colorado made a similar decision to the Williams case, the Supreme Court of the State of Florida decided against a voucher system, known as the Opportunity Scholarship Program (OSP), created by then Governor, Jeb Bush. Citing article IX, section 1(a) of that state's constitution—stating that "[a]dequate provision shall be made by law for a uniform, efficient, safe, secure, and high quality system of free public schools"—Judge Barbara J. Pariente ruled against the use of public funds to pay tuition for private education for more than 700 children in the state. Judge Pariente wrote: "It [the OSP] diverts public dollars into separate private systems parallel to and in competition with the public schools that are the sole means set out in the Constitution for the state to provide for the education of Florida's children" (Supreme Court of Florida, 2006, p. 4).

It was the Kentucky Supreme Court decision of 1989, referred to earlier, that outlined the most clear and comprehensive factors defining "adequate" education. The decision includes the following seven key factors (Minorini & Sugarman, 1999):

1. Sufficient oral and written communication.
2. Sufficient knowledge of economic, social, and political systems.
3. Sufficient understanding of governmental processes.
4. Sufficient knowledge of his or her mental and physical wellness.
5. Sufficient grounding in the arts to enable each student to appreciate his or her cultural and historical heritage.
6. Sufficient training or preparation for advanced training in either academic or vocational fields . . . to choose and pursue life work intelligently.

7. Sufficient levels of academic or vocational skills to enable public school students to compete favorably with their counterparts in surrounding states, in academics, or in the job market.

We note that in this definition of adequacy, science and technology are not specifically mentioned, nor is financial literacy, global citizenship, or environmental citizenship. Are these, then, to be considered optional, at the discretion of the school districts? Furthermore, the bedrock sufficiencies in the Kentucky decision refer only to individual knowledge and skills, and do not take into consideration the interpersonal and community dynamics that both shape individuals and are shaped by individuals and groups. Are we to assume that if each individual achieves sufficient knowledge and skill in the seven areas, we as educators have done our job?

The individualized perspective represented in these sufficiencies is only part of the picture that is needed today. The other part involves the social and cultural dynamics of the school as a living, changing organization in which leaders of all kinds play key roles. Nowhere is this more true than in urban schools, which are typically large and highly complex systems at many levels of hierarchy, with often competing goals. In a democratic and multiethnic society, such as the United States, it is crucial that educational leaders develop ways of ensuring both equity *and* adequacy, and that the indicators of adequacy are relevant to the times in which we live. In the next section, we discuss how the notions of equity and adequacy are linked to the notion of transformative leadership in a multiethnic democracy.

Transformative Leadership for a Multiethnic Democracy

In Western democracies, and the United States in particular, schools presumably play a pivotal role in forging a well-informed and educated citizenry (Apple & Beane, 1995; Barber, 1984; Dewey, 1916). This ideal premise advances the notion that schools hold the potential for people to learn how to negotiate differences, to relate to the world critically, and to resolve social conflict while also acquiring the basic habits of citizenship (Apple, 1995; Meier, 2002; Simon, 2003; Sizer, 1992).

According to this view, schools are among the few social institutions where communities often unable to communicate and/or understand each other—either at the workplace, the neighborhood, or in general public spaces—converge. Schools often provide the only chance to talk and to embrace common interests by having people share a key interest: their children's education. Furthermore, globalization and the demographic shift of the late 20th century (from predominantly European-origin immigrants to immigrants and refugees from all parts of the globe) represent the greatest opportunity for U.S. society to engender a true multiethnic, multiracial democracy.[2]

Preserving the public and secular nature of education is linked to the survival of democracy in the United States. And today's struggle for equity and adequacy in schools constitutes the arena where the future of this democracy is being decided. Transformative urban school leaders sit at the front and center in this struggle.

How can such leaders embrace a strategy of change that places adequate and equitable education at the forefront of their action? In the following section, we define transformative leaders as the key agents of school reform.

Transformative Leaders

School leaders are traditionally thought of as administrators whose central role is to manage their institutions efficiently. This paradigm emerged in the early 20th-century's push for the professionalization of education leaders. Cubberley (1916) aptly puts it this way: "The significance of this new movement is large, for it means nothing less than the ultimate changing of school administration from guesswork to scientific accuracy" (pp. 325–326). The author applies the term *scientific accuracy* to both up-to-date managerial methodologies (as in business and new industries) and to the elevation of the preparation of school leaders to the same level as that of medical, law, and other professional schools.

Although the vast and complex nature of the education system makes it hard to establish clear and definite trends in the field of school administration, Tyack (1974), Nasaw (1979), and Callahan (1962), among others, profusely documented the predominance of business models in the early 20th century, which remain with us until this day. Swayed by then popular "scientific management" (i.e., F. Taylor's 1911 work), people interested in becoming school administrators learned to direct schools following notions of efficient, centralized, corporate decision-making processes.

Throughout the 20th century, cost-effectiveness, economies of scale, and numerical measurement became enshrined and continue to prevail in this new century. Along with local state and federal restrictive policies (e.g., No Child Left Behind), the effort to redefine school administrators from business managers to transforming leaders faces seemingly insurmountable difficulties. We suggest here that viewing school leaders as active agents of change is key to surmounting these difficulties.

Agency

Agency may be defined as people's deliberate daily labor or actions organized around social systems, personalities, and cultural systems (Parsons & Shils, 2001). The first step in moving toward an agentive view of school leadership (as opposed to a managerial view) is to place the notion of agency at the center of the conversation. In this sense, agents, or people with a sense of agency, take action steeped in the cultural and social life of the institutions and organizations where they function (Castelfranchi & Conte, 1995). Agents not only operate from knowing that they can act but deliberately choose to act. As Giddens (2005) notes, agency is not about the intent of doing things but about people's "capability of doing these things" (p. 127).

Agency in school leadership operates at two levels: structures and culture. We understand structures as the various functions and systems that enable an organization to execute its plans. This is what Habermas (1987) identified as "systems world." School leaders use their agency to plan how the system of the school will operate, usually including in their plan their key objectives which, if accomplished, eventually enable the organization to achieve its mission. Culture may be defined broadly as the material, mental, social, and behavioral products that humans collectively create (Mukhopadhyay, Henze, & Moses, 2007). Each school may be considered to have its own "micro-culture," and it is to a degree intentionally shaped by those in leadership roles.

However, it is also shaped by everyone who works at and attends the school. Some cultural norms may be explicit and others implicit. Here, we focus mainly on school culture as it is carried out in the way people talk and define the way things are usually done, how people are categorized both formally and implicitly, and how relationships are sustained (Arriaza, 2004).

The second step of educational leaders as transformative agents is to have a clear but flexible set of approaches to guide their actions. We recognize the risk of prescriptive models, simply because these never work. Life and schooling are far too messy to adhere rigidly to a prescribed set of cookbook-like "recipes." We have argued throughout the previous section that urban education leaders have a duty to relentlessly pursue and provide both adequate and equitable education. In the next section of this chapter, we argue for four approaches that will help urban education leaders achieve these twin goals and successfully engage the old as well as new challenges. We are not suggesting that these are the only approaches urban leaders should consider. Our aim is to propose approaches that respond not only to the old challenges that are yet unresolved but also to what we see as new issues affecting urban schools.

Four Approaches to Guide Action

Transformative Urban Leaders Debunk Deficit Approaches and Build Students' Capital

Transformative urban leaders understand the concept of social, cultural, and intellectual capital and use this concept to guide their actions. In order to do so, they need to debunk the opposite, which is deficit attribution of school failure. According to Padilla (1976), three arguments constitute the core of the deficit attribution model: genetics, culture, and social class. Although the idea that the human species is made up of superior and inferior races has been scientifically disproved for quite a long time, the genetic argument still shows up in academic discourse (e.g., Herrnstein & Murray, 1994). Proponents of this argument state that racialized peoples are feeble-minded and genetically less intelligent than Europeans.[3]

Culture as a source of deficit has largely taken the place of biological deficit arguments among educators nowadays. Cultural deficit arguments claim that when children do not excel academically, it is because their families' cultures do not fit the culture of their schools (Valdez, 1996). According to this view, these children have not been exposed to a wide and rich range of vocabulary and linguistic expression in the dominant language (in the United States, standard English) or to the ways of behaving and believing that fit the rules and norms of schooling. Therefore, it becomes impossible for them to unlock school culture and participate in ways valued by mainstream educators and to follow social mores stemming from the European legacy of the education system's founders.

One key social phenomenon, though, tends to be ignored by cultural deficit proponents—the demographic shift caused by increased immigration to the United States during the second half of the 20th century. The new demographics have moved public education further away from a European-based student population to a third world (euphemistically called the "developing world") base, which has in turn infused significant cultural changes in schools. Furthermore, cultural deficit arguments do not address the power relations embedded in the school system.

The assumption is that the dominant culture's norms are inherently better than those of minority populations and therefore should be the target for all children, as well as their parents. Workshops for parents on middle-class styles of parenting often exemplify a cultural deficit approach, because they ignore or devalue styles of parenting that differ from those of the dominant, European American middle class.

The third explanation for low-achieving students is social class, which often overlaps with culture. Children from low-socioeconomic backgrounds tend to fail in school owing to a culture of poverty, this argument explains. Children living in economic poverty become imbued with self-defeating traditions: few reading and writing habits, limited study skills, and a poor work ethic. Children from economically poor families appear doomed from the outset in terms of academic prowess; as a result, this rationale posits, they need to be equipped with the skills and habits appropriate to their potential—for instance, learning basic thinking skills and training for low-level technical jobs.

Deficit approaches place the burden of responsibility exclusively on the children's and families' shoulders. By doing so, schools externalize their responsibility for providing effective schooling for all children. Transformative urban leaders actively lay bare deficit attributions and shift responsibility to the institution. Briscoe, Arriaza, and Henze (2009) provide detailed examples of how school leaders have used language as a key tool in contesting deficit approaches, instead framing their communication through a language of possibility.

For example, José Jacinto, a new vice-principal at a large middle school in a Northern California city, explained that although normalized labels reflect deep-seated assumptions of people using them, these labels represent an opportunity for school leaders to problematize their use and thus help users increase awareness. He observes how by using seemingly harmless labels, such as "those kids," teachers put a social distance between them and students. This labeling masks deeper misunderstandings and ignorance which, in turn, do not allow teachers to establish personalized relations, fostering instead a punitive culture. Mr. Jacinto concluded:

> Then what happens is that teachers have negative expectations. I try to let them see that . . . once they know about the student they will investigate. They usually say, "Oh, I didn't know that." A lot of people feel and are aware of labels, but they're afraid to say anything because they fear the consequences with their peers. They don't have the courage. Even if they have the skills, it might still be confrontational.

Leaders such as José Jacinto are aware of how the informal culture of a school can create labels such as "those kids," which over time develop a negative connotation. They also realize that they must use their own personal agency to contest such deficit labeling and raise awareness among the other faculty and staff members. But doing so is a delicate matter, because professional colleagues may actively resist someone exposing their own lack of awareness. José Jacinto not only points out the issue of students not having certain types of "capital" valued in the school, but also raises faculty awareness about other types of capital the students do possess. And he expects other faculty members to use their intellectual capital to investigate further about the students' experiences and background.

Other sorts of capital operate in similar ways that money capital does—we can accumulate it, transport it from place to place, and transfer it. We list here three kinds of capital: social, cultural, and intellectual. For purposes of brevity—given that the literature on the topic is quite extensive—we can provide only a limited description of each of these types.

Social Capital
Negotiating social boundaries and identifying and being part of social networks is the basis of this kind of capital. Transformative leaders help students learn how to successfully relate to others, how to connect to social networks that bring added value to their capital, and how to access, through those relationships, areas that might otherwise be inaccessible. Of vital importance here is understanding how to develop and sustain friendship groups and social status and to make explicit notions such as saving face, peer pressure, and criminalization.

Cultural Capital
An understanding of the role of identity, the cultural values of the elite, and the power of language in society constitutes this kind of capital. Transformative leaders help students by teaching them the modalities of the dominant language as it is used in formal, official settings and the difference between this use and that pertaining to informal contexts. They do not minimize the importance of maintaining the home or community language but rather engage the entire school community in developing greater awareness of how language use is governed by social situations and how power is differentially imbued in those situations (Delpit, 1995).

Children clearly distinguish between the forms of language in talking to their friends and in talking to an interviewer during a job search. They also nurture their language of origin and that of their forbears as a component of their social identity. Students learn to appreciate their origins and develop a strong sense of their position in society while also becoming skillful at negotiating power imbalances.

Intellectual Capital
This kind of capital includes the values, knowledge, and modalities of learning that students bring with them, which can support their dealings with the institutional barriers they encounter every step of the way in their schooling experience. These forms of intellectual capital originate from family and

community practices, such as primary language, artistic inclinations, study discipline, work habits, and technical knowledge. Transformative leaders help students and faculty learn how the intellectual capital students acquire at home and in their communities can be enhanced and transferred to school contexts.

Supporting the development of these forms of capital is educators' central responsibility in a democratic society. By activating their agency in the above arenas, urban school leaders can advance school reform based on a dual equity/adequacy perspective.

Transformative Urban Leaders Commit to Building Healthy Intergroup Relations

Far too many children and youth attend schools where they are fearful of bullies, afraid to speak their home language, receive little or no support in their search for identity development and group affiliations, do not feel a part of the school culture, and do not receive any explicit curricular focus on such important and life-shaping matters as race (what it is and is not, how it affects our self-perception and the perceptions of others), sexual identity, cultural identity, conflict mediation, and other matters.

Many excellent resources by scholarly practitioners in the area of social justice exist, each speaking to various aspects of intergroup relations (see, e.g., Banks & Banks, 2007; Henze, Katz, Norte, Sather, & Walker, 2002; Lee, 1998; Lindsay, Robins, & Terrell, 1999; Tatum, 1997). In general, these authors agree that having safe schools is important but not sufficient, especially since safety is often taken to mean safety from physical harm, not necessarily safety from emotional abuse. All students have the right to learn in peaceful environments where they can focus on learning. When children and youth are distracted from learning because of unsafe and unhealthy intergroup dynamics in the school, the learning goals of an adequate education cannot possibly be met. Thus we see positive intergroup relations as a floor condition that must be present in order to provide the curriculur and pedagogical elements of an adequate education.

Here, we would like to briefly touch on one model for organizing a school's efforts to advance transformative intergroup relations. This model, depicted in Figure 10.1, emerged from a 2002 study

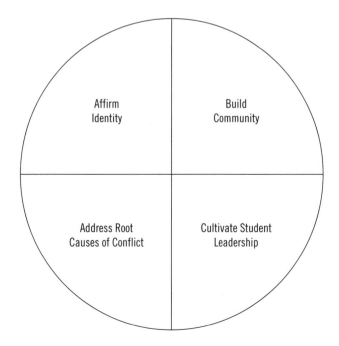

Figure 10.1 Four Principles for Improving Interethnic Relations (ABCA)

by Henze et. al. of 21 schools that were effective in developing and maintaining transformative relations among ethnically diverse student (and faculty) populations; the work of Beverly Tatum (2001) also contributed to this model.

Affirm Identity

Affirmation of identity takes place in activities that emphasize how we are all different, and that these differences are valued, important resources. Classroom examples include using readings that provide information about the demographic groups that attend the school; asking students to share information about their own places of origin (including places within the United States); constructing maps of student origins; and asking students to teach some of their home language to others. Educators should avoid simplistic overgeneralizations about particular cultures or ethnic groups and "essentializing" statements—i.e., statements assuming that certain cultural behaviors are inherent in a person's biology, or that students with Spanish surnames all share the same culture.

Build Community

This dimension emphasizes similarities, how we are the same, and how unity of purpose helps us work together toward common goals. Examples include asking students to develop an agreed-upon set of class or school-wide rules or guidelines for how people will treat each other; identifying a problem in the institution and working together to solve it; creating class matrices that display information about the class or the whole school (this can actually serve both to affirm identity to the extent that it points out differences and to build community in that it creates a sense of "us" as a group); and cooperative learning activities that require students to cooperate in order to solve a problem or complete a task.

Cultivate Student Leadership

This dimension emphasizes student voice, democratic participation, and the development of student leadership. It involves students becoming active subjects of their own histories, not just passive recipients of the history written in textbooks. Typically, only a small core of high-performing students play leadership roles; transformative urban leaders find opportunities for a wide range of students to play leadership roles.

Address Root Causes of Conflict

This dimension is essential, because if we focus only on the other three, we may never address the structural and institutional problems that cause ethnic and other kinds of intergroup conflict. For example, if some of the school staff exhibit racist attitudes, if tracking of certain groups places them in less demanding classes, or if informal segregation prevents individuals from coming to know members of other groups, transformative leaders must find ways to bring these issues to the surface and engage the school community in finding solutions (Henze et al., 2002).

Each of these dimensions is important for students' growth and for the harmonious functioning of the school community. Working on one dimension without the others will result in an imbalance. Urban leaders who use their agency to ensure that not one but all four dimensions of this framework are active in their schools find that their schools become well-functioning communities where respect is practiced on a daily basis.

Transformative Urban Leaders Commit to a Simultaneous Focus on Place, Both Local and Global

Local Relevance
In past decades, anthropologists of education have made a strong case for education to be relevant to students' communities and to draw on the types of knowledge and skills students bring to school. Using a constructivist and culturally responsive paradigm, researchers showed that when teachers bring students' local knowledge into the classroom and make it part of the curriculum for everyone, students feel more engaged with school and are able to see connections between school knowledge and home knowledge. The Funds of Knowledge project in Tucson, Arizona (González, Moll, & Amanti, 2005), is one of the best-known projects of this kind, but many others preceded and followed it. Projects such as Foxfire focused on oral history and community lore.

A number of recent projects place agency directly into the hands of students by involving them in participatory action research (PAR) to study and propose solutions to problems they and their communities face, such as lack of services for youth, unsafe school buildings, community violence, and other issues that directly affect young people (Davis, Bazzi, Cho, Ishida, & Soria, 2005; Duncan-Andrade & Morrell, 2008).

Although the push for national accountability through increased standardized testing has forced the "local relevance" argument into the background ("there is only so much time in the school day"), we argue that local relevance remains necessary. Particularly in urban areas where all one reads or hears about on the news is negative, it is important for young people to take back their communities and find meaningful and positive actions that they can take to improve their neighborhoods.

Global Connections
Local relevance is not adequate by itself (Kumaravadivelu, 2008; Luke, 2004). Education leaders need to integrate local relevance with a focus on global connections, enabling students to make connections with places far from the local. Luke calls for teachers to model for students "an agentive engagement in flows across cultures, geographies, and sites" (p. 1441).

Globalization is a term that one reads and hears everywhere now. It is a construct, a label with multiple meanings attached to certain phenomena occurring in the "real world." We cannot directly touch globalization, yet one way or another we experience its effects, even if we are not aware of them at the time. A definition we find useful in thinking about globalization and its relation to education is the following: globalization is "a multidimensional set of social processes that create, multiply, stretch, and intensify worldwide social interdependencies and exchanges while at the same time fostering in people a growing awareness of deepening connections between the local and the distant" (Steger, 2003, cited in Kumaravadivelu, 2008, p. 32). Globalization is not a new phenomenon, strictly speaking, but the speed and extent to which worldwide exchanges are taking place make this era distinct from earlier forms of globalization.

How do changes triggered by globalization affect urban schools in the United States? They do so in several ways that students and faculty directly experience. One is through the speed of Internet-based exchanges, which make possible connections that were unheard of before the current era. Another way is through the availability of technological and scientific information that does not require physical libraries. Any student with a computer connected to the Internet can research and discover knowledge that was not available before except to students in elite schools. However, counterbalancing those positive changes are negative ones: globalization (and the outsourcing of manufacturing and communications jobs, coupled with frequent economic crisis) has left countless urban communities with a shrinking income base.

Globalization affects culture. Some claim that globalization and the threat of homogenization is pushing local communities to resist and thereby strengthen their local identities, whether cultural, religious, or other types of identity. Others fear that the entire world population is adopting U.S.-style consumerism and moving toward complete homogenization.

A third or middle position, sometimes referred to as "glocalization," suggests that there is a push and pull, or creative tension, between cultural homogenization and cultural heterogenization (Appadurai, 1990, cited in Kumaravadivelu, 2008, p. 45). This tension is reproduced on a smaller scale in schools whenever we see tensions and conflicts over whose culture or which ethnic group claims to be the dominant one. Some schools veer more in the direction of universal culture ("we are all the same") and some veer more toward particularistic cultures ("we are all different"), but few schools actually find a balance that includes both sides of the coin.

Transformative urban educational leaders need to insist that graduates of urban public high schools in the United States have a minimum level of global cultural consciousness. They should have a strong understanding of geography and a personal connection to a particular community in another country, including knowledge of its history, economy, demographics, folk legends, leaders, struggles, and at least a beginning level of competency in the language of that community.

For immigrant students, this might mean developing academic knowledge of their country of origin and advanced literacy in the mother tongue. Some of this global cultural consiousness may come about naturally through social contact with diverse peers and adults, but it is up to the school leaders to ensure that curriculum and instruction are purposefully directed toward these competencies.

It is worth pointing out that the United States is one of the few places on earth where large numbers of educated people are monolingual. Throughout the rest of the globe, education comes with knowing at least one additional language. The Council of Europe's "Common European Framework of Reference," or CEFR (2001), emphasizes language study as a tool for social and economic participation. In this document, plurilingualism is emphasized: "An individual's experience of language and its cultural contexts expands from the language of the home to that of the society at large and then to the languages of other peoples (whether learnt at school or college or by direct experience)" (p. 4; cited in Larsen-Freeman & Freeman, 2008, pp. 160–161).

Definitions of language proficiency are also shifting in response to increasing global communication. Whereas old definitions of multilingualism emphasized equal proficiency in two or more languages, plurilingualism and the CEFR document "suggest that speakers of second and third languages shouldn't be compared to native speakers, but rather to highly competent non-native speakers" (Larsen-Freeman & Freeman, 2008, p. 160).

Our rapidly advancing technologies make global connections far easier and less expensive than in the past. Web-based collaborations take us far beyond the old technologies such as the mail, teletype, cable- or telephone-based. Students would wait for weeks to receive penpal letters, by which time interest had to be regenerated all over again. Now, they can "skype" or "elluminate" with peers in another country in real time or share video, photos, scanned drawings, and documents on a group Web site. Although it may be financially unfeasible to expect every high school graduate to travel to a foreign country, students, with expert guidance and oversight, can make full use of the technologies now available to shrink the space between them and their world-wide peers. Such connections have always been commonplace among the children of the elite, who attend private schools and well-funded public schools.

In an equitable and adequate school environment, every student, regardless of family income or location, would enjoy such learning opportunities. The technologies now available render old excuses about the costs of foreign travel unacceptable. Foreign travel, while desirable, is no longer a precondition for fostering global awareness and skills as global citizens.

In this section, we have emphasized the need for urban educational leaders to cultivate in their schools both local, community-based knowledge and global cultural competence. Recent decades in

U.S. education have overemphasized the local at the expense of the global, particularly in urban and low-income communities. It is time to shift that balance once again to include the global. It is worth considering here Kumaravadivelu's descriptions of two Indian state leaders, both from apparently similar religious, historical, national, and political environments.

Nehru had personal dealings with both Indian and Western cultural traditions, and these produced in him "an ambivalent, hybrid identity . . . and a feeling of spiritual loneliness . . . and ambivalence" (Kumaravadivelu, 2008, pp. 168–169). Gandhi, on the other hand, embraced both his own culture of origin and the contributions made to his identity development by his contact with other cultures—the "twin pillars of rootedness and openness" (p. 169). Gandhi stated, "I don't want my house to be walled in on all sides and my windows to be stuffed. I want the cultures of all lands to be blown around my house as freely as possible. But I refuse to be blown off my feet by any" (Gandhi, 1921, cited in Kumaravadivelu, 2008, p. 167).

Transformative Urban Leaders Commit to the Integration of Academic and Applied Preparation

In 2003, Castellano, Stringfield, and Stone wrote:

> Career and technical education has remained on the margins of secondary education since its inception and on the margins of secondary research for 30 years. However, the immense changes in the United States over the last 30 years necessitate a change . . . [and require] the integration of career preparation into the fabric of secondary education. (p. 265)

For decades, educators have been stressing the importance of preparing all students to go to college. In fact, this is the assumed sine qua non measure of a high school's success: what percentage of its graduates go on to two- and four-year colleges. Along the way to equity, which we have yet to achieve, we lost what was then termed vocational education. We lost it for good reasons. As Oakes (1994) and others amply demonstrated, vocational tracks were being used as dumping grounds for African American and Latino youth, and poor youth of all racial/ethnic groups. Not only were Black, Latino, and low-income students being encouraged to pursue a vocational path, but they were too often actively discouraged from seeking college preparation. Counselors and other school personnel were complicit in this (Erickson & Schultz, 1982).

Now, however, we have a generation of students in large cities who do not plan to go to college (even though their high schools supposedly prepared them for it) and who have no job skills that can provide them with a living wage. We seem to be caught in an either/or trap. In the past, we offered students a choice that was not a real choice because students were actively tracked; then we took away vocational preparation and claimed that we were all emphasizing college preparation. Only recently have schools begun to develop models that prepare students both to enter a two- or four-year college *and* to work in an applied field that would enable them to earn a living wage after graduation. According to Castellano et al. (2003), the current era of career/academic integration is "seriously under-researched" (p. 231) and lacks adequate outcome data to be able to confidently claim the effectiveness of the models used.

The old label *vocational* has been largely discarded since 1998 and replaced with the term *career and technical education* (CTE) (Castellano et al., 2003). The Carl Perkins Act, now in its fourth authorization (2006), has increased attention to accountability in order to measure learning outcomes both in the career area and academic subjects. The federal mandate for accountability has encouraged "new unions of CTE and academic departments in secondary schools" (Castellano et al., 2003, p. 231).

Three different approaches can be discerned in current efforts to integrate academic and CTE: "education through work, education about work, and education for work" (Stone, 2000, cited in Castellano et al., 2003, p. 244). Education through work involves learning traditional school subjects with work as the context. Education about work involves learning broad knowledge and skills relating to work, such as the democratic rights of workers, safety concerns, the labor market, team building, job seeking, and so on. Education for work targets specific jobs and prepares students for those jobs while also integrating academic content in the preparation.

Data are beginning to show positive results for the new generation of career preparation in secondary schools, both in terms of academic outcomes and earning ability. For example, the Southern Regional Education Board found that "students at schools with highly integrated, rigorous academic and CTE programs have significantly higher student achievement in reading, mathematics and science than do students at schools with less integrated programs" (cited in ACTE, n.d., p. 1). The 2004 National Assessment of Vocational Education Independent Advisory Panel Report indicated that students who took four high school CTE courses showed an average increase in earnings of $1,200 immediately after graduation and $1,800 seven years later (cited in ACTE, n.d., p. 1).

One charter school in Chicago, ACE Tech (the ACE stands for architecture, construction, and engineering), has recently completed its fourth-year evaluation. This school serves a low-income population of whom 98% qualify for free or reduced-cost lunches. ACE Tech has achieved a graduation rate of 85%, compared with the Chicago public schools' overall rate of 58%. The majority of its graduates have gone on to two- or four-year colleges, while others have gone to apprenticeship schools to become electricians, carpenters, and so on. The remaining graduates have gone immediately into paid employment. The main ingredients for success, according to Knight, Donohue, & Knight (2008), are "a focused curriculum, a well-organized management team, an engaged faculty, and an empowered student body" (p. 22). The school follows the academic standards of the Illinois Board of Education and incorporates relevant industry standards within the curriculum to ensure that students are meeting both sets of standards.

There are a number of issues that must be addressed if similar alliances of career preparation and academic content are to be more broadly successful. One is the need for teacher preparation to enable teachers to teach both academic content and applied areas, or for teachers across CTE and academic areas to develop much tighter collaborations so that they can effectively make use of planning time to provide coherent, rather than fragmented, curriculum and instruction.

Another issue is how to ensure that the careers that are infused in secondary school curricula are viable and can realistically be expected to employ students who complete high school. Because of rapid changes in the economy and rapid advances in technical fields, it is difficult to predict with any accuracy which jobs are likely to be open in the future. Some experts, such as Livingstone (2004), argue that focusing on career education without economic reform is misguided. He stresses that we should be focusing on economic reforms, such as work redistribution and workplace democratization, so that there will be jobs for future graduates. But this approach is not within the purview of urban school leaders, who still need to prepare students for viable means of earning a living.

The environmental challenges we face will lead to companies scrambling to get on board with cleaner, less environmentally damaging products and processes. Industries that respond to this urgent need may offer high school and college graduates in the United States prospects for jobs in the "green" industries. Students who graduate with a strong background in science and technology, along with environmental awareness, will be well poised either to pursue higher degrees in a related field or to go to work immediately after high school and receive further on the job training.

Conclusion

We have argued that urban education leaders in the coming decades require a different set of notions or approaches in order to realize the potential of public schooling in this multiethnic and multiracial democracy. Meeting the demand for equity and adequacy can no longer be satisfied by just monitoring compliance with state and federal mandates. To attain success requires deep examination of the personal commitment to and understanding of equity and adequacy as well as a broader set of skills to respond to present-day challenges.

From Darwin we learned that species that thrive are those capable of adapting to their environments. In the educational context, we suggest that transformative leaders who integrate into their work the four approaches outlined here will have a distinct advantage over more traditionally prepared leaders because they will be better able to adapt their leadership to a world that has become deeply interdependent, fragile, and compacted. They will be able to debunk deficit logic, forge transformative intergroup relations, establish local and global foci in curriculum and instruction, and integrate academic and applied preparation for students.

Above all, transformative leaders must understand how current "equity" policies are based on a very narrow conception of achievement. Instead, transformative leaders advance a twin approach of adequacy and equity, knowing that if the latter is to be achieved, the former must be present as well.

Notes

1. Some parts of this chapter were inspired by an in-progress piece written by Gilberto Arriaza and Arlando Smith.
2. The European-origin immigration to North America was multiethnic; when European ethnic groups converged in North America with indigenous peoples, and later with Africans imported as slaves "racial" differences were invoked to create and maintain hierarchical power relations in which the European ethnic groups were located at the top of the hierarchy. However, the lines that separate "races" are socially constructed; nature and biology do not provide any evidence of separate human races (Mukhopadhyay, Henze, & Moses, 2007). The term *multiracial* as used here invokes a socially constructed distinction rather than a biological one.
3. The history of eugenics has been widely documented. A good source is the Harvard "Facing History and Ourselves Project" (e.g., see Stoskpopf, 2002).

References

Appadurai, A. (1990). Disjunctures and difference in the global cultural economy. In M. Featherstone (Ed.), *Global culture: Nationalism, globalization, and modernity* (pp. 295–310). London: Sage.

Apple, M. (1995). *Education and power.* New York: Routledge.

Apple, M., & Beane, J. (1995). *Democratic schools.* New York: Penguin Books.

Arriaza, G. (2004). Changing schools for good: A study of school culture and systems. Melbourne, Australia. *Education and Society, 22*(2), 5–21.

ACTE (Association for Career and Technical Education) (n.d.). Fact sheet. Research demonstrates the value of career and technical education. Retrieved March 16, 2001 from: www.actonline.org/content.aspx?id=9452

Auerbach, A., & Hassett, K. A. (2002). Horizontal equity: A new measure of horizontal equity. *American Economic Journal, 92*(4), 1116–1125.

Banks, J., & Banks, C. M. (Eds.) (2007). *Multicultural education: Issues and perspectives* (6th ed.). Boston: Allyn & Bacon.

Barber, B. (1984). *Strong democracy: Participatory politics for a new age.* Berkeley: University of California Press.

Berne, R., & Stiefel, L. (1999). Concepts of school finance equity: 1970 to the present. In National Research Council, *Equity and adequacy in education finance. Issues and perspectives* (pp. 14–33). Washington, DC: National Academy Press.

Briscoe, F., Arriaza, G., & Henze, R. (2009). *The power of talk: How words change our lives.* Thousand Oaks, CA: Corwin Press.

Brown, K. M. (2005). Pivotal points: History, development and promise of the principalship. In F. W. English (Ed.), *The Sage handbook of educational leadership: Advances in theory, research and practice.* Thousand Oaks, CA: Sage.

Callahan, R. E. (1962). *Education and the cult of efficiency: A study of the social forces that have shaped the administration of public schools.* Chicago: University of Chicago Press.

Castelfranchi, C., & Conte, R. (1995). *Cognitive and social action.* London: Routledge.

Castellano, M., Stringfield, S., & Stone, J. R. (2003). Secondary career and technical education and comprehensive school reform: Implications for research and practice. *Review of Educational Research, 73*(2), 231–272.

Cubberley, E. P. (1916). *Public school administration.* Palo Alto, CA: Leland Standford Junior University.

Davis, K. A., Bazzi, S., Cho, H., Ishida, M., & Soria, J. (2005). It's our kuleana: A critical participatory approach to language minority education. In L. Pease-Alvarez & S. Schecter (Eds.), *Learning, teaching, and community: Contributions of situated and participatory approaches to educational innovation* (pp. 3–26). Mahwah, NJ: Erlbaum.

Delpit, L. (1995). *Other people's children: Cultural conflict in the classroom.* New York: New Press.

Dewey, J. (1916). *Democracy and education: An introduction to the philosophy of education.* New York: Macmillan.

Duncan-Andrade, J. M. R., & Morrell, E. (2008). *The art of critical pedagogy: Possibilities for moving from theory to practice in urban schools.* New York: Peter Lang.

Erickson, F. D., & Schultz, J. (1982). *The counselor as gatekeeper: Social interaction in interviews.* New York: Academic Press.

Giddens, A. (2005). The constitution of society. Outline of the theory of structuration: Elements of the theory of structuration. In G. Spiegel (Ed.), *Historical writing after the linguistic turn.* New York: Routledge.

González, N., Moll, L., & Amanti, C. (2005). *Funds of knowledge: Theorizing practice in households, communities, and classrooms.* Mahwah, NJ: Erlbaum.

Griffith, M. (2005). School finance litigation and beyond. *Project of school finance adequacy report for the Education Commission of the States (ECS).* Denver, CO: ECS Publications.

Habermas, J. (1987). *The theory of communicative action. Lifeworld and system: A critique of functionalist reason.* Boston: Beacon Press.

Henze, R., Katz, A. M., Norte, E., Sather, S., & Walker, E. (2002). *Leading for diversity: How school leaders promote positive interethnic relations.* Thousand Oaks, CA: Corwin Press.

Herrnstein, R. J., & Murray. C. A. (1994). *The bell curve.* New York: Free Press.

Kaye, J. (2003). *Campaign for fiscal equity inc., et al.* v. *State of New York, et al.,* Court decision no. 74. New York.

Keigwin, C. A. (1930). Origin of equity. *Georgetown University Law Journal, 18*(3), 215–240.

Kluger, R. (1977) *Simple justice: A history of Brown v. Board of Education.* New York: Random House.

Knight, E. O., Donohue, J., & Knight, P. (2008). The fourth year of CTE and academic integration. *Techniques, 83*(8), 22–25.

Kozol, J. (1991). *Savage inequalities: Children in America's schools.* New York: Crown.

Kumaravadivelu, B. (2008). *Cultural globalization and language teaching.* New Haven, CT: Yale University Press.

Larsen-Freeman, D., & Freeman, D. (2008). Language moves: The place of "foreign" languages in classroom teaching and learning. *Review of Research in Education, 32*(1), 147–186.

Lee, E. (1998). Anti-racist education: Pulling together to close the gaps. In E. Lee, D. Menkart, & M. Okazawa-Rey (Eds.), *Beyond heroes and holidays. A practical guide to K–12 anti-racist, multicultural education and staff development* (pp. 26–34). Washington, DC: Network of Educators on the Americas.

Legal Information Institute (2005). Cornell University Law School. Retrieved December 27, 2005 from: www.law.cornell.edu/wex/index.php/Equity

Lieberson, S. (1980). *A piece of the pie. Blacks and White immigrants since 1980.* Los Angeles: University of California Press.

Lindsay, R. B., Robins, K. N., & Terrell, R. D. (1999). *Cultural proficiency: A manual for school leaders.* Thousand Oaks, CA: Corwin Press.

Livingstone, D. W. (2004). *The education-jobs gap: Underemployment or economic democracy?* Toronto: University of Toronto Press.

Luke, A. (2004). Teaching after the market: From commodity to cosmopolitan. *Teachers College Record, 106*(7), 1422–1443.

Meier, D. (2002). *In schools we trust. Creating communities of learning in an era of testing and standardization.* Boston: Beacon Press.

Michelli, N. M., & Keiser, D. L. (2005). *Education for democracy and social justice.* New York: Routledge.

Minorini, P., & Sugarman, S. D. (1999). School finance litigation in the name of educational equity: Its evolution, impact and future. In H. Ladd, R. Chalk, & J. Hansen (Eds.), *Equity and adequacy in education finance. Issues and perspectives* (pp. 34–71). Washington, DC: National Academy Press.

Mukhopadhyay, C. C., Henze, R., & Moses, Y. T. (2007). *How real is race?* Lanham, MD: Rowman & Littlefield.

Nasaw, D. (1979). *Schooled to order: A social history of public schooling the United States.* New York: Oxford University Press.

National Access Network (2005). Litigation: Electronic publications of Teachers College, Columbia University. Retrieved May 16, 2011 from: www.schoolfunding.info/litigation/litigration.php3

Oakes, J. (1994). Tracking, inequality and the rhetoric of reform. Why schools don't change. In H. S. Shapiro & D. E. Purpel (Eds.), *Critical social issues in American education* (pp. 127–148). Mahwah, NJ: Erlbaum.

Padilla, A. M. (1976). Competent communities: A critical analysis of theories and public policy. Paper delivered at the Annual Community-Clinical Workshop, Lanham, MD.

Parsons, T., & Shils, E. A. (2001). *Toward a general theory of action. Theoretical foundations for the social sciences.* Cambridge, MA: Transaction Publishers.

Picus, L., & Blair. L. (2004). School finance adequacy: The state role. In L. Smith-Hansen (Ed.), *Insights.* Austin, TX: Southwest Educational Development Laboratory. Retrieved April 17, 2008 from: www.sedl.org/policy/insights/n16/insights16.pdf

Random House Unabridged Dictionary (1983). New York: Random House.

Simon, G. K. (2003). *Moral questions in the classroom: How to get kids to think deeply about real life and their schoolwork.* New Haven, CT: Yale University Press.

Sizer, T. R. (1992) *Horace's school: Redesigning the American high school.* Boston: Houghton Mifflin.

Steger, M. (2003). *Globalization: A very short introduction.* Oxford: Oxford University Press.

Stone, J. R. (2000). Editor's notes. *Journal of Vocational Education Research, 25,* 85–91.

Stoskpopf, A. (2002). *Race and membership in American history: Teaching guide.* Facing History and Ourselves. Retrieved May 16, 2001 from: http://zinnedproject.org/posts/582).

Supreme Court of Florida (2006). Opinion, case no. SC04-2323. *John Ellis "Jeb" Bush, etc., et al., appellants v. Ruth D. Holmes, et al., appellees.*

Tatum, B. D. (1997). *Why are all the black kids sitting together in the cafeteria? And other conversations about race.* New York: Basic Books.

Tatum, B. D. (2001). Which way do we go? Leading for diversity in the new frontier. *Journal of Negro Education, 68*(4), 550–554.

Tyack, D. B. (1974). *The one best system: A history of American urban education.* Cambridge, MA: Harvard University Press.

Taylor, F. W. (1911). *The principles of scientific management.* New York: Harper & Brothers.

Valdez, G. (1996). *Con respeto: Bridging the distances between culturally diverse families and schools.* New York: Teachers College Press.

11

System Leadership

A Response to the Challenges Facing Urban Schools in England[1]

Elpida Ahtaridou and David Hopkins

Schools in urban areas have been a concern in England for many years. These concerns were raised as educational performance in areas of social disadvantage was found to be lagging behind that of the national average. In particular, there were great disparities that were more prevalent in inner city schools (Smith, 1996, p. 40). In 1993, the Office for Standards in Education (Ofsted), the body responsible for education standards in English schools, in its influential report *Access and Achievement in Urban Education*, indicated the scale of the problem. Ofsted clearly stated that the residents of disadvantaged urban areas who took part in its survey were poorly served by the education system (Ofsted, 1993, p. 6).

In 2001 the then Labour government introduced a range of initiatives to support improvement in these schools, with very positive results. A key factor contributing to such improvement was the emphasis on leadership development. This chapter focuses on an emerging form of leadership, called system leadership, which, in our view, is the most promising strategy for supporting improvement in all urban schools. To clarify this strategy, in this chapter we:

- briefly discuss the challenges of urban leadership in England;
- outline recent improvements in urban schools;
- identify the leadership initiatives that have brought about improvement;
- define system leadership; and
- examine the internal and external aspects of system leadership.

Challenges Facing Urban Leaders in England

Recent work in the field of urban education advises us against making simple unidimensional distinctions in attempting to define it (Martin, McCann, & Purcell, 2003). Complex analyses are now emerging that distinguish between urban and nonurban education in terms of geography, economics, deprivation, ethnicities, and cultures, as well as in relation to areas of public policy such as housing, transport, health, and labor market policy (Dyson, 2003).

In an attempt to include such complexities, we can identify three broad categories of challenges that these schools face, much of the time simultaneously:

1. *Challenges arising from the children they serve.* In England, there are schools that have 35% of their pupils receiving free school meals (FSM) used as a proxy for deprivation (Ofsted, 2000). These schools also have very low levels of attainment among pupils on entry. This is explained by the high proportion of students from nonnative ethnic groups, many of whom have English as their second language. In some cases the low levels of attainment on entry are also explained by high levels of pupil mobility. For example:

   - Ofsted has highlighted that 95% of schools with high proportions of pupils on FSM are in urban areas (2000, p. 5).
   - In 2004, the percentage of pupils in primary and secondary schools eligible for FSM in the main urban areas ranged from 20% to 27%, when for the rest of England this figure was 13%.
   - In terms of ethnicity, in Greater London, more than 45% of pupils are other than White. This figure is 20% in all other metropolitan cities and less than 10% in the rest of England.
   - For 35% of primary and secondary pupils in Greater London and 20% of those in the West Midlands, English is believed not to be their first language, compared with just 5% for the rest of England (Department for Education and Skills, 2004).

2. *Challenges arising from the "neighborhood" they serve.* Often these schools serve many children from low-income families living in marginal housing and with little experience of education beyond compulsory early schooling. They also often serve communities where there are aspects of deprivation such as poor facilities, poor health, dislocation and disaffection, and high levels of drug and alcohol abuse (Ofsted, 2000).

3. *Challenges arising from within the school.* Such challenges include poor management, budget deficits, rundown buildings, staffing problems, low levels of pupil attainment on entry (as already noted), behavior problems, high rates of unauthorized absence and pupil exclusion, low levels of parental involvement, falling enrollment and high pupil turnover, and a lack of public confidence in the schools (NCSL, 2003).

In this context, urban leaders in England must ensure the progression of the challenging groups of students they serve, make certain that good teaching and learning is consistently employed, integrate a sound grasp of basic knowledge and skills within a broad and balanced curriculum, manage behavior and attendance, strategically manage resources and the environment, build the school as a professional learning community, and develop partnerships beyond the school to encourage parental support for learning and new learning opportunities.

In addition, a set of specific contemporary challenges face urban leaders stemming from broader social change and government-led reform (Price Waterhouse Coopers, 2007). They include the following:

- *The synergy between standards and welfare.* School leaders are asked to retain a rigorous focus on raising pupil attainment while at the same time leading improvements that enable children to be safe, healthy, enjoy and achieve, and make a positive contribution to society. The "welfare/Every Child Matters (ECM) agenda" includes the development of extended provision (including before- and after-school clubs) as well as participating in the organization of multiagency children's services. This stems partly from concerns for child safety and protection, but is also an important strand in national efforts to tackle the pervasive impact of social class on educational achievement.
- *The drive to increasingly personalize the learning experience of students.* This demands, among other things, that leaders embed assessment for learning and the use of data on pupil

achievement as whole-school professional practices in the design of learning experiences that really stretch individual pupils. In both cases school leaders will also be expected to work collaboratively to deliver the entitlement for every young person to study the new diploma qualifications by 2013. This collaborative effort will involve working with not just other schools but also with the further education sector, employers, and work-based learning providers. School leaders are further expected to recognize the importance of extended schools in delivering personalization. The challenges for improvement are both technical and cultural.

- *Implementation of England's national workforce agreement.* This agreement underpins reform, calling for the shifting of administrative tasks from teachers to support staff, limiting requirements on teachers to cover absent colleagues, and helping teachers to achieve an overall reduction in workload and a reasonable work–life balance. The challenge for urban leaders is to ensure not only that this change does not undermine stability but also that a wider range of school staff is effectively deployed to support student progression and attainment.

- *The impetus for school diversity and parental choice.* Particularly in the secondary phase, schools have been encouraged to diversify away from a common comprehensive school model toward a wide range of school types in terms of both curriculum (specialist status) and governance (trusts and federations). This has been coupled with an explicit move to provide parents with greater choice in the schools to which they send their children, in terms of both admissions procedures and the construction of new schools (academies). Both the diversity and choice agendas are seen by government as drivers of improvement. The challenge for school leaders is to make sense of these initiatives at the local level, engage with the broader system in a meaningful way while also protect their students, staff, and school ethos from uncoordinated or even unnecessary change (Higham, Hopkins, & Ahtaridou, 2007, pp. 24–25).

Improvements in Urban Schools in England

Ten years on from the 1993 "damning" Ofsted report on the quality of education in urban disadvantaged areas, significant improvements have been recorded. In 2003 the report, entitled *Access and Achievement in Urban Education: 10 Years On,* stated that urban schools had benefited from both general strategies for school improvement and specific initiatives in urban areas, and that they were improving generally. In 2006, Ofsted, in *Improvements in London Schools 2000–2006,* found London schools to have improved dramatically. For secondary schools, it noted that the depressing picture of poor pupil results in 2001 had been turned around and that at key stages 3 and 4 standards were rising faster than in schools nationally.

Similar findings were reported for other primary and secondary urban areas in terms of both quality and of performance. Although data on improvements in London and other urban areas are sporadic and not always compared nationally, we attempt to bring together some of the evidence that is publicly available below.

Quality

- In 2005–2006, Ofsted judged 59% of secondary schools and 64% of primary schools in London to be good or better in their overall performance than 49% and 59%, respectively, of schools nationally.
- 73% of London schools were judged as having leadership and management that was as good as or better than that of 51% and 58%, respectively, of all other schools in England.

- 57% of London schools were judged as having a quality of teaching and learning that was as good as or better than that of all other schools in England.
- Fewer London schools are in the lowest 25% of all schools, which is the national floor target.

Academic Achievement

- Figure 11.1 shows the gradual improvement of urban schools in England from 1997 to 2004.
- From 2006 to 2009, London's publicly supported secondary schools have outperformed the national average with 47.9% of students obtaining 5+ A*–C at GCSE, including English and math, compared with the national average of 45.9%.
- From 2007 until end of 2009, London continued to surpass the national average with 60.9% of students achieving 5+ A*–C GCSEs in all subjects, compared with 60.1% for England as a whole.
- In 2009, almost one in three maintained schools in London secured outstanding results (over 70% 5+ A*–C GCSEs in any subject). In 1997, only 36 schools reached this level (Department for Children, Schools and Families, 2008).

However, what is particularly striking is the comparatively better progress of students on FSM, especially in Inner London. In terms of progress, schools with high FSM in inner London appear to be overcoming the expected gap between pupils from advantaged versus disadvantaged families. Progress has also been recorded for pupils who have English as a second language and for ethnic minority students, whose performance has consistently been poorer—for example, immigrants of Irish, Gypsy/Romani, Black African, Black Caribbean, or Pakistani descent. Although progress has been noted for these groups, they still cause concern. In the most deprived urban areas, 52.3% of pupils achieved 5 or more A*–C grades at GCSE and equivalent in 2006–2007, compared with 69.1% of pupils attending schools in the least deprived urban areas (Department for Children, Schools and Families, 2008).

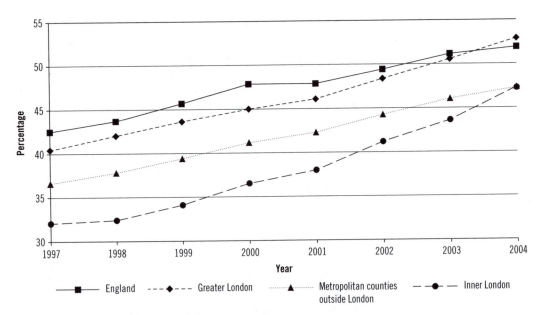

Figure 11.1 Percentage of 15-year-olds Achieving 5+ GCSEs at Grades A*–C

The improvements described above have resulted from a number of policy initiatives introduced to support schools specifically in urban areas, alongside educational reforms aiming to improve standards and the school system as a whole under the school improvement umbrella. A number of these had a specific focus on improving the quality of leadership and supporting collaboration between schools. We explore these measures in the next section.

Leadership Strategies to Improve Urban Schools in England

In 2001 urban education was given considerable attention by the Labour government, which introduced a number of initiatives designed to deal with the many challenges facing urban schools, especially in secondary education. These included the Education Action Zones, the subsequent Excellence in Cities program, and, in 2003, the London Challenge. In 2008, based on its success, the London Challenge was expanded into the City Challenge, involving London, the Black Country, and Manchester.

A key focus of these initiatives was improving the quality of leadership, especially among those urban schools where success was difficult to achieve and sustain, the Key to Success schools. The City Challenge Leadership Strategies, comprising a number of programs for secondary and primary schools in the three urban areas, which were delivered through the National College of School Leadership. These programs, among others, included:

- *Leading from the middle,* a course addressing the weaknesses in departmental and head-of-year posts in schools, which Ofsted had identified as a particular problem in London.
- The employment of *Consultant Leaders,* with primary and secondary leaders who were currently or recently in posts having shown a proven record of raising attainment in their own schools. This was probably one of the most effective City Challenge leadership initiatives (Hill & Matthews, 2008).
- Personalized *mentoring and coaching* by an established and successful head teacher for newly appointed head teachers and those who had been transferred to a new school.
- *Local and National Leaders of Education* (LLEs and NLEs), a core offer to Key to Success schools. This involves consultancy support from the best primary and secondary head teachers—heads of schools rated by Ofsted as outstanding or very good, the two highest Ofsted performance grades, including some recently retired heads. Early evidence of their impact also shows positive results (Hill & Matthews, 2008).
- *Improving Schools Programme* leadership pilot groups, an extension of the successful Improving Schools Programme (ISP) leadership pilot run in 2007 in other areas of England, which was extended to 90 schools in London. The program involves head teachers who have used the ISP successfully to raise standards in their own schools and have led a triangle of schools with a shared focus on improvements in whole-school planning and individual pupil progress alongside development of the core curriculum and the learning environment.
- The *Good to Great* programme, providing deputy head teachers in outstanding schools with the opportunity to undertake action research for six weeks in a more challenging school. Half of their time is spent teaching in either Year 2 or Year 6, targeting an underachieving group in English or mathematics. They then develop a personalized curriculum or teaching style for this group, which can be disseminated more widely throughout the school. The other half of their time is spent in gaining management experience.
- The *Teaching Schools* programme, especially for secondary schools, with schools being designated as Teaching Schools that offer a range of leadership and teaching and learning programs for teachers. These are leaders in innovation and best practice.

- *Subject specialist support*, focusing on heads of departments and other middle leaders and their teachers to improve teaching and learning in their subject areas by providing them with a mentor from a partner school.

What is striking about the examples outlined above, is the commitment of these school leaders to work and lead beyond an individual school. This collaboration is at the forefront of leadership innovation. The General Secretary of the Association of School and College Leaders in England, in his address to the National Conference of the Specialist Schools and Academies Trust (Dunford, 2005, p. 3), argued that:

> The greatest challenge on our leadership journey is how we can bring about system improvement. How can we contribute to the raising of standards, not only in our own school, but in others and colleges too? What types of leaders are needed for this task? What style of leadership is required if we are to achieve the sea change in performance that is demanded of us?

This implies a significantly more substantive engagement with other schools in order to bring about system transformation. It is being termed system leadership, which in our view it is the most effective measure for improving urban schools. Thus, it is to system leadership that we turn our attention in the following sections.

System Leadership: The Concept and the Model

"System leaders" are those head teachers who are willing to shoulder system leadership roles—who care about and work for the success of other schools as well as their own. In England there appears to be an emerging cadre of these head teachers who stand in contrast to the competitive ethic of headship that was so prevalent in the nineties. It is these educators who, by their own efforts and commitment, are beginning to transform the nature of leadership and educational improvement in this country. Interestingly, there is also evidence of this role emerging in other leading educational systems in Europe, North America, and Australia (Pont, Nusche, & Hopkins, 2008).

The proposition is simple: to improve urban schools—and all schools for that matter—policy and practice must focus on system improvement. This means that a school head must be almost as concerned about the success of other schools as he or she is about his or her own school. Sustained improvement of schools is not possible unless the whole system is moving forward.

The first thing to say is that system leadership, as Michael Fullan (2003, 2005) has argued, is imbued with moral purpose. Without that, there would not be the passion to proceed or the encouragement for others to follow. In English urban schools, for example—where the regularities of improvement in teaching and learning are still not well understood, where deprivation is still too good a predictor of educational success, and where the goal is for all urban schools to improve—the leadership challenge is surely a systemic one. This perspective offers a broader appreciation of what is meant by the moral purpose of system leadership.

We would argue that system leaders express their moral purpose in the following ways:

- By measuring their success in terms of improved student learning and increased achievement and by striving to raise both the bar and narrow the gap.
- By being fundamentally committed to the improvement of teaching and learning. They engage deeply with the organization of teaching, learning, and curriculum and assessment in order to ensure that learning is personalized for all their students.
- By developing their schools as personal and professional learning communities, with relationships built across and beyond each school to provide a range of learning experiences and professional development opportunities.

- By striving for equity and inclusion through acting on context and culture. This is not just about eradicating poverty, as important as that is. It is also about giving communities a sense of worth and empowerment.
- By realizing in a deep way that the classroom, school, and system levels all affect one another. Crucially, these leaders understand that in order to change the larger system, you have to engage with it in a meaningful way.

Although this degree of clarity is not necessarily obvious in the behavior and practice of every head teacher, these aspirations are increasingly becoming part of the conventional wisdom of our best global education leaders (Hopkins, 2007).

Building on these key capabilities and combining them with the range of identified roles, it is possible to offer a model of system leadership practice that emerges inductively from the actions of our sample leaders. This is set out in Figure 11.2. The model exhibits a logic that flows from the inside out. At the center, leaders driven by a moral purpose related to the enhancement of student learning seek to empower teachers and others to make schools a critical force for improving communities. This is premised on the argument that sustainable education development requires education leaders who are willing to shoulder broader leadership roles, who care about and work for the success of other schools as well as their own.

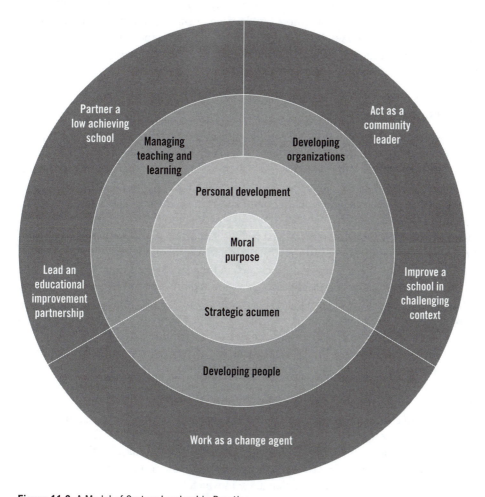

Figure 11.2 A Model of System Leadership Practice

It is also clear from research that system leaders share a characteristic set of behaviors and skills. As illustrated in the second inner ring of the diagram, these are of two types. First, system leaders engage in "personal development," usually informally through benchmarking themselves against their peers and developing their skill base in response to the context in which they find themselves working. Second, all the system leaders we have studied have a strategic capability: they are able to translate their vision or moral purpose into operational principles that have tangible outcomes.

As denoted in the third ring of the model, the moral purpose, personal qualities, and strategic capacity of the system leader find focus in three domains of the school detailed above—managing the teaching and learning process, developing people, and developing organizations.

Finally, although there is a growing number of outstanding leaders who exemplify these qualities and determinations, they are not necessarily "system leaders." A system leader needs not only these aspirations and capabilities but also must, as seen in the outer ring of the model, work to change other contexts by engaging with the wider system in a meaningful way. We have included in the outer ring the range of roles that have been identified: improving other schools, sharing curriculum innovations, empowering communities, and/or leading partnerships committed to enabling all schools to move forward (Higham & Hopkins, 2007).

The model represents a powerful combination of practices, giving us a glimpse of leadership in a new educational landscape. Realizing that landscape, however, may also require a bigger shift within the broader education system. We have attempted to describe the nature of this shift in detail elsewhere (Higham, Hopkins, & Matthews, 2009). Taking into consideration the limited space provided for this chapter, the next sections focus briefly on the internal and external aspects of system leadership.

Internal Aspects of System Leadership

A good way of focusing on the internal aspects of system leadership is to draw on Leithwood and Riehl's (2005) conceptualization of the central tenets of successful school leadership. These authors summarize this as the following four central domains: setting direction, managing teaching and learning, developing people, and developing the organization. Table 11.1 sets out these practices. This analysis reinforces the argument that the enhancement of learning and teaching is a key priority for school leadership.

In any discussion of the "internal system leadership," it is important to realize that at the heart of personalized learning is its impact not just on test scores and examination results but also on the students' learning capability. If conditions can be created in the school where the teacher can teach the students how to learn at the same time as helping them to acquire curriculum content, then the twin goals of learning and achievement can both be met. This point was made in *Models of Learning – Tools for Teaching* (Joyce, Calhoun, & Hopkins, 2002), where it was argued that it is the teacher's task not only to "teach" but also to create powerful contexts for learning.

This idea and the essence of personalized learning were expressed in this way: "Learning experiences are composed of content, process and social climate. As teachers we create for and with our children opportunities to explore and build important areas of knowledge, develop powerful tools for learning, and live in humanising social conditions" (Joyce et al., 2002, p. 7).

It is the integration of curriculum content, teaching, and learning strategies and the school culture that enhance self-confidence and provide the parameters for the work of skilled teachers. But there is a significant barrier to progress in this area: despite the contemporary emphasis on the importance of classroom practice, the language or discourse about teaching remains in general at a restricted level. There is a need for a far more elaborate language in which to talk about teaching and more sophisticated frameworks against which to reflect on practice. Even in those instances where more

Table 11.1 A Conceptualization of the Capabilities of School Leaders

Core practices	Key system leadership components
Setting direction	Total commitment to enable every learner to reach his or her potential with a strategic vision that extends into the future and brings immediacy to the delivery of improvements for students.
	The ability to translate vision into whole-school programs that extend the impact of pedagogic and curricular developments into other classrooms, departments, and schools.
Managing teaching and learning	Ensuring that every child is inspired and challenged through an appropriate curriculum and a repertoire of teaching styles and skills that support personalized learning.
	Developing a high degree of clarity about and consistency of teaching quality both to create the regularities of practice that sustain improvement and to enable sharing of best practice and innovation across the system.
Developing people	Enabling students to become more active learners, develop thinking and learning skills, and take greater responsibility for their own learning. Involving parents and the community to minimize the impact of challenging circumstances on expectations and achievement.
	Developing schools as professional learning communities, with relationships built and fostered across and beyond schools to provide a range of learning experiences and professional development opportunities for staff.
Developing the organization	Creating an evidence-based school, with decisions effectively informed by student data, with self-evaluation and external support used to seek out approaches to school improvement that are most appropriate to specific contextual needs and that build on other examples and practices in the system.
	Extending an organization's vision of learning to involve networks of schools collaborating to build, for instance, curriculum diversity, professional support, extended and welfare services, and high expectations. In so doing, building a school's capacity to support wider system leadership roles.

Source: Based on Leithwood and Riehl (2005)

precision of language is achieved, there are few operational definitions against which teachers can assess their own practice and thereby develop and expand their range of classroom practices. The key challenge for urban leaders here is to ensure that quality teaching and learning is underpinned by more elaborate and explicit frameworks for learning and teaching.

Space precludes more discussion on these frameworks, but in *School improvement for real* (Hopkins, 2001), a framework for thinking about teaching and learning is introduced. Its elements are illustrated in Figure 11.3; these, interestingly, are often regarded as being contradictory rather than complementary.

Let us briefly discuss each of these elements in turn.

- *Teaching skills.* These include the everyday classroom management skills and behaviors such as content coverage, engaged time (i.e., students learn more when they are on task for a high proportion of class time), active teaching, structuring information, wait time, and effective questioning. (See Creemers (1994) for a summary of teaching effects that is replete with cues and tactics necessary for effective teaching.)

- *Teaching relationships.* These are less technical and more related to the teacher's commitment to his or her students and belief in the power of high expectations. A supportive, rigorous, and optimistic learning environment is fundamental for high levels of student achievement. A key aspect of teaching is the teacher's ability to generate and sustain an authentic relationship with the students.

- *Teacher reflection.* This refers to the practice of teachers of combining the two elements above through a process of reflection to create an individual style. It is through reflection that the teacher harmonizes, integrates, and transcends the necessary classroom management skills and the personal aspects of teaching into a strategy that has meaning for students.

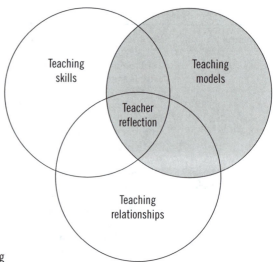

Figure 11.3 A Framework for Thinking about Teaching

It is the integration of these three elements into a distinctive individual approach that most people would regard as being the definition of a very good teacher. But, in our view, this is a necessary but not a sufficient condition for the quality of teaching required to personalize learning. What is also required is a focus on the models of teaching that simultaneously define the nature of the content, the learning strategies, and the arrangements for social interaction that create the learning environments of students.

Models of teaching are also models of learning. How teaching is conducted has a large impact on students' abilities to educate themselves. Each model has its own core purpose that relates not only to how to organise teaching, but also to ways of learning.

The purpose of this discussion of teaching for personalizing learning is to emphasize how important this focus is for urban leadership committed to ensuring that all students reach their potential and that their school is on the path to greatness. Although the impact of leadership on student achievement and school effectiveness has been acknowledged for some time, it is only recently that we have begun to understand more fully the fine-grained nature of that relationship. A reasonably elegant summary of this evidence is as follows:

- The leadership develops a narrative for improvement.
- The leadership is highly focused on improving the quality of teaching and learning (and student welfare).
- The leadership explicitly organizes the school for improvement.
- The leadership creates consistency (of the systems spread across school) and continuity (of the systems over time).
- The leadership creates internal accountability and reciprocity.
- The leadership works to change context as a key component of the improvement strategy.
- The leadership seeks to achieve clarity (of the systems established).

There are two relatively new features to this profile. The first is the emphasis on narrative and its impact on both strategy and culture. It is student learning that is the central focus of the narrative, which then presents a series of complex and interacting initiatives within a unifying story around the image of a journey. This is strategic insofar as it integrates a wide variety of initiatives and projects forward and cultural insofar as it speaks both to the individual and collective contribution and the moral purpose of schooling.

The second new feature is the emphasis on "systems" and the transferability and sustainability of best practice. It is here where we find the link with the external aspects of system leadership, and it is to this that we now turn.

External Aspects of System Leadership

As mentioned above, the emphasis on systems and the transferability and sustainability of best practice is where we find the link with the external aspects of system leadership. The characteristics of the "effective school" have been known for some time, but at a rather high level of generalization. Again, we have recently acquired a more textured understanding of what these effective practices look like and how they are combined into a "whole-school design."

We now are at a point when all of the key practices can be presented in an implementable and action-oriented form. It is these practices that provide the currency of interaction between system leaders as they increasingly engage with schools other than their own. It is the exchange of excellent and increasingly precise practices for the personalization of learning that is becoming the stock in trade of the new breed of system leaders and that informs the roles that they are adopting.

We have recently identified a variety of system leader roles that are emerging in England and are consistent with our moral purpose. At present these are as follows (Higham et al., 2009):

- Developing and leading a successful educational improvement partnership between several schools, often focusing on a set of specific themes that have significant and clear outcomes reaching beyond the capacity of any one single institution.
- Choosing to lead and improve a school in extremely challenging circumstances and change local contexts by building a culture of success and then sustaining once low-achieving schools as high-valued-added institutions.
- Partnering with another school facing difficulties and improving it, either as an executive head of a federation or as the leader of a more informal improvement arrangement.
- Acting as a community leader to broker and shape partnerships and/or networks of wider relationships across local communities to support children's welfare and potential, often through multiagency work.
- Working as a change agent or expert leader within the system, identifying best classroom practice and transferring it to support improvement in other schools.

No doubt these roles will expand and mature over time, but what is significant about them is that they have evolved in response to the adaptive challenge of systematic change. If we want to transform systems as well as schools, then the knowledge encapsulated in the previous discussion is necessary but not sufficient. It is necessary, indeed essential, because these practices are the critical currency of urban school improvement. This is inevitably the only focus of the conversations of system leaders, but it must be coupled with a strategy for system-wide change. It is important to realize, however, that this aspiration of system-wide transformation, facilitated by the degree of segmentation existing in the system, holds only when certain conditions are in place. There are two crucial aspects to this:

1. There is increased clarity on the nature of intervention and support for schools at each phase of the performance cycle.
2. Schools at each phase are clear as to the most productive ways in which to collaborate in order to capitalize on the diversity within the system.

To understand the dynamics involved, it is helpful to discuss the different categories of secondary schools in England—approximately a total of 3,313. The categories relate to the schools' effectiveness in terms of student achievement at age 16, and include:

1. *Leading schools (possibly 10% of secondary schools).* These are the highest performing schools that also have the capacity to lead others. Their route to further improvement and contribution to the system comes in at least two forms: first, becoming leading practitioners by disseminating best practice and networking and, second, by working more formally and systematically with lower performing schools through some "federation" arrangement to improve the partner school's performance.

2. *Succeeding, self-improving schools (possibly 20% of secondary schools).* These are schools that have consistently above-average levels of value added and that exhibit aspects of best practice that will benefit the system through further dissemination. Their route to further improvement and contribution to the system comes in networking their best practice in local networks using their leading teachers to mentor in other schools and to take students from local schools into their areas of specialization.

3. *Succeeding schools but with significant areas of underperformance (possibly 20% of secondary schools).* These schools, although successful on the basis of published criteria, have unacceptable numbers of underperforming teachers or departments who are masked by the averaging out of published results. Their route to further improvement and contribution to the system comes by contributing as above to other schools from their areas of strength and being the recipients of such support in their weaker areas.

4. *Underperforming schools (possibly 25% of secondary schools).* Defined as those secondary schools in the lowest value-added quartile of their distribution who may have adequate or good headline results but are consistently failing to add value to the progress of their students. Their route to further improvement is to use the data discussed with the school improvement partner (SIP) as the basis for a plan to raise the standards of a whole school. They will need sustained consultancy in the early stages of an improvement process from a school with a similar intake but far higher value added, using a modified version of "federations intervention."

5. *Low-attaining schools (possibly 20% of secondary schools).* Defined as those secondary schools below the 30% A*–C GCSE floor target but with a capacity to improve. Their route to further improvement requires sustained support through some federation arrangement or involvement, consultancy support through the National Challenge, and possibly the application of an improvement grant.

6. *Failing schools (possibly 5% of secondary schools).* Defined as being well below the floor target and with little capacity to improve. At a minimum these schools will require intervention in the form of a "hard federation" or membership in the Intensive Support Programme. If these strategies are not successful in the short term, then closure, academy status—publicly funded schools free from local authority and national government control—or a schools competition is the only other answer if adequate provision for the students involved is to be sustained.

A summary of this "segmentation" approach is set out in Table 11.2. In the right-hand column is a basic taxonomy of schools based on the previous analysis. The number of categories and the terminology will vary from setting to setting, the crucial point being that not all schools are the same and each requires different forms of support. This is the focus of the second column, where a range of strategies for supporting schools at different phases of their development is briefly described. Again, these descriptions are grounded in the English context, but they do have a more universal applicability. There are three key points here:

1. One size does not fit all.
2. These different forms of intervention and support are increasingly being provided by schools themselves, rather than being imposed and delivered by some external agency. This

Table 11.2 The "Segmentation Approach" to School Improvement

Type of school	Key strategies: Responsive to context and need
Leading schools	Become leading practitioners
	Formal federation with lower-performing schools
Succeeding, self-improving schools	Regular local networking for school leaders
	Between-school curriculum development
Succeeding schools with internal variations	Consistency interventions such as Assessment for Learning
	Subject specialist support to particular departments
Underperforming schools	Linked school support for underperforming departments
	Underperforming pupil programs: "catch up"
Low-attaining schools	Formal support in federation structure
	Consultancy in core subjects and best practices
Failing schools	Intensive support program
	New provider, such as an academy

approach to system-wide transformation relies fundamentally on school-to-school support as the basis of the improvement strategy.

3. This process can continue to evolve in an ad hoc manner or it can be orchestrated by national organizations with strong local roots.

This approach to transformation requires a fair degree of boldness in setting system-level expectations and conditions. Three implications in particular must be grappled with:

1. All failing and underperforming (and potentially low-achieving) schools should have a leading school that works with all of them in either a formal grouping as a federation (where the leading school's principal or head assumes overall control and accountability) or in a more informal partnership. Evidence from existing federations, where the approach to replication described earlier was adopted, suggests that a national system of federations would be capable of delivering a sustainable step-by-step improvement in relatively short periods of time. For example, a number of federated schools have improved their five A*–Cs at GCSE from under 20% to over 50% in two years.

2. Schools should take greater responsibility for neighboring schools, so that the move toward networking encourages groups of schools to form collaborative arrangements outside of local control. This would be on the condition not only that these schools provide extended services for all students within a geographic area but also on the idea that there would be incentives for doing so. Encouraging local schools to work together will build capacity for continuous improvement at the local level.

3. The incentives for greater system-wide responsibility should include significantly enhanced funding for students most at risk so as to counter the predictive character of poverty noted earlier.

Beyond incentivizing local collaboratives, the potential effects of large-scale long-term reform include the following:

- A more even distribution of at-risk students and associated increases in standards, with more schools seeking to admit a larger proportion of at-risk students in order to increase their overall income.
- A significant reduction in "sink schools," even where at-risk students are concentrated, as there would be a much greater potential to respond to the socioeconomic challenges (for example, by paying more to attract the best teachers or by developing excellent parental involvement and outreach services).

- A rationalization of national and local agency functions and roles to allow the higher degree of national and regional coordination for this increasingly devolved system. At present there are too many national and local organizations acting in a competitive, uncoordinated, and capricious way.

To bring system leadership to scale, however, should be the ultimate goal. The three key drivers provide a core strategy for systemic improvement through building capacity while also raising standards of learning and achievement. It is system leadership, though, that adapts them to particular and individual school contexts. This is leadership that enables systemic reform to be both generic in terms of overall strategy and specific in adapting to individual and particular situations. It needs to be made clear, however, that, as was intimated earlier, for transformation system leadership needs to be reflected at three levels:

1. *System-wide leadership at the school level*, with, in essence, principals becoming almost as concerned about the success of other schools as they are about their own.
2. *System-wide leadership at the local/regional level*, with practical principles widely shared and used as a basis for local alignment with specific programs developed for the most at-risk groups.
3. *System-wide leadership at the national/state level*, with social justice, moral purpose, and a commitment to the success of every learner providing the focus for transformation and collaboration.

In conclusion, it is important to remember that the challenge of urban education has great moral depth. It addresses directly the learning needs of our most disadvantaged students and the professional growth of teachers. It also enhances the role of the school as an agent of social equity and change. This is why, as we imagine a new future for education, we require a new way of working capable of realizing a future where every school is a great one. It is here where, as we have argued in this chapter, system leadership comes into its own. The collective sharing of skills, expertise, and experience creates much richer and more sustainable opportunities for rigorous transformation than can ever be provided by isolated institutions. It is this approach that will eventually lead toward "every school a great school" as well as "the good society."

Note

1. This chapter was written before the May 2010 General Election in England. Thus, one must consider the policy narrative included in this chapter to be that of the previous Labour government.

References

Creemers, B. P. M. (1994). *The effective classroom.* London: Cassell.

Department for Children, Schools and Families (2008). GCSE and equivalent examination results in England 2006/07 (revised). Retrieved September 15, 2010 from: www.education.gov.uk/rsgateway/DB/SFR/s000768/index.shtml

Department for Education and Skills (2004). *London schools: Rising to the challenge.* Nottingham: DfES.

Dunford, J. (2005). Watering the plants: Leading schools and improving the system. Address to the National Conference of the Specialist Schools and Academies Trust.

Dyson, A. (2003). Inaugural Lecture. December 8. Faculty of Education, University of Manchester.

Fullan, M. (2003). *The moral imperative of school leadership.* London: Corwin Press.

Fullan, M. (2005). *Leadership and sustainability.* London: Corwin Press.

Higham, R., & Hopkins, D. (2007). System leadership: Mapping the landscape, *School Leadership and Management, 27*(2), 147–166.

Higham, R., Hopkins, D., & Ahtaridou, E. (2007). *Improving school leadership: Country background report for England.* London: Department for Children, Schools and Families/Organisation for Economic Co-operation and Development. Retrieved September 15, 2010 from: www.oecd.org/dataoecd/33/45/39279379.pdf.

Higham, R., Hopkins D., & Matthews, P. (2009). *System leadership in practice.* Milton Keynes: Open University Press.

Hill, R., & Matthews, P. (2008). *Schools leading schools: The power and potential of national leaders of education.* Nottingham: NCSL.

Hopkins, D. (2001). *School improvement for real.* London: RoutledgeFalmer.

Hopkins, D. (2007) *Every school a great school.* Maidenhead: Open University Press.

Joyce, B. R., Calhoun, E., & Hopkins, D. (2002). *Models of learning – tools for teaching* (2nd ed.). Buckingham: Open University Press.

Leithwood, K., & Riehl, C. (2005). What we know about successful school leadership. In W. Firestone & C. Riehl (Eds.), *A new agenda: Directions for research on educational leadership* (pp. 22–47). New York: Teachers College Press.

Martin, D., McCann, E., & Purcell, M. (2003). Space, scale, governance and representation: Contemporary geographical perspectives on urban politics and policy. *Journal of Urban Affairs, 25*(2), 113–121.

NCSL (National College for School Leadership) (2003). *A model of school leadership in challenging urban environments.* Nottingham: NCSL.

Ofsted (1993). *Access and achievement in urban education.* Retrieved September 2010 from: www.ofsted.gov.uk/Ofsted-home/Publications-and-research/Browse-all-by/Education/Leadership/Governance/Access-and-achievement-in-urban-education

Ofsted (2000). *Improving city schools,* London: Ofsted.

Ofsted (2003). *Access and achievement in urban education: 10 years on.* Retrieved September 15, 2010 from: www.ofsted.gov.uk/content/download/1464/10372/file/Access%20and%20achievement%20in%20urban%20education%20%20ten%20years %20on%20(PDF%20 format).pdf

Ofsted (2006). *Improvement in London schools 2000–2006.* HMI: 2509. London: Ofsted.

Pont, B., Nusche, D., & Hopkins, D. (Eds.) (2008). *Improving school leadership: Volume 2: Case studies on system leadership.* Paris: OECD Press/McGraw-Hill.

Price Waterhouse Coopers (2007). *Independent study into school leadership: Main report.* London: Department for Education and Skills.

Smith, G. (1996). Urban education: Current position and future possibilities. In M. Barber & R. Dann (Eds.), *Raising educational standards in inner cities: Practical initiatives in action.* London: Cassell.

III
Accountability

Demands for accountability are shaping the work of urban educational leaders at all levels. This section focuses on the implications and challenges of this enhanced focus on accountability and addresses accountability as a tool for organizational improvement.

12

Competing Accountability
Demands in Urban School Districts

David T. Conley

Urban schools in the United States serve multiple masters. More so than perhaps any other sector of public education in the United States, urban schools are the focal point for accountability demands and the proving grounds for new approaches to and methods of educational governance and accountability. Urban schools and the districts within which they are situated end up being a primary reference point for and drivers of state and federal accountability policies and practices. They are a source of tension between and among school boards, mayors, city councils, governors, state legislatures, and state and federal education agencies. The net effect of the diffuse yet constant pressure on urban school districts that emanates from the city, state, and federal levels has been to shape and distort their functioning and to lead to the rise of a variety of educational models, structures, and strategies intended to improve urban schooling and to make urban districts and schools more responsive to the demands and needs of policymakers and, theoretically, the communities these schools serve.

Evolution of Accountability Policy

Urban schools are subject to the same forces and trends in accountability policy that have affected all U.S. schools, particularly over the past 30 years. These forces and trends result from historical precedents and practices that are relatively unique to the United States with its history of decentralized educational governance (Conley, 2003b; Fuhrman, 1999). A brief overview of previous approaches to accountability is necessary to understand the current expectations that urban districts face.

Formal, extensive state and federal accountability systems that affect schools and schooling at the local level are relatively recent phenomena. In the United States, locally governed schools has meant that states generally, and the federal government, specifically, have kept out of the business of gauging school effectiveness (Conley, 2003b; Kirst, 2004). The expectation among policymakers and the public at large was that local citizens were best equipped to judge their schools and would enforce their will largely by voting for or against local education taxes and electing school board members who reflected local values and priorities (Conley, 2003b; Cuban, 2004; ECONorthwest & Center for Education Policy Research, 2004). One major policy assumption underlying this approach to accountability was that whoever paid for education had the final right to control it, and that, if local citizens were footing the bill, local school systems might decide to pursue distinctly local educational goals and have locally determined expectations for student and school performance, provided the schools abided by fiscal and safety regulations, and promoted basic civil conformity and comportment.

The basic way that states exercised a modicum of oversight was through fiscal accounting rules and accreditation processes (Cuban, 2004). The fiscal record-keeping requirements were meant to thwart fraud. The accreditation processes were designed largely to ensure a floor of consistency by means of an inventory of educational conditions. State education agencies or regional accreditation agencies appointed committees of educators to visit schools on a designated schedule and charged them with reviewing a wide variety of educational inputs, such as the number of books in the school library, the existence of binders containing all district and state policies, a full schedule of courses that met state requirements, adequate facilities, and perhaps a check on the textbooks to ensure they were all on a state-approved list (Jennings, 2007).

Accountability in this context consisted largely of procedural compliance, something that could be addressed via reasonable planning and foresight without necessarily affecting existing educational programs or practices directly. In fact, if a school failed on one or more dimension, it was normally a simple process to correct the deficit before accreditation was ever threatened. The net effect was that essentially all schools retained state accreditation continuously, absent some sort of egregious fault or blatant mismanagement. In essence, all schools were treated the same and held to roughly the same standards, which all were capable of meeting theoretically. State accountability was really a matter of "management by exception," where only the worst problems were identified and, even then, dealt with in a very circumspect fashion in order to maintain respect for local control.

During much of this period of time, which extended past the mid-point of the 20th century, urban districts were the crown jewel of the U.S. education system. Many cities constructed magnificent temple-like high schools during the first half of the century, often dedicating individual schools to distinct purposes or goals and outfitting them with state-of-the-art equipment and resources. Schools had strong community involvement and support. Instruction, while perhaps uninspired, was nevertheless conducted in an orderly and systematic fashion. Severe discipline problems, while not unheard of, were comparatively rare.

While this somewhat bucolic characterization of these districts and their high schools overlooks a dropout rate in excess of 50% even in the early 1950s and blatant discrimination against poor, minority, and special needs students, it nevertheless reflects at least a point of view held by many policymakers and citizens that is useful in understanding why accountability for urban schools was so different 50 or 60 years ago. The urban school inevitably followed the larger trajectory of inner cities that began to change for the worse in the 1960s and accelerated in the 1970s and 1980s. Although some U.S. city centers have experienced a degree of gentrification and selective improvement since those low points, urban school systems for the most part have not been the beneficiaries of renewed interest in central cities by a new generation of city dwellers. In fact, the contrasts between the expectations of these new urban denizens and the realities of those in communities that have been been virtually trapped in the inner city for decades have helped to sharpen demands for greater accountability for city schools across the country.

The limitations of a hands-off style of accountability became more readily apparent with the sea change in attitudes toward government programs that began in the early 1980s (Conley, 2003b). The 1960s and 1970s were an era of more government social programs, aimed at solving problems in education and elsewhere. By the early 1980s, the emphasis had begun to shift toward the philosophy that government programs should achieve results, not just provide services. This occurred at least partly in reaction to the perception that many of the social programs implemented during the previous 15 years were not achieving their goals (Berman & McLaughlin, 1976; Educational Testing Service, 1971). States, particularly many in the South that had relatively centralized education authorities that were instituted immediately after the Civil War, began to look more closely at the functioning of local school districts, what was referred to as "systems approaches" to accountability (Shafer, 1975).

Two macro trends that emerged in the 1980s served to raise the stakes for school accountability generally and for urban schools in particular. One of these was the deep economic downturn of the early 1980s, following as it did on the heels of a decade of economic stagnation in the 1970s. Conventional wisdom was that the U.S. economy was no longer able to compete globally, and one of the chief reasons was the U.S. worker, who was not educated well enough to adapt to new methods and technologies or well prepared enough for new economic opportunities and enterprises (National Commission on Excellence in Education, 1983; Waxer, 2004). Without a massive improvement in the next generation of workers, analysts claimed, the U.S. would face continuing and inexorable economic decline (Doyle & Hartle, 1985; National Business Roundtable, 1988; National Commission on Excellence in Education, 1983).

The other factor was a growing awareness that urban schools were falling into crisis and a call to do something about it (Tyack, 1974). As U.S. urban cores continued to deteriorate during the 1970s, the composition of their schools changed dramatically and suddenly. Increasingly, urban schools were populated by large proportions of students from low-income families or who were members of ethnic or racial minorities that had experienced long-term discrimination. These groups had historically not performed as well in school as had students who did not have to overcome similar challenges (Bankston III & Caldas, 1996; Coleman et al., 1966; Cuban, 2004; Darling-Hammond, 2000; Rist, 1970).

While urban schools had always educated a larger proportion of the poor than their suburban counterparts in particular, the idea that schools could really do something about this gap in achievement was lent greater credence by the effective schools movement and subsequent related research (Edmonds, 1979, 1982; Teddlie & Stringfield, 1993; Wenglinsky, 2002). This research established that schools could exceed levels predicted by the socioeconomic makeup of their student population if certain conditions were met. This research was so significant because it established that demographics were not destiny, in contrast to the findings of the Coleman Report (1966), which 15 years earlier had seemed to settle the debate in favor of the inevitability of socioeconomic status, although it is worth noting that even at the time, some urban educators raised their voices to protest this conclusion (Meier, 1967).

At the federal level, the 1980s was also the era of deregulation across a range of economic sectors and, simultaneously, a time of heightened emphasis on improved government efficiency and reduced waste. An increasing demand by the public and by legislators for measures to gauge the effectiveness of government-funded activities set the stage for state lawmakers to examine public education more closely, in part because schools consumed the largest proportion of tax dollars in most states (Cuban, 2004).

The initial forms of what came to be known as outcome-based accountability gauged students' ability to pass basic skills tests of fundamental literacy and numeracy, and defined a new level of state engagement in setting expectations for local school districts (Baratz, 1977). These systems were known as "mastery learning" (Block, 1980), "management by objectives" (Schrader, 1973), and "minimum competency testing" (Wise & Darling-Hammond, 1983). Individual school districts and states with stronger histories of district-wide or state-level testing took the lead in developing such systems voluntarily. Interestingly, many urban districts implemented pioneering student-testing programs locally without state mandates to do so (Doherty, 1976).

All states had by 1980 instituted some version of a state testing program (Baratz, 1980). These first systems served a variety of purposes and did not necessarily have high stakes associated with them. They were used largely to gauge district-wide progress and to provide information for program improvement, although by the late 1970s, the majority of states had already adopted minimum competency standards for promotion, graduation, or both (Pipho, 1977).

This first phase of significant widespread accountability testing yielded data that demonstrated and confirmed the vastly differing educational outcomes students were achieving based on their geographic location and family background (Tugend, 1985). This result, combined with the imperative to improve the quality of the workforce, spurred many state legislatures to action. Even this first wave of accountability testing generally had a greater impact on urban schools than on any other type of school (Darling-Hammond, 2000).

These developments set the stage for states to adopt more complex accountability models that focused not on the educational programs provided but on the student learning that resulted (Fuhrman, 1999)—in other words, on outputs, not on inputs or even processes (Smith & O'Day, 1991). Output-driven models require more elaborate measurement and reporting framework than do input models. Academic content standards (the output goals) must be identified and implemented, and accompanying assessments (the output measures) must be designed and administered on a regular basis. The results must then be quantified and reported in a fashion that allows for meaningful comparisons over time. All of this complexity invites significantly greater state involvement and management.

This shift in accountability philosophy to output models reached full fruition in the 1990s and 2000s (Cuban, 2004) at the state level and in 2001 at the federal level with the passage of the No Child Left Behind legislation (U.S. Department of Education, 2001), which was derived from state accountability models, largely the Texas system, and went on to influence essentially all state accountability systems during the first decade of the 21st century (Hursh, 2005).

Unique Factors in Urban Schools

Urban schools in the United States are subject to a set of unique factors and expectations not faced to the same degree or magnitude by any other category of U.S. school. Historically, these schools have been the places where the children of immigrants have been socialized to U.S. values and traditions by substituting U.S. culture and language for that of the country of origin (Tyack & Cuban, 1995). Cities have borne the full brunt of the deindustrialization of the U.S. economy and the subsequent flight of workers and families to suburbs that offered new jobs and new housing (Bettis, 1996). Urban schools have gone from being the pride of the U.S. educational system, to representing the decay of the inner city that has occurred since the 1950s (Buckley, Schneider, & Shan, 2004). They faced substantial financial challenges as the costs for educating their changing student population rose dramatically, just as their tax base contracted in a similarly dramatic fashion.

These factors were then compounded by a governance web within which urban districts frequently fell that was largely an amalgam of late 19th-century practices combined with reforms initiated early in the 20th century by the Progressive Movement. The ultimate responsibility for the success of the schools was often spread among competing governmental units (Kirst, 1984; Wirt & Kirst, 1989), a characteristic of many urban districts that continues to the present.

As urban districts sank deeper into fiscal chaos in the 1980s, cities had to face the prospect of the collapse of their school systems and the potential for disruption this posed for the city as a whole (Kirst & Bulkley, 2000). This led mayors and city councils in many prominent cities to approach state legislatures with requests for the state to provide additional funding to schools to cope with their unique challenges and needs. State legislatures tend to reflect suburban and rural interests disproportionately, and urban districts often had a long history of being aloof and separate from the rest of the state's schools (Conley, 2003b). In return for the critically necessary funding, legislatures often extracted changes in the governance of urban schools, as did mayors. In some cases, these laws led to greater decentralization of governance to the school level (Cuban, 2001). In other cases, the result was greater mayoral control. Occasionally, both results occurred simultaneously (Kirst & Bulkley, 2000, 2001). The net effect was to create new and more complex governance structures in urban schools that simultaneously gave neighborhood schools greater autonomy and local control, and held the district as a whole to higher accountability standards.

Urban districts face other challenges that make it difficult for them to respond to demands for improvements and greater efficiencies. Frequent turnover in key leadership positions, although not as severe or frequent as is often characterized, still makes it more challenging to sustain reform (Reid, 2001; Yee & Cuban, 1996).

City school boards also experience significant internal conflict and frequent turnover, which directly affects the tenure of superintendents (Wirt & Kirst, 1989). A new board majority may seek to put its imprint on the district and may feel no obligation to sustain the priorities (or leadership choices) of previous boards. In addition, strong urban teachers unions are able to negotiate greater control over working conditions when districts are not able to provide money for raises or salaries competitive with suburban districts.

This tendency toward gridlock at the leadership level can increase the power of entrenched interests, both administrator and teacher, in urban school districts, which makes it increasingly difficult to change or improve educational practice within them (Elmore, 2000; Meyer & Rowan, 1977; Tyack & Cuban, 1995). Simultaneously, urban districts have hemorrhaged students over the past 30-plus years (Gehring, 2005). As these districts have contracted, the core of the existing teaching force has tended to age in place at the same time that turnover among new teachers has soared. Contracts that establish rigid hierarchies that result in the last hired being the first fired in times of budget shortfalls have exacerbated this tendency. This combination of calcification among veterans and instability at the entry level also tends to stultify innovation and make school improvement more difficult to sustain.

States and then the federal government began implementing progressively more comprehensive and stronger accountability measures in an attempt to bring about desired changes in urban schools (Conley, 2003b; Elmore, 2000). While earlier demands for well-prepared workers never completely subsided, the national focus shifted from workers attaining uniform minimal levels of literacy and numeracy to preparing a workforce and citizenry that possessed "21st century skills" (Jobs for the Future, 2005; Partnership for 21st Century Skills, 2008). The educational ante was raised from basic skills and minimum competency to proficiency, and college and career readiness (Conley, 2005a, 2005b, 2010). The old models that set the "floor" beneath student performance were gradually replaced by "ceiling" accountability systems that sought in principle to get all students to the level where they could meet challenging standards at high levels of performance (Conley, 2003a; Linn, 2005).

The federal No Child Left Behind (NCLB) legislation (U.S. Department of Education, 2001) represents the apex of accountability expectations for urban districts. While NCLB applies to all U.S. public districts that accept federal funds, its provisions are more significant for schools receiving Title I funds, which is the case for the vast majority of urban schools. Many suburban and rural schools also receive Title I funds, but these schools have been less directly affected by NCLB accountability requirements, which in some cases are far more difficult to enforce in such environments (Reeves, 2003). The impact of NCLB has therefore been disproportionately greater on urban schools (Azzam, Perkins-Gough, & Thiers, 2006).

The notion of an "achievement gap" is at the heart of the NCLB accountability model. Although evidence of systematic differences in performance between socioeconomic and racial groups had long been available from national sources such as the National Assessment for Educational Progress (Haycock, 2001; Kim, 1993; National Education Goals Panel, 1992), increasingly thorough and highly visible state testing programs have yielded data on disturbing and stubborn differences in student achievement by various ethnic and racial groups, trends that did not seem to be changing much over time (Coleman et al., 1966; Evans, 2005). These gaps are most pronounced and intractable in urban districts. Solve the problems of the urban schools, the thinking goes, and the achievement gap disappears.

Range of Regulatory Mechanisms

The state has at its command numerous potential mechanisms to control schools and schooling, only a few of which are presented in this chapter. All attempt to do basically the same thing, which is to encourage or compel the behavior of everyone within or associated with the educational system to achieve certain state-identified or mandated goals or conditions. This range of accountability mechanisms is explored in the remainder of this section before returning to a discussion of the effect of these mechanisms on urban schools.

The state can employ many regulatory policies to increase school accountability, depending on the specific goals it is attempting to achieve (Brady, 2003; Conley & Bodone, 2002). In general, these mechanisms can be characterized as existing along a continuum from less intrusive to more intrusive (Brady, 2003). At one end are data reporting systems that simply present information to policy-makers, educators, or parents. These systems function in a largely unobtrusive fashion to generate a level of accountability based essentially on public pressure to improve. The state assumes the role of providing a common and objective point of reference derived from data, and then steps back to allow local educators to make decisions. Schools are expected to be accountable because the state has provided the information necessary to make improvements, and the schools should now respond accordingly. This relatively passive approach assumes that cause-and-effect relationships will result from key triggering information, such as student performance data.

Midway through the spectrum are administrative accountability mechanisms by which the state takes an active role in the implementation and enforcement of accountability expectations and that therefore affect schools more directly. Historically, these have been in areas where the state wants to control access to or the quality of a particular factor central to schooling, such as teacher licensure or financial reporting requirements. The state establishes the rules and procedures, and local school officials are required to verify that they have followed these rules and procedures and meet the requirements. For example, with teacher license requirements, districts must ensure anyone in a teaching position has the proper license for the position they hold and maintain records that verify the status of employee licenses, which agents of the state check periodically (ECONorthwest & Center for Education Policy Research, 2004). Similar procedures exist for fiscal record keeping.

At the far end of the accountability spectrum are systems that expect schools to meet specific outcome targets for a range of subgroups by specific dates, that mandate what must be measured, and that set criteria for how learning can be assessed. The No Child Left Behind Act of 2001 sets perhaps the most demanding framework for accountability of any of the existing models (Linn, 2005; Linn, Baker, & Betenbenner, 2002). Incorporating elements from a number of state accountability systems, particularly Texas, NCLB goes beyond any individual state system by establishing a timeline by which all schools must enable all students to meet state standards via a federally approved assessment. State educational accountability became a legal obligation under NCLB, which clearly outlines requirements that states must follow when establishing standards, assessments, and consequences for districts and schools (Linn et al., 2002).

Although NCLB may constrain state autonomy, it does not eliminate it by any means. States are still responsible for adopting standards for academic content and student performance, and each state must also select an assessment system that measures its content standards and the scores students must attain to be judged to have met the state standards. States adopt a uniform set of standards and one assessment system under NCLB, which may or may not be well aligned with the needs and realities of urban schools.

Scholars and policy advocates have argued that accountability mechanisms can never achieve much beyond getting educators to comply with regulations, and regulations can only generate simple behaviors in response, not the complex decision-making necessary for the kinds of changes many believe are necessary if schools are to improve dramatically in order to achieve key social goals (Amrein & Berliner, 2002; Conley & Goldman, 2000; Meier, 2000; Sizer & Rogers, 1993). Accountability targets can be reached, it is argued, only when all participants in the policy and gover-nance process understand and share common goals, and have the resources and opportunity necess-ary to achieve them successfully (Fuhrman, 1993, 1999; Spillane, 2004). Regulatory mechanisms that help create these conditions are very difficult to craft and implement successfully.

Data-driven Accountability Systems

Data-driven accountability systems with no specific requirements regarding how to use the data are the least intrusive of accountability practices. In such a model, the state collects data uniformly in key areas, provides the resulting findings to schools, and then leaves schools on their own to make the necessary improvements. This approach, more prevalent a decade ago, is becoming less common as states increasingly use data from state assessments to make general judgments about the quality of schooling and to prescribe actions or interventions.

Data-driven accountability is premised on the assumption that, by sharing accurate, unbiased information on key aspects of system functioning, the system will improve (Fuhrman & Elmore, 2004). This improvement will result both from internal efforts undertaken in response to data results and to external pressure applied upon the system by constituents. Bureaucracies and the people who populate them abhor negative attention as well as external intervention into internal operational decisions (DiMaggio & Powell, 1983). Therefore, bureaucratic organizations, such as schools, may be more likely to respond to and change to avoid data that may reflect negatively on the organization.

Furthermore, as knowledge about how the organization is functioning becomes increasingly public, the quality of decisions made to improve the organization can be expected to improve, along with the urgency to undertake improvement efforts. Organizations theoretically get better because they can no longer continue operating in their current state without drawing public attention to the suboptimal results they are achieving. Public disapproval affects the self-esteem of members of the organization (Daly, 2009). This pressure theoretically serves to enhance motivation to improve student learning in schools (Brady, 2003).

At the heart of a data-driven accountability structure is the assumption that an effective feedback loop exists between the key large-scale performance indicators, which include assessments of student performance, and a group of responsible parties that will use this information to adjust and modify the educational delivery system until improvement goals are met (O'Day, 2002).

Collecting and reporting data for policy formulation requires accurate information in order to make useful decisions. Baker & Linn (2004) state that systems tend to operate under the premise that the data collected are accurate. The feedback loop running among student performance data, teachers, schools, and state policymakers assumes that the data collected are valid indicators, that the results will be interpreted properly, and that the actions taken will necessarily cause the desired improvement. In practice, establishing the causal relationships between the data gathered and the results desired is much more problematic than policymakers may believe (Linn, 2008).

O'Day (2002) points out the challenges with which accountability systems of all types must cope, but particularly those that use data to make high-stakes decisions about schools, students, and educators. Although the school is the unit of analysis, the individual student is the unit of action. People, administrators, teachers, and students construct the teaching-and-learning process interactively. Yet, results are reported for schools as a whole, as if the school had its own existence independent of the actions of the individuals in it. Such reporting obscures the range of strengths and weaknesses present in the school as an organization. Change ultimately must occur on the individual level, and all the school-level data do is to create a general, rather than specific, motivation for change.

A second challenge is that a data system is an external mechanism seeking to influence internal school operations. Past research suggests this mechanism may not always operate as policymakers expect (Berman & McLaughlin, 1978; Goertz, Floden, & O'Day, 1996). Finally, and most relevant, information can be both essential to schools and problematic for school improvement. While data are obviously necessary for school improvement, they are not automatically sufficient. The real issue becomes how school staffs utilize data, the capacity they have to understand data, to work with data, and modify practices based on what they have learned. In the final analysis, schools are complex organizations that can reach any of a number of possible decisions about how to react to data provided.

Data-driven accountability systms may be designed to have specific rewards or consequences for schools or not. Problems arise with this method if the right data elements are not properly selected and widely publicized. Schools as cultures have never been particularly hospitable environments into which to introduce large quantities of student-learning data because of the strong privacy norms and the subsequent difficulty interpreting the significance of information and reaching agreement on necessary changes resulting from the data (Lafee, Dawson, Alwin, & Yeagley, 2002; Little, 1990, 1995; Spillane, 2004; Spillane & Zeuli, 1999). A cultural shift of this nature requires considerable energy and effort because most school personnel are not trained to collect or interpret data (Lafee et al., 2002).

Urban schools face particular challenges accommodating and responding positively to data-driven accountability mechanisms. Although data are increasingly available in urban schools, high teacher turnover along with contracts that specify all aspects of teacher work make it more difficult to construct and implement multi-year improvement plans linked to data. The physical infrastructure of urban schools may fall short of the threshold necessary to take full advantage of data that are available online in state or district databases (Lafee et al., 2002). Finally, student mobility poses a significant challenge to data-driven accountability strategies, such as growth models, that assume students are in one school continuously. Urban schools have greater difficulty tracking students. A data-driven system in high mobility environments is less effective in part because no one takes responsibility for the learner who is moving among schools frequently, and it is more difficult to establish the value that any teacher or school is contributing to students who come and go throughout the year.

Data-driven reporting systems at the beginning of the second decade of the 21st century are still largely in early implementation stages, although states with prior histories of using state data for accountability purposes, such as Texas and Florida, have made the development of such systems a high priority. Federal funds disbursed under the Race to the Top program will also speed the development of state data systems (Achieve, 2009).

Value-added models have emerged as an approach that is being adopted by numerous states and localities (Koretz, 2008; Sanders, 1998). This method uses statistical analyses of student test scores across grade levels. The value-added methodology is designed to determine whether the degree of learning that occurs is consistent with what could or should be expected for the student, class, school, or district in question, although it is not without its challenges and critics (Doran & Fleischman, 2005; Kupermintz, 2003).

The potential effect of accountability systems driven by student testing data upon the performance of the K–12 education system is yet to be fully determined, but there are indications that these systems do have effects on student learning. For example, Carnoy and Loeb (2002) found that students in high-accountability states had greater gains on the National Assessment of Educational Progress tests in 8th grade math than states with less stringent accountability measures. Similarly, Hanushek and Raymond (2004) concluded that accountability improves student test scores. However, they did not find differences between reporting scores and attaching consequences to those scores. Selecting the kinds of data to collect, and designing the database systems to deliver and analyze this information are the major elements in debate at this time, although larger issues such as privacy rights, funding, and educator resistance are coming to the fore as well (Lafee et al., 2002; Misco, 2008).

Standards-driven Accountability Systems

Since the early 1990s, essentially all states have developed educational standards that specify what students should be expected to know and be able to do at various grade levels or upon completion of particular courses (Elmore, 2000; Fuhrman, 1999). States now utilize standards-based systems as a primary means for judging how their education systems are performing and whether they are improving (Brady, 2003). While considerable variation exists among states in terms of the scope, depth, and breadth of their standards, all states expect their standards to influence local education practice.

School districts are generally accountable to have implemented the standards and trained teachers in their use. Many states make judgments and categorize individual schools on the basis of results from standards-based assessments. This standards-based method of accountability raises the stakes of a data-driven system, but does not necessarily have individual-level effects for principals, teachers, or students. Standards-based accountability systems have been advocated as a way to create greater awareness among educators of what specifically they are expected to accomplish (Haycock, 2001).

Some argue that judging schools based on how well they achieve state standards leads to distortions in teaching practices and a decrease in teacher autonomy and creativity (Elmore, 2000; Lafee et al., 2002). The results are often used to compare schools, which some contend is arbitrary and unsupportable scientifically (Kiplinger, 2008). Schools, it is argued, are not and should not be fundamentally competitive with one another. Each should be attempting to teach students as much as possible with sensitivity to the local context (Sizer & Rogers, 1993). Student growth over time and the achievement of locally specified goals, this argument asserts, is a better measure than absolute performance in relation to a set of state standards (Betebenner, 2008; Kane & Staiger, 2002).

A standards-based system, whatever its weaknesses, does create a common reference point for judging school performance, something that had never existed previously in most states, except perhaps in the form of norm-referenced achievement tests not specifically tied to a set of desired learning outcomes (Elmore, 2000). Researchers note that all large-scale testing is subject to a series of issues and conditions that restrict the usefulness of school-level results (Baker & Linn, 2004; Kane & Staiger, 2002). Norm-referenced tests have largely fallen out of favor, in part because of the "Lake Wobegon Syndrome" (Cannell, 1988a, 1988b), the phenomenon that all children could score above average, which has the effect of rendering scores relatively useless for accountability purposes or for public ratings for schools.

The introduction of content standards and the ability to compare performance on common learning standards across schools within a state has created tremendous anxiety but also a great deal of activity within schools (Firestone, Mayrowetz, & Fairman, 1998; Koretz, Mitchell, Barron, & Keith, 1996; Moon, Brighton, Jarvis, & Hall, 2007). Evidence suggests that much, although by no means all, of this activity has led to a reexamination of assumptions about learners and the adaptation of instructional programs to meet the needs of students with skill deficiencies (Zavadsky, 2006). Many of the affected students have been members of groups that have not heretofore received direct or specialized attention from schools.

One of the key accomplishments of a standards-based accountability system, it is argued, is to raise the expectations that teachers in urban schools hold for their students (Haycock, 2001). Without external standards, local expectations may be set based largely on individual teacher assumptions about their students' capabilities (Smey-Richman, 1989). Given the skill deficiencies with which many students enter urban schools, teachers may tend to adjust expectations downward. If teachers in each successive grade level continue to set their expectations based on those of the previous teacher, a self-fulfilling prophecy can occur, in which urban students are unable to close the achievement gap because they are not exposed to material and learning challenges sufficient to enable them to catch up with their non-urban peers (Fryer & Levitt, 2004; Haycock, 2001; Kozol, 1992; Rist, 1970; Smey-Richman, 1989).

Standards-based accountability systems level the playing field to the degree to which they set comparable expectations for all students in a state or across states, as the Common Core State Standards are designed to do (Council of Chief State School Officers & National Governors Association, 2010a, 2010b). A set of standards do not, in and of themselves, address the fundamental underlying issues of opportunity to learn and of the resources necessary for urban students to have educational experiences comparable to more privileged students (Darling-Hammond, 2000; Noguera, 2001). Standards-based accountability systems may be suitable vehicles for identifying and specifying the deficiencies of urban schools, but wholesale improvements seem unlikely without a concomitant effort by states to help these schools address the issues that led to the achievement gap in the first place (Darling-Hammond, 2000).

Sanctions-driven Accountability Systems

A sanctions-driven accountability system is the next step beyond a standards-based system in terms of the degree of direct impact on schools. In a sanctions-driven system, test results and other indicators are used to rank or categorize students and schools. Based on these categorizations, students, teachers, or principals may be subject to a consequence if a specified performance level is not met (Mintrop, 2003).

The consequences for students may be the inability to be promoted or to graduate from high school. While states commonly test at a number of grade levels, students are most directly affected by high school exit examinations. Tests at other grade levels may result in student retention, but the denial of a diploma is the most severe consequence for the individual student (Lashway, 2001).

For principals and teachers, sanctions-driven accountability can result in the removal of teachers from their current position or the reconstitution of a school's entire faculty and administrative team. Superintendents or school boards are directly affected in the case of state takeovers of school districts, another consequence that may occur (Brady, 2003; Malen, Croninger, Muncey, & Redmond-Jones, 2002).

The use of state-imposed sanctions on schools is a second dimension of this form of accountability (Kane & Staiger, 2002). Principals may be removed from low-performing schools and reassigned elsewhere. Other consequences can include offering students additional options to receive tutoring or to enroll in another school in the district. Urban districts have seen large-scale replacements of principals and other sanctions implemented, including the closing of schools that persistently fail to improve (Cibulka, 2003).

Results from tests in states with sanctions-driven accountability systems can be used to intervene directly into the governance of a school district where state law permits this type of action. The most extreme forms of intervention are reconstitution or state takeover (Gill, Zimmer, Christman, & Blanc, 2007; Hall, 1998; Wong & Shen, 2001; Ziebarth, 2002). Both reconstitutions and take-overs tend to occur disproportionately more often in urban schools (Cibulka, 2003).

Sanctions-driven accountability has a certain appeal because it attempts to establish cause-and-effect relationships between governmental policy and educational performance. Legislators in many states have begun to favor strategies that leapfrog local school boards and affect students, teachers, and administrators more directly. This mechanism creates a range of reactions in schools, some desirable from the state's point of view, some not (Anagnostopoulos & Rutledge, 2007; Wong & Anagnostopoulos, 1998). Because consequences befall individual students, the general public is much more interested in such systems, as opposed to standards-driven accountability in which results are reported and sanctions enforced predominantly at a school level and somewhat out of the public eye.

The challenges created by these systems are numerous (Mintrop & Sunderman, 2009). Because they do have consequences, they tend to affect the structure and functioning of schools most directly. Sometimes the solution-seeking process yields constructive, creative reforms and new ideas. Just as often, it results in few changes in core teaching methods or courses and the addition of programs for failing students based largely on reteaching the same material in the same manner and extensive test preparation (Crocco & Costigan, 2007; Herman & Golan, 1993). Some studies and reports have demonstrated the changes in teacher behavior that occur when high-stakes accountability systems are implemented (Abrams, Pedulla, & Madaus, 2003; Crocco & Costigan, 2006; Olson, 2002; Pedulla et al., 2003). Urban teachers may be more inclined to focus on test preparation given the low scores their students achieve on state tests, leading to potentially greater effects, intended and otherwise, of state accountability policies on practices in urban classrooms (Crocco & Costigan, 2006, 2007).

Many factors are required for sanctions-driven accountability systems to work, among them the ability to measure the right things in the right ways at the right levels. If standards are set too low and tests are simplistic in design, students are not challenged, and instruction in schools focuses on the most basic of skills. If standards are set too high or if tests are poorly aligned with the desired high standards, many students fail, and the entire accountability system comes under attack while student performance does not increase significantly. Staff at the poorest performing schools may simply give up under the belief that they can do little to improve pass rates (Daly, 2009). Rarely, if ever, are the results of state accountability exams utilized by higher education or the business world, meaning that a tremendous amount of effort is devoted by teachers and students to a measure that references only itself and does not connect particularly well to subsequent opportunities (Brown & Conley, 2007).

Incentive-driven Accountability Systems

Many educators and policymakers have pointed out that punishments are not the only way to get desired results. Incentives can also work to serve that purpose (Raham, 2000). Incentive-driven accountability uses more than just educator motivation to achieve its goals. Incentives can have effects on those who achieve them and those who do not. The absence of receiving a reward can also serve to spur action to achieve the reward or recognition in the future. Incentives, then, create a more subtle but nevertheless potent pressure for schools to improve. Incentives-based systems can also create the circumstances under which schools staffs must work collaboratively, focus their efforts, and make necessary changes to gain the desired reward or recognition, thereby achieving many of the same goals sanction-driven accountability systems seek to achieve.

The current emphasis is on incentives for teachers, not schools, in the form of merit or pay-for-performance systems (Podgursky & Springer, 2007; Robelen, 2009). These would pay teachers based on student learning improvements as measured by state tests. Merit systems tend to focus teacher attention even more tightly on state testing programs.

Incentives can be problematic. The most obvious inhibiting factor can be the cost of programs that provide monetary rewards. Policymakers may resist the idea that school staff should receive rewards simply for doing what they were expected to do in the first place. Another problem has been the difficulty of deciding actually what and whom to reward. If incentives serve to reinforce desired behavior, then it is critical to target them on cause–effect relationships between the desired student learning gains and the person or persons responsible for improving the learning.

Urban schools have been the targets for incentive systems tied to improvements in student test scores. Some states have made awards to schools as a whole when student test scores improve. A few districts and states have instituted limited bonuses for individual teachers and principals based on test score improvement.

Several significant experiments have been undertaken in urban districts, including Denver's ProComp performance pay system (Gonring, Teske, & Jupp, 2007). Results of these programs have been mixed (Springer et al., 2010), and many states abandon them when finances become tighter. Those that do survive seem to have some measure of teacher involvement and buy-in along with clear, well-defined goals, and multiple measures of performance that may incorporate test scores, but also include growth measures and teacher skill acquisition (Gratz, 2009). The U.S. Department of Education's Teacher Incentive Fund (2010) has made major awards to districts with high-needs schools to develop performance compensation programs. The results of these programs and others may help define the value and effectiveness of pay-for-performance programs in urban schools.

In the final analysis, incentive programs may be a necessary component of a total set of accountability mechanisms, but no state has yet learned how to utilize incentives in ways that get anything like the same reaction as sanctions or the threat of them (Cornett & Gaines, 1992). This is not to say that incentive systems cannot be powerful policy tools, only that states have not necessarily learned how to utilize them in such a fashion to date.

Market-driven Accountability

The final major category of accountability model are those approaches that rely on some degree of choice by students and parents as a means to generate improvement in schools or, at the least, to improve the education of individual students who avail themselves of a wider range of educational options. The market-driven approaches range from vouchers to open enrollment to selective opt-out programs to alternative service providers to charter schools (Chubb & Moe, 1990; Levin & Belfield, 2003). All assume that existence of an informed "consumer" of educational services and of choices of sufficient variety and quality as to allow the "consumer" to do better by going elsewhere. Here, again, the results have been mixed and controversial (Fiske & Ladd, 2000; Ladd, 1996, 2002).

Market advocates argue that centrally planned schools lack the ability to respond flexibly to differences between regional populations and individual student bodies (Ladd, 2002). A central bureaucracy, at the state or school district level, prescribing the same organizational structure and educational offerings for all schools, tends toward solutions that may work for some students and teachers but are ineffective for many others. In the view of market advocates, centralized decision-making is inherently inefficient given the manifold needs of student bodies and the myriad resources that exist within a single district, let alone across an entire state (Kirst & Bulkley, 2000; Smarick, 2008).

Urban districts are particularly subject to criticisms of being overly centralized in their governance and of attempting to impose one-size-fits-all policies on schools that differ vastly in terms of their populations and needs. This stems in part from the history of the creation of urban districts, which occurred simultaneously with the industrialization of the United States Urban districts became large at the same time that U.S. corporations did, and they took on many of these characteristics (Jennings, 2007). The newly constituted urban districts tended to adopt current business management techniques, which advocated economies of scale, division of labor, and efficiencies of the assembly line (Kirst & Bulkley, 2000). Urban districts retained many of these organizational traits and management techniques even as the private sector began to abandon or modify them in favor of more decentralized management models that emphasized employee involvement in decision-making (Levin & Belfield, 2003). Suburban districts, for the most part, were much smaller during the early parts of the 20th century and never adopted many of the industrial management policies in the same way that urban districts did.

Urban schools have been the site for a number of market-driven accountability experiments. Most notable are the Milwaukee and Cleveland voucher programs (Peterson, Howell, & Greene, 1999; Witte, 1999), the use of private service providers in cities such as Philadelphia, and the open enrollment options that are included in the NCLB legislation. To date, these experiments have been limited in scope and effect. Considerable debate continues regarding their effectiveness (Gill et al., 2007; Levin & Belfield, 2003; Peterson et al., 1999; Witte, 1998). Charter schools and new networks of schools are currently the most widespread manifestations of market-based accountability in urban districts, and these are now growing in scope and impact, although their effects on student achievement seem to be complex and mixed (Smarick, 2008; Zimmer & Buddin, 2006).

Accountability in the Urban Context: Can it be the Solution?

No one model of accountability for urban education clearly works in all settings. In essence, districts, states, and the federal government have utilized a multiple-methods approach to holding urban schools accountable. All of the models described in this chapter have been tried with urban districts, sometimes layered one upon another within a state or an urban district. The effects on the whole have fallen short of hopes and expectations.

It is unclear how effective accountability measures alone can be in improving urban schools. One prevalent point of view is that the problems of urban schools cannot be solved simply by instituting accountability systems in isolation from other remedies (Berliner & Biddle, 1995). This more comprehensive approach argues for a broad coalition of civic organizations and private sector partners that work together in a coordinated fashion to help address issues of unemployment, health care, and social services necessary to support the creation and maintenance of functional families or stable environments where students are able to pursue educational goals successfully.

What appears most evident is that state and federal policymakers seem committed to continuing to attack the problems of urban schools and that accountability systems will be one of the primary policy tools they utilize to attempt to bring about desired changes in these schools. What also seems relatively apparent is that the problems and challenges of urban schools are longstanding and deeply ingrained into the schools and their surrounding communities. Federal "turnaround school" programs are one example of an attempt to change the culture and pattern of failure in the most highly distressed urban schools (U.S. Department of Education, 2009).

Common core standards and accompanying common assessments (Council of Chief State School Officers & National Governors Association, 2010a, 2010b) may also help address the problem of urban schools by stabilizing the accountability target and criteria. Greater stability could help urban districts to focus more consistently for sustained periods of time on what is most important to teach. Common assessments may enable urban districts across multiple states to learn from one another more directly, allowing the successes attained in one district to be duplicated in others. Common standards implemented uniformly in large numbers of urban schools may encourage publishers to develop higher quality instructional materials geared to the specific needs of these schools. The existence of quality curriculum and teachers equipped with quality materials may help urban schools to better meet accountability standards as manifested in the common assessments.

It does seem to be the case that as long as urban schools continue to perform significantly below their suburban peers that federal and state governments will continue to refine or evolve accountability policy and mechanisms in the hopes of solving the problem of the urban school. The degree to which this approach will be successful ultimately remains an open question. Urban schools seem destined to continue to serve multiple masters, local, state, and national, all of whom will seek to extract a measure of accountability from them.

References

Abrams, L. M., Pedulla, J. J., & Madaus, G. F. (2003). Views from the classroom: Teachers' opinions of statewide testing programs. *Theory into Practice, 42*(1), 18–29.

Achieve (2009). P-20 longitudinal data systems. Race to the top: Accelerating college and career readiness. Retrieved May 31, 2011 from http://achieve.org/RTTT-P20LongitudinalData

Amrein, A. L., & Berliner, D. C. (2002). *The impact of high-stakes tests on student academic erformance: An analysis of NAEP results in states with high-stakes tests and ACT, SAT, and AP test results in states with high school graduation exams.* Tempe: Education Policy Research Unit, Arizona State University.

Anagnostopoulos, D., & Rutledge, S. A. (2007). Making sense of school sanctioning policies in urban high schools: Charting the depth and drift of school and classroom change. *Teachers College Record, 109*(5), 1261–1302.

Azzam, A. M., Perkins-Gough, D., & Thiers, N. (2006). The impact of NCLB. *Educational Leadership, 64*(3), 94–96.

Baker, E., & Linn, R. (2004). Validity issues for accountability systems. In S. Fuhrman & R. Elmore (Eds.), *Redesigning accountability systems for education* (pp. 47–72). New York: Teachers College Press.

Bankston III, C., & Caldas, S. J. (1996). Majority African American schools and social injustice: The influence of de facto segregation on academic achievement. *Social Forces, 75*(2), 535–555.

Baratz, J. C. (1977). Requiring performance standards for children: What is the state's responsibility? Paper presented at the National Conference of State Legislators, Washington, DC, December.

Baratz, J. C. (1980). Policy implications of minimum competency testing. In R. Jaeger & C. Tittle (Eds.), *Minimum competency achievement testing: Motives, models, measures, consequences* (pp. 529–539). Berkeley, CA: McCutchan.

Berliner, D. C., & Biddle, B. J. (1995). *The manufactured crisis: Myths, fraud, and the attack on America's public schools.* New York: Addison-Wesley.

Berman, P., & McLaughlin, M. (1976). Implementation of educational innovation. *Educational Forum, 40*(3), March, 344–370.

Berman, P., & McLaughlin, M. (1978). *Federal programs supporting educational change. Vol. 8: Implementing and sustaining innovations.* Santa Monica, CA: Rand Corporation.

Betebenner, D. W. (2008). Toward a normative understanding of student growth. In K. E. Ryan & L. A. Shepard (Eds.), *The future of test-based educational accountability* (pp. 155–170). New York: Routledge.

Bettis, P. J. (1996). Urban students, liminality, and the postindustrial context. *Sociology of Education, 69*, 106–107.

Block, J. H. (1980). Promoting excellence through mastery. *Theory into Practice, 19*(1), 66–74.

Brady, R. C. (2003). *Can failing schools be fixed?* Washington, DC: Thomas B. Fordham Foundation & Institute.

Brown, R. S., & Conley, D. (2007). Comparing state high school assessments to standards for success in entry-level university courses. *Journal of Educational Assessment, 12*(3), 137–160.

Buckley, J., Schneider, M., & Shan, Y. (2004). *The effects of school facility quality on teacher retention in urban school districts.* Washington, DC: National Institute of Building Sciences.

Cannell, J. J. (1988a). The Lake Wobegon effect revisited. *Educational Measurement: Issues and Practice, 7*(4), 12–15.

Cannell, J. J. (1988b). Nationally normed elementary achievement testing in America's public schools: How all 50 states are above the national average. *Educational Measurement: Issues and Practice, 7*(2), 5–9.

Carnoy, M., & Loeb, S. (2002). Does external accountability affect student outcomes? A cross-state analysis. *Educational Evaluation and Policy Analysis, 24*(4), 305–331.

Chubb, J., & Moe, T. (1990). *Politics, markets, and America's schools.* Washington, DC: Brookings Institution.

Cibulka, J. G. (2003). Educational bankruptcy, takeovers, and reconstitution of failing schools. In National Society for the Study of Education (Ed.), *Yearbook of the national society for the study of education* (Vol. 102). New York: Wiley.

Coleman, J. S., et al. (1966). *Equality of educational opportunity* (No. OE–38001). Washington, DC: National Center for Educational Statistics.

Conley, D. (2003a). *Understanding university success. A report from standards for success* (No. ED476300). Eugene, OR: Center for Educational Policy Research.

Conley, D. (2003b). *Who governs our schools? Changing roles and responsibilities.* New York: Teachers College Press.

Conley, D. (2005a). College knowledge: Getting in is only half the battle. *Principal Leadership, 6*(1), 16–21.

Conley, D. (2005b). *College knowledge: What it really takes for students to succeed and what we can do to get them ready.* San Francisco, CA: Jossey-Bass.

Conley, D. (2010). *College and career ready: Helping all students succeed beyond high school.* San Francisco, CA: Jossey-Bass.

Conley, D., & Bodone, F. (2002). Measuring quality: State accountability systems, school data collection practices, and the Oregon Quality Education Model. Paper presented at the University Council on Educational Administration, Pittsburgh, PA, November.

Conley, D., & Goldman, P. (2000). Half full, half empty? Educator response over time to state-level systemic reform initiatives. *International Journal of Educational Reform, 9*(3), 249–269.

Cornett, L. M., & Gaines, G. F. (1992). *Focusing on student outcomes: Roles for incentive programs. The 1991 national survey of incentive programs and teacher career ladders.* Atlanta, GA: Southern Regional Education Board.

Council of Chief State School Officers & National Governors Association (2010a). Common core state standards for English language arts & literacy in history/social studies, science, and technical subjects. Retrieved September 6, 2010 from: www.corestandards.org/assets/CCSSI_ELA%20Standards.pdf

Council of Chief State School Officers & National Governors Association (2010b). Common core state standards for mathematics. Retrieved September 6, 2010 from: www.corestandards.org

Crocco, M. S., & Costigan, A. T. (2006). High-stakes teaching: What's at stake for teachers (and students) in the age of accountability. *New Educator, 2*(1), 1–13.

Crocco, M. S., & Costigan, A. T. (2007). The narrowing of curriculum and pedagogy in the age of accountability: Urban educators speak out. *Urban Education, 42*(6), 512–535.

Cuban, L. (2001). *Leadership for student learning: Urban school leadership – Different in kind and degree.* Washington, DC: Institute for Educational Leadership.

Cuban, L. (2004). A solution that lost its problem: Centralized policymaking and classroom gains. In N. Epstein (Ed.), *Who's in charge here? The tangled web of school governance and policy* (pp. 104–130). Washington, DC: Brookings Institution.

Daly, A. J. (2009). Rigid response in an age of accountability: The potential of leadership and trust. *Educational Administration Quarterly, 45*, 168–216.

Darling-Hammond, L. (2000). *Transforming urban public schools: The role of standards and accountability.* Stanford, CA: Stanford University School of Education.

DiMaggio, P. J., & Powell, W. W. (1983). The iron cage revisited: Institutional isomorphism and collective rationality in organizational fields. *American Sociological Review, 48*(2), 147–160.

Doherty, V. (1976). Developments in goal based measurement in the Portland public schools. Paper presented at the annual meeting of the American Educational Research Association, San Francisco, CA.

Doran, H. C., & Fleischman, S. (2005). Challenges of value-added assessment. *Educational Leadership, 63*(3), 85–87.

Doyle, D. P., & Hartle, T. W. (1985). *Excellence in education. The states take charge.* Washington, DC: American Enterprise Institute.

ECONorthwest & Center for Education Policy Research (2004). *Strenghtening accountability: Evidence on regulatory and market-based strategies to improve student achievement.* Portland, OR: The Chalkboard Project.

Edmonds, R. (1979). Effective schools for the urban poor. *Educational Leadership, 37*(1), 15–18, 20–24.

Edmonds, R. (1982). Programs of school improvement: An overview. Paper presented at the National Invitational Conference, "Research on Teaching: Implications for Practice," Warrenton, VA, February.

Educational Testing Service (1971). *Proceedings of the Conferences on Educational Accountability.* Princeton, NJ: Educational Testing Service.

Elmore, R. F. (2000). *Building a new structure for school leadership.* Washington, DC: The Albert Shanker Institute.

Evans, R. (2005). Reframing the achievement gap. *Phi Delta Kappan, 86*(8), 582–589.

Firestone, W. A., Mayrowetz, D., & Fairman, J. (1998). Performance-based assessment and instructional change: The effects of testing in Maine and Maryland. *Educational Evaluation and Policy Analysis, 20*(2), 95.

Fiske, E. B., & Ladd, H. F. (2000). *When schools compete: A cautionary tale.* Washington, DC: Brookings Institution.

Fryer Jr., R. G., & Levitt, S. D. (2004). Understanding the black-white test score gap in the first two years of school. *The Review of Economics and Statistics, 86*(2), 447–464.

Fuhrman, S. (1993). The politics of coherence. In S. Fuhrman (Ed.), *Designing coherent policy: Improving the system.* San Francisco, CA: Jossey-Bass.

Fuhrman, S. (1999). *The new accountability* (CPRE Policy Brief No. CPRE-RB-27). Philadelphia, PA: Consortium for Policy Research in Education.

Fuhrman, S., & Elmore, R. (Eds.) (2004). *Redesigning accountability systems for education.* New York: Teachers College Press.

Gehring, J. (2005). Dips in enrollment posing challenges for urban districts. *Education Week, 24*(25), 1, 12.

Gill, B., Zimmer, R., Christman, J., & Blanc, S. (2007). *State takeover, school restructuring, private management, and student achievement in Philadelphia.* Santa Monica, CA: Rand Education.

Goertz, M. E., Floden, R., & O'Day, J. (1996). *The bumpy road to education reform. CPRE policy briefs.* Philadelphia, PA: Consortium for Policy Research in Education.

Gonring, P., Teske, P., & Jupp, B. (2007). *Pay for performance teacher compensation: An inside view of Denver's ProComp Plan.* Cambridge, MA: Harvard Education Press.

Gratz, D. B. (2009). *The peril and promise of performance pay: Making education compensation work.* Lanham, MD: Rowman & Littlefield.

Hall, B. (1998). *State intervention in the Newark public schools. Occasional Paper 1997–98. Educational Policy Conversations.* New York: Institute for Education and Social Policy, New York University.

Hanushek, E. A., & Raymond, M. E. (2004). The effect of school accountability systems on the level and distribution of student achievement. *Journal of the European Economic Association, 2*(2–3), 406–415.

Haycock, K. (2001). Closing the achievement gap. *Educational Leadership, 58*(6), 6–11.

Herman, J. L., & Golan, S. (1993). The effects of standardized testing on teaching and schools. *Educational Measurement: Issues and Practice, 12*(4), 20–25.

Hursh, D. (2005). The growth of high-stakes testing in the USA: Accountability, markets and the decline in educational equality. *British Educational Research Journal, 31*(5), 605–622.

Jennings, M. (2007). Accountability and abdication: School reform and urban school districts in the era of accountability. *Educational Foundations, 21*, 27–38.

Jobs for the Future (2005). *Education and skills for the 21st century: An agenda for action.* Boston, MA: Jobs for the Future.

Kane, T. J., & Staiger, D. O. (2002). The promise and pitfalls of using imprecise school accountability measures. *The Journal of Economic Perspectives, 16*(4), 91–114.

Kim, L. Y. (1993). Factors affecting student learning outcomes: A school-level analysis of the 1990 NAEP mathematics trial state assessment. Paper presented at the annual meeting of the American Educational Research Association, Atlanta, GA.

Kiplinger, V. L. (2008). Reliability of large-scale assessment and accountability systems. In K. E. Ryan & L. A. Shepard (Eds.), *The future of test-based educational accountability* (pp. 93–114). New York: Routledge.

Kirst, M. (1984). *Who controls our schools?* New York: Freeman.

Kirst, M. (2004). Turning points: A history of American school governance. In N. Epstein (Ed.), *Who's in charge here? The tangled web of school governance and policy* (pp. 14–41). Washington, DC: Brookings Institution.

Kirst, M., & Bulkley, K. (2000). "New, improved" mayors take over city schools. *Phi Delta Kappan, 81*(7), 538–540, 542–546.

Kirst, M., & Bulkley, K. (2001). *Mayoral takeover: The different directions taken in different cities*. Philadelphia, PA: Consortium for Policy Research in Education.

Koretz, D. M. (2008). Further steps toward the development of an accountability-oriented science of measurement. In K. E. Ryan & L. A. Shepard (Eds.), *The future of test-based educational accountability* (pp. 71–91). New York: Routledge.

Koretz, D. M., Mitchell, K. J., Barron, S., & Keith, S. (1996). *Perceived effects of the Kentucky instructional results information system (KIRIS)* (No. MR-792-PCT-FF). Santa Monica, CA: Rand Corporation Institute on Education and Training.

Kozol, J. (1992). *Savage inequalities: Children in America's schools*. New York: HarperCollins.

Kupermintz, H. (2003). Teacher effects and teacher effectiveness: A validity investigation of the Tennessee value added assessment system. *Educational Evaluation and Policy Analysis, 25*(3), 287–298.

Ladd, H. F. (Ed.) (1996). *Holding schools accountable: Performance-based reform in education*. Washington, DC: Brookings Institution.

Ladd, H. F. (2002). *Market-based reforms in urban education*. Washington, DC: EPI Books.

Lafee, S., Dawson, L. J., Alwin, L., & Yeagley, R. (2002). Data-driven districts. *School Administrator, 59*(11), 6–10.

Lashway, L. (2001). *The new standards and accountability: Will rewards and sanctions motivate American's schools to peak performance?* Eugene, OR: ERIC Clearinghouse on Educational Management.

Levin, H. M., & Belfield, C. R. (2003). The marketplace in education. *Review of Research in Education, 27*, 183–219.

Linn, R. (2005). *Fixing the NCLB accountability system*. Los Angeles: National Center for Research on Evaluation, Standards, and Student Testing, University of California.

Linn, R. (2008). Educational accountability systems. In K. E. Ryan & L. A. Shepard (Eds.), *The future of test-based educational accountability* (pp. 3–24). New York: Routledge.

Linn, R. L., Baker, E. L., & Betenbenner, D. W. (2002). *Accountability systems: Implications of requirements of the No Child Left Behind Act of 2001*. Los Angeles: Center for The Study of Evaluation & National Center for Research on Evaluation, Standards, and Student Testing, University of California.

Little, J. W. (1990). Teachers as colleagues. In A. Lieberman (Ed.), *Schools as collaborative cultures: Creating the future now* (pp. 165–193). New York: Falmer Press.

Little, J. W. (1995). Contested ground: The basis of teacher leadership in two restructuring high schools. *Elementary School Journal, 96*(1), 47–63.

Malen, B., Croninger, R., Muncey, D., & Redmond-Jones, D. (2002). Reconstituting schools: "Testing" the "Theory of Action." *Educational Evaluation and Policy Analysis, 24*(2), 113–132.

Meier, D. (1967). The Coleman Report. *Equity & Excellence in Education, 5*(6), 37–45.

Meier, D. (2000). *Will standards save public education?* Boston: Beacon Press.

Meyer, J. W., & Rowan, B. (1977). Institutionalized organizations: Formal structure as myth and ceremony. *American Journal of Sociology, 83*(2), 340.

Mintrop, H. (2003). The limits of sanctions in low-performing schools: A study of Maryland and Kentucky schools on probation. *Education Policy Analysis Archives, 11*(2).

Mintrop, H., & Sunderman, G. L. (2009). Predictable failure of federal sanctions-driven accountability for school improvement – and why we may retain it anyway. *Educational Researcher, 38*(5), 353–364.

Misco, T. (2008). Was that a result of my teaching? A brief exploration of value-added assessment. *Clearing House: A Journal of Educational Strategies, Issues and Ideas, 82*(1), 11–14.

Moon, T. R., Brighton, C. M., Jarvis, J. M., & Hall, C. J. (2007). *State standardized testing programs: Their effects on teachers and students*. Stoors, CT: National Research Center on the Gifted and Talented.

National Business Roundtable (1988). *The role of business in education reform: Blueprint for action* (No. ED 302 602). Report of the Business Roundtable Ad Hoc Committee on Education. New York: National Business Roundtable.

National Commission on Excellence in Education. (1983). *A nation at risk: The imperative for educational reform*. Washington, DC: National Commission on Excellence in Education.

National Education Goals Panel. (1992). *Gauging high performance: How to use NAEP to check progress on the national education goals: Report of the NAEP technical subgroup for the National Education Goals Panel* (Report No. 92-01): National Education Goals Panel.

Noguera, P. A. (2001). Racial politics and the elusive quest for excellence and equity in education. *Education and Urban Society, 34*(1), 18–41.

O'Day, J. A. (2002). Complexity, accountability, and school improvement. *Harvard Educational Review, 72*(3), 293–329.

Olson, L. (2002). Survey shows state testing alters instructional practices. *Education Week, 21*(32), 14.

Partnership for 21st Century Skills (2008). *21st century skills education and competitiveness guide*. Tucson, AZ: Partnership for 21st Century Skills.

Pedulla, J. J., Abrams, L. M., Madaus, G. F., Russell, M. K., Ramos, M. A., & Miao, J. (2003). *Perceived effects of state-mandated testing programs on teaching and learning: Findings from a national survey of teachers.* Chestnut Hill, MA: National Board on Educational Testing and Public Policy.

Peterson, P. E., Howell, W. G., & Greene, J. P. (1999). *An evaluation of the Cleveland voucher program after two years.* Cambridge, MA: Program on Education Policy and Governance, John F. Kennedy School of Government, Harvard University.

Pipho, C. (1977). Minimum competency testing in 1978: A look at state standards. *Phi Delta Kappan, 59*(9), 585–588.

Podgursky, M. J., & Springer, M. G. (2007). Teacher performance pay: A review. *Journal of Policy Analysis and Management, 26*(4), 909–950.

Raham, H. (2000). Cooperative performance incentive plans. *Peabody Journal of Education, 75*(4), 142–158.

Reeves, C. (2003). *Implementing the No Child Left Behind Act: Implications for rural schools and districts* (No. ED475037). Naperville, IL: North Central Regional Educational Laboratory.

Reid, K. S. (2001). Chicago chief named amid urban turnover. *Education Week, 20*(42), 3–5.

Rist, R. C. (1970). Student social class and teacher expectations: The self-fulfilling prophesy in ghetto educaiton. *Harvard Educational Review, 40*(3), 411–451.

Robelen, E. W. (2009). Obama echoes Bush on education ideas. *Education Week, 28*(28), 1.

Sanders, W. L. (1998). Value-added assessment. *School Administrator, 55*(11), 24–27.

Schrader, A. W. (1973). MBO: Results oriented management in the educational setting. *Catalyst for Change, 3*(1), 15–17, 26.

Shafer, R. E. (1975). National assessment: Backgrounds and projections – 1975. Paper presented at the annual Conference on English Education, Colorado Springs, CO.

Sizer, T. R., & Rogers, B. (1993). Designing standards: Achieving the delicate balance. *Educational Leadership, 50*(5), 24–26.

Smarick, A. (2008). Wave of the future: Why charter schools should replace failing urban schools. *Education Next, 8*(1), 38–45.

Smey-Richman, B. (1989). *Teacher expectations and low achieving students.* Philadelphia, PA: Research for Better Schools.

Smith, M. S., & O'Day, J. (1991). Systemic school reform. In S. Fuhrman & B. Malen (Eds.), *The politics of curriculum and testing: The 1990 Yearbook of the Politics of Education Association* (pp. 233–267). Philadelphia, PA: Falmer Press.

Spillane, J. P. (2004). *Standards deviation: How schools misunderstand education policy.* Cambridge, MA: Harvard University Press.

Spillane, J. P., & Zeuli, J. S. (1999). Reform and teaching: Exploring patterns of practice in the context of national and state mathematics reforms. *Educational Evaluation and Policy Analysis, 21*(1), 1–28.

Springer, M. G., Ballou, D., Hamilton, L., Le, V.-N., Lockwood, J. R., McCaffrey, D. F., et al. (2010). *Teacher pay for performance: Experimental evidence from the project on incentives in teaching.* Nashville, TN: Vanderbilt University.

Teddlie, C., & Stringfield, S. (1993). *Schools make a difference.* New York: Teachers College Press.

Tugend, A. (1985). Half of Chicago students drop out, study finds: Problem called "enormous tragedy." *Education Week, 4*(24), 10.

Tyack, D. (1974). *The one best system: A history of American urban education.* Cambridge, MA: Harvard University Press.

Tyack, D., & Cuban, L. (1995). *Tinkering toward Utopia: A century of public school reform.* Cambridge, MA: Harvard University Press.

U.S. Department of Education (2001). *No Child Left Behind.* Washington, DC:. U.S. Department of Education.

U.S. Department of Education (2009). Obama administration announces historic opportunity to turn around nation's lowest-achieving public schools. Retrieved October 20, 2010 from: www2.ed.gov/news/pressreleases/2009/08/08262009.html

U.S. Department of Education (2010). Teacher incentive fund. Retrieved October 12, 2010 from: www2.ed.gov/programs/teacherincentive/index.html

Waxer, C. (2004). Lesson plan. *Workforce Management, 83*(7), 37–40.

Wenglinsky, H. (2002). How schools matter: The link between teacher classroom practices and student academic performance. Retrieved May 27, 2003 from: http://epaa.asu.edu/epaa/v10n12/

Wirt, F., & Kirst, M. (1989). *Schools in conflict: The politics of education* (2nd ed.). Berkeley, CA: McCutchan.

Wise, A. E., & Darling-Hammond, L. (1983). Beyond standardization: State standards and school improvement. Paper presented at the National Institute of Education Conference on State and Local Policy Implications of Effective School Research, Washington, DC.

Witte, J. F. (1998). The Milwaukee voucher experiment. *Educational Evaluation and Policy Analysis, 20*(4), 229–251.

Witte, J. F. (1999). The Milwaukee voucher experiment: The good, the bad, and the ugly. *Phi Delta Kappan, 81*(1), 59–64.

Wong, K. K., & Anagnostopoulos, D. (1998). Can integrated governance reconstruct teaching? Lessons learned from two low-performing Chicago high schools. *Educational Policy, 12*(1/2), 31.

Wong, K. K., & Shen, F. X. (2001). Does school district takeover work? Assessing the effectiveness of city and state takeover as a school reform strategy. Paper presented at the American Political Science Association, Seattle, WA.

Yee, G., & Cuban, L. (1996). When is tenure long enough? A historical analysis of superintendent turnover and tenure in urban school districts. *Educational Administration Quarterly, 32*, December, 615–641.

Zavadsky, H. (2006). How NCLB drives success in urban schools. *Educational Leadership, 64*(3), 69–73.

Ziebarth, T. (2002). *State takeovers and reconstitutions.* Policy Brief (No. ED473720). Denver, CO: Education Commission of the States.

Zimmer, R., & Buddin, R. (2006). Charter school performance in two large urban districts. *Journal of Urban Economics, 60*, 307–326.

13

Accountability for Equity in Postsecondary Education

Alicia C. Dowd, Robin Bishop, Estela Mara Bensimon, and Keith Witham

In an article titled "'What's good for Boyle Heights is good for the Jews': Creating multiracialism on the Eastside during the 1950s," Sánchez (2004) traced the history of racial diversity, social activism, and "multiracialism" in the Boyle Heights neighborhood of Los Angeles to the turning points when the area became populated predominantly by Mexican Americans and Mexican immigrants. Sánchez's close analysis of the documents of a variety of civic and political organizations—including the Soto-Michigan Jewish Community Center, the Community Services Organization, and the Los Angeles Committee for the Protection of the Foreign Born—shows how, during the 1950s, organizers acted to forward leftist political ideals and sustain the Boyle Heights community as a multiracial community in the face of growing pressure from the House Un-American Activities Committee and other conservative groups. Using announcements for events, meeting minutes, and news from the local press, Sánchez illustrates how activists created intercultural programming for the Japanese, Jewish, Anglo, and Latino communities and shared a struggle for workers' rights.

The demise of this multiracial coalition occurred through "a changing ideology of race and a growing lack of tolerance for social mixing" (Sánchez, 2004, p. 636). Jews and other groups previously viewed as ethnic "others" increasingly became grouped with White Protestants as "Caucasians" during a time when new racially restrictive neighborhoods were springing up to the West and North of downtown and Jews departed to pursue the ideal of middle-class assimilation. The active hand of the Federal Housing Authority in denigrating Boyle Heights in the decades that preceded this exodus is evident as, in 1939, it detrimentally characterized the neighborhood as "hopelessly heterogenous" (p. 637) and applied its lowest possible rating.

This history of the "complex transformation of the terms of racialization" (p. 637) and the "geography of difference" (p. 636), to use Sánchez's terms, is a telling one in contemplating the meaning of the term *urban education* in the postsecondary context in the United States today. Sánchez's close, street-level reading of that history is also relevant to understanding racial dynamics and racial equity in postsecondary access and outcomes. To a newcomer to Los Angeles, it might seem that Boyle Heights and East LA were always Latino neighborhoods and that South LA was always African American—that these geographies of difference are natural and irrevocable rather than socially constructed and political.

In similar terms, the lack of Latinos at elite institutions like UCLA in Westwood, and their great numbers at East Los Angeles College, El Camino College, Rio Hondo College, and other community colleges in and around Los Angeles are viewed as natural differences of geography and culture. Urban postsecondary education is not characterized by racial diversity (as many of the most urban colleges are homogeneously African American or Latino) or uniquely by linguistic diversity (as it is common for land grant universities and suburban liberal arts colleges also to boast of the many languages spoken by members of the student body and the many countries from which they hail). If any characteristics can be isolated to distinguish urban colleges and universities from their rural, suburban, and exurban counterparts, the features of stratification and inequality—greatly opposed and in close proximity—stand out.

Like Sánchez's, in our work at the Center for Urban Education (CUE) at the University of Southern California we conduct close readings of local texts to interpret racialized geographies of difference. In our case, however, of interest are the texts of colleges and universities and their state systems rather than those of political and civic organizations. Our readings are not only of written texts but of a variety of cultural artifacts represented in numerical data, data displays, language, physical space, signs, and symbols. We draw on critical race theory, cultural historical activity theory, and theories of practice and inquiry to interpret inequities among racial–ethnic groups in access to colleges and universities, participation in the various strains of the stratified whole, and outcomes in terms of major field of study, degrees awarded, and honors and awards bestowed. We do so using a range of research methodologies, including action research involving practitioners as researchers of their own policies and practices.

In this chapter, we illustrate this approach and its relevance to educational accountability in urban settings. We start with a summary of the primary concepts of cultural historical activity theory (CHAT) (Cole, 2003; Cole & Engeström, 1993; Cole, Engeström, & Vasquez, 1997; Engeström, 2001, 2008; Engeström, Miettinen, & Punamäki-Gitai, 1999; Kuutti & Engeström, 2005; Ogawa, Crain, Loomis, & Ball, 2008). The second section introduces a narrative of action research (Greenwood & Levin, 2005; Kemmis & McTaggart, 2000; Reason, 1994) conducted by CUE researchers with administrators and faculty members at Long Beach City College (LBCC), a community college located in Long Beach, California, south of Los Angeles. Subsequent sections continue the narrative interspersed with interpretation of the narrative using the CHAT framework. This illustrates how CHAT, particularly applied through social learning theory (Tharp, 1993; Tharp & Gallimore, 1988), provides the framework for guiding CUE's action research methodology, which is focused on remediating the artifacts of professional practice in colleges and universities to achieve equity in outcomes among racial–ethnic groups. Action research is validated through the actions of practitioners whose beliefs and behaviors change through the remediation of the artifacts of their practice. CHAT calls attention to the historical and dialectical construction of the language and practices of postsecondary education. The conclusion locates this case in a broader framework of action research and accountability.

Cultural Historical Activity Theory

Acknowledging the social and cultural construction of knowledge, CHAT addresses how new learning takes place within a setting that is inherently constrained by its historical legacies and the language and objects present within its culture. CHAT considers not only these verbal and physical "cultural artifacts," but also the ways that individuals interact with these artifacts in their ongoing learning on behalf of the institution. Such interaction is affected by the group memberships, goals, rules and norms, and division of labor within the setting. Therefore, the learning setting is recognized as dynamic and reflexive, characterized by various changing parts that may affect one another. As noted by Engeström (2001, p. 134), actions within these systems are "always, explicitly or implicitly, characterized by ambiguity, surprise, interpretation, sense making, and potential for change."

CHAT takes its name from four important ideas. The summary that follows emphasizes a fifth central concept—that of mediating artifacts.

Culture

CHAT acknowledges, first and foremost, that all learning takes place in the context of culture. This means that every thought or decision is inevitably influenced by the values, norms, assumptions, and expectations of the cultures—be they institutional, societal, or familial—of which we are a part. In all instances, culture affects what we see (or fail to see) and what we do (or choose not to do). Within the study of organizational change, it is necessary to address the question: what cultural factors within the institution are facilitating or hindering desired change? Despite the ever-present influence of culture, we generally fail to see how it affects us because we are constantly within it. Cole likens this to being a "fish in water," adding that, "encounters with other cultures make it easier to grasp our own as an object of thought" (Cole, 2003, p. 8).

History

Our daily actions are constrained not only by the present state of our cultures and our current forms of participation in them but also by the histories of those cultures and the legacies of prior generations. Every institution is characterized by customs or traditions, or a "way that things have always been done." These customs often go unrecognized and unquestioned, as they are transmitted—both consciously and through the subtle socialization of new members—from one generation of practitioners to the next. As we incorporate these practices and legacies into our own repertoires and they become patterns, or habits, they shape how we undertake the same actions again in the future. In essence, we project our history into an imagined future (Cole & Engeström, 1993). This can be efficient because current actions require little deliberation; however, it may also hinder change by limiting the alternatives we are able to conceptualize. Conversely, active reflection about how our current actions are situated within our history can illuminate resistance to change and allow for a conscious consideration of the benefits of "historically new" forms of action.

Activity

CHAT acknowledges that the best way to learn new information, and especially new modes of action, is in the context of a shared, mutually engaging activity. CHAT literature describes an "ideal" activity setting as one in which individuals come together around a shared activity, an activity into which they all have some input (Roth & Lee, 2007). As participants negotiate roles and rules and embark upon ways of investigating or solving the problem at hand, each brings back new discoveries. As agreements and disagreements in perspective are explored, new knowledge is coconstructed within the group.

Activity Setting

CHAT provides the opportunity to examine the social construction of practice holistically and in historical perspective. It focuses on an activity setting as the unit of analysis (Engeström, 2001). Within a given setting, multiple facets are key to the overall functioning (Table 13.1). A change in any one of these facets may bring about changes in others, and may contribute to change in the overall system in which the various settings are embedded. Such a model allows for a focus on all of these facets within an action research methodology.

Table 13.1 Facets of Activity Settings

Outcome	The ultimate goal at which the shared task is aimed.
Object	The shared productive activity around which participants have convened, an activity that is aimed at the outcome but is also an end in itself; the way in which shared meaning is made of this activity, which will ultimately inform the outcome.
Subjects	Participants who engage in the activity.
Rules	Those expectations that are explicitly stated as well as implicit norms.
Division of labor	"Who does what" among participants.
Activity setting community	The participants who have gathered around the shared productive activity.
Mediating artifacts	Aspects of the physical and spoken environment that affect how participants understand their world, including the task at hand.

Mediating Artifacts

The concept of mediating artifacts is both complex and nuanced. From the time that a person enters a given institution or environment, his or her understanding of what is valued there, what is accepted, what is celebrated, what is to be striven for (and conversely, what is not valued, accepted, celebrated, striven for) is communicated in a number of ways. These include the following: via language (what is and is not said), via signs (what is and is not visually communicated), via physical space (the arrangement and allocation of physical resources), and via tools (the materials of production and reproduction used in various activities).

"Equity for All" at Long Beach City College

As one of nine community colleges participating in a CUE-facilitated action research project named "Equity for All: Institutional Responsibility for Student Success,"[1] Long Beach City College (LBCC) engaged in a year-long process of examining data on educational outcomes disaggregated by race and ethnicity. The culmination of this project was a customized version of CUE's "Equity Scorecard," which told the college how well it was doing based on indicators of the educational outcomes of historically underrepresented students.[2] In the process of examining the transfer readiness and actual transfer of four cohorts of first-time students from the community college, the "evidence team" (Bensimon, 2004; Bensimon & Neumann, 1993; Bensimon, Polkinghorne, Bauman, & Vallejo, 2004; Bensimon, Rueda, Dowd, & Harris III, 2007) of instructors and administrators wanted to know how many students in a multiyear, four-cohort sample of 27,422 students[3] had managed to meet all the necessary transfer requirements in three years (the standard for "on-time" associate's degree completion).

On learning that only 520 students, a mere 2% of the original cohort, had achieved transfer-ready status within three years, the LBCC Scorecard team dubbed this unique group the "fast-track" transfer-ready students. The team then asked more fine-grained questions about them, particularly in regard to their transitions within the public system to the University of California (UC) and California State University (CSU) campuses. They asked, "How many of the 520 fast-track students qualified for transfer to UC?" "Of those, how many actually went to a UC?" "Did all 520 transfer to a four-year college, and of those how many went to a CSU?" Finally, at each step of the analysis, they asked, "Were differences in transfer patterns by race and ethnicity observed?"

LBCC's experience shows what an institution can learn about itself in the process of gathering data to answer questions that contextualize problems indicated by the low numbers of students who transfer. The sample for the numerical data analysis comprised the "fast-track" students, but the focus of the study quickly expanded to consider transfer opportunities for all LBCC students. The speedy completion of transfer requirements by the fast-track group suggests they were among the college's most academically prepared students, "high achievers" whose success was emblematic of the possibilities for other students whose journeys toward a college degree and the possibility of transfer would take longer and be more challenging.

As the research team examined the transfer outcomes of the fast-track students, they also became interested in understanding the kinds of information, counseling, and academic support the other 98% of their students experienced in regard to transfer opportunities. That led to a second phase of the study in which a larger group of LBCC practitioner-researchers collaborated to collect qualitative data based on interviews with students and colleagues, ethnographic observations on campus, and document analyses, all with the purpose of seeing the college from the point of view of LBCC students. The team set out to study their own transfer culture and to answer the question "How do we 'do' transfer here?" (Bensimon & Dowd, 2009; Bensimon, Dowd, Alford, & Trapp, 2007).

By focusing on the content and quality of institutional practices, the team of practitioner-researchers acknowledged, albeit implicitly, the possibility that accepted and long-standing routines of providing transfer information and preparing students for transfer might not be effective for all students, and most particularly for members of minority racial–ethnic groups. These questions— "How do we 'do' transfer here?" and by implication, "Why is the way we 'do' transfer here failing to advance the educational attainment of Latino/Latina and African American students most particularly?"—were ways of reframing a problem of institutional practices that were producing inequities. In this way, institutional practices, rather than students, became the focus for remediation.

Introducing the language of racial equity in transfer was particularly important as a strategy to mediate cultural change. Although LBCC had the required percentage of Latino and Latina students to qualify as a Hispanic-Serving Institution (HSI) and be eligible for the special federal funding designated for HSIs, its identity as an HSI was ambiguous in the sense that the symbols and artifacts of culture at LBCC did not reflect an espoused value for serving Hispanic students. Although the college had become more Latinized, the faculty were predominantly White and their assumptions about institutional practices reflected a sense of "color-blindness." The idea that an HSI might ask itself "What are our responsibilities as an HSI and how do we know whether we are meeting them?" was not part of the cultural norms of the college.

Policy studies of California's community colleges and of transfer in other states have primarily focused on gross measures of success such as retention and transfer rates. Similarly, the state system of Accountability Reporting for the Community Colleges (ARCC) is designed to monitor aggregate measures of student outcomes. Such general measures provide a snapshot of system and institutional performance, but they are too "high above the ground" to help define problems in ways college administrators and faculty can tackle. Additionally, outcome data are more likely to be reported for "all students" or for "underrepresented minorities" compared with "Whites," which reinforces the norms and ideology of being racially diverse without being racially conscious (Iverson, 2007).

When LBCC's team of practitioner-researchers delved into more fine-grained measures, disaggregated by race and ethnicity, of the transfer outcomes of their fast-track students, they moved closer to answering the questions that most interested them. These questions were not routinely asked at their college as part of strategic planning, accountability reporting, or institutional research:

- How many students in our college, by race and ethnicity, become transfer-ready within three years of enrolling?
- How many of our transfer-ready students, by race and ethnicity, actually transfer within one to three years?
- How many of our UC transfer-ready students, by race and ethnicity, actually transfer to UC or a college that is equally selective?

When LBCC's research team asked these three questions and dug into their institutional data to answer them, they uncovered gaps in transfer enrollments that most likely exist at many community colleges in California and nationally. These problems are rarely talked about in policy or research circles, however, because accountability data are typically too aggregated to reveal them. At LBCC, not only did this study of the college's own "local" data generate local, particularized knowledge of these gaps, it motivated members of the research team to do more to understand how to address them and to improve the college's transfer effectiveness more generally.

The number of LBCC transfers to the University of California (UC) in the data analyzed by the LBCC evidence team was strikingly small (only 40), despite the fact that the special fast-track subgroup who had achieved transfer eligibility in only three years was culled from a combined four-year (1999–2002) population of first-time students. As a result, the numbers transferring to a UC from any group were also extremely low, ranging from 6 African Americans and 6 Asian/Pacific Islanders to 11 Latinas and Latinos.

Remediating Accountability

The narrative above illustrates how the CHAT framework applied to action research methodology provides new understandings of the enterprise of public accountability (Burke, 2005) for equity in postsecondary outcomes (Dowd & Tong, 2007). Under monitoring and reporting strategies of accountability, college administrators and faculty are to be motivated, upon seeing data revealing poor institutional performance, by a mix of shame and professional pride to improve upon that performance. This approach may work to a limited extent, but it may also stimulate political renegotiation of accountability criteria or incentives to change the numbers being reported rather than the underlying causes of poor institutional performance (Dougherty & Hong, 2006).

Alternatively, by asking administrators and faculty to assume roles of researchers analyzing their own institutional data, the action research approach seeks to change the division of labor in knowledge construction based on the information contained in the data. The Equity Scorecard's process of collaborative data analysis creates an activity setting for a joint productive activity, which is an opportunity for the social construction of learning. Student progression and success data usually reside in the hands of institutional researchers, whose professional socialization and training provide technical and analytical competence in presenting institutional data (Terenzini, 1999). Institutional researchers are not typically asked to assume the role of teacher (Dowd, Malcom, Nakamoto, & Bensimon, in press). The activity setting of customizing and completing an Equity Scorecard for LBCC remediated the roles of the individuals involved on the evidence team. That this remediation was lasting in any sense cannot be said based on this narrative, but it is clear from the willingness of the evidence team to conduct further research that they were assuming a new role.

The low numbers of students transferring also introduced a contradiction. Surely, drawing from a dense and highly diverse urban population and 4 cohorts of new students numbering over 27,000, a greater number than 6 African Americans, 6 Asian/Pacific Islanders, and 11 Latinas and Latinos would have transferred to a UC. Several campuses are located close by, including UCLA, UC Irvine, UC Riverside, and UC San Diego. Transfer is a key component of California's master plan. Community colleges are the cornerstone of that plan and the gateway to social mobility.

Within the CHAT framework, the presentation of contradictions is viewed as facilitative, as contradictions present the opportunity for participants to question, challenge, and experience conflict, all of which engender learning (Engeström, 2000; Gutierrez & Vossoughi, 2010). As the Scorecard participants' early hunches about the reasons for such inequities were explored, a period of questioning and challenging ensued. This led to further inquiry into factors and potential solutions. Such explorations can lead to what Engeström has called "expansive transformation," as "participants begin to question and deviate from . . . established norms . . . [and] the object and motive of the activity are reconceptualized to embrace a wider horizon of possibilities" (2001, p. 136).

Stratification

Perhaps to an even greater extent than other conduits to the baccalaureate, transfer admissions requirements in California are heavily regulated and numerous bureaucratic entities exert oversight, including the State of California, the UC and CSU systems, and private college admissions offices. The hierarchies of transfer access mirror hierarchies established in the state's master plan for higher education. Students are required to follow exact procedures in order to qualify for transfer. The rules of transfer are codified in an array of legal documents, such as the Intersegmental General Education Transfer Curriculum (IGETC). Understanding the numerous technical details, regulations, and exceptions that constitute transfer requires mastery of a highly specialized language and the patience to follow very explicit rules. The regulations are not necessarily intuitive or easily fathomed. Individual community colleges set their own rules through their curriculum committees,[4] counseling services, and enrollment management functions. In addition, community colleges are in an intermediary position when it comes to the transfer requirements of the UC and CSU systems. They communicate the requirements of the upper division campuses, but do not determine them. Materials communicating these complex transfer requirements often include a "buyer beware" warning. At the time of our study, a boldface headline at the top of one of LBCC's transfer documents stated, "All information contained herein is subject to change without notice." This signaled that the regulations were variable and in flux. Students could not confidently make decisions based on printed information, yet the information governed their access to public institutions and degrees and the better life promised by more advanced degrees.

The result of multiple layers of regulation is an elaborate labyrinth of rules, constituted through a specialized transfer lexicon. For example, at the time our study was conducted, LBCC organized information about general education requirements and transfer eligibility in three curricular tracks referred to as Plan A, Plan B, and Plan C. These plans were summarized in a four-page flyer from the college titled General Education Plans, which listed degree and transfer requirements in an "at-a-glance" format. The flyer was intended only as a starting point, a quick reference guide. To determine whether a course carried credits transferrable to a UC, students also needed to refer to the LBCC course catalog. Another document, called the ABC Guide, provided notice of any changes in Plans A, B, or C. A Transfer Guide provides information distilled from four-year college catalogs and articulation agreements.

Our review of the LBCC General Education Plans summary alone highlighted for us the sheer number of specialized terms a person must understand in order to decipher transfer requirements (summarized in Table 13.2). Some are relatively common, such as credit, degree, or certificate, while others, like IGETC, ASSIST, and the "50% rule," are more specialized. The dictates of various regulating institutions are evident in the "alphabet soup" of the various curriculum categories. LBCC's Plan B, specifying the general education breadth requirements of the CSU system, relied on disciplinary categories labeled Areas A through E, with subnumbered subject or major area groupings. Plan C, on the other hand, categorized required courses in areas numbered 1 through 6, with subcategories 1A, 1B, and 1C.

Other printed resources included flyers, brochures, catalogs, booklets, guidebooks, information request postcards, and application forms. These were produced by LBCC itself, by four-year colleges and universities, or, in the case of the guidebooks, by publishing houses. These print materials were supplemented by the college's Web pages featuring transfer information, as well as a number of state, university, or private organization Web sites such as www.assist.org (California's official state guide

Table 13.2 Lexicon of Transfer Regulations and Processes

A	Counselor	L M P Q
AA/AS	Credit	LBCC Curriculum Guide
ABC Guide	Cross-listed	Limitations
Acceptance		Lower division
Areas 1A, 1B, 1C, 2–7	D	Major
Articulation	Discipline	Plan A, B, C
Arts	Double-counted credit	Private university
Assessment test	Dual major	Proficiency
ASSIST		Quarter
Associate degree	F	
	50% rule	R S T U
B		Request for graduation
Bachelor's degree	G H I	Residency
Breadth	General education	Semester
	General Education Areas A1, A2,	Schedule of classes
C	A3, B1, B2, B3, B4, C1, C2,	Student Success/Transfer Services
California State University	D1–9, D0, E	Center
Catalog	Humanities	Transfer Curriculum Guide
Catalog rights	Interdisciplinary	UCTCA
Certificate	Intersegmental General Education	Unit
Certification	Transfer Curriculum (IGETC)	University of California
Concentration		

to transfer requirements and articulation agreements), www.csumentor.org (the CSU systems on-line advising site), and www.collegesource.org (a centralized source of four-year college catalogs).

The plans reflect the bureaucratic stratification of transfer access. Plan A was designed for students interested in earning an associate's degree. Plan B provided the lower division general education breadth requirements for admissions to the CSU system. Finally, the courses included in Plan C met the requirements of the Intersegmental General Education Transfer Curriculum (IGETC) of the CSU and UC systems. Plan C was the best plan for transfer to a UC campus, but the Plan C curriculum also qualified students for transfer to a CSU. In addition to completing the IGETC curriculum, UC transfers were required to have a grade point average of 2.4 or higher, complete all courses with a grade of C or better, and demonstrate foreign language proficiency. In addition to understanding these differences, students were also required to complete four foundation courses from a selection designated in the "Golden Four" categories of English/Written Communication, Speech/Oral Communication, Mathematics, and Critical Thinking. In order to be certified as eligible for transfer under Plan B, a student was required to complete 50% of their transfer credits at the college. For Plan C, this "50% rule" was relaxed, as credits could be completed at any California community college.

Notably, such requirements pertain only to students who were not eligible for CSU and UC admissions upon high school graduation. Those who were eligible right after high school may elect to take courses at a community college and transfer based on their high school academic record. The full weight of transfer regulations, therefore, falls on students who were least academically prepared when they entered college. Compare the opaqueness of transfer regulations to the information provided by highly selective institutions, reaching out to the most academically savvy and prepared students, to recruit their freshman classes using four-color viewbooks, brochures, social media, and electronic communications targeted in niche markets. Information about complex choices in other realms, such as healthcare for example, are typically conveyed with professional graphic designs. Most community colleges, which pride themselves as open-access institutions (Dowd, 2008), are not well equipped for major marketing efforts. The LBCC budget for copying in the Transfer Center was minimal. An enterprising "do-it-yourselfer" at LBCC was able to save on the copying budget by using small type and a jam-packed design, but the resulting document was far from inviting. Other published pieces at the college, such as the course catalog, similarly revealed the challenge of including too much information in too small a space. That the burden of communicating complex requirements to first-generation students, immigrants, and others who are still learning how to navigate academic systems falls to community colleges is, therefore, suspect.

As noted above, from the time an individual enters an environment, his or her understanding of what is accepted, valued, and celebrated in that environment is mediated by artifacts in the multiple forms of language, signs, physical space, and tools. The specialized terms of the transfer lexicon and the rules and regulations governing access are the mediating artifacts defining who is valued in different sectors of higher education in the state. Such stratification characterizes urban post-secondary education in racialized ways because there is a systemic valuing of academic credentials that racially minoritized groups cannot access in ways equal to students living in dominant communities with higher socioeconomic status.

One of the findings of our study, previously reported (see Bensimon & Dowd, 2009), showed that even some of those students who were eligible to transfer to a UC campus did not, opting to enroll at less competitive institutions instead. All the signs of the bureaucracy communicated that transfer students were not valued at UC campuses. The strict stratification evident in these transfer artifacts served to constitute the "life world" (Kemmis & McTaggart, 2000) of transfer as a bureaucratic maze. The historical assumption of higher education standing in relationship to its environment—its citizenry—as a public good and a public right became subsumed by an assumption of higher education as a resource to be guarded by bureaucratic protections.

Remediating Roles

At the time of our study, students at LBCC were instructed to consult with a counselor before embarking on Plan A, B, or C. Otherwise they were at risk of misunderstanding some intricacy of transfer regulations and taking courses that would not be counted when they tried to transfer or of taking more courses than they needed. There was agreement on LBCC's evidence team that more students should make their way to LBCC's Transfer Center and receive one-on-one counseling. But the Transfer Center budget was essentially flat from 2005 through 2007 (the period of our study) and services had recently been cut, included evening transfer workshops, and in-class presentations by counselors. Even the field trips to four-year college campuses, though apparently of great importance to some students, were funded not through the Transfer Center but through the budgets of special programs such as PUENTE, a "bridge" program designed to support the college success of Latina and Latino students, and the federally funded Equal Opportunity Programs and Services (EOP&S).

To assess the culture of transfer at LBCC, LBCC faculty and staff engaged in an action inquiry. Applying the CHAT framework to action research methodology, CUE researchers provided a tool created at the Center after a national study of transfer (Dowd et al., 2006). Using CUE's Transfer Self-Assessment Inventory as a guide, an evidence team collected observational data to attempt to "see" the college's transfer culture for themselves. The results of the team's research suggested that the transfer advising information was not reaching its intended audience. The research team's observational data highlighted dust on postcards, a lack of posted information in areas outside the immediate physical space of counseling centers, a page limitation on printing from Web sites presenting transfer information, and an underutilization of transfer-planning Web sites. For example, a respondent in the counseling area commented that the www.collegesource.org site was a valuable resource but one that was seldom used, perhaps owing to a lack of advertising about its availability. An LBCC faculty member on the research team observed, based on his teaching experience, that many students would not have the computer skills to find transfer information. These comments highlighted the fact that the value of Web sites for counseling is low if only a few students use them. Poor signage made it difficult for the LBCC researchers to physically find the main transfer counseling centers on their own campuses, suggesting that students, too, would need to be persistent in their search for them.

Formal counseling appointments were difficult to schedule. Students were required to schedule their transfer advising appointments a week in advance. Transfer advising appointments were limited to students who had completed the assessment process and 24 units of transfer coursework, including at least two of the four foundation courses in English/Written Communication, Speech/Oral Communication, Mathematics, and Critical Thinking. Online and "Xpress," or 10-minute advising, was available, but it was difficult to convey the complexities of transfer requirements in a short counseling appointment or through virtual advising.

There were numerous ways in which the campus did reach out to students, including transfer fairs, transfer presentations by counselors in classrooms, and field trips to four-year colleges. Transfer workshops, at which students could get assistance in selecting their courses and completing four-year college applications, were sometimes held. Transfer fairs were a centerpiece of LBCC's efforts to reach out to students. The transfer center calendar for spring 2007 indicated that representatives from a variety of institutions in the four-year sector would participate. These included private nonprofit institutions such as Mount St. Mary's, a consortium of historically Black colleges and universities, private for-profit institutions such as Vanguard and Phoenix Universities and the DeVry Institute, as well as nearby CSUs (Long Beach, Dominguez Hills, Los Angeles, Fullerton, and Cal Poly Pomona) and UCs (Los Angeles, Irvine, and Santa Barbara). It is unclear how much participation the fairs attracted, however. One LBCC researcher who visited such a fair found very few students in attendance, but another found long lines.

There were notable differences in the level of participation of four-year institutions at the transfer fairs depending on their level of selectivity and enrollment demand. The most selective institutions acted like "choice" colleges, with the ability to select among numerous applicants, whereas those with enrollment capacity acted more like "supply" colleges. Supply colleges marketed themselves in numerous ways at the transfer fair, as illustrated by the range of activities taking place at the "Day with Dominguez Hills" event held on the LBCC quad. An LBCC researcher described what she learned through an informal interview with the university representative about how the event was planned and from observing interactions between counselors and students:

> A person in the transfer office invites both deans and faculty members from different departments to be part of the fair, so they can field specific questions regarding their department's requirements; she thinks it's having a positive impact. I saw representatives from the Music Department, Human Services, Liberal Studies, Army Reserve Officers Training, and Financial Aid (whose representative was speaking in Spanish to a student!). There were brochures available from Public Administration, English, Anthropology, and World Cultures as well.

> She also has an evaluator present, so that on-site admissions can be done. She wants to be proactive in order to increase the number of transfer students to Dominguez Hills, and also encourages her faculty to be available to make presentations in community college classrooms. Once students are at Dominguez Hills, they seem to do well, so her goal is to increase the number of transfers. As part of her proactive stance, she also makes sure that transfer fairs are held where they will be visible to the greatest number of students (near food/financial aid/the bookstore).

The LBCC researcher learned that CSU-Dominguez Hills also recruits transfer students through telemarketing, mailings, and special receptions for transfer students. A for-profit institution was similarly active in marketing itself by providing information about tuition discounts, federal and state grants (Pell and CAL), department-level contact names who could advise on selecting a major, and on-site assessment of transfer-credit eligibility. CSU-Long Beach and CSU-Dominguez Hills were the most frequent participants at LBCC transfer fairs, sending representatives to provide information on campus 15 and 12 times, respectively. There were a total of 66 visits from four-year institutions in the spring of 2007, with 40 of those requiring appointments. All of the 10 UC and Cal Poly Pomona visits required students to make an appointment, in comparison to 25 of the 35 CSU visits, suggesting that it would not be easy for a student to meet with a UC representative, and to a lesser extent a CSU representative, without advance planning.

The evidence team members discussed whether most students would know how to negotiate a transfer fair and learn what they needed to do to transfer by going to a fair. They considered which setting might feel more intimidating for students, the transfer fairs or one-on-one appointments. The evidence team considered whether it would be helpful to actually provide students with a list of questions, perhaps by posting them at the fairs, that they would know to ask each university representative and have an initial primer for how to approach them. The following two comments illustrate the discussion among LBCC evidence team members during our review of the data they had collected using the Transfer Self-Assessment Inventory:

> I wondered if students might be more likely to approach an individual at a table outside on the quad versus having to make an appointment and speak one-on-one with someone.

> The fairs are great to provide information but [how do we go about] getting the students to go to them? By giving them a list of what questions to ask? What is important? These are things to ask. What do you do with the information you received?

One researcher argued that transfer counseling and resources were available to students who knew how to find them. But "Students on campus tend to have to seek us out, rather than our being able to look out for them." The statement implies that the LBCC researcher is espousing a role for individuals who were not transfer counselors to "look out" for students. This statement stood out because in earlier conversations it was stated several times that individuals who were not transfer counselors (a formal function and role at the college) could not advise students about transfer because they could not possibly know the intricacies of the transfer regulations and requirements. After gaining a first-hand understanding of why students may not understand what is required to transfer, the idea that transfer counseling must be left to transfer counselors came under questioning. As noted above, human activity has historical precedents. Practices are sustained in artifacts that reflect the values and assumptions embedded in the culture. Through action inquiry, the LBCC evidence team members examined data about their own transfer culture. This allowed them to question "the ways things have always been done" and to think in new ways about their role in the community of practitioners whose responsibilities included transfer advising.

The transfer self-assessment inventory that we provided to the LBCC researchers did not have explicit references and indicators concerning racial inequities in transfer. As a consequence, the researchers' results were "color mute." They did not actively consider the implications of the lack of transfer advising on Latina and Latino students and African Americans, for example. However, we saw the introduction of a contradiction between the espoused ideals of the community college as the "gateway" to social mobility and collegiate attainment and the college's own data showing that 6 African Americans, 6 Asian/Pacific Islanders, and 11 Latinas and Latinos had transferred to a UC from among a four-year population of first-time students at the college of 27,422 unique cases. By bringing the researchers' attention to this contradiction and to the activity settings in which transfer took place at LBCC, the division of labor to address the problem of the low numbers of students transferring became open to negotiation.

The surprise of the researcher at the financial aid counselor's use of Spanish to communicate with the prospective transfer student reveals that such a practice was against the norm, despite the college's location in Southern California, which is home to a large Spanish-speaking population. Just as the hierarchies and stratification of transfer access to the UC and CSUs are revealed through the complexities of the transfer lexicon, the racialized assumptions of the public system are revealed by this observation. The observer's surprise shows that the prevailing cultural assumptions of the way transfer and college advising "are done" were contradicted. The social construction of public college access as a monocultural, monolingual activity is contradicted by the enterprising marketing of the CSU-Dominguez Hills representative. Just as Sánchez's 2004 article "What's good for Boyle Heights is good for Jews" reveals a history of a neighborhood that became monocultural through the social construction of multiracial mixing as "hopelessly heterogeneous," the researcher's surprise reveals the social construction of college access in "Whites only" terms. A different political history may have led to multilingual educational environments in Southern California's schools and colleges, just as a different political history may have sustained a multiracial Boyle Heights in the 21st century.

Action Research as a Process of Accountability and Change

How can colleges build both the language to talk about race and the ability to inquire systematically into causes of inequity and potential solutions? How can institutions create environments that allow higher education professionals to learn new ways of speaking about race and new ways of framing student inequities that shift responsibility to institutions? A structured setting in which a committed group of professionals meet on an ongoing basis can provide the opportunity for an evolution of a more complex understanding of race within the group. Such a process can be assisted by the presence of an outsider whose role, in part, is to help these professionals develop racially intentional language, as well as to help them to examine their own assumptions about student outcomes in a safe and deliberate environment.

These explorations require that members of a given institution are prepared and willing to actively explore racial inequities by engaging in a conversation in which race is an explicit theme, and furthermore, that upon the acknowledgment of inequities, they will be able and willing to identify and change the policies and practices that contribute to these gaps. Unfortunately, this is often not the case, due to strong taboos against racially explicit language in many education settings and to beliefs about the presence of equal opportunities. Harper and Patton (2007) note the resistance among many college educators to engage in ongoing dialogue about race, and they offer three reasons for this reluctance:

1. To commit to such a discussion requires a willingness to deal with discomfort, guilt and frustration, as well as an acknowledgment of privilege by those who might be advantaged by their racial positions on a campus.
2. Such a discussion generally leads to the acknowledgment that the problem of racism is not likely to end.
3. These discussions and ensuing realizations should lead to a compulsion to take personal responsibility.

One approach to remediating the roles and community of practice of higher education practitioners is to ask them to assume the role of action researchers and to conduct action inquiry into their own practices (Reason, 1994). As noted by Reason, a key skill for those involved in action inquiry is that of "find[ing] ways of sidestepping one's own and others' defensive responses to the painful process of self-reflection" (p. 322). The CHAT framework makes clear that in order to remediate practice it is necessary to remediate the artifacts that are the tools for the social construction of practice. In our work at the CUE, therefore, we focus on creating remediating artifacts in the form of tools for action inquiry and action research. These are referred to as a scorecard (e.g., the "Equity Scorecard"), tools (e.g., the "Benchmarking Equity and Student Success Tool"; the "STEM Toolkit"), and self-assessment inventories (e.g., the Transfer Self-Assessment Inventory).

In CUE's research, the use of language in and through the tools of action research and action inquiry is key in a number of ways:

1. In the introduction of race-conscious terms. For example, the introduction of dis-aggregated data usually requires the introduction of a new language and vocabulary that can help ease the discomfort practitioners experience when talking about race and ethnicity, and facilitate a transition among participants from that uneasiness to an intentional dialogue.

2. In the exploration of the absence of certain racially explicit language within the campus community. Many practitioners may have been socialized toward "color-blindness"; thus the introduction of new language may be accompanied by an exploration of why this language may feel "ill-fitting" and how to take ownership of it in productive ways.

3. In the use of language to reframe attributions about student inequities. A language that provides a vocabulary for discussing race allows stereotypes and false assumptions to surface so that they can be tested and invalidated. For example, instead of defaulting to generalized statements using coded terms, such as suggesting that "working" students do not care about school as much as finding a job and making money, a language that allows participants to articulate those assumptions more explicitly provides a more honest and candid inquiry into participants' empirical observations. "I see that Latino students are less likely to reach transfer level math. Where are they experiencing less success or persistence in the basic skills math pipeline? Where are they experiencing greater success and per-sistence?"

4. In the framing of inequitable outcomes as the responsibility of the institution and its practi-tioners, rather than as a result of what students lack. For example, at a given institution, African American students may have lower overall college-level credit attainment than other groups. Yet, a fine-grained examination of data may reveal that those African American students who are successfully completing basic skills courses actually have *higher* graduation rates than other groups. Thus, the question then becomes: "How is the institu-tion supporting African American students in advanced courses but not in basic skills courses?"

A wide variety of assessment activities are undertaken regularly on college campuses as part of institutional self-study, accreditation, and accountability initiatives. Remediated artifacts can be used in structured forms of professional development as part of accountability requirements. The primary method, in our work, for increasing the capacity of colleges to carry out action inquiry for equity is by convening practitioners from different functional areas to engage in collaborative assessment activities (Bensimon, 2004, 2005a, 2005b, 2007; Bensimon, Harris III, & Rueda, 2007; Bensimon et al., 2004; Bensimon, Rueda et al., 2007; Dowd, 2005, 2008; Dowd & Tong, 2007). The assessment inventories are designed to provide a productive structure for these groups. The members of the teams are viewed as providing institutional leadership and as developing their leadership capacity through teamwork (Bensimon, Harris III et al., 2007; Bensimon & Neumann, 1993).

The design of action research tools and of action inquiry activities are designed to bring estab-lished and entrenched knowledge (Tharp, 1993; Tharp & Gallimore, 1988) to the forefront of a practitioner's attention. The explicit articulation of knowledge influencing professional decision-making has the potential to make entrenched knowledge amenable to change through collaborative assessment processes. Practitioners are not always consciously aware of the social context of their work. Collaboration with peers in well-constructed professional assessment activities is sometimes necessary to articulate divergent viewpoints and practices, thereby making the social context visible. In a sense, vocal participation in collaborative assessment helps practitioners "hear themselves think," as we might say more colloquially. Therefore, accountability initiatives are likely to benefit when they engage participants in meaningful and productive activities in professional settings, purposefully designed as activity settings for social learning. The goal, if valued, motivates participants to assist each other's learning and professional development. These goals and activity settings are defined by the social systems in which participants do their work, but the culture of those settings can be remediated through purposeful use of artifacts designed to elicit reflection on the culture. The action research tools assist practitioners in observing more closely the material and social conditions of their practice. Close observation through collaborative and productive activities is intended to bring established and entrenched knowledge into relief, building on the positive aspects of the former and challenging the counterproductive aspects of the latter. By stimulating "un-learning," action research tools are designed to initiate new cycles of guided and self-guided learning (Tharp & Gallimore, 1988), leading to new established competencies.

The participants in activity settings designed to enhance institutional accountability should include college faculty, administrators, and institutional researchers. At times, the inclusion of researchers external to the college, acting as facilitators in the activity setting, will also be warranted. The participation of external facilitators is sometimes necessary for the following reasons stated by Tharp and Gallimore (1988):

- Practitioners do not always see their own social (ecocultural) context.
- Supervisors and those with bureaucratic authority mistakenly focus on assessing rather than assisting performance.
- Practitioners face real or perceived constraints on professional development and learning from authorities in their professional life.
- Habits of interaction ("interaction scripts") are unconscious, deeply embedded in professional culture, and taken as a given.
- Errors or weaknesses are not well tolerated as opportunities for learning in everyday professional life.
- In-house training programs may simply perpetuate the existing culture and strengthen counter-productive entrenched knowledge.

Based on these concepts, the key principle for designing effective professional development programs as part of accountability initiatives is to ensure that effective assistance occurs among peers, among authorities and those whose professional actions are regulated, and between external facilitators and participants in the activity setting. State and federal accountability systems often attempt to focus practitioner attention on achieving greater student educational outcomes through a variety of reporting requirements. Yet, it is questionable whether the information contained in mandated reports is meaningful to practitioners and whether public reporting requirements truly have the potential to bring about positive change in performance. The answer is unclear, but many studies suggest that accountability indicators are not meaningful to practitioners because they are measured at a highly aggregated level, far removed from the classrooms and programs in which practitioners do their work. This is not to say that the goal of increasing persistence, graduation, and transfer rates (to use several common performance indicators as examples) is not of intrinsic value to practitioners. Indeed, many, and perhaps the majority, of faculty and administrators are caring professionals who would like to increase the educational achievements of their students. The cultural norms governing educational practice often obscure opportunities for improvement. It is not possible to guarantee positive learning and increased performance among practitioners through the use of any assessment instrument or process. However, CHAT and social learning theory offer valuable and practical guidance for designing effective assessment activities.The design of accountability activities based on these theories will increase the likelihood of positive professional development, organizational learning, and public accountability for higher education.

Notes

1. A project of USC's Center for Urban Education, which was funded by the Lumina Foundation for Education and the Chancellor's Office for California Community Colleges.
2. In the context of the "Equity for All" project, the term *historically underrepresented students* refers primarily to African Americans, Latinas, and Latinos.
3. The 27,422 consisted of all first-time students who entered LBCC in the fall semesters from 1999 to 2002 and did not have a college degree at the time of enrollment.
4. California state legislation adopted in 2010, subsequent to the time we conducted our research, seeks to ensure a much greater standardization for the transfer of credits and associate's degrees to the CSU and UC systems.

References

Bensimon, E. M. (2004). The diversity scorecard: A learning approach to institutional change. *Change, 36*(1), 45–52.

Bensimon, E. M. (2005a). Closing the achievement gap in higher education: An organizational learning perspective. In A. Kezar (Ed.), *Organizational learning in higher education* (Vol. 131). San Francisco, CA: Jossey-Bass.

Bensimon, E. M. (2005b). *Equality as a fact, equality as a result: A matter of institutional accountability* (commissioned paper). Washington, DC: American Council on Education.

Bensimon, E. M. (2007). The underestimated significance of practitioner knowledge in the scholarship of student success. *Review of Higher Education, 30*(4), 441–469.

Bensimon, E. M., & Dowd, A. C. (2009). Dimensions of the "transfer choice" gap: Experiences of Latina and Latino students who navigated transfer pathways. *Harvard Educational Review* (Winter), 632–658.

Bensimon, E. M., & Neumann, A. (1993). *Redesigning collegiate leadership: Teams and teamwork in higher education.* Baltimore, MD: Johns Hopkins University Press.

Bensimon, E. M., Harris III, F., & Rueda, R. (2007). The mediational means of enacting equity-mindedness among community college practitioners. *Diversity Research, 7*(1,2), 14–15.

Bensimon, E. M., Dowd, A. C., Alford, H., & Trapp, F. (2007). *Missing 87: A study of the "transfer gap" and "choice gap."* Long Beach and Los Angeles: Long Beach City College and the Center for Urban Education, University of Southern California.

Bensimon, E. M., Polkinghorne, D. E., Bauman, G. L., & Vallejo, E. (2004). Doing research that makes a difference. *Journal of Higher Education, 75*(1), 104–126.

Bensimon, E. M., Rueda, R., Dowd, A. C., & Harris III, F. (2007). Accountability, equity, and practitioner learning and change. *Metropolitan, 18*(3), 28–45.

Burke, J. C. (2005). The many faces of accountability. In J. C. Burke & Associates (Eds.), *Achieving accountability in higher education* (pp. 1–24). San Francisco, CA: Jossey-Bass.

Cole, M. (2003). Cultural historical activity theory in the family of socio-cultural approaches. *International Society for the Study of Behavioural Development Newsletter, 1*(47), 1–4.

Cole, M., & Engeström, Y. (1993). A cultural-historical approach to distributed cognition. In G. Salomon (Ed.), *Distributed cognitions: Psychological and educational considerations* (pp. 1–46). Cambridge, UK: Cambridge University Press.

Cole, M., Engeström, Y., & Vasquez, O. (1997). *Mind, culture, and activity: Seminal papers from the Laboratory of Comparative Human Cognition.* Cambridge, UK: Cambridge University Press.

Dougherty, K. J., & Hong, E. (2006). Performance accountability as imperfect panacea: The community college experience. In T. R. Bailey & V. S. Morest (Eds.), *Defending the community college equity agenda* (pp. 51–86). Baltimore, MD: Johns Hopkins University Press.

Dowd, A. C. (2005). *Data don't drive: Building a practitioner-driven culture of inquiry to assess community college performance* (research report). Indianapolis, IN: Lumina Foundation for Education.

Dowd, A. C. (2008). The community college as gateway and gatekeeper: Moving beyond the access "saga" to outcome equity. *Harvard Educational Review, 77*(4), 407–419.

Dowd, A. C., & Tong, V. P. (2007). Accountability, assessment, and the scholarship of "best practice." In J. C. Smart (Ed.), *Handbook of Higher Education* (Vol. 22, pp. 57–119). New York: Springer Publishing.

Dowd, A. C., Malcom, L. E., Nakamoto, J., & Bensimon, E. M. (in press). Institutional researchers as teachers and equity advocates: Facilitating organizational learning and change. In E. M. Bensimon & L. E. Malcolm (Eds.), *The Equity Scorecard model in theory and practice.* Sterling, VA: Stylus Publishing.

Dowd, A. C., Bensimon, E. M., Gabbard, G., Singleton, S., Macias, E. E., Dee, J., et al. (2006). Transfer access to elite colleges and universities in the United States: Threading the needle of the American dream. Retrieved May 5, 2008 from www.jackkentcookefoundation.org (links: Grants and RFPs/Community College Transfer Initiative/CCTI Research Report/Executive Summary)

Engeström, Y. (2000). Activity theory as a framework for analyzing and redesigning work. *Ergonomics, 43*(7), 960–974.

Engeström, Y. (2001). Expansive learning at work: Toward an activity theoretical reconceptualization. *Journal of Education and Work, 14*(1), 133–156.

Engeström, Y. (2008). *From teams to knots: Activity-theoretical studies of collaboration and learning at work.* Cambridge, UK: Cambridge University Press.

Engeström, Y., Miettinen, R., & Punamäki-Gitai, R.-L. (1999). *Perspectives on activity theory.* Cambridge, UK: Cambridge University Press.

Greenwood, D. J., & Levin, M. (2005). Reform of the social sciences and of universities through action research. In N. K. Denzin & Y. S. Lincoln (Eds.), *Handbook of qualitative research* (3rd ed., pp. 43–64). Thousand Oaks, CA: Sage.

Gutierrez, K. D., & Vossoughi, S. (2010). Lifting off the ground to return anew: Mediated praxis, transformative learning, and social design experiments. *Journal of Teacher Education, 61*(1–2), 100–117.

Harper, S. R., & Patton, L. D. (Eds.) (2007). *Responding to the realities of race* (New Directions for Student Services, Vol. 120). San Francisco, CA: Jossey-Bass.

Iverson, S. V. (2007). Camouflaging power and privilege: A critical race analysis of university diversity policies. *Educational Administration Quarterly, 43*, 586–611.

Kemmis, S., & McTaggart, R. (2000). Participatory action research. In N. K. Denzin & Y. S. Lincoln (Eds.), *Handbook of qualitative research* (2nd ed., pp. 567–605). Thousand Oaks, CA: Sage.

Kuutti, K., & Engeström, Y. (2005). Activity theory. In K. Brown (Ed.), *Encyclopedia of language and linguistics* (2nd ed., Vol. I, pp. 44–47). Oxford, UK: Elsevier.

Ogawa, R., Crain, R., Loomis, M., & Ball, T. (2008). CHAT-IT: Toward conceptualizing learning in the context of formal organizations. *Educational Researcher, 37*(2), 83–95.

Reason, P. (1994). Three approaches to participative inquiry. In N. K. Denzin & Y. S. Lincoln (Eds.), *Handbook of qualitative research* (pp. 324–339). Thousand Oaks, CA: Sage.

Roth, W.-M., & Lee, Y.-L. (2007). "Vygotsky's neglected legacy": Cultural-historical activity theory. *Review of Educational Research, 77*(2), 186–232.

Sánchez, G. J. (2004). "What's good for Boyle Heights is good for the Jews": Creating multiracialism on the Eastside during the 1950s. *American Quarterly, 56*(3), 633–661.

Terenzini, P. T. (1999). On the nature of institutional research and the knowledge and skills it requires. *New Directions for Institutional Research, 104*(Winter), 21–29.

Tharp, R. G. (1993). Institutional and social context of educational practice and reform. In E. A. Forman, N. Minick, & C. A. Stone (Eds.), *Contexts for learning: Sociocultural dynamics in children's development.* New York: Oxford University Press.

Tharp, R. G., & Gallimore, R. (1988). *Rousing minds to life: Teaching, learning, and schooling in social context.* Cambridge, UK: Cambridge University Press.

14

The Limits of Desegregation Accountability

Ross E. Mitchell and Douglas E. Mitchell

For many people, desegregation means eliminating student racial isolation and creating racially balanced schools. This is consistent with the celebrated U.S. Supreme Court's *Brown* v. *Board of Education of Topeka* decisions (1954, 1955). But school desegregation also involves the complete dismantling of separate or "dual" school systems, removing such "vestiges" of ethnic apartheid as program tracking, resource inequalities, and unequal access to qualified staff. Although often seen as primarily concerned with the statutory system of Black–White segregation in the old South, segregated schools have always involved multiple ethnic groups and quickly became a major issue in the urban centers of the northern and western United States. This chapter explores how the courts, Congress, and various administrative agencies have sought to devise means to hold school systems accountable for school desegregation. We limit our discussion here to the desegregation of student enrollment, because that is the fundamental issue and serves to clarify the nature and limits of desegregation accountability.

As the Supreme Court noted more than 20 years after the *Brown* decisions, a central issue in student desegregation is whether any groups of children are "isolated by force of law from the mainstream" (*Milliken* v. *Bradley*, 1977, p. 287). The U.S. courts have made it clear that race is not the only unconstitutional basis for segregation. In addition to race, the Supreme Court has found segregation or exclusion to be unacceptable when it is based on national origin, language (*Lau* v. *Nichols*, 1974), or alienage (*Plyler* v. *Doe*, 1982). Lower courts have also found the following to be educationally indefensible: segregation or exclusion based on curriculum tracking (*Hobson* v. *Hansen*, 1967) and mental, physical, or emotional disabilities or impairments (*Pennsylvania Association for Retarded Children* v. *Commonwealth of Pennsylvania*, 1972, hereafter *PARC*; *Mills* v. *Board of Education of the District of Columbia*, 1972). Congressional policies have tackled segregation based on gender. When found guilty of segregating based on unjustified categories, school districts have been held accountable for ceasing proscribed actions and developing eventual remedies.

The development and maintenance of effective accountability systems for eliminating unacceptable segregation have proven difficult both politically and administratively. A brief review of the history of efforts to integrate the nation's public schools and our review of efforts to measure the existing segregation and plot progress toward its removal will reveal unsolved problems in both the definition and measurement of student segregation. Not only do existing measures provide confusing assessments, but the administrative and policy tools available for remedying segregation once it is identified are too often clumsy and blunt.

The Limits of Accountability

To identify the limits of accountability for desegregation, we must first clarify what the term *account-ability* means in this context. In matters of school desegregation, accountability addresses actions taken by public agencies, not the actions of private citizens. Of course, individuals are both morally and legally accountable for their private actions, but these private responsibilities are not the focus of attention when it comes to the assignment of responsibility for assuring equality of educational opportunity or securing constitutional and statutory rights. Rather, the focus of accountability for racial and ethnic desegregation is on the use of governance authority and government resources to overcome unconstitutional segregation and keep private prejudices from being used in coordinated or public ways to deprive targeted groups of their rights. Private individuals are morally responsible for fair and equitable treatment and, by law, are responsible for keeping hateful actions out of interpersonal relationships and ethnic bias out of contract agreements. The Constitution does not forbid individual citizens from holding prejudicial attitudes, but it does require public agencies to ensure that these bad attitudes are not turned into prejudicial policies or practices. Tort law holds individuals responsible by allowing claims for damages done. Beyond tort liability, however, constitutional law and statutory enforcement procedures hold public agencies accountable.

Since accountability for desegregation rests on public rather than private actors, there are but three core accountable agencies of governance whose actions can be scrutinized: the federal government, state governments, and local school boards. Much civil rights organization and agitation emphasized public consciousness raising and securing political support for needed enforcement actions. At their core, however, the civil rights organizing, litigation, and direct action are devoted to holding one or more of these three governance structures to account. Actions such as corporate boycotts, lunch counter sit-ins, or refusals to ride in the back of a bus challenge private agencies to become morally accountable. Ultimately, however, political and legal accountability rests with the agencies of civil governance that must guarantee constitutionally protected rights. Where private actors respond to moral suasion, government enforcement is not needed; but when private actors are not persuaded, the responsibility for accountability shifts directly and unequivocally to formal governance agencies—the judiciary, legislative authorities, and responsible executives.

This does not mean that accountability is concerned only with overturning bad laws. To the contrary; court cases from *Mendez* v. *Westminster* (1946) to *Keyes* v. *School District No. 1* (1973) have challenged extralegal actions by many school boards, seeking to end harmful prejudicial practices never embraced by statutory law. To be sure, beginning with the invidious racial distinction embedded in the original U.S. Constitution, our national history has been besmirched by a long line of prejudicial laws aimed at demeaning and victimizing not only African Americans but also Native Americans, Asians, Mexicans, women, citizens with disabilities, and homosexuals. At its core, desegregation accountability involves responsibility for the equitable use of government authority and public resources. Public agencies are responsible for corrective actions regardless of whether abuses are supported by unconstitutional laws or arise from the intentional abuse of equity principles by groups or individuals holding government authority.

To be accountable for its actions, a government agency must have both the authoritative jurisdiction and the fiscal resources needed to respond. In political regimes such as ours, with divided adjudicatory systems and limited government powers, it may prove difficult to fix specific responsibilities. The question of which government agencies are accountable for what desegregation actions continues to be contested both legally and politically. At the federal level, the judiciary has borne the lion's share of responsibility for action. However, it has been very difficult to hold Congress and the executive branch accountable for timely desegregation actions. Not until a massive grassroots civil rights movement sprang up and attracted mass media attention did the Eisenhower and then the Kennedy and Johnson administrations aggressively begin to pursue equal educational opportunities for minority students. Congressional action was largely stymied by North–South splits in the major political parties, with a resulting inability to produce the majorities needed to break filibustering and move legislation forward. For this reason, the best way to understand government accountability for school desegregation is to review the judicial records of state and federal courts.

A Brief History of School Desegregation Law

Over the last century, the processes of segregation, adjudication, and remedial action by government have been quite complex; nevertheless, they can be fairly characterized as making a broad swing from the principle of "separate but equal" articulated in *Plessy* v. *Ferguson* (1896) to the conviction that separate is "inherently unequal," set forth in *Brown*, and then back again to the *Plessy* perspective by the end of the twentieth century (Fairfax, 1999). This rise and fall of judicial commitment can be traced through a review of key federal court decisions that defined and then challenged de jure segregation in the schools, proceeded to endorse the elimination of de facto segregation, and then retreated to allow de facto separation of groups to proceed unchecked. In their most recent decisions, both federal and state courts have tacitly agreed to limit relief to equalizing services or resources rather than insisting on the elimination of segregated schools and classrooms. An exception to this last generalization is the courts' continuing support for federal policies requiring integrated educational experiences for children with various types of mentally or physically handicapping conditions. The dynamics of this policy evolution are driven by an ongoing tension between a view of the government's responsibility for intervening actively to protect citizen rights regardless of how they are being trampled upon, and a view that government is primarily responsible for organizing and supporting the collective interests of the majority of the citizenry. Creating public schools supports majoritarian interest, desegregating them aims at protecting private rights. The evolution of this tension has unfolded in the 14 identifiable steps described in the following paragraphs.

1. Support for state enforced segregation. When the U.S. Supreme Court handed down the infamous *Plessy* decision, it ratified state-sponsored segregation of facilities and established the doctrine of "separate but equal" for segregated railway transportation. Grounded in this decision, state-sanctioned racial and ethnic discrimination operated with impunity in public education until well after the end of World War II. Both the *Cumming* v. *Board of Education of Richmond County* (1899) and *Gong Lum* v. *Rice* (1927) decisions affirmed the right of states to define racially or ethnically "separate but equal" school systems for any two or more "races" (i.e., White separate from Negro, or Black and Chinese or colored, respectively). Thus, private prejudices were seen as legitimately codified into public policy.

2. Extralegal segregation challenged. A decade prior to the landmark *Brown* decisions, the *Mendez* decision in the federal district court, affirmed by the Ninth Circuit Court of Appeals (*Westminster* v. *Mendez*, 1947), struck the first blow at de jure school segregation. In *Mendez*, the early 20th-century tradition whereby local school districts established separate "Mexican schools" was ruled illegal, since the State of California, which had laws permitting racial separation, had not identified people of Mexican ancestry as a separate "race." Prompted by the *Mendez* litigation, then Governor Earl Warren backed the successful 1947 repeal of those provisions in the California Education Code, providing for the segregation of Chinese, Japanese, Mongolian, or American Indian public school students (Wollenberg, 1974).

3. Expanding "separate but equal" to include intangible inequalities. Three years later, the U.S. Supreme Court, in its *Sweatt v. Painter* (1950) and *McLaurin v. Oklahoma State Regents* (1950) opinions, declared that racially segregated graduate school education was inherently unequal. These decisions declared that, in addition to the tangible sources of unequal opportunity—such as libraries, faculty, facilities, and so on—segregation produced inequalities in areas that are "are incapable of objective measure" (*Sweatt*, p. 634). Such inequalities include program reputation and quality of interactions with peers, particularly, peers of another race who would otherwise never share classes, discussions, or assignments. In these decisions, a direct challenge of the *Plessy* precedent was avoided in favor of other rationales.

4. Declaring that there can be no place for "separate but equal" school systems. An unequivocal repudiation of *Plessy* came with the first *Brown* (1954) decision's unanimous opinion prepared by then Chief Justice Earl Warren:

> Any language in *Plessy* v. *Ferguson* contrary to this finding [of the detrimental effect of segregation on colored children] is rejected. We conclude that in the field of public education the doctrine of "separate but equal" has no place. Separate educational facilities are inherently unequal.
>
> > (*Brown* v. *Board of Education of Topeka*, 1954, pp. 494–495, hereafter *Brown I*; also see *Bolling* v. *Sharpe*, 1954)

5. Recognizing that remedial action requires measurable indicators tracking segregation. Remedial guidance was not provided in the 1954 *Brown I* decision. This was delayed until the second *Brown* decision (*Brown* v. *Board of Education of Topeka*, 1955, hereafter *Brown II*). Local school districts, metropolitan school systems, and states were to bear the burden of developing desegregation plans that would "effectuate a transition to a racially nondiscriminatory school system ... with all deliberate speed" (*Brown II*, p. 301; also see *Green* v. *County Sch. Bd. of New Kent County*, 1968, p. 439). Beyond the racial separation of student bodies, the district courts were advised to:

> consider problems related to administration, arising from the physical condition of the school plant, the school transportation system, personnel, revision of school districts and attendance areas into compact units to achieve a system of determining admission to the public schools on a nonracial basis, and revision of local laws and regulations which may be necessary in solving the foregoing problems.
>
> > (*Brown II*, pp. 300–301)

The bases for judging the existence of illegal school segregation identified in *Brown II* were reiterated and elaborated in *Green*, *Swann* v. *Charlotte-Mecklenburg Bd. of Educ.* (1971), and *Keyes*. School systems were further urged also to consider segregation and inequalities arising in extra-curricular activities, school facilities, and attendance catchment areas in order to, "eliminate from the public schools all vestiges of state-imposed segregation" (*Swann*, p. 15; also see *Davis* v. *School Comm'rs of Mobile County*, 1971, p. 37).

6. Positive action, beyond unfettered choice or liberal transfer policies, is required. Simply relenting on previous government-supported segregation was deemed insufficient in a series of Court rulings. State or school district reliance on freedom-of-choice plans (*Green*), private school vouchers, or other state funding of private school attendance (*Griffin* v. *School Board*, 1964; *St. Helena Parish School Board* v. *Hall*, 1962), or policies facilitating minority-to-majority transfers (*Goss* v. *Board of Education*, 1963; *Keyes*) was deemed to be an unacceptable evasion of school districts' affirmative duty to dismantle a dual (racialized) system of education. Moreover, desegregation may not be impeded by subdividing districts under court order (*United States* v. *Scotland Neck Bd. of Educ.*, 1972; *Wright* v. *Council of City of Emporia*, 1972). These sorts of actions are functionally defiant of the Court's mandates when it comes to the application of the *Brown* decisions.

7. Within-school segregation is found unconstitutional. Among the many strategies employed to evade racial or ethnic desegregation were assertions that students should be separated to serve specific educational needs. The *Mendez* decisions decried the unjustified segregation of students putatively based upon need for differentiated English language instruction. In *Hobson* (1967), a permanent system of curriculum tracking—one that sorted Black from White students based upon their initial academic assessments and then maintained this separation regardless of academic development and without equivalent academic offerings—was rejected. Educationally indefensible segregation of students, whether between or within schools, was declared to have violated their equal protection rights.

8. Requiring a showing of intentionality. For a brief period following the mandate to remove the "vestiges" of a segregationist history, it appeared that the courts would require desegregation by race and ethnicity to be undertaken regardless of how it had arisen. Before long, however, it became clear that this was not the case. Of course, when states or school districts intentionally segregate students by race or ethnicity, they violate students' equal protection and due process rights and are enacting de jure segregation (*Brown I*; *Bolling*). Any state law or school district policy that has a racially segregative purpose is illegal, and responsible government agencies are compelled to dismantle this de jure segregation on a system-wide basis, not just for a subset of affected schools within the district (see *Columbus Board of Education* v. *Penick*, 1979; *Dayton Bd. of Education* v. *Brinkman*, 1979; *Keyes*; *Swann*). As emphasized in *Swann*, however, the intentions of the policymakers are a key factor in determining constitutionality. *Swann* states the principle clearly: no remedy is required "in the situation of so-called 'de facto segregation,' where racial imbalance exists in the schools but with no showing that this was brought about by discriminatory action of state authorities" (*Swann*, pp. 17–18; but see also Justice Douglas's dissent in *Spencer* v. *Kugler*, 1972). Segregation producing racial isolation is prima facie evidence of possible intent, meriting judicial scrutiny; but the existence of segregation alone does not prove intentionality and therefore falls short of demanding state or district remedial action.

9. Restrictions on desegregation remedies begin to flow. The requirement to demonstrate intent to segregate has profound effects on the nature of a desegregation remedy. On this basis, for example, the first *Milliken* decision (*Milliken* v. *Bradley*, 1974, hereafter *Milliken I*) foreclosed on the possibility of multidistrict metropolitan-wide desegregation orders as a means by which to eliminate racial isolation in urban schools. Since only districts found to have intentionally segregated students are subject to district court intervention and supervision, there would have to be provable interdistrict collusion to justify interdistrict accountability. Soon after *Milliken I*, the redrawing of attendance areas as a means by which to remedy racial imbalance began to be limited in some jurisdictions (*Pasadena City Bd. of Education* v. *Spangler*, 1976). The second *Milliken* decision (*Milliken* v. *Bradley*, 1977, hereafter *Milliken II*) elevated remedial education programs above school desegregation as the preferred available means for removing the vestiges of state-imposed segregation.

10. Evolving mathematical formulas for desegregation planning. Because segregation was typically seen as the separation of students into separate schools or classrooms, often accompanied by similarly segregated faculty and staff, the creation of any kind of desegregation accountability required some sensible measure against which to assess progress. The *Brown* decisions focused on eliminating racially isolated schools (later to be defined as 90% or more White or non-White; e.g., see Dye, 1968).

It soon became clear, however, that this 90% rule when applied to individual schools did not adequately address many instances in which intentional segregating policies were producing significantly imbalanced school enrollments across entire school districts, particularly in large urban centers, where multiple ethnic groups were confounded with poverty and language bases for segregation. As a result, using a measure of the imbalances in district-wide student enrollment proportions by race or ethnicity for both student and faculty desegregation came to be seen as a defensible approach as long as these "mathematical ratios" did not become binding quotas (*Swann; U.S. v. Montgomery Bd. of Educ.*, 1969). As described in the next section of this chapter, several different measures of ethnic concentration were developed. None has proven entirely satisfactory, and together they create issues of substantive meaning and proper application.

11. Recognizing that multiple population groups are being simultaneously segregated. As the *Gong Lum* and *Mendez* decisions testify, separate education has never been strictly a biracial Black–White matter (also see *Keyes*). The explicit recognition of multiple group-based separation, exclusion, or unequal educational opportunity in public schooling has expanded to include very different population groups. Individuals who are mentally, physically, or emotionally impaired are identified in *Hendrick Hudson District Board of Education* v. *Rowley* (1982; also see *Mills; PARC*). Children in poverty are identified in *San Antonio School District* v. *Rodriguez* (1973, hereafter *Rodriguez*), national origin or language groups addressed in *Lau*, aliens regardless of their documented status in *Plyler*, and sex in *Communities for Equity* v. *Michigan High Sch. Athletic Ass'n* (2006; for public postsecondary cases involving sex, see *Mississippi University for Women* v. *Hogan*, 1982; *United States* v. *Virginia et al.*, 1996). Although no education-specific case has come before the federal courts for this group, due process rights based on sexual orientation have been affirmed (*Lawrence et al.* v. *Texas*, 2003). This expansion of the list of "suspect categories" of students whose interest deserve "strict scrutiny" by the courts both expanded and complicated the pursuit of an appropriate strategy for holding school systems accountable. Political changes in the country and the mind-boggling complexity of simultaneously addressing the rights of a long list of target groups probably played a significant role in judicial withdrawal from enforcement of comprehensive desegregation.

12. Courts begin declaring districts to have reached "unitary status." As states and school districts more or less complied with the terms of their consent decrees, a substantially changed and much more politically conservative Supreme Court started to raise the importance of releasing school districts from supervision and returning their operation to full local control. This required the finding of unitary status: declaring that schools are no longer under state-imposed segregation, that pupils are being assigned in a nondiscriminatory fashion, and that all vestiges of de jure segregation had been eliminated. Though these decisions were controversial (see, e.g., Chemerinsky, 2005; Orfield & Eaton, 1996) and the Court delivering slim 5–4 majority opinions in two of three cases (*Board of Ed. of Oklahoma City* v. *Dowell*, 1991, hereafter *Dowell; Missouri* v. *Jenkins*, 1995, hereafter *Jenkins*), it delivered three opinions in the 1990s that set the path for numerous partial and full unitary status declarations (*Dowell; Freeman* v. *Pitts*, 1992; *Jenkins*). The *Dowell* decision was probably the most startling because, having been declared unitary, the district was permitted to return to neighborhood school attendance zones, which guaranteed the reestablishment of racially isolated schools.

13. Declaring that racial integration is not a compelling state interest. Finally, with the *Parents Involved in Community Schools* v. *Seattle School District No. 1* (2007) decision, the Court reversed the unanimous *Swann* opinion, delivered by Chief Justice Burger, which included the statement that:

> School authorities are traditionally charged with broad power to formulate and implement educational policy and might well conclude, for example, that in order to prepare students to

live in a pluralistic society each school should have a prescribed ratio of Negro to White students reflecting the proportion for the district as a whole. To do this as an educational policy is within the broad discretionary powers of school authorities. (p. 16)

Prior to the *Parents Involved* decision, the constraining of voluntary family enrollment preferences to support desegregation goals was seen as legal and appropriate. The majority opinion in *Parents Involved* determined, however, that maintaining racial and ethnic balance ratios to serve such a pluralistic interest in Seattle, Washington, and Louisville, Kentucky, was unconstitutional. Families seeking to pursue their individual interests in a particular school placement for their children outweighed the state interest in protecting integrated enrollment patterns that reflected the city's racial and ethnic pluralism. School authorities are not granted discretionary powers as broadly defined by the Burger Court. In the absence of any vestiges of de jure segregation, a student's race or ethnicity may not be solely determinative of his or her public school assignment.

14. *A return to* Plessy-*type relief by concentrating on the "equal" part of "separate but equal."* Even as the federal courts were dismantling de jure segregation, school finance systems were being challenged in several state courts. Although the U.S. Supreme Court found no constitutional protection against inequitable school funding schemes (*Rodriguez*), state courts were beginning to invalidate state funding formulas as unconstitutional based on their own state constitutions, beginning with California's *Serrano* v. *Priest* (1971). Initial progress in the state courts was slow, but by the 1990s several states had revised their school finance laws to provide more "adequate" educational opportunities for all students (Rebell, 2009). There was no getting the states to redistribute (desegregate) students to equalize educational opportunity, which left no other recourse than to demand that all schools be provided with adequate resources to educate the children in their charge.

In sum, after 100 years of constitutional analysis and debate, we have yet to overcome "the familiar phenomenon that in metropolitan areas minority groups are often found concentrated in one part of the city. In some circumstances certain schools may remain all or largely of one race until new schools can be provided or neighborhood patterns change" (*Swann*, p. 25).

Moreover, unlike rural school systems, in "metropolitan areas with dense and shifting population, numerous schools, congested and complex traffic patterns," it is not easy to stabilize and maintain desegregated enrollment (*Swann*, p. 14). However, as we describe in the next section, instability in the definition and monitoring of enrollment segregation and lack of consensus and clarity in the measure of practically achievable desegregation has contributed to confusing accounts of progress as well as to unintended consequences.

Criteria for Desegregation Accountability Have Changed Over Time

Prior to guidelines issued under the Civil Rights Act of 1964, federal courts judged desegregation cases on their individual merits, with no uniform standard for permissible racial segregation (Dunn, 1967). Until the development of the Civil Rights Act, Title VI, guidelines, little or no progress was made in desegregating southern schools. Without measurable standards, progress could not be documented and desegregation orders could not be enforced. Measurement of the extent of segregation is a prerequisite for accountability.

Supervision and Monitoring Indices: Isolation and Imbalance

Both social scientists and public officials have contributed to the development of a number of indices of segregation. Using various criteria, these administratively and judicially defined indices have been used to hold school officials to account for desegregation. The original policy measure was a rule for identifying racially isolated schools in order to monitor the dismantling of the southern pattern of dual schools for Blacks and Whites. Other measures were needed in northern and western schools systems, where segregation did not depend on legal apartheid and multiple ethnic groups were involved. The following paragraphs examine the merits and limits of these alternative measurement systems (for technical details, see Mitchell & Mitchell, 2010; Reardon & Firebaugh, 2002).

1. *The limits and merits of the 90+% non-White school measure.* Two federal reports, those by Coleman et al. (1966) and U.S. Civil Rights Commission (1967), highlighted the measurement of racial isolation and led to the adoption of a segregation measure based on the "per cent of total Negro elementary pupils in schools which are 90–100% Negro" (Dye, 1968, p. 142). This measure of African American segregation focuses on individual schools but is usually aggregated to determine the proportion of African American children so isolated. In multiethnic states like California, where the segregation of Asian American and American Indian students had been legal until 1947, it is clear that this racial isolation index is too narrowly defined. The U.S. Supreme Court, in *Keyes*, recognized this and expanded its interpretation of racial isolation to cover all non-White students.

Although other measures have come to dominate policy debates, the identification of 90–100% concentrations of non-White students remains a useful and powerful indicator of the most serious instances of racial isolation. This index is no respecter of district boundaries; it can identify *all* schools in a district as being isolated if they are more than 90% non-White. Where eliminating racial isolation is a political priority, this measure remains an important accountability tool.

2. *The limits and merits of the racial imbalance measure.* Racial imbalance tests whether the racial or ethnic composition of any school in a district deviates by more than some set percentage from the overall ethnic composition of the district; it was affirmed as a useful approach in *Swann*. This measure is not only intuitively easy to appreciate but also directs attention squarely upon the ethnically imbalanced schools and specifies exactly what needs to be done to overcome the imbalances. Moreover, it is capable of assessing segregation for any number of racial or ethnic groups; it is not limited to binary comparison like the racial isolation approach and allows for a range of enrollment variations to be accepted as adequately desegregated.

Criteria for labeling a school as ethnically out of balance have varied from time to time and place to place. For example, California's State Board of Education adopted a 15% rule in 1969, declaring that a school was racially imbalanced if the enrollment of any of six identified racial or ethnic groups at that school was not within plus or minus 15% of the district-wide percentage for that group (Calif. Admin. Code, Title 5 § 14021(c); also see Calif. Ed. Code §§ 5002–5003, 1971; California State Department of Education, 1967; Hendrick, 1975, pp. 227, 230). Although this strict numerical rule was repealed by ballot proposition in 1972, it had been in place long enough to establish a clear sense of acceptable racial imbalance (see *National Assn. for the Advancement of Colored People* v. *San Bernardino City Unified Sch. Dist.*, 1976). Similar indices of imbalance are found in many desegregation orders across the United States (some as tight as 10% and others as liberal as 20%; see, e.g., Berger, 1983; Giles, 1977; Rossell & Armor, 1996; Smith & Mickelson, 2000; Welner, 2006).

This measure holds districts accountable and recognizes that complete integration is an unrealistic goal. It has the virtue of simplicity: every school can be evaluated as to its compliance with the imbalance rule. School districts can be told which schools to modify and by how much.

The remaining four indices are largely the result of social science researchers becoming more involved in measuring segregation following adoption of the Civil Rights Act of 1964. This work resulted in more sophisticated and generalizable measures of multiethnic segregation. Researchers sought to analyze multiethnic segregation within and across multiple cities and school districts. They also sought measures with sensitivity to the difference between random fluctuations and substantial changes in segregation on the one hand and, on the other, assessments that distinguish inter- from intradistrict segregation as well as identifying which ethnic groups are most segregated.

3. The limits and merits of Theil's information index. Reardon and Firebaugh (2002) demonstrate the technical superiority of Theil's information index (H) as a measure satisfying important social science criteria. It has a standard error measure to identify random fluctuations and is partitionable to identify which geographic areas and ethnic groups are most affected. Despite assertions to the contrary, however, Theil's H is not intuitively meaningful to most observers. Moreover, it provides little guidance to school district administrators regarding where or how to address problems. Theil's H does tell us how much we know about students' ethnicities by knowing which schools they attend. However, school records already reveal this information to district officials. Policymakers and educators interested in desegregation are more concerned with how many students need to be moved, where those students are now, and which schools should receive them. Theil's H provides little help in answering these questions.

With its ability to locate whether segregation is concentrated within rather than between school districts and its ability to clarify which groups are being victimized, Theil's H can play a very prominent role in ascertaining where responsibility for action should be located, even though it does not helpfully describe the actions needed.

4. The limits and merits of the dissimilarity index. The dissimilarity index (D) lacks the mathematical elegance of Theil's H, but it has a virtue that is important to policymakers and educators: it identifies precisely what proportion of a school district's population would have to change schools in order for all segregation to be removed. While both H and D reach zero at the same point—when each school's student composition mirrors precisely the ethnic composition of the district—H is nonlinear with respect to the number of children who would have to be relocated, while D estimates that number precisely. Thus, D estimates the effort needed to desegregate. Policymakers recognize that student mobility, housing segregation, and transportation costs make perfect desegregation impossible. However, the D statistic is weak because it does not show whether desegregation actions are directed to the most segregated schools. At quite modest levels of D, districts with several schools could be within overall desegregation guidelines while still having one or more schools that are severely isolated or imbalanced by racial isolation and imbalanced enrollment measures.

The dissimilarity index also lacks H's capacity to compare inter- and intradistrict segregation levels. Thus, while it may be helpful to district planners in addressing within-district segregation, it is not as useful as H in addressing broader governance concerns. A multiethnic D also lacks an easy way of determining whether specific ethnic groups are most subject to the ravages of segregation, making it difficult, in a multiethnic environment, to determine which groups may be moving toward successful desegregation while others remain segregated. Where longitudinal data are available, both D and H will track changes in overall district segregation. Theil's H is a superior measure, however, because it tracks regional and interethnic changes as well as overall levels of segregation.

5. The limits and merits of the Gini coefficient index. The Gini coefficient (G), named for its Italian creator, is among the oldest of social science indices. It approaches the definition of ethnic unevenness by examining the extent to which members of each ethnic group tend to be disproportionately concentrated in some schools and not in others. When only two groups are being compared, this is a reasonably powerful index because it measures the proportion of total population of both groups that are not distributed equally among the schools. Reardon and Firebaugh provide a multiethnic generalization of G, but it is much harder to give its values an intuitively meaningful interpretation and it no longer points to specific groups or schools as the source of an elevated index. Beyond its historical interest, G does not seem to add much to our ability to describe school segregation or identify how to fix it.

6. *The limits and merits of the ethnic isolation index.* The exposure index (usually labeled P*) calculates the extent to which students of each ethnic group are attending schools where they are disproportionately likely to encounter members of their own ethnic group (isolation) or members of other ethnic groups (interaction). Multiethnic isolation is calculated from the weighted sum of each group's isolation from all other groups (Reardon & Firebaugh, 2002). This index has a reasonably direct interpretation: if a student's schoolmates are drawn more from his or her own ethnic group than would happen if a school's enrollment matched district-wide ethnic proportions, then he or she is to some degree being isolated from the other groups.

While the level of ethnic isolation is typically averaged across all schools to get a measure of district-wide isolation, this index can easily be calculated for each individual school and can therefore be used to identify schools of substantial isolation short of the 90+% threshold of the earlier racial isolation index. Unlike D, however, this index does not directly specify how many students must be moved in order to overcome the isolation that exists.

No Two Indices Are the Same

No two of these six measures tell the same story. Each responds to a different model of segregation. Early indices focused on individual schools, assessing whether they were either isolating various ethnic groups from interactions with others or displaying student enrollment compositions that were out of balance with overall district averages. Indices developed by social scientists focus on more global measurement, assessing the extent of deviations in the enrollments in a collection of schools from the overall ethnic composition of a region or school district. At present, there is a clear trade-off between statistical sophistication and the development of intuitively meaningful and administratively useful measures. The development of useful and reliable measures is especially difficult when we address multiethnic school systems. If complete desegregation could be expected, the choice of a criterion measure would not matter as much; they all converge on zero as desegregation becomes complete. When district-wide composition and residential segregation eliminate any realistic hope of full desegregation, however, the selection of a criterion measure becomes vitally important, as the judgment as to whether a school, district, or region has met its accountability obligations can be very different if one index is chosen rather than another.

Limitations of Measurements and Administrative Options

The complex array of desegregation indices attends to different aspects of segregation and produces differing values in unpredictable ways, which generates significant accountability problems. Understandably, any jurisdiction charged with the responsibility of desegregating a school system wants to know which benchmark criteria will be used to judge responsibility, measure progress, and identify success. Given relentless student mobility and the tendency for housing to be quite segregated, it is unreasonable to expect complete desegregation, but that is the only point at which the various measures of desegregation converge to a common value. Faced with the substantial costs of moving students and staff, those responsible for establishing and maintaining desegregated school systems need to know not only how fast is "all deliberate speed" but also how thoroughly they must remove the "vestiges" of a dual school system and by what measure they can become a "unitary system."

In addition to knowing measurement criteria, policymakers and school administrators need to know upon whom the responsibility for action is to fall. Are all classrooms in each school to be desegregated? All schools within each district? All school districts in a region or state? Is each level to be tackled separately, or are accountability criteria to be applied to each and every level? If classrooms are to be integrated, action will have to be taken at the school level. If only classrooms within schools are to be desegregated, however, there will be precious little desegregation for the large number of schools with substantially imbalanced ethnic representation in their student bodies. If schools within a district are the target, then action at the level of the school district will be required; but even if the districts are completely successful in desegregating within their boundaries, there will remain substantial between-district ethnic imbalances that go unaddressed. If regional action is expected, some agency with a broader purview of governance than the local districts will have to become accountable. In most states there is some form of county-level governance serving a number of school districts. Except for those states that use the county boundaries to define school districts, however, these intermediate units tend to be relatively weak governance mechanisms, generally without any authority to control student assignments to schools within or between school districts.

The proliferation of charter schools further complicates any effort to produce reasonably thorough desegregation. They are not anchored to catchment areas and generally compete with regular public schools for voluntary enrollment of students. It is clear that charter schools have exacerbated more often than alleviated ethnic segregation—this despite the fact that most charters mandate enrollment criteria that would promote desegregation.

Often overlooked in the clash of segregation definitions and measurements is the fact that policy-makers and administrators have a limited set of tools with which to ameliorate school segregation, regardless of how serious it might be. Housing segregation patterns make it abundantly clear that citizens, in making private decisions, will often produce substantially segregated population centers. Apparently, desegregation can be expected to occur only if there are either substantial private incentives or binding policy decisions that allocate students to schools, in part at least, on the basis of their ethnicity. In the paragraphs below we describe the five most potent ways for school districts to take responsible action.

1. Redrawing school catchment areas. With the adoption of the *Brown* decisions by the Supreme Court, it was expected that the de jure segregation patterns in the South would be ended primarily through the redrawing of school catchment areas in ways that put Blacks and Whites into the same neighborhood schools. This was feasible because the southern school systems had enforced segregation by sending children to separate schools even though they were living in the same geographic neighborhoods. In some cases, following desegregation of the apartheid system, children were assigned to schools that were actually closer to their places of residence. It was soon recognized, however, that redrawing contiguous catchment areas would not be able to overcome much of the residential segregation of ethnic groups, particularly in the large cities of the North and West. School districts like Berkeley, California, have carried the redrawing of catchment areas to a new level by creating catchment areas that are not contiguous but pair relatively affluent with relatively less affluent and high-minority subareas to create substantially desegregated schools, even though the residential subareas composing the schools' attendance boundaries are highly segregated.

2. Creating more flexible school facilities. At the margins, it is possible to make the redrawing strategy somewhat more powerful by creating schools facilities that can substantially adjust their enrollment capacities. This is done through the relatively widespread use of temporary, portable classrooms (infamously dubbed "Willis Wagons," after the Chicago school superintendent who purportedly used them to reinforce segregation rather than to ameliorate it). School sites may double or halve school enrollments by moving portable classroom trailers onto or away from a site containing a core permanent facility. If concentrated residential neighborhoods are not too large, portable classrooms can be located in ways that facilitate ethnic integration by changing the direction children take when moving from home to school. Of course, portable classrooms are most frequently used simply to relieve population pressure on existing school facilities rather than to facilitate desegregation, but their strategic use can make the redefinition of school catchment areas a somewhat more effective desegregation strategy.

3. Transporting students. The use of school buses or public transport systems to move children from one neighborhood to another in order to facilitate desegregation is a third desegregation strategy, one that became highly controversial during the 1970s. For the most part, political resistance on the part of White and middle-class families to bussing for integration was so intense that school districts produced only "one way" bussing programs, which moved some minority children out of their neighborhoods and into predominantly White schools. Despite the imposition of travel time and inconvenience primarily on the minority students, resistance to this integration technique was strong enough to produce a spike in "White flight," thus reinforcing the long-standing trend of White families' urban exodus to the suburbs, where their children could attend schools in a different school district.

4. Magnet school programs. A number of school districts have approached desegregation by developing specialized programs expected to be attractive to White families and situating them in predominantly minority schools to reverse the one-way bussing flow of students. Concern has been expressed that this strategy has the effect of creating on-campus segregation (separating the ethnic groups into different educational programs) that undermines the purpose of producing desegregated school systems. This on-campus segregation is overcome if the entire school program becomes specialized, eliminating the residual "neighborhood" school programs that may have been left untouched by the early magnet school approaches. This has become a more prevalent approach in the last decade, especially at the secondary level.

5. Picking sites for new schools. Where relatively long-term commitment to desegregation of the schools is present, it is possible to use the planning for and locating of new school buildings to facilitate desegregation. Where school location has historically emphasized placing schools, particularly elementary schools, centrally within perceived social neighborhoods, school desegregation can be facilitated by placing these facilities closer to the boundaries between relatively segregated housing neighborhoods to make it easier to define catchment areas that are integrated.

Summary and Conclusion

The foregoing discussion supports three important conclusions regarding why accountability for public school desegregation is difficult to establish and maintain. First, the judiciary has substantially abandoned the commitment made in the *Brown* decisions to ridding the nation of ethnically separated schools. Although there is continuing support for the notion that no government agency has the right to segregate children intentionally on the basis of their race, language, educational attainment, or gender, segregation along these lines when produced by private decisions is no longer seen as constitutionally suspect. Indeed, with the *Parents Involved* decision, school boards appear to be prohibited under current judicial guidelines from even creating mechanisms that provide incentives for families to desegregate their schools voluntarily. Government-sponsored desegregation by redrawing school catchments does appear to pass muster if, as in Berkeley, California, the catchment areas do not rest on race or ethnicity alone.

Our second core conclusion is that there are serious problems with the measurement of school segregation—problems that affect both the ability to interpret the location and magnitude of school segregation, which might be addressed if there were a legal and politically supported way to do so. Although the indices that are most frequently used to assess the severity and location of segregation in the schools are in substantial agreement about when schools are totally segregated or perfectly integrated, these measures produce inconsistent assessments at any realistic degree of integration. The best measures—those founded on Theil's information-based measures of group separation— are also the most difficult to interpret meaningfully because they provide a curvilinear measure in which incremental changes in the indices do not reflect equal amounts of student group segregation. Thus, we have found that it is necessary to employ multiple measures; but even when multiple measures are used, it is not possible to be explicit about the degree of change in school segregation from one period to another when the numbers and sizes of schools within a school district are changing.

Finally, we have concluded that administrative mechanisms that have been used in attempts to facilitate desegregation are blunt tools. Many are hard to support politically and may sometimes encourage the families of advantaged students to flee school districts or even to exit the public school system entirely.

References

Berger, M. A. (1983). Neighborhood schools: The new (?) legal response to enrollment decline and desegregation. *Urban Education, 18*(1), 7–28.

California State Department of Education (1967). *Racial and ethnic survey of California public schools, part one: Distribution of pupils.* Sacramento: California State Department of Education.

Chemerinsky, E. (2005). The segregation and resegregation of American public education: The court's role. In J. C. Boger & G. Orfield (Eds.), *School resegregation: Must the South turn back?* (pp. 29–47). Chapel Hill: The University of North Carolina Press.

Civil Rights Act of 1964, Pub. L. No. 88–352, 78 Stat. 241 (1964).

Coleman, J. S., Campbell, E. Q., Hobson, C. J., McPartland, J., Mood, A. M., Weinfeld, F. D., et al. (1966). *Equality of educational opportunity.* Washington, DC: U.S. Government Printing Office.

Dunn, J. R. (1967). Title VI, the guidelines and school desegregation in the south. *Virginia Law Review, 53*(1), 42–88.

Dye, T. R. (1968). Urban school segregation: A comparative analysis. *Urban Affairs Quarterly, 4*(2), 144–165.

Fairfax, L. M. (1999). The silent resurrection of Plessy: The Supreme Court's acquiescence in the resegregation of America's schools. *Temple Political and Civil Rights Law Review, 9*(1), 1–57.

Giles, M. W. (1977). Racial stability and urban school desegregation. *Urban Affairs Quarterly, 12*(4), 499–510.

Hendrick, I. G. (1975). Public policy toward the education of non-white minority group children in California, 1849–1970 (NIE Project No. NIE-G-00-3-0082). Riverside: School of Education, University of California, Riverside.

Mitchell, R. E., & Mitchell, D. E. (2010). Assessing multiethnic school segregation: Measurement and interpretation. Paper presented at the annual meeting of the American Educational Research Association, Denver, CO, April.

Orfield, G., & Eaton, S. E. (1996). *Dismantling desegregation. The quiet reversal of Brown v. Board of Education.* New York: New Press.

Reardon, S. F., & Firebaugh, G. (2002). Measures of multigroup segregation. *Sociological Methodology, 32*, 33–67.

Rebell, M. A. (2009). *Courts and kids: Pursuing educational equity through the state courts.* Chicago: University of Chicago Press.

Rossell, C. H., & Armor, D. J. (1996). The effectiveness of school desegregation plans, 1968–1991. *American Politics Quarterly, 24*(3), 267–302.

Smith, S. S., & Mickelson, R. A. (2000). All that glitters is not gold: School reform in Charlotte-Mecklenburg. *Educational Evaluation and Policy Analysis, 22*(2), 101–127.

U.S. Civil Rights Commission (1967). *Racial isolation in the public schools.* Washington, DC: U.S. Government Printing Office.

Welner, K. G. (2006). K–12 race-conscious student assignment policies: Law, social science, and diversity. *Review of Educational Research, 76*(3), 349–382.

Wollenberg, C. (1974). *Mendez v. Westminster:* Race, nationality and segregation in California schools. *California Historical Quarterly, 53*(4), 317–332.

Legal Cases

Board of Ed. of Oklahoma City v. Dowell, 498 U.S. 237 (1991).

Bolling v. Sharpe, 347 U.S. 497 (1954).

Brown v. Board of Education of Topeka, 347 U.S. 483 (1954).

Brown v. Board of Education of Topeka, 349 U.S. 294 (1955).

Columbus Board of Education v. Penick, 443 U.S. 449 (1979).

Communities for Equity v. Michigan High Sch. Athletic Ass'n, 459 F.3d 676 (6th Cir. 2006).

Cumming v. Board of Education of Richmond County, 175 U.S. 528 (1899).

Davis v. School Comm'rs of Mobile County, 402 U.S. 33 (1971).

Dayton Bd. of Education v. Brinkman, 443 U.S. 526 (1979).

Freeman v. Pitts, 503 U.S. 467 (1992).

Gong Lum v. Rice, 275 U.S. 78 (1927).

Goss v. Board of Education, 373 U.S. 683 (1963).

Green v. County Sch. Bd. of New Kent County, 391 U.S. 430 (1968).

Griffin v. School Board, 377 U.S. 218 (1964).

Hendrick Hudson District Board of Education v. Rowley, 458 U.S. 176 (1982).

Hobson v. Hansen, 269 F. Supp. 401 (D. D. C. 1967).

Keyes v. School Dist. No. 1, 413 U.S. 189 (1973).

Lau v. Nichols, 414 U.S. 563 (1974).

Lawrence et al. v. Texas, 539 U.S. 558 (2003).

McLaurin v. Oklahoma State Regents, 339 U.S. 637 (1950).

Mendez v. Westminster, 64 F. Supp. 544 (C. D. Cal. 1946).

Milliken v. Bradley, 418 U.S. 717 (1974).

Milliken v. Bradley, 433 U.S. 267 (1977).

Mills v. Board of Education of the District of Columbia, 348 F.Supp. 866 (D. D. C. 1972).

Mississippi University for Women v. Hogan, 458 U.S. 718 (1982).

Missouri v. Jenkins, 515 U.S. 70 (1995).

National Assn. for the Advancement of Colored People v. San Bernardino City Unified Sch. Dist., 17 Cal.3d 311 (1976).

Parents Involved in Community Schools v. Seattle School District No. 1, 551 U.S. 701 (2007).

Pasadena City Bd. of Education v. Spangler, 427 U.S. 424 (1976).

Pennsylvania Association for Retarded Children v. Commonwealth of Pennsylvania, 343 F.Supp. 279 (E. D. Pa. 1972).

Plessy v. Ferguson, 163 U.S. 537 (1896).

Plyler v. Doe, 457 U.S. 202 (1982).

San Antonio School District v. Rodriguez, 411 U.S. 1 (1973).

Serrano v. Priest, 5 Cal.3d 584 (1971).

Spencer v. Kugler, 404 U.S. 1027 (1972).

St. Helena Parish School Board v. Hall, 368 U.S. 515 (1962).

Swann v. Charlotte-Mecklenburg Bd. of Educ., 402 U.S. 1 (1971).

Sweatt v. Painter, 339 U.S. 629 (1950).

United States v. Scotland Neck Bd. of Educ., 407 U.S. 484 (1972).

United States v. Virginia et al., 518 U.S. 515 (1996).

U.S. v. Montgomery Bd. of Educ., 395 U.S. 225 (1969).

Westminster v. Mendez, 161 F.2d 774 (9th Cir. 1947).

Wright v. Council of City of Emporia, 407 U.S. 451 (1972).

15

Private Provision of Education in Urban Contexts

Guilbert C. Hentschke

Expenditures for all levels of education continue to increase in virtually all countries with comparable data. In about three-quarters of these countries funding from private sources is increasing more rapidly than from public sources (OECD, 2008, p. 243). "Privately provided" education continues to grow, both absolutely and as a proportion of all formal education. This is occurring at both compulsory and tertiary levels, and in most corners of the world (Quddus & Rashid, 2000). It encompasses many different kinds of organizations, with a widening range of governance, financing, and ownership arrangements (e.g., for profit versus nonprofit and privately funded versus publicly funded), that vary by level of education, region of a country, and across countries.

Despite these important variations, privately provided education's sustained and widespread growth over several decades suggests fundamental changes in the conditions that shape schooling. At the same time, each country in the world is increasingly "urbanizing," regardless of its size, location, or stage of economic development. Like the meaning of *privately provided*, that of *urbanizing* varies greatly, influenced by a multitude of demographic, economic, political, geographic, cultural, and historic contextual factors. As a consequence, generalizations about either category should be developed with caution, and generalizations about the interactions between both—a goal of this chapter—should be made with extreme caution.

That being said, this chapter examines the factors and forces that shape the disproportionate growth and impact of privately provided education services in urban settings. It opens with an examination of "private provision" as reflected in departures from the widespread model of public (governmental) funding and provision of schooling services. What constitutes the private provision of education today, and how has that concept evolved? What are the predominant and emerging forms of private provision, and how does that vary between compulsory and tertiary sectors of education? What are the primary explanations for the growth of private provision of schooling?

Next in the chapter, I examine dimensions of urbanization that most directly bear on schooling. To what extent are the forces and trends that foster the growth of private schooling disproportionately represented in urban environments? Do those factors adequately explain the disproportionate growth of private provision of education in urban settings?

Third, in light of increased privatization and urbanization, a global sample of changes in the scope and scale of private education services is presented and evaluated. What form do private education services take in differing, especially urban, contexts? What impact does private education appear to have in general and vis-à-vis the primary governmental system of education?

Fourth, private organizations that are chartered as *for*-profit enterprises are distinct in several ways from those that are chartered as *non*profit enterprises. The fact that virtually identical services are at times provided by each of the two types of providers should not mask the distinctive features to be found in for-profit forms of business, including variations in the mission, governance, and finance. Is this problematic? What is the shape of the for-profit sector of the education industry? Where has growth been most pronounced? Why?

The final section of the chapter addresses the implications of the private provision of schooling for urban dwellers: implications for equity, access, human capital development, public policy, and a revised notion of education as a public good. Given the rise of private provision of schooling and the increasing household contribution to schooling consumption, how has the basic social contract between governments and citizens evolved with regard to education? Is the change a difference in "degree" or a difference in "kind"?

Private Provision of Education

Private provision of formal schooling is both very old and relatively new. Up to the last several hundred years, the history of formal schooling was largely "private" in that groups of individuals voluntarily organized to "school themselves." In the United States, the (private) "one-room schoolhouse" preceded the (public) "common school." As nation-states (along with subsidiary jurisdictions) emerged as the primary form of political organization, the state assumed more and more responsibility for schooling provision.

In today's world, over 85% of financial support for schooling comes from public sources. In addition, governments operate the schools that most of the children and young adults in the world attend (OECD, 2008, p. 243). In tandem with population growth, economic development, and uneven industrialization, governments in most parts of the world have assumed primary responsibility for education services, directly operating the majority of schools. Historically, old private schools, colleges, and universities remained, but they shrank substantially in proportion to public education growth, until about the last 30 to 50 years.

Factors Influencing Growth of Privately Provided Education

Within this relatively recent frame of time, a variety of forces have emerged that have fostered the growth of a variety of forms of private schooling, chief among which have been the growing recognition that "human capital" (what each of us knows and can do) has a positive value and contributes to individual and social well-being, compounded by the strengthening relationship between "learning" and "earning" as the industrialized world evolves into a "global knowledge economy" (OECD, 2008; Spring, 2009). The incentives to pursue schooling are escalating (OECD, 2008).

Beyond these "human capital" arguments, private schools are also being created as alternatives to existing public schools for philosophical and religious reasons (Agai, 2007), due in part to disagreements over the qualities of government-provided options (Astiz, Wiseman, & Baker, 2002). Many of these reasons foster demand for different *kinds* of schooling, which, if not provided by governments, translates into a demand for *more* (as well as different) schooling. This demand for (and supply of) *increased* levels of schooling is shared by households, businesses, communities, and nations, but it does not automatically follow that governments can or do provide for the *increases* in schooling services being demanded (Centre for Educational Research and Innovation, 2006). The capacity of governments to fill these needs has not kept pace with increased demands, and private (nongovernmental) forms of schooling are filling in as "demand absorbing" educational enterprises. Arguably, the growing value of and demand for education, then, is influencing the growth of private provision.

The distinction here between "private" and "public" provision of education requires some clarification, even in the United States. "Purely private" schools in the United States would include all schools operated by private nonprofit and/or for-profit organizations where governments provide no direct operating subsidies to the students or to the institution. Historically, these would have included prep, parochial, and independent schools at the K–12 level (serving about 10% of that population) and the independent (nonprofit) sector of higher education (serving about 20% of that population). Over time, public financial support of these and other education institutions has increased, and today 91.4% of total spending on U.S. K–12 and higher education comes from public sources (OECD, 2008, p. 252).

The "pure private form" of education has been supplemented by a form of "private governance with public financial support" plus increased private contributions to publicly provided schooling. This should not suggest that governments are actively seeking to privatize education by diverting their resources to privately governed entities, but this has been the result. In fact, governments appear to be subsidizing publicly provided schooling as much as they can: *public education* spending has been increasing as a proportion of *total public* expenditure (OECD, 2008, p. 257). Total funding for education has increased proportionately, and private funding serves more as a supplement, seeking to respond to excess demands for schooling, beyond that which governments can provide.

Regardless of whether "private" is defined as organizational control or as source of funding, private schooling is increasing. Today, the definition of *private* has expanded. In K–12 education, this definition would include home schooling, private schools in voucher programs, and charter schools (despite educators' arguments that charter schools are "public" because they are government-funded and are not permitted to charge for tuition). The vast majority of the 4,600 charter schools in the United States are incorporated as private, not-for-profit 501(c)3 corporations.

At the tertiary or higher education level the definition would, in addition to the traditional not-for-profit privates, include for-profit colleges and universities, such as Corinthian Colleges, the University of Phoenix, and about 3,800 other similar institutions. Much, but not all, of the growth of privately provided education has come from these (relatively) "new" K–12 and higher education institutions. *Private provider* here, then, refers to the economic sectors in which the enterprise is incorporated (nonprofit versus for profit), not the source of the operating revenues.

With the recent growth in the privatization of many government programs, the "constitutional paradigm of a sharp separation between public and private" (Metzger, 2003, p. 1367) is increasingly at odds with the blurred public–private character of modern governance. Education is no exception to this trend or to this blurring among sectors. In this gray area of private/public services the "proper" role of government is politically contested. Within a framework of governmental delegation of powers to carry out public services, it is not always clear whether relationships are adequately structured to "satisfy the demands of constitutional accountability . . . without intruding unduly on governmental regulatory prerogatives" (Metzger, 2003, p. 1367). Privatizing trends in education, as in other industries, seek such a balance. Enabling legislation (as with charter schools), coupled with regulatory oversight (as with for-profit higher education), greatly affects the shape and impact of each (partially) privatized industry. The "balance" in education amounts to more than fostering growth without losing control; it reflects as much the classic principal agent problem of the effective delegation of decision rights (Hentschke & Wohlstetter, 2004).[1]

Public Regulation of Privately Provided Education

Not all industries lend themselves equally to privatization by public policymakers (Blank, 2000, p. 34). Privatization has expanded from extractive industries such as mining to various forms of transportation, into telecommunications, electric utilities, and, most recently, social services. The social services market (which in this discussion includes education services, health, child care, and welfare) is characterized by what economists call multiple market failures—that is, where relying strictly on private markets to produce and allocate services would be counterproductive.[2]

Problems arise in these fields when consumers are concerned with quality as well as with price. If quality is readily observable, then governments can more readily regulate private providers to assure that standards are met. However, privatization may be problematic when standards of quality are difficult to observe or to agree upon, belief in government's capacity and intention is not high, equity and universalism are priorities, and difficulties arise in collecting and disseminating information on service quality (Blank, 2000). This is the broad context within which the private provision of education is located: it is in demand, growing in scope, and politically problematic.

Education, like health, is a highly regulated industry. This includes significant levels of public oversight over inputs, processes, and outputs, and legislation designed to support and/or regulate elements of the industry. Examples affecting education have included the American Recovery and Reinvestment Act of 2009, which allocated nearly $100 billion to education; the Education Jobs Fund ($10 billion); the elimination of the Federal Family Education Loan (FFEL) student loan program; and reauthorization of the Elementary and Secondary Education Act ("No Child Left Behind"), and the Higher Education Opportunity Act (HEOA). Much of what private education organizations can do is framed and delimited by the parameters of licensing, accreditation, Equal Employment Opportunity and Occupational Safety and Health Administration regulations, state education codes, and union contracts. High levels of regulation are likely to occur when a service is publicly funded and when significant benefits accrue to individuals—the case of education.

Most of these support and compliance mechanisms in education are focused on organizational inputs and processes rather than outputs, with the notable exceptions of student test scores in the K–12 segment of the industry and graduation rates applied to for-profit postsecondary institutions. Other outputs are not systematically tied to regulatory oversight. This is explained in part by the difficulty in reaching consensus about what to measure and, no less consequential, how to interpret the resulting data. Persell and Wenglinsky (2004), for example, found that graduates from for-profit colleges and universities have less "civic engagement" than graduates from traditional colleges. They could not discern whether the differences are attributable to differences in student populations or differences in experiences at the two different types of institutions. Should civic engagement be considered a legitimate output of a postsecondary education? If so, how much of it "came with" the student at the point of initial enrollment?

Privatization *within* Educational Institutions

The growth of the private provision of education is reflected not only in new private schools, colleges, and universities but also *within* existing, *traditional* public and private nonprofit educational institutions. In other words, the provision of educational services by private (nonprofit and for-profit) organizations is an increasingly integral part of *all* schools and colleges. This might seem like a surprising generalization. After all, public schools serve nearly 90% of U.S. schoolchildren and about 80% of the world's schoolchildren (OECD, 2008).

Furthermore, about three-fourths of U.S. higher education students are enrolled in public colleges and universities. At the same time, however, these traditional educational institutions are increasingly outsourcing many of their core education and support functions to private providers. Non-core outsourced functions range from custodial to endowment management services, transportation to energy management services, construction to bookstore services, food services to security services, and public relations ("communications") to legal services. Core-education services are also being increasingly outsourced, including assessment, tutoring, testing, records and data management, professional development, recruiting, course or "learning management systems" and services, curricula, and, most recently, teaching assistant services and entire programs of study (higher education only).

Privatized outsourcing is taking place in private as well as in public schools and colleges, and in education organizations in rural as well as in urban environments. In fact, outsourced forms of these services are increasingly found in all education institutions, reflecting not only a trend in the historic "buy versus make" decisions of many organizations, but also the growing capacity, efficiency, and sophistication of specialty service providers within the education industry (Hentschke, 2007).

Government Support for Privately Provided Education

Explanations for the growth of different forms of private education vary with the context. Services get outsourced (or, the opposite, in-sourced) for reasons of convenience, efficiency, organizational capacity, and the presence of viable alternatives. New schools, colleges, and universities are created for somewhat different sets of reasons. These include increases in demand in excess of government capacity (developed and developing countries), lack of government infrastructure (developing countries as well as poor and rural regions of developed countries), and increases in per capita economic growth, fueling demands for more schooling (regions with a rising middle class).

Although some of these arguments for private provision of schooling can be viewed as criticisms *of* governments, similar rationales have been developed *by* governments for fostering the growth of privately organized schooling options, especially as they (governments) compete for highly educated residents who contribute to the growth of their taxable personal and corporate income bases or seek greater efficiencies in publicly supported schooling services (Adnett, 2004). If families are dissatisfied with current school offerings in their governmental jurisdiction *and* can afford to relocate to a (more expensive) jurisdiction with better-quality schools, they may.

With increasing household mobility and private returns to schooling, the "exit threat" of this particular demographic poses a potential problem for governmental jurisdictions at all levels. It behoves governments to encourage the creation of these schooling options within their jurisdictions (at less than current costs per student) in order to increase the odds that taxpaying citizens do not relocate. In regions of the world with few or no government-provided or supported schooling options, individuals can (and do) take it upon themselves to create and participate in schooling that is largely private.

Driven by differing combinations of the reasons cited above over the last several decades, many national and regional governments across the geographical and economic development spectrum have sought to introduce various elements of market-based resource-allocation schemes into their compulsory education systems, usually including government financial support for privately operated schooling. Examples include developed countries (parts of Canada, the United Kingdom, Japan, the United States, Australia, Sweden, New Zealand, the Netherlands, and France), recently emerging economies (Qatar, Singapore, Chile, Argentina, and parts of China), and developing countries (Tanzania, Nicaragua, and Pakistan) (Brewer & Hentschke, 2009). In broad strokes, these initiatives include various combinations of public funding of private institutions, devolution of governance, increased consumer voice, and new forms of private institutional financing of public and private institutions. All cases represent a departure from the pure model of government finance and provision of schooling.

In the United States, state governments (about 40) have supported the creation and growth of charter schools through enabling legislation. The legislation and related regulations in some of these states foster the creation and growth of relatively large numbers of charter schools, e.g., California and Minnesota. Enabling charter school legislation in other states is relatively restrictive, e.g., Missouri. The details of enabling legislation, coupled with the market context of each state, significantly influence the degree of growth of privately operated schooling.

The privatization trend in compulsory schooling is reflected in tertiary education as well, although the financing, regulatory, and governance mechanisms differ. State governments are the primary engine for regulation and support in compulsory education whereas, at the tertiary education level, that role sits at the federal level of government.

Private Schooling for Whom?

Private schools and universities serve some of the most elite student populations in the world, but these enterprises (for-profit or nonprofit) are not limited to families of the "reasonably well to do." In fact, private (even for-profit) schooling enterprises have been documented in some of the poorest, least developed, largely rural but often intensely urban regions of the world. From the slums of Hyderabad in India to the largest shanty town in Africa to in the mountains of Gansu, China, large proportions of poor families (by almost any definition) are paying tuition fees to send their children to private, for-profit schools, even when government-provided, tuition fees-free options are available to them (Tooley, 2009). Parents who send their children to these schools believe that teachers in and owners of for-profit schools try harder to provide a good education, in contrast to many teachers in government schools who were frequently absent (Tooley, 2009).

> Similar results were found by others in Pakistan, where the real story . . . is not the growth in religious schooling but that in self-owned, nonreligious, for-profit private schools. This rise in private schooling is decentralized, market based, and totally unaided by government subsidies or support.
>
> (Andrabi, Das, & Khwaja, 2008, pp. 329–330)

These schools emerged in parts of the country where two conditions were present: (1) government alternatives were lacking or marginal and (2) disproportionate numbers of women high-school graduates (from government schools) were available to teach. Reports of private school growth throughout Africa reflect roughly similar circumstances (Teferra & Altbach, 2004).

The expansion of private schooling in China, on the other hand, is surfacing in regions characterized by rapidly rising incomes among families, a growing middle class that has aspirations for schooling quality above that currently provided by their (local) government, plus a desire for greater control over schooling policies and practices (Mok, 1997). Part of the support for increased private school and college alternatives stems from a belief that they provide greater opportunity for students from less well-to-do families ("deprived people") (Mok, 1997, p. 50).

Urbanization

At one level the association between the private provision of schooling and urbanization is easily understood. Schooling (at all levels) is increasingly an urban enterprise, if only because increasing proportions of the world's population are becoming urban, resulting largely from decades-long migrations from rural villages (and farming) to cities (and nonfarm employment). Based on UNESCO's estimates, 2010 marks the first time in history when the majority of the population now lives in cities (Mead, 2010). Indeed, the world is now entering its "peak urbanization" rate when the vast rural-to-urban migration will be at its fastest. Some 50 years ago, two-thirds of the world's population lived in the countryside; 50 years from now three-quarters of the world's people will live in cities. Going forward, the majority of the world's 6.7 billion people will live in cities.

Increasing Urbanization

By 2025 the proportion of people living in cities should climb to about 60%. But the "urban" of urban education is more than a quantitative dimension; it reflects a qualitative dimension that distinguishes cities from suburbs, towns, and villages. Some, but by no means all of these dimensions link cities to social problems—e.g., poverty, drugs, violence, gangs, congestion, pollution, and extreme social and economic inequality, and so on, or "public bads."

Other dimensions of urban areas are more positively viewed—e.g., a more highly educated labor force, greater employment diversity and opportunity, greater infrastructure for commerce, and so on, or "public goods." Other dimensions contribute to a mix of goods and bads—e.g., greater density, income inequality, social and racial diversity. Greater income inequality, for example, is mixed, in that it has been found to be associated with greater expenditures for education and correspondingly with improvements in distributional equity (Corcoran & Evans, 2010). Corcoran and Evans drew upon a balanced panel of more than 10,300 local school districts spanning 1970–2000 to explore the relationship between rising income inequality and fiscal support for public elementary and secondary education. In contrast with some other studies, they found that rising income inequality appears to be associated with *higher* per-student expenditure in local school districts, driven primarily by an increase in revenues from local sources. Given the redistributive nature of education, their results suggest that some of the potentially negative consequences of rising social inequality may have been counteracted by local government's ability to raise additional funds from growing incomes at the top of the distribution.

Greater proportions of individuals now live in cities, but growth and impacts are uneven. Developed nations have a higher percentage of urban residents than less developed ones. However, urbanization is occurring rapidly in many less developed countries, and it is expected that most urban growth will occur in less developed countries during the next decades. Disproportionate growth of cities is largely a function of birth rates plus migration from rural areas within a given country and, more recently, by international migration to cities from other less urban countries and by inter-city migration. In general and over a long period of time, rural-to-urban urban migration can be viewed as a "transfer of labor from a traditional, land-intensive technology to a human capital-intensive technology with an unending potential for growth, [with] . . . cities as places in which new immigrants can accumulate the skills required by modern production technologies" (Lucas, 2004, p. 29).

"Cities" with a population of more than 50,000 have been eclipsed by "megacities" with populations in excess of 5 million. Today, over 100 cities in the world are larger than 3 million, and about 20 of these are over 10 million. The fastest-growing cities are largely in the developing world, and the slowest tend to be in Europe. Quantitative growth belies qualitative evolution as the world urbanizes. It is "much more than simple population growth; it involves changes in the economic, social and political structures of a region" (*The Economist*, 2009, pp. 22–23).

The Changing Nature of Cities

Rapid urban growth is responsible for many environmental and social changes in the urban environment, and its effects are strongly related to global change issues, not the least among which are growing extremes of inequality among residents who live in close proximity to one another. Growing inequality is recorded throughout the modern world and has been linked directly to a wide variety of social problems in addition to poor education quality, including those related to physical health, mental health, drug abuse, imprisonment, obesity, social mobility, trust and community life, violence, teenage births, and child well-being (Wilkinson & Pickett, 2010).

Although associations between these problems and inequality are not limited to urban environments, inequality itself is most evident there. Further, the rapid growth of cities strains their capacity to provide services such as energy, education, healthcare, transportation, sanitation, and physical security. Because governments have less revenue to spend on the basic upkeep of cities and the provision of services, cities have become areas of massive sprawl, serious environmental problems, and widespread poverty. Nonetheless, in comparison to society at large, urban dwellers do not see their education options as uniquely problematic or inadequate (Rose & Gallup, 2003). Rather, their views of the shortcomings of schooling options are similar to those expressed by society as a whole.

At the same time, cities continue to grow and to differentiate among themselves and from nonurban areas (Roberts, 1989), in part *because of* the opportunities they provide to individuals relative to other options. For example, on average, workers in cities earn 33% more than their nonurban counterparts, suggesting that cities speed the accumulation of human capital (Glaeser & Mare, 2001), even as the very nature of employment is shifting from industrial positions in large firms toward more "informal" systems (Roberts, 1989, p. 680). Cities, like countries, are economic enterprises, each with its own levels of development, and the most developed economically are not necessarily the largest in population.

As an illustration, of the top 30 metropolitan regions in the world in terms of GDP, 12 are located in the United States, but in terms of population, only three of the top 30 cities are in the United States. By 2020, 80% of the world's largest cities by population will be in developing countries (City Mayors Statistics, 2010). Educational level and economic development are highly correlated, and cities vary on both dimensions. For individuals cities present opportunities but not security. Education is a vehicle to improve the odds of success, and private schooling arises in response to the resulting demand.

The disproportionate growth of the provision of private education in cities is a response to the stresses placed on traditional education systems, to the growth of populations pursuing schooling (all levels), and to the overall growing value of schooling to individuals, especially to those living in cities. Cities are attractive, especially in developing countries and despite their associated costs of excessive concentration, extreme income inequality, and underdeveloped or overburdened institutions (Henderson, 2002).

Growth in Privately Provided Education in Cities

As "demand-absorbing" institutions, privately provided schooling arises where the demand is—in this case, cities. Cities house an increasing proportion of potential students; their current (largely public systems) are relatively overburdened; financial support (governmental, philanthropic, and investor) for schooling there is disproportionately higher; and the labor market returns to schooling are relatively higher there. These generalizations apply to compulsory as well as tertiary education, especially in the United States. There, K–12 charter schools and for-profit higher education are usually considered as separate and distinct entities, and for good reasons. One is located in the compulsory part of our system and the other in the tertiary (voluntary) part. The private organizations that operate charter schools are a blend of for-profit and nonprofit entities, whereas for-profit colleges and universities are, by definition, all part of the former group. Despite these obvious differences, these two sets of education institutions share several common characteristics.

First, institutions in both sets are private entities, incorporated and governed as private non-profit or for-profit entities. Second, institutions in both derive very large proportions of their operating revenue from government sources. Charter schools derive their revenue from government funds designed to support K–12 schooling, and for-profit colleges and universities are aided by federal student financial assistance funds. A third shared characteristic is that individual schools and campuses in both sets seek to specialize and focus their programs rather than try to become "comprehensive," like their traditional counterparts. Public schooling in the United States has been characterized by "comprehensive" secondary schools, where students are assigned to one of a variety of "tracks," ranging from "general" to "college preparatory" to "vocational."

In contrast, the approximately 100 Knowledge Is Power Program (KIPP) charter schools spread across 20 states all offer only college preparatory programs. In like manner, program offerings at a traditional higher education institution are characterized by many, often hundreds, of specialties, majors, departments, minors, and electives. In contrast, the approximately 120 campuses of for-profit Corinthian Colleges, Inc., focus on just seven program areas: healthcare, criminal justice, business, information technology, transportation technology and maintenance, and construction trades. Most of their career-oriented programs have no electives, largely because the institution seeks to educate individuals in a highly specific field.

A fourth shared characteristic is that both sectors are "consolidating" in a roughly similar manner; a relatively small number of charter school management organizations (education management organizations, or EMOs) operate a disproportionate share of charter schools, and a relatively small number of for-profit higher education institutions (largely but not exclusively publicly traded ones) operate a disproportionate share of for-profit higher education campuses. Nearly 30% of all 4,600 charter schools in the United States are operated by slightly over 200 private organizations, each of which operates three or more campuses.[3] In like manner, among the 3,800 for-profit higher education institutions, the largest dozen account for over half of all enrollments (Silber, 2010). In both instances, increasing proportions of campuses and enrollments are found in a small number of the largest enterprises, enabling them to capture economies of scale in their operations.

The fifth, closely related, characteristic is that the larger organizations from both sectors represent a disproportionate share of the *growth* of their segments. As an illustration, Imagine Schools, Inc., the largest for-profit EMO (numbers of schools), experienced growth of somewhere between 19 and 33 schools from 2007 to 2008, and from 2008 to 2009, growing to a total of 76 schools (Molnar, Miron, & Urschel, 2009, p. 1). Similarly, among for-profit higher education institutions, the dozen largest institutions account for greater than average growth of the entire for-profit sector (Silber, 2010). What has been the shape of that growth?

Growth of Compulsory Schools (Charters)

At the *compulsory* level, options for privately operated schooling are being largely provided by charter schools. The majority of U.S. charter school students live in cities (55.7%), as opposed to those from suburbs (25%), towns (5.9%), and rural areas (13.5%) (Smith, 2009, p. 13). Overall, about 4% of the students in compulsory education are enrolled in charter schools, but cities account for much higher proportions of these students—for example, New Orleans (54%), Washington, DC (30%), Dayton (27%), Detroit (22%), Phoenix (23%), Kansas City (22%), and Philadelphia (15%) (Smith, 2009, p. 19). The largest number of charter schools in the country are in Los Angeles. The forces favoring *urban* charter schools operate on both the demand side (parents seeking preferable options) and the supply side (civic leaders, philanthropic organizations, investors who support the creation of charter schools).

Cities (with already disproportionate numbers of charter school students) continue to increase their share of charter school enrollments over time. Examples of increasing market share between 2005–2006, and 2007–2008 include all the previous examples except New Orleans, plus Oakland

(13% to 16%), Albany (10% to 14%), Columbus (10% to 14%), Indianapolis (7% to 12%), and Trenton (9% to 11%) (Smith, 2009, pp. 19–20). Demand continues to outpace the supply of charter school seats. Approximately 385,000 students were waitlisted by charter schools in 2008–2009, while 26 states plus the District of Columbia maintain state-imposed caps on the number and growth of charter schools (Smith, 2009).

Overall, charter schools serve about 1.4 million students, representing an 11% growth from the previous year (2007–2008). In general, they differ from traditional public schools in the racial composition of their student bodies (62% non-White in charters versus 45% in all public schools) and their family income levels (48% qualifying for free and reduced lunch in charters versus 45% in all public schools) (Smith, 2009).

Higher Education Growth (For-profit Colleges and Universities)

At the *tertiary* education level, for-profit higher education has grown with the same urban emphasis: most of the for-profit higher education campuses created within the last 30 years are located within large metropolitan areas. The largest for-profit higher education institutions have a dispropor-tionate presence in the top 50 U.S. metropolitan statistical areas (MSAs). The Apollo Group and ITT Educational Services, for example, each have campuses in 47 of the top 50 MSAs; they are accompanied by the other largest 11 publicly traded for-profits, averaging as a group a total of about six campuses on average in each of the top 50 MSAs (Silber, 2010).

For-profit education institutions serve students who are disproportionately urban residents, working adults, and underserved students with backgrounds that work against the odds of success-fully completing higher education programs, including being relatively poor. For-profits also focus on specific "job training," often describing their programs as preparing students for specific occu-pational specialties. Students generally are bearing increasing proportions of the cost of higher education, and these low-income students are bearing even greater proportions due to the relatively high tuitions of for-profits in comparison to public sector colleges and universities.

Despite the preponderance of risk factors among for-profit students, completion rates at for-profit schools are higher, under certain circumstances, than those at public institutions (Silber, 2010). In a 2006 study, only 43.2% of students who entered postsecondary institutions in 1995–1996 seeking a degree or certificate had, by 2001, actually earned that credential at that same institution (i.e., a 43.2% graduation or completion rate). Although 6.2% of the group were still enrolled at the same institutions six years later (i.e., had not yet completed the program), 19.2% had transferred to another institution during that period (of that 19.2%, 11.1% had completed their programs at the other institution). The remaining 31.4% had dropped out (i.e., attrition rate) of postsecondary education altogether. The for-profit sector had a higher completion rate at the first institution (60.9%) than its public not-for-profit peers (25.1% for two-year institutions and 51% for four-year institutions) (Silber, 2010). Further, the 60% graduation rate for students attending for-profit two-year institu-tions is much higher than the 21.9% rate at (public) community colleges (Silber, 2010). Because the student at a for-profit institution often incurs a large amount of debt to pay for schooling, the consequences of non-completion can be particularly problematic for those students—more so than at institutions with very low tuition rates.

Private Education in Other Parts of the World

The international higher education market is, of course, much larger than the U.S. market, but, at the same time, it is much more fragmented and with proportionately fewer private universities than is the case in the United States. International higher education has grown by 57% since 2000, compared with 20% in the United States (Silber, 2010). The U.S. share of world tertiary-level enrollments shrank to about 12% in 2007 from 28% in 1970 (Silber, 2010, p. 329). Some of the greatest gains in higher education enrollment rates have occurred in countries such as China, Brazil, and India, all associated in part with rapid urbanization, rising per capita income, and increasing access to (public and private) higher education. A brief portrait of changes in China's higher education system illustrates that growth as well as private education's role in that growth.

China enrolled roughly 10.2 million students in higher education in 2008, representing about an 11.1% annual growth rate from 1978 (Silber, 2010) and an even steeper rate of 19% per year between 1999 and 2007. Its rural-to-urban migrant population has driven much of this growth. In 2005, the Ministry of Education estimated that 100 million Chinese citizens were eligible for higher education but that the public facilities could accommodate only about 15 million students. Private institutions constituted a large part of the increase in higher education institutions in China between 1978 and 2008, to 2,263 from about 600. Many of these new private schools were vocational and technical schools.

The increasing role of private provision is reflected as much in changes in finance as in institutional control data. In China, government appropriations for higher education between 1996 and 2007 slid from 79% to 54% of all education funding, whereas funding from student tuition and other sources grew from 15% to 58% during the same time (Silber, 2010). Government funding mechanisms for private education depend on the context of the country. Salerno (2004), for example, found that in countries with newly emerging private education sectors, unclear regulations, and concerns about quality, that public funding tends to be channeled into private institutions indirectly, e.g., through tax-abatements and student financial aid. In countries where private institutions play a more substantial role, public funding is channeled to privates using direct measures as well, e.g., institutional support.

Growing cross-border provision into China has contributed to this increase, including the increased participation of U.S. for-profit higher education providers in China. One Chinese for-profit higher education institution (CIBT Education) has licensed curricula from U.S.-headquartered Apollo Group's Western International University and Corinthian Colleges' Wyotech to offer those programs in China. In 2004, Laureate Education opened a hotel management college there, and in 2007 Kaplan Inc. acquired a majority stake in Chinese-based ACE Education, which provides preparatory classes for entry into UK universities (Silber, 2010). There are, in addition to these initiatives, a number of publicly traded institutions (foreign and domestic) that provide postsecondary services in China (Silber, 2010).

Despite important differences in context in comparison with China, other countries' trends in higher education are roughly similar to those found in China: overall increases in economic development, relatively rapid increases in postsecondary enrollments, and a growing private sector presence in the industry. Examples include but are not limited to India and Brazil, Chile, and Mexico (Silber, 2010) as well as countries throughout Africa (Teferra & Altbach, 2004).

Other Education Services (to Education Institutions and Markets)

In addition to the provision of entire degree programs, a wide variety of private education providers have emerged over the last 30 years that specialize in one or more postsecondary functions and/or related services, not unrelated to the outsourced education functions discussed earlier. Services to students and parents include college planning, test prep, essay services, financial aid, and scholarship information. Services to colleges and universities include direct marketing, lead generation, lead management, enrollment management, retention services, financial aid management, and payment processing. Services to graduates and employers of graduates include resume services, career advising, job placement, internships, and loan servicing.

Although not examined in detail here, these private specialty education businesses represent a growing segment of the education industry, selling their services to other education entities (business-to-business or "B2B"), directly to consumers (business-to-consumer or "B2C"), or both. These are largely *for-profit* enterprises and, along with for-profit schools, colleges, and universities, constitute a major, but distinct subset of all privately provided education services. The growth of for-profit education is outpacing other private education, in part because of its unique access to investment capital, and for that reason warrants separate consideration here.

For-profit Education: A Distinctive Sector within "Private Provision"

For-profit organizations differ from nonprofit organizations in one fundamental respect: parties can buy and sell pieces of the for-profit organization to each other. From this fundamental difference, a wide variety of rules and regulations (e.g., tax law) have evolved that partially distinguish the two forms of organization. For-profit firms, part of the (three-sector) education industry, are worthy of separate consideration here for several reasons. This sector is the fastest growing among the three sectors; for-profit education firms evolve (live and die) more rapidly, and, as creatures of educational entrepreneurs, these firms are often innovators in the goods and services they seek to sell (Gomez & Hentschke, 2009).

As targets of potential investment capital, the most successful for-profit educational services are able to grow their firms and increase the shares of the markets in which they operate. These features derive from the ability of for-profit owners to buy and sell parts (or all) of their organizations. They can buy campuses in new territories or buy new programs in areas where they want to expand. They can sell off less productive or non-core campuses or programs in order to concentrate on higher priorities. They can liquidate and use the capital for new investments. Finally, they can sell additional shares of their organization as it grows, thereby controlling a smaller fraction of a larger enterprise. These for-profit "opportunities" provide no guarantee for growth (many fail and go out of business), but they do provide unique tactics that can facilitate growth.

Not surprisingly, the for-profit sector of education continues to gain market share as the value of added schooling gets reflected more in the marketplace and as government policies support the adoption of for-profit education services by (traditional) schools and colleges (Hentschke, 2007). Education constitutes about 8.3% of the U.S. gross domestic product (GDP). Of the $1.23 trillion spent on education in the United States in 2010, the for-profit share was still small at roughly 9.5% (nearly $118 billion). That share has steadily grown and is expected to continue to grow to about $153 billion or 9.7% by 2015 (Silber, 2010), although some parts are larger and/or grow faster than others. The four major, but unequal, parts of the for-profit education industry are early child care ($68.5 billion), K–12 education ($667.4 billion), postsecondary education ($449.6 billion), and corporate training ($50.3 billion) (Silber, 2010).

Many of the firms within these four categories are becoming large enough to offer shares of their company on the open market through an initial public offering (IPO) of their stock. Examples from the United States since 2006 include online postsecondary providers (e.g., Capella and American Public Education), online K–12 providers (e.g., K–12 and Archipelago Learning), and providers of K–12 *and* higher education and/or online *and* in-seat education services (e.g., Ambow Education, North American University) (Silber, 2010). Most of the private for-profit providers, however, are not nearly as large as the relatively few publicly traded firms. Although individual firms vary greatly, firms within each of the four categories respond to roughly similar influences. The following subsections address the first three of these four areas (corporate training is not discussed).

Early Child Care

This area is quite fragmented, with many small private nonprofit and for-profit providers. At the same time, there are a few very large private for-profit firms that provide early childhood services. Knowledge Universe, for example, serves over 226,000 children in 1,699 centers, and the Learning Care Group serves about 157,000 children in its 1,053 centers.

The largest private *non*profit child care providers are smaller than the for-profits (e.g., PLASP Child Care Services, which serves 13,113 children at 205 centers). But even the largest for-profit company has no more than a 2.3% market share, and most (67%) of the licensed child care centers in the United States in 2008 were operated as small family-run businesses (Silber, 2010, p. 30). Child care providers are increasingly specializing in various ways, including home-based versus center-based, worksite child care, and backup care.

The for-profit market is more developed in the United States than in most countries, and these services have grown up largely in those countries with relatively high levels of GDP per capita accompanied by modest to very little government funding for early childhood services in countries like the United States (Silber, 2010). Countries with significant government provision of early child care (e.g., Austria, Sweden, Singapore, and the UK) have relatively less private for-profit provision. Accountability in this sector is pursued largely though center licensure processes.

K–12 Schooling

This is the largest of the four education industry segments. Private-sector businesses here provide more than schools, including technology solutions, comprehensive student assessment tools, and supplementary education products in tutoring and college prep as well as teacher development programs, among other services. Growth of these and other for-profit K–12 education services are often fueled by a combination of government requirements and financial support. Accountability legislation, focusing largely on student performance, will continue to evolve, but its most recent formulation entails four "turnaround models" all aimed at improving the lowest 5% of schools, regardless of whether they are traditional public schools or charter schools. These remedies range from replacing the principal to closing the schools and enrolling the students who attended them in other, higher-performing schools in the district (Silber, 2010). Many of the ingredients needed to respond to government requirements for school improvement are provided by for-profit firms.

Because of the primacy accorded to testing in the accountability system, providers of testing and assessment services are disproportionately growing in size and in their contribution to K–12 schooling. Private testing and assessment providers (nonprofit and for-profit), include the College Board, Pearson Educational Measurement, Renaissance Learning, Inc., and WestEd. Continued growth in this field and the move to common standards among the states is facilitating the development of more integrated assessment tools. In addition to assessment, for-profit providers have grown in the following service areas: tutoring and test preparation, professional development, and supplemental education services as well as, more visibly, charter schools (Silber, 2010).

Since 2000–2001, the number of charter schools has grown on average roughly 13% annually (enrollments at 15% annually), clearly outpacing the less than 1% average K–12 enrollment growth over the same period. In the 2008–2009 school year, 65% of charter schools had waiting lists with an average number of 239 students, up from 59% in 2008 with an average number of 198 students (Silber, 2010). Increasing proportions of charter schools are managed and operated by for-profit educational management organizations or nonprofit charter management organizations. Among the largest of the hundreds of for-profits are Edison Learning, serving 37,574 students in 31 schools, and Imagine Schools, serving 32,316 students in 76 schools (Silber, 2010). KIPP, the largest nonprofit charter management organization, serves 17,211 in 64 schools.

Private for-profit school providers headquartered in the United States are now opening up schools in major cities in other parts of the world. Some of these offer variations of online learning models, while others are locally sensitive, "traditional" bricks-and-mortar schools. Online learning is increasingly an option provided within K–12 schooling. Public schools that offer online courses frequently contract out this service, often using multiple service providers. Indeed, fully 83% of public school districts use more than one external provider of blended and online content, while 39% use four or more providers (Silber, 2010). Private providers of online content include K12 Inc., serving 68,000 students; Connections Academy, serving 20,000 students; and Kaplan Virtual Education, serving 5,000 students.

Some private for-profit providers focus exclusively on special education students. About 6.6 million school-age children (about 13.4% of the total) in the United States receive special education services (Silber, 2010). These are offered by numerous private providers, including Aspen Education Group, Camelot Schools, Catapult Learning, Community Education Partners, and Educational Services of America. Therapeutic schools are another private provider specialty, focusing on the roughly 6% of teens age 16–19 who are neither working nor attending school (Silber, 2010). Therapeutic schools include boarding schools, outdoor behavioral health schools, and residential treatment centers.

Postsecondary Education

As of 2008–2009 roughly 19.1 million students enrolled in degree-granting postsecondary institutions; about 64% attended four-year schools and about 36% enrolled at two-year schools. These 19.1 million students are overwhelmingly enrolled in undergraduate (86%) versus post-baccalaureate or graduate (14%) degree programs (Silber, 2010). Less than 30% of the U.S. population above age 25 holds a bachelor's degree (up from 9.1% in 1964). As is the case with K–12, the overwhelming majority of students attend public institutions (72%), while private nonprofits serve 18.8% of those students and for-profits serve the remaining 9.2%.

These figures represent only institutions that participate in Title IV (U.S. government financial aid) programs. When all institutions are counted, the for-profit sector's share of students increases to 11.8% (Silber, 2010). Traditional (public and nonprofit) institutions dominate higher education, while for-profits dominate at less-than-two-year schools. For-profits tend to serve female, older, and minority students with lower academic performance prior to enrolling (Silber, 2010). For-profits have gained market share in graduate student enrollment, from 6.4% in the fall of 2004 to 9.2% in the fall of 2008, and at the undergraduate level from 5.8% in the fall of 2004 to 10% in the fall of 2008 (Silber, 2010).

Enrollment at for-profit degree-granting institutions has increased at an 11.6% compound annual growth rate (CAGR) since the fall of 1976. Between 1997 and 2008, for-profit enrollments have grown at 12% CAGR, six times the rate of growth of traditional institutions (Silber, 2010).

Tradeoffs Between Private Nonprofit and For-profit Educational Organizations

Theoretical distinctions between the comparative advantages of for-profit vis-à-vis nonprofit forms of education are not obvious, in part because there are extensive examples of both forms in all levels of schooling—from early child care, through K–12 schooling, and postsecondary education. As described earlier, one of the more visible advantages associated with for-profit forms of organization is their superior access to capital through their unique ownership rights. For-profit forms of organization in education may, however, incur other, less easily counted "agency" costs that may be disproportionately associated with for-profit forms of organization. At the risk of oversimplification, these costs are associated with the peculiar juxtaposition of for-profit business and education, i.e., where it is presumed that the business will do all it can to maximize profits *and* the outputs of education are extremely hard for consumers to measure and compare against some benchmark. The net result is "contract failure" of the for-profit form of organization (strong incentives for the owner to maximize profits over quality) and the inherent advantage of the nonprofit form of organization in protecting the interests of the consumer. Contract failure occurs when ordinary contract devices in themselves do not provide consumers with adequate means for policing the performance of producers. Specifically,

> producers can cut quality in ways that consumers either can't perceive or to which they can't respond. For profit firms are particularly dangerous to consumers in these situations because the owners of these firms benefit from whatever surplus the firms gain from their customers' losses. Consumers respond to this problem by turning to nonprofit firms who act somewhat like fiduciaries on their behalf. Nonprofit firms can serve this function because state law prohibits them from distributing profits to shareholders.
>
> (Morley, 2006, p. 1796)

Morley's analysis of U.S. charter schools suggests that for-profit charter management organizations only survive "when the economies of scale they capture through superior capital-raising offset their higher agency costs" (Morley, 2006). Certainly, there exists a degree of skepticism, perhaps justified in some instances, from some regulators, donors, and parents about the agency costs of for-profit forms of organization, especially at the K–12 and postsecondary levels. As a consequence, for-profit charter management organizations have been prohibited from holding charters (as opposed to contracting for services with charter holders) in some states, and for-profit colleges and universities have recently been *categorically* castigated as unscrupulous (albeit with modest disclaimers). The empirical evidence in education for this tradeoff, however, is not clear: charter school management companies are not larger than nonprofit ones, and for-profit higher colleges and universities are all for-profit, from smallest to largest.

Arguments for and against for-profit education extend far beyond the U.S. borders where for-profit education is growing, albeit from a more modest base (Tooley, 2009; Wildavsky, 2010). Faced with growing concerns about equitable access to education, increasing flows of resources to education, the growth in innovative, market-sensitive education services by for-profit providers and seeking to maximize the benefits from those increases, other nations are exploring policies that will more explicitly support the growth and development of private, even for-profit education services. Working against these policy initiatives in parts of the developing world are the ideology of free education (tertiary as well as compulsory) and of government provision of education services, and the opposition of the upper classes to means-tested scholarship programs (Patrinos, 1990).

Privatized Education, Urban Education, and the Public Good

The education dimensions of urban environments include: people with extremely different back-grounds and increasingly unequal circumstances all living in close proximity to each other, all facing highly variable education options, coupled with an equally diverse array of employment options, each with its own educational and experience prerequisites. The interplay of circumstances and educational opportunities itself varies greatly and is itself potentially growing more unequal (Haskins & Sawhill, 2009). The public as well as private net benefits of education have been well documented in numerous studies over more than four decades (e.g., Brewer & McEwan, 2010; Karoly & Panis, 2004), but the net impact of growing inequality of circumstances on an individual's ability to pursue those benefits is less clear (Haskins & Sawhill, 2009; Wilkinson & Pickett, 2010).

The growth of private provision and private funding of schooling up and (especially) down this "opportunity structure" reflects in part a social (non-governmental) pursuit of these private and public benefits, sanctioned if not financially supported by governments. Private provision is supported in part because of the public benefits that private education provides. Public and private benefits refer to *outcomes* and not to ownership structures. When education is "purely private," i.e., privately produced and consumed with no public subsidies to either buyer or seller, the output of schooling may still have *public* benefits or spillovers ("positive externalities"). One illustration is where the education of one person augments the productivity of others.

The public good argument has provided the justification for governments to support privately provided education, and that argument has aligned with the preferences of households, businesses, and nations to increase both the provision and consumption of schooling. The broad consensus of the value of schooling, coupled with the limited capacity of governments to respond, has fostered a variety of public/private enterprises which, in effect, have blurred the distinction between "publicly provided" and "privately provided" schooling. These historic descriptive tools are becoming increasingly inadequate, especially in light of proliferating private schooling options and growing private pay for public options. Public and private *benefits* accrue equally from among these options when holding "quality" constant.

It is increasingly problematic, then, to frame education, especially higher levels of education, as a purely, or even largely, public good, in the classic sense that (1) consuming education by one individual does not reduce availability of the good for consumption by others (non-rivalry) and (2) that no one can be effectively excluded from getting an education (non-excludability). Access to *quality* schooling opportunities may be an increasing, not a decreasing, challenge. Education is now more broadly available to people all over the world than ever before. Despite this fact, it retains significant elements of rivalry and excludability at a period in history when it is most highly valued.

Furthermore, the concept of "public" is increasingly conflated with *national* even as people live in an increasingly *global* knowledge economy. In such an environment, new levels and kinds of educational externalities emerge—both public "goods" and public "bads"—including "brain drain," "brain gain," and various socioeconomic and demographic distributional consequences (Marginson, 2007). Increases in international *student* migration, cross-border educational programming, distance (online) learning, and *household* migration reflect different attempts to overcome rivalry and excludability in education.

It is difficult to determine with any precision the degree to which private provision of education may be disproportionately an urban phenomenon or whether it is "better" or "worse" than some theoretical "purely public" alternative. That this appears to be the case is in many ways not surprising. From the "prospective student side," increasing proportions of the world's population live in cities and greater quantities and varieties of jobs exist in cities, collectively requiring greater varieties and levels of educated labor.

From the side of the "private education provider," cities are where more and more prospective students live, and their greater varieties of educational wants and needs ("market segmentation") make it especially difficult for governments adequately to provide, let alone customize, education services. Private provision (imperfectly) responds to that gap.

If, as argued here, private provision and personal financial support of education are increasing and individuals (as well as society) benefit substantially from education, then governmental education policy may benefit from a shift toward policies that more directly align public support for an individual's education with that individual's financial contribution to her/his personal education. At the compulsory level these policies would foster the growth of alternative private providers through increased incentives for school completion (rather than attendance). At the tertiary level these policies would foster access to financial credit, tying loan payback schemes more to an individual's future stream of income than to tuition differences associated with the sector location of the provider. By linking more directly the private benefits from education back to the (public and private) costs of education, economic inequality might grow less fast and economic mobility might improve somewhat.

Notes

1. Classic agency problems include adverse selection (providers with insufficient capacity and values), divergent objectives (providers pursue objectives different from directors), information asymmetry (providers' information advantage), weak incentives (directors' insufficient decision rights), and limited decision rights (providers lacking sufficient decision rights to enforce agreements). See Hentschke and Wohlstetter (2004).
2. The principal forms of market failure involve externalities, informational asymmetries, agency problems, and distributional concerns. See Blank (2000, pp. 26–37).
3. Estimated by dividing 4,600 charter schools into the sum of charter schools operated by for-profit and non-profit charter management organizations as referenced in Molnar et al. (2009) and Miron and Urschel (2010).

References

Adnett, N. (2004). Private-sector provision of schooling: An economic assessment. *Comparative Education, 40,* 385–399.

Agai, B. (2007). Islam and education in secular Turkey: State policies and the emergence of the Fethullah Gulen Group. In R. W. Hefner & M. Q. Zaman (Eds.), *Schooling Islam: The culture and politics of modern Muslim education* (pp. 149–171). Princeton, NJ: Princeton University Press.

Andrabi, T., Das, J., & Khwaja, A. I. (2008). A dime a day: The possibilities and limits of private schooling in Pakistan. *Comparative Education Review, 52,* 329–355.

Astiz, M. F., Wiseman, A. W., & Baker, D. P. (2002). Slouching towards decentralization: Consequences of globalization for curricular control in national education systems. *Comparative Education Review, 46,* 66–88.

Blank, R. M. (2000). Can public policy makers rely on private markets? *Economic Journal, 110,* 34–49.

Brewer, D. J., & Hentschke, G. C. (2009). An international perspective on publicly-financed, privately-operated schools. In M. Berends et al. (Eds.), *Handbook of research on school choice* (pp. 227–246). New York: Routledge.

Brewer, D. J., & McEwan, P. J. (Eds.) (2010). *The economics of education.* Amsterdam: Elsevier.

Centre for Educational Research and Innovation (2006). *Demand-sensitive schooling? Evidence and issues* (pp. 9–31). Paris: Organisation for Economic Co-operation and Development.

City Mayors Statistic (2010). Retrieved December 28, 2010 from: www.citymayors.com/statistics/richest-cities-2020.html

Corcoran, S., & Evans, W. N. (2010). *Income inequality, the median voter, and the support for public education.* Working Paper No. 16097. New York: National Bureau of Economic Research. Retrieved December 9, 2010 from: www.nber.org/papers/w16097

Economist, The (2009). *Pocket world in figures: 2010 edition.* London: The Economist.

Glaeser, E. L., & Mare, D. C. (2001). Cities and skills. *Journal of Labor Economics, 19,* 316–342.

Gomez, L. M., & Hentschke, G. C. (2009). K–12 education and the role of for-profit providers. In J. D. Bransford, D. J. Stipek, N. J. Vye, L. M. Gomez, & D. Lam (Eds.), *The role of research in educational improvement* (pp. 137–160). Cambridge, MA: Harvard Education Press.

Haskins, R., & Sawhill, E. (2009). *Creating an opportunity society.* Washington, DC: Brookings Institution.

Henderson, V. (2002). Urbanization in developing countries. *World Bank Research Observer, 17,* 89–112.

Hentschke, G. C. (2007). Characteristics of growth in the education industry: Illustrations from U.S. education businesses. In K. Martens, A. Rusconi, & K. Leuze (Eds.), *New arenas of education governance: The impact of international organizations and markets on educational policy making* (pp. 176–194). London: Palgrave Macmillan.

Hentschke, G. C., & Wohlstetter, P. (2004). Cracking the code of accountability. *University of Southern California Urban Education,* Spring/Summer, 17–19. Retrieved July 11, 2011 from: http:///www.usc.edu/dept/education/cegov/focus/leadership/publications.html

Karoly, L. A., & Panis, C. W. A. (2004). *The 21st century at work: Forces shaping the future workforce and workplace in the United States.* Santa Monica, CA: RAND Corporation. Summary, pp. xiii–xxxiv. Retrieved December 9, 2010 from: www.rand.org/pubs/monographs/MG164

Lucas, R. C. Jr. (2004). Life earnings and rural–urban migration. *Journal of Political Economy, 112,* 29–59.

Margison, S. (2007). *Prospects of higher education: Globalisation, market competition, public goods and the future of the university.* Rotterdam: Sense Publishers.

Mead, W.R. (2010). The American interest. Retrieved December 28, 2010 from: http://blogs.the-american-interest.com/wrm/2010/01/13/2010s-3-panopolis/

Metzger, G. E. (2003). Privatization as delegation. *Columbia Law Review, 103,* 1367–1502.

Miron, G., & Urschel, J. L. (2010). *Profiles of nonprofit education management organizations: 2009–2010.* Boulder, CO: National Education Policy Center.

Mok, K. (1997). Private challenges to public dominance: The resurgence of private education in the Pearl River Delta. *Comparative Education, 33,* 43–60.

Molnar, A., Miron, G., & Urschel, J. (2009). *Profiles of for-profit educational management organization* (Annual Report No.

11). Boulder, CO: Education and the Public Interest Center & Education Policy Research Unit. Retrieved December 7, 2010 from: http://epicpolicy.org/publication/profiles-profit-emos-2008-09

Morley, J. (2006). For-profit and nonprofit charter schools: An agency-costs approach. *Yale Law Journal, 115*, 1782–1821.

OECD (Organisation for Economic Co-operation and Development) (2008). *Education at a Glance 2008: OECD Indicators.* Paris: OECD.

Patrinos, H. A. (1990). The privatization of higher education in Colombia: Effects on quality and equity. *Higher Education, 10*, 161–173.

Persell, C. H., & Wenglinsky, H. (2004). For-profit post-secondary education and civic engagement. *Higher Education, 47*, 337–359.

Quddus, M., & Rashid, S. (2000). The worldwide movement in private universities: Revolutionary growth in post-secondary higher education. *American Journal of Economics and Sociology, 59*, 487–516.

Roberts, B. R. (1989). Urbanization, migration, and development. *Sociological Forum, 4*, 665–691.

Rose, L. C., & Gallup, A. M. (2003). Urban dwellers on urban schools. *Phi Delta Kappan, 84*, 408–409.

Salerno, C. (2004). Public money and private providers: Funding channels and national patterns in four countries, *Higher Education, 48*(1), 101–130.

Silber, J. M. (2010). *Equity research: Education and training.* New York: BMO Capital Markets.

Smith, N. (2009). *Public charter school dashboard: 2009.* Washington, DC: National Alliance for Public Charter Schools.

Spring, J. (2009). *Globalization of education: An introduction.* New York: Routledge.

Teferra, D., & Altbach, P.G. (2004). African higher education: Challenges for the 21st century. *Higher Education, 47*(1), 21–50.

Tooley, J. (2009). *The beautiful tree: A personal journal into how the world's poorest people are educating themselves.* Washington, DC: CATO Institute.

Wildavsky, B. (2010) *The great brain race: How global universities are reshaping the world.* Princeton, NJ: Princeton University Press.

Wilkinson, R., & Pickett, K. (2010). *The spirit level: Why more equal societies almost always do better.* New York: Penguin.

16

The Influence of the Second Lebanon-Israeli War on Israeli Students in Urban School Settings

Findings of the Nahariya District-wide Screening Process

**Ron Avi Astor, Heather Meyer Reynolds, Rami Benbenishty,
Ruth Pat-Horenczyk, Danny Brom, Naomi Baum, Miriam Schiff, and Kris De Pedro**

Many schools in urban settings have large numbers of students who have been exposed to traumatic events (e.g., Stein et al., 2003) ranging from natural disasters (floods, earthquakes, fires, viral or bacterial pandemics, tsunamis, hurricanes, drought, tornadoes) to man-made disasters (chemical spills, automotive accidents) to issues of violence (family violence, community violence, gang violence, terrorist acts, wars). Despite the many differences between these types of traumatic events, there are also many shared aspects. Hence, there is much to be learned from the experiences of a wide range of urban schools that have faced such experiences.

In this chapter we present a unique project that took place in the aftermath of the second Lebanon War in the urban setting of the city of Nahariya, Israel. In the year 2006, the residents of this city experienced massive rocket shelling from Lebanon. This stressful period of continual destruction, loss of human life and property, frequent and extended stays in shelters, and the evacuation of many residents to temporary camps was especially traumatic for children. In the 2007–2008 academic year following the war, the authors of this chapter applied a city-wide, school-based monitoring approach to identify schools and students who were in need of services to help with posttraumatic responses. This information was later used to provide feedback to the schools about students who reported significant problems and requested help.

Up until this pilot project, a systematic strategy to identify schoolchildren in a city suffering from the consequences of exposure to traumatic events did not exist. As illustrated below, in instances where very large numbers of children are affected, the school as a context of social support, diagnosis, rapid-response treatment, and safety net surrounding issues of trauma is an underexplored area of research and practice.

Our aim is to present this project as a prototype so that this kind of system of assessment and monitoring could be replicated in any community where a traumatic event has occurred. This chapter describes the theoretical basis, empirical support, and procedures that were developed to create a whole-school approach for an entire city, based on school and city-specific data. The empirical literature related to trauma, social support, and existing programs is also discussed.

We start with a focused review of the literature on posttraumatic stress: its causes and effects. We then discuss what is known about school-focused interventions following traumatic events and identify the gaps in current knowledge and practice that our model and project aimed to address.

What Is Posttraumatic Stress Disorder?

According to the National Institute of Mental Health (NIMH), posttraumatic stress disorder (PTSD) is an anxiety-related disorder resulting from exposure to a "terrifying event or ordeal in which grave physical harm occurred or was threatened"(NIMH, 2009). Examples of events that can trigger this disorder include "violent personal assaults, natural or human-caused disasters, accidents, or military combat" (NIMH, 2009). The key symptoms of PTSD include "persistent frightening thoughts and memories of their ordeal and feeling emotionally numb, especially with [the loss of] people they were once close to." Those who experience PTSD may also report having problems sleeping, feeling "detached or numb" and being "easily startled" (NIMH, 2009). (For the five diagnostic criteria of PTSD, see American Psychiatric Association, 2000; www.nimh.nih.gov/health/topics/post-trauma.)

Many students in urban settings experience terrifying events and ordeals. Many of these students suffer from severe symptoms that are educationally debilitating and impede academic performance, reduce school attendance, and cause many school discipline problems (e.g., suspension/expulsion, poor relationships with peers and teachers, and lack of motivation to succeed) (e.g., Stein et al., 2003).

It is important to note that the definition of PTSD in the *Diagnostic and Statistical Manual of Mental Disorders* (DSM) (American Psychiatric Association, 2000) includes several criteria that a student must meet in order to be assessed as suffering PTSD. However, as far as schools are concerned, it is possible (and quite likely) for students not to have full-blown clinical PTSD but still experience reactions to trauma that cause many personal and school-related difficulties. Compared with the extensive literature on DSM-defined PTSD, little is empirically known about these potentially life-changing but not clinically diagnosable reactions to trauma. However, some studies have found psychological distress and PTSD symptoms emerging in school-age children in the aftermath of hurricanes and other natural disasters (Evans & Oehler-Stinnett, 2006; Garrison et al., 1995; Vernberg, LaGreca, Silverman, & Prinstein, 1996).

The research literature that explores the etiology and course of PTSD examines a wide range of traumatic events. Some of these include terrorist attacks (e.g., Auger, Seymour, & Roberts, 2004; Hobfoll, Canetti-Nisim, & Johnson, 2006; Perrin et al., 2007), natural disasters (e.g., Mills, Edmondson, & Park, 2007; Perilla, Norris, & Lavizzo, 2002; Wolmer, Laor, & Yazgan, 2003), workplace violence (e.g., Pole, Best, Metzler, & Marmar, 2005), family and community violence (e.g., Stein et al., 2003), school violence (e.g., Daniels et al., 2007), and combat-/war-related violence (e.g., Pat-Horenczyk et al., 2007a, 2007b; Pat-Horenczyk, Schiff, & Doppelt, 2006; Roberts, Kitchiner, Kenardy, & Bisson, 2009; Tanielian et al., 2008). In general, although there are differences according to the type of event and exposure, there are significant similarities in the clinical picture and its development across many types of settings and traumatic events.

Traumatic Events and the Incidence of PTSD and Other Mental Health Issues

Rates of PTSD tend to vary depending on the type of disaster and the quality of the response to the disaster. The literature on the prevalence of PTSD following traumatic events is extensive and is not reviewed here; however, a few examples may be informative. A study of Hurricane Katrina evacuees predicted that between one-third to one-half of the evacuees would experience significant symptoms of PTSD two years after the event (Mills et al., 2007). Another study conducted in the year following Hurricane Katrina (which displaced over a million people) found that almost one-third of the children who returned to school in the greater New Orleans area demonstrated significant depression and/or trauma (American Psychological Association, 2006a).

In terms of terrorism, public health surveys conducted in New York City in the months following the September 11 terrorist attacks found that between 7% and 11% of residents were presenting with symptoms of PTSD (e.g., Schlenger et al., 2002). A study that documented the psychiatric health of survivors of the Oklahoma City bombing of 1995 found that approximately 34% had PTSD six months after the disaster (e.g., North et al., 1999).

It is likely that being in the middle of a war zone will drastically increase symptoms and rates of PTSD. A study by the RAND Corporation (Tanielian et al., 2008) found that 18.5% of servicemen and women returning from Iraq and Afghanistan met the clinical criteria for PTSD and/or major depression. A study that looked specifically at veterans returning from Iraq found that approximately 41% of active army soldiers and 52.2% of members of the Army Reserve/National Guard were exhibiting significant symptoms of PTSD (Milliken, Auchterlonie, & Hoge, 2007).

Chronic and severe community violence is another form of trauma that can cause PTSD. A study by Stein et al. (2003) found that 15% of urban students reported significant PTSD symptoms prior to their participation in a cognitive behavioral intervention.

Many factors appear to mediate the development, severity, and duration of PTSD symptoms, including a number of contextual factors identified in the literature and now to be explored.

Contextual Factors Affecting the Development and Course of Responses to Traumatic Events

The development of PTSD does not appear to be evenly distributed across a variety of demographic and other personal characteristics. This is an important fact to consider in developing and shaping responses/interventions (American Psychological Association, 2006a, 2006b; Brock & Cowan, 2004; Hobfoll et al., 2006; Mills et al., 2007; Pole et al., 2005). For instance, a history of mental health issues prior to the trauma, prior experiences with violence (e.g., family violence), and social class/family income (Stein et al., 2004) are significant predictors of PTSD. Research also shows that females are twice as likely as males to develop PTSD (Brock & Cowan, 2004).

In addition to personal information, there is important *contextual* information that must be considered in structuring a treatment. For instance, type and extent of exposure to the traumatic event is a major factor. Hence, the physical proximity an individual had to the traumatic event (e.g., how close the person was to the event), his or her emotional proximity to the event (e.g., did this person know someone who was injured or who died?), and his or her own level of personal injury (Brock & Cowan, 2004) are important variables to consider.

Ethnicity and Culture as Context

A number of studies have indicated that racial and ethnic groups are not equally likely to develop stress-related disorders or depression in the wake of a traumatic event (American Psychological Association, 2006a, 2006b; Hobfoll et al., 2006; Mills et al., 2007; Pole et al., 2005). A study by Pole et al. (2005) looked at the differences in rates and severity of PTSD among Caucasians, non-Hispanic Blacks, and Hispanics in a population of police officers who had been exposed to similar levels of trauma. Hispanic police officers demonstrated higher levels of stress and PTSD than either non-Hispanic Black or Caucasian officers.

Hurricane Katrina was a natural disaster that highlighted the complex interplay of trauma, poverty, and race. More specifically, there was a complex interaction of scant resources, poor social support (since evacuees were not removed from New Orleans in an organized manner—many lost touch with friends and family), prior mental health and health-related issues of the victims, and the fact that 70% of evacuees were African American and the majority of the rescue workers were European American (American Psychological Association, 2006b).

Another study conducted in Israel looked at differences in the stress-related responses (as a result of terrorism) between Jews and Palestinian citizens of Israel (PCIs) (Hobfoll et al., 2006). Results indicated that PCIs reported higher levels of stress, and more frequent and severe symptoms of PTSD than their Jewish counterparts. The authors of the study focused on the importance of the social context of terrorism in explaining these results. PCIs, as ethnic minorities in Israel, had fewer resources and greater losses of their existing resources in the wake of a terrorist act, which impeded their ability to recover.

A study conducted after Hurricane Andrew ravaged southern Florida in 1992 found significant differences between the rates of PTSD for non-Hispanic Whites (15%), English-preferring Hispanics (19%), non-Hispanic Blacks (23%), and Hispanics who preferred to speak Spanish (38%) (Perilla et al., 2002). This study uncovered links between culture and an individual's stress response, more specifically the important role of prior personal trauma, immigration stress, perceptions of external (rather than internal) control, and perceptions of racism. The authors caution clinicians to pay close attention to the complex interplay between culture and the clinical diagnosis and treatment of stress-related disorders (Perilla et al., 2002). This research points to the importance of developing and structuring interventions at the specific community level, and that interventions or treatments should differ based on the different demographic groups living in the affected community.

How Social Roles Affect an Individual's Response to Traumatic Events

Traumatic events such as hurricanes, wars, and major terror acts may engulf whole communities. Nevertheless, there are many indications that the social roles of members of these communities have a direct impact on their functioning and responses to the traumatic events. For instance, after September 11, a study that looked at rates of PTSD among rescue workers by occupation found an overall rate of approximately 12.4%, with considerable variation based on occupation (Perrin et al., 2007). Police officers who worked at the site of the World Trade Center had the lowest rates of PTSD (6.2%), followed by emergency medical workers (11.6%), firefighters (12.2%), construction workers (17.8%), and unaffiliated volunteers (21.2%). The authors of this study hypothesized the importance of rescue workers performing tasks that were common or uncommon to their occupation as a significant risk factor for developing PTSD. This study suggests that prior training and experience served as a protective factor for the development of PTSD among rescue workers.

Teachers may have a similarly important role when traumatic events hit schools. Unfortunately, we are not aware of studies focusing on the functioning and responses of teachers in traumatic situations such as school shootings and terrorist attacks. A few studies have examined the relationship between teacher-mediated interventions and students' PTSD symptoms in the aftermath of natural disasters (Baum, Rotter, Reidler, & Brom, 2009; Wolmer, Laor, Dedeoglu, Siev, & Yazgan, 2005; Wolmer et al., 2003). For instance, a study in Biloxi, Mississippi, after Hurricane Katrina looked at the the the implementation of the Building Resilience Project, a teacher-based intervention that focuses on empowering teachers to assist students in coping with stressors in the aftermath of trauma (Baum et al., 2009). The authors of this study found that after the intervention, teachers reported gains in their confidence and ability to deal with students' social and emotional needs. In the project we describe in this chapter, there was also a strong emphasis on the important role of teachers in dealing with the consequences of traumatic events for their students.

A Key Variable in the Mediation of Stress Responses: Social Networks

The impact of a traumatic event on an individual appears to be a complex interaction of the individual and the socioecological environment. Individual, family, and community factors appear to significantly affect the severity and duration of a stress response in the wake of a traumatic event

(Stein et al., 2004). Several studies have found that the presence of strong social networks have lessened the severity and duration of an individual's stress response (e.g., as noted in Steury, Spencer, & Parkinson, 2004). Conversely, those who lack social networks appear to fare worst in terms of stress and coping in the wake of a traumatic event (Steury et al., 2004). A study by Stein et al. (2004) found that 75% of respondents who were "significantly distressed" turned to friends and family members for support in the days following the attacks on September 11, 2001. Other research has pointed to social support in one's home and school as a "protective factor" for dealing with community violence (Steury et al., 2004). The key issue is that in the wake of a traumatic event of either local or national significance, social networks may be disrupted or destroyed by the event itself (e.g., the random dispersion of family members to all parts of the United States in the wake of Hurricane Katrina). Thus, interventions or responses must focus on maintaining and facilitating these social networks.

This set of findings draws attention to the significance of the school as a social network. During and following traumatic events, there is frequently a tendency to identify individuals in distress and to attend to their individual needs. This practice, in fact, reduces the healing power of the existing social network in school, the relationships with teachers and peers, and the mutual support found in keeping the basic social structures intact. Hence, an important lesson to be drawn from the literature is the necessity of combining the individual needs of extremely distressed students and teachers with the support of the social structure of the school and class, including the continuity of the roles of the principals, teachers, and students.

Interventions for Large-scale Traumatic Events

There is an extensive and growing literature on evidence-based interventions designed to address symptoms of distress following personal trauma. Far fewer interventions are designed to provide a response to large-scale disasters. The American Red Cross has developed Disaster Mental Health (DMH) interventions in the wake of a traumatic event that address the needs of both disaster victims and responders by focusing on alleviating emotional distress, supporting resiliency, promoting positive coping skills, teaching about the psychosocial impact of disasters, psychological screening, and referrals for additional or more specific treatment (Morgan, 1995). These interventions are immediate, short-term measures that focus on referring the traumatized person to the correct supportive services.

Another example of this kind of intervention is the Critical Incident Stress Management Model (CISM), an immediate, intense attempt to moderate the reactions of the victims (e.g., Morrison, 2007). CISM utilizes trained emergency service workers to provide a single-session intervention that focuses on reducing initial levels of distress in order to prevent the development of more serious long-term mental health issues, including PTSD. More specifically, victims are given the opportunity to talk about their experience and receive "supportive feedback" from a trained individual to help them normalize their responses to the traumatic event (Morrison, 2007).

Although these interventions address the need for social supports or social networks on some level, they are short-term strategies that focus on referring victims to the correct services rather than maintaining and enhancing existing social networks. Trauma-focused cognitive behavioral therapy (CBT), for instance, provides psychoeducation to children and families, and has been found to be effective. However, effective CBT requires long-term participation (Roberts et al., 2009). Even before a disaster, schools may have to prepare for the long-term consequences of traumatic events for principals, teachers, and students.

Examples of How Schools Deal with Traumatic Local or National Events

For both large- (September 11, 2001) and small-scale traumatic events, such as school shootings or community violence (e.g., Stein et al., 2003), the school is a logical base for a crisis intervention team and for counseling or other interventions. Some research has shown how schools have attempted to prepare for disasters and/or crisis.

The terrorist attacks on the United States on September 11, 2001 allowed schools to implement some sort of crisis intervention (if available), since the majority of students were in school at the time of the attacks (Auger et al., 2004). One study found that stress responses (ranging from mild to severe) were observed in both children and counselors immediately following and six months after the event (Auger et al., 2004). Additionally, it raised concerns about the unitary focus on children's mental health and the lack of concern related to staff mental health issues, particularly involving counselors (Auger et al., 2004), which in some cases appeared to interfere with their ability to address student needs. Having a school staff who are supported and prepared to deal with crisis is an important aspect of a healthy recovery for the entire school community, but it is not an issue that schools seem to address systematically.

A study by Jaycox et al. (2007) surveyed school administrators about how they were dealing with students and faculty who had been affected by Hurricanes Katrina and Rita. The study found that there were very disparate approaches to student trauma, ranging from no ongoing services once a "stabilization" phase was completed, to the ongoing availability of and coordination of mental health services for members of the school community. The biggest impediments to the establishment and implementation of more long-term and comprehensive programs related to trauma and recovery were the following, as explained in Jaycox et al. (2007):

1. a perception among school personnel that students did not need the services after the crisis intervention stage;
2. a belief in the need to return to a focus on academics;
3. a lack of prior training in crisis intervention/management;
4. a lack of resources (both financial and informational); and
5. a lack of communication between the schools and families.

A key finding was that school personnel generally appeared to lack the training and preparedness to deal effectively with a crisis and its aftermath. The case study that follows suggests ways to deal systematically with a traumatic event in the school setting while linking students and families to the appropriate services.

Another study (Loiler, 2006) looked at the issue of terrorism and why schools were not addressing this issue. A qualitative study of teachers from Los Angeles County revealed that they did not address issues of terrorism in a systematic manner. Some explanations included the emphasis on testing in certain subject areas (Tucker & Codding, 1998), a lack of training (no in-services direction or priorities from school officials), schools being viewed as a setting for crisis management in the form of psychological "first aid" (Stein et al., 2003), and a general lack of systematic research on how schools can best deal with issues of terrorism.

The School as a Social Network in the Event of Trauma or Stress

These important questions and issues related to social context, culture, and trauma are just emerging in the research literature and being taken into consideration in the study of how psychological interventions are structured. Psychological research has demonstrated the important role that one's social context plays in development, learning, sense of community, and so on (e.g., Brock & Cowan,

2004; Stein et al., 2004; Steury et al., 2004). Interventions in the wake of crisis/disasters are only beginning to address the importance of the social context in responses to traumatic events, and how psychological counselors can best intervene while also taking potential differences into account (in terms of social support, culture and other sociodemographic variables) (Steury et al., 2004).

How does the clinical model of infusing clinicians (who are likely not from the affected community) into the community after a disaster address these contextual factors? Benbenishty and Benbenishty (2007) provide a case example of a school in Israel following a major terrorist attack and show that students and teachers rejected the well-intentioned clinicians who flocked to the school to help the students. Instead, the school community reverted to its everyday social support structures, and gave both students and teachers social support within the school's daily routines and ceremonies.

Recent public health models that look at ways of dealing with the aftermath of terrorism are also recognizing the importance of considering the social context—promoting social cohesion, community well-being, and healthy community functioning as long-term interventions (Reissman, Spencer, Tanielian, & Stein, 2005).

A School-based City-wide Exemplar

Thousands of Katyusha rockets landed in northern Israel during the summer of 2006. Especially hard hit were communities in Kiryat Shmona, Haifa, Safed, and Nahariya. Schoolchildren were exposed to many stressful events, including threats of attack, being shuttled into bomb shelters, and being evacuated from homes and witnessing or hearing about loss of life. It is known that children react to these kinds of events with behavioral, academic, and psychological problems. These reactions last long after the traumatic events have passed (American Psychiatric Association, 2000). Without a system of services and interventions, exposure to the events of war can cause damage to schools, children, and their families in the long term (as evidenced by the research on the occurrence and persistence of PTSD and stress-related symptoms in the first section of this chapter).

As described in the introduction to this chapter, the scientific literature indicates that although such traumatic events have strong effects on the children exposed to them, there is much variability in the extent and severity of the resulting symptoms and difficulties. It is important, therefore, to identify those children and schools that are most affected and to describe the nature of their problems and needs for services. Thus, the objective of the city-wide school-based screening process in Nahariya was to give decision-makers at all levels systematic and exact information relevant to dealing with the educational, emotional, and psychological needs of their students. Our hope was to create a prototype that could be used in each school and school district during regional or national disasters and, over time, to create an ongoing monitoring system that could be used in urban settings that regularly experience high levels of stressful and traumatic events. For this study we used a sample from each school; in the future, however, an entire census of all children in all schools may become possible.

This project grew out of concern on the part of the heads of Nahariya's municipal and educational community regarding the welfare of the city's children. This group wanted to promote the capabilities of their local school-based and nongovernmental organizations' (NGOs) professionals, enabling them to cope in an educated way with the needs of the city's children in the aftermath of the second Lebanese War.

To this end, the city of Nahariya joined together with the Israel Center for the Treatment of Psychotrauma as well as in cooperation with the Hebrew University and the University of Southern California (with the funding of the Northern New Jersey Federation, The Israel Trauma Coalition, and United Jewish Communities) to apply a city-wide identification and screening process so as to identify the condition of Nahariya's children. The objective of the process was to provide up-to-date, systematic data that would enable schools to identify the needs of Nahariya's students, target these specific needs, and identify the resources available to them in the aftermath of the war.

Hence, during the 2007–2008 academic year (a year after the war), 1,062 students from 11 elementary schools (481 students from the fourth through sixth grades) and 2 junior high schools (581 students from the seventh through eleventh grades) took part in the screening process. The students answered questionnaires within a classroom period and each questionnaire was coded and linked to the student's name, which did not appear on the questionnaire. This ensured the anonymity of the student but also allowed researchers and professionals to identify students who were in dire need of services based on their responses to the questionnaire. To our knowledge,.this is the first time such a method was used.

Our conceptual model was based on the school violence work conducted by Benbenishty and Astor (2005), which looked at school variables moderating and mediating external variables surrounding victimization. This model, shown in Figure 16.1, was adapted to address exposure to war or terrorism. This conceptual model takes into account many of the commonly explored external ecological influences that contribute to trauma responses, but it also includes the school social setting as moderating and, in some cases, mediating these outcomes. Furthermore, this model goes beyond the concept of PTSD alone, since it includes academic, social, and psychological outcomes that would affect functioning at the school level.

Based on this ecological model, which puts the school at the center, and on the review of the literature in the introduction to this chapter, schools are seen as essential networks for children and their families. Hence, although this project screened individual students, it focused on the school as a whole. Consequently, our approach was unique in the sense that data were structured so that they would be available at the city level (all schools combined), individual school-site level, and for each child who participated in the survey (although each survey was confidential and coded not to reveal a child's identity unless he or she asked for help or PTSD levels were very high).

The current project, which focused on creating a system to gather information and use it as a basis for interventions at all levels (students, schools, and the city educational system as a whole), was based on our monitoring model (Astor, Benbenishty, Marachi, & Meyer, 2006; Astor, Benbenishty, & Meyer, 2004; Benbenishty & Astor, 2007; Benbenishty, Astor, & Zeira, 2003). The model identifies several stages at which the data serve different functions.

For example, the way data are used for assessment and planning may be different from the actual intervention phase or reassessment phases. Findings for each school could be used for the implementation and site processes at each model level. Each level in the model (Figure 16.2) involves achieving certain implementation tasks, goals, and products. In this model there are successive stages that represent the processes of gathering data, making use of the data, creating plans of action, implementing the plans, reassessing the progress made by these programs, and continuing the cycle. This process would be similar to those studying data-driven school reform efforts (e.g., Datnow, Hubbard, & Mehan, 2002; Park, 2008), but this has not been utilized to study and assess students' level of posttraumatic stress-related outcomes. Our model strongly supports viewing the data from the local monitoring surveys as the collective voices of youth, teachers, and parents. Data from the surveys could be used to educate psychologists, principals, and teachers about their community and to advocate based on their school's data at each stage.

Within every stage level (as presented in Figure 16.2), information from each school can be used to explore efforts to create opportunities regarding the allocation of resources that are relevant to posttrauma needs and to data-driven policy decisions (see Datnow et al. (2002) on how such processes help in the implementation of academic school reform). One of the most important advantages of this localized monitoring system is the potential ability to modify existing instruments to improve the level of responsiveness to the immediate needs of the community and to future directions at the reassessment stage.

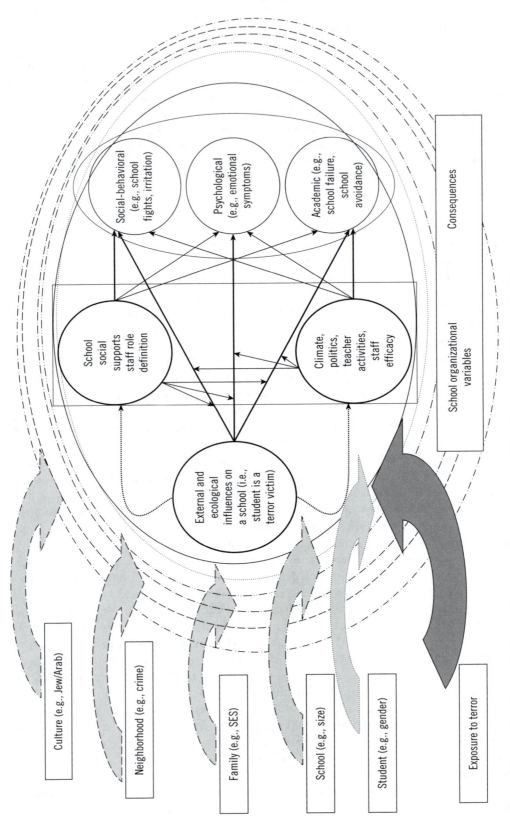

Figure 16.1 A Model of Social–Ecological Influences on Student Outcomes of War or Terrorism with School as Mediator

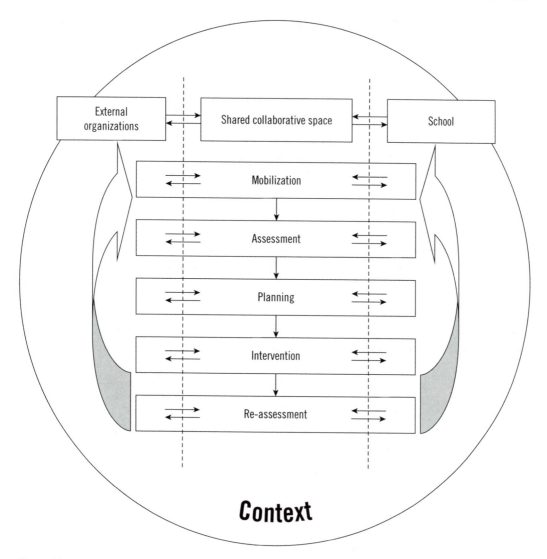

Figure 16.2 Use of Trauma and School Survey Data Procedure

The model identifies the three following areas, on which one can focus to better clarify implementation of school-based trauma intervention programs:

1. the school internal processes;
2. the partner organizations' internal processes; and
3. a shared, collaborative space that brings together both partners (this could be district-level pupil personnel workers).

Hence, professionals within and outside the setting explore how each trauma-related task within each stage of the model is achieved in this shared space. That is, the interactions between the school and these partner community organizations or school district support departments are the core focus of inquiry.

These shared collaborative spaces for data were accessible to public leaders, professional municipal staff members, each of Nahariya's school principals and his or her teaching staff, and all residents of Nahariya, including parents. This information also served as a reliable factual infrastructure in dialogue with outside factors (such as governmental factors, nonprofit organizations, and benefactors) interested in promoting the welfare of the residents of Nahariya. These processes facilitated the allocation of resources and preparation for interventions that build resilience. Resources could be allocated for individualized psychological treatment for children in particularly severe distress or for group treatment for all children and adolescents within the schools. In parallel, workshops for teachers, school counselors, and educational psychologists could be held for training in the areas of personal coping with stress, and building resilience in the classes and schools. This could be done to help promote local professionals' abilities to handle trauma situations. Teachers' lack of training/ preparedness is one of the biggest impediments to their ability to deal with a traumatic event in the school setting (e.g., Auger et al., 2004; Jaycox et al., 2007).

Conceptual Model for Instruments

We created a broad-based instrument that covered various dimensions related to the social ecological environment and trauma. This included questions surrounding the details of individual exposure to the traumatic events, posttrauma-related behaviors, academic and school-related behaviors, and help-seeking behaviors. The instrument included the students' perceptions of support in their school, family, community, and circle of friends, which research demonstrates is critical to recovering from a traumatic event (e.g., Stein et al., 2004). It was critical to identify the feelings of the students and their attitudes as well as the students' level of skills surrounding coping patterns, and risk and protective factors. Figure 16.3 represents the conceptual model underlying the instruments.

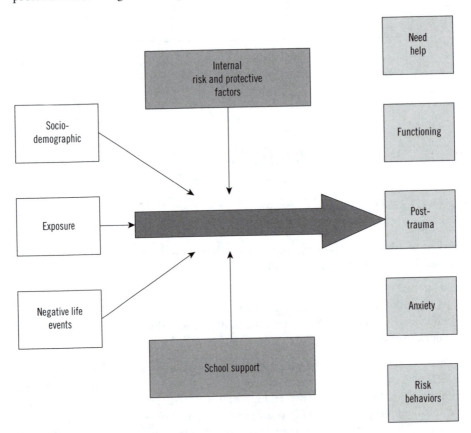

Figure 16.3 Conceptual Model for the Creation of the Instrument

School District-wide Findings from the Survey

Having a city-wide perspective was critical from an epidemiological and resource advocacy/policy perspective. Knowing how many students were exposed to the range of traumatic events during this period of trauma was a vital first step in understanding the scope of the problem for the city and school district. The following are the specific results from this survey of students who were affected by these bombings.

Exposure to Missiles, Shelters, and Evacuations

Students were given a list of specific questions about the events they had experienced during the war. No significant differences were found between elementary school students and junior high school students except for the fact that 8% of the elementary school students reported that a friend of theirs had been wounded or killed by falling missiles, compared with 3.1% of the junior high school students. Table 16.1 describes the war experiences of all the students.

The data from Table 16.1 made it evident to policymakers and educators that a high percentage of students in Nahariya schools had had close experiences with a variety of traumatic incidents as a result of the war. Over 86% of the students were in the vicinity when sirens were sounded or where missiles fell, and more than three-quarters of the students heard the shrieking of falling missiles. About half of the students (54.4%) reported feeling the shock waves of falling missiles, and 37.8% were present when missiles fell but were not injured. Many students also had relatives and friends who experienced war-related events. About one-quarter of the students (27.7%) knew someone (other than a relative) who was killed or injured by a missile. About 12% were eyewitnesses to a wounding, 7.5% reported that a relative had been wounded, 5.3% said that a friend had been injured or killed by a falling missile, and 2.5% reported that a family member had been killed by a falling missile.

Exposure to traumatic events is sometimes exacerbated by the need to evacuate. This was evident during Hurricane Katrina, where thousands of children were separated from their parents and not found until months later (e.g., American Psychological Association, 2006b). In Nahariya, over half of the students stayed in shelters or in security rooms at least once a day, while 29.3% spent time there at least four times a day. About half of the students slept in shelters, and most of them slept there for more than four days. Approximately 85% of the students in Nahariya left their homes because of the

Table 16.1 Exposure to Events of the War

Survey item	Once %	More than once %
You were present when a missile fell	1.3	0.4
A relative of yours was killed by a falling missile	2.0	0.4
A friend of yours was wounded or killed by a falling missile	5.2	0.1
A relative of yours was wounded by a falling missile	6.4	1.1
Your house was hit by a falling missile	10.2	1.5
You saw people being wounded (in reality, not on TV) when a missile fell	8.9	3.1
Someone you know (not a relative) was wounded or killed when a missile fell	23.0	4.7
A friend of yours was there when a missile fell but was not wounded	24.0	10.4
You were present when a missile fell but you were not wounded	21.0	16.8
Someone you know (not a relative) was there when a missile landed but was not wounded	35.0	14.5
You felt the shock wave of a falling missile	27.7	26.7
The house or other property (car, store, etc.) of someone you know was hit by a falling missile	44.4	23.7
You heard the shrieking of a falling missile	27.6	48.3
You were nearby when the sirens sounded or when a missile fell	25.2	61.4

Note: N = 1043–1060

war. Only a few were evacuated alone (2.5%); three-quarters of the students left with their entire families. This may have provided support to the students who were forced to leave their homes. However, of those who left, 76.3% had to move between several places. Of those who stayed in several places, 58.4% stayed in three or more places. Approximately 43.6% reported staying with family or friends, and about 13.5% stayed in hotels or tent camps. In many cases, they did not leave home to arrive at another stable and supportive setting. Instability in the students' lives, which has been evident in other large-scale crises (e.g., Hurricane Katrina), was a critical issue that needed to be factored into any posttrauma intervention system for Nahariya.

Students' Emotional and Behavioral Reactions to the War

In this particular study, it was important to find out how students viewed the events of the Lebanon War one year after the trauma. In general, elementary school students reported having more severe reactions to the war than did the junior high school students. Many of their fears were powerful enough that their academic work was affected negatively.

Fear of Death and/or Injury

About two-thirds of the students had been afraid that someone in their family might have died or would die, and over half (52.6%) feared that someone from their family had been physically wounded. Table 16.2 shows the percentage of junior high school students and the specific fears fueling their anxieties. Students assessed their levels of fear as well as their feelings of helplessness and shock during the event. A high percentage of students said that they were afraid during the event (41.5% to a great or very great extent) and a lower percentage felt helpless (30.8%) or reported that they were in shock (25.1%).

Psychological Functioning

Table 16.3 indicates that over 30% of the elementary school students reported that they sometimes did dangerous things ("a bit," 24.8%, or "a lot," 6.5%), and that they had a hard time studying

Table 16.2 Anxieties of Junior High School Students

Survey item	Yes %
Were you afraid that someone in your family was dead or would die?	66.5
Were you afraid that someone in your family was physically wounded?	52.6
Were you afraid that you might be physically wounded?	49.6
Were you afraid that a close friend (your best friend) would be physically wounded?	46.5
Were you afraid that a close friend (your best friend) was dead or would die?	46.3
Were you afraid that you might die?	39.4

Note: N = 544–553

Table 16.3 Problems with Functioning as a Result of the War Among Elementary School Students

Survey item	A bit %	A lot %
I sometimes do dangerous things	24.8	6.5
I find it harder to study	26.1	5.0
I take part less in after-school activities	18.4	8.7
I fight more with my friends	20.8	4.6
I fight more with people in my family	17.4	6.3
I do more things that are forbidden	18.6	5.0
I get punished more	13.0	4.8

Note: N = 460–463

(31.1%). In addition, over a quarter of the students reported that they were less likely to take part in after-school activities (27.1%) and were more likely to fight with their friends (25.4%) as a result of their war experiences.

Compared with primary school students, fewer junior high school students reported functional problems because of the war (see Table 16.4). Many junior high school students reported that they felt they had no such functional problems. However, 38.3% reported some sort of decrease in academic achievement and 5.9% reported that their achievement had declined to a great degree. Similarly, 28% reported that they found it harder to do their academic assignments than in the past. In addition, many junior high school students reported that relationships with their friends had deteriorated following the war (20.9%). Table 16.5 organizes the data a little differently in order to show a comparison of the number of functional problems reported by students in elementary and junior high schools in Nahariya. About one-fifth of the students in elementary schools reported functional declines in three or more areas (in junior high schools, the rate was 15.5%).

Anxiety and Depression
About 42.5% of the students said that they often still worry that something bad will happen to their parents. Almost half of the students reported that they are afraid to be alone at home (sometimes true and frequently true, 47.9%), that they go with their mother and father wherever they go (45.7%), and that they have nightmares about something bad happening to them (39.3%). Almost one-third of

Table 16.4 Problems with Functioning Among Junior High School Students, One Year After the War

Functional problem	Not at all				To a great extent
	1	2	3	4	5
Your academic achievements have declined	61.7	20.2	7.5	4.7	5.9
It is harder for you to complete your school assignments	72.0	14.8	7.5	2.6	3.1
Your relationship with friends has deteriorated	79.1	14.1	4.0	1.9	0.9
You find it harder to get along with your family	82.6	9.2	4.2	2.6	1.4
Your relationship with your family has deteriorated	83.8	9.2	2.4	2.8	1.7
You find it harder to deal with friendships	85.7	8.0	4.3	1.0	0.9
You find it harder to take part in extracurricular activities	87.3	7.5	3.1	0.5	1.6

Note: N = 574–575

Table 16.5 The Number of Functional Problems as a Result of the War Among Elementary and Junior High School Students

No. of problems	Elementary (N = 481)		Junior High (N = 581)	
	%	Cumulative rate	%	Cumulative rate
0	34.9	34.9	45.1	45.1
1	19.8	54.7	17.6	62.7
2	17.5	72.1	13.4	76.1
3	9.8	81.9	8.4	84.5
4	8.1	90.0	7.4	91.9
5 and more	10.0	95.2	8.1	100.0
	M	SD	M	SD
	1.73	1.83	1.46	1.81

the students reported that they are afraid to sleep at home (32.1%) and that they are afraid when sleeping away from home (31.6%). In a breakdown of students by their level of anxiety, 11.9% were evaluated as having a severe level of anxiety and another 7.1% with a *very* severe level of anxiety. Among junior high school students, 8.4% were presenting high levels of depression, and another 5.5% were demonstrating *very* high levels of depression.

PTSD-related Symptoms Resulting from Exposure to Trauma

Among elementary school students, more than one-third indicated that they feared that the traumatic events would recur (39.2%); that they became frightened easily when hearing a loud noise or if surprised suddenly (31.2%); or that when something reminds them of the war they become worried, frightened, or sad (30.0%). Junior high school students reported fearing that the events would happen again (23.7%); becoming frightened easily (23.7%); being worried, afraid, or sad when something reminds them of the events (15.5%); and being apprehensive and tense about danger (16.0%).

Table 16.6 shows the percentage of students who met the criteria for a diagnosis of PTSD. There was a high percentage of students who "met the criteria" in elementary schools (particularly regarding reliving the traumatic events and avoidance). It can also be seen that the areas of reliving and hyperarousal are more common than avoidance.

Table 16.7 presents the condition of the students according to their symptom severity. Approximately 11.1% of the elementary school students and 9.0% of the junior high students were in distress. Of these, slightly fewer than 3% had also been diagnosed with PTSD as well as with particularly high levels of anxiety (among elementary school students) or depression (among junior high school students).

We also asked a novel help-seeking question. We were curious to know how many children wanted help in dealing with these symptoms. We asked: "There are students who feel they would like to get help from an adult who knows how to help children and young people who are in distress because of the experiences they went through in the war. Would you like someone to contact you to help you deal with these things that may be bothering you?" To our knowledge, students are rarely asked this question in surveys following a traumatic event. Table 16.8 presents the students' answers.

Table 16.8 indicates that over a quarter of the elementary school students and 5.6% of the junior high school students said they would like someone to contact them to help them cope with their

Table 16.6 Percentage of Students who Meet One or More of the Criteria for Posttraumatic Stress Disorder

Criterion	Elementary (N = 481)	Junior high (N = 581)
Reliving the event	40.5	20.3
Avoidance	10.2	3.8
Hyperarousal	26.4	15.8

Table 16.7 Percentage of Students who have been Identified with Mental Health Impairments as a Result of the War in Elementary and Junior High Schools

Impairment	Elementary (N = 481)	Junior high (N = 581)
PTSD and anxiety or depression	2.9	2.8
Only PTSD	4.0	3.4
Only anxiety or depression	4.2	2.8
Total rate of identified	11.1	9.0

Table 16.8 Percentage of Students who would like Someone to Contact them to Help them Cope

Response	Elementary ($N = 467$)	Junior high ($N = 568$)
No	43.3	71.0
Not sure	31.0	23.4
Yes	25.7	5.6

experiences. Additionally, about one-third of the elementary school students and about a quarter of the junior high school students reported that they were "not sure." There was a clear connection between the severity of the symptoms reported by the student and the call for help. The overall mental health of the students asking for help was much worse than that of other students. In addition, the students who were not sure appeared to be in a much worse psychological state than those who reported that they did not want help. An examination of these data demonstrates that students who are not sure that they want to seek help have many more mental health/stress-related issues than those who report that they want help or who do not want help.

Particularly Vulnerable Schools

As mentioned, our approach puts the school in the center of our model. Hence, following the individual screening we asked: "Are the problems reported by the students equally distributed between schools or is it possible to identify schools that are especially vulnerable?" From Tables 16.9 and 16.10, it can be seen that there are large differences between schools with regards to the rates of students reporting emotional problems and their desire to be contacted and helped. Among the elementary schools, school 3 was identified as having a particularly high rate of reported postevent trauma and anxiety, and the rate of students wishing to be contacted approached 50%. In school 8, by contrast, there was a relatively low rate of students reporting symptoms, and there were no students who were identified as having high levels of anxiety; yet about one quarter of the students asked to be contacted for help in dealing with the war. Similarly, in school 50, the rate of junior high school students identified as having mental health issues and wishing to be contacted was almost double that of school 11, and the rate of students who had PTSD as well as depression was three times as high.

The appropriate educational and municipal authorities—including the principals, counselors, and support services NGOs—participated in a process that revealed the identity of the schools

Table 16.9 Percentage of Students who have Emotional Problems in Elementary Schools (by School)

Elementary school	Students identified as having problems	PTSD and anxiety	PTSD only	Anxiety only	Very severe anxiety	Asked for help
1	17.9	5.1	2.6	10.3	15.8	25.6
2	4.8	3.2	1.6	0.0	3.2	19.4
3	23.7	5.3	7.9	10.5	15.8	45.9
4	7.0	0.0	1.4	5.6	5.7	26.8
6	8.2	0.0	4.1	4.1	4.4	13.6
7	14.0	7.0	5.3	1.8	8.8	30.4
8	5.3	0.0	5.3	0.0	0.0	25.5
9	12.5	4.2	0.0	8.3	12.5	39.1
10	12.0	2.0	4.0	6.0	8.0	16.3
13	11.1	0.0	11.1	0.0	0.0	35.3
15	20.0	13.3	6.7	0.0	16.7	14.3

Table 16.10 Percentage of Students who have Emotional Problems in Junior High Schools (by School)

Junior high school	Students identified as having problems	PTSD and anxiety	PTSD only	Anxiety only	Very severe anxiety	Asked for help
11	9.4	1.4	2.2	12.3	2.5	4.0
50	16.7	5.0	5.4	17.0	3.2	8.3

corresponding to the school codes (schools, like students, received codes to preserve their anonymity and allow the allocation of resources based on need). The codes of students who requested help and those who were identified as being in significant distress were shared in an organized process with district-level school psychologists and guidance counselors for follow-up interviewing and referral to treatment.

Figure 16.4 is an example of the type of coded report that was provided to school-based mental health professionals. These reports were anonymous summaries of individual students who were identified as needing and/or requesting help. Parental and student consent was sought confidentially before the psychologists or counselors made any contact. This was coordinated by the central district office through the mental health unit of psychologists and counselors.

This process was important for several reasons. First, these students reported severe mental health and negative educational outcomes and requested help. Second, without reaching out and involving

Request help	Functioning	Anxiety	PTSD	Gender	Student ID	Class	Grade	School
Yes	19	Very high	Yes	Female	7	1	9	15
Not sure	11	Very high	Yes	Female	6	2	6	11
Not sure	16	High	Yes	Male	3	2	7	6
Yes	10	Moderate	Yes	Female	15	1	4	7
Yes	17	High	Yes	Male	3	2	5	6
Not sure	10	Moderate	Yes	Male	12	2	5	11

Figure 16.4 Individual School Report Identifying Specific Students Anonymously by Codes for Support Referrals

the psychologists and counselors, it was very possible that many of these students would be mis-diagnosed or treated for what seemed to be personal behavioral problems. For example, truancy, referral to special education, suspension, and school failure are possible results of the reported psychological symptoms. Identifying and helping students with severe PTSD, anxiety, or depression-related issues could avoid negative school outcomes by treating the actual source of the problem. Finally, in an era of enhanced focus on academic standards, these types of mental health data could be very useful in studying school settings that have high concentrations of students with symptoms of posttraumatic stress. Schools with students who demonstrate high levels of PTSD or other mental health issues due to trauma will perhaps require different strategies to help their students become mentally and emotionally prepared to go on with their studies.

Implications of the Data for this Population and Others Suffering from Trauma

In part, these data were used with the National Ministry of Education's psychological services to lobby and advocate for another 4,000 hours of psychological counseling in the affected areas during the years following the war. There have also been high-level Ministry of Education discussions about administering posttrauma questionnaires to all of Israel's youth through their national biannual monitoring system (called the *Meitzav*). Although this has not happened yet, the prototype demon-strated that monitoring could help to identify schools with high concentrations of students who are suffering and experiencing psychological and/or academic difficulties due to trauma, and providing services responsive to the specific needs of individual students and schools.

NGOs, the Israel Center for the Treatment of Pyschotrauma, in particular, utilized these data to create interventions surrounding

1. working with teachers on building resilience;
2. building the resilience of parents;
3. the implementation of school-based interventions;
4. identifying and training school mental health personnel;
5. working with local government authorities in order to build community capacity and ensure sustainability; and
6. the continuous monitoring of the evolving needs and effectiveness of the various com-ponents.

In a detailed chapter (Pat-Horenczyk et al., 2011) the authors articulated the process used to implement and train professionals after the initial screening of students was complete. This group has developed programs and curriculums, mentioned in that chapter, that address each of the populations mentioned above.

Perhaps most importantly, these data were able to show NGOs, school counselors, psychologists, parents, and principals which schools needed the most help. With limited resources, identifying where the greatest need is could maximize the number of students being served. This process allowed individual students to be spared a misdiagnosis of attention-deficit disorder or learning disabilities because they were provided with the treatment they needed, which focused on recovering from trauma. This prototype showed that it was possible to educate district and municipal authorities to prepare for future emergencies in order to minimize the trauma for students, school personnel, and families. Preparations of this kind are likely to strengthen the ties between education and welfare organizations in delivering solutions to the most vulnerable populations.

According to our model (Figure 16.2), the monitoring process continues over time, so that the reassessments take place after interventions have been implemented. In this project we were able, in some cases, to return to the schools and reassess the students. Unfortunately, given that this process took place two years after the war, we were not able to secure the resources and collaboration required to fully implement the model. Thus, although there was a consensus that the long-term effects of the war did not disappear, the immediate needs of a very stressed municipal and educational system took precedence. Clearly, urban settings that are exposed to the effects of long-term, ongoing stressors must plan for a more complete implementation of the model. Also, even though school personnel, researchers, and others expended great effort to reach children experiencing trauma, there will be cases where there is no response because of some parents' refusal to allow their children to participate in a monitoring system. This challenge suggests that education and/or government leaders should consider, at least in high-risk areas, institutionalizing the sort of data collection described in this model.

In addition, this prototype has implications for schools across the globe. It can be utilized in the cases of natural disaster such as earthquakes, fires, mudslides, hurricanes, and other kinds of traumatic events (mass shootings, wars, bombings). Schools can then help to bring the appropriate evidence-based programs, local resources, and services to the correct locations and to the students who need the most of help. This program can be used in school districts that have high levels of community violence, gang violence, crime, or drug trafficking. In some states and cities—such as California, New York, Massachusetts, and Chicago—monitoring systems that utilize surveys are already in existence in each school and can be easily modified to include posttrauma questions which can help to identify vulnerable students. Most importantly, by not collecting this type of information, some schools may be failing academically merely because they have large numbers of students with mental health issues or, more specifically, students with high levels of stress resulting from trauma.

This kind of assessment can enable teachers, principals, students, and parents to advocate for the types of mental health interventions and social supports that are needed by students who have lived through trauma. In addition, by understanding the specific experiences and needs of their own students, schools and school personnel will be better prepared to deal with traumatic events. Given that social supports have proven to be so important in the mediation of trauma, this kind of intervention would facilitate social support for those who ask for it as well as those who need it. Having the school as the center of this network means that, in the wake of a traumatic event, students can be in a familiar and stable environment, working with people they already know.

Additional Resources

Educators for Social Responsibility

Educators for Social Responsibility (ESR) focuses on creating safe, caring, and respectful classroom environments. This is accomplished by promoting discussions on global issues—e.g., war, terrorism—(Educators for Social Responsibility, 2009). A few examples of the resources provided by ESR (2009) include:

- A discussion guide for teachers entitled *Talking With Children About War and Violence* and *Responding to Violent Events by Building Community: Action Ideas for Students and Schools.*
- Lessons entitled *Understanding, Discussing, and Analyzing War; Teaching About the Iraq Crisis; Analyzing the Middle East;* and *Discussing North Korea.*

National Association of School Psychologists

The National Association of School Psychologists (NASP) has developed *The Safe and Responsive Schools* model, outlining a violence-prevention planning process for schools. More specifically, this model outlines strategies for school personnel to develop a detailed violence-prevention plan tailored to the needs and resources of each individual school (National Association of School Psychologists, 2009). NASP also provides:

- Resources related to therapeutic responses to violence and crisis situations.
- Responses in terms of plans and procedures following a crisis.
- Interventions for students at risk or in need of support.
- Materials related to war/terrorism, suicide, natural disasters, and trauma.
- Crisis materials targeted for educators and parents.

American Red Cross

The American Red Cross offers terrorism-specific materials including *Terrorism: Preparing for the Unexpected* (American Red Cross, 2001). This curriculum includes:

- preparedness;
- prevention;
- response information.

The American Red Cross also offers many community disaster education materials, designed for implementation in the classroom, about natural hazards. For example, The *Masters of Disaster* curriculum was created to help teachers integrate fundamental disaster safety instruction into their regular core subjects (American Red Cross, 2007). *Facing Fear* is a curriculum developed immediately following September 11 that supplements the *Masters of Disaster* curriculum. *Facing Fear* focuses on:

- Helping children in uncertain times, especially man-made disasters.
- Reinforcing a sense of security in young people.
- Facilitating a discussion of thoughts and feelings.
- Educating about misinformation and misperceptions.
- Helping them to respond to past events and plan for future events and uncertain times.

Elements specific to terrorism and war are incorporated in this curriculum (American Red Cross, 2004).

Jane's School Safety Handbook

Jane's School Safety Handbook is a tool designed for teachers, school administrators, and other agencies to prepare for, respond to, and recover from school safety and security incidents (Jane's, 2001). This particular handbook focuses on safety in schools in the United States and includes:

- safe school planning and training;
- crisis management and communications;
- threat assessments;
- sheltering-in-place/lockdown;
- recognizing warning signs.

Cognitive–Behavioral Intervention for Trauma in Schools (CBITS)

CBITS is a 10-week intervention designed specifically to address trauma in inner-city school mental health clinics, using a cognitive behavioral therapy model. This particular intervention focuses on facilitating the following to groups of five to eight students:

- identifying symptoms of stress and trauma;
- relaxation training;

- discussing thoughts and feelings;
- combating negative thoughts;
- using imagination/drawing/writing to address stress;
- learning social problem-solving skills;
- relapse prevention.

This particular intervention has proven to be effective in lowering self-reported symptoms of PTSD three months after the intervention (Stein et al., 2003).

Building Resilience in Preschool Children

Building Resilience in Preschool Children is a teacher's manual comprising resilience-building activities in the preschool classroom. Teachers are encouraged to construct activities that address the trauma of young students exposed to terrorist attacks (Jane's, 2001). Resources for workshops include information pages, articles, classroom activities, and worksheets for multimodal resiliency-building activities focusing on the following strategies (Baum, Bamberger, & Anchor, 2005):

- mind–body connection;
- expressing feelings and coping with fears;
- developing personal resources;
- meaning making and hope.

References

American Psychiatric Association (2000). *Diagnostic and statistical manual of mental disorders* (4th ed., text revision). Washington DC: American Psychiatric Association.

American Psychological Association (2006a). One year after Katrina, more is known about its mental health effects; storm's widespread effect on people of color and children and the need for culturally competent mental health services are evident. Retrieved September 13, 2009 from: www.apa.org/news/press/releases/2006/08/katrina.aspx

American Psychological Association (2006b). APA's response to international and national disasters and crises: Addressing diverse needs. *American Psychologist, 61*, 513–521.

American Red Cross (2001). *Terrorism: Preparing for the unexpected.* Retrieved September 13, 2009 from: www.redcross.org/www-files/Documents/pdf/Preparedness/AreYouReady/Terrorism.pdf

American Red Cross (2004). *Facing fear: Helping young people deal with terrorism and other tragic events.* Retrieved September 13, 2009 from: www.redcross.org/portal/site/en/menuitem.d229a5f06620c6052b1ecfbf43181aa0/?vgnextoid=749bf655c099b110VgnVCM10000089f0870aRCRD

American Red Cross (2007). American Red Cross Masters of Disasters education materials. Retrieved September 2, 2009 from: www.redcross.org/disaster/masters

Astor, R. A., Benbenishty, R., & Meyer, H. A. (2004). Monitoring and mapping student victimization in schools. *Theory into Practice, 43*, 39–49.

Astor, R. A., Benbenishty, R., Marachi, R., & Meyer, H. A. (2006). The social context of schools: Monitoring and mapping student victimization in schools. In S. Jimerson & M. Furlong (Eds.), *Handbook of school violence and school safety: From research to practice* (Chapter 15). Mahwah, NJ: Lawrence Erlbaum.

Auger, R., Seymour, J., & Roberts, W. (2004). Responding to terror: The impact of September 11th on K–12 schools and schools' responses. *Professional School Counseling, 7*, 222–230.

Baum, N., Bamberger, E., & Anchor, C. (2005). *Building resilience in preschool children.* Jerusalem: Herzog Hospital.

Baum, N., Rotter, B., Reidler, E., & Brom, D. (2009). Building resilience in schools in the wake of Hurricane Katrina. *Journal of Child and Adolescent Trauma, 2*(1), 62–70.

Benbenishty, R., & Astor, R. A. (2005). *School violence in context: Culture, neighborhood, family, school, and gender.* New York: Oxford University Press.

Benbenishty, R., & Astor, R. A. (2007). Monitoring indicators of children's victimization in school: Linking national-, regional-, and site-level indicators. *Social Indicators Research, 84*(3), 333–348.

Benbenishty, A., & Benbenishty, R. (2007). *Managing for hope: From the disco bombing to the President educational prize.* Jerusalem: Geffen Publishing [in Hebrew].

Benbenishty, R., Astor, R. A., & Zeira, A. (2003). Monitoring school violence at the site level: Linking national, district and school-level data. *Journal of School Violence, 2*(2), 29–50.

Brock, S., & Cowan, K. (2004). Preparing to help students after a crisis. *Principal Leadership, 4*, 9–13.

Daniels, J., Bradley, M., Cramer, D., Winkler, A., Kinebrew, K., & Crockett, D. (2007). In the aftermath of a school hostage event: A case study of one school counselor's response. *Professional School Counseling, 10*, 482–489.

Datnow, A., Hubbard, L., & Mehan, H. (2002). *Extending educational reform: From one to many.* New York and London: RoutledgeFalmer.

Educators for Social Responsibility (2009). *Elementary school programs.* Retrieved September 13, 2009 from: www.esrnational.org/otc/view_lessons.php?action=grade&gradeid=24

Evans, L., & Oehler-Stinnet, J. (2006). Children and natural disasters: A primer for school psychologists. *School Psychology International, 27*(1), 33–55.

Garrison, C. Z., Bryant, E. S., Addy, C. L., Spurrier, P. G., Freedy, J. R., & Kilpatrick, D. G. (1995). Posttraumatic stress disorder in adolescents after Hurricane Andrew. *Journal of the American Academy of Child & Adolescent Psychology, 34*(9), 1193–1201.

Hobfoll, S., Canetti-Nisim, D., & Johnson, R. (2006). Exposure to terrorism, stress-related mental health symptoms, and defensive coping among Jews and Arabs in Israel. *Journal of Consulting and Clinical Psychology, 74,* 207–218.

Jane's (2001). *Jane's school safety handbook* (2nd ed.) Retrieved September 11, 2009 from: http://catalog.janes.com/catalog/public/index.cfm?fuseaction=home. ProductInfoBrief&product_id=98448

Jaycox, L., Tanielian, T., Sharma, P., Morse, L., Clum, G., & Stein, B. (2007). Schools' mental health response after Hurricanes Katrina and Rita. *Psychiatric Services, 58,* 1339–1343.

Loiler, M. (2006). The role of school in responding to and educating about terrorism. Doctoral dissertation. University of Southern California.

Milliken, C., Auchterlonie, J., & Hoge, C. (2007). Longitudinal assessment of mental health problems among active and reserve component soldiers returning from the Iraq War. *JAMA, 298,* 2141–2148.

Mills, M., Edmondson, M., & Park, C. (2007). Trauma and stress response among Hurricane Katrina evacuees. *Research and Practice, 97,* S116–S123.

Morgan, J. (1995). American Red Cross disaster mental health services: Implementation and recent developments. *Journal of Mental Health Counseling, 17,* 291–300.

Morrison, J. (2007). Perception of teachers and staff regarding the impact of the Critical Incident Stress Management (CISM) model for school-based crisis intervention. *Journal of School Violence, 6,* 101–120.

National Association of School Psychologists (2009). *School safety and crisis resources.* Retrieved September 13, 2009, from www.nasponline.org/resources/crisis_safety/index.aspx

National Institute of Mental Health (NIMH) (2009). *Posttraumatic stress disorder.* Retrieved September 11, 2009, from: www.nimh.nih.gov/health/topics/post-traumatic-stress-disorder-ptsd/index.shtml

North, C., Nixon, S., Shariat, S., Mallonee, S., McMillan, J., Spitznagel, E., et al. (1999). Psychiatric disorders among survivors of the Oklahoma City bombing. *JAMA, 282,* 755–762.

Park, V. (2008). Beyond the numbers chase: How urban high school teachers make sense of data use. Doctoral dissertation. University of Southern California.

Pat-Horenczyk, R., Schiff, M., & Doppelt, O. (2006). Maintaining routine despite ongoing exposure to terrorism: A healthy strategy for adolescents? *Journal of Adolescent Health, 39,* 199–205.

Pat-Horenczyk, R., Brom, D., Baum, N., Benbenishty, R., Schiff, M., & Astor, R. (2011). A city-wide school-based model for addressing the needs of children exposed to terrorism and war. In V. Ardino (Ed.), *Posttraumatic syndromes in children and adolescents.* London: Wiley/Blackwell.

Pat-Horenczyk, R., Peled, O., Daie, A., Abramovitz, R., Brom, D., & Chemtob, C. (2007a). Adolescent exposure to recurrent terrorism in Israel: Posttraumatic distress and functional impairment. *American Journal of Orthopsychiatry, 77*(1), 26–85.

Pat-Horenczyk, R., Peled, O., Miron, T., Brom, D., Villa, Y., & Chemtob, C., (2007b). Risk-taking behaviors among Israeli adolescents exposed to recurrent terrorism: Provoking danger under continuous threat? *American Journal of Psychiatry, 164,* 66–72.

Perilla, J., Norris, F., & Lavizzo, E. (2002). Ethnicity, culture, and disaster response: Identifying and explaining ethnic differences in PTSD six months after Hurricane Andrew. *Journal of Social and Clinical Psychology, 21,* 20–45.

Perrin, M., DiGrande, L., Wheeler, K. Thorpe, L., Farfel, M., & Brackbill, R. (2007). Differences in PTSD prevalence and associated risk factors among World Trade Center disaster rescue and recovery workers. *American Journal of Psychiatry, 164,* 1385–1394.

Pole, N., Best, S., Metzler, T., & Marmar, C. (2005). Why are Hispanics at greater risk for PTSD? *Cultural Diversity and Ethnic Minority Psychology, 11,* 144–161.

Reissman, D., Spencer, S., Tanielian, T., & Stein, B. (2005). Integrating behavioral aspects into community preparedness and response systems. *Journal of Aggression, Maltreatment & Trauma, 10,* 707–720.

Roberts, N. P., Kitchiner, N. J., Kenardy, J., & Bisson, J. I. (2009). Systematic review and meta-analysis of multiple-session early interventions following traumatic events. *The American Journal of Psychiatry, 166,* 293–301.

Schlenger, W., Caddell, J., Ebert, L., Jordan, B., Rourke, K., Wilson, D., et al. (2002). Psychological reactions to terrorist attacks: Findings from the National Study of Americans' Reactions to September 11th. *JAMA, 288,* 581–588.

Stein, B., Jaycox, L., Kataoka, S., Wong, M., Tu, W., Elliott, M., & Fink, A. (2003). A mental health intervention for schoolchildren exposed to violence: A randomized controlled trial. *JAMA, 290,* 603–611.

Stein, B., Jaycox, L., Elliott, M., Collins, R., Berry, S., Marshall, G., et al. (2004). The emotional and behavioral impact of terrorism on children: Results from a national survey. *Applied Developmental Psychology, 8,* 184–194.

Steury, S., Spencer, S., & Parkinson, G. (2004). The social context of recovery. *Psychiatry: Interpersonal and Biological Processes, 67*(2), 158–163.

Tanielian, T., Jaycox, L., Schell, T., Marshall, G., Burnam, M., Eibner C., et al. (2008). *Invisible wounds of war: Summary and recommendations for addressing psychological and cognitive injuries,* Santa Monica, CA: RAND Corporation, MG-720/1-CCF, 2008, 64 pp., available at http://veterans.rand.org

Tucker, M., & Codding, J. (1998). *Standards for our schools: How to set them, measure them, and reach them*. San Francisco, CA: Jossey-Bass.

Vernberg, E. M., LaGreca, A. M., Silverman, W. K., & Prinstein, M. J. (1996). Prediction of posttraumatic stress symptoms in children after Hurricane Andrew. *Journal of Abnormal Psychology, 105*(2), 237–248.

Wolmer, L., Laor, N., & Yazgan, Y. (2003). School reactivation programs after disaster: Could teachers serve as clinical mediators? *Child and Adolescent Psychiatric Clinics of North America, 12*(2), 363–381.

Wolmer, L., Laor, N., Dedeoglu, C., Siev, J., & Yazgan, Y. (2005). Teacher-mediated intervention after disaster: A controlled three-year follow-up of children's functioning. *Journal of Child Psychology and Psychiatry, 46*(11), 1161–1168.

17

Fiscal Accountability in Urban Schools and School Districts

Lawrence O. Picus

Fiscal accountability for school districts helps assure that money is both accounted for properly and that the budget is balanced—i.e., it ensures that spending on individual line items does not exceed the budget for that line item and that revenues and expenditures are tracked. As a result, accounting systems in school districts offer information on spending by *object* (type of expenditure, such as teacher salaries, all personnel benefits, instructional materials, etc.), *function* (general areas, such as instruction, instructional support, administration, operations and maintenance), and in some cases *program* (elementary instruction, middle schools, special education).

However, those accounting systems rarely link fiscal elements of the system to personnel counts and even less often to measures of student performance and teacher quality. And while information on the resources available to each school in a district is generally available, it is rarely used to budget strategically so as to focus those resources on strategies that can lead to improved student performance in a cost-effective way.

This chapter argues that whereas managing the often complex accounting functions of today's urban school districts is essential, it is not sufficient if we are to be sure that our schools offer educational programs that enable all students to receive a high-quality education (defined here as meeting their state's student proficiency standards). Doing so requires a fiscal accountability system that not only tracks revenues and expenditures but also supports recruitment and retention of the best human capital and ensures that its personnel receive the support they need to continuously improve instruction for all children. The chapter also argues that districts must work to ensure schools establish routines that use resource and time efficiently to maximize opportunities for students to learn.

Although these additional responsibilities may seem beyond the role of a typical school district business office, fiscal accountability requires the participation of all school district staff to focus on and support strategies that will improve student learning. This is particularly important in today's urban school systems, which are often plagued with low student test scores, high dropout rates, and myriad other problems that impact student learning. This chapter tracks the issue of fiscal accountability by starting with a brief historical context for school funding and the way money has been accounted for in the past. Following that, there is a discussion of current trends in school finance, with an emphasis on how resources are distributed to individual schools within a district. It then argues that simply providing funds to schools and districts is not enough to ensure high student performance and suggests that, in looking at the use of that funding, it is essential to move beyond the analysis of dollars and cents and also look at how personnel are used, how time is spent in providing instruction on a daily basis, and who is teaching what curriculum to students.

The chapter considers alternative approaches to distributing funds to schools and districts, arguing that if schools are to be held accountable for student performance, the distribution mechanism under which funds are sent to districts and then to schools is less important than correctly estimating how much is needed and how those resources are actually used. The chapter concludes by suggesting that a district's fiscal system can be used to help school leaders focus resources on identified priorities for improving student learning.

Historical Context of Urban School Funding

School finance in the United States has had three distinct periods. Each will be described in the subsections below.

Equalization

School finance initially focused on what can best be characterized as taxpayer equity issues, making sure school districts had equal levels of resources for equal tax effort. It often also established roughly equal levels of per-pupil spending across school districts. Today, all state school finance systems include an equalization component designed to equalize both property tax effort and per-pupil spending across school districts (Odden & Picus, 2008).

These systems are designed to offer equal levels of resources to all school districts regardless of local tax-raising ability. Local effort is measured through the per-pupil taxable property wealth of a district. Districts with high property wealth per pupil generate more local resources than districts with low property wealth per pupil, and state aid is provided to districts in inverse relation to their property wealth.

Because urban districts often have high concentrations of students from low-income households, it is frequently assumed that urban districts benefit from these equalization schemes in state aid formulas. In fact, though, urban districts in most states are often above average in property wealth compared with rural and most suburban areas because of their greater commercial and industrial property base. Consequently, they do not benefit from large increases in equalization aid from the state as much as one might expect.

Categorical Funding

In the latter part of the 20th century there was a movement to improve, or at least understand productivity in education. This led to numerous studies that attempted to show how money mattered in producing student outcomes. Although today few argue that less money is better than more money, considerable research has not succeeded in clearly identifying a systematic relationship between spending and student learning as measured through test scores and completion of high school (see, e.g., Hanushek, 1997). What did emerge from this work is a nearly universal agreement that some students needed more support from the education system than others. In particular, it became clear that schools need to devote more effort to helping students from low-income families and children who come to school with limited English-language skills.

To address these needs, categorical funding programs were established. Typically focused on a specific student characteristic or need, categorical grants provide additional funds to support the students who generate those funds. The Federal Title I program, which provides additional funding to states and school districts to serve children from low-income homes, is the largest and probably the most familiar of these programs.

Categorical programs typically come with a number of spending requirements such that the funds must be spent on the students with characteristics that generated the funding and that the funds supplement, not supplant, other state and district funding. This was done to ensure that the money would be spent on the children who needed the extra support and that districts did not shift local funding to students who did not qualify for the categorical grant funding. As a result, over time, a number of complex accounting requirements have developed to make sure that categorical resources are used as intended (for a review of categorical programs, see Odden & Picus, 2008).

Adequacy

In recent years, a third trend in school finance has emerged—adequacy. This term can best be defined as providing a level of resources that will ensure that all children are able to meet their state's learning standards. This is a high standard, and there remains considerable debate over how best to estimate what an adequate level of resources might be. To date, researchers have identified four general approaches to estimating adequacy (see, e.g., Baker, Taylor, & Vedlitz, 2008; Odden & Picus, 2008). Two of those approaches seek to estimate an appropriate funding level based on the spending patterns of districts that meet a certain performance standard, whereas the other two determine the programmatic elements needed at a school to establish with confidence that all or almost all students will be able to reach a given level of performance and then to estimate the costs of those elements.

In the first group, the *successful district approach* identifies school districts that meet state-defined criteria for high performance and use the per-pupil expenditures of those districts as the base for adequacy, adjusting individual district funding levels based on student and district characteristics (Alexander, Augenblick, Driscoll, Guthrie, & Levin, 1995; Fermanich et al., 2006). The *cost function method* uses econometric modeling techniques to identify a per-pupil spending level sufficient to produce a given level of performance while adjusting for characteristics of students and other socioeconomic-status characteristics of districts (Imazeki & Reschovsky, 2006; Reschovsky & Imazeki, 1998, 2001).

The two approaches that identify the elements needed to produce student learning are *professional judgment* and *the evidence-based approach*. Professional judgment studies bring together groups of educational professionals to identify program elements needed at schools and school districts for an adequate program (Augenblick & Myers, Inc., 2001a, 2001b; Chambers, Levin, & DeLancey, 2006; Guthrie et al., 1997). The evidence-based method relies on research findings to identify the program elements of an adequate educational program and estimates the costs of those resources (Odden & Archibald, 2009; Odden & Picus, 2008).

Each method has been used in a number of states to estimate the cost of adequacy; in some instances, these approaches have been used to structure state school finance systems. Whereas all provide a standard of adequate resources, none ensures that student performance will improve unless accompanied by efforts on the part of districts and schools to utilize the funding available to purchase and support the resources (people and materials) necessary for success. The unique characteristics of urban school systems are identified below; then the ways in which resources can be deployed efficiently to create student learning are described.

The Challenges Facing Urban School Districts

Urban school districts pose particularly significant challenges to school funding systems and the provision of adequate education. They are by far the largest districts in most states; their enrollments often include large numbers of children from low-income homes, many of whom face daily challenges outside of school that make teaching and learning harder; and many suffer from years of management and fiscal challenges. In 2008–2009 (the most recent year for which comparison data are available), there were 13,976 school districts in the United States, of which only 27 had more than 100,000 students. These districts represented 0.2% of the school districts, yet they educated 6.4 million students, or 13.1% of the nation's 48.6 million K–12 public school enrollments (Sable, Plotts, & Mitchell, 2010).

Looked at another way, Sable et al. (2010) report that each of the 100 largest districts in the United States enrolled 47,400 or more students and that the 11.8 million students in those districts represent almost one quarter (22.3%) of all K–12 students in the United States. Moreover, the 100 largest districts have an average of 169 schools per district, compared with a national average of 6.6 schools per district.

The schools in the largest districts tend to be larger than average as well (673 students per school, compared with 514). These 100 districts served 35% of students in the United States who are Black, Hispanic, Asian/Pacific Islander, and American Indian/Alaska Native; only 12% of the students identified as White (Sable et al., 2010). In 99 of the 100 largest districts that reported free and reduced-price lunch eligibility, 56% of the students qualified for this program, compared with a national average of 45% in all districts. Interestingly, 13% of the students in these districts had Individualized Education Programs (IEPs) for special education, the same percentage found in all districts.

Data were available to compute the Average Freshman Graduate Rate (AFGR) for 2007–2008 in 93 of the 100 largest districts. The AFGR for those districts was 65%, compared with 75% for all school districts. Moreover, dropout rate from grades 9 through 12 was 5% for the 99 districts reporting dropout rates (Sable et al., 2010).

The median pupil/teacher ratio in the 100 largest districts was 15.3:1 (compared with a national average of 15.0:1), and total per-pupil spending was just over $12,500 in 2007–2008 (Sable et al., 2010). This is more than $2,200 greater than the national average per-pupil spending of $10,297 for the same year (Zhou, 2010).

Funding Mechanisms for Urban Schools

Although urban districts have somewhat more money for each student, the challenges they face to educate each of them to their individual state standards are considerable. Simply ensuring that the available resources are accounted for in the appropriate categories (something that has challenged more than a few large school districts in recent years) is not enough. Districts must find ways to use the resources available to them in order to employ a qualified teacher workforce that can implement learning strategies that research shows will help students learn to high standards. More often than not, schools with fewer low-income and/or minority children benefit from having a more stable and senior teacher force—one that is more expensive as well.

One of the first fiscal issues large school districts deal with is simply distributing the resources they have fairly across all of the schools in the district. On one level, this could be as simple as making sure each school has the same dollars per pupil as every other school in the district. Although simple on the surface, achieving such a goal—if it were desirable—is nearly impossible because of factors like teacher salary schedules—which reward teachers on the basis of experience and education—and union contracts that often give transfer priority to senior teachers. The result is more "desirable" schools in a district may have a disproportionate number of more experienced teachers increasing the per-pupil expenditures at that school, a factor that may or may not be linked to measures of teacher success. Roza (2010) has shown substantial variation in per-pupil expenditures across schools within a district. Moreover, the use of detailed school-level expenditure data also finds that many elective courses are more expensive to operate on a per-pupil basis than are core math and English classes. This finding is a function of both more options being available to senior (and more expensive) teachers as well as the frequently smaller sizes of elective classes.

What can education leaders do to reverse this apparently "backward" process, whereby more resources are devoted to the schools attended by the most advantaged children? Funding allocation schemes in school districts generally follow one of three patterns: use of pupil/teacher ratios, use of weighted students, or some combination that funds basic classes and provides categorical funding to meet specific student needs. Although all have the potential to direct resources toward student need, this goal is often mitigated by political opposition, union contracts, and other factors that appear to limit the ability of school leaders to implement changes that will lead to improved learning. Each funding approach is described below.

Pupil/Teacher Ratios

This approach, used by many school districts, establishes a fixed class-size ratio (which often varies by school level) and then assigns teacher resources to schools based on student enrollments. It works well to distribute teaching resources evenly, but—absent some variation in the ratios based on student characteristics—it often leaves the most needy schools with class sizes the same as or larger than those of more successful schools. An alternative way to distribute resources under this model would be to provide additional staff to schools based on the count of at-risk students. For example, the funding model could provide one teacher per 25 students and then fund an additional teaching position for every 100 students identified as being at risk, using a proxy such as the number of students receiving the free and reduced-price lunch. This would focus additional resources to schools with large concentrations of children from low-income households, but it does not on the surface provide any help with what those teachers might do. Some schools simply use the additional teachers to reduce existing class size, with little evidence that this alone will improve learning. Others use those teachers to provide pull-out or other tutoring services to the neediest students at the school.

Weighted Pupil Models

Rather than focus on the distribution of teachers, weighted pupil models focus on the individual characteristics of students, offering additional funding (weights) for students who enroll in school with characteristics that research shows require additional resources. Like the teacher ratio approaches, schools can use the additional funds to purchase additional teacher or aide positions to help students. A number of large urban districts have implemented weighted pupil systems to varying degrees of success (see, e.g., Ouchi, 2009). Roza (2010) argues that this approach works well in focusing resources efficiently and fairly on student needs. The problem with this method is that it works best when the base pupil amount as well as the weights are adequate to meet student needs—a number that is both hard to identify and often not fully funded. Thus, a weighted pupil system that does not provide adequate resources to fund the programs identified by school officials as successful will not necessarily work better than other options. And, of course, there is still the question of whether or not the resources that reach the school are focused on those children whose identified needs generated the flow of funds in the first place.

Categorical Grants

Many state funding systems rely on the use of categorical funding systems (resources generated on the basis of an identified student need and then required to be utilized to serve those children). The Federal Title I program, which provides additional funds to school districts serving high proportions of low-income children, is perhaps the best example of these categorical grants. Such grants often come with strings attached and require the district or school to use them in very specific ways, often limiting flexibility of local school leaders. They also have a certain level of funding uncertainty from year to year, making it more difficult for schools to employ teachers who have long-term contract protections using funds that may not be available in two or three years.

What this very brief discussion of funding allocation strategies highlights is that funding is important, but how the resources generated are used to produce learning is more critical and certainly the focus of today's educational accountability systems. Rather than debate the level and distribution of resources, the balance of this chapter argues that what is more important is to use the resources that are available toward strategies that have a high likelihood of success for student learning. There are many examples of how schools have improved student learning and many models that educators can follow (Chenoweth, 2008; Miles & Frank, 2008; Zavadsky, 2010). What is important is to have a strategy about how children will be served and then to allocate and use resources to achieve those goals.

Financing Human Capital and Time-use Strategies

The next sections identify human capital and time-use strategies that can help to improve student performance and offer ways to finance these systems in the current context of urban finance.

Understanding How Fiscal Resources Link to Accountability

It is unlikely that the simple provision of more dollars will lead to improved student outcomes, the hiring of better teachers, or more and better training for teachers. Obviously, the classes and support offered to students can make a difference in how well students learn. Research from evidence-based adequacy models has shown that attracting high-quality teachers, providing them with useful and regular professional development (both learning opportunities and coaching support in their schools) and giving them with opportunities for collaboration with other teachers in the school can lead to improved student learning.

In addition, students who are enrolled in relatively small classes (15 in grades K to 3 and 25 in other grades) and who have an opportunity to focus on core subjects with strategies to support them when they are struggling (e.g., RTI Tier 2 type assistance) have demonstrated improved outcomes. The key is to find the appropriate human capital and learning opportunities to implement these strategies.

Work with a number of urban districts has found that even when they feel they are constrained by finances, labor contracts, and growing expenses outside of their control, principals who focus on allocating what resources they have on the best possible strategies have been able to improve student outcomes in their schools (Odden & Archibald, 2009). Outlined below are some of the personnel and time alternatives schools could consider in finding ways to focus resources on improving student learning.

Human Capital—A Critical Resource

Over half of the full-time employees of a school district are teachers; in the largest urban districts, certified teachers represent 52% of the FTE employees, compared with 51% of all districts (Sable et al., 2010). Given the more than ample evidence that teacher quality has the largest impact on improved student outcomes (see, e.g., Hanushek & Rivkin, 2006), it is critical that urban districts employ strategies to attract and retain the best teachers available.

Urban districts often lag behind their suburban counterparts in attracting the best and brightest new teachers to their districts. It was once thought that teaching in such environments was undesirable, but today many college graduates are eager to teach in urban settings—witness the success of Teach for America and the New Teacher Project (Aportela & Goetz, 2008; Goetz & Aportela, 2008). The problem often lies in attracting and hiring the top new teacher talent before these people seek employment elsewhere.

The Strategic Management of Human Capital (SMHC) project identified 10 strategies to accomplish the goal of improving teacher quality in large urban districts. These include the following (SMHC, 2008):

1. Expand the talent pipeline to seek out top teacher and principal talent.
2. Strengthen screening for the selection of new teachers and give school sites more autonomy to hire teachers who fit the school's instructional vision.
3. Place top talent in high-need schools.
4. Develop new intensive induction and mentoring programs for teachers.
5. Provide high-quality professional development on an ongoing basis.
6. Have a strong evaluation system to measure teacher performance.
7. Manage teacher performance to improve teacher quality and student achievement.
8. Reward, promote, and retain effective teachers and principals.
9. Restructure human resources departments to manage human capital strategically so as to hire and support teachers, provide professional development, collect data, and ensure accountability—all focused on improving student achievement.
10. Implement a relevant, comprehensive, and easy-to-use data system.

Thus, fiscal accountability is far more than just making sure a school district's human resources (HR) department balances its budget; it includes operating a strategic HR department whose primary focus, like that of the entire district, is aimed at improving student achievement. SMHC (2008) offers evidence that some large urban districts have been successful in speeding up their interviewing and hiring process so that they can compete for the very best teachers' college graduates each year and that, in the process, they have been able to focus more effectively on improved student performance. Groups like Teach for America (TFA) and the New Teacher Project have had substantial success in recruiting the best and brightest college graduates to teaching, and TFA has recently released its findings on what they think are the most important characteristics of a good teacher (Farr, 2010).

Urban districts often have higher salary schedules than surrounding districts, so in theory they should be able to retain the best of the teachers they recruit. However, simply paying teachers more than other districts has not been enough to retain then. But even with the best teachers in place, strong instruction along with the effective use of time is important to maintaining high student standards.

The Use of Time for Instruction in Our Schools

How instruction is provided is critical to academic success. How schools use the teaching resources available to them is as important as ensuring that the resources are in the school. It is argued here that a successful school will allocate resources to provide for small classes to the extent possible but will also ensure that teachers have time for individual planning as well as time to collaborate on instruction and curriculum design (DuFour, DuFour, & Eaker, 2008). Schools also need instructional coaches to help teachers improve instruction; they must also use data to focus their teaching on the needs of students.

Additionally, schools need professional staff to work with students who are struggling with the curriculum. Odden and Archibald (2009) demonstrate that certified teachers serving as tutors who work with students one to one or in very small groups—with a goal of returning the student to the regular classroom as soon as possible—is a strategy that has been very successful at improving student achievement. Finding ways to meet student needs through such tutors is often a highly efficient way to improve learning. The key is to seek out options that make these teaching positions available in a school.

At the secondary school level, one possible strategy is to reduce the number of elective offerings. High school students typically take six or seven classes a day, and most secondary school teachers teach five. If a school's goal is to maintain class sizes of, say, 25, then a school that offers six periods with teachers teaching five will need approximately 20% more teachers. A school with a seven-period day and five periods of teaching requires 33% more teachers. Moreover, the typical school day is 6.5 hours long, with 30 minutes for lunch. Assuming 5-minute passing periods, a school can offer six 55-minute periods or seven 42-minute periods. Thus, not only does the school need more teachers (or conversely have larger classes), but it also has less instruction time for each class including important core courses like math, English, social studies, and science.

At the elementary school level, where class sizes are often even smaller, the challenge is often to find time for both planning and collaboration among teachers. In most elementary schools, teachers have approximately one hour each day (out of six) where their class participates in music, art, or physical education taught by a specialist. Some of this planning time could be used for collaboration or, alternatively, classes taught by specialists could be larger, providing more free time for regular classroom teachers to collaborate.

Class-size Trade-offs

There is a general view (supported to some extent by research) that smaller classes are better. It is hard to argue this point; it is also difficult to observe substantial differences in teaching and learning when class sizes fluctuate by one or two students. Yet, simply allowing smaller class sizes to drive resource allocation is often observed. There is evidence (see, e.g., Chenoweth, 2008; Odden & Archibald, 2009) that instructional coaches with a regular presence in a school can often make a difference in improving instruction. In an elementary school with 20 regular classrooms, each with 15 students, increasing the class size to an average of 16 or 17 would free enough resources to hire a coach. Similar trade-offs are possible at secondary schools as well.

Impediments to Changing Resource Allocation Strategies

One of the complaints heard frequently among school leaders, particularly in urban districts, is that they cannot enact substantial change in the use of teachers because of contract restrictions. Contracts may require that when a class exceeds, say, 25 students, another teacher must be hired. This is either very inefficient (as there are now two classes averaging 12 or 13 students) or the school will be forced to move around a large number of children in many grades (possibly creating multigrade classrooms) simply to balance class loads. Both are disruptive to learning. Similar contractual requirements are those requiring that when a class reaches a certain size, the teacher gets an aide to help with the students. There may, instead, be more efficient uses of resources that could enable a school to employ tutors to help struggling students and/or a coach to help teachers plan and deliver high-quality instruction. Again, more flexibility in setting class sizes may enable schools to deploy strategies that, according to the evidence, lead to improved student performance.

Other Factors Schools Can Consider

In our work in a large suburban district in a fiscally strapped state, we sought to develop a zero-based strategic budget. Each school's resources were combined into a model that allowed simulation of alternative class size options as well as alternative support programs for teachers and struggling students. We found that, by using the district's student/teacher ratios to distribute certified teaching staff to the schools, we allocated the same 1,600 teachers to the core and specialist functions that the district had allocated. What we observed was that our strategy left the district with another 700 certified teaching positions that could be used to implement district priorities. Moreover, following our initial analysis, we worked with the district to establish a set of instructional goals and priorities for the students. This included service to English language learners, special education students, and others who were struggling. It also emphasized additional collaborative time for teachers.

What we noted when we ran our initial simulations was that many of the 700 certified teachers who were not part of the core and specialist teacher ranks were doing things very differently from the stated priorities of district. In effect, the reallocation of resources within and across the schools in the district could serve to help implement strategies that had been deemed as conducive to improved learning. The district also realized that its five comprehensive high schools were operating on three completely different class schedules and that a substantial number of students in the district were transferring between high schools each year. That is, the district's management realized that, by shifting to the same schedules, many students would be better able to keep up with the standard curriculum as they moved from school to school—and this in a district that had, up to that point, highly valued school-based decision-making.

Conclusion: Fiscal Resources for Accountability Can be Found in Any District

In a time of growing fiscal constraint, school districts continue to cut back and reduce services to all parts of the education program but often work to minimize the reductions in core teachers, all with an eye to keeping class sizes as small as possible. Yet research suggests that there are a number of more resource-efficient strategies to support teachers and students in their learning that can be implemented without additional personnel or costs. Often, small increases in class size, coupled with increased support from instructional coaches or more highly focused interventions for struggling students, can help improve the quality of instruction and learning, and help keep students from falling further and further behind.

Finding ways to identify these options is the first step to making substantial improvements in student learning. Implementing them in urban school systems is often hard because of political and contractual constraints; but with leadership and effort, it is often possible to demonstrate the potential of cost-effective strategies that enhance school district efficiency and at the same time help students meet state-established performance goals.

References

Alexander, K., Augenblick, J., Driscoll, W., Guthrie, J., & Levin, R. (1995). *Proposals for the elimination of wealth-based disparities in public education*. Columbus, OH: Department of Education.

Aportela, A., & Goetz, M. (2008). *Strategic management of human capital: The new teacher project*. Madison, WI: Strategic Management of Human Capital. Retrieved August 1, 2010 from: www.smhc-cpre.org/resources

Augenblick & Myers, Inc. (2001a). *Calculation of the cost of an adequate education in Maryland in 1999–2000 using two different analytic approaches*. Report prepared for the Maryland Commission on Education Finance, Equity, and Excellence.

Augenblick & Myers, Inc. (2001b). *A procedure for calculating a base cost figure and an adjustment for at-risk pupils that could be used in the Illinois school finance system*. Report prepared for the Education Funding Advisory Board.

Baker, B. D., Taylor, L. L., & Vedlitz, A. (2008). *Adequacy estimates and the implications of common standards for the cost of instruction*. Washington, DC: National Academy of Sciences, National Research Council.

Chambers, J., Levin, J., & DeLancey, D. (2006). Efficiency and adequacy in California school finance: A professional judgment approach. Palo Alto, CA: American Institutes for Research. Retrieved May 17, 2011 from: http://irepp.stanford.edu/documents/GDF/STUDIES/19-AIR-ProfessionalJdgmet/19-AIR-PJP-Report(3-07).pdf

Chenoweth, K. (2008). *It's being done*. Cambridge, MA: Harvard Education Press.

DuFour, R., DuFour, R., & Eaker, R. (2008). *Revisiting professional learning communities at work*. Bloomington, IN: Solution Tree.

Farr, S. (2010). *Teaching as leadership*. San Francisco, CA: Jossey-Bass.

Fermanich, M., Mangan, M., Odden, A., Picus, L. O., Gross, B., & Rudo, Z. (2006). *A successful-districts approach to school finance adequacy in Washington.* Analysis prepared for the K-12 Advisory Committee of Washington Learns. Retrieved May 17, 2011 from: www.washingtonlearns.wa.gov/materials/SuccessfulDistReport9-11-06Final_000.pdf

Goetz, M., & Aportela, A. (2008). *Strategic management of human capital: Teach for America.* Madison, WI: Strategic Management of Human Capital. Retrieved August 1, 2010 from: www.smhc-cpre.org/resources

Guthrie, J. W., Hayward, J. W., Smith, J. R., Rothstein, R., Bennett, R. W., Koppich, J. E., et al. (1997). *A proposed block grant model for Wyoming school finance.* Davis, CA: Management Analysis and Planning, Associates, LLC.

Hanushek, E. A. (1997). Assessing the effects of school resources on student performance: An update. *Educational Evaluation and Policy Analysis, 19*(2), 141–164.

Hanushek, E. A., & Rivkin, S. G. (2006). Teacher quality. In E. A. Hanushek & F. Welch (Eds.), *Handbook of the economics of education* (pp. 1051–1078). Amsterdam: Elsevier.

Imazeki, J., & Reschovsky, A. (2006). Does No Child Left Behind place a fiscal burden on states? Evidence from Texas. *Education Finance and Policy, 1*(2), 217–246.

Miles, K. H., & Frank, S. (2008). *The strategic school.* Thousand Oaks, CA: Corwin Press.

Odden, A. R., & Archibald, S. J. (2009). *Doubling student performance . . . and finding the resources to do it.* Thousand Oaks, CA: Corwin Press.

Odden, A. R., & Picus, L. O. (2008). *School finance: A policy perspective* (4th ed.). New York: McGraw-Hill.

Ouchi, W. G. (2009). *The secret of TSL.* New York: Simon & Schuster.

Reschovsky, A., & Imazeki, J. (1998). The development of school finance formulas to guarantee the provision of adequate education to low-income students. In W. J. Fowler (Ed.), *Developments in school finance 1997* (NCES 98-212). Washington, DC: National Center for Education Statistics.

Reschovsky, A., & Imazeki, J. (2001). Achieving educational adequacy through school finance reform. *Journal of Education Finance 26*(4), 373–396.

Roza, M. (2010). *Educational economics: Where do school funds go?* Washington, DC: Urban Institute Press.

Sable, J., Plotts, C., & Mitchell, L. (2010). *Characteristics of the 100 largest public elementary and secondary school districts in the United States: 2008–09* (NCES 2011-301). Washington, DC: U.S. Department of Education, National Center for Education Statistics.

Strategic Management of Human Capital (SMHC) (2008). *Taking human capital seriously.* Madison, WI: Strategic Management of Human Capital. Retrieved August 1, 2010 from www.smhc-cpre.org/resources

Zavadsky, H. (2010). *Bringing school reform to scale.* Cambridge, MA: Harvard Education Press.

Zhou, L. (2010). *Revenues and expenditures for public elementary and secondary education: School year 2007–08 (fiscal year 2008)* (NCES 2010-326). Washington, DC: U.S. Department of Education, National Center for Education Statistics. Retrieved August 1, 2010 from: http://nces.ed.gov/pubsearch/pubsinfo.asp?pubid=2010326

18

Ethics in Urban Educational Accountability

Kenneth A. Strike

In recent years, educators have come to see accountability largely as a matter of state or national governments holding educators responsible for raising achievement test scores. I will refer to this view of accountability as *the common model*. It is the heir to the reform movement that began with *A nation at risk* (National Commission on Excellence in Education, 1983), passed through systemic reform and *Goals 2000* (Goals 2000: Educate America Act, 1993), and, for the moment, has become the main event in the attempt to improve public education. It is the picture of accountability that produced No Child Left Behind (NCLB Act, 2002). It appears to be alive and well in the Obama administration's Race to the Top. It is rooted in the conviction that education can be improved by a centralized governmental apparatus that monitors compliance and outcomes and rewards or sanctions effective behavior.[1] It sees accountability largely as a state matter and seeks to use the power and funding of the U.S. government to leverage state effort.

Much of the current debate about accountability concerns how to get the common model right. It is less common to ask whether this is the kind of accountability we want or whether the emphasis on accountability should occupy such a central place in school reform. Instead, we focus on whether we need better standards or whether we should use value added measures to evaluate teachers.

Nor is there much discussion concerning whether the common model is normatively appropriate. In this chapter I argue that the common model is seriously flawed, in part because it creates perverse incentives for miseducative, unethical, and ineffective behavior and, in part, because it is "normatively unbalanced." I also argue that its defects are likely to be felt most strongly by urban schools. We should not try to tinker it into success. I develop several alternative models of accountability that are rooted in normative considerations and give more weight to what might be called democratic localism as well as to professionalism. These models should be viewed as ideal types. The trick to having an effective and normatively justified system of accountability is not to choose among them but to find principled ways to balance them.

How to Think about Accountability

A model of accountability can be specified by how it answers three questions and how it justifies its answers to these questions. The questions are:

1. Who is accountable and under what description?
2. To whom are they accountable?
3. For what are they accountable?

If it is to be justified, a model of accountability must be both effective and normatively appropriate. Effectiveness can be judged by whether a view of accountability helps us realize the full range of desired and desirable goals, by the plausibility of what I call its theory of action, by its cost-effectiveness, and by whether it has undesirable side effects. Normative appropriateness can be judged by whether the goals aimed at are worthy and legitimate, whether actors are treated fairly, the just distribution of its outcomes, and the adequacy of its view of legitimate authority. In what follows I emphasize the theory of action and the view of legitimate authority assumed by different models.

A theory of action explains why one would believe that an accountability system would be effective. It will typically involve assumptions about matters such as how the view of accountability leads to desired and effective behavior, and about how these things result in the improvement of education. Moreover, any view of accountability gives some people authority over others. This authority must be justified. Thus, a view of accountability can be judged by the moral legitimacy of its view of authority. The way authority is distributed also has consequences for the effectiveness of a scheme of accountability. Thus, for practical purposes, it is also part of its theory of action.

The Common Model: A Critique

The common model (in theory) begins with curricular content standards. These standards are generally created by state governments in consultation with teachers, subject matter experts, and others. Hearings may be held. The process can be described as democratic (see O'Day & Smith, 1993; and, for discussion, Strike, 1997). Curricula and tests are expected to be aligned with these standards (although it is common for states to use "off-the-shelf" tests to measure reading and mathematics for No Child Left Behind (NCLB) purposes). The results of these tests are used to establish benchmarks for students, educators, schools, school districts, and even states. It has been common to judge individual schools by whether an adequate percentage of their students are proficient. Proficiency is a somewhat arbitrary standard (Rothstein, 2004; Rothstein, Jacobson, & Wilder, 2008) of what constitutes satisfactory performance. Whether benchmarks are met may affect the allocation of resources, but most commonly benchmarks are used to decide whether a school is a failing school and to determine remedies based on this assessment. The threat of such remedies is thought to "incentivize" educators. How does the common model address my three questions and what is its justification?

Who is Accountable?

Here the primary answer is that educators (teachers and administrators) are accountable. They are typically accountable as members of their schools, since most sanctions for inadequate performance are applied at the school level. If test scores are used to determine pay or retention, teachers and principals may also be accountable as individuals. Where high-stakes tests are used for such matters as promotion or graduation, students may also be accountable. I emphasize educators as the primary targets of accountability. Of course, educators will be accountable on any view of accountability. What is distinguishing is the description under which they are accountable. On the common model, they are accountable as employees of public agencies. It should be noted that although teachers are often isolated from direct consequences of accountability by collective bargaining agreements that protect job security and prevent merit pay, teachers seem greatly motivated by their desire to avoid such a stigma and the sanctions of having their school labeled a failing school.

To Whom are Educators Accountable?

They are accountable to one or more legislatures and their agents. Typically, accountability is to state legislatures although Race to the Top may involve some degree of nationalization of accountability. Test-based information may also be used to inform the local public about the performance of its schools. This might be viewed as a form of citizen empowerment. If it is to function in this way, there must be effective mechanisms that allow for citizen participation. Often there are not, and the release of test data functions largely as a kind of public shaming.

For What are Educators Accountable?

On the common model, educators are accountable for meeting benchmarks for student achievement. These benchmarks are defined by scores on standardized tests. There is now considerable interest in using value-added benchmarks so as to reduce the unfairness to schools that teach difficult-to-educate students or that work under adverse circumstances. Valued-added benchmarks would very likely reduce much of the pressure on urban schools and would add to the capacity to hold individual teachers accountable (McCaffrey, Koretz, Lockwood, & Hamilton, 2003). Schools may also be accountable for graduation rates. Accountability is for results, not for inputs or process.

What is the Theory of Action?

The common model seems intended to do three things. First, it generates information about student achievement. Legislatures can use this information to make and evaluate policy. Citizens may use it to evaluate their schools. Schools may use it to evaluate teachers and to improve instruction. Second, it creates incentives. Accountability programs are now accompanied by rewards and punishments. These are supposed to "incentivize" schools and their employees to improve instruction. These incentives may be in the form of building-level sanctions—schools may be labeled failing and subject to various consequences on that account—or they may be used to reward individual teachers through merit pay or other personnel decisions. Third, it may affect the flow of resources and attention. Districts may attempt remediation of schools to avoid their being labeled failing or to improve them when they are. Often it is the remedies for failure that are experienced by educators as punishments and function as negative incentives.

Accountability information systems are designed, however, to serve the interests of policymakers more than teachers. The features of test-based information systems are driven by costs, the requirements of test validity, the need to compare schools on a common metric, and the need for interpretability by nonexperts. The information such tests provide to teachers is of limited use for improving instruction. It is not timely, does not typically provide information about the progress of individual students, may not be well aligned with what is taught, and does not judge real performance. Teachers need timely and student-specific information on the success of their lessons and students need timely feedback on their performance. Pedagogically, useful information often requires interpretation by someone with expertise in the subject being taught. Information of this sort is probably best provided by good teacher-created tests or by teacher-judged student performance. The tests used for accountability rarely provide such information. That they have great value for instructional improvement is thus doubtful. They have a cost in instructional time. Whether their use displaces teacher-created tests is unclear.

What the common model is attempting to do can best be described as creating a system that emphasizes monitoring of results and rewarding or punishing effective behavior. Accountability is to be achieved through bureaucracy. It tends to assume that performance can be improved through incentives more than by assisting people to gain competence. Advocates may compare these systems to the behavior of successful corporations. Detractors may compare them to the Soviet Union's five-year plans.

Legitimate Authority

The central political norms assumed by the common model are three. The first is that the central meaning of democracy is the sovereignty of an elected legislature. The second is that education is substantially a public good appropriately subject to democratic decision-making. The third is that education should be the responsibility of states or of the national government. This last point has a legal justification rooted in the 10th Amendment to the U.S. Constitution, but the version of the claim of most interest here is that the increasing authority of state legislatures and of Congress and the diminishing authority of the local school district and local community is justified by the fact that the many of the consequences of education are no longer born locally and by the widespread perception that democracy at the district level is dysfunctional (Bryk, Sebring, Kerbow, Rollow, & Easton, 1998) and inadequate to create workable accountability systems (Rothstein et al., 2008). These perceptions are especially strong concerning urban school systems.

The common model has a number of inherent weaknesses. Four of these are discussed in this section: goal distortion, gaming, problematic authority relationships, and unjust distributions of resources and outcomes. Other critical points are made in considering alternative models.

Goal Distortion

There are three types of goal distortion. They are goal displacement, goal reduction, and goal redefinition (Strike, 2006).

Goal displacement is the tendency of those who are held accountable to emphasize those goals for which they are held accountable and to deemphasize others that may be valued but not monitored. Goals may be valued but not monitored because they are more difficult or costly to measure or because they are not seen as priorities. In a test-driven system, schools may come to emphasize reading and mathematics, and to deemphasize other subjects such as social studies, art, and music. Presumably, most Americans have broader aspirations for their children than that they should be able to read and compute (Rothstein, 2002). Of course, it may be argued that reading and mathematics are central to anything else schools may wish to accomplish, so that an increased emphasis on them is warranted especially in those schools where there are high failure rates in these subjects.

Goal reduction concerns what is taught within a given subject matter area. It is the tendency for educators to emphasize those aspects of a subject that are tested for and to deemphasize those that are not. Goal reduction may occur because tests that meet the criteria of validity and affordability may emphasize factual content over more ambitious goals such as comprehension, critical thinking, and problem solving. If the appraisal of writing is involved, what will be appraised may often be a few brief paragraphs, and these may be judged by criteria that have more to do with the organization of writing than with critical analysis or sound reasoning.

It is difficult for a standardized test to ask for a real performance. Here, I understand a performance to be the application of the knowledge and skills involved to an authentic context. In music, it is playing or appreciating music; in science, it is solving a scientific problem in a research-like context; in history it is researching a topic and writing up the results. As tests come to approximate performance, they are more faithful to their subjects, but they are also likely to require expert judgment to evaluate. They are more expensive and less reliable. The paradigm case of goal reduction is teaching to the test. Teaching to the test will distort goals to the degree that tests are not faithful to the full content of the subject for which they test.

Goal redefinition is the least noticed but perhaps, ultimately, the most important way in which the common model can distort goals. We all (presumably) want an education with high standards, one that is rigorous and excellent. What do these terms mean? If we think about these concepts apart from the lens of the common model, what we want our schools to produce is students who can read and appraise a complex text; who love and can appreciate good literature; whose writing is elegant, or beautiful, or persuasive, or revealing; who can understand and produce mathematical proofs where the reasoning is sound, original, and elegant; who can perform and appreciate music and art in a manner that is beautiful and insightful; and who can understand and produce history that is not only well researched, informative, and revealing, but also suggests lessons for civic life. We want an educational system that enriches lives and produces good citizens as well as one that produces human capital and encourages consumption. An educational system that encourages students to aspire to such performance can be described in terms such as these; that it would enrich the lives of our students would therefore be considered rigorous and excellent. When educators expect performance with these characteristics they hold students to high standards. I suspect that, prior to the dominance of the "standards" movement and the emphasis on test-based accountability, this is what most people meant by *standards, rigor,* and *excellence.*

But this is not what the common model means. The common model defines a good education by test score results. An education is rigorous if it requires high scores on demanding tests. It is excellent if a high percentage of students pass such tests. It has high standards if it judges student performance by rigorous tests.

The common model invites us to confuse the meaning of a good education with the measure of a good education. It employs measures that involve both goal displacement and goal reduction. But we do not notice, because we no longer really look at what our students can actually do, whether they reason well, write well, can do research, or can think through complex issues. We know that they are doing well if they have high scores and that they are not doing well if they have lower scores. We know these things because the common model has redefined and corrupted the very concepts of standards, rigor, and excellence. Goal redefinition is the mask worn by goal displacement and goal reduction. It has the power to dramatically change what we understand a good education to be and to do so in a way that is corrosive of good education.

Gaming

Gaming occurs when people find ways to meet the benchmarks set for them, apart from succeeding on the underlying goals these benchmarks were intended to measure. In education, the most obvious form of gaming is cheating—giving students the answers to test questions or altering their scores. There are many other forms. Deliberate goal displacement and goal reduction are forms of gaming. Shifting resources away from students who are unlikely to pass or unlikely to fail and focusing them on "bubble kids" is a form of gaming. Push-out (getting poor performing students out of school and off the records) is a form of gaming. Manipulating student classifications is a form of gaming. Nichols and Berliner (2007) have provided extensive (if anecdotal) documentation of these forms of gaming. They use these instances to argue for what they call Campbell's law (Campbell, 1976): "The more any quantitative social indicator is used for social decision making, the more subject it will be to corruption pressures and the more apt it will be to distort and corrupt the social processes it is intended to monitor" (p. 49). Amrein and Berliner (2002) refer to this as the uncertainty principle. Rothstein et al. (2008) provide an extensive discussion suggesting that Campell's law has been a problem in most areas where quantitative indicators have been used as the sole basis of decision making.

Authority Relationships

The central principle of legitimate authority of the common model is the sovereignty of demo-cratically elected legislatures over public matters. The common model aims to improve education, which it views as a public matter, by a bureaucratic system of monitoring and incentivizing outcomes. As legislatures are bound to do when they make policy for large and complex systems, it rules through bureaucracy (Strike, 1993). Since much educational literature tends to juxtapose bureaucracy and democracy, it is important to note that this is incorrect. Bureaucracy is, in fact, an extension of legislative sovereignty. It is how distant legislatures ensure faithfulness to policy in large organizations.

At the same time it should be noted that a commitment to legislative sovereignty does not itself require the centralization of function authority in a state bureaucracy. Legislatures can delegate. Whether, how much, and to whom they delegate is likely to be a function of their theory of action and of additional principles of legitimate authority they may try to accommodate.

The common model has tended to displace locally elected school boards as the primary agencies to whom educators are accountable and to replace them with state governments and Congress. Local school districts are more likely to be held accountable than to hold their employees accountable. As test results work their way into teacher evaluations, the common model has the tendency to centralize even local decision-making over teacher retention and salaries.

The common model thus has the consequence of centralizing authority over educational decision-making and taking responsibility out of the hands of locally elected officials, local schools, and those who do the work. It is reasonably clear, when content standards are set at the state level, that goal setting is taken out of the hands of educators (Strike, 1997, 1998). When educators are held accountable for test results, the consequences may be broader. When the state determines the "what" of education (University of the State of New York, 1994) and holds educators accountable for it, local discussions about goals and standards tend to lose their point, and educators will stop asking themselves questions about what constitutes a good education and the means they can employ to provide it; instead, they will start asking themselves how to raise test scores. To the extent that Campbell's law is true, these are different questions. One is more likely to get goal distortion and gaming than better education. Moreover, it is an easy step from measuring achievement to mandating how to raise it. States may mandate programs or practices. Educators shift from reflection on their work to compliance.

This shift may be accompanied by a decline in morale. Teachers are, in effect, being deprofessionalized. Such a situation will have potential consequences for teacher retention (Crocco & Costigan, 2007).

Unjust Distribution of Outcomes and Consequences

NCLB disaggregates test results by demographic categories and requires schools to show progress in each. This might be thought of as an attempt to prevent a kind of gaming—one where schools compensate for the poor performance of some populations by concentrating resources on those who give more achievement "bang for the buck." This provision of NCLB seems to me to be reasonable. It does, however, invite a different form of gaming. Schools may attempt to move high-performing students into low-performing categories or low-performing students into high-performing categories so as to reduce the risk of failing to meet a benchmark in each group. This kind of demographic gerrymandering is most likely in areas (such as special education) where there can be some discretion in how children are classified. As a result, some children may receive inappropriate or inadequate resources.

A second issue concerns the consequences of accountability for the allocation of resources. NCLB provides some incentive for districts to provide more resources for schools that are most at risk of being considered low-performing. It would be an especially attractive feature of the common model were it to lead districts to abandon seniority provisions in teacher contracts that allow senior teachers to opt out of low-performing schools. These provisions are especially problematic in large districts.

A third concern is that any negative impact of accountability efforts that express the common model will probably be visited most severely on those schools most likely to fail to meet some benchmark. Schools that are seen as being in danger of failure will be under the most pressure to raise test scores. Although this may mean that they will be under pressure to adopt instructional strategies that are successful in raising test scores, it also means that they are most likely to face and to succumb to perverse incentives. If the common model produces goal reduction or goal distortion, these ills are apt to affect potentially failing schools. If there are perverse incentives that lead to gaming, these are most likely to affect potentially failing schools. If there are penalties that are destabilizing, failing schools will be their victims. If there are declines in morale, these will be felt most strongly in potentially failing schools. In effect, this means that negative consequences of the common model are likely to be felt most strongly in those schools that serve many poor and minority students. This is the case both because these children typically perform less well and because diverse schools serve more demographic groups with which they must succeed. These schools are disproportionately urban schools.

A related concern is that schools that are found to be failing or that are perceived as in danger of failing are most likely to be subjected to externally imposed mandates intended to improve their performance. However, it has been argued (Anyon, 1997) that numerous and conflicting mandates are themselves causes of failure. Chubb and Moe (1990) argue that the loss of autonomy is also a cause of failure.

A final concern with the common model is that it expresses and sustains an ideology that misdirects attention from the real causes of urban school failure and supports a schools-only approach to inequality. The evidence that schools are not able to overcome the educational consequences of poverty and that real educational gains by poor urban students require a broader approach that addresses the circumstances of poor children's lives seems to me to be compelling (Anyon, 2005; Berliner, 2006; Rothstein, 2002, 2004). As Anyon (1997, p. 168) suggests, "Attempting to fix inner city schools without fixing the city in which they are embedded is like trying to clean the air on one side of a screen door." Indeed, although socioeconomic status (SES) is not destiny, the evidence for the substantial effects of SES on achievement has been persuasive ever since the Coleman report (Coleman, 1968; Coleman et al., 1966). The common model is a part of a larger view of school reform that is sustained by clichés such as "no excuses," and "the soft discrimination of low expectations." When policy persistently runs counter to evidence, it is reasonable to view it as ideological (Strike, 2005).

Many of the problems with the common model concern the perverse incentive generated for miseducative behavior. How serious are these concerns? The critique I have made is somewhat hypothetical. Is there evidence to support the claim that these problems are real problems rather than theoretical ones? There is much commentary on these issues; yet much of the evidence is anecdotal or based on surveys. Some of the best recent discussions of accountability suggest that these concerns are quite serious. Rothstein et al. (2008) provide a detailed account of the negative impact of a few quantitative indicators to make policy and personnel decisions in a number of areas. Nichols and Berliner (2007) provide an extensive documentation of the negative consequences of high-stakes testing in education. Other studies have shown the consequences of the common model for urban schools. Crocco and Costigan (2007, p. 512) summarize the results of their New York City study of the consequences of high-stakes testing:

> Under the curricular and pedagogical impositions of scripted lessons and mandated curriculum, patterns associated nationwide with high-stakes testing, the No Child Left Behind Act of 2001, and the phenomenon known as the "narrowing of curriculum," new teachers in New York City (NYC) find their personal and professional identity thwarted, creativity and autonomy undermined, and ability to forge relationships with students diminished—all critical factors in their expressed job satisfaction. These indirect consequences of accountability

regimen as it operates in NYC may exacerbate new teacher attrition, especially from schools serving low-income students.

Amrein and Berliner (2002) have done a systematic examination of the overall effectiveness of the common model as expressed in high-stakes testing. They document a range of the negative behaviors and undesirable consequences that have resulted, and they note that because high-stakes tests for graduation are used disproportionately by states with high percentages of minority students, these students are disproportionately affected by the resulting negative consequences. Amrein and Berliner (2002) summarized the results of their analysis of data from 18 states as follows:

> Evidence from this study of 18 states with high-stakes tests is that in all but one analysis, student learning is indeterminate, remains at the same level it was before the policy was implemented, or actually goes down when high-stakes testing policies are instituted. Because clear evidence for increased student learning is not found, and because there are numerous reports of unintended consequences associated with high-stakes testing policies (increased drop-out rates, teachers' and schools' cheating on exams, teachers' defection from the profession, all predicted by the uncertainly principle), it is concluded that there is need for debate and transformation of current high-stakes testing policies.

Of course, as far as assessing the consequences on high-stakes testing on achievement is concerned, there are numerous studies and metastudies done with varying degrees of rigor. As is the case in many areas of educational research on complex matters, their results are, to say the least, inconsistent, and one can always find studies to support one's views, whatever they may be. Nevertheless, there is plenty of evidence pointing to the validity of the claim that accountability strategies that depend on high-stakes testing are not especially effective in raising achievement and that, in fact, they have many undesirable consequences. We should therefore, at the very least, be motivated to look at alternatives.

Accountability and Legitimate Authority

What are the roots of these problems? I want to point to two connected factors. I think that the theory of action, relying as it does on incentivizing educators, is substantially wrong and that the political norms it assumes are unbalanced. I have suggested that there are three norms of legitimate authority that inform the common model: the central meaning of democracy is the sovereignty of an elected legislature, education is substantially a public good appropriately subject to democratic decision-making, and education should be the responsibility of states or of the national government.

When we add to this mix a theory of action that emphasizes incentives, considerable suspicion of the efficacy of local government, and legal understandings that make education a state responsibility, the result is an attempt to design a management system for education that rewards effective behavior and sanctions ineffective behavior. This system is mandated and managed by the U.S. government and the states in some combination. These entities must determine desired outcomes, find suitable and cost-effective ways to decide whether they have been met, and, when they are not, find ways either to assist or incentivize.

The crucial difficulties with a system of this sort are, in my judgment, first, that educational systems are too complex and the outcomes we want from them too varied and subjective to be managed in this way, and, second, that a culture of local competence and responsibility is undermined.

My critique of the three political principles underlying the common model is not that they are wrong; it is that they are unbalanced. Legislatures, after all, can delegate and forbear from exercising the authority they have. A more decentralized system of accountability is consistent with the three principles. But if we are to consider a more decentralized system we will have to articulate additional norms of legitimate authority.

What I offer here is a rather aphoristic characterization of four views of legitimate authority. I then show how an alternative view of accountability can be generated from each of these views. In the final section I discuss what a reasonable balance looks like.

The following are four views of legitimate authority together with an aphorism that captures its spirit:

- **Legislative sovereignty** Democratic authority means the sovereignty of an elected legislature over those matters that are properly viewed as public matters. (*All power to the legislature.*)
- **Consumer sovereignty** In free societies it is the choices of consumers that should determine what is produced. Consumers and producers should engage in free exchanges without undue government regulation. (*All power to the market.*)
- **Professionalism** Decisions should be made by those with the appropriate knowledge and skill to make them wisely. (*Those who know should rule.*)
- **Democratic localism** Decisions should be made by local communities of those most directly affected by them and through fair, discursive, consensus-seeking forums. (*All power to the people.*)

Legislative Sovereignty

The view of legitimate authority here is Lockean (Locke, 1960; Strike, 1993). Human beings, claims Locke, are naturally free and equal. This being the case, no one is entitled by nature to rule and no one is a natural slave. The authority of the government, therefore, must rest in the consent of the governed. That consent is expressed through elections and results in the sovereignty of a properly elected legislature. The authority of this government is, however, limited by rights that individuals continue to possess. It is this view—together with a Weberian vision of how the authority of the legislature is to be exercised as well as the presumption that education is a matter of public concern more than a matter of individual liberty—that supports the common model of accountability.

Consumer Sovereignty

The idea of consumer sovereignty can be expressed as two claims, one normative and one empirical. The normative claim is that, other things being equal, people have a right to want what they want and to express their preferences through their choices in the market. Preferences, as one commentator (Monk, 1990) notes, have moral force. If this is the case, then governments should not gratuitously interfere with the market and may do so largely only to secure public goods. Public goods are commonly understood to be those goods that, because of externalities or neighborhood effects, are not adequately secured by the market. Some philosophers (e.g., Nozick, 1974) have argued that justice requires an economic system in which goods are distributed through free transactions among willing participants.

The second claim is that markets are a more efficient means of satisfying consumer preferences than government provision or regulation. An economic system in which providers are free to offer such goods and services as they wish on the market and in which consumers are free to choose those they wish to buy creates a society in which producers succeed by satisfying the wants of consumers. In the famous words of Adam Smith, social welfare is secured "as by an invisible hand." Milton Friedman (1958) characterizes the market as creating "cooperation without coercion." These assumptions have been applied to education in a now classic chapter by Friedman (1962), who argues that although there are public goods associated with education (largely the need for shared values), these public goods make a case only for public financing of education but not for public provision. Education would be more efficiently provided by markets than by a public bureaucracy.

Professionalism

Professionalism can be viewed as the expression of the Platonic aphorism "Those who know should rule." The essential idea is that authority should be put in the hands of those who have the knowledge and skill required to make just decisions, set proper goals, and carry their plans out competently. Those who emphasize professionalism in education (Darling-Hammond, 1985) typically claim that there is an esoteric knowledge base that educators must master if they are to practice competently.

Professions are held to be self-regulating in several ways. First, professionals are held to be entitled to considerable autonomy in their practice. Second, individual practitioners are held to be motivated and guided by professional standards and by a client-centered ethic. Regulation is self-regulation. Third, professionals have a role in legitimating the standards that govern their practice. Fourth, when practice is collective and collaborative, professionals deliberate with one another to determine what constitutes best practice. They form a kind of collegium. Fifth, professionals set standards for the education and certification of new members of the profession. Finally, professionals may be involved in disciplining those who are guilty of unprofessional conduct.

Gutmann (1987) has argued for a somewhat different conception of professionalism that deemphasizes the importance of an esoteric knowledge base and places more emphasis on the role of teachers in developing a critical perspective among their students. It is the need to protect teachers in the performance of this role that warrants some measure of autonomy.

Democratic Localism

I represent this view as a synthesis of three related ideas. The first comes from what is called discourse ethics or deliberative democracy (Gutmann & Thompson, 1996, 2004; Habermas, 1990; Young, 2000). Habermas characterizes just decisions as arising from an open and undominated discourse in which all interested speakers can argue their views and all relevant views can be heard and considered. Just decisions express the power of the better argument and express a consensus that those who are affected can accept. Just decisions reconcile autonomy with governmental authority in that they shape the will, such that people wish to do what they ought to do. Gutmann (1987) expresses a similar view in *Democratic Education* through her emphasis on the principles of nonrepression and non-discrimination. Deliberative democracy has often distinguished itself from what Young (2000) calls aggregative democracy, which sees the role of democracy as vectoring interests so as to maximize the satisfaction of preferences without critiquing these interests. Nussbaum (1997, p. 19) captures the zeitgeist of deliberative democracy in the following:

> Socratic argument . . . is essential to a strong democracy and to any lasting pursuit of justice. In order to foster a democracy that is reflective and deliberative, rather than simply a marketplace of competing interest groups, a democracy that takes thought for the common good, we must produce citizens who have the Socratic capacity to reason about their beliefs . . . To unmask prejudice and to secure justice, we need argument, an essential tool of civic freedom.

A second feature of this view of democracy is the idea that democratic political participation is an intrinsic good that deserves a place in any individual citizen's conception of a good life.

A third idea is that these values are best expressed where possible through local democratic forums. Local democratic participation cultivates competence, responsibility, and democratic character.

Alternative Models of Accountability

An ideal/typical view of accountability might be developed through an emphasis on each of the last three views of legitimate authority. (Recall that the common model captures legislative sovereignty.) Again, these are ideal types. The point is not to choose one of them but to get a better picture of the values a reasonable view of accountability needs to accommodate and to determine how to balance these values in an effective system.

In each case, I consider how an ideal type constructed on the basis of each view might answer the three questions I have used to characterize a model of accountability and what its associated theory of action might be like. I also discuss a potential line of criticism of the common model from the perspective of each view.

Consumer Sovereignty

Consumer sovereignty is typically expressed through a choice scheme of some sort in which quasi-markets and competition are created.

1. **Who is accountable?** Here, as with the common model, educators are accountable. Here too they are typically accountable as members of an individual school, but now they are accountable under the description of service providers.
2. **To whom are they accountable?** Educators are responsible to consumers who "vote with their feet," their choices, or (indirectly, since under most choice schemes money follows the student) their dollars.
3. **For what are they accountable?** Ultimately, consumer sovereignty makes educators accountable for satisfying the preferences of consumers, or more accurately, for satisfying the preferences of some segment of the education market that they are able to attract to their school.

The Theory of Action

The theory of action that follows from the idea of consumer sovereignty has two main features. First, an education system that permits choice among diversified educational options is more likely to be a better educational system simply because it satisfies the diverse preferences people actually have. Here it should be noted that the preferences likely to be satisfied are not necessarily those of the children who attend but are those of their families who make the choice of a school for their children. This suggests that the range of options available in a choice system should be constrained not only by some notion of the public good but also by a conception of the basic interests of the child (Brighouse, 2000).

Second, the competition among providers requires them to make efficient and effective use of their resources so as to attract sufficient students to fund their operation. Competition, thus, aligns the interest of educational producers and consumers.

Critique of the Common Model

Two main lines of criticism of the common model follow. First, the common model is not responsive to the diversity of consumer preferences. In fact, the common model, because it needs educational standards for an entire educational system (typically created at the state level) tends to standardize the content of an educational system. Its test-driven curriculum will reflect a vision of education that is politically negotiated. It will also be influenced by the needs of the accountability system itself, since that system requires the ability to compare different schools.

It should be noted here, however, that advocates of choice often do not reject state-generated standards and the testing regimes rooted in them. They are, however, more likely to see these testing regimes as means to provide consumers with information than they are as a management tool to be employed by state bureaucracies.

The second implied criticism of the common model that follows from the idea of consumer sovereignty is that markets are a more efficient way of incentivizing educators than are the incentives that public bureaucracies are able to generate. Advocates of choice and educational markets may see goal distortion and perverse incentives to game the system as confirmation of this view. They are also likely to claim that teachers' unions and the bureaucracies of school districts will find ways to protect their interests against any incentives that the common model attempts to impose. Here it is worth noting that the incentives generated by NCLB typically do not threaten teachers either with loss of salary or position.

Professionalism

Educators are viewed as forming a kind of self-regulating guild.

1. **Who is accountable?** Professional educators are accountable. They are, however, accountable under the descriptor "professional," which serves to grant them some level of autonomy in their practice and accords their judgments some measure of respect.
2. **To whom are they accountable?** Educators are accountable to themselves individually and collectively. The assumption is that professionals are internally motivated to make judgments rooted in professional standards and that they will act in the best interests of their "clients." They are accountable to one another in that professionals legitimate professional standards, some decisions concerning professional practice are made collectively, and because professionals have a role in socializing and disciplining one another.
3. **For what are they accountable?** Educators are accountable for regulating their practice by those professional standards that should govern practice and for following the norms of a client-centered ethic.

The Theory of Action

Ceding considerable authority to professional educators individually and collectively might be justified on the following grounds. First, the decisions required to teach effectively require expertise to make them competently. These decisions cannot be made by individuals without the proper training and experience. Nor can they easily be captured by rules or systems. They require complex judgments made in situ and that take into account many context factors. Second, good teaching is difficult to incentivize by any system of reward and punishments. It is better to rely on intrinsic motivation. Teachers must care about ideas, the quality of their work, and their students. Good schools are places that create a professional culture where newer teachers are socialized into norms that encourage professionalism and professional collaboration.

I have not found the claims that professionals possess a body of expertise about teaching that grounds their practice convincing (Strike, 1990, 1993). Such a body of knowledge would need to be generally agreed upon by the profession, and it would be difficult or impossible to practice if one did not possess it. But theories about pedagogy are notorious for producing durable disagreements, and it seems that there are many fine teachers who manage to practice competently without possessing the kinds of esoteric knowledge that have been claimed to ground their practice. There is nothing about pedagogical knowledge that grounds pedagogical practice in the same way as the body of accumulated medical knowledge grounds medical practice. Moreover, professionalism is undemocratic. It seeks to ground authority in expertise rather than in the consent provided by democratic participation. We should be especially suspicious of claims of professionalism in education where the promotion of democratic norms is particularly important and where proposals to professionalize the field seem likely to enhance the power of teachers' unions more than to promote the rule of reason.

These comments should not, however, be taken to mean that the wisdom and experience of accomplished teachers should be devalued. Nor does it suggest that the academic study of teaching has no point. Theories that are not known to be true nevertheless can provide concepts that enhance perception and judgment. Moreover, the role of teachers in teaching subject matter with integrity and teaching so as to enhance the critical capacity of their students is central to their role. These considerations do justify some forms of autonomy for teachers in their professional roles.

Moreover, it is important that teachers function as what I have called a collegium. When teachers in a given school function as a collegium, they cooperate in planning, implementing, and evaluating their school's educational programs. They hold themselves accountable one to another. The discussions of a collegium help to share a pool of collective wisdom and ideas and to mentor new teachers. A well-functioning collegium is also important in creating and maintaining a task-oriented professional work environment. It performs a crucial socializing role.

Critique of the Common Model

The theory of action suggests several criticisms of the common model. It may undermine intrinsic motivation by making educators subservient to bureaucratically generated incentives rather than their own best judgment. It may also undermine the effective working of a collegium by separating the process of monitoring from implementation. These things are especially likely if the common model produces goal reduction or gaming. The common model may incentivize some collaboration toward meeting benchmarks, but unless its incentives align well with teachers' considered judgments about the nature of a good education, it is unlikely to promote a sense of professionalism and attention to the requirements of a client-centered ethic. It may, instead, produce an alienated work environment where teachers feel that their professionalism and competence are not respected.

Democratic Localism

Democratic localism[2] sees the school as a democratic community and emphasizes deliberative processes where all members of the community have opportunity to be heard and to influence decisions.

1. **Who is accountable?** Here, as in other views, educators are accountable, but other members of the community, students, and parents are also accountable. They are accountable as members of a community united in the pursuit of self-chosen common goods.
2. **To whom are they accountable?** Members of democratic communities are accountable to one another.
3. **For what are they accountable?** They are accountable for fulfilling their roles in achieving collectively self-chosen goals. These goals include not only typical academic goals but also creating democratic citizens, respecting the equal dignity of members of the community, and helping to maintain democratic norms and practices.

The Theory of Action

The theory of action of this model of accountability emphasizes that importance of participation in creating a sense of community, commitment to its goals, respect for its decisions, and trust. Members of communities are not alienated from the work of their communities because they see it as their work. They are able to trust one another because they see other members of the community as committed to the same goals to which they are committed. They are able to deliberate effectively with one another on planning and evaluating their mutual efforts because they have a core of agreement about what their shared goals are and how to pursue them. Their deliberations function not only as ways to make decisions, resolve disagreements, and assess progress toward goals, but also to help socialize members to value the norms and goods of the community, and they build competence and skill concerning how shared goals may be effectively pursued. To put the point in a somewhat different way, deliberative, democratic communities tend to build social capital.

Critique of the Common Model

From the perspective of local/participatory democracy, the common model undermines democratic deliberation by taking much of the deliberation that should take place within the community and centralizing it in a way that removes it from the local community. As a consequence, members of the local community are no longer pursuing self-chosen goals. They are, instead, seeking to comply with externally imposed mandates and expectations. The result is likely to be the loss of intrinsic motivation and an alienated work environment for teachers, students, and their families. Trust is likely to diminish as people see themselves as working toward incentives that are not rooted in shared goals.

What Would a Synthesis Look Like?

Where does this take us? I have argued that the common model of accountability encourages goal distortion and gaming, and I have suggested that its implicit view of educational authority has become unbalanced in that it is not attentive to the norms of other views. Although I have not been able in the space of a chapter to argue for much of what I have suggested, and this warrants some modesty in making strong claims about future directions, nevertheless I think the various positions taken do point toward certain goals. The following are some of the conclusions I believe we should entertain.

First, education has three characteristics that make centralized goal formation, monitoring, and incentivizing problematic. Its goals are "soft." They are difficult to measure by inexpensive tests, their expression often depends on context, and judgments as to whether they have been accomplished often require an expert observer. It is very difficult to capture them well in a test-driven accountability system without producing goal distortion and gaming. Bureaucratic control over complex systems with soft goals is likely to lead to results that look more like those of the Soviet Union's five-year plans than it is to produce truly useful educational systems.

Second, although reasonable people can disagree both about the kinds of choice we should have in the United States and about why we should have it, I am hopeful that we might agree at least that some diversity in educational goals and pedagogical approaches is important if we are to serve all of our children well. We want schools that reflect local needs and that fit different kinds of students. We do not want to aim at the one best system. While there are also some reasons why some standardization of curriculum is useful—for example, in a mobile society, children must be able to transfer from one school to another without great difficulty—there are no good educational reasons why every school should offer the same program in the same way as every other school. We should not create such a system merely because the effective monitoring of outcomes requires it.

Third, although teachers may not be professionals only because they possess a body of esoteric knowledge that warrants substantial authority over education, they do bring training, experience, and subject matter expertise to their work. This wisdom is not just about pedagogical techniques. It includes conceptions of how the goals of a good education are to be understood. This means that teachers need to be empowered to reflect on, evaluate, and make decisions about their work. An accountability system that transfers monitoring of the quality of teachers' work to remote others is disempowering. Moreover, intrinsic motivation is important to the success of schools. People rarely become teachers because they wish to become rich. They become teachers because they care about ideas and about children. Systems of accountability that emphasize external monitoring and centralized goal formation and that focus on creating incentives for performance tend to undermine intrinsic motivation.

Finally, the families that send their children to a given school need the opportunity to participate in the deliberations of the schools on fair terms. What counts as fair terms is a complex matter and must reflect the different levels of responsibility between parents and teachers, and the different level of maturity between students and adults. Nevertheless, this right to participate should go beyond the right merely to be informed and to comment. Families should be viewed as a part of the school's educational community, and mechanisms should be created whereby they can participate in its deliberations.

I believe that the implications of these views can be succinctly stated as follows. Accountability should not be viewed as a process in which schools are held responsible for objectives that are defined by the legislature and its agents through a bureaucratic process that monitors outcomes and incentivizes performance. Rather, accountability should be a process in which the members of educational communities are accountable to the community by means of deliberative practices through which they choose and refine goals, create programs, assess them regularly, and seek to improve them on an ongoing basis. The focus of accountability should be how to create and maintain schools that do this well.

This is not to say that the state has no role. The legislature remains the sovereign authority, but its role should be differently conceived and executed. It should first of all establish the goal of creating educational communities that take effective responsibility for their programs as its first priority in creating an accountable educational system. It needs to grant the required autonomy, develop models of effective school governance, and provide training and resources. I do not suggest that the legislature should altogether abandon its role of monitoring the effectiveness of its schools. Educators are, after all, human beings. They will screw up. When they do, the state should take notice. However, monitoring should not create a test-driven system. Monitoring should include inspections and discussions with educators as well as some testing. The first objective should be school improvement through appropriate kinds of assistance. Before a school is closed or reconstituted, the state should assure itself that all reasonable remedies have been tried, but there should not be a system of penalties linked to system-wide benchmarks. Test data should trigger an inquiry, not penalties.

Here are some principles that should govern a balanced, community-oriented, and flexible system of accountability:

1. *Accountability should primarily be to the community, its students, and to professional standards, especially those that define high-quality teaching and learning.* It should be only secondarily to an educational bureaucracy or a legislature and its agents.
2. *Accountability should enhance community, local responsibility, and local governance.* Accountability should contribute to an environment in which those who do the work of educating take responsibility for the quality and effectiveness of their work. It should create a sense of ownership for educational programs within the community. Democratic localism should not be undermined. Accountability should not be alienating. Socialization for responsible community membership should be emphasized over monitoring and incentivizing.
3. *Educational goals should be chosen prior to and independently of the selection of the instruments of accountability.* Goals should be chosen because they are what we want schools to accomplish and because there are good reasons for them. They should be chosen by the local school within a framework developed by the state. They should not be chosen because they are easily measured or quantified or because they satisfy the needs of policymakers.
4. *All goals should be assessed.*

5. *Goals should be assessed in ways that are appropriate to their character.* When goals involve capacities that are best expressed through performance, they should be assessed by the observations of performances that are as close as is feasible to the normal expression of these capacities.
6. *Goals should not be assessed in ways that distort the curriculum or teaching.*
7. *Accountability should aim to inform the community and provide evidence that is relevant to instructional improvement.*
8. *Accountability should aim to assist rather than to coerce.* An acceptable view of accountability should aim first of all to improve education by providing information useful to those who do the work of educating concerning how instruction can be improved. It should be formative rather than summative.
9. *Accountability schemes should not have perverse incentives.* They should not "incentivize" gaming.
10. *State governments should assist schools to function as self-monitoring, self-improving communities. They should also monitor their success through inspections as well as some testing.* Tests should not be high-stakes tests. They should trigger an inquiry. Governments should aim first and foremost to help. Coercive measures should be a last resort.

What vision of accountability meets these criteria? I suggested earlier in this chapter that views of accountability can be defined by answers to three questions as well as their theory of action. Here is my alternative to the common model.

1. **Who is accountable?** Educators are accountable, but they are not accountable primarily as employees. They are accountable as professionals and as community members. Other members of the school community are accountable for fulfilling their roles as community members.
2. **To whom are educators accountable?** Educators are accountable primarily to the school community, to students and their families, and to their professional communities.
3. **For what are educators accountable?** They are accountable for effectively providing the educational program that the members of the school community have chosen, for teaching to high standards, and for maintaining the community.

Modern views of school reform and accountability have often been seen as responses to the failure of local government to adequately monitor the quality of education (Bryk et al., 1998; Rothstein et al., 2008). Here the local government that was seen as failing was the local school district. Large urban schools systems were viewed with special concern. They were seen as overly bureaucratic, inflexible, and largely unresponsive to the needs of children. The proposed solution was to centralize some functions of educational governance at the state level while devolving others onto the local school. The state would set standards but local schools would have considerable autonomy to figure out how to meet these standards. The expression "the state determines the 'what' and the local school determines the 'how'" is the canonical expression of this view.

This is not how it has worked out. Few schools, especially urban schools, have received the autonomy that was promised. They have continued to be plagued with conflicting mandates and intense bureaucratic scrutiny, which is as often as not the expression of the desire of officials to maintain their fiefdoms. The standards movement as it is now expressed through accountability systems that emphasize high-stakes testing seems to have increased the bureaucratization of school systems. Urban schools are more likely to be victims of this system than beneficiaries. We need an accountability system, the first objective of which is to restore responsibility for their work to those who do it.

Notes

1. For a critique of the underlying assumptions of current school reform efforts and an elaborated alternative, see Strike (2010).
2. The term *democratic localism* is used by Bryk et al. (1998) to characterize the philosophy underlying the Chicago School Reform Act of 1988. They view it as part of a larger picture of urban reform that seeks to reinvigorate urban communities through democratic participation.

References

Amrein, A. L., & Berliner, D. C. (2002). High-stakes testing, uncertainty, and student learning (electronic version). *Education Policy Analysis Archives, 10*. Retrieved May 17, 2011 from: http://epaa.asu.edu/epaa/v10n18

Anyon, J. (1997). *Ghetto schooling: A political economy of urban educational reform.* New York: Teachers College Press.

Anyon, J. (2005). *Radical possibilities: Public policy, urban education, and a new social movement.* New York: Routledge.

Berliner, D. C. (2006). Our impoverished view of educational research. *Teachers College Record, 108*(6), 949–995.

Brighouse, H. (2000). *School choice and social justice.* Oxford, UK: Oxford University Press.

Bryk, A. S., Sebring, P. B., Kerbow, D., Rollow, S., & Easton, J. Q. (1998). *Charting Chicago school reform.* Boulder, CO: Westview Press.

Campbell, D. T. (1976). *Assessing the impact of planned social change.* Dartmouth, NH: The Public Affairs Center, Dartmouth College.

Chubb, J. E., & Moe, T. M. (1990). *Politics, markets, and the American school.* Washington DC: Brookings Institution.

Coleman, J. (1968). The concept of equal opportunity. *Harvard Educational Review, 38*, 7–22.

Coleman, J. S. et al. (1966). *Equality of educational opportunity.* Washington, DC: U.S. Department of Health, and Welfare, Office of Education/National Center for Education Statistics.

Crocco, M. S., & Costigan, A. T. (2007). The narrowing of curriculum and pedagogy in the age of accountability: Urban educators speak out. *Urban Education, 42*(6), 512–535.

Darling-Hammond, L. (1985). Valuing teachers: The making of a profession. *Teachers College Record, 8*(2), 205–218.

Friedman, M. (1958). Introduction to I Pencil. In *I, Pencil: My family tree as told to Leonard E. Read.* Irvington-on-Hudson, NY: The Foundation for Economic Education.

Friedman, M. (1962). *Capitalism and freedom.* Chicago: University of Chicago Press.

Goals 2000. Educate America Act (1993). Retrieved May 17, 2011 from: www2.ed.gov/legislation/GOALS2000/TheAct/index.html

Gutmann, A. (1987). *Democratic education.* Princeton, NJ: Princeton University Press.

Gutmann, A., & Thompson, D. (1996). *Democracy and disagreement.* Cambridge, MA: Harvard University Press.

Gutmann, A., & Thompson, D. (2004). *Why deliberative democracy.* Princeton, NJ: Princeton University Press.

Habermas, J. (1990). *Moral consciousness and communicative action* (C. N. Lenhardt, Shierry Weber, Trans.). Cambridge, MA: The MIT Press.

Locke, J. (1960). *Two treatises of government.* New York: Cambridge University Press.

McCaffrey, D. F., Koretz, D., Lockwood, J. R., & Hamilton, L. S. (2003). *Evaluating value-added models for teacher accountability.* Santa Monica, CA: RAND Corporation.

Monk, D. H. (1990). *Educational finance: An economic approach.* New York: McGraw-Hill.

National Commission on Excellence in Education (1983). *A nation at risk.* Washington, DC: U.S. Department of Education.

Nichols, S. L., & Berliner, D. C. (2007). *Collateral damage: How high-stakes testing corrupts America's schools.* Cambridge, MA: Harvard Education Press.

No Child Left Behind Act (2002). Executive Summary. Retrieved May 17, 2011 from: www2.ed.gov/nclb/overview/intro/execsumm/html

Nozick, R. (1974). *Anarchy, state, and utopia.* New York: Basic Books.

Nussbaum, M. (1997). *Cultivating humanity: A classical defense of reform in liberal education.* Cambridge, MA: Harvard University Press.

O'Day, J. A., & Smith, M. S. (1993). Systemic reform and educational opportunity. In S. H. Fuhrman (Ed.), *Designing coherent educational policy* (pp. 250–312). San Francisco, CA: Jossey-Bass.

Rothstein, R. (2002). *Out of balance: Our understanding of how schools affect society and society affects schools.* The Spencer Foundation 30th Anniversary Essay. Chicago: The Spencer Foundation.

Rothstein, R. (2004). *Class and schools: Using social, economic, and educational reform to close the Black–White achievement gap.* New York: Teachers College Press.

Rothstein, R., Jacobson, R., & Wilder, T. (2008). *Grading education: Getting accountability right.* New York and Washington, DC: Economic Policy Institute and Teachers College Press.

Strike, K. A. (1990). Is teaching a profession: How would we know? *Journal of Personnel Evaluation in Education, 4*, 91–117.

Strike, K. A. (1993). Professionalism, democracy, and discursive communities: Normative reflections on restructuring. *American Educational Research Journal, 30*(2), 255–275.

Strike, K. A. (1997). Centralized goal formation and systemic reform: Reflections on liberty, localism, and pluralism. *Educational Policy Analysis, 5*(11). Retrieved July 11, 2011 from: http://epaa.edu/ojs/article/viewFile/612/734

Strike, K. A. (1998). Centralized goal formation, citizenship, and educational pluralism: Accountability in liberal democracies. *Educational Policy, 12*(1&2), 203–215.

Strike, K. A. (2005). Review of Richard Rothstein: Class and schools: Using social, economic, and educational reform to close the Black–White achievement gap. *American Journal of Education, 11*(3), 414–420.

Strike, K. A. (2006). *Ethical leadership in schools: Creating community in an environment of accountability.* Thousand Oaks, CA: Corwin Press.

Strike, K. A. (2010). *Small schools & strong communities: A third way of school reform.* New York: Teachers College Press.

University of the State of New York (1994). *A new compact for learning.* Albany, NY: The State Education Department.

Young, I. M. (2000). *Inclusion and democracy.* Oxford, UK: Oxford University Press.

IV
Learning and Motivation

Learning and motivation underlie the core work of educational institutions. This section focuses on the variety of ways that current work on teaching, learning, and motivation is tackling the special issues confronting urban schools, particularly with respect to their increasing racial, ethnic, linguistic, and social class diversity.

19

Motivation for Academic Achievement in Urban American Schools

Cynthia Hudley and Vichet Chhuon

Much has been written about the pervasive disengagement of students in urban schools, an observation that has a direct bearing on motivation for academic achievement. The following selective review examines the evidence on levels of student motivation in urban American schools. To establish the context of our review, we must first define and delimit our use of the construct *urban schools*. Although the term *urban* can be associated with culture, refinement, and highly developed civilization, as in *urbane*, the phrase *urban schools* in education research typically has a negative valence (Leonardo & Hunter, 2007). In an educational context, *urban* typically refers to a metropolitan area confronting a broad range of social problems, including a lack of employment opportunities and commercial services, high levels of criminal activity, substandard housing, and poor and disadvantaged residents, most of whom are members of ethnic minority groups. The term *urban schools* typically refers to institutions in these metropolitan areas that serve largely low-income students of color (i.e., African American, Latino, and Southeast Asian students), and the schools in these areas are perceived as the site of social problems. While the populations and social and economic challenges in some suburban areas and small cities are similar to those in large metropolitan areas (Foster, 2007), our review of motivation in urban schools will confine itself to large metropolitan districts. Although we use this more restrictive definition, we remain cognizant of the fact that urban schools are defined more often by racial and socioeconomic characteristics than by geographic location.

Demographic data (Council of the Great City Schools, 2008) help to further clarify our use of the term *urban schools*. Schools in cities with populations over 250,000 or districts with student enrollment over 35,000 represent 12% of the schools, 14% of the teachers, and 15% of the students in public school in the United States. Yet they enroll 32% of African American students, 29% of English language learners, and 26% of all minority students in public schools. In schools comprising this category (i.e., urban American schools), an average of 64% of all students receive free or reduced price lunches, indicating that their families are near or below the national poverty level. Most important for our discussion, all students in urban schools are often represented in the education literature as poorly motivated and "at risk" for school and social failure. However, we would be remiss in ignoring the reality that students in urban schools who struggle academically are more often seen as unmotivated or conduct-disordered, while struggling affluent, White children receive services (e.g., counseling, tutoring) to improve learning (Bowles & Gintis, 1976). Such services are less often freely available in urban schools and economically out of reach for low-income, minority parents who might wish to purchase such services from commercial providers.

Institutional Effects

A substantial portion of the motivation literature has examined a range of psychological variables including goals, self-perceptions, and the perceived environment. Because theories guiding academic research on achievement motivation have come primarily from psychology, there has been a tendency in the past to view motivation at school as a within-child phenomenon that is entirely under the volitional control of the student. However, recent literature has more closely examined the role of school conditions and school culture (Hudley & Gottfried, 2008) in shaping student achievement and motivation. Before turning to the relatively larger body of work on psychological variables, we therefore begin with a selective review of the impact of school environments on academic achievement motivation in urban schools.

The School Quality

Unequal schooling is an insidious contributor to social inequality; this is a particular problem in urban schools and a predictor of both student achievement and student engagement (Uline & Tschannen-Moran, 2008). The U.S. Department of Education reported a decade ago that physical conditions in urban schools are predictive of academic engagement and performance (Lewis, Parsad, Carey, Farris, & Smerdon, 1999). However, these authors conclude that basic materials—including textbooks, science equipment, and even desks—are generally in disrepair or absent in urban schools. The academic quality of urban schools has also been questioned, as the proportions of certified teachers (Shen & Poppink, 2003), beginning rather than veteran teachers (U.S. Department of Education, 2003), and college-preparatory or advanced placement offerings (Freel, 1998) lag significantly behind suburban schools and those serving more advantaged populations. Research has examined a number of motivational consequences of these physical and academic conditions.

A body of literature has documented the suppression of student motivation and aspirations by underfunded, poorly resourced urban schools. Simple structural conditions such as dirty bathrooms, structural decay, vermin, and overcrowding that are rampant in many urban schools have severe psychological and motivational costs for students. Theories of stress and coping when applied to educational settings find that these stressors undermine students' ability to concentrate and to learn, particularly the comprehension of complex and difficult material (Lepore & Evans, 1996). Lack of concentration, or poor "on-task behavior," is one of the universally agreed upon signs of low motivation and disengagement in students. Decrepit conditions also create in students, particularly high school students, a powerful sense of alienation and abandonment (Fine, Burns, Payne, & Torre, 2004; Kozol, 1991). Primarily qualitative data reveal that urban, low-income secondary school students of color are deeply aware of the systemic inequity that leaves them but not their more affluent White peers in schools that are physically decayed, filthy, overcrowded, and lacking in basic tools of learning (e.g., science labs, gyms, technology). Some students in blighted urban schools believe that the poor quality of school facilities indicates that society wishes to move them toward low-wage occupations on the margins because somebody has to fill the needs of the more affluent (Kozol, 1991). For others, the blight leads to very low expectations of schools and society at large, coupled with self-blame and self-defeating attitudes that lead rapidly to school disengagement and a more general sense of alienation from civic life and responsibility (Fine et al., 2004).

The School Climate

In addition to the physical conditions, the perceived atmosphere or psychological climate of school is an important influence on student motivation. One body of research has examined a fundamental human psychological need (Baumeister & Leary, 1995), variously labeled "school belonging," "school relatedness," "school community," or "school bonding." Whatever the label, this construct refers to students' sense of trust, acceptance, and personal relatedness at school (Goodenow & Grady, 1993) as well as feeling safe, respected, and supported in the school environment (Osterman, 2000). Correlational findings from low-income students in urban middle schools (Goodenow & Grady, 1993) revealed that a sense of belonging in school was significantly related to students' valuing of education and overall school motivation (i.e., "schoolwork is worthwhile and important") but not to self-reported effort. School belonging was also related to students' expectations for academic success, but the relationship was stronger for urban Hispanic and White students than for urban African American students and stronger for girls than for boys. Although students generally reported levels of achievement motivation equal to their suburban peers, almost half of the participants reported a low sense of school belonging. More recent research (Brown & Evans, 2002) suggests that extracurricular activities (i.e., sports and youth groups) are positively related to a sense of school belonging and thus an indirect influence on motivation at school. However, correlational findings cannot determine whether positive achievement motivation and student activities lead to feelings of belonging, or if a sense of belonging facilitates achievement motivation and higher rates of school participation.

Research using statistical modeling techniques has begun to unpack the processes that link belonging and motivation, and work with urban students has examined multiple dimensions of both belongingness and achievement motivation (Faircloth & Hamm, 2005). This research measured students' perceptions of teacher relations, social networks at school, participation in extracurricular activities, and perceptions of discrimination at school, to comprise a latent variable for feelings of belonging. Attributions for success and failure, perceptions of competence, self-reported effort, and valuing of schoolwork tapped student motivation. The authors conclude that a feeling of belonging at school fully mediated the relationship between student motivation and student achievement, suggesting that a sense of belonging is an important and necessary amplifier of achievement motivation, particularly for the academic success of urban African American and Latino students.

In addition to the interpersonal climate, a school's academic climate has been implicated in motivation and achievement in urban schools. *Academic press*, defined as an emphasis on academic achievement, the application of rigorous standards and expectations to behavior and achievement, and the agreement among the entire school community that academics are a top priority, has sometimes been set in opposition to social support as a means of improving student engagement and achievement. A strong press for academic achievement has long been identified as an important characteristic of effective schools for urban and ethnic minority students (Edmonds, 1979), initially at a time when these students were often handicapped and held back by low expectations and negative stereotypes of low intelligence. Research on urban school reform using a broad national sample (Shouse, 1996) as well as a specific look at urban Chicago schools (Lee, Smith, Perry, & Smylie, 1999) has demonstrated the complementary nature of academic press and social support for student motivation, engagement, and achievement. Stated simply, low-income urban students are most successful when both a strong sense of belonging and a strong academic press are apparent at the schools they attend.

A reform model referred to as "nativity schools" has also demonstrated the combined power of academic press and social support. These parochial middle schools provide low-income urban minority students an elite education at relatively little cost. Such schools also maintain their relationships with students and families long after they go on to high school and beyond, providing support and guidance for accessing a high-quality high school and college education. A comprehensive assessment of nine nativity schools in urban areas across the United States (Fenzel & Monteith, 2008) revealed that students reported a significantly stronger sense of belonging but did not rate themselves higher in intrinsic motivation than students in traditional parochial schools. However, for all students, intrinsic motivation predicted academic achievement, and students in nativity schools improved their scores on standardized achievement tests at rates double those of comparison students. The nativity model seems to establish that the effort and engagement typical of high levels of intrinsic motivation is normative rather than an unusual occurrence. If this interpretation is correct, such beliefs will serve these students well as they persevere in academic pursuits. Unfortunately, far too often students in the poorest, largest, and lowest-achieving public schools are the least likely to enjoy high levels of academic press and social support (Lee et al., 1999), although they are most in need of exactly this kind of school climate. While the broad school climate is clearly a significant influence on student motivation, understanding how specific school practices affect student motivation requires a more fine-grained examination of the characteristics of schools—a topic to which we now turn.

The Student–Adult Interface

The effort to understand specific social relationships as determinants of student motivation represents a substantial and rapidly growing segment of the literature on academic achievement motivation. The past two decades of research have established important connections between adult–student relationships at school and academic motivation and achievement (e.g., Juvonen & Wentzel, 1996; Martin & Dowson, 2009). These social interactions can lead to either positive or negative perceptions of the school and the classroom environment, and also exert important influences on students' self-perceptions. Ultimately, social interactions with adults in urban schools, as is true in every school, have much to do with students' achievement motivation.

In addition to the negative effects of physical and structural deficiencies, urban schools can sometimes be characterized by interactions among students and adults in the school setting that do not support student motivation and engagement (Wehlage & Rutter, 1986). For example, low-income ethnic Korean high school students in inner-city New York perceived their teachers to be ineffective and uncaring, and their counselors to be hostile to students' educational aspirations (Lew, 2006). Many of the participants described classrooms that were simply out of control, with noisy students who constantly disrupted learning. Teachers were perceived as not teaching at all and holding extremely low expectations for students. Students reported that counselors accused them of poor motivation, encouraged them to leave school, and were unwilling to provide counseling services to support students' self-reported aspirations for academic success. Perhaps unsurprisingly, participants, who were typically considered members of a model minority, had dropped out of schools that they perceived to be warehouses where students were neither allowed nor expected to achieve. Qualitative investigations that capture Latino and African American students' voices also reveal that urban minority students, both high-achieving and struggling, want teachers, counselors, and other adults in school to support their aspirations, recognize their abilities, and care about them as individuals. When that does not happen, and when teachers and counselors treat them or their friends differently based on race and ethnicity, they are quite aware that their motivation and engagement in school fall off precipitously (Howard, 2003). Quantitative data provide partial support for these findings, revealing that students are more engaged in medium-sized but not large urban high schools if relationships between adults and students are positive (Lee & Burkham, 2003).

The Classroom

The literature on classroom-specific effects on student motivation and engagement has converged around similar themes, demonstrating, across multiple student populations, the importance of student–teacher relationships and classroom climate on academic achievement motivation (for reviews of the general literature, see Martin & Dowson, 2009; Osterman, 2000). While chaotic schools and condescending adults can lead urban students to drop out, specific classroom practices and environments can have equally detrimental or highly positive effects on the beliefs and values that support achievement motivation in urban students.

Teachers arguably represent the most central relationship for students in the classroom. Teachers provide support for students' academic aspirations, establish the classroom environment in which students should be motivated to succeed, and manage the pedagogy that should engage students in learning. Those who study classrooms have defined teacher support as a nurturing, respectful attitude toward students that conveys a personal interest and expectations for success (Wentzel, 1997). Thus, teacher support comprises both emotional and academic dimensions. Perceptions of teacher support are related to academic motivation, particularly for urban ethnic-minority adolescents (Hudley, 1995, 1997; Murdock, 1999). Work with urban middle-school students has demonstrated that perceived teacher support partially mediates the relationship between status variables (race and socioeconomic status (SES)) and motivational variables, defined as engagement in assignments, attendance, and the presence or absence of disciplinary problems (Murdock, 1999). This effect was especially strong for low-income African American students, suggesting that positive relationships with teachers have the greatest motivational impact on the groups at highest risk for school failure.

Unfortunately, as we have described earlier, urban minority students may more often perceive their teachers as having low expectations, and these perceptions of differential treatment are borne out by teachers' self-reports. Data reveal that teacher judgments can be affected by students' social class and ethnicity. Research in multicultural education has found that some teachers across all grade levels may perceive African American and Latino students as more behaviorally disturbed (i.e., discipline problems), affectively turned off (i.e., not caring about education), and unmotivated than other groups regardless of objective similarities in behavior across groups (Kalin, 1999; Katz, 1999). Evidence for a similar bias has been found among preservice teachers as well (King, 1991).

The classroom environment established and maintained by the teacher has also been persuasively linked to students' achievement motivation. A comparison of classroom structures in urban middle schools enrolling low-income minority students, for example, revealed that student ratings of intrinsic motivation for reading, math, science, and social studies were significantly influenced by specific kinds of classroom features (Hudley, 1997). Self-contained classrooms in which teachers held high expectations for students, gave students some autonomy in selecting academic activities, provided individualized and hands-on activities, and were governed by a minimum of behaviorally stated, visible rules had more positive motivational consequences than departmentalized, remedial classrooms that emphasized lecture, memorization, peer tutoring, and discipline that relied on individual reprimands. These findings are consistent with cognitive evaluation theory (Deci & Ryan, 1987), which specifies that intrinsic motivation is related to the perceived context. Intrinsic motivation for a given activity is supported in contexts perceived as supporting order, personal autonomy, interpersonal relatedness, and personal competence. Conversely, contexts experienced as controlling, uncaring, chaotic, or containing messages of personal incompetence tend to diminish intrinsic motivation (Deci & Ryan, 1992). These effects have been shown to hold for students from all backgrounds and social circumstances.

Grounded in goal theory, the study of classroom goal structures has been another fruitful approach to understanding achievement motivation for the past two decades. Achievement goal theory assumes that all students pursue individual goals in academic settings and is concerned with the reasons why students approach academic tasks and the motivational consequences of their goals (Kaplan, Middleton, Urdan, & Midgley, 2002). In general, achievement goals are grouped in two classes: task, mastery, or learning goals emphasize intellectual learning and improvement, while ego, performance, or ability goals stress competition and peer comparison (Ames, 1992). Goal structures (Midgely & Urdan, 2001) are the perceived objectives emphasized in the classroom or the school and may be determined by how instruction is delivered, how grades and evaluation are determined, and the degree of public evaluation and social comparison emphasized in the school environment. Although most research has been conducted with White middle-class samples, the few studies that have been conducted with urban students reveal that perceived goal structures are significantly related to motivation. Among urban elementary school students, a perceived classroom focus on performance rather than mastery goals predicted lower motivation to achieve in the form of self-handicapping behaviors, including failure to complete homework, reduced effort in academic tasks, and increased off-task behavior in class (Urdan, Midgley, & Anderman, 1998). Results suggest that students use self-handicapping strategies in the face of highly salient ability goals in the classroom if they are doubtful of their own ability and wish to protect themselves against judgments of low ability.

In a comparison of urban and rural middle-school classroom goal structures, students in urban middle schools reported lower levels of perceived mastery goal structures in their classes and lower levels of personal mastery goals (Freeman & Anderman, 2005). In addition, increases in personal mastery goals from sixth to seventh grade were significantly lower for students in urban schools. These differences were related to urban classroom characteristics that included less respectful communication between teachers and students, more negative teacher talk, more whole-group instruction, a more teacher-dominated management system, and less on-task behavior. These results also strongly suggest that in all schools, perceived classroom goals have an impact on student motivation, student behavior, and interactions between students and teachers. In urban schools, the absence of perceived mastery or task goal structures occurs along with students' lack of academic achievement motivation and behavioral engagement. Overall, this very limited research base suggests that the motivational impact of perceived classroom goal structures and interpersonal interactions in classrooms is consistent across all student populations.

Finally, the pedagogic choices that teachers make also have important influences on student motivation in urban schools. Low-achieving high school students in an urban school reported (Lee, 1999) that lectures and individual worksheets rather than group projects or activities were boring and led them to disengage from class work and often to cut class. In these teacher-centered classrooms, students felt that there was very little explanation or help with learning, and teachers did not provide individual help of any kind. Conversely, when teachers offered challenging work that was patiently and clearly explained, and creatively presented through a variety of discussions, activities, and media (e.g., music, visuals), students were much more motivated to engage, learn, and complete classwork and homework. For these urban high school students, one of the primary determinants of motivation was a balance in favor of novelty, and active rather than passive participation in the classroom.

Research with urban middle-school students has reached similar conclusions. An interesting experimental classroom governed by self-worth motivational theory (Covington, 1992) examined the efficacy of teaching strategies to change student motivation over time (Teel, Debruin-Parecki, & Covington, 1998). The theory posits that student motivation, engagement, and behavior in school are determined largely by a sense of academic self-worth, and students will refuse to engage in academic work if they anticipate failure a threat to their academic self-worth. In an urban classroom with low-achieving students, the project implemented pedagogic strategies that were hypothesized to support self-worth by supporting students' positive perceptions of their abilities. Grading was based on effort, various modes of performance (e.g., oral or artistic rather than written) were acceptable, students were given more responsibility and choice in determining the curriculum, and specific attention was paid to each student's cultural heritage. Over time, these strategies led students to increase their participation in class discussions, demonstrate more effort in their schoolwork, spend more time on tasks, and cooperate more willingly with one another and with the teacher. This experimental intervention convincingly demonstrated a causal relationship between classroom pedagogy, and student behavioral engagement and motivation in urban classrooms.

Not surprisingly, findings from studies of low-income urban elementary schools diverge somewhat from those of secondary schools. Relative to classrooms with lower levels of student self-reported motivation, classrooms with more motivated students have teachers who interact directly and more frequently with students, provide more independent and individualized projects, and present more written assignments (Waxman & Huang, 1997). Although the passive nature of student participation in the classroom may be a concern for the development of students' self-management, help-seeking skills, and social competence, the younger students' developmental needs for teacher attention and approval were more effectively met in the classrooms with higher levels of teacher interaction. As well, students seemed to perceive greater task orientation and clarity of rules in classrooms that were more motivating. Again, clearer boundaries and expectations coupled with greater teacher attention may be developmentally appropriate for motivating elementary school students. This interpretation is consistent with our earlier discussion of the multiplicative power of academic press and social support at the whole-school level to facilitate motivation among relatively older students. The specific characteristics of classroom social and academic relationships and expectations appear to function similarly as important influences on student motivation. These environmental influences are translated into motivational outcomes largely through their impact on individual student characteristics. We now turn our attention to a discussion of critical student variables that have been implicated in motivational outcomes for urban students.

Student Characteristics in Social Context

The examination of individual characteristics of urban students' achievement motivation represents a decidedly psychological perspective on student motivation, engagement, and achievement in school. In this section we briefly review literature concerning self-beliefs and student perceptions of societal circumstances that have been assessed in urban students. Although self-beliefs are characteristics of individuals, they are strongly shaped by cues in the environment. We have previously discussed the role of the classroom environment in shaping student achievement goals and intrinsic motivation. Classroom contexts can also shape self-beliefs that are directly related to academic achievement motivation.

Research with low-income, predominantly ethnic-minority urban students examining self-beliefs has revealed significant relationships among perceptions of the classroom, beliefs about self, motivation, achievement, and persistence in school (Close & Solberg, 2008). Three motivational variables—autonomous and controlled motivation as described by self-determination theory (Ryan & Deci, 2000), and self-efficacy—were examined in this study. Autonomous motivation, which has been positively associated with academic self-beliefs and achievement, implies free choice to engage in a behavior, while controlled motivation implies coercion, including internal (guilt) or external pressure. Academic self-efficacy (Bandura, 1997), defined as the confidence to perform school-related activities, is also consistently and positively associated with achievement (Multon, Brown, & Lent, 1991). Urban students who reported a greater sense of relatedness to teachers and peers in their classes also reported significantly greater feelings of autonomous motivation; self-reported motivation positively predicted self-efficacy and achievement. Efficacy beliefs negatively predicted feelings of distress (agitation, somatic complaints, sleep disturbance) and positively predicted achievement.

Importantly for high school students, feelings of distress positively predicted school dropout. These findings yield valuable information for teachers and teacher educators. A sense of connection, particularly toward teachers, has the power to make students feel more positive about themselves as students, a self-belief that has a significant impact on student motivation, engagement, retention, and achievement.

Academic self-concept or perceived academic competence, a motivational construct related to self-efficacy, comprises perceptions and attitudes about one's academic abilities, and has been conceptually distinguished as a unique dimension of the self in multidimensional models of self-concept (e.g., social, physical, emotional, global) (Harter, 1999; Marsh & Shavelson, 1985). This construct has been investigated among urban students over the past several decades and has shown a relationship to student motivation and achievement. Research on multidimensional models of motivation and self-concept in an urban middle school revealed significant relationships between self-perceived academic competence and intrinsic motivation (Hudley, 1997). Academic self-concept associated with a specific subject (i.e., reading and math) related significantly to self-reported intrinsic motivation for the same subject. The results were particularly strong for math self-concept and math intrinsic motivation.

Similar work with urban elementary school students has revealed that self-perceptions of academic competence were positively related to a self-reported preference for challenging tasks (Marchant, 1991). Cluster analyses of these data demonstrated significant connections between academic self-concept and three dimensions of motivation (curiosity, preference for challenge, and mastery motivation), and a measure of attendance, which can be considered an indicator of school engagement. Data connecting self-beliefs, self-reported motivation, and school engagement have also been reported for urban high school students (Fisher, 2000). Together, these studies suggest that self-perceptions are important contributors to achievement motivation for urban students, as is true for all students, and these results are robust across development.

The Social Context

Our discussion of self-beliefs would be incomplete if we did not consider the social context in which urban low-income ethnic-minority students must develop their self-beliefs and achievement motivation. Family wealth is arguably the most powerful key that unlocks access to the opportunity structure across the globe (Nonoyama-Tarumi, 2008) and for students from all backgrounds (Lew, 2007; Malecki & Demaray, 2006). Thus, urban minority students are often at a disadvantage due to limited family economic and social resources. This dynamic is often not lost on urban students, who must sustain positive self-beliefs and achievement motivation in the face of systemic inequality.

Research that has examined urban African American male students' motivation (Irving & Hudley, 2005) found that a belief that the opportunity structure (e.g., schools, the justice system, employment opportunities) is biased in favor of the dominant society—also known as cultural mistrust—was inversely related to students' expectations about the future benefits of academic success and their valuing of academic pursuits. Thus, individual differences in students' beliefs about access to the opportunity structure explained differences in student motivation. A follow-up study (Irving & Hudley, 2008) linked academic expectancies and the valuing of academics to academic achievement. Although urban and low-income students consistently express high aspirations (Kao & Thompson, 2003; Solorzano, 1991), the belief that access to the opportunity structure is biased against them is often negatively related to both motivation and achievement for some low-income, urban students. For other students, however, a clear understanding of bias serves as a challenge rather than a threat (Blascovich, Mendes, Hunter, & Lickel, 2000). Research that conveys the voices of diverse high-achieving and gifted urban students—a seriously understudied population— consistently finds these students to be highly motivated in the face of an inequitable opportunity structure. Such high school students report that they maintain high aspirations, a firm commitment to academic achievement and higher education, and a strong belief in their own abilities to overcome obstacles, of which they are very aware (Griffin & Allen, 2006; Hébert & Reis, 1999).

These data suggest that the relationship between the perception of societal bias and individual student motivation may be moderated by achievement levels. However, the direction of effects between achievement and social perceptions remains unclear. Does high achievement lead students to maintain their achievement motivation and view systemic bias as a challenge, or does the perception of systemic bias as a threat suppress student motivation and achievement? This question requires urgent attention from both research and practice, as the answers will have much to say about supporting and increasing academic motivation and high achievement among students in urban schools.

Another dimension of the social context that has received considerable attention in the literature has been the influence of peers in urban settings. In some instances, peers exert negative pressure on high-achieving ethnic-minority students to adopt an oppositional identity toward school. High achievers of all ethnicities may be labeled "acting White" for achieving and being motivated in school (Fordham & Ogbu, 1986; Lew, 2006). More recent research has challenged the "acting White" hypothesis (Tyson, Darity, & Castellino, 2005) and revealed that academically successful African American middle and high school students do not suffer from "acting White" taunts. Mexican American adolescents who reported high levels of peer academic support place a higher value on school success (Gonzalez & Padilla, 1997), and urban early adolescents who associated with high achieving peers were more likely to consider the opinions of their peers before adopting behaviors that undermine school achievement (Wentzel & Caldwell, 1997). Finally, studies of very high achieving and gifted urban students reveal that a strong network of supportive and motivated peers is one of the primary hallmarks of academic motivation and success for this group irrespective of student ethnicity (Chhuon, Hudley, Brenner, & Macias, 2010; Griffin & Allen, 2006; Hébert & Reis, 1999; Hudley et al., 2009). Although attention is more often given to negative influences from peers in urban settings, peer support can also serve as a powerful source of strength and motivational support.

Conclusions and Directions for Future Research

Our examination of research on achievement motivation in this population leads us to conclude, unsurprisingly, that motivational characteristics of urban students are consistent with the literature on student motivation in other populations (e.g., rural, middle class, suburban). Motivational issues uniquely relevant to urban students relate to societal conditions that have the power to affect motivation. The deplorable conditions that constrict not only motivation but also opportunities to learn in some urban schools are a pressing and obvious concern that will require significant reordering of economic priorities in our society. The persistent bias and stereotyping evident in our society (Hudley & Graham, 2001), which militates against motivation and academic expectancies among low-income young people of color, will require serious reflection on our national character and a shift in the nation's willingness to respect and care for all of our children and families. As we move more rapidly into the most significant demographic changes in the nation's history, we must maximize the nation's human capital by refusing to minimize the importance of academic and social success for all children.

Research on urban education in the United States has a long and substantial history. It is not surprising that the research base has been less than successful in ameliorating the host of societal problems that plague urban schools and the students they serve. However, the research has been more successful in documenting inequity, helping schools and families move toward best practices, and giving voice to the young people who represent an important component of our national future. With that in mind, some areas of research on urban education remain noticeably underrepresented in the academic literature.

Most important, research on high-achieving and gifted children is sorely needed. The presumption that all students in urban schools are low achieving and at risk for school failure is an incomplete, inadequate picture. Gifted children in the inner city may lack the resources afforded their more affluent peers, but that does not diminish their intellectual promise according to the limited research base that has examined this population (Van Tassel-Baska, 2010). Rather, it shames those all the more who have created and continue to benefit from a stratified system of education that will not meet the needs of all the students it claims to serve. Understanding the unique strengths and resilience of high-achieving and gifted students in urban schools will be a significant contribution that can guide efforts to improve the educational outcomes for all students.

A body of knowledge already exists on best practices for encouraging student engagement, motivation, and achievement at the school level (Edmonds, 1979; Sizemore, 1990), in classroom organization (Waxman & Huang, 1997), and student and teacher beliefs and behaviors (Hudley, 1997). We have reviewed a sample of the work here to demonstrate that motivational theory and research can be applied in classrooms to successfully motivate students. Unfortunately, translating that knowledge broadly to teacher and administrator preparation, in-service training, parent education, and school policy has been a more difficult and slow process. Thus, research on translation and dissemination is another area of urgent need. Our knowledge is by no means perfect, but there is sufficient evidence that changes in adult behavior, school practices, and student beliefs can lead to changes in student motivation and behavior. Urban education, indeed all education, will benefit greatly from advances in knowledge about how best practices in motivating students can be effectively implemented in preprofessional and professional training. It will also benefit from learning how information can best be communicated to the broad community of stakeholders in public education (policymakers, administrators, students, parents, the business community). In closing, we remain optimistic about the prospects for engaging urban students in urban schools, but only if significant attention is paid to the need to improve resources and reduce societal risk factors that work against student motivation and achievement. The world, including the United States, is moving ever more rapidly in the direction of increasing urbanization and increasing diversity among populations, leaving little choice but to commit to providing the best education possible for everyone.

References

Ames, C. (1992). Classrooms: Goals, structures, and student motivation. *Journal of Educational Psychology, 84*, 261–271.

Bandura, A. (1997). *Self-efficacy: The exercise of control.* New York: Freeman.

Baumeister, R. F., & Leary, M. R. (1995). The need to belong: Desire for interpersonal attachments as a fundamental human motivation. *Psychological Bulletin, 117*, 497–529.

Blascovich, J., Mendes, W., Hunter, S., & Lickel, B. (2000). Stigma, challenge, and threat. In T. Heatherton, R. Kleck, M. Hebl, & J. Hull (Eds.), *The social psychology of stigma* (pp. 307–333). New York: Guilford Press.

Bowles, S., & Gintis, H. (1976). *Schooling in capitalist America.* New York: Basic Books.

Brown, R., & Evans, W. (2002). Extracurricular activity and ethnicity: Creating greater school connection among diverse student populations. *Urban Education, 37*, 41–58.

Chhuon, V., Hudley, C., Brenner, M., & Macias, R. (2010). The multiple worlds of successful Cambodian American students. *Urban Education, 45*, 30–57.

Close, W., & Solberg, S. (2008). Predicting achievement, distress, and retention among lower-income Latino youth. *Journal of Vocational Behavior, 72*, 31–42.

Council of the Great City Schools (2008). *Urban School Statistics.* Retrieved June 15, 2009 from: www.cgcs.org/about/statistics.aspx

Covington, M. (1992). *Making the grade: A self-worth perspective on motivation and school reform.* New York: Cambridge University Press.

Deci, E., & Ryan, R. (1987). The support of autonomy and the control of behavior. *Journal of Personality and Social Psychology, 53*, 1024–1037.

Deci, E., & Ryan, R. (1992). The initiation and regulation of intrinsically motivated learning and achievement. In A. Boggiano & T. Pittman (Eds.), *Achievement and motivation: A social–developmental perspective* (pp. 9–36). Cambridge, UK: Cambridge University Press.

Edmonds, R. (1979). Effective schools for the urban poor. *Educational Leadership, 37*, 15–18.

Faircloth, B., & Hamm, J. (2005). Sense of belonging among high school students representing four ethnic groups. *Journal of Youth and Adolescence, 34*, 293–309.

Fenzel, L. M., & Monteith, R. (2008). Successful alternative middle schools for urban minority children: A study of nativity schools. *Journal of Education for Students Placed at Risk, 13*, 381–401.

Fine, M., Burns, A., Payne, Y., & Torre, M. (2004). Civics lessons: The color and class of betrayal. *Teachers College Record, 106*, 2193–2223.

Fisher, T. (2000). Predictors of academic achievement among African American adolescents. In S. Gregory (Ed.), *The academic achievement of minority students: Perspectives, practices, and prescriptions* (pp. 307–344). Lanham, MD: University Press of America.

Fordham, S., & Ogbu, J. U. (1986). Black students' school success: Coping with the "burden of acting White." *The Urban Review, 18*, 176–206.

Foster, M. (2007). Urban education in North America: Section editor's introduction. In W. T. Pink & G. W. Noblit (Eds.), *International handbook of urban education* (pp. 765–778). New York: Springer.

Freel, A. (1998). Achievement in urban schools: What makes the difference? *Education Digest, 64*, 17–23.

Freeman, T. M., & Anderman, L. H. (2005). Changes in mastery goals in urban and rural middle school students. *Journal of Research in Rural Education, 20*(1), 1–13. Retrieved July 16, 2009 from: www.jrre.psu.edu/articles.html

Gonzalez, R., & Padilla, A. (1997). The academic resilience of Mexican American high school students. *Hispanic Journal of Behavioral Sciences, 19*, 301–317.

Goodenow, C., & Grady, K. (1993). The relationship of school belonging and friends' values to academic motivation among urban adolescent students. *Journal of Experimental Education, 62*, 60–71.

Griffin, K., & Allen, W. (2006). Mo' money, mo' problems: High achieving black high school students' experiences with resources, racial climate, and resilience. *Journal of Negro Education, 75*, 478–494.

Harter, S. (1999). *The construction of the self: A developmental perspective.* New York: Guilford Press.

Hébert, T., & Reis, S. (1999). Culturally diverse high-achieving students in an urban high school. *Urban Education, 34*, 428–457.

Howard, T. (2003). A tug of war for our minds. *The High School Journal, 87*, 4–17.

Hudley, C. (1995). Assessing the impact of separate schooling for African-American male adolescents. *Journal of Early Adolescence, 15*, 38–57.

Hudley, C. (1997). Teacher practices and student motivation in a middle school program for African American males. *Urban Education, 32*, 304–319.

Hudley, C., & Gottfried, A. (2008). *Academic motivation and the culture of school in childhood and adolescence.* New York: Oxford University Press.

Hudley, C., & Graham, S. (2001). Stereotypes of achievement striving among early adolescents. *Social Psychology of Education: An International Journal, 5*, 201–224.

Hudley, C., Moschetti, R., Gonzalez, A., Cho, S., Barry, L., & Kelly, M. (2009). College freshmen's perceptions of their high school experiences. *Journal of Advanced Academics, 20*, 438–471.

Irving, M., & Hudley, C. (2005). Cultural mistrust, academic outcome expectations and outcome value among African American males. *Urban Education, 40*, 476–496.

Irving, M. A., & Hudley, C. (2008). Cultural identification and academic achievement among African American males. *Journal of Advanced Academics, 19*, 676–698.

Juvonen, J., & Wentzel, K. (1996). *Social motivation: Understanding children's school adjustment.* Cambridge, UK: Cambridge University Press.

Kalin, W. (1999). How white teachers perceive the problem of racism in their schools: A case study in "liberal" Lakeview. *Teachers College Record, 100*, 724–750.

Kao, G., & Thompson, J. (2003). Racial and ethnic stratification in educational achievement and attainment. *Annual Review of Sociology, 29*, 417–442.

Kaplan, A., Middleton, M., Urdan, T., & Midgley, C. (2002). Achievement goals and goal structures. In C. Midgley (Ed.), *Goals, goal structures, and patterns of adaptive learning* (pp. 21–54). Mahwah, NJ: Lawrence Erlbaum.

Katz, S. (1999). Teaching in tensions: Latino immigrant youth, their teachers, and the structures of schooling. *Teachers College Record, 100*, 809–840.

King, J. (1991). Dysconscious racism: Ideology, identity, and the miseducation of teachers. *Journal of Negro Education, 60*, 133–146.

Kozol, J. (1991). *Savage inequalities: Children in America's schools.* New York: Crown.

Lee, P. (1999). In their own voices: An ethnographic study of low-achieving students within the context of school reform. *Urban Education, 34*, 214–244.

Lee, V., & Burkham, D. (2003). Dropping out of high school: The role of school organization and structure. *American Educational Research Journal, 40*, 353–393.

Lee, V., Smith, J., Perry, T., & Smylie, M. (1999). *Social support, academic press, and student achievement: A view from the middle grades in Chicago.* Chicago: Chicago Annenberg Research Project.

Leonardo, Z., & Hunter, M. (2007). Imagining the urban: The politics of race, class, and schooling. In W. T. Pink & G. W. Noblit (Eds.), *International handbook of urban education* (pp. 779–801). New York: Springer.

Lepore, S., & Evans, U. (1996). Coping with multiple stressors in the environment. In M. Zeidner & N. Endler (Eds.), *Handbook of coping: Theory, research and applications* (pp. 350–377). New York: Wiley.

Lew, J. (2006). *Asian Americans in class: Charting the achievement gap among Korean American youth.* New York: Teachers College Press.

Lew, J. (2007). A structural analysis of success and failure of Asian Americans: A case of Korean Americans in urban schools. *Teachers College Record, 109*, 369–390.

Lewis, L., Parsad, B., Carey, N., Farris, E., & Smerdon, B. (1999). *Teacher quality: A report on the preparation and qualifications of public school teachers.* Washington, DC: U.S. Department of Education, Office of Educational Research and Improvement.

Malecki, C., & Demaray, M. (2006). Social support as a buffer in the relationship between socioeconomic status and academic performance. *School Psychology Quarterly, 21*, 375–395.

Marchant, G. (1991). A profile of motivation, self-perception, and achievement in black urban elementary students. *Urban Review, 23*, 83–99.

Marsh, H., & Shavelson, R. (1985). Self-concept: Its multifaceted, hierarchical structure. *Educational Psychologist, 20*, 107–123.

Martin, A., & Dowson, M. (2009). Interpersonal relationships, motivation, engagement, and achievement: Yields for theory, current issues, and educational practice. *Review of Educational Research, 79*, 327–365.

Midgley, C., & Urdan, T. (2001). Academic self-handicapping and achievement goals: A further examination. *Contemporary Educational Psychology, 26*, 61–75.

Multon, K. D., Brown, S., & Lent, R. (1991). Relations of self-efficacy beliefs to academic outcomes: A meta-analytic investigation. *Journal of Counseling Psychology, 38*, 30–38.

Murdock, T. (1999). The social context of risk: Status and motivational predictors of alienation in middle school. *Journal of Educational Psychology, 91*, 62–75.

Nonoyama-Tarumi, Y. (2008). Cross-national estimates of the effects of family background on student achievement: A sensitivity analysis. *International Review of Education, 54*, 57–82.

Osterman, K. (2000). Students' need for belonging in the school community. *Review of Educational Research, 70*, 323–367.

Ryan, R., & Deci, E. (2000). Self-determination theory and the facilitation of intrinsic motivation, social development, and wellbeing. *American Psychologist, 55*, 68–78.

Shen, J., & Poppink, S. (2003). The certification characteristics of the public school teaching force: National, longitudinal, and comparative perspectives. *Educational Horizons, 57*, 130–137.

Shouse, R. (1996). Academic press and sense of community: Conflict, congruence, and implications for student achievement. *Social Psychology of Education, 1*, 47–68.

Sizemore, B. (1990). The Madison Elementary School: A turnaround case. In K. Lomotey (Ed.), *Going to school: The African-American experience* (pp. 155–180). Albany: State University of New York Press.

Solorzano, D. (1991). Mobility aspirations among racial minorities: Controlling for SES. *Sociology and Social Research, 75*, 182–188.

Teel, K., Debruin-Parecki, A., & Covington, M. (1998). Teaching strategies that honor and motivate inner-city African-American students: A school/university collaboration. *Teaching and Teacher Education, 14*, 479–495.

Tyson, K., Darity, W., & Castellino, D. (2005). It's not "a black thing": Understanding the burden of acting White and other dilemmas of high achievement. *American Sociological Review, 70*, 582–605.

Uline, C., & Tschannen-Moran, M. (2008). The walls speak: The interplay of quality facilities, school climate, and student achievement. *Journal of Educational Administration, 46*, 55–73.

Urdan, T., Midgley, C., & Anderman, E. (1998). The role of classroom goal structure in students' use of self-handicapping strategies. *American Educational Research Journal, 35*, 101–122.

U.S. Department of Education (2003). *Contexts of elementary and secondary education: Beginning teachers.* Washington, DC: U.S. Department of Education: National Center for Education Statistics.

Van Tassel-Baska, Joyce L. (2010). *Patterns and profiles of promising learners from poverty.* Waco, TX: Prufrock.

Waxman, H., & Huang, S. (1997). Classroom instruction and learning environment differences between effective and ineffective urban elementary schools for African American students. *Urban Education, 32*, 7–44.

Wehlage, G. G., & Rutter, R. A. (1986). Dropping out: How much do schools contribute to the problem? *Teachers College Record, 87*, 374–392.

Wentzel, K. (1997). Student motivation in middle school: The role of perceived pedagogical caring. *Journal of Educational Psychology, 89*, 411–419.

Wentzel, K., & Caldwell, K. (1997). Friendships, peer acceptance, and group membership: Relations to academic achievement in middle school. *Child Development, 68*(6), 1198–1209.

20

Competence Formation
Resilience in Educational Contexts

Dena Phillips Swanson and Margaret Beale Spencer

Adapting to the developmental demands of adolescence requires negotiating perceptions of the self within the constraints of contextual expectations. Adolescents are confronted with a range of psycho-social tasks (e.g., identity formation) and environmental shifts (e.g., school transitions). Their inter-actions with the outside world increase, allowing them to further integrate cognitive skills, social skills, and emotions. Adapting to these normative developmental demands requires balancing aspects of the self (e.g., problem-solving skills or self-esteem) with the social environment (e.g., the avail-ability of social support) (Dupree, Spencer, M. B., & Fegley, 2007; Swanson, 2010).

Children and adolescents who are less proficient at integrating their knowledge of self and internal reality with knowledge of the environment and external reality exhibit more emotional and behavioral problems. Educational successes provide a domain for competence formation—the ability to effectively interact in an academic context. Adaptive strategies are important independent of the developmental period; however, the possible negative or problematic consequences are particularly relevant during adolescence as their implications extend into adulthood.

This chapter explores (1) developmental considerations in examining competence formation and educational outcomes as risks posed by educational inequities, (2) the framing of educational resilience as an emerging context-specific domain within resilience research, and (3) their implica-tions, discussed in terms of the role of adults in providing contexts that are culturally competent as well as the importance of encouraging greater collaborative initiatives that offer sustainability.

The review incorporates studies on the role of adaptation (i.e., competence) and development for interpretations of academic and behavioral outcomes. There is an emphasis on youth's academic and psychosocial coping processes and outcomes within an educational context. The focus affords a strategy for highlighting poignant daily experiences accrued by individuals as they transition across broad contexts. Further, the conceptual strategy reaffirms the legitimacy and salience of symbolic processes experienced by individuals as each transitions (i.e., psychologically alone) across time and place. Attendant and unavoidable perceptions become apparent given normative developmental processes, particularly as linked to cognitive maturation.

The combination of factors has important implications for self-appraisals, social perceptions, and competence pursuits. The noted conceptual relationships are relevant during the preschool through middle-childhood periods; however, cognitive maturation, perceptual insights, and broadening social experiences heighten the vulnerability of adolescents (i.e., suggesting greater risk than protective factors available and/or accessible).

Development and Educational Experiences

There is consistent evidence that adolescents are disengaging from formal education (e.g., *Education Week*, 2007), while stressful experiences compromise the academic success of those remaining engaged at any level (Cunningham, Hurley, Foney, & Hayes, 2002). Youth living in poverty, in particular, are more likely than their peers from more economically stable homes and communities not to graduate from high school. Youth providing familial support in caring for siblings or helping parents with addictions, mental health, or physical disabilities are also at increased risk of poor academic outcomes. These outcomes are often attributed to absences or lack of focus when they are able to attend school. The impact of this disengagement is further exhibited in chronic truancy, low levels of participation in school activities, delinquency in the form of school violence and vandalism, and eventually dropping out of school (Kearny, 2007; Slaughter-Defoe & Rubin, 2001). The problem of keeping adolescents in school is particularly urgent in large urban areas where ethnic minority adolescents in public schools are concentrated (Spencer, M. B., Swanson, & Edwards, 2010).

Research over the past two decades has examined processes relevant to understanding resilience during adolescence (Spencer, M. B., et al., 2006). Resilient youth demonstrate positive outcomes in their academic trajectories and psychosocial processes (Luthar, 2006). Resilience is defined as "a dynamic process encompassing positive adaptation within the context of significant adversity" (Luthar, Cicchetti, & Becker, 2000, p. 543). Outcomes associated with resilience are broadly identified as factors contributing to success under adverse conditions.

Although dropout rates have declined across the country in recent years (U.S. Department of Education, 2010), African American students continue to drop out of school at a higher rate than the population as a whole. These rates are particularly high for adolescents living in urban inner cities, where many African Americans and Latinos attend predominately segregated schools. Despite the increases in high school graduation rates, many African Americans, particularly males, still fall far behind their cohorts in educational attainment and basic literacy skills (Dupree et al., 2007; Harper, 2006). Large numbers of youth continue to be incarcerated, become victims of violent crimes, fail to graduate secondary school, have lower college entry rates, or are enticed by illicit activities. The retention rate among middle and high school students is alarming; for over two decades, males, in particular, have consistently been retained an average of 1.5 years before reaching ninth grade. This level of retention seriously impedes school-related performance and affects future job marketability.

To understand the impact of school-related stressors and variations in youth's coping responses, it is necessary to explore the normative adaptive accommodations youth make to the social environments in which they live (Bronfenbrenner, 1992). Each context provides resources through which youth come to know themselves in relation to the opportunities and limitations of their social world. As a contextualized process, they develop and adapt through interactions that occur within particular environmental settings. The following section explores research on adolescent identity development and academic outcomes.

Identity Processes and Academic Achievement

The impact of environmental stressors on individual growth and development varies, depending on the psychological characteristics of the person (Bronfenbrenner, 1992). Various factors contribute to students' academic achievement and success; these might include teacher expectations, parental involvement, and changing demographics (e.g., family composition, neighborhood conditions, and national economics, which influence socioeconomic status). These factors, however, vary in the extent to which they influence achievement. As such, identity formation is determined or influenced by cognitive maturation, current contextual and situational conditions, and prior socialization influences, in conjunction with available coping strategies (Swanson, 2010). Social and cognitive functioning is especially relevant during the middle- and high school years. Relationships between identity processes and academic performance have implications for the development of individual coping strategies and a personal sense of competence.

Students with low evaluations of their academic competence and general self-worth tend to perform poorly in school, to lose interest in academic activities, and are also likely to be truant. According to the National Center for School Engagement (2007), truant students experience academic, social, and emotional issues that can affect their relationships in and out of school. Factors that contribute to truancy (i.e., unexcused absences) can be found within all age, socioeconomic, and ethnic groups; however, higher truancy rates are found among children and youth living under economically disadvantaged conditions. Research has also established lack of commitment to school and truancy as risk factors for substance abuse, teen pregnancy, and delinquent behavior in addition to dropping out of school (Spencer, A. M., 2009). Truancy is often a symptom of other problems the student is facing; however, it is an early indicator of academic disengagement. As with many negative outcomes, students with multiple risk factors are more vulnerable to the use of truancy as a coping option.

Independent of gender, it is a general observation that underachievement during childhood is causally related to subsequent antisocial activity. Underachievement and hyperactivity are often linked during grade school, with hyperactivity being predictive of later delinquency. However, in general, support is weak for a direct path from low achievement to delinquent behavior. Yet delinquency rates decline when adolescents are not in school (e.g., during school vacations or after school dropout). In addition, some children with reading difficulties and no adverse behavioral characteristics develop delinquency by late adolescence. Both of these findings suggest that school failure may predispose some students to reactive (i.e., "acting out") behavior.

Using an ecological approach, among other social and academic associations, Vosler and Proctor (1990) found that (1) children's social and academic competence is strongly associated with fewer behavior problems, (2) African American children have significantly lower levels of behavior problems than White children when income, family structure, and total social–environmental stress are controlled, and that (3) family competence (the family's ability to deal with stress and to cope both with crisis events and normative transitions and change) as well as (4) total social–environmental stress as opposed to any specific stressor matter for the character of youth outcomes.

For African American adolescents, academic self-esteem is consistently a better predictor of academic achievement than general self-esteem (Swanson, Cunningham, Youngblood, & Spencer, M. B., 2009). Self-esteem emerges from feelings of competence in domains of greatest significance to the individual (e.g., academic, social, or athletic). As children enter adolescence, they navigate sources of support across their peer group, school, family, and neighborhood, which can help mitigate the negative, debilitating effects of an adverse situation or context (Phelan, Davidson, & Cao, 1991).

Various studies have examined the impact of experiencing several life transitions simultaneously during early adolescence (Burchinal, Roberts, Zeisel, & Rowley, 2008; Masten et al., 1995; Simmons, Burgeson, Carlton-Ford, & Blyth, 1987). They analyzed the effect of multiple life changes (school transition, pubertal development, early dating, residential mobility, and family disruption) on students' self-esteem, academic grade point average, and participation in extracurricular activities. These studies consistently report the youth most at risk for problem outcomes are those who must simultaneously cope with several major transitions while also confronting normative developmental (and challenging) tasks (Havighurst, 1953). More specifically, responding to normative tasks for a particular developmental period is difficult and requires more coping (i.e., both short-term reactive coping and more internalized and stable coping associated with identity processes) when accompanied by copious risks.

Coping Responses and Identity Development

Adolescents are confronted with numerous events that are normative (i.e., puberty, school transitions) but differentially experience many that are nonnormative (i.e., community violence). The incongruence between environmental or contextual demands and youth's ability to effectively manage them constitutes stress (Swanson, 2010). The extent to which a stressful experience is chronic or uncontrollable affects the individual's ability to manage the event or its consequences. The presence of coping skills, social supports, and positive self-esteem has been found to offset the risk of emotional and social problems posed by high stress and/or physical vulnerability in children and adolescents. The absence of these coping mechanisms increases the likelihood that emotional or behavioral disorders will occur even under conditions of moderate stress and no physical vulnerability.

In response to the uncertainties of their environment, many African American adolescents have developed coping responses and adaptive behaviors that compensate for marginalized experiences resulting from their minority status. Anxiety for these youth may be triggered by academic problems, family conflict, community violence, interpersonal relationships, or employment/career issues. Behaviors such as hyperactivity, acting out, and aggression in younger adolescents suggest the presence of unaddressed anxiety, while delinquent activity, substance abuse, and sexual promiscuity are potential responses to underlying anxiety or depression among older adolescents. These behaviors reflect coping responses that enable youth to adapt to impoverished or oppressive lifestyles, but are yet maladaptive for success in mainstream society (Swanson et al., 2003). While tertiary prevention is necessary for students experiencing an emotional or behavioral crisis, mitigation of the presenting problem should be the immediate goal but not the long-term goal. The focus of long-term goals will include preventing future occurrences of the presenting problem *and* addressing the developmental needs.

Competence formation is the development of attributes that permit an individual to effectively interact with the environment (White, 1959). The process is attained through interaction, interfacing, or negotiating and highlights the need for understanding not only psychosocial influences on outcomes, but also the context in which these influences occur. Aspects of general competence have been addressed and outlined for children that are also considered appropriate for adolescents (Anderson & Messick, 1974): A competent child should be able to (1) initiate action and direct behavior within given environmental constraints and (2) recognize that different roles are required in different situations and contexts; thus the child should demonstrate behavior that reflects the incorporation of these expectations. Although these are general features of competence, they have implications for developmental outcomes. The ability to interact with the environment is attained through accumulated experiences. Historically, the cultural experience of minorities in American society has required some level of biculturalism in which the individual is capable of demonstrating competence both in the larger society and within their ethnic group. Additionally, experiences of social injustice have resulted in inconsistent expectations given one's social status. Youth are capable of assessing and negotiating environmental constraints when it is clear that an identified approach will result in the expected outcomes. For ethnic minority youth of color, particularly attending urban schools, the potential for individual impact on environmental constraints is elusive. Development, however, is partially determined by the opportunities, limitations, and expectations that society makes available to individuals. Experiences of success increase a sense of personal empowerment (i.e., competence) and the likelihood of future successes in subsequent tasks. Given the developmental tasks associated with adolescence, issues of competence are compounded by one's culture as well as one's status in the larger society.

The sociocultural context facing youth has potential for enhancing or compromising developmental outcomes. In recent years, many empirical investigations concerned with positive youth development have addressed the previous abundance of studies concerned with maladaptive outcomes. However, given the breadth of studies that relate environmental stressors to adaptation during adolescence, and the conceptual framing of these experiences around positive youth development, negative outcomes continue to be interpreted as deviant or pathological adolescent behavior within educational contexts. For adolescents, poor academic achievement is often attributed to characteristics of the student (e.g., disinterested, no future aspirations) that result in negative outcomes such as school dropout or delinquency. While empirical work on positive youth development has expanded within the social science research community, the implications of this broadened, contextualized framing remains elusive within applied contexts where academic interventions or mental health factors are considered (Spencer, M. B., Fegley, & Dupree, 2006). Given such issues, there is a need to incorporate development and context when examining behavioral outcomes. This is especially relevant considering the long-term stigmatizing assumptions associated with behaviors such as aggressiveness and the underestimated influence of withdrawn or anxious symptoms on future adaptation. An understanding and interpretation of such outcomes requires an integrated knowledge of adaptation, both normative and nonnormative (i.e., maladaptive), in the context of development (Masten et al., 1995).

Cultural values represent an important aspect of accrued knowledge because they afford the adolescent information necessary to interpret and proactively respond to environmental experiences and stereotypic messages concerning minority status (Spencer, M. B., 2006). With development, there is greater awareness of group membership and the expectations, privileges, restraints, and social responsibilities that accompany that membership. Within a broad social context, group membership has implications for the ongoing experiences of youth of color as they interpret or make meaning of social inequities or injustices (i.e., inequitable treatment). Competence, therefore, is not only rooted in prior experiences of success but also in one's culture.

Chestang (1972) asserts the existence of environmental conditions that are socially determined and institutionally supported that characterize the experiences of ethnic minorities. He proposes that social policies are infused with inconsistencies (i.e., institutionalized disparity between the mission/purpose and supportive initiatives/efforts) that represent such conditions. In the academic arena, disparities exist when there is incongruence between what schools say they provide for all students and what is actually done. When the disparity is subjectively experienced by students or interpreted as the rejection of denied educational opportunities, the cumulative effect creates obstacles for personal efficacy and achievement outcomes. This effect is described as an individual's sense of powerlessness to influence the environment. For example, notwithstanding the legitimacy of concerns regarding implementing and evaluating the No Child Left Behind Act, the institutionalized reactivity may suggest to youth that schools are, in fact, fine with leaving many students academically behind and disengaged. The inferences youth draw from their experiences influence their coping responses and their emerging identity (Spencer, M. B., 2006).

In summary, competence permits an increasingly differentiated awareness of one's personal needs and an assurance in one's ability to shape or influence external reality. The capability to modify the environment depends on being enabled or empowered to engage in behavior that influences the environment (Bronfenbrenner, 1992). This process of acquiring and confronting external and internal reality continues throughout life, but is particularly critical during childhood and adolescence. If the expression of these basic abilities is viewed as threatened or challenged by environmental or social constraints, the response capability of the individual to cope with the demands will greatly influence the type of behavior expressed. Adaptive strategies are of importance for racial and ethnic minorities individuals independent of developmental stage. However, the possible negative or problematic consequences are particularly relevant during adolescence. The extent to which African American adolescents experience competence in academic endeavors is critical for establishing a foundational framework for their future aspirations. This foundation offers support for a more productive and fulfilled future in a society that offers racial and ethnic minority youth inconsistent or limited support. The following section explores educational resilience and school-relevant supports toward expanding opportunities for competence and identity formation during adolescence.

Educational Resilience: An Adaptive Coping Strategy

As an emerging concept, educational resilience has begun to draw attention as a domain-specific concept. In exploring multiple components of resilience, educational resilience represents a specific domain where youth have positive educational adaptations and outcomes within the context of significant adversity; few things have been as adverse as the impact of slavery. As described by Spencer, M. B., et al. (2006), African Americans have always seen education as an opportunity for demonstrating resilience. In fact, Spencer, M. B., Cross, Harpalani, and Goss (2003) synthesize historical analyses by Cross as well as his identity analysis, which together suggest that the Black community's valuing of education resulted in an early and critical number of educated leaders, teachers, and potential educational administrators soon after leaving slavery. This review of Cross's analysis includes a consideration of Du Bois's estimate that 150,000 of 4 million slaves were able to read and write; literacy was not surprising among free Blacks (Du Bois 1935, p. 638); crossing into freedom by ex-slaves appeared to include "educational designs" as a critical source of change (Spencer, M. B., 2006, pp. 879–880).

Education continues to represent a primary impetus toward social and economic mobility as well as a mechanism for redressing societal inequalities (Spencer et al., 2010). Yet the difficulties many youth face in educational systems contribute to disengagement from the educational process. Disengagement is displayed in the form of poor academic performance and little or no educational goals (Swanson, Spencer, M. B., & Petersen, 1998). Academically disengaged youth (a) withdraw both socially and emotionally from the school climate, (b) interact minimally with others, (c) fail to find their niche in the academic system, and (d) do not develop adequate levels of commitment to the institution of learning. When compared with other groups, African American males have higher suspension rates, lower attendance, and lower standardized test scores, all of which contribute to higher dropout rates. The high school dropout rate among African American adolescent males continues to be a serious concern. In response to high dropout rates among this group, Fram, Miller-Cribbs, and Van Horn (2007) suggest a closer, constructive approach that would shift the focus from disengagement to "factors that keep African-American students engaged" (p. 1).

Resilience research consistently identifies the significance of a supportive adult in differentiating resilient from nonresilient youth developing under high-risk conditions (see Swanson, 2010). These significant adults provide critical support in facilitating positive developmental outcomes for youth by buffering the effects of negative circumstances. In classifying protective and risk factors associated with Latino and African American high school students' academic outcomes, Solberg, Carlstrom, Howard, and Jones (2007) identified several student profiles, including disengaged and resilient characteristics. Resilient youth reported higher availability of family support, interpersonal school relationships, academic self-efficacy, and intrinsic motivation than their academically disengaged peers.

Similar to Solberg et al. (2007), Wang, Haertel, and Walberg (1997) suggest several factors associated with educational resilience. Key factors include students' exposure to significant adversity (e.g., negative life events, low teacher expectations, or race-related stressors) and the combined positive influence of exemplars such as their home environment, teacher expectations, and classroom climate. Such students are more likely to have high reports of teacher or school support, high expectations from parents and significant adults (i.e., teachers), high academic self-esteem, and high parent involvement and/or parental monitoring. The importance of considering both challenges and supports has been carefully described by Spencer, M. B. (2006, p. 835). She suggests that deficit views about diverse youth of color focus on risks alone without *also emphasizing and exploring the presence of protective factors*. In addition, the traditional focus on risks and their linkages to problems unintentionally encourages culturally narrow social scientists to assume only unproductive and homogeneous outcomes and labels such as castelike minorities (see Fordham & Ogbu, 1986; Ogbu, 1985; Spencer, M. B., et al., 2003, 2006). The problematic viewpoint and concomitant deviant perspectives fuel deterministic assumptions, which may reinforce stereotypes. This conceptual conundrum is infrequently assumed for privileged youngsters (i.e., middle-income Whites). Our alternative view is that all humans are vulnerable at some level (i.e., burdened with risks and buoyed by protective factors).

Education and Youth Stressors

Youth who develop strategies for coping with stressful experiences acquire a set of coping responses for facing future stressors (Swanson et al., 2003). These strategies can result in positive resolutions, which contribute to the development of an effective repertoire of responses. Adaptive strategies are important independent of the developmental period; however, the possible negative or problematic consequences are particularly relevant during adolescence, as the implications extend into adulthood. The extent to which youth experience competence in their efforts to change their circumstances is critical for establishing a foundational framework for future challenges. Some stressors that challenge competence are adolescent-dependent, in that they are events unique to adolescence (i.e., pubertal changes, school transitions). Most of the normative stress that adolescents encounter is inevitable and uncontrollable: they are encountered by most youth and include day-to-day hassles encountered in different social environments. Life-event stressors in urban environments are often associated with exposure to community violence as well as typical adolescent stressors (e.g., conflicts with parents).

Explicit strategies for addressing adversities such as exposure to negative events, both communicated and modeled, shape youth's perspective of the challenges they may encounter and actions required to mitigate them. O'Connor (1997) explored characteristics of six African American students who were a subsample of a study on 46 students' perception of American opportunity structures and the students' optimism regarding the impact on their future aspiration. The resilient students "had (a) strong evidence of their personal competence, (b) concrete experiences which conveyed that individuals could defy racial barriers, and (c) social interactions which communicated strategies that would allow them to negotiate the financial limitations of their households in their pursuit of upward mobility" (p. 622). These attributes were considered incomplete in accounting for the optimism expressed by the educationally resilient youth.

Maturationally, most students are cognitively capable of recognizing systemic challenges—relative to their status as minority members and associated with race, class, and gender—that could potentially frame their perspectives of life opportunities as limited (Swanson et al., 2009). According to O'Connor (1997), however, the challenges for some students are not identified as limiting their options and they subsequently defy the odds by demonstrating defiance. Gordon (2004) defines defiance as "acts of active resistance to a challenge and pushing against obstacles standing in the way of personal achievement" (p. 124). As such, in contrast to students who recognize systemic challenges, students identified as academically resilient also recognize and explicitly respond to social injustices; they are not resolved to accept systemic challenges without struggle or action. O'Connor (1997) further noted that

> [T]he social experiences of these resilient students, while heightening their awareness of structural constraints, did not represent them as indomitable structures which could not be defied, negotiated, or in fact altered. This transmitted potential for change may have additionally created the space for these youths to be optimistic about their futures and exhibit continued effort in school. (p. 623)

As previously noted, individual attributes develop as a function of behaviors or beliefs that reflect an active, selective, structuring orientation toward the environment. The ability to modify, select, and reconstruct the environment, however, depends on conditions that enable or empower youth to engage in behavior that influences the environment (i.e., competence) (Bronfenbrenner, 1992). Social structures and conditions, such as expectations at home and school, provide relevant experiences that interact with psychological processes resulting in adaptive behaviors. Many adolescents exhibiting problem behaviors are likely to be among those with limited supportive opportunities or inadequate educational experiences contributing to appraisals of "disempowerment." Without the necessary supports, even "defiant" youth can be identified as problems, impeding the impact of their individual efforts to "overcome the odds." Prior research underscores the significance of positive academic experiences and competencies for producing positive, and preventing negative, outcomes (Swanson et al., 2003). Research, for example, of stress exposure to school-based competence shows that youth with less positive family support were less competent and more likely to be disruptive at high stress levels (Burchinal et al., 2008; Solberg et al., 2007).

Teachers and School Climate

Examining the school context is crucial when describing educational resilience from a positive youth development perspective (Baker, Duly, Aupperlee, & Patil, 2003). Similarly, Slaughter-Defoe and Rubin (2001) emphasize the influential role of school officials in establishing a school's climate and providing continuity of support for adolescents. Their longitudinal study of Head Start eligible children demonstrates the magnitude of change occurring from elementary to middle school; as children grow older, teachers' influence on achievement patterns and outcomes is stronger than that of parents. The classroom structure and school climate shape the contextual and educational experiences of students.

Patrick, Turner, Meyer, and Midgley (2003) identified supportive classroom environments as encompassing school-based factors that foster resilience. The school environment provides critical protective factors for fostering educational resilience. These factors include developing caring relationships that teach social skills while providing a culture of care, respect, and support; setting high, achievable, and explicit expectations for academic performance and classroom behavior; and providing opportunities to actively engage in meaningful learning experiences. Patrick et al. (2003) studied sixth-grade teachers to distinguish between supportive, ambiguous, and non-supportive environments. In contrast to supportive classes, teachers who create non-supportive environments are authoritarian in that they stress teacher power and control, convey low expectations, and utilize extrinsic motivation to engage students. Ambiguous environments reflect teachers who are generally supportive but do not connect with students in a personal way. While potentially setting high expectations, they are inconsistent in demanding student effort and respect, subsequently diminishing their efforts.

In differentiating resilient and nonresilient students, Waxman, Huang, and Padron (1997) examined the classroom context and individual attributes of Latino middle-school students in math classes. Resilient students had significantly higher perceptions of academic involvement, satisfaction, self-concept, and aspirations than nonresilient students. Although nonresilient students were comparable to national reports of academic aspirations, the resilient youth were significantly higher. Academic settings provide resources that facilitate students' sense of responsibility and connection to the school. Newmann, Rutter, and Smith (1989) evaluated expectation and efficacy as relevant factors affecting school climate. They defined expectations as "teachers' perception of the extent to which the students are capable of learning the material that teachers try to teach" (p. 224). Expectations set the standard for the desired goals and criteria for reaching them, encompassing actions, language, and interactions with other members of the school. Consistent and explicitly communicated high expectations create an environment that conveys the necessity of joint responsibilities in achieving desired goals.

Additionally, Newmann et al. (1989) assert that "[a] sense of efficacy refers to the teacher's perception that his or her teaching is worth the effort, that it leads to the success of students and is personally satisfying" (p. 223). This concept has a twofold dimension: teachers must feel fully capable and equipped, and must have structural support to assist students academically. The second aspect is that students must feel as though the teachers are invested in their craft of teaching and personally feel as though there is progress in their academic success. This dual interaction creates a universal expectation for both members. The combination of teachers and students provides more of an active role in decision-making, creates a greater sense of belonging and community–teacher empowerment; thus, it elicits stronger school affiliation and a strong bond to the success of students. The influence of teachers, as supportive adults in facilitating resilience, is well established in the literature (see Osterman, 2000). The contextual support they need within the school community, however, is less frequently acknowledged. While students' truancy, for example, is attributed to various community, school, and family factors, school factors that incorporate classroom considerations are often the focus of interventions. Common school factors include inconsistent policy implementation and limited opportunities for school engagement among culturally and academically diverse students. Individual student factors vary depending on developmental level, but there is often a lack of basic academic skills or lack of connectedness to schools among older students (Spencer, A. M., 2009).

Schools with a strong sense of community provide the necessary foundation to produce an academically sound community. They utilize resources that allow students to address personal issues in an environment that is conducive to academic and personal growth. The climate of a school community is a significant factor not only in contributing to student performance and academic outcomes but also in critically influencing members' sense of commitment. In contrast to the classroom climate, the school is an academic community that provides (and supports) expectations and shared values for all school members in facilitating interactions that set the foundation for academic standards congruent with the school values and beliefs. According to Cohen, McClosky, and Pickeral (2009), the school climate is shaped by the interpersonal relationships within the school that reflect the norms, goals, and values of the school. This framing highlights the significance of various relationship interactions in a school's climate and suggests the relevance of a shared school identity rather than a framing where norms and goals are framed around rules and consequences. Relationships have a direct impact on the perceptions and beliefs regarding the school and connectedness to it.

A positive school climate sets an atmosphere where members are able to effectively function, feel comfortable sharing their concerns, and celebrate accomplishments. This sense of community is not only reflected in the standards but also embedded in daily activities and interactions. A positive school climate illustrates shared values, cohesiveness among teachers, school staff, and administrators in demonstrating the prioritization of issues such as supports for academic engagement or academic achievement.

A significant consideration for school members to note, however, is the concern with establishing expectations and shared values shaped solely from the perspective of those whose own cultural or socioeconomic background is different from their student body, families, and communities. Schools are a context conducive for dynamic interactions that represent behavioral coping strategies; adult and student members rely on personal experiences and coping histories in their interactions with each other. Deficit perspectives of urban youth remain pervasive and the potential for administrators and teachers to alienate other members of the school community (i.e., students, parents) is exacerbated (see Seaton, Dell'Angelo, Spencer, M. B., & Youngblood, 2007). This form of alienation undermines the purpose of ensuring a strong school climate. Issues of cultural competence and community collaborations serve to decrease the potential of "blaming" students and their families for continued problems in schools and for poor achievement outcomes. The opportunity for schools to produce a climate conducive to a welcoming and personable environment is likely to minimize discontentment and resistance. Loukas and Murphy (2007) found that quality school climates perceived as cohesive and generally satisfying protect some adolescents from emotional and behavioral problems by providing a sense of belonging and connectedness to the school. Expectations developed through cultural competence set a climate of opportunity for members to examine the information and how it is communicated and perceived, celebrate and maintain identified community strengths, and offer opportunities for continuous improvement.

Implications

Phelan et al. (1991) demonstrate the importance of effective interaction in various domains within one's environment. It is noted, for example, that behavior problems may become more pronounced with increased adaptational difficulties. Of primary relevance, however, is the potential struggle facing minority adolescents in negotiating and constructing their realities across family, peer, and classroom contexts. This highlights the need for youth to obtain experiences that provide some continuity with their lived experiences to reduce their vulnerability and maximize opportunities for positive outcomes. To mitigate youth vulnerabilities, sufficient supports are required to enhance academic competence leading to academic resilience (Trask-Tate & Cunningham, 2010). The supports reduce risks in areas that are most likely to directly impact academic performance and intellectual curiosity. Part of the solution lies within the connection between youth and influential adults. "The extent to which adolescents can demonstrate competence often depends on their access to a range of legitimate opportunities and long-term support from caring adults" (Swanson, Spencer, M. B., & Petersen, 1998, p. 19). Relationships with safe, supportive adults during adolescence provide opportunities for interpersonal exchanges that facilitate development through exposure to the values of others, which oftentimes includes adults in their community. Two key implications for expanding youth's resilience, with a developmental focus, are framed in the contextualizing opportunities provided by adults in the academic context: the significance of cultural competence and the role of collaborative initiatives.

Cultural Competence

For racial and ethnic minority students, competence and identity formation also must incorporate their cultural identity. Minority status represents an inextricable aspect of the student that provides a framework for defining parameters for life course choices and opportunities. As previously noted, the extent to which African American adolescents, for example, experience competence in academic endeavors is critical. The significance of cultural "synchronization" between minority students and teachers on academic achievement has been well documented (see Gay, 2000; Irvine, 1990). Racial identity, therefore, represents an integral aspect of minority development and competence formation. Although school administrators remain concerned with students' intellectual achievements, social and behavioral problems are the primary predictors of grade retention and dropout rates (Cohen et al., 2009).

Culturally competent adults in the lives of children and youth exercise a major influence on their cultural attitudes and development. They are knowledgeable adults who are comfortable exploring a youth's cultural history, norms, and contemporary issues. To facilitate the academic engagement and maximize youth's educational opportunities, an integration of culturally relevant formal and informal exchanges is necessary within the school *and* classroom contexts. This ability to be culturally engaging must be central to the training of individuals working with youth from backgrounds different from their own first to mitigate personal biases and secondarily in being validated as an educational asset for youth. The detailing of key issues of culturally relevant educational environments is beyond the scope of this chapter, but this topic is covered extensively in other resources (e.g., Gay, 2000). What is important to explicitly discuss here, however, is the need for every individual to obtain two key experiences as precursors to the strategies and considerations outlined elsewhere. The first is an opportunity to examine one's own family of origin. This entails a review and reflection of family values and attitudes, customs and traditions, cultural expressions of race/ethnicity, social class and gender dynamics, and responses to life course events such as births and deaths, marriages, problems with individual members, and so forth. The second key experience for adults working with youth and families from cultures or backgrounds different from their own is to spend some time immersed in a different culture or lifestyle. These experiences provide the basis for engaging students in culturally relevant educational opportunities that incorporate their cultural and lived experiences. As eloquently stated from a practice and culturally sensitive perspective, Chestang (1972) notes the everyday impact of microaggressions, particularly for those without training. Administrative support for teachers and staff to explore and integrate these experiences into their interactions with students will facilitate an engaging school climate fostering educational resilience among students (Seaton et al., 2007).

Collaborative Initiatives

As a final brief note, it is worth acknowledging the impact of collaborative efforts to maximize the impact on youth outcomes. As this chapter has focused on the school context in which youth negotiate educational and psychosocial processes, the issues raised are not the sole responsibility of schools. Schools, as well as community members, should invite or establish initiatives that allow collaborations with others interested in the educational experiences of youth. Although there are institutions that provide needed services or resources for schools, they do not (necessarily) participate in shared decision-making and activities characterizing collaborations. The wealth of research on parental involvement, for example, is replete with strategies and considerations that suggest parents' role in school engagement is primarily as resources for meeting school needs, in contrast to collaborators who facilitate in defining the needs and exploring strategies for addressing them (Sanders, 2005).

Collaborations across school, family, and community organizations offer the opportunity for collectively addressing challenges and providing supports toward enhancing youth's educational resilience and academic engagement that cannot be singularly achieved (Bryan, 2005). According to Cohen et al. (2009), school climate can "promote meaningful staff, family and student engagement and enhance the social, emotional, ethical, civic, and intellectual skills and disposition that contribute to success in school and in life" (p. 45). In establishing collaborations, there are increased opportunities to express concerns but also to develop strategic plans. Building shared and established common goals show the strength and likeness of community members that can include, for example, students, teachers, parents, school counselors, administrators, owners of small businesses, and members of faith-based institutions or media organizations. Each member's knowledge of his or her role and contribution within the collaboration toward achieving specified student outcomes is critical to the success of the efforts. Successful collaborations are fostered when the creation of mutual respect, shared trust, and clear vision is well planned and executed. A shared mission, identified goals, and periodic evaluations of the goals and the process help to further facilitate the engagement necessary for success.

Conclusion

The major thesis of this paper has been to address competence formation generally and identity formation more specifically in interpreting educational resilience among adolescents. As also noted from the review, the relationship between competence, development, educational resilience, schooling contexts, and supports shapes the developmental trajectory for many urban ethnic minority youth. Given the theoretical position posited by Chestang (1972) regarding the potential impact of societal inconsistencies, conditions remain favorable for exacerbating adverse outcomes for some youth. With contextual experiences and effective environmental interactions undergirding competence formation, adverse experiences and ineffective interactions would undermine competence, thereby influencing identity processes and impacting behavioral outcomes. Consistent with the perspective that individuals value domains of personal competence, youth come to value areas in which they excel and have control and discount or devalue areas where competence cannot be obtained or expressed (e.g., educational success).

As schools provide an environment critical to the psychosocial development of adolescents, students' academic experiences within this context can either support or undermine developmental processes. Early educational preparation is significant for future career consolidation and subsequent adult roles. Academic achievement and positive school experiences are therefore necessary to ensure healthy identity development and a sense of competence. It is from this sense of self, associated with the ability to effectively impact the environment, that academic outcomes are exhibited facilitating adverse or productive outcomes.

References

Anderson, S., & Messick, S. (1974). Social competency in young children. *Developmental Psychology, 10*(2), 282–293.

Baker, J. A., Duly, L. J., Aupperlee, J. L., & Patil, S. A. (2003). The developmental context of school satisfaction: Schools as psychologically healthy environments. *School Psychology Quarterly, 18,* 206–221.

Bronfenbrenner, U. (1992). Ecological systems theory. In R. Vasta (Ed.), *Six theories of child development: Revised formulations and current issues* (pp. 187–249). London: Jessica Kingsley.

Bryan, J. (2005). Fostering educational resilience and achievement in urban schools through school–family community partnerships. *American School Counseling Association, 8,* 219–227.

Burchinal, M. R., Roberts, J. E., Zeisel, S. A., & Rowley, S. J. (2008). Social risk and protective factors for African American children's academic achievement and adjustment during the transition to middle school. *Developmental Psychology, 44*(1), 286–292.

Chestang, L. W. (1972). *Character development in a hostile environment* (Occasional Paper, No. 3). Chicago: University of Chicago, School of Social Service Administration.

Cohen, J., McCloskey, M., & Pickeral, T. (2009). Assessing school climate. *Educational Leadership, 74,* 45–48.

Cunningham, M., Hurley, M., Foney, D., & Hayes, D. (2002). Influence of perceived contextual stress on self-esteem and academic outcomes in African American adolescents. *Journal of Black Psychology, 28,* 215–233.

Du Bois, W. E. B. (1935). *Black reconstruction.* New York: S. A. Russell.

Dupree, D., Spencer, M. B., & Fegley, S. (2007). Identity as coping in diverse levels of context: Adolescents' developmental challenges and opportunities. In R. K. Silbereisen & R. M. Lerner (Eds.), *Approaches to positive youth development* (pp. 111–131). Thousand Oaks, CA: Sage.

Education Week (2007). *The last word: The best commentary and controversy in American education.* New York: Wiley.

Fordham, S., & Ogbu, J. U. (1986). Black students' school success: Coping with the "burden of 'acting White.'" *Urban Review, 18*, 176–206.

Fram, M. S., Miller-Cribbs, J. E., & Van Horn, L. (2007). Poverty, race, and the contexts of achievement: Examining educational experiences of children in the U.S. South. *Social Work, 52*(4), 309–319.

Gay, G. (2000). *Culturally responsive teaching: Theory, research, and practice.* New York: Teachers College Press.

Gordon, E. W. (2004). Defiance: variation on the theme of resilience. In R. L. Jones (Ed.), *Black psychology* (4th ed., pp. 117–127). Hampton, VA: Cobb & Henry.

Harper, S. R. (2006). Peer support for African American male college achievement: Beyond internalized racism and the burden of "acting White." *Journal of Men's Studies, 14*(3), 337–358.

Havighurst, R. J. (1953). *Human development and education.* New York: McKay.

Irvine, J. J. (1990). *Black students and school failure: Policies practices, and prescriptions.* New York: Greenwood Press.

Kearny, C. (2007). Forms and functions of school refusal behavior in youth: An empirical analysis of absenteeism severity. *The Journal of Child Psychology and Psychiatry Allied Disciplines, 48*(1), 53–61.

Loukas, A., & Murphy, L. J. (2007). Middle school perceptions of school climate: Examining protective function on subsequent adjustment problems. *Journal of School Psychology, 45*, 293–309.

Luthar, S. S. (2006). Resilience in development: A synthesis of research across five decades. In D. Cicchetti & D. J. Cohen (Eds.), *Developmental psychopathology, Vol. 3: Risk, disorder, and adaptation* (2nd ed., pp. 739–795). Hoboken, NJ: Wiley.

Luthar, S. S., Cicchetti, D., & Becker, B. (2000). The construct of resilience: A critical evaluation and guidelines for future work. *Child Development, 71*, 543–562.

Masten, A. S., Coatsworth, J. D., Neemann, J., Gest, S. D., Tellegen, A., & Garmezy, N. (1995). The structure and coherence of competence from childhood through adolescence. *Child Development, 66*(6), 1635–1659.

National Center for School Engagement (2007). *Pieces of the truancy jigsaw: A literature review.* Denver, CO: Division of Colorado Foundation for Families and Children.

Newmann, F. M., Rutter, R. A., & Smith, M. S. (1989). Organizational factors that affect school sense of efficacy, community, and expectations. *Sociology of Education, 62*, 221–238.

O'Connor, C. (1997). Dispositions toward (collective) struggle and educational resilience in the inner city: A case analysis of six African-American high school students. *American Educational Research Journal, 34*, 593–629.

Ogbu, J. (1985). A cultural ecology of competence among inner-city Blacks. In M. B. Spencer, G. K. Brookins, & W. R. Allen (Eds.), *Beginnings: The social and affective development of Black children* (pp. 45–66). Hillsdale, NJ: Lawrence Erlbaum Associates.

Osterman, F. K. (2000). Students' need for belonging in the school community. *Review of Educational Research, 70*, 323–367.

Patrick, H., Turner, J., Meyer, D. K., & Midgley, C. (2003). How teachers establish psychological environments during the first days of school: Associations with avoidance in mathematics. *Teachers College Record, 105*, 1521–1558.

Phelan, P., Davidson, A. L., & Cao, H. T. (1991). Students' multiple worlds: Negotiating the boundaries of family, peer, and school cultures. *Anthropology and Education Quarterly, 22*, 224–250.

Sanders, M. G. (2005). *Building school–community partnerships: Collaboration for student success.* Thousand Oaks, CA: Sage.

Seaton, G., Dell'Angelo, T., Spencer, M. B., & Youngblood, J. (2007). Moving beyond the dichotomy: Meeting the needs of urban students through contextually-relevant education practices. *Teachers Education Quarterly, 34*(2), 163–183.

Simmons, R., Burgeson, R., Carlton-Ford, S., & Blyth, D. A. (1987). The impact of cumulative change in early adolescence. *Child Development, 58*(5), 1220–1234.

Slaughter-Defoe, D. T., & Rubin, H. H. (2001). A longitudinal case study of Head Start eligible children: Implications for urban education. *Educational Psychologist, 36*, 31–44.

Solberg, V., Carlstrom, A. H., Howard, K. A., & Jones, J. E. (2007). Classifying at-risk high school youth: The influence of exposure to community violence and protective factors on academic and health outcomes. *The Career Development Quarterly, 55*(4), 313–327.

Spencer, A. M. (2009). School attendance patterns, unmet educational needs, and truancy: A chronological perspective. *Remedial and Special Education, 30*(5), 309–319.

Spencer, M. B. (2006). Phenomenology and ecological systems theory: Development of diverse groups. In W. Daman & R. Lerner (Eds.), *Handbook of child psychology, Vol. 1: Theoretical models of human development* (6th ed., pp. 829–893). New York: Wiley.

Spencer, M. B., Fegley, S., & Dupree, D. (2006). Investigating and linking social conditions of African-American children and adolescents with emotional well-being. *Ethnicity & Disease, 16*(2), 63–67.

Spencer, M. B., Swanson, D. P., & Edwards, M. (2010). Sociopolitical contexts of development. In D. P. Swanson, M. Edwards, & M. B. Spencer (Eds.), *Development in a global era* (pp. 1–27). London: Elsevier.

Spencer, M. B., Cross, W. E. Jr., Harpalani, V., & Goss, T. N. (2003). Debunking the "acting White" myth and posing new directions for research. In C. C. Yeakey & R. D. Henderson (Eds.), *Surmounting all odds: Education, opportunity, and society in the new millennium* (pp. 273–304). Greenwich, CT: Information Age.

Spencer, M. B., Harpalani, V., Cassidy, E., Jacobs, C., Donde, S., Goss, T., et al. (2006). Understanding vulnerability and resilience from a normative development perspective: Implications for racially and ethnically diverse youth. In D. Cicchetti & D. J. Cohen (Eds.), *Developmental psychopathology, vol. 1: Theory and method* (2nd ed., pp. 627–672). Hoboken, NJ: Wiley.

Swanson, D. P. (2010). Psychosocial development: Identity, stress and competence. In D. P. Swanson, M. C., Edwards, & M. B., Spencer (Eds.), *Adolescence: Development in a global era* (pp. 93–121). Boston, MA: Elsevier.

Swanson, D. P., Spencer, M. B., & Petersen, A. (1998). Adolescent identity formation: 21st century issues and opportunities. In K. M. Borman & B. Schneider (Eds.), *Youth experiences and development: Social influences and educational challenges* (pp. 18–41). Chicago: University of Chicago Press.

Swanson, D. P., Cunningham, M., Youngblood, J., & Spencer, M. B. (2009). Racial identity during childhood. In H. A. Neville, B. M. Tynes, & S. O. Utsey (Eds.), *Handbook of African American psychology* (pp. 269–281). New York: Sage.

Swanson, D. P., Spencer, M. B., Dupree, D., Harpalani, V., Noll, E., Seaton, G., & Ginzburg, S. (2003). Psychosocial development in diverse groups: Conceptual and methodological challenges in the 21st century. *Development and Psychopathology, 15,* 743–771.

Trask-Tate, A., & Cunningham, M. (2010). Planning ahead: The relationship among school support, parental involvement, and future academic expectations in African American adolescents. *The Journal of Negro Education, 79,* 137–150.

U.S. Department of Education (2010). *The condition of education 2010* (NCES 1010–028, Indicator 20). Washington, DC: Institute of Education Sciences National Center for Education Statistics.

Vosler, N. R., & Proctor, E. K. (1990). Stress and competence as predictors of child behavior problems. *Social Work Research & Abstracts, 26*(2), 3–9.

Wang, M. C., Haertel, G. D., & Walberg, H. J. (1997). Fostering educational resilience in inner-city schools. In H. J. Walberg, O. Reyes, & R. P. Weissberg (Eds.), *Children and youth: Interdisciplinary perspectives* (pp. 119–140). Thousand Oaks, CA: Sage.

Waxman, H. C., Huang, S. L., & Padron, Y. N. (1997). Motivation and learning environment differences between resilient and non-resilient Latino middle school students. *Hispanic Journal of Behavioral Sciences, 19,* 137–155.

White, R. (1959). Motivation reconsidered: The concept of competence. *Psychological Review, 66,* 297–333.

21
Teacher Learning for Instruction of Second Language Learners

Aída Walqui and Lucinda Pease-Alvarez

Education in the United States, especially in urban settings, is changing dramatically. The need for an educated citizenry is changing even more. Currently, with few exceptions, schools within urban systems are producing workers for jobs that no longer exist, in which following orders, reading minimally, and recalling a few facts would be considered enough. Instead, the 21st-century workplace requires individuals who can think critically, read with the ability to understand and respond appropriately and purposively to a wide variety of texts, collaborate with others, be creative, solve problems flexibly, and be resilient.

How do we change this situation and think systemically about the education and professional development of teachers charged with the task of realizing the potential of English language learners and all other urban students? In this chapter we offer a heuristic to organize how and what an accomplished urban 21st-century teacher needs to learn to create learning opportunities that will enable his or her students to be productive, responsible, and compassionate members of the communities in which they live and work.

Demographics

English learners (ELs) make up a growing percentage of our school-age population. More than 5.5 million, or 10%, of all U.S. students lack sufficient proficiency in English to participate in academic engagements without support. In the decade between 1995 and 2005, the number of ELs in the United States grew by 56% while the general school-age population grew by just 2.6% (Batalova, Fix, & Murray, 2007). In the coming decade, ELs are predicted to represent over 30% of all schoolchildren (Fix & Passel, 2003).

In the first decade of the 21st century, the majority of ELs lived in economically stressed situations. Nationwide, two-thirds of elementary ELs lived in homes with incomes below 185% of the poverty level (Capps et al., 2005). In California, which represents 40% of the nation's EL population, 85% of the state's EL students were eligible for free and reduced-price lunches, the state's proxy for low income (Legislative Analyst's Office, 2008).

To make matters more complex, ELs were concentrated in urban areas. Some 60% of the nation's ELs live in 20 metropolitan areas, with the Los Angeles Unified School District and New York City

Public School District serving a larger number of ELs than all the other districts in the nation (Swanson, 2009). As Swanson reports, ELs tend to be enrolled in schools that are considerably larger, more urbanized, and racially and economically segregated than their non-EL counterparts. Adolescent ELs are concentrated in large, urban, impoverished comprehensive high schools with low teacher qualifications and little teacher stability. This segregates them from native English-speaking peers and good models of English (Gándara & Hopkins, 2010). Equally important, they lack access to a more experienced and stable teaching force.

ELs attending these schools face enormous academic challenges. After more than a decade of educational policy aimed at high expectations, emphasis on standards, and increased accountability, the achievement of ELs remains consistently low (Gandara & Contreras, 2009; Garcia, Kleifgen, and Falchi, 2008; Maxwell-Jolly, Gándara, & Méndez Benavides, 2007; Public Policy Institute of California, 2004). National and state measures of mathematics achievement reveal persistent patterns of underachievement for ELs. The National Assessment of Educational Progress (NAEP) in mathematics shows that only 7% of eighth-grade ELs are proficient in mathematics and over 69% score below the basic level nationwide. In California, a state that scores in the bottom five jurisdictions tested in the NAEP, 96% of ELs scored at the basic level or below (National Center for Education Statistics, 2009).

It had been assumed for a long time that ELs were newcomers to the United States and that they therefore needed English language development; during the last five years, however, it has become evident that most of them are, in fact, second- or third-generation U.S. citizens. Estimates put the presence of second- or third-generation ELs in elementary schools at 76% (Goldenberg, 2008) and in middle and high schools at 57% (Batalova et al., 2007). Demographers have calculated that the projected growth of the EL population will come mostly from second- and third-generation EL students, with the second generation growing by 83% and the third by 36% (Passel, 2008); see Figure 21.1. The pedagogical assumption is that what works for one EL works for all, but important

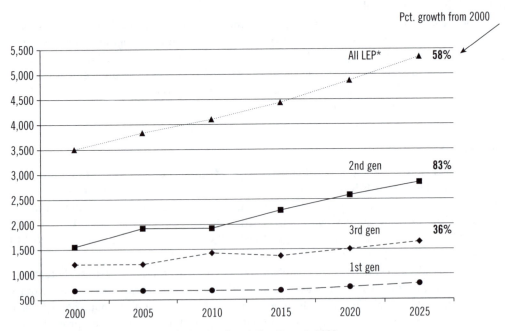

Figure 21.1 Projected Growth of the EL Student Population through 2025

Source: Pew Hispanic tabulation, from Census 2000 (Passel, 2008).
* LEP, Limited English Proficient, is the federal designation for EL students.

differences exist between these two groups of students. Teachers need to study these differences in order to decide how to teach their ELs in the most appropriate ways.

For example, first-generation immigrant students—those who were born in another country and moved to the United States—constitute a very diverse population, from recent immigrants to long-term ELs (defined as students who have been identified with limited English proficiency for seven years or more). They may include students who are literate and up to par academically as well as refugees, undocumented immigrants, and/or transnational students who have experienced little formal schooling prior to their arrival in the United States. Many of these students identify themselves as bilingual, and they have oral skills in their native language. They display different degrees of proficiency in conversational and academic encounters. In contrast to popular perceptions, many are enthusiastic students who behave well in school. Further, many identify strongly with their countries of origin.

Second- or third-generation students were born in the United States, so most of them are American citizens. They have conversational proficiency in English, although they may have little experience in using English for academic purposes. Their scores on tests of English language proficiency indicate that many have reached an intermediate level of proficiency and that they do not seem to advance past this point. They experience high rates of academic failure and perform poorly on assessments. As a consequence, schools continue to categorize them as ELs. For many of these students, English is their only language; they struggle with issues of identity and have developed oppositional attitudes to school. According to Goldenberg (2008) and others, they are at high risk of dropping out of school.

To be effective, then, teachers need to realize that ELs are not a monolithic group. In addition to understanding their histories and experiences, teachers must engage in extremely complex pedagogical work. Lowering of the academic expectations and supports, which is what tends to happen, is not a good response to this situation. Instead, teachers need to be supported in designing powerful lessons, where the tasks students are invited to participate in are robust enough that the learning will be substantive and generative but also flexible, so that students with a wide variety of strengths can participate and derive benefit from their participation.

Context

Urban teachers work in challenging contexts. When compared with schools in other settings, urban schools tend to have fewer material resources, woefully inadequate facilities, students who do not do well on tests of academic achievement, and greater concentrations of students living in poverty. We have found that many programs for teacher education and new teacher induction do little to prepare teachers for these challenges.

The educational policy environment is one aspect of this context that many teachers of ELs find particularly challenging. Nowhere is this more apparent than in California, home to 40% of all ELs nationwide, where interpretation of the federal No Child Left Behind (NCLB) Act of 2001 has contributed to a longstanding tendency to provide low-income ELs with inadequate educational experiences (Gándara & Baca, 2008). Although NCLB has directed the public's attention to the need to enhance the academic achievement of all students, including those who have been traditionally underserved by schools and society, the accountability and testing measures that NCLB has enacted in California enforced a one-size-fits-all approach to teaching literacy in the elementary grades. As a result, the academic needs of underserved children have been overlooked, thereby constraining their opportunities to learn in school. Although NCLB requires that ELs who have attended school in the United States for three or more consecutive school years be tested in English for reading/language arts, California requires that *all* ELs be tested in English, regardless of how long they have been in the country. Not surprisingly, ELs often do not meet the required benchmarks on these tests and consequently tend to be enrolled in program improvement (PI) schools and districts that rely on standardized or one-size-fits-all approaches to instruction in hopes of improving their performance on tests (Harper, de Jont, & Platt, 2008; Walqui, Koelsch, & Hamburger, 2010). In addition to mandating the use of commercial ELD (English Language Development) and literacy programs throughout the grades, many schools and districts in California insist that teachers adhere to pacing and testing schedules designed to enforce teachers' implementation of these programs with fidelity (Pease-Alvarez & Samway, 2008).

Throughout the United States, we are now seeing that when poor children, including those who live in urban settings, do not achieve desired benchmarks on tests of academic achievement, teachers are blamed and threatened with removal from their teaching positions. The turnaround model of educational reform, which consists of firing or threatening to fire teachers in so-called under-performing schools, is gaining a strong foothold in today's educational policy landscape. Despite a long tradition of research that attests to the complexities associated with explaining the pernicious phenomena of differential achievement in the United States, this simplistic solution to the achievement gap is one that has garnered many supporters.

We advocate a different solution—one that invests in teachers as well as students. If we wish to ensure equity in education, it is imperative that we address the achievement gap for ELs. To accomplish this objective, the crucial variable is a teaching force that is knowledgeable about the contexts in which they practice and who can enact that knowledge in robust, enticing pedagogical practice (Darling-Hammond, 2000; Walqui & van Lier, 2010). Despite the need for a highly capable workforce, teachers feel underprepared to meet the needs of ELs (Gándara, Maxwell-Jolly, & Driscoll, 2005). Tragically, few theoretically informed professional development efforts focus on the specific needs and circumstances of ELs. Increasingly, teachers of ELs rely on standardized curricula originally developed for native English speakers or focus their instruction on discrete features of English (Walqui et al., 2010). As a result, ELs continue to find their opportunities to learn in school severely constrained and their curricula devoid of meaningful content.

A Model of Teacher Learning for English Language Learners

This chapter focuses on what it means to develop accomplished teachers of ELs. We describe what teachers need to know and how they develop that knowledge. We begin by highlighting the sociocultural perspective on learning that we endorse, followed by a description of the domains that constitute the knowledge, dispositions, and practices that accomplished teachers of ELs draw on in their work. Although our description sometimes separates the "how" and "what" of teacher learning, it is important to keep in mind that the dimensions of teacher development we describe are interrelated. How one learns comprises what one learns and vice versa. To help the reader envision the model of teacher learning that we describe here, we will reference our experiences as teacher educators, which are grounded in the theories of learning, teaching, and knowing described in this chapter.

Sociocultural Perspective on Teacher Learning

We advocate a sociocultural perspective on learning, including the learning of teachers, that highlights the connections between learning, doing, and social context. Unlike traditional approaches, which focus on psychological processes that reside in the individual, sociocultural perspectives situate learning and knowing in the cultural and historical experiences and contexts of individuals. According to this perspective, individuals transform their roles, relationships, identities, and understandings through their participation in the everyday activities of their communities, institutions, and societies. This perspective on learning conceives of context and learning as mutually constitutive. Context shapes learning, and learning ultimately affects context. Thus, the development of teacher expertise is shaped and defined by the dynamic and interacting macro- and microsocial contexts in which they live and work. Further, teachers themselves draw on what they learn to transform these contexts.

Traditional perspectives on development assume that learning can be successful only when learners demonstrate that they possess the competence and abilities that position them as developmentally ready to learn. In contrast, a sociocultural perspective conceives of development as following learning, meaning that individuals learn when they are engaged in activities that are just beyond their current competence, or in their zone of proximal development (ZPD). As learners engage in joint activity focused on academic skills and concepts, they engage in interaction through which they learn those skills and concepts with the support of others. Often this support takes the form of carefully scaffolded exchanges in which a more expert individual supports a novice participating in a given activity. At other times, the support is characterized by learners observing more accomplished members of their communities or by working in collaboration with other learners. As learners engage in an unfamiliar activity with the support of others over time, they assume greater independence in contributing to and accomplishing that activity, ultimately appropriating it into their repertoire of cultural practices. Underlying the discussion of the roles social interaction and activity play in learning is the assumption that learning proceeds from the social to the individual (Rogoff, 2003). As Vygotsky (1987) aptly explains, "What the child is able to do in collaboration today he will be able to do independently tomorrow" (p. 211).

Domains of Teacher Learning

The domains of teacher expertise described below have been adapted from the work of Shulman (1987) and Shulman et al. (1995). They consider five categories along which teachers develop over a life of study and practice: vision, motivation, knowledge, reflection, and practice. In the following discussion of these interacting dimensions, we reference specific learning processes that draw on the sociocultural perspectives described above. We do not intend to provide an exhaustive description of each dimension. Rather, we highlight aspects of teacher knowledge related to the education of ELs that have been overlooked in other accounts or models of teacher learning, including knowledge about what it means to know, learn, and teach language and subject-matter content to multilingual and second-language learners.

Vision

Vision is a dispositional cluster of attributes that includes the goals, hopes, and dreams a teacher has for her teaching and for her students. We propose a short-term vision for the microlevel notion of how teaching and learning could ideally operate in a classroom, and what students can accomplish in a class. At the macrolevel, vision encompasses both the teacher's aspirations to reach a level of excellence individually and collectively, and the goal of students to be able to perform their roles as active, contributing members of society at the conclusion of their studies. This vision focuses proleptically not on who students are today but on who they can be tomorrow as a result of effective learning and teaching.

Motivation

Drawing on the sociocultural perspective to teacher learning that we advocate, we do not conceive of motivation as simply an attribute or characteristic that resides within the individual. Instead, it is inextricably connected to the various dimensions of teachers' experience and the contexts in which these experiences are embedded. Aspects of the social environment in which teachers live and work assert an important influence on teachers' motivation and sense of efficacy. These include the networks of relationships that contribute to teachers' and students' motivation and engagement in academic tasks. Whereas Hudley and Chhuon (Chapter 19, this volume) emphasize the role teachers play in supporting student motivation, we have found that teachers' relationships with others (e.g., students, other teachers, administrators, families, and community members) affect their ability to establish the pedagogical learning environment that promotes student achievement and motivation. The way in which teachers are treated in a school and the opportunities they are afforded to collaborate around the specifics of their work, make it possible for them to draw on these same collaborative contexts in their classes. It is difficult for teachers in an authoritarian environment to teach collaboratively (Nadelstern, 2004). Furthermore, the larger institutional contexts, including the current set of curricular policies that determine how and what teachers teach, not only threaten teachers' sense of self-efficacy and autonomy, but also their motivation and desire to continue to pursue a career in teaching.

Knowledge

This dimension of our model refers to the range of understandings that accomplished teachers of ELs must possess in order to effectively meet the needs of their students. Drawing on an adaptation of Shulman's model of teacher expertise (Walqui, 2010), these understandings may be categorized in the following domains:

- pedagogical knowledge;
- subject-matter knowledge;
- pedagogical content knowledge;
- knowledge of students.

Pedagogical knowledge refers to general understandings about learning and teaching that are foundational to teachers' work across subject areas and students. Knowledge about how youngsters learn and principles of curriculum and instruction—including the linkages between instruction and assessment, curricular planning, and classroom organization—are just some of the understandings that fall in this category.

Subject-matter knowledge comprises the teacher's knowledge of main concepts and relationships in a given subject area or discipline as well as the approaches used to generate subject-matter knowledge, including, for example, the canons of evidence and proof shared by subject-matter communities. Subject-matter knowledge also includes knowledge about what it means to know languages, including the language practices and genres used to express and negotiate meanings related to specific disciplines. As sociolinguists have demonstrated over the last 30 years, language is more than an inventory of discrete forms and skills. It is a semiotic tool individuals use to communicate with one another shaped by the social and cultural contexts in which they live, work, and learn. In considering the interface between language and disciplinary knowledge, it is important to be alert to how language works in all subject-matter areas.

Pedagogical content knowledge is the knowledge teachers possess about *how* to teach a specific subject, including concepts and themes thought to comprise a subject, to specific groups of students. In considering the needs and circumstances of ELs, pedagogical subject matter knowledge as it relates to the learning of language and content includes the following understandings about language variation, bilingualism, and second-language learning.

Given our goal of supporting the learning of individuals who are, to varying degrees, bilingual and multicultural, we must be cognizant of the variable nature of bilinguals' language proficiency and practice. Because children deemed to be ELs often live in communities where they have access to multiple language varieties, their language proficiency is distributed across these varieties. Unlike balanced views of bilingual competence driven by a view of the ideal bilingual as an individual who has native-like proficiency in each language, children growing up in communities characterized by the use of multiple varieties often "translanguage," meaning that they draw on one or the other or both of their languages to construct meaning, which may entail using different languages for different modalities or functions (Garcia, 2009). For many of these children, the very act of switching language conveys meanings that are unattainable via the use of a single language. By privileging a standard monolingual native-speaker norm, schools and classrooms often obfuscate children's ability to translanguage. Thus, instead of holding students to a monolingual native-speaker norm, schools should aim to develop students who become "successful multicompetent speakers" (Cook, 1999, p. 204).

Research also indicates that instruction in the child's home language is a valuable resource for English learners' acquisition of content and English (Greene, 1997; Ramirez, Yuen, & Ramey, 1991; Thomas & Collier, 2002; Willig, 1981–1982, 1985). Further, a well-established body of research has found positive relationships in ELs' learning of specific aspects of literacy in their first and second languages (Dressler & Kamil, 2006; Nagy, Garcia, Durgunoglu, & Hancin-Bhatt, 1993; Proctor, Carlo, August, & Snow, 2006; Royer & Carolo, 1991; Verhoeven, 1994). In addition, several researchers have found that cross-linguistic transfer operates in two directions, moving from students' second language to their first language as well as from their first language to their second language (e.g., Barrera, 1983; Edelsky, 1986; Hudelson, 1984; Reyes, 2001) Moreover, students who are allowed to access their first language while engaging with English texts or concepts may also use it as a means to reflect on, negotiate, and better understand those texts or concepts (Lantolf & Thorne, 2006; Moll & Diaz, 1987). Dworin (2003), as quoted in Garcia (2009), highlights the bidirectional aspect of bilingual children's literacy development and language use practices in characterizing biliteracy development as the "dynamic, flexible process in which children's transactions with two written languages mediate their language learning for both languages" (p. 345).

As many scholars have documented (Valdés, 2004; Valdés, Bunch, Snow, Lee, & Matos, 2005), ELs tend to be enrolled in classrooms where the emphasis is on the learning and teaching of English, usually via an atomistic presentation of grammar and vocabulary and/or a sequential approach that first focuses on listening followed by speaking, reading, and finally writing. Despite this pervasive trend, researchers have demonstrated that a mastery of linguistic form is not a prerequisite for engaging in academic activity in the second language (e.g., Bunch, Lotan, Valdés, & Cohen, 2005; Valdés, 2004). Not having so-called native-like ability in a language does not preclude using that language to express complex concepts and ideas (Alvarez, Valdés, & Capitelli, 2010; Ballenger, 1997, 2005; Merino & Hammond, 2002; Rosebery, 1997; Warren, Ballenger, Ogonowski, Rosebery, & Hudicourt-Barnes, 2001).

Over the last 20 years, researchers and educators have argued for pedagogical approaches that enhance the academic language development of ELs (e.g., Pease-Alvarez & Hakuta, 1992; Valdés, 1998). Although the exact academic language needs of this student group have been the subject of some debate, leading scholars agree that schools have not been successful in involving ELs in using language for a range of academic functions (e.g., Bunch, 2006, in press; Valdés, 2004; Walqui et al., 2010). They argue that learning academic language entails engaging students in a range of academic tasks in which they use an extensive repertoire of oral and written language abilities, including a variety of genres and registers associated with different academic disciplines. What is key for ELs' development of academic content and academic language is their participation in academic activity that entails the use of their full range of semiotic resources.

Research on first- and second-language acquisition conceives of interaction as a key context for the development of language (Bruner, 1983; Ellis, 1994; van Lier, 1996; Walqui & van Lier, 2010). In regard to second-language acquisition, researchers have focused on various dimensions of inter-action, including the use of verbal moves, such as paraphrases and requests for elaboration or clarification that a second-language learner's interlocutor uses to support the learner in extending or rewording verbal contributions (Walqui & van Lier, 2010). Also, when second-language learners are required to produce verbal contributions, often termed *language output,* within the context of communicative exchanges, they process and ultimately learn to produce language that would not be available to them if they only listened to the language of others (Swain, 2005). Educators drawing on classroom interaction studies have identified a number of ways in which teachers can support or scaffold ELs' development of oral language, literacy, and content in their second language (Gibbons, 2002, 2009; Walqui, 2007, 2010). In addition, classroom language studies involving second-language learners have alerted us to various aspects of interaction among peers that benefit their learning of language and content (Bunch, 2006, in press).

Knowledge of students is crucial. Not surprisingly, researchers have underscored the variable nature of ELs' language, literacy, and content development (e.g., August & Hakuta, 1997; August & Shanahan, 2006). Given the complexities of classroom life, there is no guarantee that paying attention to and enacting the principles mentioned up to this point will directly translate into positive learning environments and improved student outcomes. Indeed, some researchers have found that teachers with commitments to one or more of these pedagogical principles may foster classroom environ-ments that may be detrimental to children's learning and social well-being (e.g., Ernst-Slavit, 1999; Gutiérrez, 1995). That is to say, teachers' "good" intentions do not necessarily match the reality of the classroom environments in which they work. For this reason, knowledge of principles such as those mentioned here does not suffice when it comes to developing classrooms that are productive and equitable learning environments. Teachers of ELs must also constantly monitor, assess, and evaluate the learning and teaching that goes on in their classrooms. This must include not only examining ELs' academic work and outcomes but also ELs' participation in classroom activities. Recent accounts of teacher research focused on ELs' learning and classroom participation describe revisions to classroom instruction that appear to improve EL students' opportunities to learn (Gonzalez, Moll, & Amanti, 2005; Willett & Rosenberger, 2005; Willett, Harman, Hogan, Lozano, & Rubeck, 2008).

Further, numerous studies have documented the cultural practices that are part of the socializa-tion of ELs in their social networks outside of school (Baquedano-Lopez, 2000; Gonzalez, 2001; Orellana, 2009; Solsken, Willett, & Wilson-Kennan, 2000; Valdés, 2003; Vasquez, Pease-Alvarez, & Shannon, 1994). Inspired in part by the work of Gonzalez et al. (2005), there is a commitment among many educators to make sure that the cultural practices that are part of ELs' everyday lives and social networks are viewed as instructional resources. However, in achieving this goal, it is important not to draw on monolithic and essentialist views that attribute a practice or disposition to a group, particularly in light of the variable, dynamic, and hybrid nature of ELs' participation in their cultural communities (Gutiérrez & Rogoff, 2003). Instead, in planning learning opportunities in their classroom, teachers are advised to engage in inquiry focused on the cultural practices that are available to ELs outside of school.

Reflection

Teachers become fully conscious of their own understandings, performances, and dispositions when they reflect metacognitively with the purpose of learning and deliberately strengthening the opportunities they provide their students to learn and develop. We find that three kinds of reflection are important in teaching (van Manen, 1991). In the case of *anticipatory reflection*, teachers deliberately consider and decide among options to follow in their teaching, anticipating consequences, deliberating as to which pedagogical road may work best for the specific students they teach. *Interactive reflection* relates to the "thinking on their feet" that teachers engage in, as they enact decisions, monitor their impact, and decide on variations to their plans to contingently respond to students' emerging needs. *Recollective reflections* occur when teachers revisit past events and decisions to learn for future application. Reflection is the engine that drives teacher expertise as they deliberately interrogate situations and consider optimal and less appropriate choices to guide their teaching.

Practice

Teachers may have ambitious goals for their students, they may possess knowledge of their disciplines and how to teach them, they may be motivated to do a good job, and still, as they enact lessons, they may not be able to translate all their knowledge, dreams, and skills into practice that is robust, well supported, and responsive to the needs of students. In an ideal situation, teachers apprentice how to translate knowledge into appropriate (situated in the particulars of a class) plans and then into good enacted lessons. This apprenticeship could begin during their clinical experience as they codesign lessons and team teach with master teachers. It could then continue through their first years of practice through coaching, intervisitations, lesson-planning sessions, lesson study, or analysis of the artifacts that students produced during a lesson.

Given the immense complexity of American classrooms and the multiple needs of varied English learners, schools must provide teachers with structures and time to collaborate with each other, learning together how best to serve their students. In most European and Asian countries, teachers spend less than half of their working time teaching; the rest of the time they work on tasks related to teaching (Wei, Darling-Hammond, Andree, Richardson, & Orphanos, 2009).

Applying the Model

The approach to teacher learning we describe here has important implications for the education of teachers who are prepared to meet the needs of ELs living in urban settings. Here, we elucidate a set of themes that describe key processes integral to the professional development of prospective and practicing teachers.

The Collaborative and Situated Nature of Teacher Education

We conceptualize teacher learning as most productively evolving over a professional life sustained by collaborative structures and actions that have been deliberately created to increase the impact of their work. Ideally, preservice and practicing teachers participate in professional learning communities where they are constantly expected to connect the theoretical with the practical as well as to theorize from practice. However, unlike traditional models of preservice education, in which prospective teachers take coursework on college campuses and participate in student teaching placements for a few hours of the day in public school classrooms, we endorse an approach to teacher education that is situated within schools and communities. Teacher education faculty along with other members of school communities directly support the learning of prospective students as they negotiate the activity of teaching. They work around a model of learning and teaching where every course, every meeting, and every action is designed to build teacher expertise to provide ELs and all other students with high levels of challenge and support.

Once they assume positions as practicing teachers, novice teachers are productively served within the context of these learning communities, in which a good part of their support comes from colleagues who regularly visit them in their classrooms and jointly reflect on classroom events. Within the context of these collaborative communities, accomplished teachers provide novices with disciplinary and pedagogical support.

Unlike novice teachers, experienced teachers are more comfortable teaching the various subject areas and are able to better negotiate the cultures of their school communities. They continue to work collaboratively with their peers as they themselves enhance their expertise to meet the challenges of an ever-changing educational environment. When compared to novice teachers, these teachers contribute more to the schoolwide agenda, including the development of schoolwide policies and norms, the pedagogical vision of the school community, and the administration of the school site.

Learning through Doing

In providing the appropriate support to teachers throughout their careers, teachers work collaboratively to develop and enact the understandings and practices that comprise this instructional model. Based on our experience as teacher educators, this is done in two important ways. First, it is necessary to engage teachers in the activities that they expect their students to appropriate, accompanied by reflection and analysis that ultimately supports them in designing, implementing, and revising these activities in their own classrooms. Second, as they reflect on and analyze their enactments of these activities in their own classrooms, with the support of other more knowledgeable teachers, they appropriate these practices into their teaching repertoire. Thus, not only do teachers engage in authentic collaborative learning/teaching activities, in which they draw on the support of others to learn concepts that they plan to teach, they also engage in authentic learning/teaching activity with their students, supported by more knowledgeable teachers.

Teacher as Policymaker

A synergistic relationship exists between teacher learning and the policy contexts in which teachers live and work. Simply put, teachers are not mere conduits of educational policy, including those described in this chapter. They learn and transform as they negotiate the policy environment. In addition, the policies that they are expected to enact often transform. As teachers work with students, their interpretations and implementations of policy initiatives may emanate from deeply held principles about learning and teaching (e.g., Achinstein & Ogawa, 2006; Datnow & Castellano, 2000; Joseph, 2006; MacGillivray, Ardell, Curwen, & Palma, 2004; Pease-Alvarez & Samway, 2008). In many cases this has resulted in adapting practices that are part of curricular mandates. In a few cases, teachers have been part of collective actions that have led to new or revised policies and/or policy recommendations (Compton & Weiner, 2008; Pease-Alvarez & Thompson, 2011). In addition, their understandings about learning, teaching, and knowing also change as they attempt to enact, mitigate, and/or resist policy mandates (Pease-Alvarez & Samway, 2008).

In line with this perspective on policymaking, we advocate supporting teachers in assuming a generative role in the policymaking process in ways that enable them to draw on their pedagogical understandings and first-hand experiences with ELs as they dialogue with other educational stakeholders. An important aspect of this dialogue includes teachers working with others (e.g., researchers and teacher educators) to investigate how curricular policies are affecting their students' opportunities to learn in classrooms (Willett & Rosenberger, 2005; Willett et al., 2008). For example, in their description of an M.A. degree for teachers that involves them in research on their classroom practices with professors, district administrators, other teachers, and parents, Willet et al. (2008) describe a collaborative that enabled teachers to transform standardized practices emanating from curricular mandates. Interestingly, in this case, a professional development initiative provided an institutionally approved venue through which the collaborative negotiation and renegotiation of curriculum and policy occurred. Moreover, an important aspect of this work was the generation of important knowledge about teaching and learning that informed teachers' classroom practices.

In our work as teacher educators, we have participated in other collaborative efforts to influence policy. For example, we have worked with a group of teachers known as Educators Advocating for Students (EAS) that has successfully advocated for teachers' voices in setting district policies (Pease-Alvarez & Thompson, 2011). EAS first emerged as an opportunity for teachers of English learners to get together on a regular basis to share professional concerns about and experiences with standardized approaches to instruction and assessment that were mandated by their local district. Over time, EAS, which merged with a subcommittee of the local teachers' union, engaged in a variety of activities, including writing letters to local newspapers describing teachers' concerns about state and district mandated testing and assessment policies; appearing on local community television programs describing these concerns; and participating in collective bargaining efforts that led to including a clause in their contract requiring the district to seek teacher input on testing and assessment policies. Members of EAS were compelled by a set of pedagogical principles, including a commitment to balanced education (i.e., teaching science, social studies, art, and music, in addition to reading and mathematics), a reduction in time and resources spent on standardized testing, focusing on students' development of biliteracy, and a view of teacher as an active and vital participant in instructional decision-making.

How does a school with limited expertise to serve their English learners, even among their veteran teachers, arrive at the communities of teachers who continuously learn together outlined above? An example is provided by the work of the Quality Teaching for English Learners (QTEL) implementation in Austin, Texas (Walqui & van Lier, 2010). All educators in a high school engage in professional development for three years through a multiple embedded model in which work starts with the educational leadership, which is intended to help support the program and enable teachers to take on the roles of the professional developers. Each year administrators and teachers receive six days of professional development in their discipline, focused on how to develop the disciplinary uses of English. The curriculum weaves activities that address issues of vision, knowledge, and pedagogy, and engages participants in multiple reflections around their specific school situation. A subset of teachers in each subject area receives coaching support to focus on the translation of ideas into practice, and in reflection on lessons planned and enacted. These are the teachers who will first open their classrooms to school colleagues to observe and reflect on practice together during the second year of implementation. An even smaller number of teachers, self-selected from the group of teachers who are coached, prepare to be professional developers, the teachers at the school who will be able, at the end of three years, to apprentice new colleagues to the school culture and the ways of working with academic rigor and deliberate support in teaching ELs and all other students. During the third year, teachers who have been coached and then prepared to coach join the QTEL team in coaching, thus expanding coaching support for all teachers at the school.

This model creates collective capacity at a school; it is guided by the same vision of excellence for all students. It also creates coherence of approaches to the education of ELs and other students because it is anchored in disciplinary work. Furthermore, it fosters a growing sense of internal accountability (Elmore, 2006). Rather than firing most teachers at a school to turn it around, similar models of teacher professional development can be created to address the great needs of students and teachers in our schools. In the end, unless teachers are involved in collaborative, well-supported opportunities to grow, they will not be able to design these opportunities or enact them with their students.

References

Achinstein, B., & Ogawa, R. T. (2006). (In)fidelity: What the resistance of new teachers reveals about professional principles and prescriptive educational policies. *Harvard Educational Review, 76*(1), 30–63.

Alvarez, L., Valdés, G., & Capitelli, S. (2010). What is the role of accuracy in English language proficiency assessments? Paper presented at the annual conference of the American Association of Applied Linguistics, Chicago.

August, D., & Hakuta, K. (Eds.) (1997). *Improving schooling for language minority children.* Washington, DC: National Academy Press.

August, D., & Shanahan, T. (Eds.) (2006). *Developing literacy in second-language learners: Report of the National Literacy Panel on language-minority children and youth.* Mahwah, NJ: Lawrence Erlbaum Associates.

Ballenger, C. (1997). Social identities, moral narrative, scientific argumentation: Science talk in a bilingual classroom. *Language and Education, 1*(1), 1–14.

Ballenger, C. (2005). "I would sing everyday": Skepticism and the imagination. In L. Pease-Alvarez & S. R. Schecter (Eds.), *Learning, teaching, and community: Contributions of situated and participatory approaches to educational innovation* (pp. 27–46). Mahwah, NJ: Lawrence Erlbaum Associates.

Baquedano-Lopez, P. (2000). Narrating community in doctrina classes. *Narrative Inquiry, 20*(2), 429–452.

Barrera, R. (1983). Bilingual reading in the primary grades: Some questions about questionable views and practices. In T. H. Escobedo (Ed.), *Early childhood bilingual education: A Hispanic perspective* (pp. 164–184). New York: Teachers College Press.

Batalova, J., Fix, M., & Murray, J. (2007). *Measures of change: The demography and literacy of adolescent English Learners—A report to Carnegie Corporation of New York.* Washington, DC: Migration Policy Institute.

Bruner, J. (1983). *Child's talk: Leaning to use language.* New York: W. W. Norton.

Bunch, G. C. (2006). "Academic English" in the 7th grade: Broadening the lens, expanding access. *Journal of English for Academic Purposes 5,* 284–301.

Bunch, G. C. (in press). The language of ideas and the language of display: Expanding conception of "academic language" in linguistically diverse classrooms. In K. Rolstad (Ed.), *Rethinking school language.* Mahwah, NJ: Lawrence Erlbaum Associates.

Bunch, G. C., Lotan, R., Valdés, G., & Cohen, E. (2005). Keeping content at the heart of content-based instruction: Access and support for transitional English learners. In J. Crandall & D. Kaufman (Eds.), *Content-based instruction in primary and secondary school settings* (pp. 11–25). Alexandria, VA: Teachers of English to Speakers of Other Languages.

Capps, R., Fix, M., Murray, J., Ost, J. Passel, J., & Hirontoro, S. (2005). *The new demography of America's schools: Immigration and the No Child Left Behind Act.* Washington, DC: Urban Institute.

Compton, M., & Weiner, L. (2008). *The global assault on teaching, teachers, and their unions: Stories for resistance.* New York: Palgrave Macmillan.

Cook, V. (1999). Going beyond the native speaker in language teaching. *TESOL Quarterly, 33*(2), 185–209.

Darling-Hammond, L. (2000). Teacher quality and student achievement: A review of state policy evidence. *Education Policy Analysis Archives, 8*(1), 1–44. Retrieved October 2009 from: http://epaa.asu.edu/epaa/v8n1

Datnow, A., & Castellano, M. (2000). Teachers' responses to Success for All: How beliefs, experiences, and adaptations shape implementation. *American Educational Research Journal, 37*(3), 775–799.

Dressler, C., & Kamil, M. (2006). First- and second-language literacy. In D. August & T. Shanahan (Eds.), *Developing literacy in second-language learners: Report of the National Literacy Panel on language-minority children and youth* (pp. 197–246). Mahwah, NJ: Lawrence Erlbaum Associates.

Dworin, J. (2003). Insights into biliteracy development: Toward a bidirectional theory of bilingual pedagogy. *Journal of Hispanic Higher Education, 2,* 171–186.

Edelsky, C. (1986). *Writing in a bilingual program: Había una vez.* Norwood, NJ: Ablex.

Ellis, N. (Ed.) (1994). *Implicit and explicit learning of languages.* London: Academic Press.

Elmore, R. (2006). Leadership as the practice of improvement. OECD. Paper presented at the international conference on Perspectives on Leadership for Systemic Improvement, sponsored by the Organisation for Economic Cooperation and Development (OECD, London).

Ernst-Slavit, G. (1999). Come join the literacy club: One Chinese ESL child's literacy experience in a 1st-grade classroom *The Free Library.* Retrieved May 20, 2011 from: www.thefreelibrary.com/Come+Join+the+Literacy+Club%3a+One+Chinese+ESL+Child's+Literacy...-a078356243

Fix, M., & Passel, J. (2003). *U.S. immigration trends and implications for schools.* Washington, DC: Urban Institute.

Gándara, P., & Baca, G. (2008). NCLB and California's English language learners: The perfect storm. *Language Policy, 7,* 201–216.

Gándara, P., & Contreras, F. (2009). *The Latino education crisis. The consequences of failed social policies.* Cambridge, MA: Harvard University Press.

Gándara, P., & Hopkins, M. (2010). Forbidden language: The changing linguistic landscape of the United States. In P. Gándara & M. Hopkins (Eds.) *English learners and restrictive language policies* (pp. 7–19). New York: Teachers College Press.

Gándara, P., Maxwell-Jolly, J., & Driscoll, A. (2005). *Listening to teachers of English learners.* Santa Cruz, CA: Center for the Future of Teaching Learning.

García, O. (2009). *Bilingual education in the 21st century: A global perspective.* Malden, MA: Wiley-Blackwell.

García, O., Kleifgen, J., & Falchi, L. (2008). *From English language learners to emergent bilinguals.* New York: Teachers College Campaign for Educational Equity.

Gibbons, P. (2002). *Scaffolding language, scaffolding learning.* Portsmouth, NH: Heinemann.

Gibbons, P. (2009). *English learners, academic literacy, and thinking: Learning in the challenge zone.* Portsmouth, NH: Heinemann.

Goldenberg, C. (2008). Teaching English language learners. What the research does and does not say. *American Educator,* Summer, 8–21. Retrieved May 20, 2011 from: www.aft.org/pdfs/americaneducator/summer2008/goldenberg.pdf

Gonzalez, N. (2001). *I am my language: Discourses of women and children in the borderlands.* Tucson: University of Arizona Press.

Gonzalez, N., Moll, L., & Amanti, C. (2005). *Funds of knowledge: Theorizing practices in households, communities, and classrooms.* Mahwah, NJ: Lawrence Erlbaum Associates.

Greene, J. P. (1997). A meta-analysis of the Rossell and Baker review of bilingual education research. *Bilingual Research Journal, 21*(2/3), 1–22.

Gutiérrez, K. D. (1995). Unpacking academic discourse. *Discourse Processes,* 19, 21–37.

Gutiérrez, K. D., & Rogoff, B. (2003). Cultural ways of learning; Individual traits or repertoires of practice. *Educational Researcher, 32*(5), 19–25.

Harper, C. A., de Jont, E., & Platt, E. J. (2008). Marginalizing English as a second language teacher expertise: The exclusionary consequence of No Child Left Behind. *Language Policy,* 7, 267–284.

Hudelson, S. (1984). Kan yu ret an rayt en Ingles: Children become literate in English as a second language. *TESOL Quarterly, 18*(2), 221–238.

Joseph, R. (2006). "I won't stop what I'm doing": The factors that contribute to teachers' proactive resistance to scripted literacy programs. Paper presented at the annual meeting of the American Educational Research Association.

Lantolf, J. P., & Thorne, S. L. (2006). *Sociocultural theory and the genesis of second language development.* Oxford, UK: Oxford University Press.

Legislative Analyst's Office (2008). *Analysis of the 2007–08 budget: English learners.* Sacramento, CA: Legislative Analyst's Office.

MacGillivray, L., Ardell, A. L., Curwen, M. S., & Palma, J. (2004). Colonized teachers: Examining the implementation of a scripted reading program. *Teaching Education, 15*(2), 131–144.

Maxwell-Jolly, J., Gándara, P., & Méndez Benavides, L. (2007). *Promoting academic literacy among secondary English language learners: A synthesis of research and practice.* Davis: University of California, Davis, Linguistic Minority Research Institute.

Merino, B. J., & Hammond, L. (2002). Writing to learn: Science in the upper-elementary bilingual classroom. In M. C. Colombi & M. J. Schleppegrell (Eds.), *Developing advanced literacy in first and second languages* (pp. 227–244). Mahwah, NJ: Lawrence Erlbaum Associates.

Moll, L. C., & Diaz, E. (1987). Change as the goal of educational research. *Anthropology and Education Quarterly, 18*(4), 300–311.

Nadelstern, E. (2004) Interview with Aida Walqui. San Francisco, CA: WestEd.

Nagy, W., Garcia, G. E., Durgunoglu, A. Y., & Hancin-Bhatt, B. (1993). Spanish-English bilingual students' use of cognates in English reading. *Journal of Reading Behavior, 25*(3), 241–259.

National Center for Education Statistics (2009). *The Nation's Report Card (NAEP): State profiles.* Washington, DC: U.S. Department of Education, Institute of Education Sciences. Retrieved May 20, 2011 from: http://nces.ed.gov/nations reportcard/states

Orellana, M. F. (2009). *Translating childhoods: Immigrant youth, language, and culture.* Piscataway, NJ: Rutgers University Press.

Passel, J. (2008). Projections from the Census 2000. Power point presentation to the Annie E. Casey Foundation, June.

Pease-Alvarez, L., & Hakuta, K. (1992). Enriching our views of bilingualism and bilingual education. *Educational Researcher, 21*(2), 4–7.

Pease-Alvarez, L., & Samway, K. D. (2008). Negotiating a top-down reading program mandate: The experiences of one school. *Language Arts, 86*(1), 32–41.

Pease-Alvarez, L., & Thompson, A. (2011) Teachers organizing to resist in a context of compliance. In K. Davis (Ed.), *Critical qualitative research in second language studies: Agency and advocacy* (pp. 277–295). Charlotte, NC: Information Age Publishing.

Proctor, C. P., Carlo, M. S., August, D., & Snow, C. (2006). The intriguing role of Spanish language vocabulary knowledge in predicting English reading comprehension. *Journal of Educational Psychology, 98*(1), 159–169.

Public Policy Institute of California (2004). *How are immigrant youth faring in California?* San Francisco, CA: Public Policy Institute of California.

Ramirez, J. D., Yuen, S. D., & Ramey, D. R. (1991). *Final report: Longitudinal study of structured immersion strategy, early-exit, and late-exit transitional bilingual education programs for language-minority children.* San Mateo, CA: Aguirre International.

Reyes, M. L. (2001). Unleashing possibilities: Biliteracy in the primary grades. In M. L. Reyes & J. J. Halcon (Eds.), *The best for our children: Critical perspectives on literacy for Latino students* (pp. 96–121). New York: Teachers College Press.

Rogoff, B. (2003). *The cultural nature of human development.* Oxford, UK: Oxford University Press.

Rosebery, A. S. (1997). Appropriating scientific discourse: Findings from language minority classrooms. *The Journal of Learning Sciences, 2*(1), 61–94.

Royer, J. M., & Carolo, M. S. (Eds.) (1991). Transfer of comprehension skills from native to second language. *Journal of Reading 34*(6), 450–455.

Solsken, J., Willett, J., & Wilson-Kennan, J. (2000). Cultivating hybrid texts in multicultural classrooms: Promise and challenge. *Research in the Teaching of English, 35*, 179–211.

Shulman, L. (1987). Knowledge and teaching: Foundations of the new reform. *Harvard Educational Review, 57*, 114–135.

Shulman, L. et al. (1995). Fostering a community of teachers and learners. Unpublished progress report to the Mellon Foundation.

Swain, M. (2005). The output hypothesis: Theory and research. In E. Hinkel (Ed.), *Handbook of research in second language teaching and learning* (pp. 471–484). Mahwah, NJ: Lawrence Erlbaum Associates.

Swanson, C. B. (2009). *Perspectives on a population: English-language learners in American schools.* Bethesda, MD: Editorial Projects in Education.

Thomas, W. P., & Collier, V. P. (2002). *A national study of school effectiveness for language minority students' long-term academic achievement.* Berkeley: University of California, Center for Research on Education, Diversity and Excellence.

Valdés, G. (1998). The world outside and inside schools: Language and immigrant children. *Educational Researcher, 27*(6), 4–18.

Valdés, G. (2003). *Expanding definitions of giftedness: The case of young interpreters from immigrant communities.* Mahwah, NJ: Lawrence Erlbaum Associates.

Valdés, G. (2004). Between support and marginalization: The development of academic language in linguistic minority children. *International Journal of Bilingual Education and Bilingualism, 7*(2–3), 102–132.

Valdés, G., Bunch, G., Snow, C., Lee, C., & Matos, L. (2005). Enhancing the development of students' languages. In L. Darling-Hammond & J. Bransford (Eds.), *Preparing teachers for a changing world: What teachers should learn and be able to do* (pp. 126–161). San Francisco, CA: Jossey-Bass.

van Lier, L. (1996). *Interaction in the language curriculum: Awareness, autonomy, and authenticity.* London: Longman.

van Manen, M. (1991). *The tact of teaching: The meaning of pedagogical thoughtfulness.* Albany: State University of New York Press.

Vasquez, O. A., Pease-Alvarez, L., & Shannon, S. M. (1994). *Pushing boundaries: Language and culture in a Mexicano community.* New York: Cambridge University Press.

Verhoeven, L. T. (1994). Transfer in bilingual development: The linguistic interdependence hypothesis revisited. *Language Learning, 44*(3), 381–415.

Vygotsky, L. S. (1987). Thinking and speech. In R. W. Rieber & A. S. Caron (Eds.), *The collected works of L. S. Vygotsky* (N. Minick, Trans.) (pp. 37–285). New York: Plenum.

Walqui, A. (2007). Literacy for adolescent English learners: Building capacity for quality programs. Paper presented at the National High School Center Summer Institute, Washington, DC.

Walqui, A. (2010). The growth of teacher expertise for teaching English language learners: A socioculturally based professional development model. In T. Lucas (Ed.), *Teacher preparation for linguistically diverse classrooms: A resource for teacher educators.* London: Taylor & Francis.

Walqui, A., & van Lier, L. (2010). *Scaffolding the academic success of adolescent English language learners: A pedagogy of promise.* San Francisco, CA: WestEd.

Walqui, A., Koelsch, N., & Hamburger, L. (2010). *What are we doing to middle school English learners? Findings and recommendations for change from a study of California EL programs* (Research Report). San Francisco, CA: WestEd.

Warren, B., Ballenger, C., Ogonowski, M., Rosebery, A. S., & Hudicourt-Barnes, J. (2001). Rethinking diversity in learning science: The logic of everyday sense-making. *Journal of Research in Science Teaching, 38*(5), 529–552.

Wei, R. C., Darling-Hammond, L., Andree, A., Richardson, N., & Orphanos, S. (2009). *Professional learning in the learning profession: A status report on teacher development in the United States and abroad.* Dallas, TX: National Staff Development Council.

Willett, J., & Rosenberger, C. (2005). Critical dialogue: Transforming the discourses of educational reform. In L. Pease-Alvarez & S. R. Schecter (Eds.), *Learning, teaching, and community: Contributions of situated and participatory approaches to educational innovation* (pp. 191–213). Mahwah, NJ: Lawrence Erlbaum Associates.

Willett, J., Harman, R., Hogan, A., Lozano, M. E., & Rubeck, J. (2008). Transforming standard practices to serve the social and academic learning of English language learners. In L. Stoops Verplaetese & N. Migliacci (Eds.), *Inclusive pedagogy for English language learners: A handbook of research-informed practices* (pp. 16–54). Mahwah, NJ: Lawrence Erlbaum Associates.

Willig, A. C. (1981–1982). The effectiveness of bilingual education: Review of a report. *NABE Journal, 6*(2/3), 1–19.

Willig. A. C. (1985). A meta-analysis of selected studies on the effectiveness of bilingual education. *Review of Educational Research 55*(3), 269–317.

22

Effects of Ethnically Segregated Learning Settings in the United States and Germany

Julia Eksner and Petra Stanat

In the United States and in many European countries, urban schools are characterized by relatively high rates of students from disadvantaged families, nondominant groups,[1] and homes in which the language spoken is not the language of instruction in schools. Because many youth in urban schools attain below-average scores on standardized achievement tests (Lippman, Burns, & McArthur, 2004), research on institutional determinants of student achievement has explored whether the composition of the student body in these schools affects achievement.

The underlying idea of research on composition effects is that an individual student's success is influenced by the extent to which students in his or her school share certain background characteristics. Most of this research has focused on students' mean socioeconomic status and mean prior ability or achievement as class or school-level determinants of achievement outcomes (Hattie, 2002; Thrupp, Lauder, & Robinson, 2002). As the proportion of youths from nondominant groups—including immigrant youths—has increased in urban schools in most Western countries, the role of immigrant status as well as ethnic or language background of the student body has attracted growing attention during recent years.

Research on ethnic composition effects explores the question whether students' immigrant status and ethnic or language background at the aggregate level of classrooms or schools impacts their educational success.[2] As this chapter describes in some detail, studies in different countries and educational systems have yielded contradictory results. Some of the more recent and methodologically sophisticated investigations indicate that there are, in fact, school composition effects of students' social and ethnic or language background as well as level of prior achievement. However, the interplay among these factors is not sufficiently understood. A series of studies performed in Germany indicate that ethnic or language background effects tend to disappear when the social composition and prior achievement levels of the student body are controlled.

In this chapter we first frame research on ethnic composition effects historically, and critically discuss the concept of ethnicity as diversely employed in this line of research. We then introduce the German case by describing the historical, social, and educational context of ethnic segregation in schools in Germany, and then describe and juxtapose theory and assumptions underlying research on ethnic composition effects as they are discussed in the United States and Germany. Subsequently, we present current empirical evidence on ethnic composition effects in Germany, and close with a discussion of these findings and questions to be addressed by future research.

Framing Research on Ethnic Composition Effects

Early research on composition effects performed in the United States was strongly influenced by the political and social climate of the mid-1960s, in which the Civil Rights Movement was at its height and Congress passed the Civil Rights Act, mandating school desegregation. School segregation was regarded through the principle that "separate is inherently unequal" (Ladson-Billings, 2004). Based on achievement outcomes of students in segregated schools in the southern United States, educational research at this time was fueled by the view that the separation and segregation of students from nondominant and dominant groups leads to increased disadvantage of the former (Siddle Walker, 2000). Research that focused on composition effects was strongly influenced by this idea and investigated the hypothesis that racial school segregation impedes minority members' access to educational resources and their ability to acquire communication patterns or a more general *habitus* acceptable to members of the dominant society (Caldas & Bankston, 1998; Hawley & Smylie, 1988). Simultaneously, educational sociology applied theory about the relationship between individuals and social structure to the question of composition effects in schools (Coleman, 1966; Dreeben & Barr, 1988; Rumberger & Willms, 1992).

In Germany, educational research has begun to explore the question of composition effects much more recently, as segregated school settings have become an issue only during the last 10 to 20 years. For a long time, schools in Germany were considered to be composed of homogeneously German student bodies.[3] With about 25% of children and youths in Germany coming from immigrant families, however, German schools are highly diverse today, leading to an increasing interest in ethnic composition effects in schools.

As in the United States, the dominant theoretical approach to ethnic composition effects in Germany comes from the sociology of education, which investigates the effects of the social environment on students' educational pathways. This approach is influenced by an ecological perspective (Bronfenbrenner, 1979): schools as social and ecological settings of youth development and learning are viewed as important determinants of students' educational pathways and as specific ecological settings in which everyday activities and practices structure the development and learning of young people (Baumert, Stanat, & Watermann, 2006; Bronfenbrenner, 1979; Cole, 1996; Rogoff, Baker-Sennett, Lucasa, & Goldsmith, 1995). The attendance of a particular school (and, within the German tracking system, a particular type of school[4]) then implies differential opportunities for development independent of and in addition to a young person's individual intellectual, cultural, social, and economic resources (Baumert et al., 2006).

Current research in both Germany and the United States explores whether ethnic composition is a significant determinant of students' achievement outcomes. In order to investigate ethnic composition effects, it is necessary to define the category of ethnicity at a conceptual and operational level. In addition, it requires theoretical assumptions on how ethnic composition effects may unfold. As our review will show, research conducted in the United States and Germany differs in how the category of ethnicity and the underlying processes have been conceptualized.

Ethnicity as a Research Category in the United States and Germany

Ethnic composition effects have been operationalized by various types of group membership in different research traditions. In the United States, "ethnicity"—the identification with population groups characterized by common ancestry, language, and custom (American Anthropological

Association, 1997)—and "race" are the central categories used to define group membership in educational research. The federal standards for the reporting of "ethnicity" and "race" issued by the U.S. government define these categories in terms of social and cultural characteristics as well as biological ancestry.[5] They are generally assessed via self-identification of respondents. These self-reported categories are widely used in U.S. educational research today.

Educational research in Germany (as well as in Switzerland and Austria) does not have comparable guidelines, nor does the category "ethnicity" occupy a similarly central role in research on immigrants and their descendants as it does in the United States. In Germany, as elsewhere, people are thought to belong to ethnic or national groups. However, until recently the official position denied that Germany is an immigration country with ethnocultural diversity (see below). Official ethnicity categories do not exist and empirical data sets including the ethnic background of respondents were almost nonexistent until the early 2000s (the data of the Socio-Economic Panel (SOEP) being the only exception). Therefore, educational research in Germany was, until very recently, forced to operationalize ethnic group membership based on citizenship.[6] Immigrants from a range of different sending countries were most commonly agglomerated into the single composite category of "foreigner"—that is, noncitizen. Although this category strictly represents citizenship, it possesses an ethnic aspect because of the implicit correspondence between ethnicity and citizenship that was codified in German citizenship law until its revision in 2000. The dichotomist model of noncitizen "foreigner" as opposed to "German citizen" was very visible in government publications as well as public discourse from the 1970s to 1990s and continues to be used today (Bundesministerium des Inneren, 2007; Engelmann, 1984; Fennell, 1997; MBBBA, 1995; Seifert, 1998; Statistisches Bundesamt, 2008). Because of a fast-growing population of immigrants, with increasing numbers of students in German schools being born to immigrant parents who themselves have German citizenship, however, the limitations of this approach became more and more apparent. As a result, the categories most commonly employed by researchers today are based on other proxies of ethnicity as well on theoretical assumptions about the processes determining immigrant youths' educational outcomes. These indicators include the child's, the parents', and the grandparents' country of birth (i.e., first, second, or third immigrant generation (Portes & Rumbaut, 2001, 2005)) and the language spoken at home or the first language acquired, respectively.

While currently these are the categories most commonly used for analyses in educational research, segmented patterns of outcomes and processes for the largest immigrant populations in Germany have been identified (e.g., Segeritz, Walter, & Stanat, 2010). As a result, the use of the composite category will most likely decrease and "ethnicity" (defined by the specific country of birth or language spoken at home) will be used instead.

The German Case

There are three trends that make the question of ethnic composition effects in German schools a timely one for educational researchers: first, a large increase in the number of children and youths from immigrant families growing up in Germany, giving rise to increasing patterns of ethnic segregation in schools; second, findings of international studies on student achievement showing that children and adolescents from immigrant families living in Germany experience educational inequity particularly harshly, thus indicating that structures and processes particular to the German setting might contribute to this inequity; and third, a concern with the evolving patterns of interethnic segregation in German schools that work along horizontal (i.e., school choice) as well as vertical (i.e., school type) lines. In order to better understand the particular focus and findings of German studies on effects of segregated school settings, the following sections introduce the historical, social, and educational context in which immigrant youths come of age in Germany.

Immigrant Youth in Germany

Currently, more than 15 million people (18.7%) in Germany have an immigrant background (Statistisches Bundesamt, 2008). Large-scale immigration flows between 1953 and 1973 brought so-called guest workers from southern and southeastern European countries to Germany. The expectation of the German government as well as of the immigrants themselves was that they would return to their home countries after a three-year sojourn in Germany. However, as employers needed skilled and experienced workers, many work permits were extended. As a consequence, guest workers often brought their families from their home countries to stay with them in Germany.

After 1973, when guest workers were no longer recruited by the German government and labor immigration stopped, the incoming flow of relatives who were joining their families in Germany continued, and the percentage of children and youth from immigrant families increased noticeably during this period. Nevertheless, the social and educational provisions made for the children of immigrants in Germany continued to be largely absent or insufficient. The presence of children and youth from immigrant families was not a central issue addressed by governmental policy.

The growing concern with the social and educational equity for immigrant youths in German society is indeed a fairly recent development. At the turn of the millennium, there was a noticeable shift from affirmations that Germany "is not an immigration country" to one in which the successful "integration" of immigrants into German society became—and it continues to be—one of the most heatedly discussed topics in politics and the media. As a result of this debate, the reform of German naturalization law in the year 2000 made it easier for immigrants and their children born in Germany to obtain German citizenship, whereas it had been very difficult to impossible before.

The reform of the naturalization law coincided with the publication of the sobering results of the first and second Programme for International Student Assessment (PISA) studies in 2000 and 2003 (Baumert et al., 2001; Stanat & Christensen, 2006). The findings shook Germany's political and academic landscape, because PISA was the first investigation to present achievement results for the entire population of 15-year-olds with an immigrant background regardless of citizenship. Basic assumptions were now overturned.

It became clear that immigrants made up more than 20% of the population and not only 9%, as census data based on citizenship had suggested for a long time. Moreover, PISA revealed that students from immigrant families in Germany scored significantly lower than their nonimmigrant peers in all achievement domains. These findings jump-started a national agenda to understand and address the educational disparities between students from immigrant families and students from native families, as well as an interest in the effects of the ethnic composition of classrooms and schools.

Today, most Germans with an immigrant background are second- and third-generation immigrants with German citizenship; only about 9% of the population are immigrants without citizenship. In 2007, the nine largest immigrant groups came from the following countries: Turkey, 14.2%; the Russian Federation, 9.2%; Poland, 6.9%; Italy, 4.2%; Romania, Serbia, and Montenegro, each 3%; Croatia, 2.6%; Bosnia Herzegovina, 2.3%; and Greece, 2.2%.

Germany's immigrant populations cluster in its urban centers, especially in Stuttgart (40% of the population there are immigrants), Frankfurt (39.5%), and Nuremberg (37%) (Statistisches Bundesamt, 2008). In six cities more than 60% of the children under the age of five have an immigrant background, including Nuremberg (67%), Frankfurt (65%), Dusseldorf, and Stuttgart (each 64%). Across Germany, including its rural areas and the eastern states, where very few immigrants live, about 30% of the children under the age of five have an immigrant background (Statistisches Bundesamt, 2008); in some urban school districts, they make up the majority of the student body.

The social and historical context of immigration to Germany presents specific challenges for immigrant communities in establishing access to institutional networks and resources (Caglar, 1995). Immigrants can be found at all levels of society, yet many immigrant families are positioned at the lower socioeconomic levels. Immigrants in Germany are twice as likely as other Germans to have incomes that are below the poverty line (32% of immigrants), have higher exposure to crime and violence (Pfeiffer & Wetzels, 2000), are three times as likely to be unskilled workers (44% of immigrants), experience twice the rate of unemployment (29% of immigrants), are 2.5 times as likely to drop out of high school (17.5% of immigrant students),[7] and show a distinct pattern of lower educational achievement than students from families without immigrant background (Kristen, 2008; Ohliger & Raiser, 2005; Schwippert, Bos, & Lankes, 2004; Stanat & Christensen, 2006).[8]

These data mirror the low symbolic, cultural, and educational capital of immigrants in Germany (Bourdieu, 1977; Maaz, Baumert, & Cortina, 2008). Thus, immigrants' social positioning in Germany is characterized by disadvantage, even as ongoing demographic change is slowly eroding the formerly clear-cut majority–minority relationship.

Educational research shows that for students from immigrant families there is a consistent, albeit segmented, achievement gap (e.g., Baumert et al., 2001; Schümer, 2004; Stanat & Christensen, 2006). In 2008, some 40% of immigrant students were attending the lowest track of the German education system, as opposed to only 15% of ethnically German students. Almost half of the students without an immigrant background (45%) but only a fifth of immigrant students (21%) were in the highest track (A-level courses) (Bundesministerium des Inneren, 2007). The pronounced overrepresentation of immigrant students in the lowest track coincides with a large achievement gap (Kornmann, 2006; Müller & Stanat, 2006; Stanat, 2009; Stanat & Christensen, 2006). The PISA studies also revealed that immigrant students in Germany fare worse compared with their peers from nonimmigrant families than in most of the other 43 countries participating in the PISA studies (Stanat & Christensen, 2006). These results have focused research attention on the structural and institutional conditions that led to this strong educational inequity for immigrant youths in Germany (Alba, Handl, & Müller, 1998).

Ethnic Segregation in German Schools

Currently, there are no large-scale data on school segregation in Germany or its urban centers. The available findings are based on case studies of schools that are considered representative of "segregated" schools in Germany's urban neighborhoods (Baur & Häussermann, 2009; Radtke, 2007). Based on these cases, several processes that are hypothesized to lead to school segregation in the German context have been discussed. Theory building on the processes leading to ethnic school segregation in Germany and the United States has developed along different lines, mainly because of distinct empirical realities giving rise to these processes.

There is a reality of inequality along the lines of ethnicity and social class in both the United States and Germany. School composition effects must be viewed in light of these patterns of inequality. Findings for the United States indicate that housing and employment patterns create conditions that promote the development of urban communities, in which predominantly disadvantaged families live. In such residentially segregated contexts, school segregation will also be a reality (Ladson-Billings, 2004; Powell, Kearney, & Kay, 2001). The current trend toward the resegregation of U.S. schools, despite continued government effort to desegregate, is a reflection of this process (Frankenberg & Lee, 2002; Orfield & Yun, 1999).

In Germany, a trend toward segregation along the lines of neighborhood contexts seems to exist as well, although it is much less pronounced than in the United States. The patterns of segregation in Germany's urban schools must be understood as the result of varied and perhaps different processes. Current theory and research on school segregation in Germany considers residential segregation as only one of several determinants of school composition, along with the central role of the tracked school system and school selection processes of middle-class parents. There might then be different processes at work in different national settings that are defined by different sets of social and educational structures. Ethnic segregation in German schools today is considered to be the result of a range of factors, including the tracking system, the quality of life in the neighborhood, the pedagogical profile of the school, selection practices, the quality of neighborhood schools, and the preferences of parents choosing a school for their children (Kristen, 2002; Radtke, 2007).

Although public discourse perceives a steady increase in segregation between Germans and immigrant groups and the development of an immigrant "parallel society," the available data are sparse and contradictory. Some studies suggest that segregation in Germany exists and is strongest for Turkish and Moroccan citizens (Friedrichs, 2008). Recent analyses indicate, however, that the residential segregation between Germans and immigrants *without* German citizenship—and particularly immigrants with Turkish citizenship—appears to have *decreased* since 1976. However, a methodological problem in the interpretation of these findings is that they are based on citizenship (i.e., German citizen vs. noncitizen) and fail to include second- and third-generation immigrants with German citizenship.

In fact, there are no data available on segregation patterns for immigrants *with* German citizenship. Thus, the "German" category includes all immigrants with German citizenship, who in the second and third generation make up a considerable proportion of the population. Consequently, the increased integration reported in this study might be an artifact of increased naturalization rates. Nevertheless, overall census data indicate that even those neighborhoods in urban centers that are considered most segregated have heterogeneous population structures with both German and immigrant residents. Furthermore, the sociostructural characteristics of exclusion and risk are not at all comparable with those found in the urban ghettos of the United States (Wacquant, 2007). Residential segregation of nondominant groups in Germany is generally much less pronounced than in the United States.

Although strong patterns of residential segregation are absent in Germany, there is nevertheless an established pattern of interethnic segregation or preference for friendship homophily. A recent study based on survey data of the Federal Institute for Population Research explored the homogeneity of friendship networks of Germans, German Italians, and German Turks aged 18–30. The overall finding was that friends are most often selected within ethnic groups. Nevertheless, interethnic friendship exists. Interethnic friendship with Germans and members of other ethnic groups is more frequent among immigrants (more than 40%) than among Germans (23%) (Haug, 2003, 2006).[9] Other studies have also identified a generational effect (Esser, 1990; Wimmer, 2002).

Segregation in the German School System

Historical and Vertical Tracking

Despite differences in degree, urban schools in both the United States and in Germany reflect a "hypersegregation" (Ladson-Billings, 2004) that is more pronounced than the pattern found in the cities' overall populations. Some research suggests that schools—not neighborhoods—may be the primary sites for the ethnic separation of Germany's youth.[10] Prior to the recruitment of immigrant workers, who subsequently had their families move as well, schools in Germany were largely integrated, comprising only small percentages of children of immigrants.

In the 1970s, the temporary creation of "regular foreigner classes" (*Ausländerregelklassen*) in some urban centers, such as Berlin, led to government-regulated ethnic segregation. These classes included only "foreign" (i.e., noncitizen) students. The underlying rationale for this policy was that the students would soon return to their home countries; hence, there was no need to integrate them into the German school system. Instead, lessons in their mother tongue (*Muttersprachlicher Unterricht*) prepared them for their return "home." In Berlin, the proportion of immigrant children and youth in regular classrooms was limited to 30% or 50% (Gogolin & Niedrig, 2001; Pfaff, 1991). These quotas were abolished during the mid-1990s (Baur & Häussermann, 2009).

Another mechanism of ethnic segregation in schools works *vertically* via educational stratification processes. As pointed out above, approximately 40% of immigrant students are assigned to the lowest track of the three-tier school system (Maaz, Watermann, & Baumert, 2007; Solga & Wagner, 2001, 2004). Especially in urban areas, the lowest track is characterized by a relatively homogeneous social structure—a large percentage of the students come from families of low socioeconomic status. Therefore, the composition of the student body in these schools involves an agglomeration of risk and stress factors, such as parents' lack of educational capital and frequent unemployment (Baur & Häussermann, 2009).

Parental School Choice

According to Radtke (2007), the segregation of urban schools in Germany is primarily caused by middle-class German as well as immigrant parents, who opt out of neighborhood schools deemed insufficient and who have the necessary social and cultural capital to realize their preferences for their children's schooling (Radtke, 2007). As a result, schools in Germany do not simply mirror the social composition of the neighborhood. Instead, because middle-class parents living in neighborhoods with higher proportions of immigrants tend to pull their children out of these schools, low-income urban neighborhood schools tend to be more homogeneously composed of students from families of low socioeconomic status and low educational capital. Social problems then appear to be even more concentrated in the schools than in the neighborhoods in which they are located (Baur & Häussermann, 2009; Solga & Wagner, 2004).

These two processes—stratification within the tracked educational system and middle-class parents' flight from neighborhood schools in urban centers—lead to the concentration of students from families of low socioeconomic status and low educational capital in urban neighborhood schools and lower tracks. The question research has been asking then, is whether the existing patterns of school segregation and, as a result, the ethnic composition of the student body, affect school achievement.

Theoretical Models and Empirical Findings

Researchers in both the United States and Germany are currently trying to move from simply determining the extent, to which a relationship between the ethnic composition of the school and achievement outcomes exists, to identifying the processes underlying this relationship. Research has explored social composition and prior achievement as determinants of achievement outcomes at the school level (see the review of empirical findings below). In the U.S. setting, the organizational, curricular, pedagogical, and cultural arrangements of the school have been proposed to be responsible for ethnic composition effects. For instance, families from ethnic minorities are often disproportionally represented in poor neighborhoods. Schools in these neighborhoods have been found to attract lower funding levels and less motivated teachers (Dreeben & Barr, 1988; Rumberger & Willms, 1992). This, in turn, should influence the academic, social, and disciplinary climate in the school, resulting in lower achievement levels.

In Germany, it is especially students' language competency that is thought to cause ethnicity effects (Esser, 2001). This assumption has probably become the most influential model of ethnic composition effects in Germany today. The idea is that in ethnically segregated learning settings there are fewer opportunities for interethnic contact and therefore fewer opportunity structures for using the language of instruction (Esser, 2006). This restricted "time on task" is thought to impair the acquisition of the language of instruction, which in turn is assumed to result in lower achievement across all school subjects. Some of the empirical studies reviewed below build on this conceptualization and conduct analyses of segmented educational achievement patterns for students whose families immigrated from Turkey or the former Soviet Union—families that represent the largest immigrant groups in Germany.

The Role of Peer Group and Teachers

Thus far, systematic analyses of the role that peer groups and teachers play in the ethnic composition effects are lacking. Yet a few analyses have explored the extent to which peer-group and teacher characteristics may contribute to the emergence of social composition effects. Because of the overlap between ethnic and social composition, the processes identified in these studies may help to explain ethnic composition effects as well.

First, the achievement and behavioral norms of the peer group as well as competition, emulation, or identification with the peer group were suggested to mediate social composition effects (Baumert et al., 2006). Peer groups and (ethnic) youth subcultures may be hypothesized to influence students' academic attitudes and behaviors (Bottrell, 2009; Louie, 2006; Silbereisen & Titzmann, 2007). The general "attitude" or "school climate" in ethnically segregated schools may be determined by these peer group norms (Thrupp et al., 2002). However, a study by Baumert et al. (2006) exploring this mediator failed to reveal any effects.

Second, it has been argued that the expectations and behaviors of teachers may mediate student outcomes as students' internalize or react to adults' view of themselves; that is, identity development is influenced by teacher expectations (see, e.g., Burns & Mason, 1995; Caldas & Bankston, 1998; Hattie, 2002; Westerbeek, 1999). In schools in which the majority of students are subject to negative teacher expectations (because of stereotypes about the scholastic aptitude of students from minority groups), internalization processes could lead to lower scholastic achievement of the student body.

Thus, several mechanisms can be assumed to cause ethnic composition effects in classrooms and schools. The question, then, becomes whether such effects do, in fact, occur. As the next section shows, the research evidence on this issue is mixed.

Empirical Findings on Ethnic Composition Effects

Again, most research carried out so far has explored effects of the *social* composition of the student body in schools or classrooms. Noticeably fewer studies have analyzed effects of *ethnic* composition or the percentage of children from immigrant families attending a school. Although potential costs and benefits of segregated learning settings are discussed in Germany as well as in other countries, conclusive empirical research is limited. Most importantly, there is a dearth of research on the potentially underlying mechanisms discussed in the literature.

The pioneering study by Coleman (Coleman, 1966), based on data of the Equality of Educational Opportunity Study, indicates that the social composition (i.e., mean socioeconomic status of students in a school) influences achievement outcomes more than any other factor. His findings also suggest that African American students would benefit from integrated schooling with a majority of White students in the classroom. Methodological concerns about the validity of these findings were raised early on, however (Hauser, Sewell, & Alwin, 1976), pointing out that the conclusions of the Coleman report were questionable.

More recently, social composition effects have been explored in a range of studies in Europe, the United States, and Australia, some of which also examined the effects of ethnic composition (Fekjaer & Birkelund, 2007; Hattie, 2002; Lee, H., 2007; Rumberger & Willms, 1992; Stanat, 2006; Stanat, Schwippert, & Gröhlich, 2010; Thrupp et al., 2002). The findings of these studies are contradictory (Stanat, 2006; Thrupp et al., 2002), primarily due to inconsistent conceptualizations of ethnic composition and methodological problems. For the identification of composition effects, longitudinal study designs that allow for a control of students' prior achievement or ability are necessary. More specifically, it is necessary to assess students' competencies at the time they enter the more or less segregated school setting in order to estimate the extent to which learning development over time is affected by compositional factors. This was possible in one of these studies (Stanat et al., 2010). Other investigations with cross-sectional designs used general cognitive ability as a proxy for prior achievement, which is not optimal but seems to result in reliable estimates as well (Baumert et al., 2006).

Empirical Findings on Ethnic Composition Effects in Germany

Since large-scale data for Germany have become available during the last 10 years, researchers investigated social and ethnic composition effects with increasing methodological sophistication. The large-scale character of these studies allowed for analyses of the relationship between students' social and ethnic backgrounds as well as of their prior achievement or ability levels. The analyses described below were conducted chronologically and build on each other.

In one of the first German studies, Kristen (2002) analyzed fourth-grade classrooms in six elementary schools and found that a higher proportion of students with an immigrant background in a classroom was associated with a reduced likelihood of making the transition to the higher tracks of secondary schooling. A limitation of these analyses was that the study controlled for grades in German and math as a proxy for prior achievement. In studies involving several schools, however, grades are poor indicators of achievement levels, as teachers tend to grade students by comparing the individual child to the social reference frame of reference within each classroom. This limits the interpretability of the results.

In analyses of the PISA 2000 data, a test of general cognitive ability was used as an indicator for students' prior achievement (on the validity of this indicator, see Baumert et al., 2006) and students' immigrant background was operationalized with the language spoken at home (Stanat, 2006). The findings of hierarchical linear modeling confirmed the hypothesis that, within the lowest track of the school system (*Hauptschulen*), a higher percentage of immigrant students speaking a language other than German at home is associated with lower achievement levels (Stanat, 2006).

For each percentage point increase in the proportion of immigrant students within a school, reading competency levels on average decreased by half a point on the PISA scale. Further analyses revealed that in schools, in which 40% or more of the youths did not speak German at home, students' scores on the PISA reading test were on average 25 points lower than the scores of students in schools where less than 5% of the youths did not speak German at home. This difference is equivalent to an achievement lag of about one year (Baumert & Artelt, 2002).

Although this result seemed to confirm the existence of an ethnic composition effect, further analyses complicated the findings. In schools with many students from immigrant families, the mean socioeconomic status of the student body also tends to be low. Similarly, students from immigrant families show lower scores on assessments of mean ability. After controlling for these characteristics at the school level, the effect of ethnic composition disappeared.

A second series of analyses conducted with the PISA 2003 data confirmed that the effects of a high percentage of immigrant students may not be specifically associated with the ethnic composition of the student body. Again, after socioeconomic status and mean ability were controlled at the school level, no significant ethnic composition effects remained (Stanat, 2006).

As pointed out earlier, language plays a central role in German theory building on ethnic composition effects. According to the theoretical model of Esser (2006), a high proportion of students from immigrant families at the school level should lead to disadvantage when the group is ethnically homogeneous and the language of everyday interaction is not the language of instruction, as is the case in many schools in the U.S. school system as well as in a number of urban schools in Germany. Thus, the percentage of immigrant students in schools should primarily affect the achievement of students from immigrant families.

However, estimates of cross-level interactions between the percentage of students speaking in a language other than German at home at the school level and the language spoken at home at the individual level did not reveal the predicted differential effects (Stanat, 2006). The results showed that students speaking another language and students speaking German at home were equally affected by the composition of the student body. The findings from the PISA 2000 data, then, could not confirm Esser's hypothesis (Stanat, 2006).

Walter and Stanat (2008) further investigated Esser's hypothesis by analyzing segmented patterns for youths from different immigrant groups using the PISA 2003 data. For youths whose families came from the former Soviet Union, the results did not reveal a significant composition effect. For youths whose families immigrated from Turkey, however, a significant composition effect was identified. In schools with less than 40% of students from Turkish immigrant families, this effect was no longer significant after students' socioeconomic status and ability levels at the school level were controlled. Yet in schools with more than 40% of students from Turkish immigrant families, the composition effect remained significant even when socioeconomic status and ability levels were held constant. This latter finding is disconcerting and will require further research to explore the underlying mechanisms that account for the ">40% effect."

Another study by Kristen (2008) focused on school choice processes and how they contribute to ethnic school segregation. Mechanisms that may account for ethnic differences in school choice were analyzed based on the primary school choice of families of Turkish and German origin. The results revealed that children with Turkish as their first language are more likely than children with German as their first language to enter a school with relatively higher proportions of students of immigrant background—a pattern that in the aggregate seems to contribute to an increasing ethnic separation at the school level. This study, however, did not find evidence for an independent effect of ethnic school composition on achievement outcomes. When average cognitive ability of the student body was controlled, there was no association between the percentage of immigrant students who spoke German as their first language and their reading and math achievement. There also was no significant effect for German Turkish students in particular. This study thus contributes further evidence indicating that it is the mean prior achievement of the student body that influences the development of learning in these settings, while ethnic composition characteristics appear to be secondary (cf. Baumert et al., 2006; Thrupp et al., 2002).

The strength of the evidence described so far was limited, however, because the studies are based on cross-sectional data and used only proxies of prior achievement in their analyses. Walter and Stanat (2008) were the first to present a longitudinal analysis, which investigated competency development from the end of ninth grade to the end of tenth grade based on data from PISA 2003. When students' average cognitive ability and average socioeconomic status were controlled, these analyses also failed to yield an independent ethnic composition effect. However, the observation frame of one year was relatively short, and most students had already been exposed to the composition characteristics of their classrooms for several years. For an optimal assessment of composition effects, it is necessary to assess cognitive ability and prior achievement *before* students enter the classroom or school and to model their competency development over a longer period of time.

With data of the longitudinal KESS study (*Kompetenzen und Einstellungen von Schülern und Schülerinnen*—Competencies and Attitudes of Students; Bos et al., 2006), which assessed school-related competencies of children from the fourth through ninth grades, such analyses have become possible. The most recent study based on these data analyzed student competencies in reading at the beginning of grade 7 while controlling prior achievement at the end of grade 4 (Stanat et al., 2010). Initially, these analyses showed a linear negative effect on reading achievement of the percentage of students who do not speak German at home.

After controlling for the social composition of the student body (operationalized as the average socioeconomic status of their families), this effect decreased. When average prior achievement was controlled for as well, the ethnic composition effect was no longer significant. A similar pattern was found in separate analyses for students who spoke Turkish at home. After controlling for social and prior achievement composition of the classrooms, there was no significant ethnic composition effect for Turkish-speaking students. However, the effect of mean socioeconomic status on achievement outcomes remained in these analyses even after controlling for mean ability. These findings indicate once more that ethnic composition effects can, for the most part, be accounted for by the mean socioeconomic background and prior achievement levels of the student body in classrooms (Kristen, 2008; Stanat, 2006; Walter, 2006; Walter & Stanat, 2008; Westerbeek, 1999).

Discussion

The findings for the German case reviewed in this chapter converge on the central finding that lower student achievement in schools with a high percentage of immigrants is not specifically associated with the ethnic composition of the student body. After prior achievement is controlled for longitudinally, which is necessary for a correct estimation of composition effects, no independent effect of the proportion of immigrant students in a school on competence development could be observed. Similarly, controlling for mean socioeconomic status of students tends to reduce the size of ethnic composition effects considerably.

Whereas the findings of the studies discussed in this chapter all point in a similar direction, there are patterns in the empirical data that remain unexplained and that require future analyses. In particular the ">40% effect" requires further investigation. Although this effect has not been identified consistently, at least one recent study showed that in schools with more than 40% of students from Turkish families, the effect of ethnic composition remained significant, even when mean socioeconomic status and ability levels were controlled (Walter & Stanat, 2008). If this effect is replicated in future studies, analyses exploring the underlying mechanisms should be carried out.

More generally, there is a dearth of research on the processes underlying ethnic and social composition effects, and efforts aimed at identifying the underlying mechanisms should be increased.

In addition, future research should consider not only the risks but also potential benefits of neighborhood and school settings that are characterized by ethnic and social homogeneity. Most of the literature on context effects studies potentially negative effects of social and ethnic segregation in neighborhoods and schools. This perspective has been challenged by U.S. practitioners and educational researchers interested in instructional approaches based on positive ethnic and racial identity in voluntarily segregated school settings.

The curricula of these schools challenge the traditional focus on detrimental effects of segregated schools and provide voluntarily segregated learning environments for students from nondominant groups in order to positively impact the processes thought to affect student achievement, such as language acquisition and use, peer-group processes, identity development, or curricular and cultural arrangements in the school. These learning environments (such as the Afrocentric Betty Shabazz International Charter School in Chicago) provide developmental settings that are segregated yet differ in striking ways from marginalized segregated schools in urban low-income communities (Lee, C.D., 2007).

Initial outcomes documented in these schools indicate that it is possible to reach high levels of achievement in segregated learning settings. This adds to the existing evidence and suggests that it is not membership in a nondominant group per se that leads to lower average achievement in schools. Instead, the context and climate (norms and values, curricula, resources) in segregated school settings move into the center of attention, as these contribute to how students view themselves, and the positive, protective, or stigmatizing identities they come to develop.

A range of recent studies has adopted this perspective and suggests that attending schools, which are predominantly composed of students from one's own reference group may, under some circumstances, have beneficial effects on identity development and school achievement[11] (cf. Portes & Hao, 2004, for segmented patterns). Schools in which negative racialization experiences are minimized (Chavous, Rivas-Drake, Smalls, Griffin, & Cogburn, 2008; Neblett, Philip, Cogburn, & Sellers, 2006) and in which a strong and positive identity orientation is part of the curriculum (Chavous et al., 2003) seem to positively influence achievement outcomes.

In a similar vein, research has established that the spatial concentration of poverty, unemployment, and low educational status in urban neighborhoods creates conditions that disadvantage children and youth over and above their individual burden of disadvantage (Berton & Stabb, 1996; Spencer et al., 2006; Brenner, Graham, & Mistry, 2008). However, there are also findings that point to ethnic enclaves and neighborhoods functioning as resources for dealing with everyday concerns. In these neighborhoods, close local networks built along the lines of ethnicity, family, and friendship provide valuable support networks (Cook, Herman, Phillips, & Settersten, 2002; Elwert, 1982; Zhou & Bankston, 1994).

Findings for the German case provide some evidence for this hypothesis, as immigrants have been found to have higher social capital—indicated by integration into social networks and social support—than ethnic Germans (Haug, 2006; Nauck, Kohlmann, & Diefenbach, 1997), which may buffer some of the effects of structural disadvantage as immigrants. Educational policy and research must consider both of these perspectives (i.e., disadvantages as well as advantages associated with the formation of ethnic enclaves) concurrently as it attempts to address the equity issue and in particular the question of how ongoing societal processes promote the emergence of ethnically delineated, residentially and educationally segregated segments in society—a relatively recent phenomenon, at least in Germany.

Notes

1. We use the term *nondominant* to refer to ethnolinguistic minorities and immigrant populations. The term *nondominant*, in our view, adequately describes the social and structural positioning of the populations we discuss in this chapter. It does so better than the term "minorities" because in some urban settings these youths are de facto not the minority but the majority; and better than the term "immigrants" because of the difficulties of employing the term *immigrant* to youths whose parents or grandparents already immigrated to the host country. In discussing theoretical models that focus on analyzing the processes contributing to ethnic composition effects and the sample selection criteria of empirical studies, we use more specific terms that identify nondominant group characteristics along the lines of immigrant status, first language spoken, and citizenship.
2. Composition effects are estimated by aggregating the group mean of the independent variable in question (e.g., socioeconomic status or prior ability) or by calculating the proportion of students with a certain background characteristic (e.g., immigrant status).

3. The heterogeneity of students in German schools has partially been masked by the notion of what counts as ethnically German in the available census data. The population of ethnic Germans who lived in Eastern Europe and the former Soviet Union for several generations and who immigrated to Germany since World War II were subsumed under the "German" category and could therefore not be identified.

4. Although the number of private schools is currently increasing, secondary education in Germany is largely public. The public school system includes four main types of schools. Students are assigned to these school types based on their academic achievement at the transition from grade 4 to grade 5, or from grade 6 to grade 7, depending on the German federal state. In the *highest* track (*Gymnasium*) students are prepared for university studies and finish with the *Baccalaureate* diploma after grade 12 or 13 (comparable to British A-levels); in the *middle* track (*Realschule*) students finish with an intermediate diploma (*Mittlerer Schulabschluss*) after grade 10 (comparable to British GCSE); in the lowest track (*Hauptschule*) students are prepared for vocational education and finish after grade 9 or 10. In addition, comprehensive schools (*Gesamtschule*) combining the three tracks exist in some Länder. It should be noted, however, that a reform process is currently under way in Germany, involving a reduction of school types from three to two tracks in many states.

5. The official designations for "race" are "American Indian or Alaskan Native," "Asian or Pacific Islander," "Black or African American," and "White." The designations for "ethnicity" used in the United States are "Hispanic origin" or "not of Hispanic origin."

6. Until 2000, German citizenship was almost exclusively determined by inheritance from parents and not by place of birth. A child born to a German citizen parent automatically acquires German citizenship regardless of the place. Conversely, children born to immigrants without German citizenship did not acquire German citizenship at birth. Since 2000, these children acquire both citizenship of their parents' country of origin and German citizenship, and have to decide for one or the other between the age of 18 and 23. An exception to this rule is the group of ethnic German immigrants (*Aussiedler*) from the former Soviet Union and Eastern Europe who came to Germany in the 1990s. While integration policies and social supports were offered to ethnic German returnees, labor immigrants had to largely take care of themselves.

7. This value is based on data for students without German citizenship (as opposed to those with an immigrant background regardless of citizenship).

8. For all of these outcomes, there are segmented patterns for different immigrant groups. Immigrants with a Russian or Polish background are typically better off than immigrants with a Turkish or Italian background.

9. Very similar findings for younger fourth-grade children in a multicultural school were reported in a study carried out in Austria. The findings showed that 77% of friendship networks of children with German as a native language consisted of other German mother-tongue children. Their friendship networks were more segregated than the friendship circles of children with Turkish, Serbo-Croatian, and other immigrant languages as a first language (Strohmeier, Nestler & Spiel, 2006).

10. The demographic shift that led to schools in which students from nondominant groups represent the majority is relatively recent; therefore, there is no official classification, such as that of the U.S. National Schools Board Association, that assigns German schools the status of being segregated or not.

11. Using data from the *Children of Immigrants Longitudinal Study (CILS)*, Portes and Hao (2004), explored composition effects on grades and high school dropout rates as well as mathematics achievement. They identified a segmented pattern of ethnic composition effects in schools: students from Asian families showed higher achievement in schools with a smaller percentage of students with an Asian background. Conversely, students from Mexican families, who overall showed lower achievement levels, reached higher achievement in schools with a higher percentage of Mexican students. However, this study, like most research on this issue, had methodological limitations, as it did not control for the influence of ability level and social background.

References

Alba, R. D., Handl, J., & Müller, W. (1998). Ethnic inequalities in the German school system. In P. H. Schuck & R. Münz (Eds.), *Paths to inclusion: The integration of migrants in the United States and Germany* (pp. 115–154). New York: Berghahn Books.

American Anthropological Association (1997). *Response to OMB Directive 15: Race and ethnic standards for federal statistics and administrative reporting.* Arlington, VA: American Anthropological Association.

Baumert, J., & Artelt, C. (2002). Untersuchungsgegenstand, Fragestellungen und technische Grundlagen der Studie (Research objective, questions, and technical background of the study). In J. Baumert, E. Klieme, M. Neubrand, M. Prenzel, U. Schiefele, et al. (Eds.), *PISA 2000—Die Länder der Bundesrepublik Deutschland im Vergleich* (pp. 11–38). Opladen, Germany: Leske und Budrich.

Baumert, J., & Klieme, E., Neubrand, M., Prenzel, M., Schiefele, U. et al. (2001). *PISA 2000—Basiskompetenzen von Schülerinnen und Schülern im internationalen Vergleich* (*PISA 2000. Basic competencies of students in international comparison*). Opladen, Germany: Leske und Budrich.

Baumert, J., Stanat, P., & Watermann, R. (2006). Schulstruktur und die Entstehung differenzieller Lern- und Entwicklungsmilieus (School structure and the emergence of differential environments for learning and development). In J. Baumert, P. Stanat & R. Watermann (Eds.), *Herkunftsbedingte Disparitäten im Bildungswesen: Differenzielle Bildungsprozesse und Probleme der Verteilungsgerechtigkeit. Vertiefende Analysen im Rahmen von PISA 2000* (*Educational disparities and family background: Differential educational pathways and problems of just allocation*) (pp. 1–94). Wiesbaden, Germany: VS Verlag für Sozialwissenschaften.

Baur, C., & Häussermann, H. (2009). Ethnische Segregation in deutschen Schulen (Ethnic segregation in German schools). *Leviathan, 37*(3), 353–366.

Berton, M. W., & Stabb, S. D. B. (1996). Exposure to violence and post-traumatic stress disorder in urban adolescents. *Adolescence, 31*(122), 489–499.

Bos, W., Bonsen, M., Gröhlich, C., Guill, K., May, P., & Rau, A. (2006). *KESS 7—Kompetenzen und Einstellungen von Schülerinnen und Schülern—Jahrgangsstufe 7 (Competencies and attitudes of students in grade 7)*. Hamburg, Germany: Behörde für Bildung und Sport.

Bottrell, D. (2009). Dealing with disadvantage: Resilience and the social capital of young people's networks. *Youth & Society, 40*(4), 476–501.

Bourdieu, P. (1977). *Language and symbolic power*. Cambridge, MA: Harvard University Press.

Brenner, A. D., Graham, S., & Mistry, R. S. (2008). Discerning direct and mediated effects of ecological structures and processes on adolescents' educational outcomes. *Developmental Psychology, 44*(3), 840–854.

Bronfenbrenner, U. (1979). *The ecology of human development: Experiment by nature and design*. Cambridge, MA: Harvard University Press.

Bundesministerium des Inneren (2007). *Migrationsbericht 2006 (Migration report 2006)*. Nuremberg, Germany: Bundesamt für Migration und Flüchtlinge.

Burns, R. B. & Mason, D. A. (1995). Organizational constraints on the formation of elementary school classes. *American Journal of Education, 103*(2), 185–212.

Caglar, A. S. (1995). German Turks in Berlin: Social exclusion and strategies for social mobility. *New Community, 21*(3), 309–323.

Caldas, S. J., & Bankston, C. III. (1998). The inequality of separation: Racial composition of schools and academic achievement. *Educational Administration Quarterly, 34*(4), 533–557.

Chavous, T. M., Bernat, D. H., Schmeelk-Cone, K., Caldwell, C. H., Kohn-Wood, L., & Zimmerman, M. A. (2003). Racial identity and academic attainment among African American adolescents. *Child Development, 74*(4), 1076–1090.

Chavous, T. M., Rivas-Drake, D., Smalls, C., Griffin, T., & Cogburn, C. (2008). Gender matters, too: The influences of school racial discrimination and racial identity on academic engagement outcomes among African American adolescents. *Developmental Psychology, 44*(3), 637–654.

Cole, M. (1996). *Cultural psychology: A once and future discipline*. Cambridge, MA: Belknap Press of Harvard University Press.

Coleman, J. S. (1966). *Equality of educational opportunity*. Washington, DC: U.S. Department of Health, Education and Welfare.

Cook, T. D., Herman, M. R., Phillips, M., & Settersten, R. A. Jr. (2002). Some ways in which neighborhoods, nuclear families, friendship groups, and schools jointly affect changes in early adolescent development. *Child Development, 73*(4), 1283–1309.

Dreeben, R., & Barr, R. (1988). Classroom composition and the design of instruction. *Sociology of Education, 61*(3), 129–142.

Elwert, G. (1982). Problem der Ausländerintegration—Gesellschaftliche Integration durch Binnenintegration (Problems in the integration of foreigners—societal integration via interior integration). *Kölner Zeitschrift für Soziologie und Sozialpsychologie, 34*, 717–731.

Engelmann, B. (1984). *Du deutsch? Geschichte der Ausländer in unserem Land (You German? History of foreigners in our country)*. Munich: C. Bertelsmann Verlag.

Esser, H. (1990). Interethnische Freundschaften (Interethnic friendships). In H. Esser & J. Friedrichs (Eds.), *Generation und Identität Theoretische und empirische Beiträge zur Migrationssoziologie (Generation and identity: Theoretical and empirical perspectives on the sociology of immigration)* (pp. 185–205). Opladen, Germany: Westdeutscher Verlag.

Esser, H. (2001). Integration und ethnische Schichtung (Integration and ethnic stratification). In *MZES Arbeitspapiere 40 (MZES Working papers 40)*. Mannheim, Germany: Mannheimer Zentrum für Europäische Sozialforschung.

Esser, H. (2006). *Sprache und Integration. Die sozialen Bedingungen und Folgen des Spracherwerbs von Migranten (Language and integration: The social conditions and consequences of language acquisition of immigrants)*. Frankfurt am Main, Germany: Campus.

Fekjaer, S. N., & Birkelund, G. E. (2007). Does the ethnic composition of upper secondary schools influence educational achievement and attainment? A multilevel analysis of the Norwegian case. *European Sociological Review, 23*(3), 309–323.

Fennell, B. A. (1997). *Language, literature and the negotiation of identity: Foreign worker German in the Federal Republic of Germany*. Chapel Hill: University of North Carolina Press.

Frankenberg, E., & Lee, C. (2002). *Race in American public schools: Rapidly resegregating school districts*. Cambridge, MA: The Civil Rights Project, Harvard University Press.

Friedrichs, J. (2008). Ethnische Segregation (Ethnic segregation). *Kölner Zeitschrift für Soziologie und Sozialpsychologie, 48*, 380–411.

Gogolin, I., & Niedrig, H. (2001). Länderbericht Berlin (State report Berlin). In I. Gogolin, U. Neumann, & L. Reuter (Eds.), *Schulbildung für Kinder aus Minderheiten in Deutschland 1989–1999. Schulrecht, Schulorganisation, curriculare Fragen, sprachliche Bildung (Education for children from minority groups in Germany 1989–1999. School law, school organization, curricular issues, language education)*. Münster, Germany: Waxmann.

Hattie, J. A. C. (2002). Classroom composition and peer effects. *International Journal of Educational Research, 37*(5), 449–481.

Haug, S. (2003). Interethnische Freundschaftsbeziehungen und soziale Integration. Unterschiede in der Ausstattung mit sozialem Kapital bei jungen Deutschen und Immigranten (Interethnic friendship ties and social integration. Differences in social capital between young Germans and immigrants). *Kölner Zeitschrift für Soziologie und Sozialpsychologie, 55*, 716–736.

Haug, S. (2006). Interethnische Freundschaften, interethnische Partnerschaften und soziale Integration (Interethnic friendships, interethnic couples, and social integration). *Diskurs Kindheits- und Jugendforschung, 1*(1), 75–91.

Hauser, R. M., Sewell, W. H., & Alwin, D. F. (1976). High school effects on achievement. In W. H. Sewell, R. M. Hauser, & D. L. Featherman (Eds.), *Schooling and achievement in American society* (pp. 309–341). New York: Academic Press.

Hawley, W. D., & Smylie, M. A. (1988). The contribution of school desegregation to academic achievement and racial integration. In P. A. Katz & D. A. Taylor (Eds.), *Eliminating racism: Profiles in controversy* (pp. 281–297). New York: Plenum Press.

Kornmann, R. (2006). Die Überrepräsentation ausländischer Kinder und Jugendlicher in Sonderschulen mit dem Schwerpunkt Lernen (Overrepresentation of foreign children and youths in schools for special needs children with the focus on learning). In G. Auernheimer (Ed.), *Schieflagen im Bildungssystem (Tilts in the educational system)* (pp. 71–85). Opladen, Germany: Leske und Budrich.

Kristen, C. (2002). Hauptschule, Realschule oder Gymnasium? Ethnische Unterschiede am ersten Bildungsübergang (Lowest, middle, or upper track? Ethnic differences at the first transition in the school system). *Kölner Zeitschrift für Soziologie und Sozialpsychologie, 54*, 534–552.

Kristen, C. (2008). Primary school choice and ethnic school segregation in German elementary schools. *European Sociological Review, 24*(4), 495–510.

Ladson-Billings, G. (2004). Landing on the wrong note: The price we paid for Brown. *Educational Researcher, 33*(7), 3–13.

Lee, C. D. (2007). *The role of culture in academic literacies: Conducting our blooming in the midst of the whirlwind.* New York: Teachers College Press.

Lee, H. (2007). The effects of school racial and ethnic composition on academic achievement during adolescence. *The Journal of Negro Education 76*(2), 154–172.

Lippman, L., Burns, S., & McArthur, E. (Eds.) (2004). *Urban schools: The challenge of location and poverty.* NCES 96–184. Washington, DC: U.S. Department of Education, National Center for Education Statistics.

Louie, V. (2006). Second-generation pessimism and optimism: How Chinese and Dominicans understand education and mobility through ethnic and transnational orientations. *International Migration Review, 40*(3), 537–572.

Maaz, K., Baumert, J., & Cortina, K. S. (2008). Soziale und regionale Ungleichheit im deutschen Bildungssystem (Social and regional disparities in the German educational system). In K. S. Cortina, J. Baumert, A. Leschinsky, K. U. Mayer, & L. Trommer (Eds.), *Das Bildungswesen in der Bundesrepublik Deutschland. Strukturen und Entwicklungen im Überblick (The education system in the Federal Republic of Germany)* (pp. 205–243). Reinbek bei Hamburg, Germany: Rowohlt.

Maaz, K., Watermann, R., & Baumert, J. (2007). Familiärer Hintergrund, Kompetenzentwicklung und Selektionsentscheidungen in gegliederten Schulsystemen im internationalen Vergleich. Eine vertiefende Analyse von PISA Daten (Familial background, competence development, and educational decision-making in tracked school systems in international comparison. An in-depth analysis of PISA data). *Zeitschrift für Pädagogik, 53*(4), 444–461.

MBBBA (1995). *Mitteilungen der Beauftragten der Bundesregierung für die Belange der Ausländer: Die Diskussion über "kulturelle Überfremdung"—eine Erklärung oder erklärungsbedürftig? (Announcements of the federal government's commissioner for the concerns of foreigners: The discussion on "cultural infiltration"—an explanation or something to be explained?).* Bonn, Germany: MBBBA.

Müller, A. G., & Stanat, P. (2006). Schulischer Erfolg von Schülerinnen und Schülern mit Migrationshintergrund: Analysen zur Situation von Zuwanderern aus der ehemaligen Sowjetunion und aus der Türkei (Academic achievement of immigrant students: Analyses on the situation of immigrants from the former Soviet Union and from Turkey). In J. Baumert (Ed.), *Herkunftsbedingte Disparitäten im Bildungswesen: Differenzielle Bildungsprozesse und Probleme der Verteilungsgerechtigkeit (Educational disparities and family background: Differential educational pathways and problems of just allocation)* (pp. 223–255). Wiesbaden, Germany: VS Verlag für Sozialwissenschaften.

Nauck, B., Kohlmann, A., & Diefenbach, H. (1997). Familiäre Netzwerke, intergenerative Transmission und Assimilationsprozesse bei türkischen Migrantenfamilien (Family networks, intergenerational transmission, and assimilation processes in Turkish immigrant families). *Kölner Zeitschrift für Soziologie und Sozialpsychologie, 49*(3), 477–499.

Neblett, E. W. Jr., Philip, C. L., Cogburn, C. D., & Sellers, R. M. (2006). African American adolescents' discrimination experiences and academic achievement: Racial socialization as a cultural compensatory and protective factor. *Journal of Black Psychology, 32*(2), 199–218.

Ohliger, R., & Raiser, U. (2005). *Integration und Migration in Berlin. Zahlen—Daten—Fakten (Integration and Immigration in Berlin. Numbers—Data—Facts).* Berlin: Der Beauftragte des Senats von Berlin für Integration und Migration.

Orfield, G., & Yun, J. (1999). *Resegregation in American schools.* Cambridge, MA: The Civil Rights Project, Harvard University.

Pfaff, C. W. (1991). Turkish in contact with German: Language maintenance and loss among immigrant children in Berlin (West). *International Journal of the Sociology of Language, 90*, 97–129.

Pfeiffer, C., & Wetzels, P. (2000). Junge Türken als Täter und Opfer von Gewalt. (Young Turks as perpetrators and victims of violence). *DVJJ-Journal, 11*(2), 107–113.

Portes, A., & Hao, L. (2004). The schooling of children of immigrants. Contextual effects on the educational attainment of the second generation. *Proceedings of the National Academy of Science, 101*, 11920–11927.

Portes, A., & Rumbaut, R. G. (2001). *Legacies: The story of the immigrant second generation.* Berkeley: University of California Press.

Portes, A., & Rumbaut, R. (2005). Introduction: The second generation and the children of immigrants. Longitudinal study. *Ethnic & Racial Studies, 28*(6), 983–999.

Powell, J. A., Kearney, G., & Kay, V. (2001). *In pursuit of a dream deferred: Linking housing and education policy.* New York: Peter Lang.

Radtke, F.-O. (2007). Segregation im deutschen Schulsystem (Segregation in the German education system). In W.-D. Bukow, C. Nikodem, E. Schulze, & E. Yildiz (Eds.), *Was heißt hier Parallelgesellschaft? (What do you mean by, "Parallel Society"?).* Wiesbaden, Germany: VS Verlag für Sozialwissenschaften.

Rogoff, B., Baker-Sennett, J., Lucasa, P., & Goldsmith, D. (1995). Development through participation in sociocultural activity. *New Directions for Child and Adolescent Development, 67*, 45–65.

Rumberger, R. W., & Willms, J. D. (1992). The impact of racial and ethnic segregation on the achievement gap in California high schools. *Educational Evaluation and Policy Analysis, 14*(4), 377–396.

Schümer, G. (2004). Zur doppelten Benachteiligung von Schülern aus unterprivilegierten Gesellschaftsschichten im deutschen Schulwesen (On the multiple disadvantage of students from underprivileged social strata in the German educational system). In G. Schümer, K. J. Tillmann, & M. Weiß (Eds.), *Die Institution Schule und die Lebenswelt der Schüler. Vertiefende Analysen der PISA-2000-Daten zum Kontext von Schülerleistungen (The school as institution and the life world of students. In-depth analyses of the PISA 2000 data on the context of student achievement)* (pp. 73–114). Wiesbaden, Germany: VS Verlag für Sozialwissenschaften.

Schwippert, K., Bos, W., & Lankes, E.-M. (2004). Heterogenität und Chancengleichheit am Ende der vierten Jahrgangsstufe in den Ländern der Bundesrepublik Deutschland und im internationalen Vergleich. (Heterogeneity and equity at the end of grade four in Germany and in international comparision.) In W. Bos, E. M. Lankes, M. Prenzel, K. Schwippert, R. Valtin, & G. Walther (Eds.), *Iglu: Einige Länder der Bundesrepublik Deutschland in nationalen und internationalen Vergleich (Several federal states of Germany in national and international comparison)* (pp. 165–190). Münster, Germany: Waxmann.

Segeritz, M., Walter, O., & Stanat, P. (2010). Muster des schulischen Erfolgs von jugendlichen Migranten in Deutschland: Evidenz für segmentierte Assimilation? (Patterns of educational success of young immigrants in Germany: Evidence for segmented assimilation?). *Kölner Zeitschrift für Soziologie und Sozialpsychologie, 62*(1), 113–138.

Seifert, W. (1998). Social and economic integration of foreigners in Germany. In P. H. Schuck & R. Münz (Eds.), *Paths to inclusion: The integration of migrants in the United States and Germany* (pp. 83–113). New York: Berghahn Books.

Siddle Walker, V. (2000). Valued segregated schools for African American children in the South, 1935–1969: A review of common themes and characteristics. *Review of Educational Research, 70*, 253–285.

Silbereisen, R. K., & Titzmann, P. F. (2007). Peers among immigrants: Some comments on "Have We Missed Something?" In R. C. M. E. Engels, M. Kerr, & H. Stattin (Eds.), *Friends, lovers and groups* (pp. 155–166). West Sussex, UK: John Wiley & Sons.

Solga, H., & Wagner, S. (2001). Paradoxie der Bildungsexpansion. Die doppelte Benachteiligung von Hauptschülern (The paradoxes of educational expansion. The doubled disadvantage of lower-track students). *Zeitschrift für Erziehungswissenschaft, 4*(1), 107–127.

Solga, H., & Wagner, S. (2004). Die Zurückgelassenen—die soziale Verarmung der Lernumwelt von Hauptschülerinnen und Hauptschülern (The left-behind—The social impoverishment of learning environments of lower track students). In R. Becker & W. Lauterbach (Eds.), *Bildung als Privileg: Erklärungen und Befunde zu den Ursachen der Bildungsgleichheit (Education as privilege: Explanations and findings on the causes of eduational disparity)* (pp. 187–215). Wiesbaden, Germany: VS Verlag für Sozialwissenschaften.

Spencer, M. B., Harpalani, V., Cassidy, E., Jacobs, C. Y., Donde, S., Goss, T. N., et al. (2006). Understanding vulnerability and resilience from a normative developmental perspective: Implications for racially and ethnically diverse youths. In D. Cicchetti & D. J. Cohen (Eds.), *Developmental psychopathology: Vol. 1. Theory and method* (2nd ed., pp. 627–672). Hoboken, NJ: John Wiley & Sons.

Stanat, P. (2006). Schulleistungen von Jugendlichen mit Migrationshintergrund: Die Rolle der Zusammensetzung der Schülerschaft (Educational achievement of adolescents with an immigrant background: The influence of the social composition of the student body). In J. Baumert, P. Stanat, & R. Watermann (Eds.), *Herkunftsbedingte Disparitäten im Bildungswesen: Differenzielle Bildungsprozesse und Probleme der Verteilungsgerechtigkeit (Educational disparities and family background: Differential educational pathways and problems of just allocation)* (pp. 183–213). Wiesbaden, Germany: VS Verlag für Sozialwissenschaften.

Stanat, P. (2009). Heranwachsende mit Migrationshintergrund im deutschen Bildungswesen (Adolescents with immigrant background in the German education system). In K. S. Cortina, J. Baumert, A. Leschinsky, K. U. Mayer, & L. Trommer (Eds.), *Das Bildungswesen in der Bundesrepublik Deutschland (The education system in the Federal Republic of Germany)*. Reinbek, Germany: Rowohlt.

Stanat, P., & Christensen, G. (2006). *Where immigrant students succeed—A comparative review of performance and engagement in PISA 2003.* Paris: OECD.

Stanat, P., Schwippert, K., & Gröhlich, C. (2010). Der Einfluss des Migrantenanteils in Schulklassen auf den Kompetenzerwerb: Längsschnittliche Überprüfung eines umstrittenen Effekts (The influence of the percentage of immigrants in school classrooms on competency development: Longitudinal analysis of a debated effect). *Zeitschrift für Pädagogik, 55* (Supplement), 147–164.

Statistisches Bundesamt (2008). *Bevölkerung und Erwerbstätigkeit. Bevölkerung mit Migrationshintergrund—Ergebnisse des Mikrozensus 2007 (Population and employment: Population with immigrant background—Results of the Micro-Census 2007).* Wiesbaden, Germany: Statistisches Bundesamt.

Strohmeier, D., Nestler, D., & Spiel, C. (2006). Freundschaftsmuster, Freundschaftsqualität und aggressives Verhalten von Immigrantenkindern in der Grundschule (Patterns and quality of friendship and aggressive behavior of immigrant children in elementary school). *Diskurs Kindheits- und Jugendforschung, 1*, 21–37.

Thrupp, M., Lauder, H., & Robinson, T. (2002). School composition and peer effects. *International Journal of Educational Research, 37*, 483–504.

Wacquant, L. (2007). French working-class banlieu and Black American ghetto: From conflation to comparison. *Qui Parle, 16*(2), 1–34.

Walter, O. (2006). Die Entwicklung der mathematischen und der naturwissenschaftlichen Kompetenz von Jugendlichen mit

Migrationshintergrund im Verlauf eines Schuljahres (The development of mathematical and science competency of adolescents with immigrant background across one year of schooling). In M. Prenzel, J. Baumert, W. Blum, R. Lehmann, D. Leutner, M. Neubrand, et al. (Eds.), *PISA. 2003—Untersuchungen zur Kompetenzentwicklung im Verlauf eines Schuljahres (PISA 2003 Analyses of competence development across one school year)* (pp. 249–275). Münster, Germany: Waxmann.

Walter, O., & Stanat, P. (2008). Der Zusammenhang des Migrantenanteils in Schulen mit der Lesekompetenz: Differenzierte Analysen der erweiterten Migrantenstichprobe von PISA 2003 (The relationship between percentage of immigrants in schools and reading competency: Differential analyses of the extended immigrant sample of PISA 2003). *Zeitschrift für Erziehungswissenschaft, 11*(1), 84–105.

Westerbeek, K. (1999). *The colours of my classroom. A study into the effects of the ethnic composition of classrooms on the achievement of pupils from different ethnic backgrounds.* Florence, Italy: European University Institute.

Wimmer, A. (2002). Multikulturalität oder Ethnisierung? Kategorienbildung und Netzwerkstrukturen in drei schweizerischen Immigrantenquartieren (Multiculturalism or ethnicization? Category formation and network structures in three Swiss immigrant neighborhoods). *Zeitschrift für Soziologie, 31*(1), 4–26.

Zhou, M., & Bankston, C. L. III. (1994). Social capital and the adaptation of the second generation: The case of Vietnamese youth in New Orleans. *International Migration Review, 28*(4), 821–845.

23

Immigrant Learning

Mariëtte de Haan

Students in migrant settings, particularly in large urban centers, confront multiple sociocultural worlds and traditions. These include both mainstream cultural practices and the migrant cultures that students encounter in the neighborhoods in which they have settled. As a result, an important part of their socialization is to learn to navigate between these multiple worlds and negotiate their diverse semiotic and normative frames. Besides, the trusted paths, networks, traditions, and knowledge present in the families of these students are contested and have to be reinvented. Immigrant parents and children alike are pushed into pioneering work to help the family survive or move up the social ladder. Learning becomes focused on fulfilling immediate knowledge needs rather than on trusting and teaching already-established paths. Who counts as the expert in this case is based on who brings in valuable experience and knowledge rather than on pre-established positions in which older generations pass down knowledge to the younger generation. Such processes always have been true for immigrants, but newer developments now are significantly affecting immigrant learning and socialization. In particular, increasing travel possibilities and students' use of new media mean that the spaces of socialization no longer are confined to the person's location of residence. Immigrants still must navigate among diverse spaces on-location and deal with the particular majority–minority histories that characterize these locations. However, increasingly, their learning is defined by the multiple navigation possibilities in the virtual and material world. This can allow immigrant learners both to continue their affiliations with their networks back home and to build new networks at a variety of geographical scales involving multiple affiliations and sociocultural worlds.

Importantly, these changes are affecting everyone and are not unique to immigrant communities. Most people now find that their social worlds are highly defined by connectivity and increased cultural contact. These highly connected spaces are characteristic both of urban centers and online networks of people located in diverse locations across the world.

"Urban" in this chapter therefore refers to the conditions of highly connected places. This chapter is intended to generate insights that generalize beyond the learning of immigrants in the sense of relatively recent settlers and that tell us something of the learning that more and more is characteristic of our current era. The chapter takes the perspective of immigrants, who often inhabit urban education settings, focusing on their informal *learning* at the levels of individuals, families, and communities.

Learning, Migration, and Diversity

Migrant Condition and Education in the 21st Century

Growing mobility and new communication technologies have increased the rhythm of exchange between different communities and individuals. New media and mass migration have had interconnected and related effects on these developments (Wired Up, www.uu.nl/wiredup/index.htm) and have led to new forms of mobility and connectedness. As Appadurai (1996) argues, social life has become defined by the constant flows of ideas and ideologies, people and goods, images and messages, technologies and techniques; a vision of the social and cultural as being in flux has replaced that of social life as stationary, closed, and stable.

This new mobility, with its variety of flows at a global level, has led to an acceleration of cultural exchange and cultural transformation, and has fundamentally changed the nature of culture, heritage, or tradition and how these relate to places. Cultural meanings and identities are no longer tied to one particular location, as intensified travel and new communication technologies disentangle cultural forms from specific locations (Hannerz, 1992).

It is no longer true that a culture is the unique worldview a particular community, rooted in a particular place, has generated over time. Instead, given the focus on mobility and increasing connectivity between people from different geographical locations, cultural heritages are more defined by histories of travel through multiple and diverse spaces instead of by a history that leads back to one single place. Rather than culture as place-of-origin or as "the root" of meaning-making, travel relationships, encounters, and connections between spaces have become foregrounded (Clifford, 1997). The detachment from a territory, or deterritorialization has been associated with the nomadic quality of being constantly "on the move" and with the image of the migrant, the stranger, or the exile by Deleuze and Guattari (1986).

Deterritorialization has been adopted by authors like Braidotti (1994) who not so much refer to becoming detached from particular places in a literal sense as to the distantiation of conventions and to developing a critical position to the "canonical," which the nomadic position through it multi-perspectivity allows (Papastergiadis, 2000). Living within or moving between these highly connected heterogeneous spaces has been referred to as the *migrant condition*, indicating both a state of passing through multiple and diverse social and cultural spaces, as well as the need to take distance from the existing cultural paradigms while reconsidering and recreating them. Here, I will use the idea of the migrant condition mostly to refer to the condition of passing through multiple, often connected, heterogeneous spaces without exclusively referring to the live conditions of immigrants.

Living with the heritages or simultaneous presence of multiple, diverse communities creates particular challenges. These include the management of identities associated with multiple traditions or places and creating forms of belonging to a variety of communities. The consequences for how young people learn and how we educate the younger generation in a globalizing world which is increasingly defined by a high degree of connectivity and the confrontation of multiple heterogeneous heritages are only beginning to be addressed (see, e.g., Gardner, 2004; de Haan, 2009; Leander, Phillips, & Taylor, 2010; Suàrez-Orozco & Qin-Hilliard, 2004; Weisner & Lowe, 2005).

Children's social worlds become increasingly diverse and the possibilities they are offered to develop, learn, and expand with these different optional worlds increase. Globalization has led to an explosion in the variety of sources of information available, to greater community heterogeneity, and to participation in multiple, overlapping communities (although these effects vary considerably depending on local conditions (Weisner & Lowe, 2005)). As culture itself is becoming more mobile, cultural reproduction likewise will become more defined by trajectories, both through time and through different locations, as well as by the accelerated exchange possibilities between the different locations involved (Appadurai, 1996). This mobile, non-sedentary reproduction of culture, or cultural reproduction "in flux" happens in multiple spaces that parents and children do not necessarily share, and which often represent contradictory and opposing worldviews. As the studies reviewed in this chapter will show, this has particular consequences for families "in migration," but cultural reproduction "in flux" is certainly becoming less of an exceptional case.

How to Conceptualize Learning in Migration

Most studies on how immigrant populations have developed over time have focused on how well they have adapted to mainstream populations. But this research has been conducted from a majority position in which minority populations are judged in terms of their adaptation process, operationalized as school results or economic success. There is even a tendency to pathologize the acculturation process of immigrants as many studies investigate its effect on (mental) health issues. Terms such as "acculturative stress" and the "stress-buffering potential of ethnic identity" exemplify this, which might be the result of the disciplines who have adopted these topics (psychiatry, clinical psychology) (Berry, Phinney, Sam, & Vedder, 2006).

Instead of focusing on how immigrant populations become more like mainstream populations, I would like to address these developmental processes as learning processes that are defined by highly heterogeneous settings. In a number of ways, this perspective allows us to conceive immigrant learning as an example of a practice of learning that is becoming more important in times in which mobility and increasing cultural contact are becoming defining elements of how we understand social life.

In my attempt to explore such a perspective, I will draw upon two particular perspectives on learning. The first of these is the perspective that the sociocultural is an inherent part of the learning processes. I will argue that, given the focus of culture "as travel," in the elaboration of such a theoretical perspective the encounter between cultures needs to be more foregrounded. The second perspective is one on learning as situated in larger semiotic systems and collectivities, in which change at the individual level is always interrelated with processes of change at these larger, collective, or structural levels.

A Sociocultural Perspective on Learning

Despite the growing awareness of the need for broader units of analysis and sociocultural perspectives on learning (Bransford et al., 2006; Sawyer, 2006), the learning sciences long have been based on a vision of learning that is non-contextual and non-cultural. According to sociocultural perspectives on learning, intelligent actions take place in the midst of a culturally defined, complex environment and depend on the joint actions with others as well as on complex tool systems (Cole, 1996; Hutchkins, 1995; Lave & Wenger, 1991; Rogoff, 2003).

In this perspective, learning is not seen as lifted out of its sociocultural context but is inherently interwoven with it. Learning and culture are mutually constitutive processes, which means that learning is inherently interwoven with the cultural practices that are appropriated, identified with, or mastered (de Haan, 1999). I consider learning, as opposed to development (which can be seen as more automatic) as the intentional (though not necessarily conscious or rational) engagement with social others or cultural artifacts to reach particular kinds of transformations.

These transformations are not located only in individual minds but happen, in accordance with a perspective on the distributed nature of cognition, across individual minds, bodies of people, and cultural tools or artifacts. As cognition, interaction and learning are the result of historically formed and culturally informed technologies, texts, and tool systems; they are inherently cultural in nature. This means that learning experiences, as cultural practices, are not socially neutral or semiotically empty, but represent a particular world vision and a history of ways of acting upon the world.

However, just as much as there is a need to reconsider the nature of culture, given its uprooted condition and the constant travel through a diversity of sociocultural worlds, there is a need to reconsider how learning and culture are related. Instead of considering how particular world views are an inherent part of learning and participating in particular communities, we should shift our attention to the questions of (a) what it means to learn to participate and move through multiple different worlds and (b) what learning means as a process of transformation while participating in these cultural heterogeneous spaces. These questions draw attention to the multiplicity of learning experiences and to the fact that not only each repertoire or competence also at the same time represents a particular view on the world, characterized by its own meanings, purposes, and values but that learning how to move and mediate successfully through these multiple spaces becomes the focus issue. Traditional notions of learning do not account for this cultural heterogeneity and how heterogeneity also poses important intellectual problems and involves key learning skills. This is a particularly relevant lens to study immigrant learning, for knowing how to deal with a diversity of cultural worlds is an important condition that characterizes their learning.

In this chapter, with the following question in mind—what is particular about their learning in general?—I will review studies on immigrant learning while paying specific attention to the heterogeneity of immigrants' life worlds and how this might affect their learning. I will first review the literature on immigrant children's informal learning through brokering, as well as studies on the learning of immigrant parents and families. In the second part I will address the learning of immigrant families as related to conditions of globalization, paying attention to child raising in transnational settings and immigrant youth learning online. Finally, I will come back to the theoretical issues raised around the conceptualization of immigrant learning while asking the question how the studies reviewed in the chapter can inform and contribute to these issues.

Immigrant Learning

What are the particularities of (informal) learning practices of immigrant youth and their parents in the family setting? What can be said about the learning that takes place between generations, from the older to the young but perhaps also vice versa? And how does migration shape these learning experiences?

Immigrant Children's Brokering and How It Shapes their Learning

The literature confirms that migration puts serious pressure on families and the role divisions between the generations. One important factor in this pressure is the so-called "uneven rhythms of acculturation" between the generations (Hernandez & McGoldrick, 1999). Children often acquire all kinds of skills faster than their parents during the early settlement period in their new location; this is especially true of literacy and language skills. Children spend large parts of their time in contexts for socialization, such as schools, after school programs, sport and other leisure clubs, which help them to learn key skills and knowledges faster than their parents.

As a result, children are asked to serve as intermediaries to bridge the gap between the family and all kinds of institutional settings (Martinez, McClure et al., 2009). Parents rely on their children for (language) brokering in important settings such as medical consults, parent–teacher conferences and help with financial or other official documents, as well as taking over parenting roles for younger siblings (Birman, 2006; Orellana, 2001; Valdés, 2003; Valenzuela, 1999). Several studies have shown that the many adult-like responsibilities of children who broker on a regular basis pushes the social and cognitive development of children (Buriel, Love, & De Ment, 2006). Shannon (1990) found that children who acted as language brokers acquired complex sociolinguistic skills, as they had to take on the position of an adult when representing their parents while talking to professionals and at the same time maintaining the dignity of their parents.

Malakoff and Hakuta (1991) in their study of 68 Spanish/English child translators, found that the skills these children developed were beyond a simple surface level decoding and involved meta-linguistic awareness and translation strategies necessary to manage the complexities of the translin-guistic and transcultural situations with which they had to cope. McQuillan and Tse (1995) report from interviews with children who brokered that these children not only had developed their language skills but also their self-confidence, relational skills, and problem-solving skills. Besides, children gained knowledge and experience of multiple social worlds, and how these relate to each other, resulting from the constant need to mediate between them.

On the negative side, the McQuillan and Tse study reported that the respondents' responsibilities for their families limited them to spend time with friends or to invite people in at home, thus curbing their possibilities in other domains. Buriel, Perez, De Ment, Chavez, & Moran (1998) found that social self-efficacy and academic performance were positively associated with language brokering in settings in which adolescents had to interact with adults. Orellana (2009) demonstrated how translation situations can be socially and cognitive demanding learning experiences, ones that involve complex communicative, linguistic, transcultural and relational skills. She also found that active translators had higher academic scores on reading and math tests while controlling for their initial scores on these topics.

In sum, the studies on learning of immigrant children related to their brokering activities suggest that the constant need to mediate between languages, and cultural experiences stimulates and develops not only the language skills of children but also their intercultural competences and social (linguistic) skills. In terms of intergenerational learning, the migration setting enhances the possi-bilities for exploring new knowledge and enables to learn to take responsibility in high stake-settings, but it limits the possibilities to learn and play in adult-led designed spaces, released of responsibilities, so typical for Western middle-class childhoods.

Immigrant Parents' Learning

How do parents who have recently migrated develop their parenting in the migration setting? And how might this also be related to the learning of the younger generation? I will address these questions both from a review of the literature as well as from first-hand knowledge; that is, from my own research on how parenting is shaped through migration in the Netherlands. My own work with immigrant families in the Netherlands focuses on how caregiver arrangements were reshaped and/or maintained since migration, and how this was related to the different traditions of parenting they encountered (de Haan, 2008, in preparation).

In a qualitative interview study with 29 immigrant parents, mostly of Moroccan origin, parents were asked if and how their parenting strategies had changed since migration and what other traditions the parents used to reflect upon when evaluating their own parenting practices. The results show that parents struggle with the different traditions of parenting they come across as they attempt to identify the right kind of parenting in the migration setting.

Mostly, parents find that their own parenting traditions are confronted with "Dutch" parenting, but sometimes with other immigrant cultures as well. Parents developed different kinds of responses toward this "being in the midst of multiple traditions" and in particular had different attitudes toward what difference or heterogeneity meant for the continuation of their own parenting. One response from parents was to complain that the new environment countered and threatened their efforts to educate their children and that this either paralyzed their parenting efforts or led to parenting that was primarily "protective" as they then attempted to keep children as much as possible in controlled spaces away from culturally external influences.

In these cases, parents would stress the distance between traditions of parenting in the Netherlands and back home, as well as the difficulty to overcome this distance. Parents would complain, for example, that they were not allowed, by law, to exert the harsh, direct forms of disciplining that they were used to in their country of origin, and that this caused problems in their child raising. Children lose respect toward parents when they know they will not be punished in a culturally appropriate way.

Also, parents often reported that, as a result of the differences in the amount of freedom children were granted between the home and other socializing spaces such as the school but also the public sphere, they had started to curb the child's freedom of movement and to monitor their children more than before. The "outside" spaces of socialization were considered to be risky and to represent regimes of upbringing against which they wished to protect themselves. Often, these negative evaluations were inspired from a moral model of parenting in which showing the child what is right and wrong was a central principle.

Both the countering effects of a too diverse socialization environment as well as the increased monitoring as a response to migration have been found in other studies on immigrant parenting, mostly in the United States but also in the Netherlands (Jonkers, 2003; Pels, 1991). For instance, Bacallao and Smokowski (2007) and Reese (2002) found that Mexican immigrant parents in the United States became more authoritarian and held their children under a stricter regime compared to when they were in the pre-migration setting. Also, the negative evaluations of socialization regimes in the country of arrival and that these other regimes are seen as problematic for the continuation of the parenting of immigrants have been documented for other immigrant groups, for instance, by Delgado-Gaitan (1994), Suàrez-Orozco and Suàrez-Orozco (2001) and by Perreira, Chapman, and Stein (2006) for Mexican immigrants in the United States; Kibria (1993) found the same for Vietnamese immigrants in the United States.

A second type of response parents in my study expressed was that they embraced the possibility to learn from other parenting traditions, while at the same time remaining critical toward them and weighting them against each other. Older parenting traditions (those of their own parents back home) were sometimes criticized as well. For example, some questioned the collective parenting in which children are left to the care of multiple caregivers, and in which multiple older family members could interfere in the decision-making on children of one "nuclear" family.

Parents also would acknowledge that care-taking strategies that worked in the old setting did not work in the new setting. These included, for example, the collective monitoring of children in the public sphere on which they could rely in the pre-migration setting; neighborhoods were too diverse and lacked the social trust needed to re-establish such collective arrangements. The invented alternatives often blended and remixed different models of child raising. For instance, one mother told me she had developed a style of child-centered, but close and morally informed monitoring, which seemed to blend the child-centered attitude of Dutch parenting with a more religiously informed guidance of showing "the right way."

Whereas the development of new parenting skills that are more in accordance with those of the country of arrival has been widely documented (see e.g. Delgado-Gaitan, 1994; Pels, 1998; Pels & de Haan, 2006; Perreira et al., 2006), few studies account for how this happens in the midst of a diversity of models of parenting. Among the few to have done so are Kağıtçıbaşı and Ataca (2005), who examined how new family models develop through the confrontation of different models of parent-ing in translocal migratory settings, and Jonkers (2003) and van der Zwaard (1992), who studied how contradictions between traditional caregiving arrangements and professional healthcare destabilizes immigrant practices. A fourth such study was that of Nsamenang (1992), which focuses on how local disciplining practices in Cameroon became unstable through confrontation with Western-oriented parenting.

I have found that immigrant families, in their search for new competences and knowledge, function as flexible learning communities in which expert roles can shift from parents to children and vice versa. Both parents and children constantly gain new responsibilities and take on new roles. For instance, making use of school knowledge, children learn to act as cultural mediators and translators for their parents, while parents develop new identities as negotiators and decision-makers with respect to their children's school career. Older siblings gain new responsibilities as mediators between the school, their parents, and their younger siblings.

In adopting these new responsibilities, immigrant families often adopt unorthodox arrangements which do not fit in child-raising models based on middle-class cultures. The following example can illustrate this:

> In a Dutch-Moroccan family, S., the oldest sister, takes care of her siblings' school career and has negotiated a task division between herself and her mother. Although S. initially helped out with all her mother's tasks, at a certain point they decided to specialize. As the older sister, S. now takes care of the other children's education the mother takes care of the household tasks. However, this task division is still in development as the mother learns more about the Dutch schools and the Dutch society. S. explicitly works on transferring this knowledge to her mother so that in time the mother can take over part of S.'s task when she will leave the house to build her own family. The task division seems to develop and shift as a consequence of the constant confrontation of existing with new practices informed by culturally "external" knowledge.
>
> S. considers herself the bridge between what is happening "outside," with its alternative child-raising practices and the "home," which is more dominated by the traditions brought along and also the place where different models can be confronted and contested. She is aware of the effects this bridging function has on her mother who has started to adopt a more child-centered view on parenting and has started to communicate more directly and frequently with her youngest children (whereas before her communication was more indirect and she saw parenting less of a conscious effort to influence the child's development).

Children's roles in bringing knowledge from "the outside world," which then has a socializing effect on adults in migration settings, has been documented elsewhere as well. Schieffelin and Cochran-Smith (1984) found that a nine-year-old Sino-Vietnamese student, V., translated and mediated for the family, which had a socializing function for other family members. But parents also act as mediators between the old and the new. Perreira et al. (2006) report how parents not only are aware of the need to develop bicultural skills themselves to manage their children's upbringing, but also consciously train their children to develop bicultural skills. Parents taught their children to acknowledge how the cultural practices they encountered differed from those of their home countries and talked about the best strategies to adapt to them, while still being aware of their roots. The reorganization of support relations in the family can be found in other studies as well, most of which have focused on assuring specific developmental outcomes of the younger generation that in the new situation are not as evident as in the pre-migration situation (Delgado-Gaitan, 1994; Reese, 2002). Other studies also document the extent to which immigrant families operate as teams that jointly strive to reach their common goals (Orellana, Reynolds, Dorner, & Meza, 2003; Valdés, 2003).

In sum, these studies show that the development of parenting during migration is highly varied and seems particularly to depend on how parents experience (a) the confrontation with other models of parenting and (b) its impact on the important socialization spaces their children function in. The diversity they encounter in the environment that defines their learning or the reconstruction of their parenting seems to provoke protective reactions in which discontinuity between cultural models of parenting "blocks" successful parenting.

On the other hand, such diversity leads to the creative reassembling of traditions. In contrast with the studies on brokering, in the studies on how parents learn and develop in these migratory settings there seem to be more emphasis on the negative, disenabling side of the confrontation with diversity, although such effects also have been reported for children in studies on multi-ethnic classrooms (see for an overview, de Haan & Elbers, 2009). In the studies reported so far, the pressure exerted on immigrant families to reorganize themselves in knowledge-intensive environments has come mostly from their participation in key institutions in the guest country (e.g., schools or health centers), although public media and the Internet also play a role in immigrant families' learning (Liu, 2008). In the globalizing era, it is to be expected that the importance of online media resources will grow. In the next section, we will turn to what it means for immigrant families to reorganize their learning and socialization in the globalizing age.

Transnational Families and the Impact on Socialization and Learning

Bailey, Blake, and Cooke (2004) point to the complex geographical organization of families who migrate over larger distances in post-industrial societies. Using the concept of linked lives, they show how immigrant families can be conceived as networks of connections that stretch out over larger geographical distances while maintaining or addressing care relationships. For instance, families make decisions about mobility or immobility based on care responsibilities (e.g., not willing to move during crucial socialization times of their children or moving back to places of origin to take care of elders). Moreover, new communication possibilities and low-cost air travel enable immigrant families to maintain transnational care relationships after migration.

What does it mean that households maintain transnational ties and socialize their children across at least two different nations? Pribilsky (2004), based on a qualitative study with immigrant Ecuadorian migrants working in Queens, New York, described how the migration of fathers directly affected the socializing possibilities in the country of origin. Income generated in the United States allowed the children of these families to attend school in Ecuador, to wear the latest North American fashions, and to be freed from the burdens of agricultural labor. Fathering at a distance changed the traditional authoritarian style into a variety of styles, but overall the distance led them to develop a more "modern" style, based on emotional ties and less on "respecto," which is often associated with parenting styles of agricultural, traditional communities.

The changing parenting style together with the economic change resulted in different kinds of childhoods for these children compared to non-immigrant children. The study also described how communication possibilities increased the ability to be closely involved in childcare at a distance. For instance, Pribilsky described how a father was intensely involved in the organization of the first communion of his daughter, both by sending money and through his daily involvement in the organization of the party using the Internet and the telephone.

Sanchez (2007), in an ethnographic study on second-generation Mexicans in California, provided evidence of how the transnational experiences of these youngsters help them develop global lifestyles and the interpersonal skills necessary to bridge several communities. Her study reveals how the participation in two distinct places, a U.S. urban center and a rural Mexican village, provides students with what she termed "world learning": experiences, knowledge, and an understanding of what it means to be a global citizen—i.e., someone who shares membership with and can empathize with multiple communities that cross local and national borders. From these experiences, youngsters learn to be culturally flexible and to develop interpersonal communication skills and identities that both bridge these communities and help them respond to larger transnational processes.

Rodríguez's (2009) study of transnational Dominican families raises the question of how experiences of transnationalism shape the worldview of immigrants' and their children, as well as the way they experience family, community, and school. She showed how immigrant children gain knowledge of multiple language communities through the constant visits of and to family members across national borders, and how this generates multiple experiences and expectations as well as the use of multiple cultural resources.

Moreover, she showed how the Dominican adolescents were able to experience schooling in two contexts, in the United States and in the Dominican Republic, and how this helped them to be critical and take more distance toward both schooling systems and their own positions in them. For instance, it helped them to take a position against the experienced "Americanization" in the Dominican Republic and see their experience of discrimination in the U.S. school from a different angle. Both Sanchez and Rodríguez take the position that the complex connections these students have to multiple places, cultures, and languages, and the transcultural experiences and skills these generate are rarely acknowledged in the urban schools they visit, while these experiences hold many unacknowledged promises for their school learning.

In the next section I will focus on how these transnational connections are defining immigrant youth's learning online. What kind of learning is induced in informal learning spaces online? How is this specific to bicultural/immigrant children?

Immigrant Youth Learning Online

Transnational populations have been eager adopters of new media, for instance, to maintain transnational lifestyles or to expand their social spaces beyond the boundaries imposed by host societies (Panagakos & Horst, 2006). Research is beginning to show how immigrants create new spaces for social interaction and identity through chat rooms, message boards, and self-created Web sites, but much less attention has been given to how these new spaces also form new learning ecologies for immigrants, and how these are specific to the learning needs and learning strategies of immigrants.

Kenner (2005) showed how bilingual homes in the United Kingdom form hybrid semiotic environments for the informal literacy productions of children through the engagement with new (and older) media. Children in her study moved beyond existing in two or more worlds to experience the diverse social worlds with which they are simultaneously connected. She claimed that these children learn to make these connections mainly through the world of popular culture, which stands in sharp contrast with their monolingually and monoculturally oriented schooling experience.

Lam (2004) also examined how learning online enables different practices compared to learning at school, focusing on the literacy and learning practices of teenage Chinese immigrants in a chat room. The chat room provided an additional context of language socialization that is different from the literacy context for learning in their schools. It provided a space in which relationships were established around the globe and in which a diversity of language resources were remixed.

These spaces served as a welcome learning ecology for these youth to build their language skills outside the more strict learning regime of schools. The chat room provided a globally oriented space in which they were able to gain a new identity as language learner that did not follow the social categories of English-speaking Americans versus Cantonese-speaking Chinese. Whereas at school these immigrant students could not take advantage of the peer-to-peer interaction with their English-speaking classmates, on the Internet they were able to identify and speak English with other young people of Chinese origin in different parts of the world, based on a mixed-code variety of English. The study clearly shows how the global networks that have opened up in these more open spaces are used to shape alternative ways of using and learning language.

In a study of Web sites for Japanese animation-based fan fiction, where immigrant youth participate in an online transnational community of peers focused on the production of fan fiction, Black (2006) found that the production of these texts relied on a shared semiotic repertoire which crossed cultural historical and linguistic backgrounds. Moreover, these sites served to develop links between traditional print-based skills and "informal" learning skills such as technology skills, knowledge of popular media and fan culture. She argued that these Web-based spaces display valued forms of expertise and provide opportunities to engage in peer-based learning, develop positive identities, and make new connections. In contrast to school learning, these spaces allow youth to be engaged in learning spaces that are highly diverse both in the sense of the language, the origin of information flows, and the cultural practices that are valued. They also acknowledge various forms of expertise.

Reconsidering Immigrant Learning

What can be said about immigrant learning in the diversity of situations this review of the literature has brought together? What might count as a common element, despite the apparent diversity? How do the theoretical notions of learning put forward at the beginning of this chapter inform or challenge what is known about the learning of immigrants? And what, from this overview, can be learned in terms of the particular challenges for the learning of immigrants, and which elements that characterize their learning are also perhaps becoming more central, also for other groups who inhabit highly connected and heterogeneous settings?

The sections on the brokering of immigrant children and on immigrant parenting show that settlement in a new country simultaneously disrupts traditional patterns of learning and socialization and creates possibilities for new, different ones. Furthermore, these studies show how difficult it is to retain the position of expert, or socializing agent, when the traditions and support networks on which one could once rely, become less valuable, out of reach, or unsupported by the social environment that once sustained them.

For instance, disciplining traditions that were once valuable means to hold on to positions of authority are not supported by local authorities, and parents also lack knowledge of the rules and traditions of key socialization spaces in which their children spend large parts of their time. However, these same contradictions and culturally heterogeneous spaces also lead both to new traditions of parenting and to new learning opportunities for children who are removed from the traditional adult-led, protected socialization spaces. These difficulties and possibilities can be seen as the consequence of the confrontation of (sometimes too) diverse traditions "on location"—i.e., of settling in one location with its traditions while attempting to continue traditions formed and learned elsewhere.

The sections on transnational families and youth learning online show how the location of socialization has become more geographically extended and scattered over different locations, both through travel and life online. This means that the effects of resettlement and the consequences of the confrontations between different regimes and traditions can be "softened," or at least have become more unpredictable as immigrants do not depend only on what happens on location. Through their online engagement, immigrant children can escape minority–majority tensions and engage in more globally oriented spaces, and overcome limiting schooling experiences on location.

Because these same effects also apply to other families, part of what has shaped immigrant learning is becoming more mainstream. The diversity of socialization spaces, the experience of constantly moving through these spaces, as well as the fact that generations do not necessarily share the same socialization space now is becoming a condition of education in our current era, with the difference that these spaces and relationships are more spread out over different geographical scales. This means that the "unit" in which children are socialized and learn is no longer the location of residence of the (nuclear) family, but the network of (transnational) relationships, as Bailey et al. (2004) describe.

These networks of relationships expose children to people, linguistic and cultural forms, and information streams from a variety of geographical origins. New skills might be learned with the help of others, or knowledge and information that are available through online transnational or translocal networks. The broadening of the location of socialization makes clear how a distributed view on learning and a vision of learning as networked is necessary to understand learning in settings where learners need to cross-cut many different spaces at different geographical scales, which nowadays applies to both migrants and non-migrants. As already pointed out, such a perspective provides a lens—offered by scholars' online learning (e.g., Ito et al., 2008; Jones & Dirckinck-Holmfeld, 2009; Steeples & Jones, 2002; Ünlüsoy, de Haan, & Leander, 2010)—through which to look at learning as relational and distributed over networks of people as well as cultural objects.

At the same time the distribution of socialization over a variety of spaces underscores the need to reconceive learning. For instance, studies cited in this chapter show that childcare in transnational families is managed from different locations in the world and that it relies on different models of childhood. Others show that immigrant youth draw on different cultural resources, from a variety of cultural communities in their online literacy productions.

Moreover, other studies have shown that crossing through multiple heterogeneous spaces both challenged and helped children (a) to develop skills to combine and integrate a variety of resources with different cultural origins, and (b) to participate in, to manage and act as a mediator between contradictory semiotic frameworks, (c) while also developing more distanced, global perspectives. Especially in the brokering studies, the learning effects of these mediating activities are well documented.

The learning and socialization processes that take place in these migration settings challenge learning and socialization theories that depart from an idea of learning as local, predefined, and stable, and that is clearly bounded to one territory. The learning that takes place in culturally heterogeneous settings becomes more centered around the comparison, confrontation, and translation of traditions, as well as on the ability to move through multiple sociocultural worlds and build multiple repertoires. These repertoires are not neutral but an inherent part of sociocultural worlds and so are associated with a particular worldview. Being able to use these repertoires requires flexibility and "inter-semiotic" skills in order to define what is true, valuable, and effective for specific occasions. It also requires the ability to distance from local realities and develop a more global orientation in which multiple local realities are included.

From the perspective of parenting, this heterogeneity and the lack of one shared and mono-interpretable space between parents and children contradicts the pedagogic principles based on the adult controlled and designed environments for learning and development advocated in the modernistic ideal. Educators will have to rethink their positions based on only partly shared spaces and points of reference with children (de Haan, 2009), and will have to stimulate the development of "inter-semiotic" skills for their children.

In the learning sciences, the transitory, innovative or "travel through" element has recently gained some attention. Nasir, Rosebery, Warren, and Lee (2006), for instance, while arguing for a cultural view on learning, draw attention to the concept of "adaptive expertise" as the ability to move to and become expert in multiple contexts which initially are unfamiliar. In the learning sciences, adaptive experts are distinguished from routine experts (Bransford et al., 2006). Both types of experts continue to learn through their lifetimes, but routine experts develop a set of core competences which they deepen with time. Adaptive experts expand their competences and move to new areas where they function as "intelligent novices" even if they initially struggle with the learning of new things. But, as

Bransford et al. suggest, adaptive experts are driven by an awareness of their distinctive roles and the balance between the value of innovation versus the costs in terms of efficiency.

The importance of the ability to understand how contents or concepts function in new contexts as a major developmental process has also been stressed from work on science education. Learning is seen in these studies as the ability to differentiate between frameworks, as understanding how the concepts in these frameworks change and function within new settings. Learning then becomes a matter of expanding the repertoires in which these concepts can be used, and different uses of concepts can co-exist, be applied and contextualized (Caravita, 1994).

Addressing the demands of a postmodern and information technology-driven society with its multi-disciplinarity and heterogeneity, Lankshear and Knobel (2003) argue that learners need to adopt new operational, critical, and cultural "knowledges" in order to be able to access new forms of work, civic, and private practices in their everyday lives. The innovative character of these knowledges will come from their ability to cross multiple disciplines and expertises: "the people best fitted to thriving in the world of postmodern knowledge . . . will include people who have strong multi- and cross-disciplinary expertise, who can cross-dress conceptually, theoretically and methodologically in order to come up with new rules and games" (Lankshear & Knobel, 2003, p. 176).

A similar argument is made by Suàrez-Orozco and Qin-Hilliard (2004) and also by Gardner (2004) who, while pointing to the importance of being able to cope with difference in the 21st century, stress the ability of multi-perspectivity. Managing difference requires the ability to acknowledge, consider, and negotiate multiple perspectives and to critically (re)consider both old and new positions. Cognitive and interpersonal skills such as the ability to take on multiple perspectives and the ability to work in interdisciplinary, intercultural teams therefore will likely move up in the educational agenda. Gardner (2004), who also points at the increasing importance of the ability to learn to think interculturally and interdisciplinary, stresses that this needs to be accomplished from a firm grounding in one's own discipline.

It is to be expected, based on the transformations in social life sketched earlier in this chapter, that these skills, which seem always to have been at the heart of intelligence and learning, will be brought to the foreground as key competences and given more importance in learning and teaching efforts. As the studies on immigrant learners reviewed in this chapter have shown, the knowledge on the informal learning practices of immigrants can serve as a source of information in this respect.

However, based on Appadurai, I argue that immigrant socialization is a typical but also special case of how cultural reproduction can take place in a world in motion. This so-called "uprooted socialization" in highly unstable settings might not only be a condition of migration but one that is increasingly part of late modern life. Learning in stable and culturally uniform settings might become the exception rather than the norm. Immigrant families, though, are special cases through their recent settlement process as well as through their position as minorities. In many of the studies it was clear that moving through different worlds also meant dealing with minority–majority relationships. For instance, immigrant parents changed their parenting practices, in part, as a felt-need to respond to or justify themselves against middle-class parenting practices with which they were becoming acquainted.

Also, studies showed how the urban schooling experiences of immigrant youth were defined by their relations with majority cultures, and how they were able to partly escape from these through their transnational relationships. The studies that were reviewed in this chapter show that in going from more place-based studies to studies that focus on transnational learning relationships these relations have a continued presence in their learning experiences. However, the initial results of empirical work also indicate that the possibility to escape their local contexts, shapes new possibilities for immigrant learning.

References

Appadurai, A. (1996). *Modernity at large: Cultural dimensions of globalization.* Minneapolis: University of Minnesota Press.

Bacallao, M., & Smokowski, P. R. (2007). The costs of getting ahead: Mexican family system changes after immigration. *Family Relations, 56,* 52–66.

Bailey, A. J., Blake, M. K., & Cooke, T. J. (2004). Migration, care, and the linked lives of dual-earner households. *Environment and Planning A, 36,* 1617–1632.

Berry, J. W., Phinney, J. S., Sam, D. L., & Vedder, P. (Eds.) (2006). *Immigrant youth in cultural transition: Acculturation, identity and adaptation across national contexts.* Mahwah, NJ: Lawrence Erlbaum Associates.

Birman, D. (2006). Adaption of children and adolescents with immigrant background: Acculturation or development? In M. H. Bornstein, & L. R. Cote (Eds.), *Acculturation and parent–child relationships: Measurement and development* (pp. 97–112). Mahwah, NJ: Lawrence Erlbaum Publishers.

Black, R. W. (2006). Language, culture, and identity in online fanfiction. *E-Learning, 3,* 170–184.

Braidotti, R. (1994). *Nomadic subjects.* New York: Columbia University Press.

Bransford, J. D., Barron, B., Pea, R. D., Melthoff, A., Kuhl, P., Bell, P., et al. (2006). Foundations and opportunities for an interdisciplinary science of learning. In K. Sawyer (Ed.), *The Cambridge handbook of the learning sciences* (pp. 19–34). Cambridge, UK: Cambridge University Press.

Buriel, R., Love, J. A., & De Ment, T. L. (2006). The relation of language brokering to depression and parent–child bonding among Latino adolescents. In M. H. Bornstein and L. R. Cote (Eds.), *Acculturation and parent–child relationships: Measurement and development* (pp. 249–270). Mahwah, NJ: Lawrence Erlbaum Associates.

Buriel, R., W., Perez, W., De Ment, T., Chavez, D. V., & Moran, V. R. (1998). The relationship of language brokering to academic performance, biculturalism and self-efficacy among Latino Adolescents. *Hispanic Journal of Behavioral Sciences, 20,* 283–297.

Caravita, S. (1994). Re-framing the problem of conceptual learning. *Learning and Instruction, 4,* 89–111.

Clifford, J. (1997). *Routes, travel and translation in the late twentieth century.* Cambridge, MA: Harvard University Press.

Cole, M. (1996). *Cultural psychology: A once and future discipline.* Cambridge, MA: Harvard University Press.

Deleuze, G., & Guattari, F. (1986). *Kafka: Towards a minor literature.* Minneapolis: University of Minnesota Press.

Delgado-Gaitan, C. (1994). Socializing young children in Mexican-American families: An intergenerational perspective. In P. Greenfield & R. R. Cocking (Eds.), *Cross-cultural roots of minority child development* (pp. 55–86). Hillsdale, NJ: Lawrence Erlbaum Associates.

Gardner, H. (2004). *How education changes.* In M. M. Suàrez-Orozco & D. Baolian Qin-Hilliard (Eds.), *Globalization, culture and education in the new millennium* (pp. 235–258). Berkeley: University of California Press.

Haan, M. de (1999). *Learning as cultural practice: How children learn in a Mexican Mazahua community: A study on culture and learning.* Amsterdam: Thela Thesis.

Haan, M. de. (2008). Opvoeding, migratie & cultuur (Education, migration & culture). In W. Koops, M. de Winter, & B. Levering (Eds.), *Opvoeding als spiegel van de beschaving: Een moderne antropologie van de opvoeding* (*Education as a mirror of civilization: A modern anthropology of education*) (pp. 75–90). Amsterdam: Uitgeverij SWP.

Haan, M. de (2009). *Culturele reproductie in een wereld in beweging* (Cultural reproduction in a world in motion). Inaugural speech. Utrecht, The Netherlands: University of Utrecht.

Haan, M. de (in preparation). *The reconstruction of parenting after migration: A perspective from cultural translation.*

Haan, M. de, & Elbers, E. (2009). From research to practice: What the study of multi-ethnic classrooms has to offer. In M. César & K. Kumpulainen (Eds.), *Social interactions in multicultural settings* (pp. 171–202). Rotterdam/Tapei: Sense Publishers.

Hannerz, U. (1992). *Cultural complexity: Studies in the social organization of meaning.* New York: Columbia University Press.

Hernandez, M., & McGoldrick, M. (1999). Migration and the family life cycle. In B. Carter, & M. Goldrick (Eds.), *The expanded family life cycle: Individual, family and social perspectives* (pp. 169–184). Needham Heights, MA: Allyn & Bacon.

Hutchkins, E. (1995). *Cognition in the wild.* Cambridge, MA: MIT Press.

Ito, M., Host, H. A., Bittanti, M., Boyd, D., Herr-Stephenson, B., Lange, P. G., et al. (2008). *Living and learning with new media: Summary of findings from the digital youth project. Series on digital media and learning.* Retrieved April 11, 2009 from: http://digitalyouth.ischool.berkeley.edu/report

Jones, C., & Dirckinck-Holmfeld, L. (2009). Analysing networked learning practices. In L. Dirckinck-Holmfeld, C. Jones, & B. Lindström (Eds.), *Analysing networked learning practices in higher education and continuing professional development* (pp. 1–28). Rotterdam: Sense Publishers.

Jonkers, M. (2003). *Een miskende revolutie: Het moederschap van marokkaanse vrouwen* (An unacknowledged revolution: Motherhood among Moroccan women). Amsterdam: Aksant.

Kağıtçıbaşı, Ç., & Ataca, B. (2005). Value of children and family change: A three decade portrait from Turkey. *Applied Psychology: International Review, 54,* 317–337.

Kenner, C. (2005). Bilingual children's uses of popular culture in text-making. In J. Marsh (Ed.), *Popular culture, new media and digital literacy in early childhood* (pp. 73–87). London: RouteledgeFalmer.

Kibria, N. (1993). *Family tightrope: The changing lives of Vietnamese Americans.* Princeton, NJ: Princeton University Press.

Lam, W. S. E. (2004). Second language socialization in a bilingual chat room: Global and local considerations. *Language, Learning & Technology, 8,* 44–65.

Lankshear, C., & Knobel, M. (2003). *New literacies: Changing knowledge and classroom learning.* Buckingham, UK: Open University Press.

Lave, J., & Wenger, E. (1991). *Situated learning: Legitimate peripherical participation.* Cambridge, UK: Cambridge University Press.

Leander, K. M., Phillips, N., & Taylor, K. (2010). The changing social spaces of learning: Mapping new mobilities. *Review of Research in Education, 34,* 329–394.

Liu, L. W. (2008). New home, new learning: Chinese immigrants, unpaid housework and care work. In D. W. Livingstone, K. Mirchandani, & P. Sawchuk (Eds.), *The future of lifelong learning and work* (pp. 275–286). Rotterdam: Sense Publishers.

Malakoff, M., & Hakuta, K. (1991). Translation skill and metalinguistic awareness in bilinguals. In E. Bialystok (Ed.), *Language processing in bilingual children* (pp. 141–166). Cambridge, UK: Cambridge University Press.

Martinez, C. R. J., McClure, H., et al. (2009). Language brokering contexts and behavioral and emotional. Adjustment among Latino parents and adolescents. *The Journal of Early Adolescence, 29*(1), 71–98.

McQuillan, J., & Tse, L. (1995). Child language brokering in linguistic minority communities: Effects on cultural interaction, cognition, and literacy. *Language and Education, 9,* 195–215.

Nasir, N. S., Rosebery, A. S., Warren, B. D., and Lee, C. D. (2006). Learning as a cultural process: Achieving equity through diversity. In R. K. Sawyer (Ed.) *The Cambridge handbook of the learning sciences* (pp. 489–504). New York: Cambridge University Press.

Nsamenang, A. B. (1992). *Human development in cultural context: A third world perspective.* Newbury Park, CA: Sage.

Orellana, M. F. (2001). The work kids do: Mexican and Central American immigrant children's contributions to households and schools in California. *Harvard Educational Review, 71,* 366–389.

Orellana, M. F. (2009). *Translating childhoods. Immigrant youth, language, and culture.* New Brunswick, NJ: Rutgers University Press.

Orellana, M. F., Reynolds, J., Dorner, L., & Meza, M. (2003). In other words: Translating or "paraphrasing" as family literacy practice in immigrant household. *Reading Research Quarterly, 38,* 12–34.

Panagakos, A. N., & Horst, H. A. (2006). Return to Cyberia: Technology and the social worlds of transnational migrants. *Global Networks, 6,* 108–124.

Papastergiadis, N. (2000). *The turbulence of migration: Globalization, deterritorialization and hybridity.* Cambridge, UK: Polity Press.

Pels, T. (1991). *Marokkaanse kleuters en hun culturele kapitaal: Opvoeden en leren in het gezin en op school* (*Moroccan pre-school children and their cultural capital: Child rearing and learning in the family and at school*). Amsterdam/Lisse: Swets & Zeitlinger.

Pels, T. (1998). *Opvoeding in Marokkaanse gezinnen in Nederland: De creatie van een nieuw bestaan* (*Child rearing in Moroccan families in the Netherlands: The creation of a new existence*). Assen: Van Gorcum.

Pels, T., & Haan, M. de. (2006). Socialization practices of Moroccan families after migration: A reconstruction in an "acculturative arena." *Young, 15*(1), 69–87.

Perreira, K., M., Chapman, M. V., & Stein, G. L. (2006). Becoming an American parent: Overcoming challenges and finding strength in a new immigrant latino community. *Journal of Family Issues, 27,* 1383–1414.

Pribilsky, J. (2004). "Aprendemos a convivir": Conjugal relations, co-parenting, and family life among Ecuadorian transnational migrants in New York City and the Ecuadorian Andes. *Global Networks, 4,* 312–334.

Reese, L. (2002). Parental strategies in contrasting cultural settings: Families in Mexico and "el norte." *Anthropology and Education Quarterly, 33*(1), 30–59.

Rodríguez, T. (2009). Dominicanas entre la gran manzana y quisqueya: Family, schooling, and language learning in a transnational context. *The High School Journal, 92,* 16–33.

Rogoff, B. (2003). *The cultural nature of human development.* Oxford, UK: Oxford University Press.

Sanchez, P. (2007). Cultural authenticity and transnational Latina youth: Constructing a meta-narrative across borders. *Linguistics and Education, 18,* 258–282.

Sawyer, R. K. (2006). Introduction: The new science of learning. In R. K. Sawyer (Ed.), *The Cambridge handbook of the learning sciences.* New York, Cambridge University Press.

Schieffelin, B., & Cochran-Smith, M. (1984). Learning to read culturally: Literacy before schooling. In H. Goelman, A. Oberg, & F. Smith (Eds.), *Awakening to literacy* (pp. 3–23). London: Heinemann Education.

Shannon, S. M. (1990). English in the barrio: The quality of contact among immigrant children. *Hispanic Journal of Behavioral Sciences, 12,* 256–276.

Steeples, C., & Jones, C. (2002). *Networked learning: Perspectives and issues.* London: Springer.

Suàrez-Orozco, C., & Suàrez-Orozco, M. M. (2001). *Children of migration.* Cambridge, MA: Harvard University Press.

Suàrez-Orozco, M. M., & Qin-Hilliard, D. B. (2004). *Globalization: Culture and education in the new millennium.* Berkeley: University of California Press.

Ünlüsoy, A., Haan, M. de, & Leander, K. (2010). Netwerken van jongeren als nieuwe leeromgeving (Youth networks as new learning ecologies). *Pedagogiek, 30,* 43–57.

Valdés, G. (2003). *Expanding definitions of giftedness: The case of young interpreters from immigrant communities.* Mahwah, NJ: Lawrence Erlbaum Associates.

Valenzuela, A. (1999). Gender roles and settlement activities among children and their immigrant families. *American Behavioral Scientist, 42,* 720–742.

Weisner, T. S., & Lowe, E. (2005). Globalization and the psychological anthropology of childhood and adolescence. In C. Casey & R. Edgerton (Eds.), *A companion to psychological anthropology: Modernity and psychocultural change* (pp. 315–336). Oxford, UK: Blackwell Publishers.

Zwaard, J. van der (1992). Accounting for differences: Dutch training nurses and their views on migrant women. *Social Sciences & Medicine, 35,* 1137–1144.

24

Intercultural Learning and the Role of Suggestions in a Culture Laboratory Intervention

Marianne Teräs and Yrjö Engeström

People living in urban settings encounter a certain complexity and diversity in their everyday lives. When they open the door in the morning and step outside, the street is in front of them and there is constant movement. They share the street with a diversity of people, and this encounter could be a source for learning about and with diversity. Kiasma, the Museum of Contemporary Art situated in Helsinki, organized an exhibition called "Fluid Street," in which the participants explored urban life and evolution through contemporary art and texts (Jaukkuri & Vanhala, 2008). One of the artists, Vesa-Pekka Rannikko (2008, p. 139), describes the overall theme of the exhibition in his own work:

> For me, the street is an opportunity for change and encounter, a kind of laboratory of processes where defined and planned actions are juxtaposed with random, undetermined actions. Encounters like that give rise to combinations and meanings that cannot be created intentionally. Such activity is inherent to streets, a kind of urban evolution . . . What interests me about the street is also its transitory and evolving nature. People, traffic, spatial structures, together these create a criss-crossing, layered web of time where things come together and something new can emerge.

Urban education as a term and a concept is not common in Finnish educational discourse. As Gordon (2007, p. 447) writes: "In the context of Nordic countries, issues around urban education have somewhat different inflections than those . . . for example, in the U.S." She adds that neoliberal politics and policies have eroded the idea of the welfare society in the Nordic countries. In spite of this, equality of education is still a strong principle in Finland.

An interesting aspect of Finnish education is the level of performance exhibited by Finnish students, also those who are not native born. The success of both native and immigrant Finnish adolescents reported in the PISA Survey (The OECD Programme for International Student Assessment) has aroused growing international interest in the Finnish education system. Finnish adolescents have scored at the top level in all measured areas, including reading and literacy as well as science and mathematics.

The reasons for this have been examined; it has been suggested (*Interpreting the results*, n.d., para. 1) that equality is the key:

The most remarkable reason for Finland's success in the PISA Survey is educational equality: the entire school system is based on it. Equality means that every citizen has an equal possibility to get education regardless of age, domicile, economic status/wealth, gender or mother tongue.

The number of foreign citizens living in Finland has grown significantly during the last 15 years, from 21,000 in 1990 to over 140,000 in 2008. Nevertheless, the number of immigrants is still very low—only about 3% of the Finnish population—and, despite its rapidity, this growth is proportionally the lowest among the EU countries. The largest groups of immigrants come from Russia, Estonia, and Somalia (Population Structure, 2008). People coming from Russia are mostly Ingrain Finns with Finnish ancestors.

Furthermore, whereas other Western European countries face challenges associated with second- or third-generation immigrants, Finland is currently dealing with the first generation. As elsewhere, big cities seem to attract people moving within or into a country, and over 40% of the total immigrant population of Finland lives in the metropolitan area of Helsinki (Joronen, 2005). The total population of the Helsinki region is approximately 1.3 million, which is about 25% of the total population of Finland and has been growing steadily for decades. This type of population expansion and growth in urban areas is a common phenomenon all over the world: cities attract people. Of the Helsinki population, 87% are Finnish-speaking, about 6% are Swedish-speaking, and about 7% speak other languages (Helsinki and the Helsinki Region, 2008, p. 55).

The Helsinki region is depicted as a dynamic world-class center for business and innovation, providing high-quality services, art and science, and creative activities for its people. It could be described as sophisticated and cosmopolitan, "urbane" rather than "urban" (cf. Manninen, 2008). Compared with other parts of Finland, it indeed seems to be more advantaged. For example, the capacity for work and long-term sickness rates are lower in that area than in other parts of Finland. The people living there also enjoy better health than those in other parts of the country, even though there are some regional differences (Sairastavuusindeksi, 2009). However, the accumulation of poverty and disadvantage inside the Helsinki area as well as increasing income inequality, especially after the recession of the 1990s, have been acknowledged (cf. Keskinen, Laine, Tuominen, & Hakkarainen, 2009). The spatial concentration of immigrants and the differentiation of areas inside Helsinki are also evident (cf. Vilkama, 2006).

This chapter describes a formative intervention process (Engeström, Y., 2007) developed for immigrant students, their teachers, and researchers, who came together to examine and improve their educational practices. We focus on how the students' voices were heard and listened to during the process. Our argument is that the voices of marginalized minority groups are of major importance. As Rannikko (2008, p. 139) puts it, "Encounters like that give rise to combinations and meanings that cannot be created intentionally."

We will demonstrate how one student's simple suggestion launched an innovative process in which students and their teachers gathered together to discuss and develop the preparatory immigrant training. First, we introduce the research site, the Helsinki City College of Social and Health Care (henceforth, the College), and then we describe the Culture Laboratory method and its implementation in the program. Next, we consider the suggestions made by the students and teachers in the Culture Laboratory, and finally we present our conclusions.[1]

The Research Site

The College is a secondary-level vocational school for social and health care; between 1,500 and 1,800 students are enrolled in vocational programs each year. The diploma course in practical nursing is the most popular choice. Other options include courses of study qualifying graduates to work as pharmaceutical assistants and special-needs assistants in educational institutions, for example. The school staff comprises around 170 teachers and around 40 other personnel. About 12% of the students at the College are immigrants (Opetusvirasto, 2008).

The preparatory immigrant training program was introduced in 1999 in different sectors of secondary-level vocational education in Finland. It was specifically developed for immigrant students who wanted to continue their education on the vocational level but whose language skills and knowledge of the Finnish study culture were not yet sufficient to enable them to cope with mainstream studies. The length of the training varies from six months to one year, and the aim is to improve language and other skills before the students embark on vocational education and training, which is mainly conducted in Finnish or Swedish (*Immigrant education*, n.d.). The program offered at the College takes one year of full-time study and includes 4–6 weeks of on-the-job training. It attracts about 40–60 students annually from different countries, predominantly Russia, Estonia, and Somalia.

The Culture Laboratory Intervention

Interventions are widely used in development and research work across various practices and disciplines. According to Long (2001), they have traditionally been seen as the linear execution of a plan of action with expected outcomes. However, an intervention is a much more complex and multifaceted process. It is not a separate, discrete project in time and space but rather a complex set of evolving social practices and struggles, and an intermingling of differing flows of events and interests. It is "an ongoing, socially constructed, negotiated, experiential and meaning-creating process" (Long, 2001, pp. 25–34).

This intervention study serves as an example of how immigrant students were active participants and agents in developing the preparatory immigrant training. Thus, collaboration and cooperation are seen as a multivocal and participatory practice. In fact, the students had knowledge and experience that most of the staff did not have: learning in different countries and cultures and being part of a new learning culture at the College.

The Culture Laboratory is an application of the generic Change Laboratory method, which is a special form of intervention developed in the framework of developmental work research. It is conducted in workplaces, and practitioners and researchers collect empirical material that they then bring to it. The empirical material is discussed, and new tools and solutions to existing problems and challenges are sought and created in collaboration with researchers and practitioners. These new means are tested and used in actual working practices and then brought back to the laboratory for monitoring (Engeström, Y., 2007; Sannino, 2008; Virkkunen, Engeström, Y., Helle, Pihlaja, & Poikela, 1997).

Mediating working tools are used to help participants in reflecting on past, present, and future working practices. The sessions are led by a chief interventionist. Prior to the Change Laboratory sessions, so-called mirror data are collected describing a current work situation—possibly a problematic situation or work disturbance. The data are then used in the sessions to facilitate reflection or to illustrate a particular aspect of the work. The theoretical tools used include modeling, in particular the activity-system model and the expansive cycle (cf. Engeström, Y., 1987).

The main practical working tool is a "board" with three tables: the mirror, ideas/tools, and models. The tables may also incorporate the time dimensions of the work: past, present, and future. A participant acts as "scribe" and makes notes of the ongoing discussions on the board. A "memo" serves as a reminder for the participants, and memos are written after each session. The participants carry out tasks related to development work between the sessions (Virkkunen et al., 1997).

As stated above, the Change Laboratory evolved within developmental work research (Engeström, Y., Virkkunen, Helle, Pihlaja, & Poikela, 1996). It is an approach that originated in Finland in the early 1980s. It combines scientific inquiry as well as the developing of practices and learning called expansive learning (Engeström, Y., 2005). The theory of expansive learning was introduced in 1987 by Engeström (Engeström, Y., 1987). He argued that most theories of learning concentrated on knowledge and skills that already existed, while he proposed a theory focused on searching for something that did not exist at the beginning of the learning process.

This means that learning is created as the process is going on. As Engeström states, people at work in contemporary workplaces are in constant need to learn something that is not stable, not even defined or understood. The object of expansive learning is typically the whole activity system. Expansive learning is often depicted as a cycle, which is manifested through specific epistemic or learning actions that illustrate a process known as "ascending from the abstract to the concrete." These actions form an expansive cycle or spiral. Typical actions are described as a seven-step process: questioning, analyzing, modeling, examining the model, implementing the model, reflecting on the process, and consolidating the new practice. The development of working practices requires many kinds of innovations, some of which may be single working instruments or practices, and other working processes comprising many phases. Expansive learning requires demanding and purposeful work from all participants (Engeström, Y., 1999; Engeström, Y., Lompscher, & Rückriem, 2005).

Change Laboratories have been implemented in many kinds of workplaces, including industrial facilities, hospitals, newsrooms, and schools (see Engeström, Y. et al., 2005). The Culture Laboratory developed and used in this study is an application of the generic Change Laboratory method for situations in which the emphasis is on cultural or ethnic variety and diversity among participants, instruments, and circumstances. Thus, a Culture Laboratory is an application of the Change Laboratory in "multilingual and multicultural" settings. It shows and explores the dynamic movement of intercultural encountering, and how this situation can enrich learning and development.

The participants of the Culture Laboratory in the work described here comprised of a group of 17 students who were natives of 8 different countries (Estonia, Russia, Somalia, Iraq, Chile, Italy, Afghanistan, and Japan), teachers and other staff, project personnel, one researcher, and the chief interventionist. The empirical material comprises the nine sessions of the Culture Laboratory between November 2001 and April 2002. Each session lasted for 2–3 hours, and there was a break of 1–6 weeks between them. The sessions covered 20 hours all together; they were both audiotaped and videotaped. The Culture Laboratory intervention was embedded in the preparatory immigrant training course of the students.

Each session had a theme, such as differences in cultural practices of learning. The sessions were not only multicultural but also multilingual. Finnish was the main language used, but Russian, Estonian, Somali, and Arabic languages were also spoken. Typical of the discussions were language difficulties, such as problems in understanding words and meanings. Between the sessions the participants carried out specific tasks related to the topic covered. They wrote about their native cultures, for example, and their work was jointly discussed. Each session was monitored, either in a group discussion or by asking the participants to fill out an evaluation form.

The Culture Laboratory was not involved in the straightforward execution of a planned intervention. It was rather a fragmented and powerful field with multiple tensions and interests that were manifested in disturbances. However, it was considered an interesting forum as well as a form of intervention because it offered new perspectives on the diverse cultures involved and on the everyday practices of the preparatory immigrant training.

Suggestions, Perspectives, and Social Languages

During the sessions, the participants made numerous suggestions concerning the training. It was striking how the students made suggestions actively from the very first Culture Laboratory session;

by the end of it, the participants had a long list of suggestions for developing the preparatory immigrant training. This was one of the reasons why we wanted to focus on the suggestion-making process more thoroughly. For analytical purposes, we employed the concepts of suggestion, perspective, and social languages.

In the context of this project a suggestion means an idea or a viewpoint concerning the preparatory training offered for consideration by someone. It indicates or influences something within the training. *Webster's dictionary* (1986) defines a suggestion as follows: "a means or process of influencing attitudes and behavior, a slight indication or touch, or the process by which one thought leads to another, especially through an association of ideas." Here, the notion is used to separate suggestions from other kinds of remarks the participants made during the Culture Laboratory. Suggestions are realized in the form of concrete individual utterances, which, for practical reasons, are simply called suggestions. Such utterances also served as a basic unit of analysis in this study. Suggestions were made and usually discussed further during the Culture Laboratory, and some of them were implemented.

A perspective could be understood as a point of view about something. We utilized the concept of perspective in order to analyze the viewpoints the participants expressed in their suggestions concerning the Finnish language. For example, Boland and Tenkasi (1995) explored and presented a process of perspective making and perspective taking in organizations, which they called "communities of knowing." They argued that producing new knowledge in order to make innovations in modern firms required not only a strong perspective within a community but also the ability to take the perspective of another into account. They called the former "perspective making" and the latter "perspective taking" (Boland & Tenkasi, 1995).

Bakhtin (1981) developed the concept of social languages. He emphasized the fact that languages are divided not only into linguistic dialects but also into socioideological groups. By this he meant that people use different historically evolved social languages in different situations: when speakers use their voices to act, they blend in with previous voices that used those particular words. Social languages emerge within social groups (Bakhtin, 1981). They also represent multivoicedness and potentiality, as in the emergence of new social languages, for example (see Engeström, R., 1995). One might assume that in the context of education teachers have their own social languages, and students have theirs. Furthermore, between and within countries students and teachers have different historically and locally constructed social languages, which they use in talking about instruction and learning.

Identifying Suggestions

The first step in the analysis was to gather a content log of talk in the Culture Laboratory; then we focused on the suggestions. Second, we separated the suggestions from other kinds of speaking turns among the participants, at the same time defining the concept of a suggestion. Suggestions were linked to each other and formed a special kind of communication sphere. The boundaries between them were twofold. The main criterion was a change of speaker, but in a few cases another participant interrupted the speaker before she or he had finished. In this case the two utterances were fused into one suggestion utterance because the first speaker had clearly put the suggestion forward.

On the other hand, in some cases the speaker was reporting on group work and included more than one suggestion in his or her turn, and each one was separated. In the third step we identified the first suggestion made in the Culture Laboratory that concerned the Finnish language. We then classified all further suggestions concerning Finnish in terms of perspective. This enabled us to look more closely into the process of suggestion making—how one suggestion lived and was transformed during the sessions. Moreover, the process revealed which suggestions were supported and which ones were rejected. We ended up with 81 suggestions concerning the training in general and 212 specifically concerning the Finnish language.

A total of 81 suggestions about the training course were made during the eight Culture Laboratory sessions. The frequency varied from 0 to 19, with no instances recorded during the second session. The content covered teaching and studying practices. Some of the suggestions concerned how teachers should teach: they should speak at a normal pace, not too slowly or too quickly, and should organize instructional games for the students. Others referred to the organization of the training, such as the length of the school days, and to the inclusion of students in the planning of the course. The students were active in making suggestions: they came up with 31 against the 4 put forward by the teachers.

Most of the suggestions (44) were made during the group work, and most of these were initiated by students, which is obvious from the content. Participants other than students and teachers made two suggestions. Some students were more active than others, even though the group work tended to facilitate the participation of all. Most of the suggestions (76) were addressed to the teachers, and 5 to the students. Many of them were explicitly formulated, including words such as *teachers* and *teaching* if addressed to teachers and *students* and *studying* if addressed to students.

Suggestions, History, and Social Languages

When a participant made a suggestion, it was assumed that historically and culturally it was a grounded way of speaking about learning and training—a historically evolved social language. Table 24.1 shows the emergence of four social languages. The 81 suggestions concerning the training were divided into eight categories on the basis of two factors: who was the active subject (either a teacher, a student in the group, or both), and what the suggestion referred to (practices inside or outside the school).

Here it should be pointed out that the suggester was not necessarily the active subject of the suggestion: students made suggestions in which teachers were the active subjects and vice versa. For example, students pointed out that it was bad practice for the teachers to give homework on an irregular basis—many assignments on one day and none on another. On the other hand, the teachers expressed the opinion that the students could also learn from each other and not only from them.

As shown in Table 24.1, some 80% of the suggestions referred to practices inside the school. Teachers were active subjects in almost 50% of them, and students in a little less than 20%. In almost 15% of them, the subject was a joint activity involving both teachers and students, and in 17% the active subject was an "outsider," such as the Finnish students in the school, other immigrants, or practitioners in the work placement locations.

Table 24.1 The Emergence of Social Languages

Who →	Teacher	Together	Student	Outsider: other students, other people	Total
Where ↓					
Inside school	39 Traditional teaching	11 Teaching and studying together	13 Traditional studying	2	65
Outside school	–	1	3 Learning outside school	12	16
Total	39 (48.1%)	12 (14.8%)	16 (19.8%)	14 (17.3%)	81 (100%)

Four types of social language emerged: traditional teaching, traditional studying, teaching and studying together, and learning outside school. "Traditional teaching" refers to classroom practices in which the teacher explains, speaks, teaches, and demonstrates in the classroom. Most of the suggestions (48%) employed this social language. Both teachers and students made suggestions reflecting traditional teaching. The following example is characteristic of the traditional teaching type of social language. It is from the sixth session, and the student expresses the wish that the teachers would explain more when the students did not understand. There were many suggestions indicating that the primary task of teachers was to explain unclear or new things to the students.

Excerpt 1
Student: Yeah, the student didn't understand what it was and what the teacher was saying, and it could be that the student didn't understand this thing at all, and also the teacher should always explain important things, the main issues, and write them on the board.

It was not surprising that the immigrant students wanted this type of teaching, because teacher-centered teaching was more familiar to them than the student-centered practices employed at the College.

The third type of social language that emerged was "teaching and studying together," which refers to classroom practices in which teachers and students act together. There were 12 (15%) suggestions in this category. Furthermore, only one suggestion reflected outside classroom activities (specifically, excursions). In the example below, which is from the fourth session, the student is referring to practices involving collaboration, which she liked because everybody had a chance to speak.

Excerpt 2
Student: We'd put an emphasis on group work, too, we like it because everybody has a chance to speak.

We interpreted this example as the "teaching and studying together" type of social language because the student emphasized group work. This was a minor surprise to us because, at the beginning of the preparatory immigrant training, the students usually shunned group work and wondered why such practices were employed at the College. On the other hand, those in the Culture Laboratory were now accustomed to more interactive study practices: it was not the first phase of the training for them.

The fourth type of social language that emerged was "learning outside school," representing suggestions in which students learn in their daily lives from the people around them or in the workplace during their practical training, for example. There were 15 suggestions in this category, which represents almost 20% of the total. The following example, from the fourth session, reflects this type of social language: the student emphasizes learning during the work placement periods.

Excerpt 3
Student: Then we think that learning in workplaces is important because workplace learning, because there we can improve our Finnish-language skills, and then we get to know about professions and then we can talk to Finnish people.

This example reflects the "learning outside school" category because the student supported learning in workplaces. This is a traditional type of learning practice in vocational education and training. However, it extended the boundaries of the Finnish-language classroom. The students thought that was a good way to get to know about different professions and to learn Finnish at work.

Next we present the two suggestions that fell outside of this categorization of social language, both of which were made by students. In the first one, from the first session, the student said that she wanted to have more instruction together with Finnish students, and in the second, from the seventh session, the student suggested that teachers could invite other immigrants into the classroom to tell "their story." We perceive both to open up a perspective that points away from the classroom on the one hand, and invites "outsiders" in on the other. Furthermore, this could create hybridity in terms of instruction by transcending the boundaries of classrooms and the College.

Excerpt 4

Student: Why don't we have working groups together with Finnish groups?

Student: May I make a suggestion? There are lots of immigrants in Finland. Is it possible to sometimes invite an immigrant here?

These suggestions pointed in an important direction. Interaction between all students at the College is essential: it strengthens good ethnic relations and supports immigrant students' learning. Inviting immigrants in would set a good example and therefore help students to cope with Finnish society.

What happened to all these suggestions is also interesting. Were there any changes in classroom practices? This was a subject the chief interventionist brought up in the sixth session: did the suggestions matter? Indeed, the teachers had taken into account some of the ones that students had made. One of them referred to her own subject matter: "suggestions the students have made, then we have tried to follow them and implement them."

Another teacher pointed out how one student's suggestion about special training for immigrants aiming at a certain profession was positively taken up by the management of the school. Students also commented on how the teachers had changed their lessons. For instance, one of them said "when we talked about how there should be more IT [computer lessons], now our teachers do it." Furthermore, the same student recalled how the teachers now organized more trips, as was suggested in the Culture Laboratory. Suggestions did matter.

Suggestions as an Expanding Process

We return here to the suggestions concerning the Finnish language because they seemed to form an interesting chain. The initial suggestion remains, but it is supplemented with another point of view, and this reveals the process. We focused on the process of one particularly interesting suggestion in order to better understand the trajectory. Figure 24.1 shows the model for this analysis. The first step

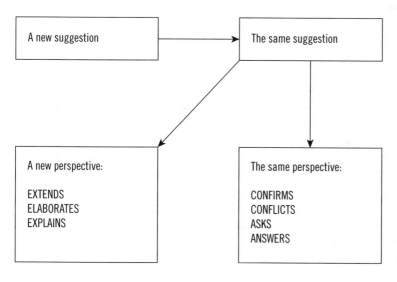

Figure 24.1 Suggestions Concerning the Finnish Language: The Process

was to recognize the new suggestion, and the next to establish whether the next one also concerned the Finnish language. If it did, was the perspective new, or was it the same?

Seven types of suggestion concerning the Finnish language emerged, three of which were the expanding type, and four the maintaining type. Perspective-expanding suggestions—extending, elaborating, and explaining—throw new light on previous suggestions, whereas perspective-maintaining suggestions—confirming, conflicting, asking, and answering—do not. The different categories are defined below, and Figure 24.2 shows the extent of their occurrence. Examples from the empirical material are given later in conjunction with the analysis of the trajectory of these suggestions. The suggestion-making process started with a new suggestion: one that is made for the first time and has not been discussed before, nor does it refer directly to any other suggestions.

Perspective-expanding Suggestions

- An *extending suggestion* extends or enlarges the one that preceded it. It offers a new perspective on a previous suggestion.
- An *elaborating suggestion* challenges a previous suggestion and opens up a new perspective.
- An *explaining suggestion* gives reasons for a previous suggestion and initiates another perspective.

Perspective-maintaining Suggestions

- A *confirming suggestion* supports or repeats a previous suggestion. It does not include minimum feedback markers such as "yeah," which could indicate that the person is listening but does not necessarily support it.
- A *conflicting suggestion* rejects a previous suggestion.
- An *asking suggestion* requests more information or assurance about a previous suggestion. The difference between this and an elaborating is that it does not open up a new perspective.
- An *answering suggestion* gives a response to or more information on the previous suggestion or revises it.

Figure 24.2 depicts the occurrence of the seven types of suggestion. There were a total of 212 suggestions concerning the Finnish language. The most common were of the confirming type (over 33%) and the most rare were the conflicting type. There were 90 instances of perspective-expanding suggestions (43%) and thus 121 perspective-maintaining suggestions, or 57% of the total.

On one hand, perspective-expanding suggestions are potentially helpful in development work, feeding the process and even escalating it at the same time. Perspective-maintaining suggestions, on the other hand, and especially confirming suggestions, created an atmosphere in the Culture Laboratory in which new ideas flourished. Even though these confirming suggestions did not open up new perspectives, they seemed to be strategically important to the process. We therefore examined them more closely.

The students articulated 26 confirming suggestions, the teachers 27, the chief interventionist 12, and others 5. Thus, both students and teachers were active in this respect. This broke up the traditional interaction and power relations between students and teachers, according to which teachers mostly approve and support what the students propose. Thus, confirming suggestions created a hybrid learning space in that the rich number seemed to result in the breaking up of traditional power relations between teachers and students. The students took the teacher's traditional role of a supporter and accepter of students' ideas. They made almost as many confirming suggestions as the teachers, thereby blending students' and teachers' tasks in the classroom.

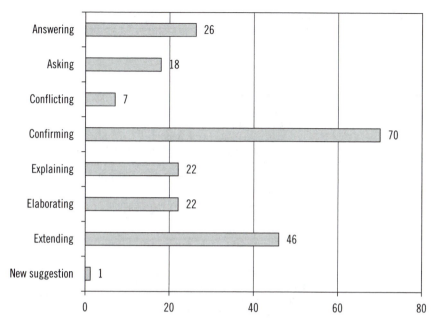

Figure 24.2 The Occurrence of the Different Types of Suggestion

The following table shows the overall trajectory of the suggestions concerning the Finnish language. The trajectory illustrates the process: how the suggestion arose, was responded to, transformed, and concluded. It also outlines the evolving and dialogic nature of the conversations in the Culture Laboratory.

The teachers made 80 suggestions (38%) and the students made almost as many, 77 (36%). The chief interventionist made 28 (13%), and 15 were the result of group work. Other staff made 3 suggestions and the researcher made 9. The whole process started when one student said that there was too little Finnish-language instruction at the College.

There were 38 episodes in 6 sessions, the length varying from 1 to 14 suggestions. Episodes turned into discussions when the same topic was further talked about in the same or subsequent Culture Laboratory sessions. The total number of discussions was 8, varying in length between 2 and 6 episodes. However, not all episodes turned into a discussion: some topics were only discussed on one occasion. We labeled the discussions from A to H according to the content and topic and separated the episodes by numbers. For example, A1 was the first episode in discussion A, A2 was the second episode, and so forth.

Excerpt 5 below is from discussion A, which we called "More Finnish language." It consisted of six episodes (A1 to A6) and 35 suggestions. We do not give all 35 here but focus on different perspectives that illustrate the process and flow.

The new suggestion is extended and then confirmed by other students, as shown in excerpt 5 (1–3). The discussion continued in the fourth session. Again, the students placed heavy emphasis on the importance of learning Finnish in the preparatory immigrant training. The teacher reacted to this by making an elaborating suggestion (4). This was supported and explained by another student (5). Then the teacher extended the suggestion (6): foreigners have to learn the different inflections by heart. The topic continued: the students wanted more Finnish lessons. The teacher repeated her suggestion (7) that classroom practice could be changed so that vocational teachers would cover the inflections, or the lessons could be better integrated.

Table 24.2 The Trajectory of Suggestions Concerning the Finnish Language

No. of suggestions	Episodes (no. of suggestions in an episode)	Discussion	Contents and topics	CL session
1–9	1 (9)	A1	More Finnish lessons	1
10–15	2 (6)		Change of Finnish-language teacher	1
16–18	3 (3)		Finnish is important for further training	3
19–23	4 (5)	B1	Condition of admission: better Finnish language-level	3
24–34	5 (11)	C1	Correcting student's language	3
35–38	6 (4)	D1	Condition of admission: language test. It is difficult that the group is so heterogeneous	3
39–47	7 (9)	D2	Placement test at the beginning, heterogeneous group	3
48–52	8 (5)	D3	Heterogeneous group, students also learn from one another	3
53–57	9 (5)	C2	Correcting student's language	3
58	10 (1)	E1	Content and language integrated instruction	3
59–65	11 (7)	C3	Correcting student's language	3
66–71	12 (6)	A2	More Finnish language, inflections	4
72–73	13 (2)	E2	Content and language integrated lessons	4
74–81	14 (8)	A3	More Finnish language, inflections	4
82–87	15 (6)		Written language and spoken language	4
88–91	16 (4)	A4/E3	More Finnish language, integrated lessons or inflections	4
92–95	17 (4)	F1	What is Finnish-language teaching?	4
96–103	18 (8)	E4	Content and language integrated teaching	4
104–117	19 (14)		How many credits are there for Finnish in the curriculum?	4
118–123	20 (6)	A5	More Finnish: expanding vocabulary and preparedness from comprehensive school	4
124–129	21 (6)	F2	What is Finnish-language teaching?	4
130–139	22 (10)		A whole year of Finnish, then? What should the student be able to do?	4
140–146	23 (7)	G1	How to learn more Finnish: one has to study hard	4
147–154	24 (8)	E5	Why are other lessons not good for Finnish learning? Integrated learning, teachers' ideas	4
155–158	25 (4)	G2	How to learn more Finnish	4
159	26 (1)	B2	Condition of admission: a better Finnish-language level	4
160–163	27 (4)	G3	How to learn more Finnish	4
164	28 (1)	B3	Condition of admission: a better Finnish-language level	4
165–168	29 (4)	G4	How to learn more Finnish	4
169–170	30 (2)	A6	More Finnish, it is involved all the time	5
171–177	31 (7)	G5	How to learn more Finnish: integration	5
178–179	32 (2)	H1	Did you learn Finnish during the practical training?	8
180–186	33 (7)		Speaking one's own mother tongue and Finnish	8
187–189	34 (3)	H2	Did you learn Finnish during the practical training?	9
190–194	35 (5)		Learning language in school or outside school	9
195–205	36 (11)		What helped you during the practical training?	9
206–208	37 (3)		Evaluating the CL sessions	9
209–212	38 (4)		Finnish grammar	9

By integration she meant that a vocational teacher and a Finnish-language teacher would plan, implement, and evaluate the lessons together. This suggestion had been brought up earlier. Discussion E focuses on this particular topic. A student again brought up the same point: we need more Finnish lessons. The teachers offered other perspectives. One of them further suggested (8) that students could learn 10 new words a day, and another extended this suggestion (9), which concentrated on vocabulary, to cover conceptions and the all-around education provided for children in Finnish comprehensive schools. The topic was brought up for the last time by students in the fifth session: we need more Finnish. The teacher confirmed her previous response that all the training was in Finnish (10).

Excerpt 5
A new suggestion (1)

Student 2: And in this school here there's only a little Finnish language but learning Finnish first is important.

An extending suggestion (2)

Student 1: We can, we need to have more lessons to learn the Finnish language.

A confirming suggestion (3)

Student 9: More Finnish.

An elaborating suggestion (4)

Teacher 3: Should the vocational teachers always give examples then? Of course, they could give the basic form of the words, genitive in the singular.

An explaining suggestion (5)

Student 14: At the same time then we'd study the Finnish language.

An extending suggestion (6)

Teacher 3: And the foreigner has to remember what the ending is and what kind of ending is affixed to what kind of stem.

A confirming suggestion (7)

Teacher 3: Then it must be integrated instruction or then instruction that you [vocational teachers] also learn the inflections of words and tenses and types of verbs.

An extending suggestion (8)

Teacher 3: I've always said that the vocabulary, it's what it is, it tends to be rather limited and narrow, so if you could increase it by ten words a day.

An extending suggestion (9)

Teacher 2: Vocabulary is more than just words if we think that Finnish vocational instruction is based on the Finnish comprehensive school, and then the same kinds of modes and other things like that. When you learn the words and other things at the same time, you kind of learn how these things are understood in Finland.

A confirming suggestion (10)

Teacher 2: I still say that, well, the Finnish language is involved in the instruction all the time. And I think this is also something that is worth discussing and thinking about, that we don't study these subjects in other languages, that you learn in every subject how to utilize the Finnish language.

This showed how one discussion (A) progressed, and how the suggestions varied in the different sessions. It started with a student's suggestion that there was too little Finnish-language teaching, and ended up with the teacher's response that the Finnish language was involved in all of the training. The suggestions made in between illuminated the various perspectives on this important issue, and expanded the idea of Finnish-language learning. For example, the participants considered where language learning could take place, who would teach it, and how it could be studied.

As Table 24.2 shows, all the other discussions (B–H) were intertwined with this central theme. Furthermore, the students offered other solutions to language problems, for example that one condition of admission should be a good command of Finnish (discussion B), and another should be a language test (discussion D). Teachers should correct mistakes in students' language (discussion C). For their part, the teachers suggested the integrated teaching of both content and language (discussion E). They also asked the students what Finnish-language teaching actually consisted of in the light of the fact that all of the training was conducted in Finnish, and what made Finnish-language lessons so desirable (discussion F). The participants also talked about how to learn Finnish (discussion G). The episodes that were individual and thus did not constitute a discussion also concerned the topic of learning the Finnish language.

Conclusions and Discussion

At the beginning of this chapter we argued that the voices of marginalized minority groups are of major importance because development work needs multiple voices—multivoicedness. In the analyses we found that students actively made suggestions and thus contributed to the development of their training. This implies that the Culture Laboratory offered them both the opportunity and the space to participate in the development of the preparatory immigrant training, and through this these immigrant students found that their view—their voice—was appreciated and listened to. Thus, the Culture Laboratory increased multivocality at the College. Furthermore, this kind of participatory method supported students who were threatened by marginalization. We therefore claim that it also promoted equality at the College.

We focused on suggestions as a reflection of historically grounded ways of speaking about learning, and on their hidden potential. Both teachers and students primarily used the "traditional teaching" type of social language (see Bakhtin, 1981) when they made suggestions (concerning how to explain new issues to students, for example). Thus, their suggestions predominantly reflected traditional ways of speaking about teaching and studying. In the light of previous research (e.g., Jackson, 1990; Lortie, 1975), this finding is by no means new: a school appears to be a place with strong traditions and high resistance to change.

However, the way of learning that is characteristic of vocational institutions—"learning outside school"—also emerged in the suggestions, as did "teaching and studying together" (cf. Johnson, Johnson, & Holubec, 1994; Resnick, 1987). This emphasizes the importance of transcending classroom and school boundaries, especially in immigrant training because immigrant students are not familiar with Finnish everyday and working life, as they pointed out during the discussion. Furthermore, daily life offers a meaningful and fruitful source of learning in opening up a new horizon and a hybrid space.

In our analysis of the suggestion-making process we followed one dominant topic, suggestions concerning the Finnish language, throughout the Culture Laboratory. It was found that a simple suggestion started an innovative, expanding process. It was not necessarily just an individual, separate idea produced by someone who wanted to improve the training, but triggered a fruitful discussion. Furthermore, the suggestions served as vehicles for students and teachers aiming to improve their daily practices.

This expands the traditional concept of a suggestion as an individual contribution to an expansive cycle, and reflects the collective nature of the suggestion-making process. Elaborating, exploring, and extending suggestions offer the potential for expansive learning (Engeström, Y., 1987). Furthermore, a single suggestion sometimes triggered an escalating and cumulative process or chain. On one hand the students needed to learn, and they had fresh perspectives and ideas related to the training, and on the other hand the teachers had the power to implement the suggestions, and the project staff contributed to the development work. All three parties were required and they all had complementary needs and competences. This broke up the traditional power relations between students and teachers.

We believe that teachers should pay more attention to students' suggestions about their training. Suggestions open up new perspectives on everyday work, and a new hybrid space for learning. Just as Rannikko (2008) wrote when he described his way of working that the street offered an opportunity for change and encounter, we have demonstrated that suggestions made in the Culture Laboratory provided a sounding board for future improvements. They reveal something about a person's history and way of talking about learning. Their contents shed light on the current state of the training, and participation in the developmental process could empower immigrant students. In any case, as we have demonstrated, suggestions matter.

Note

1. The empirical part of this paper is a section of the first author's dissertation, "Intercultural Learning and Hybridity in the Culture Laboratory" (2007). Helsinki: University of Helsinki, Department of Education. Also available on http://oa.doria.fi/handle/10024/19237

References

Bakhtin, M. M. (1981). The dialogic imagination: Four essays by M. M. Bakhtin (C. Emerson & M. Holoquist, Trans.). Austin: University of Texas Press.

Boland, R. J., & Tenkasi, R. V. (1995). Perspective making and perspective taking in communities of knowing. *Organization Science, 6*(4), 350–372.

Engeström, R. (1995). Voice as communicative action. *Mind, Culture, and Activity, 2*(3), 192–214.

Engeström, Y. (1987). *Learning by expanding: An activity–theoretical approach to developmental research.* Helsinki: Orienta-Konsultit.

Engeström, Y. (1999). Innovative learning in work teams: Analyzing cycles of knowledge creation in practice. In Y. Engeström, R. Miettinen, & R.-L. Punamäki (Eds.), *Perspectives on activity theory* (pp. 377–404). Cambridge, UK: Cambridge University Press.

Engeström, Y. (2005). *Developmental work research expanding activity theory in practice* (Vol. 12). Berlin: Lehmanns Media.

Engeström, Y. (2007). Putting Vygotsky to work: The Change Laboratory as an application of double stimulation. In H. Daniels, M. Cole, & J. V. Wertsch (Eds.), *The Cambridge companion to Vygotsky* (pp. 363–382). Cambridge, UK: Cambridge University Press.

Engeström, Y., Lompscher, J., & Rückriem, G. (Eds.). (2005). *Putting activity theory to work contributions from developmental work research* (Vol. 13). Berlin: Lehmanns Media.

Engeström, Y., Virkkunen, J., Helle, M., Pihlaja, J., & Poikela, R. (1996). The Change Laboratory as a tool for transforming work. *Lifelong Learning in Europe, 1*(2), 10–17.

Gordon, T. (2007). Urban citizenship. In W. Pink & G. Noblit (Eds.), *International handbook of urban education* (Part I, pp. 447–462). Dordrecht: Springer.

Helsinki and the Helsinki Region (2008). Key figures and some international comparisons. January 1. City of Helsinki, Urban facts. *Helsinki Quarterly, 2,* 54–57. Retrieved September 25, 2009 from: www.hel2.fi/tietokeskus/kvartti/2008/Kvartti_08_Quarterly.pdf

Interpreting the results. (n.d.). Retrieved October 8, 2009 from: www.pisa2006.helsinki/fi

Immigrant education in Finland (n.d.). Retrieved September 25, 2009 from: www.oph.fi/english/education/language_and_cultural minorities/education_for_immigrants

Jackson, P. W. (1990). *Life in classrooms.* New York: Teachers College Press.

Jaukkuri, M., & Vanhala, J.-P. (Eds.) (2008). *Notkea katu: Yksin yhdessä* (*Fluid street: Alone together*) (M. Garner et al., Trans.). Museum of Contemporary Art Publication 111. Helsinki: Museum of Contemporary Art Kiasma.

Johnson, D. W., Johnson, R. T., & Holubec, E. J. (1994). *Cooperative learning in the classroom.* Alexandria, VA: Association for Supervision and Curriculum Development.

Joronen, T. (2005). Maahanmuuttajatyö onnistunut kohtalaisen hyvin pääkaupunkiseudulla (Integration of immigrants has succeeded tolerably well in capital region). *Kvartti, 4,* 41–48.

Keskinen, V., Laine, M., Tuominen, M., & Hakkarainen, T. (Eds.) (2009). *Kaupunkiköyhyyden monet kasvot: Näkökulmia helsinkiläiseen huono-osaisuuteen* (*Many faces of urban poverty: Approaches to disadvatage in Helsinki*). Helsinki: Helsinki City Urban Facts.

Long, N. (2001). *Development sociology: Actor perspectives.* London: Routledge.

Lortie, D. C. (1975). *Schoolteacher: A sociological study.* Chicago: University of Chicago Press.

Manninen, A. (2008). Research, innovation and quality of life. City of Helsinki, Urban facts. *Helsinki Quarterly, 2,* 3–4. Retrieved September 25, 2009 from: www.hel2.fi/tietokeskus/kvartti/2008/Kvartti_08_Quarterly.pdf

Opetusvirasto (2008). Statistics provided by the City of Helsinki, Department of Education.

Population Structure (2008). Official statistics of Finland: Population structure 2008. Retrieved September 25, 2009 from: www.stat.fi/til/vaerak/2008/vaerak_2008_2009-03-27_en.pdf

Rannikko, V.-P. (2008). Vesa-Pekka Rannikko. In M. Jaukkuri & J.-P. Vanhala, *Notkea katu: Yksin yhdessä* (*Fluid street: Alone together*) (T. Snellman, Trans.). Museum of Contemporary Art Publication 111. Helsinki: Museum of Contemporary Art Kiasma.

Resnick, L. B. (1987). Learning in school and out. *Educational Researcher, 16*(9), 13–20.

Sairastavuusindeksi Helsingissä ja peruspiireittäin 2007 (2009). Tilastoja 19 Helsingin kaupungin tietokeskus (Statistics 19 Helsinki City Urban Facts). Retrieved October 8, 2009 from: www.hel2.fi/tietokeskus/julkaisut/pdf/11_02_23_tilasto_8_Haapamaki.pdf

Sannino, A. (2008). From talk to action: Experiencing interlocution in developmental interventions. *Mind, Culture, and Activity, 15*(3), 234–257.

Vilkama, K. (2006). Asuntopolitiikka ja vieraskielisen väestön alueellinen keskittyminen Helsingissä vuosina 1992–2005 (Housing policy and regional concentration of non-native population in Helsinki between 1992 and 2005). Unpublished Master's thesis, University of Helsinki. Retrieved August 7, 2009 from: www.doria.fi/handle10024/2803

Virkkunen, J., Engeström, Y., Helle, M., Pihlaja, J., & Poikela, R. (1997). The Change Laboratory – A tool for transforming work. In T. Alasoini, M. Kyllönen, & A. Kasvio (Eds.), *Workplace innovations – A way of promoting competitiveness, welfare and employment* (pp. 157–174). Helsinki: Ministry of Labour.

Webster's dictionary (1986). *Webster's third new international dictionary of the English language unabridged.* Springfield, MA: Merriam Webster.

Index